1 6 7 6

1 6 7 6

THE END OF
AMERICAN
INDEPENDENCE

Stephen Saunders Webb

Syracuse University Press

First Syracuse University Press Edition 1995

95 96 97 98 99 00   6 5 4 3 2 1

This book is published with the assistance of the John
Ben Snow Foundation. Originally published in 1984.
Reprinted by arrangement with Alfred A. Knopf, Inc.

Designed by Sara Reynolds

The paper used in this publication meets the minimum
requirements of American National Standard for Information Sciences—Permanence of Paper for Printed
Library Materials, ANSI Z39.48-1984. ∞™

Library of Congress Cataloging-in-Publication Data
Webb, Stephen Saunders, 1937–
1676, the end of American independence / Stephen
Saunders Webb.
p. cm.
Originally published: New York : Knopf, 1984.
Includes bibliographical references (p.   )
and index.
ISBN 0-8156-0361-4 (pbk.)
1. Bacon's Rebellion, 1676. 2. King Philip's War,
1675–1676.
3. Indians of North America—Government relations
—To 1789.
4. United States—Politics and government—
To 1775. I. Title.
F229.W36 1995
973.2'4—dc20   95-23883

Manufactured in the United States of America

For Linda

Stephen Saunders Webb was born in Syracuse, New York, in 1937. He received a B.A. from Williams College and an M.S. and a Ph.D. from the University of Wisconsin. He has taught at St. Lawrence University, The College of William and Mary, and Syracuse University, where he is currently Professor of History. He has been a Fellow of The Institute of Early American History and Culture; The Charles Warren Center, Harvard; The National Endowment for the Humanities; and the John Simon Guggenheim Memorial Foundation. His book *The Governors-General; The English Army and the Definition of the Empire, 1569–1681* was published in 1979, and *Lord Churchill's Coup: The Anglo-American Empire and the Glorious Revolution Reconsidered, 1667–1701* in 1995.

Contents

BOOK ONE

BACON'S REVOLUTION

BOOK TWO

THE WORLD VIEWED FROM WHITEHALL

BOOK THREE

THE ANGLO-IROQUOIAN EMPIRE

I. "The Prince and the Orator": Garacontié of Onondaga

II. Edmund Andros, English Imperialist

III. The Covenant Chain

CONCLUSIONS

A Note on Dates

In England and Ireland, during the period of this study, the calendar year began on Lady Day (the feast of the Annunciation), 25 March. In Scotland, on the continent, and in the minds of many colonists, the year began on 1 January. Dates which fell between 1 January and 25 March are written here (as many contemporaries wrote them), 1 January 1675/6, 2 February 1676/7, 25 March 1677/8, etc. Days of the week and of the month are those found on the documents cited in the notes to 1676.

Illustrations

Maps

Preface

A noted reviewer of *1676* remarked that the work presents "in several senses an Empire State interpretation, the view from Lake Onondaga," and so this new edition (by the premier publisher of books on New York and on the Onondaga Iroquois) is especially appropriate.[1] The protagonists of *1676*—Daniel Garacontié, the Onondaga sachem; Edmund Andros, the governor of New York; and James Stuart, the duke of York and Albany and proprietor of the province—allied themselves through the agency of the Covenant Chain, thus making their linked dominions the center of empire in America. So doing, these hitherto "unsung," "unlikely," and "unexpected" protagonists broke the prior preeminence in English America of puritan Massachusetts and planter Virginia.[2] They began to shift the focus of European attention to North America from the Caribbean. Their immediate successors opened the hundred years war with France for America, and the decisive outcomes of that enormous war made North America the lasting domain of English language and institutions. Such was the abiding strength of the Longhouse League, however, that, to this day, the Grand Council of the Iroquois still meets at Onondaga.

The leadership of Daniel Garacontié and Edmund Andros, under the aegis of James Stuart, produced the treaties of the Covenant Chain. These are thrice remarkable. First, they were unique examples of a native people's imposition of their institutions on the European invaders. Second, the Covenant Chain drew the first American frontier, six hundred miles from Maine to Carolina. Third, the Covenant Chain survived, unbroken, as the oldest alliance of the English crown, until 1982. In 1676, the unlikely troika of the sachem, the soldier, and the

---

1. Richard R. Johnson, *American Historical Review* 90 (1985): 751–52; *idem.*, "The Imperial Webb: The Thesis of Garrison Government in Early America Considered," *William and Mary Quarterly*, 3d ser., 43 (1986): 408–30, esp. 412; and a reply by Stephen Saunders Webb, "The Data and Theory of Restoration Empire," *ibid.*, 431–59, esp. 459.
2. William S. McFeely, "Realpolitik in Colonial New England," *New York Times Book Review*, June 24, 1984, 13.

sovereign prince were able to impose their will on their dependents —red and white, aboriginal and colonial—whom they linked to the Covenant Chain because the older "culture hearths" of Virginia and New England were decimated by war and demoralized by revolution; because the English crown had won sufficient security at home to spare the monarchical attention and the military resources that were required to extend its sway in America; and because the Five Nations of the Hodenosaunee, "the Iroquois," chose this moment to capitalize on a generation of conquest to advance their influence south from Onondaga down the Susquehanna River. The Iroquoian expansion pinned their great rivals, the Susquehanna (after whom the river is named), against the banks of the Potomac. This compression of peoples sparked the frontier fighting that, in turn, ignited Bacon's Revolution in Virginia and exposed the frontiers of the Cheasapeake colonies to the attentions of the Iroquois as they hunted down the surviving Susquehanna. So too, Iroquoian raids to the east checked the great Algonquin uprising in New England called "King Philip's War." As Virginia was shattered by revolution and New England was weakened by war, the aggressive imperialists of Onondaga, New York, and Whitehall combined in the Covenant Chain to capitalize both on the debility of the older colonies and on the destruction of the native peoples of the Fall Line, those Algonquin nations ground down between the millstones of the English and the Iroquois. These two imperial powers were left face to face at Albany to divide northeastern America between them.

In 1676, the royal personage most important to the Anglo-Iroquoian alliance was James Stuart, duke of York and Albany, and brother of King Charles II (whom James would succeed on the imperial throne of England in 1685). The cover of *1676* is an oil sketch of James by Sir Godfrey Kneller. This portrait was never finished because it all too accurately depicts its harsh and inflexible, brutal and bigoted prince subject. Yet the positive products of James's force and focus—his administrative ability, his determined royalism, and his imperial ambition—put him, and so New York, at the center of that royalization of Anglo-American governance which was the consequence of the conflicts and covenants of 1676. New York was James's own property. Since he had acquired the colony by conquest from the Dutch in 1664, James had followed their commercial example, and his soldier-executives' military recommendations, to build an alliance with the Iroquois. Once forged, the Covenant Chain led James to order his viceroy to protect the Iroquois against French Canadian invasion in 1684. James reiterated that order, despite his entente with France, on the eve of his own ouster in 1688. That deposition was, in no small measure, a consequence of King James's contradictory concessions to France in the 1686 Treaty of American Neutrality, a treaty whose destructive impact on the Iroquois and on English interests from the Hudson Bay to the Leeward Islands is detailed in *Lord Churchill's Coup: The Anglo-American Empire and the Glorious Revolution Reconsidered.*[3]

In that volume as in this one, James Stuart and his household officers (headed by John, Lord Churchill, afterwards earl and duke of Marlborough) are shown to have been the chief agents of Anglo-American empire. It was these officers who formed a "shadow cabinet" which coordinated the royal military and corporate investments in American governance and commerce and briefed its principal, James. He dominated the deliberations of his brother the king's privy council's committee for the plantations. The reassembled records of that committee— and its executive counterpart, the committee on foreign affairs—are the essential evidence from which the worldview from the royal palace of Whitehall has been reconstructed in 1676. The initial crisis faced by the privy council and James's household in that year was Bacon's Revolution in Virginia. When the western Iroquois nations (all "Senecas" to the Chesapeake colonists) pushed the formidable Susquehanna south to the Potomac, the pressure on frontier populations, red and white, exploded into a war which the aged governor and corrupt council of Virginia could not counter. So Virginia's frontiersmen turned to Nathaniel Bacon. Usurping the military prerogative of the governor, Sir William Berkeley, Bacon found himself initially at the head of a political reform of caste-ridden Virginia, then at odds with the authority of the imperial crown, and finally the champion of a shadowy and short-lived—but long remembered—colonial coalition aimed at American independence.

In 1676, as contrasted to 1776, the royal response to an assertion of American independence was swift, overwhelming, and constructive. The duke of York's subordinates in the household and the admiralty (for the duke was lord high admiral) launched a powerful punitive expedition. The commissioners in command—a First Guards officer, the duke's naval flag captain, and Virginia's agent to the crown—were ordered not only to repress the revolution in Virginia but to redress the political oppression, the social selfishness, and the military weakness which had provoked Bacon's Revolution. The results, detailed in *The Governors-General,* underlay a hundred years of royal rule and anglicanization, the imperial period of American history.[4]

---

3. New York, 1995.
4. Stephen Saunders Webb, *The Governors-General: The English Army and the Definition of the Empire, 1569–1681* (Chapel Hill, 1979, 1987).

   The duke of York took an equal interest in New England. There, the most destructive war in American history, at least in proportion to population, was decimating the English colonists and destroying the Algonquin cultures. Both the English crown and the Longhouse League exploited the weaknesses that King Philip's War revealed in the autonomous colonies of New England. The crown sponsored the investigations by customs officials and naval officers which informed the revocation of the New England charters of government. The crown's agent in New York, Edmund Andros, moved the Mohawks (who in turn recruited their nephews, the Oneidas, and their brothers, the Onondågas) to make the attack on King Philip's winter camp which turned the tide of war in New England against the Algonquin alliance. The resulting Algonquin diaspora was an Iroquoian opportunity to re-cruit the clans depleted by conversion to Catholicism and removal to New France. For his part, James, as soon as he became king, imposed upon the demoralized and diminished colonies the Dominion of New England, which (under the command of Sir Edmund Andros, newly knighted for his accomplishments in the command of New York) per-manently altered the institutions and attitudes of the old puritan prov-inces and ended, for a century, their previous independence.

   These imperial enlargements, Iroquoian and English, are personi-fied in two pioneering biographies in 1676. Daniel Garacontié of Onon-daga was the greatest American diplomat of the seventeenth century. The senior sachem of the Bear Clan, of the Onondaga Nation and of the Iroquoian League, Garacontié confronted the enormous issue of Amerindian accommodation to European culture for his peoples by his unequaled diplomacy and for himself by becoming a Christian—"the best of our Iroquois Christians," so the Jesuits settled at Onondaga declared. As an intercultural figure, Garacontié was able to obtain the endorsement of colonial agents from every colony between Maine and Carolina for the Iroquoian sphere of influence, of which he was the chief architect. Such was his influence, as an Onondaga sachem and a Christian convert, that the Iroquoian condolence council was accepted as the institutional form of the Covenant Chain alliance. Thus, Gara-contié linked the Longhouse League to the English crown in the last act of a life which was the very pattern of Iroquoian aristocracy.

   The English author of the Covenant Chain was Edmund Andros. Like Garacontié he was a cosmopolitan soldier and aristocratic diplo-mat. Andros had prepared himself for this redefinition of America by a military education in the Netherlands and fighting in Scandinavia; by personal attendance in the Stuart courts of The Hague and Whitehall; by military service to the English crown in islands an ocean apart, Guernsey and Barbados; by his defense of the English Antilles from the French and the Dutch; and by the negotiations with the Caribs in the Leeward Islands, which anticipated his transactions with the Five Nations in New York. He went on from New York to govern both New England and Virginia before retiring to the government of Guernsey, thus serving four successive Stuart sovereigns. Sir Edmund Andros personified the shaping forces of empire and authority in this formative period of American history.

The great achievement of Daniel Garacontié and Edmund Andros was the interethnic, intercolonial, and international Covenant Chain. In 1676, the sachem and the soldier presided over the creation of the first American frontier. This boundary between the coastal colonies of the English and an interior Iroquoian sphere split eastern America along a line from the Penobscot to the Dan. This Anglo-Iroquois frontier was first the mechanism of Iroquoian empire, then the vehicle of English conquest, and finally the matrix of American expansion. Ever since 1676, the concept of the frontier has controlled our understanding of the character and culture of the United States. What has been forgotten is that the first American frontier was a shared enterprise of Amerindians and Europeans, of the Iroquois and the English. For a century after 1676, the Iroquois and the English redefined the American frontier which separated their domains in periodic "rebrightenings" of the Covenant Chain. That moving frontier marked the stages of English expansion, American development, and Iroquoian decline. Nevertheless, this alliance served the interests of both the English and the Iroquois signatories; so much was symbolized by their continuing adherence to the Covenant Chain. Not until 1982, on the occasion of the patriation of the Canadian Constitution, was the Covenant Chain at last broken by an act of the British Parliament. But when the royal yacht *Britannia* sails across "the Beautiful Lake," Ontario, and up the Bay of Quinte, to anchor off what was in 1676, and still is today, Iroquois territory, the sovereign is greeted by "the faithful Mohawk." Attired in gostoweh and trade cloth, the chiefs of the Mohawk Nation carry the communion service and the prayerbooks given to their predecessors by Queen Anne down to the waterside. On the upturned canoe which serves as an altar, sovereign and subject celebrate their shared anglican faith and the ancient alliance of the Iroquoian League with the English crown. In 1676, that Covenant Chain in 1676 defined the futures of both their empires in America.[5]

Before Anglo-American empire could be achieved, American inde-

5. I am indebted to Chief Melville Hill of Tynendenaga for his hospitality, for his accounts and records of the royal visit, and for an opportunity to see those of Queen Anne's gifts in his custody.

pendence had to be ended—whether that independence took the form
of fifty years of puritan polity in New England, a Dutch dominion
between the Hudson and the Delaware, the autonomy of Sir William
Berkeley's cavalier Virginia, or the independence asserted by Na-
thanial Bacon's Chesapeake confederation. Only when the first era of
American independence was closed by war, revolution, and reaction
could the redefinition of social elites, the construction of institutions of
authority, and the formation of provincial polities lay the foundations
for maturing, anglicizing provinces of England in America. Given
elites, institutions, and acculturation, the Americans were empowered
first to capture and then to reconstitute as their own the empire defined
by the English and the Iroquois in 1676. By describing the beginnings
of this process of conquest and colonization, acculturation and expansion, 1676 is designed to widen the field of view of the "telescope"
engineered by The Governors-General.[6] Together, the English army
administrators and the Iroquois viceroys would organize the campaigns
which drove the French from the Old West. In this, the era of the
imperial wars, the Amerindians were accomplished historical actors
in history, not just history's victims. Obviously, the Iroquois, as in-
digenous imperialists, are essential to the ongoing epic of American
conquest and colonization of the continent. This was first the work
of the Amerindians themselves, both before and after the European
invasion.[7]

But 1676 also reconstitutes an important episode in the history of
these first peoples and, as part of that history, sketches the biography
of a seventeenth-century Onondaga. Both this segment of the long history of the Great League and the life story of its senior sachem are
offered to reintroduce Iroquoian history. History is the time-driven,
ever-changing narrative of events, ideas, and accomplishments, both
individual and group, and these accomplishments were interconnected
with those of other peoples and places, even across the Atlantic. But
the Iroquoian peoples, in some senses, have been denied their past by
the freeze-frame techniques of anthropology: timeless, static, communal, and isolating. Ahistorical, anthropology directs and inspires immense amounts of invaluable research, but it tends to rigidify,
compartmentalize, and isolate its subjects. Capitalizing on anthropo-
logical achievement, we must also recall "the Real People" to history
if their ongoing place in American life is to be more fully assessed and
appreciated as the shaping force it always has been.

6. J. G. A. Pocock, "The Limits and Divisions of British History: In Search of the Unknown Subject," American Historical Review 78 (1982): 329.
7. Pauline Maier, "Second Thoughts on Our First Century," New York Times Book
Review, July 7, 1985, 1, 20.

In 1676, the homeland of the Five Nations, Stuart New York, extended from the Connecticut to the Delaware. It is the forgotten parent of the mid-Atlantic colonies and states. Their separate histories underplay the influence of the administrators who laid down their institutions and sheltered them within an Anglo-Iroquoian empire. The duke's deputies in New York inaugurated English forms of law and governance in the entire region now divided into four states. In that framework, these polities achieved unequaled prosperity and became the homes of an astounding variety of social, political, and religious experiments. The peoples of the middle colonies enjoyed their peaceable kingdoms undisturbed only because of the shield held over them by the Covenant Chain allies. Thus, the heartland of America for two centuries to come grew and prospered as part of the shared vision of Edmund Andros, Daniel Garacontié, and—for he was their landlord, tolerant yet imperial—James Stuart as well.

In 1676, Stuart New York is added to the case studies of garrison government in Cromwellian Jamaica and cavalier Virginia offered in *The Governors-General*. That work detailed the imperial outcomes of royal repression of Indian war and civil war in the Old Dominion of the crown. In 1676, Bacon's "rebellion" itself is treated as a revolution. It appears that commonwealth ideology had been domesticated in Restoration Virginia; from it had grown ideas of popular government and provincial independence. The larger geopolitical environment of ultimate independence was also clear in 1676. The North Atlantic competition for empire had hardened into the rivalries of France, the Netherlands, and England, and the American colonies had become trump cards in the great game. The royal response to that fact fostered the repression that brought American independence to an end in 1676. But Bacon's Revolution had sown the ideological seeds, illuminated the class hatreds, and revealed the international competition for empire that would germinate in 1776.

The century between these two episodes of independence constituted America's *ancien regime*. That era of anglicanization in America was attributable to the escalation of English military power and administrative purpose. In all European states, and in their empires, armies were the essential agents of authority. The ratios of twenty-two army officers to each navy officer in the governor-generalships of the royal provinces in America (nine-tenths of these executives were military men) bespeaks the military education of the crown's proconsuls in America. Armies and administrations were increasingly identified, whether in imperial capitals or in American colonies. So much is made clear in *The Governors-General*. However, standing navies were second only in importance to standing armies in the articulation of empire, so 1676 reintroduces Sir John Berry, the prototypical imperial admiral. Berry was trained on the Jamaica station of the royal navy; he was employed in the government and defense of Newfoundland and Tangier, and captained the convoys which connected them with each other and with England; he commanded the expedition which took Major Andros and his Barbados Regiment out to the Lesser Antilles. Berry's decisive victory in Nevis roads saved the Leeward Islands for England. A fighting commander in the Dutch wars (fought for control of the Narrow Seas and so of communications with America), Berry was the favorite naval captain of James, duke of York and lord high admiral. Berry rescued James both from battle and from shipwreck, and the duke commissioned Berry to lead the expedition to Virginia in 1676. That expedition epitomized the imperial force and function of the royal navy.

1676 also makes it clear, however, that the Baconian garrisons— idealists, servants, and slaves—were actually annihilated by the estuarian, amphibious campaign conducted by captains of the royal naval reserve, commanded by Captain Thomas Grantham of the *Concord*. The *Concord*, and the other heavily armed ships of the tobacco fleet, were manned by tough and multi-talented crews, men who were at need sailors, soldiers, or gunners. So the tobacco ships became the floating fortresses of the counterrevolution in Virginia; next only to the infantry company, such armed ships were the chief tools of empire. Thirteen sections of 1676 and several rare ship portraits detail the American expression of that imperial fact and picture its beautiful instruments.

These "Leviathans," as contemporaries called them, transported a terrible truth to America: the absolutism which Thomas Hobbes called "The Leviathan" and which was being realized all across Europe came to the colonies in 1676. Its armed authoritarians were ruthless realists, politically forcible and instrumental, materially exploitative and metropolitan exponents of the absolutist sovereignty personified by James Stuart at Whitehall, administered by Edmund Andros from Fort James, and recognized by Daniel Garacontié at Onondaga. Indeed, the League of the Iroquois can be seen as an Amerindian response to French and English absolutisms in America. Absolutism had been defined by reactions against civil war in Europe. It came as a shock to statesmen whose sense of public life had been formed in the period prior to the English civil wars, including the older generation of colonists. These Virginians, Barbadians, and New Englanders now faced unprecedented challenges to their civic freedom from the centralizing state. The state's armed agents embodied a cold-eyed *Realpolitik*. Domestically, absolutism was authoritarian; internationally, it was economically exclusive; both at home and abroad, it was politically belligerent. Absolutism saw war as the periodic and unavoidable adjuster of the international disputes that inevitably resulted from territorial expansion, elaborating alliance systems, exclusive mercantilism, and dynamic or nationalistic ambitions. These, the social stigmata of the modern world, appeared on the body politic of early America in 1676.[8]

This fact, unwelcome to provincial populations (and many of their historians) on both sides of the Atlantic and of the American frontiers, is not intended to contradict religious and ethnic, communal and mercantile, demographic and social analyses of this, the shaping period of our past. Rather, the forcible fact of imperialism overarches, connects and relates these otherwise isolated entities. This imperial argument has hitherto been restricted by being expressed largely in terms of a uniquely parochial form of mercantilism, the "commercial and colonial" connection. European commentators, however, have long observed that mercantilism everywhere focused on war. The first system of modern economic thought tried to define the means to achieve a net balance of trade sufficient to support the military and stockpile strategic materials, and it advocated state action abroad to shut rival state economies out of lucrative overseas trades, especially by monopolizing the commerce of colonies. All of mercantilism was aimed at physically strengthening the state so that it could conduct the wars inevitable in a system of unending and escalating rivalries.[9]

As befits a revisionist work which has been credited with "the rediscovery of war" as the shaping force of America's ancien regime, the footnotes of 1676 are not only an acknowledgment of the manuscript sources on which the narrative is based, but are also signposts to the sort of fresh materials that await a researcher emancipated from the colonial and commercial considerations hitherto dominant in the discourse about our imperial period.[10] Likewise, the literary style, the biographical method, and the episodic organization of 1676 are also designed to emphasize its argument. The chapter form is replaced by three locationally and culturally distinct Books subdivided into a hundred brief sections, each with a descriptive and distinctive subhead. Listed in the Contents, the titles of these subsections are designed to supply an analytical table of the revisionist arguments and illustrative episodes of 1676. A single chronology is also eschewed; instead, the Books are designed to express the simultaneity of events in 1676 and

8. McFeely, "Realpolitik."
9. Michael Roberts, *The Military Revolution, 1560–1660* (Belfast, 1956), 29. See also Stephen Saunders Webb, "Army and Empire," *The William and Mary Quarterly*, 3d ser., 34 (1977): 1–31.
10. Maier, "Second Thoughts."

of their trans-Atlantic effects. The year itself is stretched by exploiting the contemporary (Julian) calendar to add three months to our (Georgian) year. Moreover, the events which, beginning in 1675, culminated in 1676, are described in the narrative, as are the outcome of the events of 1676 in 1677. This effort to stretch historical time is a small part of the revisionist program of *1676*.

STEPHEN SAUNDERS WEBB
Washington, D.C.
May 25, 1995

Preface to the Original Edition

Two purposes impel me to write about 1676. First, the tale of 1676 is worth the telling as the saga of the statesmen and women, the warriors and the workers of three races who laid the provincial foundations of American society. That is, 1676 shaped today. As "man's accidents are God's purposes," so the peoples of 1676 created, sometimes consciously, more often not, the structures of politics, administration, and ideology that still mold our governmental institutions and direct our imperial aspirations. Much of our unwillingness to face the contemporary fact of American empire and to acknowledge that we are constituents of a world culture lies in our ignorance of the imperial origins of our politics and of our world view. Yet our state structure and our ideology were substantially dictated by the revolutions and counterrevolutions, the colonial causes and the imperial outcomes of 1676.

In 1676, the American colonies lost—and lost for a century to come —their political independence. It had been well established. The colonies had first asserted their governmental autonomy in the later 1630s. With varying success, they had defended their political freedom against the English commonwealth and protectorate in the 1650s. For more than a quarter of a century after the execution of Charles I in 1649, however, the major American colonies had mostly governed themselves. Then, in 1676, a concatenation of disasters destroyed the autonomous elites of the American colonies. Storm and plague, Indian insurrection and civil war shattered the colonial oligarchies. Insecure and therefore oppressive, inflexible and therefore unresponsive, the old order in each of the American colonies failed to provide the leadership required by English settlements in America if they were to overcome nature and natives, social immaturity and rival empires.

It was in 1676, more than in any year since "the starving times," the beachhead years of the European invasion of North America, that the English came closest to being driven from the continent. Just the fighting in 1676—not to mention human casualties from epidemics "cousin german to the plague," crop failures and livestock losses—cost more lives, in proportion to population, than any other war in American history. In 1676 was wiped out an entire generation of settlement (many of the towns and plantations destroyed in 1675–76 had not yet been substantially reoccupied in 1705). The wars eliminated so much of the capital invested in colonization by the two founding generations that per-capita income did not achieve 1675 levels again until 1775. Indeed, some sources suggest that not until 1815 did average levels of welfare again reach the levels enjoyed by Americans before 1676. In this crisis, many of the American colonists rejected the rule of their autonomous elites and either sought or had forced upon them the administrative attentions of the English state: royal, national, imperial.

Before 1676, the empire had just two disciplined provinces, as distinct from autonomous colonies. The Cromwellian garrison government of Jamaica, as I observed in *The Governors-General,* provided the institutional models of militarization and centralization for the reshaping of American government after 1676. New York, the personal property of England's leading imperialist, James duke of York, was the center from which red-white and Anglo-American relations were reoriented during the year of disaster, 1676.

In 1676, the crown, its modernized, militarized institutions, and haut-bourgeois backers, first made its authority felt throughout England's American dominions. Because the structures of American autonomy were fractured by the forces of 1676, the crown could now apply in America the forceful men and absolutist measures with which it had taken control of the three British kingdoms during the previous decade. These measures, field-tested in Jamaica, and such men, particularly the governor-general of New York, were deployed to meet the American demands for civil order, economic reorganization, and physical protection evoked by the battles, plagues, and depressions of 1676. In a single decade, the emissaries of empire—governors and generals, proconsuls and admirals, bureaucrats and investigators, merchant seamen and imperial statesmen—made direct government by the English state supreme in America. They planted in the soil of the colonists' search for security and stability the roots of those imperial aspirations and institutions, loyalties and practices, that ended American independence for a century after 1676.

The crises of 1676 afflicted every English man and colony in America and the West Indies, and all of their native neighbors and allies, subjects and enemies as well. Rather than treat them all, superficially and inhumanely, this work narrates two tragic episodes, both in some detail and both from novel perspectives based on manuscript and documentary sources. These two episodes are Bacon's so-called "rebellion" in Virginia, actually Bacon's Revolution, and King Philip's War in New England, which was actually a widespread Algonquin resistance movement decided by the Mohawk Iroquois and New York's governor-general. Bacon's Revolution and the Algonquin resistance are equally famous and equally misunderstood crises of the formative years of the English empire and the United States.

The first episode of 1676, Bacon's Revolution, was centered in but not confined to Virginia. It has often been described: usually as a frontier feud; sometimes as a clash of personalities; occasionally as evidence of the colonies' social disorder; once, briefly and brilliantly, as an episode in the failure of traditional European institutions in an American environment. It was all of these things. More, however, the outbreak of 1676 was a civil war. It was fought by every class and race of the Chesapeake region. It was repressed by English merchant ships and seamen. It was defeated by English soldiers and sailors. They concluded that they faced not just a colonial civil war but a double revolution. The first Chesapeake revolt of 1676 was a rising against the old regime in the Bay colonies. It developed into a revolution against dependence on England, economic or political. Bacon's Revolution destroyed the colony's autonomous old regime, asserted the revolutionary government's independence, and thereby exposed the oldest of American dominions and the precursor of American independence to the purview of the new English empire.

Two imperial strands connect Bacon's Revolution to the Algonquin insurgency called King Philip's War. Not only did both these American outbreaks of 1676 require and receive English imperial remedies because of the weakness of America's *anciens régimes* and the autonomy of colonial leaders, but also both the Chesapeake and the New England wars were rooted in the imperial aspirations of the Great League of Peace. The Iroquoian League's perpetual war for universal peace was directed by ancient ideology but, by 1676, it was also dictated by the dynamics of trans-Atlantic trade, settlement, and rivalry. All of these Atlantic world factors lured the league ever more deeply into the affairs of its coastal neighbors, both red and white. From the river of the Penobscot and Maine to the Dan River and the Carolinas, Iroquoian interests meant league intervention. In 1676, the advances of the second generation of English settlers and the rising resistance of natives caught between the English and the Iroquois involved the League of Peace in war all along the upper reaches and tributaries of both the Chesapeake Bay and the Connecticut River. Here were located the Iroquoian sources of both Bacon's Revolution and the Algonquin insurgency. The heartland of the Iroquoian League, the ancestral homes of its five constituent nations, the focus of both red and white imperial designs in the America of 1676, was in today's New York State. The capitol of the league and so the political center of eastern North America was the Council House at Onondaga. The exclusive agent of English diplomacy with the league was the governor-general of New York. The Algonquin insurgency is therefore described not from the perspective of King Philip's Mount Hope or from the New Englanders' capital of Boston, but rather as it was seen from the headquarters of two empires—the Council House at Onondaga and Fort James in New York City—and as it was viewed by two visionary statesmen, Daniel Garacontié and Edmund Andros.

It is the task of 1676 to pay tribute to these and other founders of the Anglo-Iroquoian, Anglo-American empire which determined our destiny. In the words of the great Iroquoian hymn which reverberated through the most meaningful moments of 1676, and which echoes still in Onondaga,

> I come again to greet and thank the League;
> I come again to greet and thank the kindred;
> I come again to greet and thank the warriors;
> I come again to greet and thank the women.
> My forefathers—what they established!

STEPHEN SAUNDERS WEBB
Onondaga County
New York
9/10/83

Acknowledgments

Early in 1976, Bernard Bailyn waded through the snows of Cayuga country to give the Becker Lectures at Cornell University. His subject was the historian's craft. He observed that its masters characteristically attributed unexpected importance to uncelebrated dates. They sought to attach general movements to particular moments. After the lecture in question, Professor Bailyn's editor at Alfred A. Knopf, Inc., Jane Garrett, and I shared the cheering warmth of the lovely Tudor fireplace of the occasion's impresarios, Michael and Carol Kammen. It was natural for an editor to ask what signal date and what great process of our past this author would raise from undue obscurity, given the chance. *1676: The End of American Independence* is the answer to Jane Garrett's question.

To her, and to the others just named, thanks are due not only for initial inspiration but for subsequent assistance in the development of *1676*. In the composition of the work I incurred a great debt to my former student, Mary Lou Lustig. She has commented (with a tactful balance of criticism and appreciation) on almost every page of several drafts of this study. The copy editing of Anne T. Zaroff, and of Peggy Rauch at Knopf, has been both painstaking and thoughtful. Betty Anderson and Sara Reynolds tastefully evolved handsome designs from the decorative elements on the maps of the *Blathwayt Atlas*, edited by Jeannette D. Black and published by the Brown University Press for the John Carter Brown Library. At the Library, I am indebted to the former librarian and director, Thomas R. Adams, and to his successor, Norman S. Fiering, as well as to the bibliographer of the *J.C.B.*, Everett C. Wilkie, Jr., for permission to use maps and their decorations from the *Blathwayt Atlas*.

Credits for the additional pictures and portraits in each Book of *1676* are included in the three essays on illustrations. In their composition, the advice of Margaret E. Marsh has been extraordinarily helpful. Other constructive comments were generated by the excerpts from *1676* presented to academic audiences at Syracuse University and at the universities of Rochester, Edinburgh, and Hull. I am especially grateful to Robert I. Crane, Perez Zagorin, Rhodri Jeffreys-Jones, Owen Dudley Edwards, and W. A. Speck, for their astute observations on these presentations.

This old-fashioned—some may say "reactionary"—production is the work of many hands. Typing by the staff of the dean of the Maxwell School, Syracuse University (Dorothy Smith and Eleanor Boyle, most notably), and by Cheryl Wood and Anne Adams, is acknowledged with thanks. The index is the work of Anne Eberle.

Institutions are also owed many thanks for their support of this study. Completion of 1676, and the advancement of the larger work of which it is a part, would have been greatly retarded save for a generous and timely fellowship award by the John Simon Guggenheim Memorial Foundation. The support of the Guggenheim Foundation would have been unavailing, however, without the leave of absence granted by Syracuse University. With pleasure and gratitude I present 1676 to these sponsors.

In the interval which elapsed before an inspiration in 1976 produced this study of 1676, all the members of my immediate family made helpful contributions to the work. I am especially grateful to Stephen M. Webb for the materials reflected in the introduction to Book II. To Linda M. Webb, in gratitude for twenty-five years of partnership, 1676 is dedicated.

BOOK ONE

BACON'S
REVOLUTION

Introduction

POPULATIONS

The story of Bacon's Revolution is that of three peoples and their quarreling subdivisions. First on the land were the Amerindians. Their defense of their homelands was fundamental to the events of 1676. It was a Doeg attack on the encroaching English settlers of Virginia's Northern Neck that incited the mistaken assault by the frontier militias of Virginia and Maryland on the Susquehanna fort at the falls of the Potomac. Susquehanna revenge cut up the Chesapeake frontiers. It exposed the military debility of the old colonial oligarchies. It excited the popular movement that chose Nathaniel Bacon as its leader. It also exposed the Susquehanna themselves to the fatal attentions of the Five Nations of the Iroquois.

In 1676, the Iroquois terrorists broke the Susquehanna, the greatest of the Peoples of the Fall Line, and damaged their Algonquin allies, most of whom had also been allies of the old regimes of Virginia and Maryland. The Iroquois also inflicted incidental, but numerous, casualties on the European frontiersmen caught in the crossfire of this war. The war on the Susquehanna frontier made changes in the aboriginal balance of power that were to last for a hundred years, but it was only a fraction of the fighting and it led to but a portion of the diplomatic settlement by which the Five Nations made their League of Peace and Power pre-eminent in the interior of northeastern America. West from the Berkshires and Alleghenies to the river of the Illinois, south from the Ottawa's river to the

The quotations in this introduction are taken from the text that follows and are there annotated, with the exception of Berkeley's anatomical analogy on page 6 (Colonial Office, Class 1/Group 21, fol. 111v, British Public Record Office), the imperial bureaucrat's quotation

Tennessee, the "Hodenosaunee" extended their lodge. In 1676, therefore, at the series of strategic points from the falls of the Housatonic and the Hudson to those of the Delaware and the Potomac, the edges of the Iroquoian sphere met the frontiers of the English empire.

This meeting was fatal to the peoples caught between the Iroquois warriors and the English frontiersmen. Along the plantation perimeter of Virginia and Maryland, the premise and context of Bacon's Revolution was the vain resistance of the buffer tribes—Doeg, Ocaneechi, Nottaway, Meherin, and even the famous and formidable Susquehanna—to the simultaneous aggression of the Iroquois and the English. Defeated, they became the tributaries of one of the two imperial peoples or were entirely absorbed by them. In their last battles, however, the Peoples of the Fall Line not only hit hard at their enemies, both red and white, but involved them in fighting with each other. The disastrous result was that the four western nations of the Iroquois lost almost as many warriors as the English of Virginia and Maryland lost settlers. For the latter, the casualty estimates ranged up from five hundred killed to double that number. Both an Iroquoian and an Anglo-American generation were decimated in 1676.

The upshot of their costly conflict was the American frontier. The fall-line frontier of the seventeenth century disappeared with its native defenders in 1676. It was replaced by a negotiated frontier, a "semipermeable membrane" between the Iroquoian and English spheres, the classic frontier of our legendary past. So extensive was the 1676 war and so comprehensive its subsequent settlement, the Covenant Chain treaties, that their signatories periodically, peaceably, renegotiated the American frontier along the westward lines of successive Iroquoian warriors' paths from 1676 to 1796.

These outcomes of 1676 were not only wide-ranging and lasting, they were also extra-colonial and imperial, so that neither the author of the old Virginia frontier, Sir William Berkeley, nor its eliminator, Nathaniel Bacon, appear to have had large parts to play in determining the American frontier of the future. That determination, as Bacon's Maryland allies made clear early on in the Chesapeake revolution, lay in the hands of the Iroquois, led by Daniel Garacontié, and the imperialists, led by Edmund Andros. Indeed, after reading these pages, it may appear that both the

---

on page 7 (William Blathwayt to Col. William Stapleton, 25 January 1680, Blathwayt Papers, Volume 37, Folder no. 2, Colonial Williamsburg, Inc., Williamsburg, Va.), and a bit of Andrew Marvell's verse.

By annotating only the direct quotations in the text, I intend to give an economical indication of the manuscript sources on which this study is based. Also cited are those modern works to which the text is directly indebted, usually for contemporary quotations. A select list of other secondary studies is appended to each Book of 1676.

governor and the rebel, both Berkeley and Bacon, were simply lightning rods for social currents. They were attractive objects, the magnets around which various sorts of hitherto unsung English men and women organized the revolution which destroyed the old order in the "Old Dominion" and shaped the reaction to it, the "Old Empire" of 1676–1776.

Women led both the Berkeleyan and the Baconian camps. The drain "Lady Berkeley" (as she was called) put on Sir William's aging energies, her rebuff to the New Kent volunteers, her greed—personal and pecuniary, physical and proprietary—all were marked by contemporaries as causes of the revolution. After she fled to London aboard the *Rebecca*, Lady Berkeley's lobbying at Whitehall helped to excite the punitive purposes of the imperial crown. On her return to Virginia with the ensuing expedition, Frances Culpeper Berkeley became the vindictive goddess of Berkeleyan revenge. She would, she said, remember "ye Canvase Linnen ye Rebells said they would make me glad of." Despite her recent experience of Whitehall's determination to rule as well as to reign in Virginia, Lady Berkeley also led the irreconcilable elite, "the Green Spring Faction," in their resistance to direct royal government. By way of showing Berkeleyan contempt for English bureaucrats, she even replaced the royal commissioners' postilion with the Green Spring executioner. This was, as those horrified officers exclaimed, "an affront not only to ye Reverence due to his Maties great Seale; but to us in our Private persons as Gentlemen."

Other gentlewomen were victims of the revolution. So the "white aprons," the human shields of the rebel entrenchments before Jamestown, dramatically demonstrated. But the women of the Baconian camp were more numerous, and more influential, than were the Berkeleyan ladies. As Mrs. Grindon, Mrs. Stagg, and Mrs. Cheezeman exemplify, the origins of the revolution lay not in the frontier militiamen led by Nathaniel Bacon but, first, in their wives' persuasion of the men of "the better sort" to lead the militia against the Indians. And in Bacon's own case, the letters of his wife, Elizabeth, to her sister display the horrified reactions to upcountry massacres and downcountry sloth which drove frontier leaders to act against the Indians.

When upcountry self-defense encountered Berkeleyan condemnation, it was the Baconian "news wives" who organized public opinion against the government, who "told hundreds" that Sir William Berkeley was an Indian-lover. When opposition became revolution and revolution approached independence, it was Sarah Drummond who summarized the distractions of English politics and declared to the convention, "I fear the power of England no more than a broken straw." Women like Mrs. Hanyland propagated and connected the centers of the ensuing revolutionary government by traveling "poste up & downe the Country."

When at last that government was defeated, garrison by garrison, the women who had helped to organize and operate it suffered. Mrs. Grindon was robbed by Berkeleyan bandits. Mrs. Cheezeman was humiliated at the trial and execution of the husband she had persuaded to join the revolution. Mrs. Lloyd was so abused that she went into premature labor and died. That the counter-revolution spared the revolutionary women outright execution was but the clement counterpart of its denial to all women of that public life which had flared up in the revolution of 1676 and which died with it, not to be rekindled for a century. Then the revival of women's roles signaled that once again revolution had fertilized the American body politic.

That body was badly battered in Berkeleyan Virginia. "Consider us," Sir William told the king in 1667, "as a people press'd at our backes wth Indians, in our Bowills with our Servants . . . and invaded from without by the Dutch." Berkeley correctly calculated that any external distractions of the masters would excite an internal revolution: a quest for freedom by black slaves and white servants; an effort to expropriate the master class.

Among the servants were commonwealth and Cromwellian veterans, determined not just to win freedom for themselves or even to overturn Virginia society but also to attack monarchical government and to secure a republic in Virginia by winning independence from England. The sworn determination to defend the resulting revolutionary regime against the crown among aspirant servants, seasoned soldiers of English revolution, and their Maryland associates in republican politics was explicitly based in their interregnum experiences. The revolutionary forms of committee and district, oath and association, convention and ordinance, applied alike in 1642, 1676, and 1776, attested to the perennial republican and revolutionary legacy available to Anglo-American laborers, an ideology of the underclass. These revolutionaries' renewed servitude and the execution of their leaders ended social as it did political revolution in the Chesapeake for a century to come. Yet renewed revolution would reassume the ideology of the interregnum, and that of 1676.

As their degradation was deeper than that of the English servants, so the commitment of the African slaves to the revolution was stronger and longer. At least 10 percent of Virginia's slaves served in the revolution's "Choice and Standing Army" during the winter of 1676, whereas no more than 7 percent of the servants remained with the Baconian colors in winter quarters. Of the last one hundred holdouts among the Baconian headquarters guard, eighty were black. The eighty, and most of the revolution's other black soldiers, were returned to slavery, even in instances where they had been promised their freedom as the price of laying down their arms. Not just slaves, but free planters of African descent—"Edward

Lloyd, a Mulatto," and his unfortunate wife, for example—suffered pro-
foundly from the Berkeleyan revenge, even if they had done no more
than most Virginians and merely sought to be neutral to preserve their
hard-won property and status. At best, these survivors of loyalist extortion, like their counterparts in Maryland, would have to "shuffle and cut
amongst the great ones to begin againe." Not until 1776 would the loyalists give the blacks what they received from the revolutionaries of 1676:
a chance to fight for their freedom.

ANGLICIZATION

Not the ownership of humans but the owners seemed reprehensible to
the recent English emigrants who constituted the historically recognized
leadership of "Bacon's Rebellion." The ideologues, generals, and diplomats of the Chesapeake revolution of 1676 were, for the most part, metropolitan, educated, wealthy, and well-bred Englishmen or anglicized
Britons. This Jamestown clique, centered on Richard Lawrence, criticized the *nouveaux-riches*, disreputable and irresponsible, uneducated
and ill-bred, who prevailed among the Berkeleyans: "the unworthy Favorites and juggling Parasites." In fact, Virginia's colonial regime was
incorrigibly corrupt, inhumanely oppressive, and inexcusably inefficient,
especially in war, the ultimate test of seventeenth-century governments.
Englishmen themselves had measured the success of Cromwell and the
failure of Charles II by the outcome of England's most recent wars. English immigrants to Virginia applied the same standard to the colonial
oligarchy. They found it utterly wanting, as Whitehall did afterwards.

Revolutionaries and royalists alike agreed that heavy and inequitable
taxation for coastal forts "made out of mud," for public magazines emp-
tied of the arms sent out by the king, for frontier stockades "on great
men's lands" and for their protection, all properly outraged the Chesapeake colonists. They were overtaxed and undefended, yet only protection can command obedience. To all protests, however, popular or elitist,
and to all admonitions, royal or local, the old colonial regimes between
the Albemarle and the Kennebec responded at best by sending agents to
England in search of accessions of autonomy, authority, and acreage all,
as Maryland's protesters put it, "as if the king's Majesty in England hath
nothing to doe there." But the colonial agents inadvertently alerted the
awakening imperialism of the crown to their principals' autonomy at the
same time that the addition of agency taxes stimulated fresh colonial
criticism of the old oligarchies. Revolution and counter-revolution alike
took aim at the self-sufficiency of the American regimes. Indeed, the new
breed of imperial bureaucrats blamed Bacon's rebellion on Berkeley's
silence: lack of "any communication between His [Majesty's] Governors

and His Ministers has lately produced a Rebellion and other unhappy effects." The agents were forced to supply the information about colonial isolation from the crown that Sir William and his ilk would not, and the enemies of the colonial *anciens régimes* revolted against their oppression and inefficiency. Thus both agents and enemies of the autonomous oligarchies incited the crown to substitute "the Emperial Armes and supremacy of England" for the practical independence of the American governments of 1676.

Forcible anglicization was required to modernize American government because the old order in the colonies could only resist either commonwealth or crown criticisms. Provoked by popular protests against their selfish attitudes and their isolation from English imperial norms, the proprietary party in Maryland allegedly "prevailed with the Virginians to have their best common wealths men out of the waye by advysing Sir Will Barkly to doe as they did with Davis"—that is, to hang the commonwealth critics of colonialism. Censured by the crown, the colonial leaders replicated this response as closely as redcoated circumstances permitted: Lady Berkeley put in the hangman to guide the crown commissioners' coach.

Whether resisting or insisting on anglicization, both reactionaries and rebels made the recent English civil wars and revolution their common reference and resource, thus refreshing and advancing the identity of English and American political culture. The Baconians argued for the rationality of the English Revolution (and so of theirs). The Berkeleyans remarked on its ultimate failure (and its immediate destructiveness). The revolutionaries cited the interregnum in England to prove that kings "had Noe Right but what they gott by Conquest and the Sword." So they contended that conquest authenticated their command of Virginia. The reactionaries countered that the restoration of Charles II had demonstrated divine support for Stuart monarchy. They added that King Philip's War now confirmed God's wrath towards republican regicides.

That might, not right, determined sovereignty was the central lesson of the interregnum, Berkeleyan piety notwithstanding. Therefore, realists among both reactionaries and revolutionaries feared that the imperial state which had emerged during the commonwealth and the protectorate and had merged with Stuart sovereignty at its restoration would be forcibly visited on Virginia, as it had so often been on Ireland. And so it was.

REVOLUTION

Anglicization first incited and then overwhelmed revolution, but "revolution" there was, in the modern sense of that term, in Virginia in 1676. It was intended, if not achieved, everywhere else in the Chesapeake region.

"Conventions" of delegates from Virginia's counties, Maryland's Protestants, and the Albemarle settlements met at the "Middle Plantation" (Williamsburg) in August and at Green Spring in September 1676. The delegates swore allegiance to a revolutionary regime which immediately assumed the government of Virginia, denounced its former officers as "Traytors to the People," and seized their property.

For government by oligarchy, the revolutionaries substituted the rule of a political party, the "Associators" who had sworn their allegiance to the revolution and its general. These partisans governed through central, district, and county committees. They anticipated that these revolutionary institutions would be confirmed by an assembly elected on a broad franchise. The assembly was also to extend the program of popular political reform begun by the "June Laws" and make General Bacon Governor-General Bacon.

During the course of the convention, it became clear to the bulk of the Baconians that it was as treasonous to attempt to achieve their minimum program of elected governors and popular government in America as it was to undertake a thoroughgoing revision of Virginia society and establish a republican government. The Baconians therefore opted for confederation in defense of the revolution (by support for revolts in Maryland and Carolina and by alliance with New England). They planned to defend the revolutionized region by that irregular warfare based on broken terrain, malaria, and civilian support which we know as the "guerrilla." They prepared to seek the support of England's imperial rivals, France and the Netherlands, the price being the planters' defiance of England's economic monopoly of American trade. At last, the revolutionaries determined on independence.

In the sequence and sum of these stages, Bacon's Revolution in 1676 forecast the American Revolution of 1776. It would be organized by a convention which was convened on the same site and which followed precisely the same pattern in moving from reform to revolution to confederation to foreign alliance to free trade and, finally, to independence. The identities of 1676 and 1776 were dictated by the maturation in the mid-1670s of international and imperial rivalries, of the circum-Atlantic economy, of the opposed ideologies of imperial monarchy and republican state. The shaping forces of the Atlantic world and of Anglo-American politics did not change significantly in the succeeding century—save that the French replaced the Dutch as the chief external enemies of English empire and so as the most important foreign support for American independence. In the course of a century, therefore, there were no changes in the options before those who, when the wounds to American property and republican politics which were inflicted in 1676 had healed at last, once again sought American independence.

Apart from the unchanged imperial and ideological environments of 1676 and 1776, there remains the vexed question of the living legacy of Bacon's Revolution within Virginia. To begin with, "Bacon's Rebellion" did not die with its first general in October 1676, as is usually asserted. A successor was chosen by the army, the surviving civil leadership of the revolution remained intact, and the civil and social war in the Chesapeake was fought out for more than a year after its outbreak in April of 1676. In February 1676/7, the royal commissioners on the scene concluded that, unless imperial discipline was immediately imposed by force and royal justice was equitably administered in the province, the Virginians would continue to be "ill Qualified as to their Obedience and incouraged at soe remote a Distance from England to cast off the Yoke. . . ." It was three more years before the royal army concluded its mopping-up exercises in the southside refuges of the Baconians and in the heartland of revolution on the James River frontier. It was another three years—not until 1683—before the Berkeleyan opposition to royal government was finally crushed by the new-model imperial government imposed by the crown.

A struggle of such duration and intensity bred bitter and lasting memories. They appear sporadically across the popular and political history of the succeeding century, recalled by old revolutionaries and new governors-general until, in 1769, on the eve of another revolution, a provincial newspaper reprinted the story of 1676. And even in the revolution of 1776, the Lees—gentlemanly descendants of Berkeleyan barons— were reviled as having been oppressors of the people in 1676. Certainly, the revolutionary legacy of 1676 was long-lived, its effect incalculable.

Yet Bacon's Revolution failed to win political independence from England, and it could not sustain social revolution around the Chesapeake, because in 1676 even the oldest English colonies were as yet too underdeveloped economically to survive a year without English supplies. Beyond necessities, as the revolutionary convention heard, "here are many people in Virginia that receive considerable benefits, comforts and advantages" from England. There were located Virginians' hopes for future inheritance as well as present prosperity. The Chesapeake colonies were also too immature socially to avoid anarchy in the absence of English norms. As a Maryland observer of upper-class gouging and lower-class sedition put it, "the Country is but in a feeble minority." Finally, Virginia institutions collapsed when squeezed between an oligarchy contemptuous of public good and revolutionaries determined upon an insupportable independence. The fact of institutional failure itself suggested that, as yet, the colonists could not politically "subsist without their prince." Then it became apparent to the modestly established planters, the middling sort socially, the company-grade militia officers, that not self-defense or even political reform but independence from England was the ultimate aim of the revolution. That aim was immediately opposed by metropolitan and royalist representatives. Then the Baconian cause was abandoned by the vital cadres of any government: the revolution of 1676 survived only as long as it retained the support of "the middling sort." The revolution of 1776 triumphed because it never quite lost their support.

The immediately effective opponents of revolution were the sea captains whose ships commanded the underdeveloped colonies' indispensable communications with England. When the Baconians lost their only ships on the Eastern Shore, they not only isolated the revolution, they also lost their last chance to capture Sir William Berkeley and his tiny cadre of loyalists. Commissioned by a governor still at large and free to act, assisted by his lieutenants, metropolitan merchantmen and ships such as the *Young Prince* and the *Concord* were ordered and able to win the civil war for the loyalists. Meanwhile, the *Rebecca* and her sisters, escaping half-laden from the assaults of the rebels, carried news of the revolution home to Whitehall. The royal response took the form of six warships and eight transports whose officers, batteries, and troops secured the colony for the crown. The most advanced technological systems of the age, all these oceangoing ships were "A Fleet of Worlds, of other Worlds in quest," mobile and self-sufficient, economically essential and militarily powerful. Ships were the shelters of the loyalists, the jails of the rebels, the fortresses of the crown in the Chesapeake.

Of all the neglected principals in the drama of 1676—women, servants, slaves, revolutionaries, Indians—perhaps the most important individuals were English sea captains and their crews. William Carver for the rebels, Thomas Larrimore for the loyalists, Robert Morris on the James, Thomas Grantham on the York, Sir John Berry the royal commissioner—these few men did more than any others to determine the outcomes of the Chesapeake revolution. Londoners to a man, the loyalist captains fought for metropolitan hegemony, political as well as economic. They fought not just against the rebellious Virginians but against their New England, Irish, and outport backers. Naturally, no Berkeleyan or Baconian contemporary, nor any patriotic Virginia historian, ever gave these seagoing English enemies of Virginia's autonomy and independence the slightest credit for winning the civil war in the Chesapeake, but, as the crown commissioners concluded, "what signall services were done as to the suppressing this Rebellion must bee justly laid to the incessant toyle, Courage & good success of these few Sea Captains."

King Charles appreciated that the colony had been saved for his crown by the ships' captains. He paid every one of them a bounty. He had each of their names enrolled on the roster of prospective royal officers. He ordered the ships' owners paid above the standard freight for the many months their vessels were "employed in his Maties Service att Virginia." He paid to restock each ship's armory and provision store. Generally, King Charles rewarded both captains and owners because he knew that their capitalism would support the imperial absolutism he aimed at (the marriage of capitalism with absolutism is what is termed "mercantilism"). Specifically, this ship-designing, yacht-racing sailor-king appreciated that ships—concentrations of capital, technology, and professional skill—were the sinews of empire. Empire it was that sailed to, conquered, and took command of Virginia in 1676.

Hard pressed to decide whether Baconian independence or Berke-leyan autonomy was more inimical to royal rule, the king and his cabinet sent out fourteen royal ships carrying thirteen hundred regular troops and three crown commissioners to eliminate both. Autonomy and independence were subdued and replaced by an imperial executive, headed by the Grenadier Guards captain, Colonel Herbert Jeffreys. He executed royal orders through an administrative, executive, legislative, and judicial council. Its members were named by the crown, purged of Berkeleyan diehards, and staffed instead with London-linked loyalists or ex–Bacon-ian officers (who proved that there is one conservatism greater than that of successful revolutionaries).

Yet this counter-revolutionary imperial executive responded to the same stimuli as had the revolutionary leadership: the grievances of the people against the Berkeleyans. The only difference between the inde-pendents and the imperialists was the latter's more systematic and assid-uous collection of popular protests and their more effective, constructive, and durable responses to them. Informed by Sir William Berkeley him-self of the "Universal Mutiny" against the "whole Assembly" system of governance, the crown understood that, in addition to the military repres-sion (which it could not afford to continue indefinitely), the king must arrange "a fitt and speedie Redress" for popular problems and that he must institutionalize the continued application of the "Royal Pitie and Compassion."

Royal redress was ordered and princely pardons pronounced in response to the grievances collected by the king's order in the Vir-ginia counties. These catalogues of complaint are a unique record of seventeenth-century American expectations, oligarchical oppressions, and imperial possibilities. Taxation, inequitable and misappropriated, by an assembly expensive and unrepresentative, had failed to secure de-fense either speedy or effective. This was the primary popular protest, the basic cause of Bacon's Revolution. Oligarchical engrossment of land, exaction of fees, exemption from taxation, expropriation of the people's produce, labor, and weapons were the settlers' secondary grievances. For both sets of complaints, the crown commissioners provided or promised royal redress. The upshot was that, for a century to come, the fact of imperial protection procured provincial obedience. As long as its protection seemed essential to settlers in America, obedience would be offered to the English crown. So the ousted oligarchs (and not just in Virginia) correctly anticipated that absolutism was inherent in the symbiosis of popular grievance and royal redress, that autonomy would be eliminated by the interaction of "the Court and the Mob." The ultimate outcome of Bacon's Revolution would be the end of American independence.

Antagonists

At daybreak on Tuesday, 6 June 1676, a sizable sloop wound its way down the James River from "the Curles," bound for Jamestown, the capital of Virginia. On board was the sloop's owner, the frontier hero Nathaniel Bacon (the younger), his crew, and forty of his bodyguards. For leading the unauthorized attacks on the Indians which had made him the idol of his neighbors, Bacon had been ejected from the council of Virginia and declared a rebel. When, victorious against the Ocaneechi, Bacon and his frontier militia emerged from the forest, their grateful countrymen mobbed the county court to prevent the reading of the governor's proclamation outlawing Bacon. Instead, they acclaimed Bacon as their burgess, the representative of Henrico County in the Virginia legislature. The colonial assembly had been convened to deal with the Indian problem, about which Bacon was the frontier expert, but his backers suspected that their outlawed representative might not be welcome in a tidewater town, the capital of an alarmed old governor. Forty of Bacon's soldiers picked up their muskets and a bag of cornmeal apiece and joined their general in his voyage downriver to Jamestown.

General Bacon assured his men that their fears for him were groundless. He had written ahead to the governor, Sir William Berkeley, to say that he counted the governor's "Magistracy Sacred, and the justness of your authority a Sanctuary." Bacon's frontier fighters replied with evidence of the governor's "falsehood, cowardice, Treachery." They reminded Bacon that, when three of his servants had been killed by marauding natives, the governor had said that Bacon had hidden the men in his cellar, as an excuse to plunder innocent Indians. Worse, Bacon's men said, the very weapons used by the murdering natives had been provided by traders licensed by the governor. In order to preserve this unholy exchange, the governor not only denied the frontiersmen permission to protect themselves, or so they said, but warned the Indians of their impending attack. When that attack was organized anyway, the angry governor had declared the militiamen "rude, dissolute & tumultuous outlaws." He had led three hundred upper-class cavalrymen up "to the heads of James and Yorke Rivers, [to] prosecute, pursue, attack, & punish the said mutinous & rebellious psons." Naturally, the English frontiersmen had concluded that Berkeley valued the beaver skins he received from the natives more highly than he did the lives of Englishmen. While they thought of the Indians only in terms of plunder and genocide, the governor dealt with native nations by trade and diplomacy. Now, the frontiersmen joined Bacon in his voyage to Jamestown to see him commissioned by the governor as their general against the Indians and to have themselves enlisted by act of assembly to "ruine and extirpate all Indians in Generall." The governor, however, saw that the frontiersmen aimed as much at his government's authority as at the lives of the Indians. He saw Bacon as a rebel and his guards as a force coming "to surprise me" and to compel the assembly to enact a political revolution under the guise of an Indian war.[1]

The fearful governor was in his seventieth year in 1676. Sir William Berkeley still saw himself, however, and he can still be seen in his portrait, as an active officer of the English civil wars. That portrait, by Lely, still hangs where

> Berkeley's towers appear in martial pride
> Menacing all around the champaign wide

in that famous castle which was the heart of Gloucestershire loyalism in the English Revolution. The Severn sandstone shell of the great keep

1. "A True Narrative of the Rise, Progresse, and Cessation of the Late Rebellion in Virginia," in Charles M. Andrews, ed., *Narratives of the Insurrections 1675–1690* (New York, 1915, 1967), 112, 113–14, here quoted from the original manuscript, Samuel Wiseman's Book of Record, Pepysian Library 2582, Magdalene College, Cambridge, n.p. In Pepys 2582 see Henrico County Grievances, nos. 1, 2, 4. These grievances also appear in British Public Record Office, Colonial Office, Class 1, Group 39, fols. 238–39 (hereafter cited as C.O. 139, 238–39). Proclamation "By his Maties: Governr: & Capt. Genll: of Virginia, 6 May 1676, C.O. 1/37, 1–2. Berkeley [to Thomas Ludwell], 1 July 1676, in Papers Relating to Virginia, Barbados, and Other Colonies, vol. II, September 1675–February 1677, Coventry Manuscripts, Longleat House, Warminster, fol. 144 (hereafter cited as Coventry Ms. 77, 144).

rises red from the rock ridge above the green water meadows of the Doverte Brook. Gap-toothed, broken by Cromwell's cannon, the ancient stronghold of the Berkeleys commemorates the destruction of their traditional rule and that of their aristocratic ilk. The ruin evidences the power of the modern state's impersonal authority. From England's modernizing civil wars Sir William Berkeley had fled to the Old Dominion of Virginia. The statist revolution finally found him there in 1676. His heavy features and a long nose emphasized by a slight mustache and a curly wig, Sir William was patently proud of his Berkeleyan birth, his royalist past, and his present place. With one big hand he clung to a symbol of military command, the baton, while the long fingers of the other hand pointed to his sword. He wore an officer's half-armor and sash. In his early maturity, he had written the frivolous plays and statesmanlike pamphlets suited to his quality. Not so suitable were the vile and vindictive temper, the coarse and abusive language, and the arrogant and overbearing manner of Sir William's nonage.[2]

The governor's excuse for every excess was what he called the "mutinies" of "his subjects." These became more frequent as the successful second generation of Virginia settlers found themselves confined and their futures limited by the fall-line frontier of powerful native nations, by the economic strictures of the Plantations Act of 1673 (which tightened English monopoly of the tobacco trade), by the political rigidification of the Berkeleyan power structure (both at county and colonial levels), and by the defensive costs and shipping losses of the latest of England's wars with the Dutch for Atlantic empire. Fired by the cost of the third Dutch war, county tax revolts erupted at least three times in the three years before 1676. The political importance of these outbreaks was emphasized by the Berkeleyans because, ever since 1663, when the ex–Cromwellian soldiers sold into servitude in Virginia plotted against their masters on the eve of the second Dutch war, Sir William and his coadjutors (the colonial councilors and the county burgesses who, with the governor, constituted "the Grand Assembly") assumed that any foreign invasion of Virginia, by sea or by land, by Europeans or by natives, would excite the laboring classes, both servile and free, to rise against their masters and exploiters.

The Berkeleyans' fears seemed fact when, on 20 September 1673, Cornelius Evertsen's Dutch raiders burned six ships and captured eight of the English tobacco convoy assembling in the James River. Only the desperate valor of the outnumbered English naval escort permitted the bulk of the fleet to escape upriver. For Berkeley and his barons, the

2. Michael Drayton's poem is quoted in V. Sackville-West, *Berkeley Castle* (Derby, n.d.), 2.

loss of their crop cargoes was bad, but the situation ashore was worse. Their efforts to muster the militia against a Dutch landing had demonstrated "our particular disadvantages and disabilities to entertain a Warr." A colony penetrated by four great rivers and bounded by the Chesapeake Bay, and by hundreds of miles of Indian frontier, left Virginia's commanders with many "more Miles to Defend, then wee have men of trust to Defend them, for . . . Wee leave at our backs as Many servants (beside Negroes) as their are freemen to defend the Shoars and all our Frontiers [against] the Indians." Six thousand servants and two thousand slaves composed the unfree laboring population, most of it male. Free adult males numbered about six thousand. A third of these were either single workers "whose labour Will hardly maintaine them" or hopelessly indebted small farmers. The governor and his aides expected slaves, servants, laborers, and small farmers to join any invader "in hopes of bettering their Condition by Sharing the Plunder of the Countrey"—that is, by seizing the property of the large planter-elite patronized and exemplified by Sir William Berkeley.[3]

The Indian invasion of 1676 gave the underlings their long-awaited chance. "How miserable that man is," Governor Berkeley exclaimed, "that Governs a People when Six parts of Seaven at least are Poore Endebted Discontented and Armed and to take away their Armes now the Indians are at our throates were to rayse an Universal Mutiny." Sir William Berkeley realized that "Universal Mutiny" was incipient even as Nathaniel Bacon was out in the woods chasing Indians. The young man's unauthorized attack on the old governor's Indian allies and trading partners was not just a rebuff to Berkeleyan Indian policies and defense schemes but also an assault on the entire established order.[4]

So much became clear after 10 May 1676. First, only men of property obeyed Berkeley's order to desert Bacon's army. Then, the governor's proclamation of Bacon's outlawry so excited the people's hostility that Berkeley had to call the first general election in fourteen years. He even promised to resign the governorship as soon as the king could send out a successor. Finally, on 15 May 1676, the lame-duck governor acceded to the call of his council, withdrew from the falls of the James River, where he had waited with several hundred men to arrest Bacon, and joined the colonial councilors at Green Spring. There, on 29 May 1676, the governor

3. Sir William Berkeley, "An answer to ye inquiries of ye Rt Honble Lords Comrs for forraigne Plantations To ye Govor of Virginia," Pepys 2582. C.O. 1/30, 114–15, quoted in Edmund S. Morgan, *American Slavery American Freedom: The Ordeal of Colonial Virginia* (New York, 1975), 241–42. Morgan's study of the plight of Virginians in 1676 is unequaled.
4. Berkeley to [T. Ludwell], 1 July 1676, Coventry Ms. 77, 145. [Berkeley?] to the sheriff of Rappahannock County, 10 May 1676. C.O. 1/36, 137. See also Additional Manuscripts 38, 694, fol. 9b, British Library (hereafter cited as Add. Ms. 38694, 9b).

threw himself on the mercy of the country. In a defensive declaration Berkeley contrasted Bacon's treason with his own long and distinguished Virginia service. Berkeley did not wait to see if this declaration would influence the assembly elections (one of which indeed sent Bacon down the river from Henrico to Jamestown). Instead, on 1 June 1676, Governor Berkeley put his beloved young wife, Frances née Culpeper, and his treasury of gold and silver plate, on board a ship bound for the safety of London. With Lady Berkeley the governor sent a letter describing the onset of revolution.

"A Young fellow one Bacon," Sir William wrote, "Massinello like infused into the People the great Charge and uselessness of the forts wch our Assembly has most wisely founded to resist the Enemies and tis wonderful What monstrous number of the basest of the People declared for him in lesse than ten dayes in al parts of the Country." The governor recognized that the whole structure of government was under attack by the rebels. "The Rebellion is the more formidable," he wrote, "because it has no ground and is not against any particular Person but the whole Assembly." Berkeley publicly had admitted that "I whom am head of the Assembly may bee their greatest grievance." Now he emphasized his exhaustion and age, and the rising revolution, and concluded, "I am so over wearied with riding into al parts of the Country to stop this Violent Rebellion *that I am not able to support my self at this Age six months longer and therefore on my knees I beg his sacred majesty would send a more Vigorous Gouernor.*"[5]

Tax Revolt

The old governor's description of the growing rebellion was at once overpersonalized—Berkeley versus Bacon—and overgeneralized— the assembly versus the rabble. It was money rather than men, and a specific grievance rather than general social discontent, that triggered the Chesapeake revolution. When the Long Assembly of 1662–75 learned that royal grants of land and authority in Virginia to English proprietors had

5. Berkeley to Coventry, 3 June 1676, Coventry Ms. 77, 103. Italics in original. "Sir William Berkeley's Declaration," 29 May [1676], *ibid.*, 181. See also Egerton Manuscripts 2395, 537, British Library.

challenged the property and power of "the Grand Assembly of the Governor, Councill and Burgesses," it decided to finance an agency to buy out the proprietary claimants. To this end, the assembly levied a head tax of 60 pounds of tobacco per poll. This was the tax that "occasioned the first Discontents among the People," because of both its amount and its misappropriation. By June 1676, the "agency" tax had raised between £5,000 and £7,000 sterling. About £5,000 of this money was allocated by Berkeley's assembly to the governor's personal use or to the use of assemblymen and other allies of the Berkeleyan regime, not to the agency in England. At the most generous estimate, less than £2,000 of the head tax was actually spent for its lawful and public purpose: to buy back Virginia from the proprietors. In fact, none of the money was needed for that purpose, since the vacation of the proprietary grants was ordered by James duke of York without cost to the colony. The commons of Virginia neither knew the details of the misappropriation of their taxes nor had heard of the duke's bounty in June 1676, but they already, universally, correctly suspected that "the said 120 lb Tobacco Tax p. pole was a Cheate and Oppressive."[6]

"Oppressive" the 60-pound tax was, for it was the highest single item in the regressive and repressive poll-tax system. It exceeded even the cost of keeping a county's burgesses (and their servants) drinking and drabbing in Jamestown, that "little sodom" on the river. Together with the agency tax and their own expenses, the Long Assembly's session for March 1675 had also authorized the third most hated Virginia tax, the fort levy. The taxpaying planters observed that these forts "were made of mud and dirt & soe of noe use or Continuance yet of great charge to ye People yt paid for ym" and of equal profit to their cheating contractors (invariably assemblymen) and to their absentee commanders (ditto).[7]

In June of 1676, crown counselors in London observed Virginians' "annual taxes to be very high." Those taxes had been increased every year in every jurisdiction, "publique [i.e., colony], countie & parishe." Only the poorer planters were so burdened, however, for the governor, the councilors, and the clergy of the Church of England all were exempt from poll taxes on themselves, their sons, their servants, and their slaves. The burgesses each received from tax revenues some combination of salary, expense account, gift, contract, and militia officer's pay which much exceeded their poll taxes. The basic county levy, which averaged 250 pounds of tobacco per poll, was paid by unprivileged planters for

6. Virginia agents to the king, 19–23 June 1675, "Heads [for] a Charter for Virginia," "Reasons . . . which caused the Assembly of that Government to Send their Agents," 23 June 1675, C.O. 1/34, 200, 205, 207. Gloucester County Grievances, C.O. 1/39, 243. Thomas Ludwell to Coventry, 21 November 1676, Coventry Ms. 77, 299.
7. Stafford County Grievances, 8 [?] March 1676/7, C.O. 1/39, 205.

themselves, for each of their sons over the age of sixteen, for all male servants they might possess, and for every slave.[8]

Oppressive in amount, misappropriated in practice, the tax burden was doubled by the Berkeleyan method of assessment. The justices of the peace (appointed by the governor to govern the counties, to hold virtually every civil and military office of influence, and so to be the natural monopolists of assembly seats) valued the tobacco offered as tax payments by poor planters at only 8 shillings per hundredweight, then sold the tax tobacco at the market price of 16 shillings. The county chieftains doubled the nominal tax rate, for the planter had to pay twice as much tobacco to make up the levy; and the assessment method quadrupled the tax income at the government's disposal, for doubled payments were sold at doubled prices.

Tax after tax "which wee groan under this many years being not further able to bear it" bore down on the unprivileged planters in 1676. Agents' and burgesses' allowances, fort taxes, fees for the colonial secretary and the county sheriff, clerk, and coroner, the parish levy, the county tax, militia fines, and powder dues all were direct taxes on the planter for the benefit of the ruling class of Berkeleyan officeholders. Then there were the indirect taxes, assessed in Virginia, supposedly to support the colonial government, certainly at the planter's cost. These included the 2 shillings per hogshead and the penny per pound both paid on tobacco exported, and the castle duty assessed on incoming ships. Supposedly this duty was paid in gunpowder for Virginia's defense. Actually it was paid in "Shoes Stockens Linnen and other merchantable goods" which the collectors sold as the profit of their office. Finally, crushingly, most Virginians must have known that the crown collected more customs duties on their crop in England than they received for it in Virginia.[9]

The domestic taxes alone amounted to something between one-quarter and one-half of the average planter's income. They were exacted from men who, in the drought year of 1676, could not grow tobacco enough to buy clothes for their families. Perhaps they could not feed them. These ordinary planters had been close to starvation as recently as 1674. Then "mutinies" against the agency tax broke out, provoked, as the indignant Sir William Berkeley wrote, by "villaines" who told "the People that there was nothing entended by the fifty [sic] pound leavy but the enriching of some few people." In the next two years, Indian attacks had prevented upcountry planters from making anything like a full corn crop,

8. Virginia agents, "Exp. to 7th Head" of the charter, Coventry Ms. 77, 48. "Considerations upon the present troubles in Virginia," [April 1676,] C.O. 1/36, 113–14. "James Citty County Grievances Presented (by Col. Robt. Holt & Mr. William Sherwood)," 15 March 1676/7. C.O. 1/39, 194. New Kent Grievances, 2 April 1677, ibid., 233.
9. To the citations in note 8, add: Isle of Wight Grievances, n.d., C.O. 1/39, 228.

and the New England grain that had carried the Virginians through the famine in 1674 was lost to King Philip's warriors in 1675.[10]

Even in good years, peaceful years, the ordinary planter subsisted mostly on hand-mortared Indian corn and water. Occasionally beef was available after midsummer, "when the beasts have some meat on their backs." Planters butchered a bit of pork in the fall and killed some game during the winter to augment their stored corn. Nevertheless, in the winter season at least, Virginia's laborers, free or not, were not "allowed meate three dayes in the week" and so fared worse than West Indian slaves. Without money enough to buy food themselves, the planters could not afford to pay their rulers' taxes. Even the gentlemen, the rich outsiders and newcomers, who led Virginia's revolution in 1676 and who were tax-exempt or benefited, agreed that, as the bulk of their followers, small planters oppressed by Berkeleyan privilege, put it, "the cause of our rising" was "to have our taxes lowered."[11]

Writing as of 1 July 1676, Sir William Berkeley reiterated the relation of taxation to revolution. The commons were ready to mutiny over the 60- (Berkeley again said "50-") pound agency tax. They had little stake in the outcome of the agency. The loss to English proprietors of ungranted land (and fees and offices connected with land grants) which the agency was supposedly to prevent was of little concern to men at or below subsistence level. They were not in the land market, nor did they hold office. Taxing them to preserve the landed and official ambitions of the oligarchy merely added new fiscal injury to existing economic degradation. Then too, Berkeley wrote, the overtaxed and impoverished commons were alarmed by news of New England's devastation by the Indians: they were fed from the north; they preferred Yankee peddlers and low-priced goods to big planter shops and London shoddy; they rejoiced in the small-lot purchases and high prices paid by the New Englanders (who bought for European markets and evaded English customs); they feared that the great Indian insurrection would spread south from New England.

Governor Berkeley thought that it had. Therefore, Baconian agitators told the people, the fearful old executive would have the assembly authorize a frontier fort tax assessed at 1,000 pounds of tobacco per poll. "If they had not Tobb[acco] enough to pay these new taxes," Sir William was quoted as saying, "they had Cowes and porker herds sufficient to discharge their leavies." Such agitators or "News wives" as Mrs. Grindon

---

10. Berkeley [Thomas Ludwell, 1 April 1676], C.O. 1/36, 67, 16 February [1675/6], Coventry Ms. 77, 56. "An abstract to the governor," 16 February 1675/6, *ibid.*, 144. Berkeley [to Thomas Ludwell], 1 July 1676, *ibid.*, 145. For printed versions of these materials, see *The Virginia Magazine of History and Biography* 20 (1912): 243–46, 247, 248–49 (hereafter cited as V.M.H.B.), and *The William and Mary Quarterly*, 3rd ser., 14 (1957): 403–13.

11. Lancaster County Grievances, C.O. 1/39, 217. Isle of Wight Grievances, *ibid.*, 223.

and Mrs. Stagg "told hundreds," as Berkeley complained, "that I was a greater friend to the Indians than to the English," loving the fur trade more than he did planter lives, and therefore unlikely to spend the new fort levy any more effectively than he had the old ones. The result of the agency tax, of the Indian insurgency spreading south from New England, of the feared costs of its repression by the corrupt and inefficient government of Virginia, of the political direction given all this by Baconian news wives, was, as Sir William wrote, social revolt by the poor against the privileged: "through the whole Country and in every part the Rabble so threatened the better sort of people that they durst not step out of their house." Bacon had organized an army from the people whom his agitators had taught to say "damne al leavies and forts and Assembles not Chosen by the People but by a few men." Protests against taxes became a revolt against government. Both were intensified by a military crisis.[12]

Militia Mutiny and Indian War

If the first face of Virginia's revolution was a tax revolt, primarily a protest by coastal counties against a gouging government, its other aspect was a military mutiny, the frontier counties' response to antique and inequitable defense policies. The government that cannot protect its people cannot command their obedience. Berkeley's government could not protect Virginians in 1676 so they overthrew it.

Sir William's prior popularity was premised on his share of Virginia's victory in the second war with the Powhatan Confederacy, 1644–49. In twenty-one subsequent years he learned nothing and forgot nothing. His assembly's defense act of March 1675 simply repeated the protective program of 1644: neighboring natives were to be subdued by extending the plantation line across their territory; this extension was to be based on land grants and fort subsidies; land and cash were to attract the brutal energies of planter-entrepreneurs and the militant manpower of their servants and clients; their new plantations were to be the bases of a fortified-hamlet defense system. Once again, the governor thought, planter-captains and servant-soldiers would conduct search-and-destroy missions against the fields and villages of agrarian, sedentary natives.

Berkeley could not successfully repeat this prescription from 1646–49

12. Berkeley [to Thomas Ludwell], 1 July 1676, Coventry Ms. 77, 144–45.

A Mapp of Virginia Mary-land, New-Jarsey, New-York, & New England. By John Thornton at the Sundyall in the Minories and by Robert Greene at ye Rose and Crowne, in Budg-rowe. London.

in 1675–76 because of the changed nature both of Virginia's plantation frontier and of the natives it now confronted. Yet, in 1675 as in 1644, the governor pledged public payments to finance frontier forts and to subsidize their garrisons. Now, however, the population was more highly taxed and more politically active than that of 1644. The fort-building entrepreneurs, if not actually more privileged politically and less useful militarily than their predecessors had been, were described as such by their new competitors: well-financed, liberally educated, English-connected immigrants, most of them newly established either in the colonial capital or near the heads of settlements on every river.

Apart from the domestic challenge of an aggrieved population led by ambitious and accomplished newcomers, the Berkeleyan barons had also to resist a novel, mobile, native enemy, against whom the static defense of forts and fortified plantations was of no avail. Back in 1644, the agrarian Algonquins of the coastal plain had been vulnerable to seasonal attacks on their fields and villages by the colonial garrisons of palisaded plantations. By 1675, however, the English plantations had spread beyond the defensible necks and peninsulas of the Tidewater and had approached "the warriors' road," the great north-south trail network across the Virginia Piedmont along which natives traveled to fight and to hunt, to trade and to negotiate. Of these sophisticated, mobile, materialist, and aggressive peoples, the most dangerous were Iroquoian.

On the northern and western reaches of the Chesapeake's tributary rivers, the Susquehanna Iroquois were fighting their last campaign as "the bloodiest fighters" and greatest traders of the east. Greatest of the Peoples of the Fall Line ("Susquehannock" means "people at the falls" or "roily water people"), the Susquehanna had entered written history as John Smith's "giant like people" in 1609, as Samuel de Champlain's allies against the Five Nations of the Iroquois in 1615, and as the middlemen of the New Amsterdam trade from 1626 on, in competition with their kinsmen, the easternmost of the Five Nations, the Mohawk Iroquois. When the Dutch conquered New Sweden in 1655, the Susquehanna took over the trade of the Delaware. This removed them from direct competition with the Mohawk, with whom the Susquehanna now made peace after forty years of fighting over access to European trade. Their need for furs and markets among the tribes of the Ohio Valley and the Lake Erie Plain, however, forced the Susquehanna to challenge the claims on this commerce made by the remaining four nations of the Iroquoian League of Peace. These four fires of the league's longhouse were known collectively to their European contemporaries as the "Cinnique," or Seneca, afterwards a name reserved for the most numerous nation of the longhouse people.

Decades of desperate fighting with the collective "Seneca"—during

the last of which the Susquehanna drove the two smallest league nations
north right across Lake Ontario but were themselves besieged repeatedly
in their riverine capital—combined with a shift southward to the Chesapeake of the major sources of their trade goods, finally led the Susquehanna to accept the invitation of Maryland's deputy governor (and
proprietor-to-be), Charles Calvert, to move their main village to the site
of a substantial fort recently evacuated by Maryland's allies, the Piscataway, sited where the creek of that name joins the Potomac River, near
the falls of the Potomac. This southward migration of the Susquehanna,
at the invitation of a colony they had defeated only twenty years earlier,
brought them into collision with the Potomac frontiers of both Maryland
and Virginia settlement as these reached the fall line. The "Seneca"
pursuit of the Susquehanna into this debated zone made likely conflict
into inescapable war, for the northern nations expected unquestioning
hospitality from all the Susquehanna's neighbors, red and white. Instead,
the Chesapeake peoples, European and Indian alike, resisted this southward expansion of the league's sphere of influence. Both were attacked
by the Seneca war parties.[13]

Imperial frontier wars unprecedented in Virginia required military
remedies new to the Old Dominion, although the required tactics had
been in use for nearly a generation in Europe, where the ambitious
immigrants of Nathaniel Bacon's ilk had been educated. Marshal Tu-
renne's tactics in the French civil war of the Fronde—a mobile army led
by an active general and his regional deputies—were called for by the
frontier fighters. So organized and led, they hoped to subdue local Algonquin aliens and to resist vengeful Iroquoian raiders. But the mobilization
of the frontier militias by General Bacon and his Cromwellian confederates had been labeled rebellion by Governor Berkeley and his councilors.
"Oh Heavens! what a sad Dilemma!" wrote the Baconian frontiersmen;
"if to unite and meet or find out ye Enemy with a Considerable Body of
troops, and do what is requisite thereunto for our present Necessary
Preservation Safety without the ye Governors Order . . . shall be censured [as] a Mutiny or Rebellion and disobedience, when on the other
side to lay down our Guns and disperse . . . Expos'd ye Lives and fortunes of ourselves and families to ye merciless Power of a most bloudy
and Barbarous Enemy." No lawful course was to be found between revolt
against the governor and ruin by the Indians.[14]

By May of 1676, to make security legal, the Baconian army moved

13. Francis Jennings, "Susquehannock," in William C. Sturtevant, gen. ed., *Handbook of
North American Indians,* vol. 15, *Northeast,* ed. Bruce G. Trigger (Washington, 1978); see
especially 363. See Book III, below, for additional discussion of the Susquehanna.
14. "The Virginians Plea for Opposing ye Indians without ye Governors Order," C.O.
1/37, 29.

from fighting to politics. "We cannot deny but that we have vented our Discontents," the army spokesmen admitted, "in complaints of other Grievances also too great to be wholly Smother'd." Fort frauds and the fur trade, legislative salaries and county misgovernment were added to Berkeleyan failures of command "yt tended to protect and cherish ye Enemy and hinder our opposing them," in the litany of the volunteer soldiers' protest. Yet the army disclaimed any intent to "relieve our Selves by ye Sword from any Pressures in Government (much less to alter it) as Some would charge us most unjustly with." Every grievance not connected with defense they referred to the determination of the "Governor and Grand Assembly of Parlmt." To it they sent their spokes-man, General Bacon. Once the assembly reformed county and colonial politics, deregulated the fur trade, and provided for defense by legiti-mizing the frontier army and persuading the governor to commission Nathaniel Bacon as its general, the soldiers promised to demonstrate that they abhorred "all Mutiny and Rebellion or Opposition and Disturbance to Government and Magistracy whose authority we Revere as Sacred." And the frontiersmen promised that their loyalty would extend beyond a reformed and militarized colonial government to the defense of the em-pire itself—that is, of "His Maty's Right in this Colony of Virginia." [15]

Conspirators

A popular general and his politicized bodyguard, their demands for reform and their pledges of loyalty, freighted Nathaniel Bacon's sloop as she carried the half-tide eddy downriver around Swan's Point and, late on the afternoon of 6 June 1676, anchored across the river from Jamestown, meetingplace of the "Governor and Grand Assembly of Parlmt.," and of the conspirators against both.

Some of Bacon's crew rowed a boat over to the colonial capital to ask if their leader might safely take his seat in the assembly. They did not return, but the cannon of Jamestown's Brick Fort answered their ques-tion. Bacon's men cut the anchor cable and their sloop was carried up-stream on the first of the flood. As the sloop slipped past Sandy Bay, the anchorage above Jamestown, some of the ships moored there fired their

15. *Ibid.*

"great guns" at her, but Bacon and his men escaped unscathed into the evening. When the tide turned, Bacon brought his sloop back downriver. They rode the ebb tide right into Sandy Bay. Thence small boats landed the general and his guards on the beach outside Jamestown.

In the first hour of Wednesday, 7 June 1676, Nathaniel Bacon and his bodyguards walked uptown, through the Market Square, to the fine house of Richard Lawrence, the Oxford-educated burgess for Jamestown. Lawrence's education, his mercantile skill, his cynicism about Sir William Berkeley and his colonial coterie—for he "had been partially treated at Law for a Considerable Estate on behalf of a Corrupt favourite"—combined with his hospitality to attract the "best Quality" of burgesses to stay at Lawrence's house in "public times." So many legislators stayed there that the Lawrence mansion is remembered as an inn. Certainly it was the resort of the new generation of well-connected English emigrants whose path to power seemed blocked by the antiquated or provincial cronies of the old governor. A "country" opposition to the Berkeleyan "court" was formed (in the paradoxically urban way that "country" oppositions had) in the Lawrence town house. A politically astute visitor to Jamestown observed that Lawrence "made his Converse Coveted by Persons of all Ranks, so that, being Subtile, and having those advantages [of education and wealth, hospitality and hostility] he might with less Difficulty discover mens Inclinations and Instill his Notions where he found these wou'd be imbib'd with greatest Satisfaction." [16]

William Drummond was one of those who "imbib'd with greatest Satisfaction" Lawrence's notions about the cultivated qualities and virtuous conduct which country theory required of able and just rulers, notions which Lawrence's faction found lacking in the Berkeleyan courtiers. A Scot who had governed the Albemarle region of Carolina from 1664 to 1667, Drummond had quarreled with Sir William Berkeley (a proprietor of the province) about Berkeley's speculative land grants in Albemarle. Then Drummond had retired to Jamestown, where he had challenged Berkeley's corrupt contracts for the coastal "forts" (which were paid for by the people but never built by the Berkeleyans). Drummond had not lost touch with the Albemarle anti-Berkeleyans either. John Culpeper, their leader, was seen in Jamestown, conferring with Drummond, just a few days before Drummond joined Lawrence and Bacon during the early-morning hours of 7 June 1676. Like Lawrence, Drummond was an attractive political leader. In him, it was said, "wis-

16. T[homas] M[athew], "The Beginning, Progress, and Conclusion of Bacon's Rebellion, 1675–1676," in Andrews, ed., *Narratives*, 27, 40–41.

dom and honisty" were "contending for superiority." Certainly Drummond would contend with Berkeley in the assembly, in which he, with Lawrence, represented Jamestown.[17]

The new representative from Henrico, Nathaniel Bacon, fit perfectly into the Lawrence set of well-educated, well-to-do, well-spoken dissidents. "Tall, slender, blackhaired," his face full of foreboding, Bacon was a reserved man. When he spoke, however, he revealed a pragmatism so extreme that his elders in Virginia called him an atheist. The biting particularity of his language—contemporaries called it "precision"—revealed to them Bacon's "imperious and dangerous hidden Pride of heart." The old standers in Virginia were wounded by this young man's superiority. They accused him of "despising the wisest of his neighbours for their Ignorance." Bacon was, they said, at once "ambitious and arrogant."

His was the arrogance of ancient privilege and the ambition bred of its frustration. Nathaniel Bacon had been born to a most eminent East Anglian family in 1647, that too-brief year of truce between the first and second English civil wars. He grew up in the rambling structures of Freestone or "Friston" Hall, surrounded by his father's ample Suffolk estates and the ideas of his kinsmen and namesake (a leading country theorist in the struggle against King Charles I's court) who was Oliver Cromwell's master of requests, and whose discourse on the government of England was reissued in London in 1676 to unite the "country" programs of the English and the Virginian enemies of Stuart sovereignty.[18]

In May 1660, Cromwell and his patronage chief having died, Charles Stuart was restored to his father's throne and Nathaniel Bacon followed his father to Cambridge. Bacon matriculated at St. Catherine's Hall and studied there for two and a half years. Then, "having broken into some extravagances," Bacon was withdrawn from Cambridge. The eminent young scientist and linguist John Ray, who was retained as his tutor at Freestone Hall, found Bacon bright but inattentive and, after a winter of study, Ray took Bacon, two older students, and their attendants off for a grand tour of Europe in April 1663. Three years later, en route to Rome after an exhaustive tour of the Netherlands, the principalities of the Rhine, and the cities of Austria and northern Italy, Bacon, aged nineteen, contracted smallpox at Bologna. Although he recovered and rejoined his party at Venice in February 1666, Bacon's father took the occasion of the

17. [Richard Lee,] "The History of Bacon's and Ingram's Rebellion, 1676," in Andrews, ed., *Narratives*, 97.
18. The Royal Commissioners, "A True Narrative," in Andrews, ed., *Narratives*, 110; Privy Council Register 2/66, 137, Public Record Office (hereafter cited as P.C. 2/66, 137), calendared in John Neville Davenport, comp., *Bacon's Rebellion Abstracts of Materials in the Colonial Records Project* (Jamestown, Virginia, [1976]), 191. And see Book II, note 49.

illness to recall his son and set him to complete the traditional curing of
Bacons. After two further years of study at Cambridge, Bacon took his
M.A. degree in 1668, then he moved his residence to Gray's Inn, London.
There he followed his famous forebear, the lord chancellor, on the list of
the forty-eight Bacons who had read law at the Inn. "By his long study in
the Inns of Court," Nathaniel Bacon, to his title of "gentleman . . . added
that of Esquire." [19]

Adorned with many elaborate qualifications, the young squire returned home to court Elizabeth, daughter of Sir Edward Duke. They
married in May of 1670. Such was Sir Edward's aversion to Bacon that
immediately he disinherited his daughter and never spoke to her again.
Sir Edward's worst suspicions about his son-in-law were soon confirmed:
Nathaniel Bacon became a confidence man. He was exposed and exiled
to Virginia. As one discreet contemporary put it, young Bacon "could not
contain himself within bounds; which his careful Father perceiving, and
also that he had a mind to Travel (having seen divers part of the World
before) consented to his inclination of going to *Virginia*, and accommodated him with a Stock for that purpose, to the value of 1800 £
Sterling. . . ."

Now aged twenty-seven, Bacon, with bride and baggage, landed in
August 1674 at King's Creek, York River, Virginia, the home of Bacon's
fifty-four-year-old cousin and namesake, the Virginia councilor and colonel Nathaniel Bacon. Before the end of the month Colonel Bacon arranged his kinsman's purchase (from another councilor and colonel,
Thomas Ballard) of an old plantation at "Curles Neck," a high and healthy
freshwater homesite some 40 miles up the James River from the pestilen-
tial colonial capital. Bacon also bought undeveloped lands farther
upriver. The westernmost of these were at the Falls of the James, the
frontier of English settlement in Virginia and the site of present-day
Richmond. On 3 March 1674/5, only six months after Bacon took up his
residence on the narrow, winding reaches of the upper James, Sir William
Berkeley named him "to be of the Council." Three days later, Bacon took
his seat in the statehouse. This was an astounding elevation, for the
twenty-eight-year-old newcomer entered a regime afflicted with rigor
mortis. Bacon took little advantage of his place, however. He missed
altogether the council meetings of June 1675. He sat for but one day in
the September session, and only half a day longer in March 1675/6. It was

19. The quotations here are taken from "Strange News from Virginia" (London, 1677), 8–9,
reprinted in Harry Finestone, ed., *Bacon's Rebellion The Contemporary News Sheets* (Charlottesville, Va., 1956), but I must also acknowledge my deep indebtedness to the master of
Virginia's seventeenth-century history, Thomas Jefferson Wertenbaker, and to his much-
maligned study, *Torchbearer of the Revolution, The Story of Bacon's Rebellion and Its
Leader* (Princeton, 1940; Gloucester, 1965).

then that Bacon heard Sir William Berkeley announce the policy of forti-
fying the frontier against the Susquehanna.

Whatever Bacon thought at first about this revival of the ancient policy
of plantation by privileged proprietors to penetrate, conquer, and develop
Indian lands, its futility against the hostile, homeless, militant Susquehanna was brought home to him within the month. First, these Indians
murdered Bacon's overseer at the Falls farm. Then they killed three of
his servants. Bacon's terrified neighbors asked him to give them the leadership against these Indians that Sir William Berkeley had denied them.
The governor's subsequent refusal to commission Bacon, added to his
unwillingness to muster the frontier militia against the natives, both provoked the young man's thwarted ambitions and challenged his ruling-
class responsibility. Bacon led his neighbors against the Indians. For this
latest episode in a life determined by defiances of authority, Bacon was
outlawed by Berkeley.

Raised in an atmosphere of country resistance to the court, personally
"heedless" and defiant, a sophisticated young man of cosmopolitan education exiled to the frontiers of the English empire, frontiers which he
found misgoverned by the Berkeley geritocracy and its cloddish, corrupt,
colonial courtiers, Nathaniel Bacon summarized the challenges which
cast down the American colonial autarchies in 1676. With Lawrence and
Drummond, Bacon embodied Governor Berkeley's fears about reading
and rebellion, fears about the transition from traditional to modern societies which came to colonial America, late but irreversibly, in 1676. "I
thanke God . . . there is noe free schooles nor printing" in Virginia, Sir
William had written, "and I hope wee shall not have these hundred
yeares, for learninge hath brought disobedience and herisie and Sects
into ye World, and printing has divulged them and Libells against ye best
Government. God keep us from both." The governor could prevent public education and printing in the colony of Virginia, but he could not
forever exclude the educated men and political texts of England. In 1676
they brought the principles of the English Revolution to the Old Dominion.[20]

Insisting on reformed and responsible government, these "country"
principles gave national and radical shapes to the past thirteen years of
sporadic armed opposition to Berkeleyan taxation and dictation, corruption and privilege. This necessary and proper opposition, the conspirators
at Lawrence's house agreed, now had been propelled into a popular
rebellion by the failure of the colonial elite to defend the people from

20. Berkeley's report of 21 June 1671, "An answer to ye inquiries," Pepys 2582, has been
often remarked—most recently, and in terms that would have pleased Wertenbaker, by
Richard L. Morton, in *Colonial Virginia* (Chapel Hill, 1960), I, 224.

the worst war with the natives in thirty years. "Frequent, Horrid and barbarous Murthers" had been committed "by the pfidious Indians," and "the Manifold Rapine and depredations by them" were known to everyone but the governor. "Still Expectinge releife," the people found "noe order taken" by Berkeley's government to protect them, save the outmoded policy of fortified hamlets.[21]

The Indian war had consumed Virginians by the hundreds, the conspirators believed, but the governor's only response to the slaughter had been to approve the construction of "forts back in the woods upon Severall great mens Lands, under pretence of service for us against the Indians." These were useful, the dissidents agreed, only as the centers of new plantations, paid for by an already overtaxed public, to benefit the governor's "Corrupt favourites," "the Grandees." Against these provincial grafters, the conspirators measured themselves: some were newly arrived from England, most were men of wealth and education, but now that Bacon had been outlawed, all were excluded from the inner circle of the old governor's favorites. The outsiders considered what reforms might be achieved under their principled "country" leadership by the legislature now assembling, the first newly elected assembly in fourteen years. All of its members had been chosen by the freemen—not just the landowners—of Virginia's counties, and the freemen were boiling over with resentment against hostile Indians and exploitative planters, failed defenses and high taxes.[22]

A revolutionary agenda was set by such free men, even before the assembly of June 1676 met, for they composed the volunteer army. They had volunteered when Bacon "raised forces by beat of drum." They called him "Generall." From their first enlistment, the volunteers' objectives for General Bacon's army were not just military, to kill Indians, but also, as the Berkeleyans thought, political and social. By overawing the legislature, Bacon's army would achieve "ye subvercon of the Laws and to Levell all." The old order knew itself to be in mortal danger from the new forces in Virginia politics, the freshly elected burgesses, the frontier army, and its general. General Bacon had come to Jamestown to fulfill the program of his troops: "the Rabble giveing out they will have their owne Laws demanding ye Militia to be settled in ym with such like rebellious practices." Rebellion was manifest not only in criticism of the assembly's insulation from the people and in condemnation of the governor's military command, but by a demand for thoroughgoing reform of the Berkeleyan county regimes: "all authority Magistracy are by ye rab-

---

21. New Kent Grievances, 2 April 1677, C.O. 1/39, 233.

22. Isle of Wight Grievances, C.O. 1/39, 223, 226. See also Nancymond First Grievances, *ibid.*, 246; "Nathaniel Bacon Esqr. his manifesto concerning the Present troubles in Virginia," C.O. 1/37, 178.

ble contemmed." So fearing, the governor and his advisers had armed themselves, garrisoned Jamestown, and waited for the rebel general to sail into their hands. They would seize him when he tried to take his assembly seat and make him "answer to the great charge agt him with his life."[23]

Flight and Forgiveness

D espite this danger, the first light of 7 June 1676 found Bacon still at Lawrence's house. He fled dawn and discovery along the Great Road towards Sandy Bay. As he hurried towards his boats, Bacon's guards fell in around him. They heard the drums beat the alarm in the town behind them. In the flat calm of dawn, Bacon boarded the sloop while his men in the oared boats tried to tow it upriver towards the safety of the Baconian backcountry. Before they could clear the bay, however, Major Howe, the sheriff of James City County, appeared on the deck of the ship *Adam & Eve* of London (Thomas Gardiner, master) with the governor's warrant for Bacon's arrest in his hand. At the sheriff's order, a ragged broadside fired at Bacon's sloop from the *Adam & Eve* forced her to anchor. In the face of her crew of armed frontiersmen, however, there was some hesitation about seizing the rebel general. Finally, late in the afternoon, two English sea captains, Thomas Gardiner and Hubert Farrill, led their boats' crews aboard the sloop, having given the fugitives time to realize that, under the guns of the tobacco fleet, they had no choice but to surrender or to be sunk. That evening the prisoners were rowed to Jamestown. When, on the morning of Thursday, 9 June 1676, Thomas Mathew, a burgess from Northumberland County, concluded his week-long voyage from the Potomac to Jamestown, he "was welcomed with the strange Acclamations of 'All's over Bacon is taken.' "[24] But the shots from the *Adam & Eve* had begun, not ended, Virginia's revolution.

Before noon on Friday, 10 June 1676, Virginia's burgesses assembled in their second-floor chamber in the statehouse. As was customary, in Virginia as in England, the legislators elected the executive's nominee as their speaker. Then they trooped downstairs to the general court chamber to hear Governor Berkeley's opening address. He berated the northern

---

23. William Sherwood to Joseph Williamson, [1] June 1676, *V.M.H.B.* 1 (1893): 169.
24. M[athew], "Bacon's Rebellion," in Andrews, ed., *Narratives,* 22.

burgesses, for their attack on the Susquehanna had begun the Indian war. He warned all the burgesses against the machinations of "two evil men" among them (he meant Lawrence and Drummond). He then called in the rebel prisoner, Nathaniel Bacon. Before the burgesses and council of Virginia, Sir William accepted Bacon's confession, delivered on his knees, "that I have been Guilty of diverse low (unlawful mutinouse) Rebellious Practices Contrary to my duty to his most Sacred Maties Governor of this Country, vizt beating up of drums raising of men in Armes, marching with them." Berkeley then accepted Bacon's bond for £2,000 to keep the peace and promised Bacon that, if he behaved himself for a fortnight after the assembly ended, the governor would then commission him to raise and lead forces against the Indians. Finally, as if to seal his pardon and his promise, Sir William Berkeley restored Nathaniel Bacon to his council.[25]

The burgesses were astounded by the governor's leniency. They soon realized, however, that Berkeley had pardoned Bacon only because the local militia had been slow to reinforce the Jamestown garrison while Bacon's followers had swarmed to town "armed and resolute to rescue him out of our hands," as Berkeley wrote. Learning that their leader was pardoned, the countrymen left Jamestown as quickly as they had come. Yet "Great comotions, wch now Grew high & ffierce," continued to stir the counties towards revolution and to agitate the counsels of the elite assembled in Jamestown.[26]

Berkeley's defense against revolution, like Bacon's advocacy of it, focused on the assembly. First, Berkeley hoped that by restoring Bacon to its upper house, the council, he could, as he did, inveigle Bacon's armed supporters away from the capital, control their general's legislative action in the council, and separate the popular leader from the newly elected lower house. After he isolated Nathaniel Bacon, the governor exerted his legislative prerogative, stopping the burgesses' investigation of his government's fiscal records, and denying the legislators' furious demands that he permit them to revise the poll tax. He ordered them instead to debate only defense measures. To direct the defense debate, Berkeley dispatched selected members of his council to sit with the burgesses. The governor's men secured a bill that declared war against enemy Indians only (not against all natives, as the frontiersmen had asked), to be fought by troops drafted from the county militias (not by volunteers, as the upcountrymen had insisted), and which would be financed by poll taxes, paid in tobacco, assessed by the governor's justices

25. "A List of ye Names of those [of] . . . approved Loyalltie, Constancy and Courage," Pepys 2582. Bacon's confession, 9 June 1676, Coventry Ms. 77, 116.

26. Berkeley [to Thomas Ludwell], 1 July 1676, Coventry Ms. 77, 144–45. Philip Ludwell to Joseph Williamson, 28 June 1676, C.O. 1/37, 37, printed in V.M.H.B. 1 (1893): 183.

of the peace, and collected by his sheriffs (rather than, as the dissidents demanded, financed by estate taxes, payable in produce, assessed by locally elected boards, and collected by newly commissioned, single-term sheriffs). With the war bill, Berkeley defused the opposition by making a show of defense, captured control of the newly elected burgesses through his own commands and his councilors' committee-work, and reaffirmed the old order in its poll taxes, county offices, and militia structures. Virginia's *ancien régime*, it seemed, had triumphed. It only remained to deal with "General" Bacon.

Nathaniel Bacon saw that, with his backcountry bodyguard and backers dismissed from Jamestown and the governor in control of the assembly, as soon as Sir William could prorogue the legislature, he would be rearrested and condemned to death by that "Old Treacherous Villain." So sure was Berkeley that he had the situation in hand that he moved up his murderous timetable. On the evening of 11 June 1676, the governor wrote out the warrant for Bacon's arrest and dispatched messengers by horse and boat to order the militia colonels on both sides of the lower James River to march or ship their men to Jamestown to protect the capital from the rebellion that surely would follow Bacon's execution. Before daybreak on 12 June, Berkeley's men broke into Lawrence's house to arrest Bacon for treason, but he had been forewarned by his cousin and namesake, Berkeley's trusted councilor. At daybreak "a Brult ran about the town, 'Bacon is fled, Bacon is fled.' " Learning that he had struck too late, Sir William Berkeley had his Jamestown treasury ferried out to join his wife and his plate aboard Captain Christopher Evelyn's *Rebecca* in Sandy Bay, and he booked passage for himself. He planned to sail for England within ten days, hoping to escape the "approaching Conflagration." [27]

Coup

The governor had underestimated by half the speed at which the flames of revolution were approaching the colonial capital. Just five days after Bacon's escape from Jamestown, word reached it "that Mr. Bacon was 30 Miles up the River, at the head of four hundred Men." Only

27. M[athew], "Bacon's Rebellion," in Andrews, ed., *Narratives*, 27. Philip to Thomas Ludwell, 13 June 1676, Coventry Ms. 77, 121.

a day later, Bacon's "greate number of necessitated and desp'ate p'sons" was put at five hundred and they were reportedly marching east on Jamestown. Fearing that the frontiersmen's politics were as radical as their poverty was deep—that their "fortunes & Inclinations were equally desperate"—the Berkeleyans assumed that Bacon's men intended to "have all magistracy & government taken away and set up one themselves." Even worse than a political revolution was an economic one, and the governor's men were told that the upcountry army "talk openly of sharing men's estates among themselves."[28]

Sir William Berkeley's movable estate was already on board the *Rebecca*, but she was not ready for sea. So the landlocked governor prepared to defend his capital. He ordered four cannon, palisades, and a garrison transferred from the Brick Fort and the magazine in Jamestown onto the sandy isthmus that linked Jamestown to the mainland. He sent out scouts to locate the revolutionary army. They did not return. When, early on the morning of Friday, 23 June 1676, Sir William rode out to see whether the cannon were mounted at the isthmus trenches, he was received with the cry "Armes, Armes, Bacon is within two Myles of the Towne!" The governor's military situation was hopeless. Besides the men of his own riding household and the retainers of the loyalists among his council, Sir William had under arms only thirty men of Colonel Robert Holt's James City County militia. Even they were "inclined to Bacon's faction rather than our safety." No other militiamen or officers had obeyed Berkeley's repeated orders to garrison Jamestown, "the whole Country being poysoned by specious pretences," revolutionary propaganda. Unwilling to provoke what he could not resist, the governor ordered the newly mounted guns to be "throwne off their carriages," told his followers to put up their arms, and retired with his councilors to the statehouse to await the arrival of Nathaniel Bacon and his army.[29]

At two o'clock on the afternoon of 23 June 1676, Bacon and his men entered Jamestown. They numbered "at least 400 foote they ye Scum of the Country, and 120 horse," men of a somewhat higher class. Whatever their class, on the statehouse green both Bacon's infantry and his cavalry formed up in ranks as "regular as Veteran Troops." From their main body the invaders detached files to guard the isthmus trenches, the Brick Fort, the James River docks, ferry, and shore. Other detachments disarmed every potential opponent of the Baconian brigade, both those in the town and new arrivals. Hardened veterans of European civil wars appreciated Baconian military skill. "Having entered the Towne," they observed,

---

28. Philip Ludwell to Joseph Williamson, 28 June 1676, C.O. 1/37, 37; printed in *V.M.H.B.* 1 (1893): 183.
29. *Ibid.* See also [Lee,] "Bacon's and Ingram's Rebellion," in *Narratives*, 55.

Bacon "Seises and secures the Principal Places and avenues, setts Senti-
nells and sends forth scouts, so that noe Place could be more Securely
guarded."[30]

Bacon's coup exemplified the forceful techniques of garrison government common to a century of revolution. They were brought to Bacon's
service by the old Cromwellians who were now the rebels' infantry captains and horse troopers. Men such as Captain Anthony Arnold held, as
that good Cromwellian Nathaniel Bacon had done, that kings "had Noe
Right but what they gott by Conquest and the Sword." That such violent
realists were masters of the military basis of revolutionary politics they
proceeded to prove in Jamestown.[31]

Half an hour after the army occupied the capital, a drum demanded
the assembly's meeting. Before another hour passed, "Mr. Bacon came
with a file of Fusileers on either hand" to the door of the statehouse. He
sent in a captain to call out the governor and council. From them Bacon
required a commission, not just as leader of a force of frontier volunteers
against the Indians but, so fast had the revolution advanced, as dictator:
"to be Genll of all the forces in Virginia agt ye Indians with such large
expressions in it, as I think have been seldom Granted by any." Certainly
not by Sir William Berkeley. Beside himself with rage, the aged governor
tore open his shirt and cried, "here! Shoot me foregod, fair Mark, Shoot!"
"No May it please your honor," Bacon politely replied, "We will not hurt
a hair of your Head, nor of any other Man's." Raging, Berkeley challenged
Bacon to settle the issue by single combat, sword to sword, there, on the
green, in the space between his councilors and Bacon's army. Shouting
now himself, Bacon reminded Berkeley that "We are come for a Commission to save our Lives from the Indians, which you have so often
promised and now We will have it before we go."[32]

Berkeley's only reply was to turn his back on Bacon. The governor
walked beside the statehouse block towards his apartment, followed by
the members of his council, by Nathaniel Bacon, and by a detachment of
Bacon's troops. Some of the councilors told Bacon that the burgesses' bill
to draft a thousand men from the militia, to pay their expenses from
county levies, and to have them commanded by the governor's appointees, had now been engrossed as an act for the governor's signature
and so could not be changed. Confronted by this example of assembly

30. M[athew], "Bacon's Rebellion," in Andrews, ed., Narratives, 28. The Royal Commissioners, "A True Narrative," in ibid., 116; also in Pepys 2582 and C.O. 5/1371, 187–216.
William Sherwood to [Joseph Williamson], James Citty Virginia, 28 June 1676, C.O. 1/37, 39–
40, printed in V.M.H.B. 1 (1893): 171.

31. Royal Commissioners to Williamson, 27 March 1677, C.O. 1/39, 180. See p. 150.

32. M[athew], "Bacon's Rebellion," in Andrews, ed., Narratives, 28, 29. Philip Ludwell to
Joseph Williamson, 28 June 1676, C.O. 1/37, 37; printed in V.M.H.B. 1 (1893): 184.

contempt for popular demands and backed by the volunteer army ranked
behind him on the statehouse green, Bacon warned the Berkeleyans that
his men had "come for a redresse of ye peoples grievances" and that the
files of fusiliers who followed him would shoot every official in sight at
the first sign of resistance. Outraged by this "insolency," Sir William
Berkeley turned at the top of his lodgings' stairs to shout that "his hands
should be cut off" before he so much as signed a commission for Nathaniel Bacon. It must be grounded, Berkeley declared, either in Bacon's
loyalty to the king, which was nonexistent, or in his popularity with the
people, which was revolutionary.[33]

So saying, Berkeley stormed into his apartment and Bacon turned his
physical force against targets more malleable and more numerous. He
drew up one hundred musketeers beside the statehouse and ordered
them to present their weapons at the burgesses watching from the windows upstairs. He called up to the burgesses that if they refused to grant
him a general's commission on the spot, "he would immediately pull
down ye house and have all our Bloud." Cocking their muskets, Bacon's
men called for their general's commission: "We will have it We will have
it!" Led by Baconian sympathizers, the threatened legislators capitulated:
"You shall have it, You shall have it." Accepting the burgesses' surrender,
Bacon's musketeers uncocked and ordered their arms and stood silent
until their commander sent back "to their Main Body" all but a bodyguard. With his guards around him, Nathaniel Bacon climbed up the
statehouse stairs to dictate his demands, and those of his soldiers, to the
cowed House of Burgesses.[34]

This was the crucial moment of Bacon's Revolution. It was that Bacon
and his army, in June 1676, did "inviron & Besiege the Governor and
Assembly" that constituted their treason in the subsequent judgment of
the king. It was Bacon's entrance into the House of Burgesses, accompanied by his guards, that so forcibly reminded Virginians of Oliver
Cromwell's entrance into the House of Commons, backed by his redcoats. The burgesses now expected in Virginia a dictatorship like Cromwell's. "Oliver Bacon," the militant politician was called to his face.[35]

Being compared to Oliver Cromwell did not inhibit Nathaniel Bacon's

33. Sherwood to Williamson and Philip Ludwell to Williamson, 28 June 1676, C.O. 1/37, 37,
40; printed in V.M.H.B. 1 (1893): 172, 184.
34. M[athew], "Bacon's Rebellion," in Narratives, 29. The Royal Commissioners, "A True
Narrative," in ibid., 117.
35. "By the King. A PROCLAMATION For the Suppressing a Rebellion lately raised
within the Plantation of Virginia," 27 October 1676, C.O. 1/38, 10. [Sherwood,] "Virginias
Deploured Condition: Or an Impartiall Narrative of the Murders comitted by the Indians
there, and of the Sufferings of his Maties Loyall Subjects under the Rebellious outrages of
Mr Nathaniell Bacon Junr: to the tenth day of August Ao. Dom 1676," Collections of the
Massachusetts Historical Society, 4th ser., IX (1871): 174.

demands on the burgesses. As to the first of these, everyone knew that it was not the burgesses' business to issue military commissions. That was the governor's unquestioned prerogative as the king's representative. The burgesses also knew, however, that if Bacon and his under-officers were not commissioned by the governor to lead the largest possible army, of volunteers as well as conscripts, against "all Indians whatsoever," the troops encamped outside the statehouse would choose officers from among themselves. To such popular officers and trooper-electors the property of every oligarch in Virginia would be forfeit: "Gentlemen must either Command, or be Commanded." This the burgesses in a body told the councilors who sat with them. The councilors in turn pressed the burgesses' demand on the governor, saying that "unlesse I would yield to inimitable necessity they and their wives and children were al undone." Berkeley wanted to resist, but the burgesses—newly elected by freemen fearful of the Indians or angry about corruption—saw this as futile. They even denied the governor's request for a guard of a hundred gentlemen ("for the rabble I durst not trust"). Once he realized that both the burgesses and the council backed Bacon's and the army's demands, knowing as well that he had no military strength, the governor concluded that "I could do the King little service by dying for him." The only other option Berkeley could think of was an apparent submission. So Sir William agreed that General Bacon and his advisers might write military commissions, in whatever terms they liked, to whomever they chose, and he would sign them. After he signed the first thirty or so, however, the governor's hand grew as weary as his spirit. He ordered unlimited blank commissions issued. Bacon conscripted unwilling penmen from the burgesses to address these commissions to the potential commanders of "the Army of Virginia." These were identified by the burgesses, county by county, from Westmoreland on the Potomac to Nansemond on the Carolina border.[36]

In the meantime, Bacon's problem was not to defend the capital he had seized but to keep the politicians in it until they had done his bidding. His guards had twice turned back a fleeing Sir William Berkeley before the morning of 24 June 1676, when General Bacon took his political program up to the waiting burgesses and councilors. First, Bacon demanded that the governor's favorites and flunkies be forbidden to hold

36. "Sir William Berkeley to Sir Henry Coventry from Sir John Berry's ship 2d February 1676/7," Coventry Ms. 77, 352. Berkeley was much criticized, subsequently, for failing to stop the career of force by dissolving the assembly. "Thus as it seemed to be Bacon's force upon ye Assembly; soe it appears to be ye Assembly's force upon ye Governor" that elicited from Berkeley the commission that authorized Bacon's revolutionary army. This "might have been prevented, had he [Berkeley] att a word dissolved ym" (The Royal Commissioners, "A Brief Narrative," Pepys 2582 [not in the C.O. 5/1371 text used by Andrews]. M[athew], "Bacon's Rebellion," in Andrews, ed., *Narratives*, 31).

public office. Second, he insisted that the letters presumably sent by the governor to England with Lady Berkeley on 1 June—describing Bacon as a rebel and calling for military aid—be contradicted by the entire assembly, the governor included. Third, Bacon ordered that Captain Gardiner of the *Adam & Eve*, already "secured by the soldiers," be fined for the loss of Bacon's sloop subsequent to her capture and that he be imprisoned by the assembly for interfering with a burgess's (Bacon's) right to travel unmolested to represent the people in the legislature. Fourth, Bacon declared that the defense bill must be reshaped so as to authorize the operations of a volunteer as well as a conscript army. Then his followers could, as they afterwards did, plead that "as for our being in armes wee was commanded thereto by an Act of Govr counsel and assembly." To avoid signing this or any other revolutionary act, Sir William Berkeley sent his lieutenant general and deputy governor, Sir Henry Chicheley, to request General Bacon's permission for the governor to retire to Green Spring. Bacon refused: "now tagg ragg & bobtayle carry a high hand, a Guard is sett upn the Govr, & the rabble are appointing new [laws and] Councellors." So the acts demanded by General Bacon were quickly voted, signed, and sealed by the burgesses, councilors, and the governor himself as the quickest way to get "the Army of Virginia" out of the capital and off to the Indian wars.[37]

June Assembly

O n Sunday, 25 June 1676, the "house of Burgesses met to prepare business to Mr. Bacon's dispatch." Their first bill declared war "against the barbarous Indians" and referred to Nathaniel Bacon as "generall and commander in chiefe of the force raised" by this authority. The second bill responded to the rebel charge that it was the governor's monopoly of trade with the Indians that led him to defend the natives and denounce their English attackers. "No bullets can pierce beaver pelts," was the rebel slogan. The burgesses therefore eliminated the governor's control of the Indian trade and forbade all commerce with enemy aliens. Third, the burgesses junked the fort scheme of the Long Assembly. In-

37. "Characters of ye Severall Comdrs of Ships," Pepys 2582. Isle of Wight Grievances, C.O. 1/39, 223. Sherwood to Williamson, 28 June 1676, C.O. 1/37, 40, printed in *V.M.H.B.* 1 (1893): 178.

stead, they proposed that the war be fought by a mobile army supported by the sale of conquered natives and their lands. The purchasers of Indian slaves and lands would necessarily be oligarchs. The Baconians hoped that such cheap opportunities for frontier development would distract the ruling class not only from the fort scheme but also from what the dissidents saw as the Berkeleyan councilors' plan to make "rebel forfeitures loyal inheritances"—that is, to confiscate the lands of the very frontiersmen whom the Berkeleyans had driven into rebellion by neglecting effective colonial defense. This plan of expropriation, the upcountry planters contended, had been the material meaning behind Berkeley's outlawing of the Baconian volunteers in April of 1676. Now, in June, the dissidents had made their self-defense legal, and they tried to buy off the oligarchs with the land and labor of the Indians whom the commoners hated.[38]

More than frontier defense and development were on the reformers' agenda. General Bacon had already insisted that fiscal corruption must be redressed by legislation. Customs receipts, county levies, assembly allowances, all required reform. As Sir William Berkeley had forbidden reform at the colonial level—despite Nathaniel Bacon's demand for redress of the "Grievances and Calamities of that Deplorable Country"—the burgesses determined to popularize politics in their own "countries," the counties of Virginia. If, as has been so powerfully argued, counties were the most effective governments in the Old Dominion, then real revolution lay in the seven bills by which the burgesses of 1676 undid the political practices of the Berkeleyan barons for the oppression of the county commons.[39]

The county executives—the sheriffs—were now limited to a single year in office, constrained in the times when they could collect taxes, and ordered to accept tobacco at the market price in lieu of all levies. The fees of the sheriffs, court clerks, coroners—in fact, of all the appointees of the governor and council in the counties—were restricted. All proceedings of county officials were to be made public. The burgesses of 1676 further attacked the county authority of the Berkeleyan oligarchy by excluding councilors from seats in the county courts and by subjecting them to county taxes, and to all other levies as well. The burgesses next provided that the justices who were appointed to the county courts by the governor were to be balanced by an equal number of representatives chosen by the county electorate. Encouraged in these unprecedentedly popular measures by a lower-class and republican army encamped on the

38. Sherwood to Williamson, 28 June 1676, C.O. 1/37, 40; printed in V.M.H.B. 1 (1893): 178. William Waller Henning, [ed.,] The Statutes at Large; Being a Collection of the Laws of Virginia . . . (New York, 1823, Charlottesville, 1969), II, 341, 349.

39. M[athew], "Bacon's Rebellion," in Andrews, ed., Narratives, 30.

statehouse green, the burgesses also prescribed that the trustees of religion and welfare in the counties, the parish vestrymen of the Church of England, be elected by the parishioners, and that the ministers of the church be subject to taxation.

The burgesses' stress on the county electorate's control of local agencies of government came naturally to legislators elected in 1676, for these burgesses themselves were the products of the only popular election in Virginia between 1619 and 1776. Moreover, they were uniquely exempt from executive influence. Only five of the thirty-one burgesses of 1676 are known to have held lucrative offices in Sir William Berkeley's gift. Freely elected and thus free to prefer the interests of their electors to those of the executive, the burgesses not only called for elected justices and vestrymen, they also decreed that freemen as well as freeholders could vote in both the parish and the county. Under popular pressure to reverse his 1670 exclusion of freemen from the polls, Sir William Berkeley himself had authorized them to vote for burgesses in May 1676. Now every man who owned his own labor, as well as those who owned land, could vote for parish and county, as well as colonial, representatives. The House of Burgesses reflected the electoral revolution in the counties. There, in May 1676, as the Baconians rejoiced, "every free borne mans voat was heard in Election," and the royal commissioners added that the laws passed by the burgesses so elected demonstrated that "freemen were both chose and chosen Burgesses."[40]

The burgesses concluded their work with "An act of general pardon and oblivion" designed to protect all the authors of the political revolution of 1676. This act prohibited prosecutions for crimes committed between the date of the first attack by the northern militia leaders (now burgesses) on the Indian enemy, in March 1675, to the present moment, 25 June 1676. After Sir William Berkeley signed this act and all the rest, at the urging of burgesses equally anxious to escape from Jamestown's political dangers and to protect their families from the Indian raids, the governor dissolved the assembly of June 1676. A century passed before such a revolutionary legislature met again in Virginia.[41]

40. Nancymond First Grievances, C.O. 1/39, 246. Commissioners' reply to Rappahannock request (no. 14) for freeholder franchise, C.O. 1/39, 187. See also Pepys 2582.
41. Henning, [ed.,] *Statutes*, II, 363–64.

Recruits and Elites

As the burgesses hurried home, "General Bacon (as he now began to be Intitled)" by most Virginians, reluctantly left the capital and the work of cleaning the Berkeleyan stables. He had to do so because, at the climax of the assembly's last session, at noon on 25 June 1676, a courier had reported eight colonists killed in New Kent County, only 23 miles from Jamestown and 40 miles within the frontier line. Bacon's men, many of them from New Kent, insisted that he move against the raiders. So the general was forced to end "the June Assembly" without compelling it to complete the political revolution above the county level. Instead, he marched west with his little army to rally the county militia drafts against the Indian enemy. The governor's party, momentarily relieved, nonetheless expected that "it will not be long ere we heare of him againe."[42]

General Bacon and the Army of Virginia moved west out of Jamestown, north across the York River at West Point, and then east down into the Berkeleyan heartland of Gloucester County, the most recently developed and most prosperous area of Virginia. There, the more debased their status the more readily the commons enlisted in Bacon's army. General Bacon's recruiting officers offered to servants, slaves, and freemen an exciting escape from labor. Bacon's officers promised the recruits plunder from the army's Indian victims and meat from the master class' livestock. Men of small property, however, resisted the social degradation of army service alongside servants, slaves, and freemen. These freeholders also feared that their abandoned families would be killed by native raiders and that their unprotected property would be seized by Berkeley's grandees.

The grandees had grown to dominant size by engorging the land, livestock, servants, and goods of their lesser neighbors whenever public emergency promised private gain. Now, no fewer than five of Berkeley's council, "in his maties name," ordered the small planters of their counties to enlist in Bacon's force, required them "by press or otherwise to procure" provisions for it from their neighbors, and encouraged the planters'

42. "An Account Of Our Late Troubles In Virginia. Written In 1676, By Mrs. An. Cotton, Of Q. Creeke," in Peter Force, ed., *Tracts And Other Papers* . . . (Washington, D.C., 1835–36), I, 5. Philip Ludwell to Joseph Williamson, 28 June 1676, C.O. 1/37, 38, printed in *V.M.H.B.* 1 (1893): 185.

wives to propagandize for the revolutionary army. If these small planters
died in the army, their property would be easy prey to the grandees:
councilors-coroners-sheriffs-justices-colonels. If the conscripted freeholders survived the Indian and civil wars, they would find that the great
men of their counties had switched sides, had become the most vindictive of loyalists, and would prosecute their smaller neighbors for "the
rebellion" (ordered by these same prosecutors) until the small planters
surrendered their property to escape hanging.[43]

By such maneuverings had Virginia's ruling class been built in gen-
erational crises between 1622 and 1662. In 1676, another such crisis arrived. Once again victims both red and white were to provide the land
and goods and labor by which the oligarchs of 1676 had achieved that
material and political eminence so resented by ordinary Virginians, and
of which they seemed so unworthy in the eyes of better-bred English
emigrants. Bacon spoke for both poor planters and privileged newcomers
when he suggested that they "trace these men in Authority and Favour
to whose hands the dispensation of the Countries wealth has been com-
mited; let us observe the sudden Rise of their Estates compared with the
Quality in which they first entered this Country Or the Reputation they
have held here amongst wise and discerning men, and lett us see whether
their extractions and Educations have not been Vile . . . see what
spounges have sukt up the Publique Treasure and whether it hath not
bin privately contrived away by unworthy Favourites and juggling Parasites whose tottering Fortunes have bin repaired and supported at the
Publique chardg."[44]

Those of the Berkeleyans—"unworthy Favourites and juggling Parasites"—whom they found in Gloucester County (Majors Lawrence Smith
and Thomas Hawkins chief among them) the Baconian army arrested and
imprisoned, ironically enough in the Berkeleyan forts. General Bacon
then dispatched armed emissaries elsewhere to recruit upper-class men
to head an alternative government to that of Sir William Berkeley, a
government pledged to support the "Army of Virginia" and obey its general.

One burgess of the June Assembly, Thomas Mathew, had sought refuge on his Potomac plantation. He wanted neither to add to the assistance
he had unwillingly given General Bacon in Jamestown (when impresssed
to write army commissions) nor to multiply the "frowns" and "marks"

43. [Councilor and Colonel] "Thomas Ballard to Capt. Tho. Young, James Citty," 6, 10 July
1676, C.O. 1/37, 82, endorsed "Young was hang'd for Executing this Warrt. and commanding
the Company which he was compelled to by Col. Ballard Col of ye [Countie]." See also
notes 178–80, below.
44. "Nathaniel Bacon Esqr his manifesto concerning the Present troubles in Virginia," C.O.
1/37, 178; printed in *V.M.H.B.* 1 (1893): 55–58.

this had earned him from Governor Berkeley. Nonetheless, Bacon's aide "Major Langston with his Troop of Horse" rode north from the army's base in Gloucester "and Quartered Two Nights at my house," Mathew reported. "After high Compliments from the Generall," Major Langston told Mathew that "I was desired to Accept the Lieutenancy for preserving the peace in the 5 Northern Counties betwixt Patomack and Rappahannock Rivers," the Northern Neck. Nothing in the law, not even in the June Laws of 1676, authorized General Bacon to commission regional lieutenants (on the model of Cromwell's major generals), pledged to obey the people's general, not the king's governor. To do so indicated that Bacon was parlaying his military organization into a revolutionary government. Knowing this, Mathew pleaded that he was a mere merchant and struggling planter, neither warrior nor politician. Bacon's troopers promised to report Mathew's refusal to their general, who would remember it. So the governor had "marked" Mathew's penmanship. Such is the plight of a neutral in a revolution.[45]

Military as well as political doubts about General Bacon plagued other northern leaders. They feared not only that Bacon's army was aimed at domestic political enemies but also that recruiting for it would leave them without men enough "to fight the battles of the Republicque" against the Indians. Therefore, Rappahannock Fort and the county magazine were held against Bacon's lieutenants and they faced open "hostility in ye County of Westmoreland." Finally Bacon turned to another aspiring newcomer to Virginia, the widely known Indian killer Colonel John Washington. The colonel would bequeath to his grandson the leadership of the Northern Neck militia, both in provincial revolution against a tyrannical governor and in imperial war against the Iroquois. As the notorious grandfather, John, was the nemesis of the Susquehanna, so the famous grandson, George, would be the "Town Destroyer" of the Seneca: "to this day when that name is heard our women look behind them and turn pale and our children cling close to the necks of their mothers."[46]

45. M[athew], "Bacon's Rebellion," in Andrews, ed., *Narratives*, 32–34, 34–35. See the parallel case of John Baxter, "A True Relation of Colonel Hills malitious Cruelty," 17 June 1677, C.O. 1/40, 233–38.

46. Rappahannock Grievances, 13 March 1676[/7], C.O. 1/39, 197. Favor from Berkeley was no bar to recruitment by Bacon, as the names of Washington and Ballard on the 1676 2-shilling tax collectors' list attests (C.O. 1/37, 42v–43). For their collections, see "The Publk. Accot.," C.O. 1/37, 42–44. Act of the Middle Plantation Convention, 3–4 August 1676, C.O. 1/37, 131. Cornplanter to George Washington, 1790, quoted in Barbara Graymont, *The Iroquois in the American Revolution* (Syracuse, N.Y., 1972), 192. Bacon to Washington, 4 August (recruitment), 5 August (the engagement), C.O. 1/37, 133. See also Phi. Lanyon [to Secretary Williamson], Plymouth, 14 April 1676, State Papers Domestic 29/380, fol. 242 Public Record Office (hereafter cited as S.P. 29/380, 242): "Colonel Washington comanded a body who mett the Indians, he fought them, beat them, and drove them into there garrisson, wch he tooke, and put all in it to the Sword."

It was Bacon's reputation as the Indian "Town Destroyer" of 1676 that won him the support of other northerners besides Colonel Washington. They feared that if Indian attacks kept white farmers from their cornfields through the summer of 1676, upcountry Virginians would starve the next winter. Therefore Captain Giles Brent led a thousand men from the Northern Neck south across the Rappahannock to join General Bacon in Gloucester. When they reached his camp in mid-July 1676, the northerners found that Bacon and his new staff had done what Berkeley and his councilors had said was impossible: they had collected two months' provisions, armed six hundred infantry, and mounted seven hundred cavalry, all "for carrying on a warre against the barbarous Indians."[47]

Brent's arrival forced Bacon to act on the racist premise of the revolutionary movement and march against the natives. Much of Bacon's southern army and most of Brent's northern troops considered Indian-fighting to be their main mission. Moreover, so large a body of troops had to act before they began to starve. In the last days of July 1676, "the Army of Virginia against the Indians" marched west and south out of Gloucester County to the Falls of the James. Thence the army was at last to begin its campaign against the Indians.

Gloucester Petition and
Loyalist Flight

No sooner had the revolutionary and racist armies moved out of tidewater than the Gloucester Berkeleyans still at large, led by Lieutenant General Sir Henry Chicheley, Colonel Philip Ludwell, and Major Robert Beverley, presented to Sir William Berkeley a paper they mistitled "the Gloucester Petition." It was "not knowne to ten though in ye name of ye whole country." This "petition" protested Bacon's political and economic aggression, carried on under pretense of raising forces and supplies against the Indians. The purported petitioners wrote that, although Gloucester was not a frontier county, they had obeyed the act of assembly to raise men and supplies to secure their western neighbors against the heathen. They had sent what they raised to Nathaniel Bacon

---

47. Giles Bland to Thomas Povey, 8 July 1676, Rec'd 28 August 1676, C.O. 1/36, 109. Henning, [ed.,] *Statutes*, II, 341–50.

in obedience to his authority under the governor's commission. Bacon had quartered his troops in Gloucester County anyway. Those troops "took what horses and arms they pleased" and drafted men as well. That is, Bacon's troopers disarmed those they deemed disaffected to the revolution and ignored draft exemptions. Worse, they respected no one. "One Matthew Gale," a Baconian captain, even dared to point a pistol at "Coll. Matthew Kemp Commander of all the horse in this County." Surely such lèse-majesté was "contrary to all law, either civill or military," the "petitioners" exclaimed. This Gale was just as disrespectful to God Almighty as he was to Colonel Kemp, for he swore great oaths when opposed in his illegal demands. Finally he made a threat, all too terrible to those who remembered the English civil wars, to "goe to his General Bacon and, in a very short time returne with an hundred horse, and ruin the County." So scared were the Gloucester "petitioners" and so sure were they that their good governor would have granted no such authority, that they had appealed to Sir William Berkeley for relief as soon as Bacon's army left Gloucester.[48]

The governor immediately rode for Gloucester County to tell its people that Bacon "never had any Commission from me, but what with armed men he extracted from the Assembly." Berkeley then called up the militias of Middlesex and Gloucester counties "to goe out agt. the Indians." When they had mustered, some twelve hundred strong, Sir William "proposed to them to follow and Suppress that Rebel Bacon." The armed masses visibly stirred in their ranks, remembering that "their Countrymen Neighbours & friends" had marched into the wilderness with "Squire Bacon" to fight the heathen foe. In the face of the governor, his deputy and lieutenant general, and their own officers, the militiamen began to mutter, "Bacon, Bacon, Bacon, and all Walked out of the field, Muttering as they went Bacon, Bacon, Bacon." Sir William Berkeley, sick with humiliation, "fainted away on Horseback in the Field." When he recovered consciousness, Berkeley found at his side fewer than a dozen officers, and no men.[49]

"How unhappy unsuccessfull and how fatale this avocation" of Berkeley and the "Gloucester petitioners" had been. As royal commissioners afterwards observed, "Bacon (then the hopes of the People) was just on the point of marching out, and nothing could have called him back, or

48. "To the Rt: Honble: Sr. William Berkeley Knt: Governr. and Capt: Genll. of Virginia. The humble peticon of the County of Glocr:," *Collections of the Massachusetts Historical Society*, 4th ser., IX (1871): 181–83.
49. "The Governrs. Answere To Yt. Peticon:," *ibid.*, 183–84. Grievances of Isle of Wight County, 5 March 1676/7, C.O. 1/39, 223; printed in *V.M.H.B.* 2 (1894): 380–92. M[athew], "Bacon's Rebellion," in Andrews, ed., *Narratives*, 34. Marginal note to the Royal Commissioners, "Narrative of the Rise, Progresse, and Cessation of the late Rebellion in Virginia," Pepys 2582; see also the text in Andrews, ed., *Narratives*, 119.

turned the sword of a civill warr into the heart and bowels of the country but soe ill-tymed a Project as this Prov'd." On 29 July 1676, General Bacon learned of Governor Berkeley's counter-revolutionary Gloucester project. He had, the general said, expected nothing better from Indian-lovers and traders by whom "soe much blood of our dear Brethren [had been] bought and sold." Bacon's army broke camp and marched from the Falls of the James down the spine of the Peninsula to the Middle Plantation (afterwards Williamsburg). Seven miles from Jamestown, the Middle Plantation had been the military focus of Virginia since 1634. From his camp there, General Bacon sent cavalry patrols "through every County" to take pledges of allegiance to his cause from the local elites and to capture the leading Berkeleyans. Twenty of them Bacon proscribed as "Traitors to the People." This, the ultimate revolutionary charge, justified the general in ordering his troopers to confiscate the "Traitors' " property. With that confiscation, the social revolution of 1676 began in earnest.[50]

It met little opposition. As soon as he heard that Bacon had marched from the Falls, Sir William Berkeley fled downriver from Green Spring. Only four loyalists sailed with him. During August 1676, however, twenty more of the old elite fled from Bacon's horsemen and from the people's "cryeing out upon their extortions from widows and orphans." The Berke-leyans carried with them into exile the corpse of Virginia's old order, no man knew where. Some thought that the loyalists had sailed for Nevis. Others suspected that the governor was among the fugitives hidden on the London-bound tobacco ships. It was even rumored that Sir William was dead. In fact, the governor had escaped across Chesapeake Bay to Virginia's Eastern Shore.[51]

The two counties of the Eastern Shore, "the Territory of Accomack" and Northampton, were quite distinct from "Yor'Maties Colony or Plantation of Virginia." They were unaffected by the Indian war and they were dominated by powerful colonels and councilors of old families— William Spencer, John Custis, Argyll Yeardley, the Scarboroughs and the Littletons. These *hobereaux* were unchallenged in their Chesapeake isolation and English outport trade by the recent English immigrants or by their London bureaucratic and mercantile connections. Although these county chieftains' petty tyrannies—"the Corruption practiced heretofore on our Eastern shore"—angered their countrymen, they were at first little

50. Royal Commissioners, "A True Narrative," in Andrews, ed., *Narratives*, 120. M[athew], "Bacon's Rebellion," in *ibid.*, 34. "Nathaniel Bacon Esqr his manifesto," C.O. 1/37, 178. "Declaration of the People," C.O. 1/37, 129; printed in *V.M.H.B.* 1 (1893): 55–61, and in Merrill Jensen, ed., *English Historical Documents*, vol. IX, *American Colonial Documents to 1776* (New York, 1955), 581–85.

51. Berkeley to Coventry, 2 February 1676/7, Coventry Ms. 77, 353. Nancymond First Grievances, C.O. 1/39, 247. Isle of Wight Grievances, *ibid.*, 224. [Lee,] "Bacon's and Ingram's Rebellion," in Andrews, ed., *Narratives*, 62. S.P. 29/386, 329.

troubled by a revolution "hatched and acted on the Western Shore by Nath. Bacon."[52]

When Sir William Berkeley's loyal officers joined him, most fleeing from homes in Gloucester County and along the lower reaches of the York, they brought with them the arms and ammunition stockpiled for the Indian war at York Fort ("the ffort at Tindale Point") and from the Gloucester County militia magazine. These thefts gave the loyalist exiles weapons against the revolution but they also proved Bacon's contention that the Berkeleyans had sabotaged the race war against the murdering Indians in order to conduct a civil war against tax-paying Virginians. As the royal commissioners pithily put it, "The Provisions rais'd by act of Assembly to supply ye Indian warr, is by ye Governor's Party forceably taken awaye to maintaine a civill war against ye givers of itt."[53]

Revolutionary Convention

The Gloucester Petition, Berkeley's attempt to raise troops against Bacon, the governor's flight, and his followers' looting of the York River arsenals, simultaneously declared civil war and abandoned the government. The Berkeleyans had left mainland Virginia to Bacon, as the lawful commander of the Army of Virginia, and to the regional regimes he and the army had raised. To military authority the successful rebels would add civil government. The general, himself a member of the colonial council of state, was backed by four other councilors and so commanded a majority of the executive body. These councilors summoned an unprecedented, revolutionary convention to meet at the Middle Plantation on 3 August 1676, there to form a new government for the Old Dominion.

The convention met as scheduled. Composed of the council majority and company-grade militia officers from most of Virginia's counties, the convention agreed with General Bacon that Sir William Berkeley had first declared war on his people and then vacated his government. Bacon,

52. Virginia and Accomac agents to the king, 19–23 June 1675, C.O. 1/34, 200. Accomac Grievances, 11 March 1676/7, C.O. 1/39, 216. Petition of Northampton householders and freeholders to their burgesses, n.d., *ibid.*, 214.
53. Marginal note to Royal Commissioners, "A Narrative," Pepys 2582; text in Andrews, ed., *Narratives*, 131.

the convention declared, had "to move to the suppressing of forces by evill disposed persons raised against the said General Bacon purposely to foment and stirr up Civill Warre amongst us." And the people of Virginia, the convention concluded, had to turn to General Bacon for leadership. Governor Berkeley had fled "whether we knew not and left us as Sheep without a Shepherd to the mercy of the heathen Yet under the comand of Nathaniell Bacon."[54]

To secure their new government for Virginia, "under the comand of Nathaniell Bacon," the members of the revolutionary convention took an oath of allegiance. It condemned the principal Berkeleyans as "Traytors to the People." It pledged its takers to seize the persons and the property of these traitors, the latter for the use of the revolutionary government. Having declared that those officers whose authority derived from the crown were traitors to the people, the revolutionaries had committed treason. Therefore the Middle Plantation oath bound its subscribers to resist the royal army and navy until the crown conceded satisfactory terms to the Virginians. The leading members of the convention, led by the four councilors, took this oath, "Bacon's Oath," before the general and the army. Then they returned to their counties to offer the oath to both county officers and electors.[55]

The revolutionary intent testified to by the Middle Plantation oath was made even clearer on 11 August 1676. Then General Bacon and his four fellow councilors of state proclaimed that, "whereas Sir Wm Berkeley Kt, late Governor, hath absented himself from ye Governmt & Care of this his Maties distracted Country of Virginia," an assembly, elected by "all ye housekeepers and freemen," should meet at Jamestown on 4 September 1676 to legislate further redress for Virginia's "Blood & Confusion." This revolutionary replacement for the colonial assembly did not meet (although Bacon's successor as general, Lawrence [or Joseph] Ingram, may have convened a second convention or "Nominated Parliament" on the Cromwellian model) but the civil government of the revolution was nonetheless established in most mainland counties of Virginia by members of the Middle Plantation Convention and according to its directives.

The convention ordered that every civil officer in Virginia be offered "Bacon's Oath" by those who, having already taken it, constituted a revolutionary "Association" (a concept that the Virginia revolutionaries of 1676 borrowed from the English revolutionaries of the 1640s and which was again revived by the American revolutionaries of 1776). Anyone re-

---

54. Acts of the Middle Plantation Convention, 3–4 August 1676, C.O. 1/37, 130–31. Isle of Wight Grievances, C.O. 1/39, 223.
55. Acts of the Middle Plantation Convention, 3–4 August 1676, C.O. 1/37, 130–31.

fusing the oath was to be deposed from office and exposed to the hatred of the people.

The struggle about oath and association which followed the convention defined the parties in Virginia's revolution. Both loyalists and revolutionaries justified their positions by reference to the English Revolution. Berkeley's men refused the oath, contending that, although ultimately the rebellion it bespoke "would fall like the rebellion in England," in the meantime "the Governmt & gentlemen of the County would be ruined" if the rebel associators took power. The Baconians replied that "the people of England had some reason for some of theire rebellion," as Virginians did for theirs, so they threatened recalcitrant officials with the mob. One such officer was told that, if he took the oath and joined the association, "I should gaine the love of the people, Otherwise I should have their hate." Examples were made: an obstreperous supporter of the old order was shot "through the body leaving him Rithing in his blood." News of the oath and the association, of arguments and examples, were spread through the counties by the Baconian news wives. For example, Mrs. Hanyland, "an excellent divulger of News," was "sent poste up & downe the Country as Bacon's Emissary to carry his declarations & papers." [56]

Bacon's authority and his army, the prestige of the convention's members and the opportunity its orders, oath, and association gave for settling old scores and righting old wrongs in every county, the rapid erection of revolutionary regional government and the widespread issuance of its propaganda, the undeniable emergency of the Indian war, and the apparent abdication of Sir William Berkeley and his hated henchmen, all combined to lead both civil and military officers—"commissioners"—in the counties to join the association and to impose "Bacon's Oath" on their countrymen. The men of Nansemond County stated "That our Pol[itical] and malitia offiers under whom wee Served, Summon'd us by severall pre[ce]pts: to meet at severall places in our Respective p'ishes, & theire Administered to us an oath, to be trew to Bacon, And those who should refuse the same, theire names to be remitted to him ye said Bacon, & though by some of us refused, yett [the oath] being taken by our Commissioners was ye motive to induce the most pt of us to take itt . . . soe yt by ye said oath wee weare obleidged to bee true to Bacon." [57]

In the forms of the oath and the association, the Middle Plantation Convention had given General Bacon the political weapons to fight the two-front war for which it called: against the Indian enemies of all Virgin-

---

56. Edward Hill's defense addressed to the Royal Commissioners, n.d., C.O. 1/40, 152, 155.
57. Writs for Bacon's assembly, 5, 11 August 1676, Coventry Ms. 77, c. 185. Nancymond First Grievances, C.O. 1/39, 246. "Inhabitants in . . . Nanzemond to the Cmrs.," *ibid.*, 250 (no. 3). Hill's Defence, C.O. 1/40, 152, 155.

ians and against the Virginia enemies of the revolution. The economic
revolution was accomplished on 8 August 1676. Nathaniel Bacon, "Generall, by the Consent of the People," occupied Sir William Berkeley's
"Green Spring," the greatest plantation and mansion in Virginia. On that
day also fell to the army of the revolution the estates of Virginia's leading
civil officer, Secretary Thomas Ludwell, and its major general, Thomas
Smith, both absent in England as the agents of the Berkeleyan assembly.
So too the estates of Colonel Daniel Parke and of the twenty Berkeleyan
"Traitors to the Cominality" proscribed first by the general and then by
the convention, were occupied by the army on 8 August 1676. The Egyp-
tians had been spoiled by the army of their bondsmen. The domestic war
was pushed forward militarily as well as economically. During August
1676, Berkeley's deputy governor and lieutenant general, Sir Henry Chicheley, was locked up with other Gloucester Berkeleyans in Mehickson
Fort and every fortification on either the James River or the York was
seized by the revolutionaries. Triumphant on the land, the rebels turned
to the water, capturing the sloops and ships they required to support the
revolution in the Tidewater counties and to export it to the Eastern
Shore.[58]

Giles Bland

B acon and his lieutenants did not intend to exempt the Eastern Shore
from Virginia's revolution. They named Giles Bland, the royal customs collector turned Baconian political commissar, as the agent of Accomac's radicalization and of Sir William Berkeley's capture. Bland was
another English newcomer to Virginia. He had come over to enforce the
parliament's Plantation Act of 1673 and to recover his father's large estate
from the hands of Sir William Berkeley's favorites, Colonels Thomas and
Philip Ludwell. That Bland's father, John, had quarreled violently (as
mayor of Tangier) with Berkeley's friend Colonel Henry Norwood, treasurer of Virginia and governor of Tangier, and that the Ludwells, the

58. The declaration of the people, the engagement, the call for administration and election,
all dated at Middle Plantation, 23–24 August 1676, C.O. 1/37, 129–31; also in the Blathwayt
Papers, Colonial Williamsburg, Inc., vol. 13, no. 1, and the Blathwayt Papers, Huntington
Library, San Marino, California, 83, are calendared in W. Noel Sainsbury, ed., *Calendar of
State Papers, Colonial Series, America and West Indies, 1675–1676* . . . (London, 1893), no.
1010 (hereafter cited as *C.S.P.C.*). See also note 50, above. N.B.: the text of the "Declaration"
varies substantially from source to source. C.O. 1/37 is quoted here.

former of whom was the secretary of Virginia, were both Berkeleyan councilors, both relatives of Berkeley by marriage, and both born in Berkeley's native parish of Bruton, Somerset, only begin to suggest the Anglo-American interconnections and the imperial bitterness that led first to Berkeley's downfall and then to Bland's execution.

Giles Bland began his Virginia career badly. He insisted that the Ludwells restore the plantations, belonging to his father and worth "neer ten thousand pounds," which they had extorted from the custody of Bland's widowed aunt. They refused, and they were backed by Berkeley. Young Bland thereupon began to "pry" into the "secrets" of the Berkeleyans, or so they said. Certainly he reported their misappropriation of the king's customs to royal officials in London. Worse followed when, in October 1675, Philip Ludwell failed to show up for a duel with Bland. Giles tacked a note condemning the coward to the statehouse door, while the assembly was in session. This "scandalized" the Berkeleyans and, so they said, the entire Long Assembly. The governor's cronies grew angrier yet when they learned that Bland had reported to the lord treasurer their illegal trade, their appropriation of the crown's customs, and, in particular, their connivance with a crooked shipmaster in the "wrecking" of a richly laden ship, the *Phoenix* of London. The governor and council condemned its cargo for violation of the acts of trade, pocketed a large part of its £12,000 value for themselves, and neglected either to inform the treasury in London or to credit any of the money to Virginia's public account. Doubly provoked by Giles Bland's complaints of their private and public corruption, Berkeley and the council, moved by Philip Ludwell, had Bland arrested and jailed on charges of sedition, declared him guilty, fined him the unheard-of amount of £500, and suspended him from his royal customs collectorship (which last they had no authority to do).[59]

Undeterred, Giles Bland continued his reports to the king's ministers and in the spring of 1676, like those of so many alienated Virginians, his concerns moved from finance to defense and thence to politics. Virginians, the collector told Secretary Williamson, were in danger "not only from their Enemies but from . . . the Government, which all readie has so little Reverence Paide them, that a Considerable Bodie of the Countrie have armed themselves, without Comission, against theire Enemies, and for Redresse of their Grievances." The only remedy for Berkeleyan misgovernment, Bland wrote, was direct royal rule: "the immediate applica-

59. "To the Kings Most Excellent Matie:, The Humble Petition of Sarah Bland," C.O. 1/36, 86. Thomas Ludwell's reply to this "dirt wch is thrown upon the whole government of Virginia," 15 June 1676 (C.O. 1/37, 14–15), and his personal defense, 9 November 1676 (C.O. 1/38, 81–82); Order of Council, James City, 17 October 1675 (C.O. 1/35, 245), and the *Phoenix* case (C.O. 1/47, 48; C.O. 391/4, 1–2, 124–26, 132–34) are all calendared in Davenport, comp., *Bacon's Rebellion*, 99–100. See also the Royal Commissioners to the lord treasurer, 27 March 1677, C.O. 5/1371, 91–92.

tions of his Matie and his Councells; not only as this is a Colonie of English Men Subject to his Maties. Government but as it affords more than a hundred Thousand Pounds of yearly Revenue to his Matie."[60]

Besides these compelling fiscal and political reasons, an institutional aspect of the growth of English imperialism led Bland to appeal with confidence to the crown against Berkeley and his council. Bland's collectorship was but one small extension of the authority of the crown to America during the 1670s and particularly that of the lord treasurer, the earl of Danby, the most "thorough" minister of the Restoration. Bland, it appeared, was an agent of that nationalized, metropolitan, and bureaucratic imperialism which was to prove anathema to the oligarchical, autarchical, Sir William Berkeley and his colonial councilors. Of course the Berkeleyans hated Bland. As Sir William Berkeley explained, it was Bland, even more than Bacon, who forced him to resign his government to the crown in May 1676, "for Armed with my Lord High Treasurers Authority never man did such things extra ordinarily and Extraofficially as he does and I have beene severely checkt out of England lately for not obeying and seconding his Actions indeed every thing here is now deplorable and three young men that have not beene two yeares in the Country absolutely Governe it, Mr. Bacon Mr. Bland and Mr. Ingram."[61]

Bland, as Berkeley tells it, was not content with collecting the plantation duty. Rather, he enforced England's monopoly of Virginia's trade. He actually boarded all ships clearing the colony, examined their manifests, took bonds for delivery of their tobacco in England, and asked awkward questions about the collection of the tobacco export tax, the castle dues, and the smuggling of French luxury goods by the governor and his cronies. Most menacing of all, Bland reported to England that for less than half of Virginia's tobacco exports were customs duties ever paid to the crown. The crown, Bland said, lost £100,000 per annum to Berkeleyan evasions. This was indeed "a great part of his [Majesty's] Revenue betrayed and Sacrificed to private Interests," revenue with which "the imperial crown of England" intended to bolster its authority at home as well as overseas.[62]

Bland intended to sail for London to detail Berkeleyan corruption, but even as he prepared to board ship the military emergency deepened.

60. Giles Bland to Joseph Williamson, 28 April 1676, enclosing "Considerations upon the present troubles in Virginia," C.O. 1/36, 109; 111–12.

61. Berkeley [to T. Ludwell], 1 July 1676, Coventry Ms. 77, 145. Bland's influence at court is testified to in *ibid.*, 325, and he is seen as the key to the revolution in "Memoirs for his R.H." (*ibid.*, 346). Yet Bland had ridden west to the Falls of the James with Berkeley in May 1676 in pursuit of Bacon and his frontier militia.

62. "Considerations upon the present troubles in Virginia," C.O. 1/36, 111. The Bland agency subscription circular, C.O. 1/37, 86. See Book II, p. 188, on the imperial intentions for Virginia's revenues.

Virginia was "under the greatest distractions, that it hath felt since 1622, when the Indians in one night murdered so many, that they left not 500 alive in the whole colony." The governor's military weakness forced "persons of the greatest quality here," young Englishmen of family, like Bland himself, to take command of the county volunteers. From them, the young gentlemen learned that, for nine years, the fiscal grievances of the people had gone unredressed by an assembly unsupervised from England and a council half of whom were disenchanted with "the aged governor" and his henchmen but all of whom had been appointed without the constitutionally required royal approval. Naturally, Bland said, such an incompetent, even illegal government "wants that reverence that should enable it to protect it self and the publick." Finally, Bland agreed to represent General Bacon and the army in England, sharing their (correct) conviction that royal reform would follow the people's censure of the old regime. A public subscription for the costs of his agency was opened and his instructions were ready when the naval actions provoked by the governor's flight put Bland in command of the revolution's first maritime campaign.[63]

Eastern Shore

Berkeley's escape and its potential consequences impelled the revolutionaries to turn some of their attention from the land frontier, its defense, politics, and economy, to the sea frontier, naval strength, and Anglo-American government and trade at the end of July 1676. Giles Bland's own concerns had long faced seaward. Other dissidents had to acknowledge trans-Atlantic interests when they learned that the governor, Philip Ludwell, and other Berkeleyans had added to Berkeley's plate aboard Captain Christopher Evelyn's ship the *Rebecca* a set of letters which described to the assembly agents in England the military and political revolution of the three preceding months. In late July 1676, another of the proscribed Berkeleyans, William Sherwood, also got aboard Evelyn's ship, carrying his own narrative and additional dis-

---

63. Giles Bland to Charles Berne, "From James-Town," 20 April 1676, quoted in John Burk, *The History Of Virginia* (Petersburg, Va., 1805), II, 247–49. Charles City County Grievances, "Att Westover," 10 May 1677, C.O. 1/40, 141–47. For the fate of Bland's representations, see Book II, pp. 202–5.

patches. Some sources said that Sir William Berkeley himself was hidden aboard the *Rebecca*. In any case, if the *Rebecca* reached London, General Bacon and his young English associates knew—far better than Governor Berkeley did—that redcoats and warships would be sent out with orders to suppress the rebellion first, and ask about grievances afterwards. If Evelyn's *Rebecca* could be captured, however, she and her sisters from the tobacco fleet would make the revolutionaries masters of the whole Chesapeake. Chesapeake consolidation and coalition would provide the revolution with a strong position from which the army's agent, Giles Bland, could bargain with the crown for a reformed, popular government in Virginia as well as for a more equitable economic relation with England.

If the revolution's trans-Atlantic politics were Bland's concern, its Chesapeake tactics were those of Captain William Carver, "a valient stout man" even in Berkeley's estimation. This retired English sea captain had turned merchant and planter and become sheriff of Lower Norfolk County. Captain Carver had appeared at the June Assembly "to wait on the General for a commission and [to declare] that he was resolved to adventure his old bones against the Indian Rogues." It was Carver's seamanship, not his racism, however, that was wanted by General Bacon. The general named Carver captain, and Bland commissar, of the seagoing revolution. They gathered some three hundred men, put them aboard a flotilla of small craft, and, on 1 August 1676, attacked the tobacco ships anchored in the James River.

The captains of these ships had delayed their sailings long past their usual spring departures to try to purchase more tobacco from the disordered Virginia markets for their half-freighted ships, even though they had had explicit warning of the coming storm in a circular signed by Joseph Ingram "in the names of the people." It had demanded that the sea captains surrender everything put on board their ships by the proscribed Berkeleyans (Spencer, Isaac Allerton, and Richard Lee were particularly named). All the captains ignored this request but some took their half-laden ships to sea immediately. The merchantmen still anchored close to Jamestown were attacked by the rebels led by Carver and Bland. John Moore's *Honor & Dorothy* and Thomas Larrimore's *Rebecca* were captured. Their batteries were augmented with guns taken from the Brick Fort and their crews were ordered by the Baconians to sail downstream in pursuit of Christopher Evelyn's *Rebecca*, bound for London with her cargo of Berkeleyan treasure, tobacco, refugees, and dispatches.[64]

---

64. M[athew], "Bacon's Rebellion," in Andrews, ed., *Narratives*, 33. Joseph Ingram to Mr. Smith, "in ye name of ye People," n.d., Coventry Ms. 77, 331.

Captain Evelyn, warned of his ship's danger by someone in the rebel headquarters, was already out of Bland and Carver's reach. "Forced to make his Escape having no more than halfe his Loading on bord," Evelyn's was a quick crossing. The dispatches brought by the *Rebecca* reached London on 13 October 1676. Their news, that a rebel general, officers, and army had driven into exile Governor Berkeley "and most of the better sort" of Virginians, and that rebel cavalry were riding into Maryland to carry the revolution to that colony, excited the exit from the Thames, in just over a month, of the vanguard of an expeditionary force of eight transports, four men-of-war, two fireships, and thirteen hundred Guards, recruits, officers, staff, and royal commissioners of investigation. It took almost ten weeks for the leading ships of the punitive expedition to fight their way westward across the winter North Atlantic to Virginia. In the interim, the civil war in Virginia was decided by English sea captains, their sailors, ships, and sloops already in the James or York River or en route to the Chesapeake.[65]

The first significant Chesapeake action was that of the revolutionary squadron under Carver and Bland's command. They had missed Evelyn's *Rebecca,* but they located Sir William Berkeley. He had bought the Eastern Shore planters' protection by promising them twenty-five years' exemption from provincial taxation. His refuge was "Honest Jack" Custis' "Arlington" on Old Plantation Creek, Northampton County. There, after their sweep of the Lower Bay (which added two ships and a variety of small craft to the navy of the revolution), Carver and Bland found Berkeley.[66]

Majesty still surrounded the old vice-regent. Perhaps it led "this Carver," whom Berkeley had commissioned sheriff and whom he thought "an able stout seaman and soldier," to negotiate with the exiled governor. Berkeley's own opinion was that it was "the mercy of God" which brought Captain Carver and one hundred guards, "under pretence of treating with me," to the Custis plantation on 1 September 1676. Alternatively, Berkeley wrote, Carver may have wished "to corrupt or Case my Guard." While talks or corruption went forward, the wind shifted. Carver's boats were now wind-bound in Old Plantation Creek. Observing this from the *Rebecca,* Captain Larrimore (who may himself have suggested the Carver-Berkeley conference) saw that he could turn the tide of success, for the first time, against the revolutionaries. By midnight,

65. Berkeley [to Coventry], 3 June 1676, Coventry Ms. 77, 103. Morgan Lodge to Joseph Williamson, Deal, 12 October, Re[ceived] 13, 1676, S.P. 29/386, no. 160. Captain's log, *Bristol,* Admiralty, Class 51, Group 134, Part III, Public Record Office (hereafter cited as ADM 51/134, Part III).
66. Accomac petition, C.O. 1/34, 200. Accomac Grievances, 11 March 1676/7, C.O. 1/39, 216.

Larrimore managed to contact Berkeley. The captain urged the governor to keep Carver and his troops ashore somehow and in the meantime to send some of his own men out to the *Rebecca*. With their aid, Larrimore promised that he and his crew would recapture the flagship of the revolution. The Berkeleyans agonized over the decision. There were so few of them. The operation might be a rebel trick to take these last loyalists. There seemed to be no other escape from ultimate surrender to Carver and Bland, however, so Colonel Philip Ludwell offered to lead a boarding party.[67]

In the predawn hours of 2 September 1676, Colonel Ludwell and twenty-six men in two wherries rowed out to the *Rebecca*. Some of Larrimore's English seamen were waiting to let them on board through the gun-room ports. Together, Ludwell's and Larrimore's men crowded up the ship's companionways and overpowered the rebel soldiers on the decks of the *Rebecca*. Ludwell himself captured his old enemy Giles Bland.

Ashore, "Assisted by the juice of the Grape," Sir William Berkeley had pleasantly prolonged his conference with Captain Carver. Finally, however, one of Carver's guards told him that wherries had been sighted going alongside the *Rebecca*. The captain hurried on board a small boat and was rowed towards the ship. He was within musket shot of the *Rebecca* before he could tell who had won the fight on her deck, so he was himself compelled to surrender. Climbing as a captive onto the *Rebecca*'s deck, the captain tore off his wig in a rage at Bland. Giles was, Captain Carver said, a careless coward who had lost the revolution when he lost the *Rebecca*. With her went command of the Bay, the rivers, and the Eastern Shore refuge of the Berkeleyans. And Carver's head followed his wig: he was hanged by Berkeley three days after the *Rebecca* was captured. Carver's pinnace, his landing craft, their crews, and the one hundred soldiers of Carver's bodyguard, were now trapped by the *Rebecca*'s command of the Old Plantation Creek. Hungry but afraid to scatter to forage, they all surrendered to the Berkeleyans, whom they greatly outnumbered. In one more of these recapitulations of the English civil wars so characteristic of the Chesapeake revolution, the surrendered Baconians took "the Oathes of Allegeance and Supremacy . . . as the Parliament soldiers used to doe in England."[68]

In the next three days, Captain Larrimore and the *Rebecca* ran down and captured all the other major elements of the rebel squadron, making

67. Berkeley to Coventry, 27 February 1676/7, Coventry Ms. 77, 353.
68. Ludwell to Chicheley, 28 March 1678, C.O. 1/39, 96–97. M[athew], "Bacon's Rebellion," in Andrews, ed., *Narratives*, 36–37. And [Lee,] "Bacon's and Ingram's Rebellion, 1676," in *ibid.*, 65.

the loyalists invulnerable in their base on the Eastern Shore (as the inter-
ception of all subsequent invaders demonstrated and the public execution of their leaders effectively reconfirmed). Larrimore's command of
the only organized naval force in the Chesapeake gave the Berkeleyans
an opportunity to launch their own invasion of the mainland just as the
Baconians were scheduled to meet in revolutionary assembly at Jamestown.

Jamestown

L ate on the afternoon of 7 September 1676, the ship *Rebecca*, of 265
tons burden, mounting twenty guns, and carrying the governor of
Virginia, a crew of twenty-six men, and eighty armed Berkeleyans, led a
little fleet of ships and sloops up the James River. Their recapture of the
Rebecca from the rebels had given "the Loyal party a great reputation in
the Country." It enabled Sir William Berkeley to raise something between two hundred and six hundred mercenaries from the Eastern Shore,
for he promised them an equally easy capture of Jamestown and shares
in the property there of such rebels as Lawrence. These mercenaries
Berkeley placed under the command of the two dozen loyalist gentlemen
who had shared his exile, and he ordered the whole force to board the
Rebecca, her three consorts, and six sloops. En route across the Bay to
the mouth of the James, Berkeley's fleet encountered three more sloops
carrying a hundred mainland loyalists to his aid. The combined squadron
stood up the river atop the flooding tide, tacked around the rebel stronghold of Hog Island, hardened up to clear Archer's Hope, and stood westward towards Jamestown Island.[69]

Before the ships could fetch Jamestown Island, the tide slackened in
the deep channel and they had to anchor, but the more weatherly sloops
carried their lighter draft to the northern shore and played the James
River's half-tide eddy around the island's eastern end. Opening on their
starboard hand, the sloops' crews saw a series of broad ridges each end-

---

69. Berkeley to Coventry, 2 February 1676/7, Coventry Ms. 77, 354. M[athew], "Bacon's
Rebellion," in Andrews, ed., *Narratives*, 36n. "Characters of ye Severall Comdrs of Ships,"
Pepys 2582. Berkeley's force is variously estimated. [Lee,] "Bacon's and Ingram's Rebellion," in *ibid.*, 65, records "5 ships and 10 sloops, in which (as it is saide) was about a
thousand soulders." Petition of Sir Thomas Gould (owner) and Captain Thomas Larrimore,
captain of the *Rebecca*, 22 October 1677, ADM 1/3548, 271.

on to the water, the merlons of Jamestown Island's riverfront. Each of these ridges supported a farmstead and fields. Each was separated from its neighbor to the west by a cedar swamp. The westernmost of these swamps was drained by the Orchard Run. Beyond it the sloops' crews could see a broad plain, gridironed with the streets of the colonial capital's elite eastern suburb, the "New Town."[70]

Seen from the water, this eastern end of Jamestown was dominated by half a dozen brick mansions. Each great house faced the river and was made the more impressive by a red tile roof which doubled the height of the façade and glinted in the glare of the setting September sun. Kitchen gardens, fig, apple, and peach orchards, stable yards, chicken coops, and ice houses all dignified the mansions and divided them from their humbler, frame neighbors. These, the dwellings of artisans, tapsters, and retailers, wore weathered clapboards and mossy shingles. They were little noticed by observers, then or since, and they made themselves felt on the land only by the massive brick chimneys which punctuated their gable ends.

These buildings of the New Town appeared almost deserted when the sloops carried their crews westward past them. The heads of the mansion households and their menservants were out in arms, some on board Governor Berkeley's fleet, more with General Bacon's army. The mistresses and maidservants of the New Town mansions had fled from the contentious capital to the presumed safety of their families' upcountry plantations. Even from the "Country House," the triple unit of old offices on the New Town waterfront, only a few men emerged to watch the sloops sail by. The two taverns adjacent to the country house seemed to be without customers. (Jamestown had one tavern for every ten inhabitants, about the same as the notorious Port Royal, Jamaica. And the politicians who drank in Jamestown were every bit as rapacious as the pirates who sotted in Jamaica: the legislators' barroom "committee" meetings cost their constituents 25 shillings per burgess-day.) Even the low, pentagonal earthworks of the New Town Fort were scantily manned.

70. Apart from the scanty documentary descriptions (Andrews, ed., *Narratives*, 69–70, being most detailed), this account of Jamestown rests on the archeological work of twenty-five years, most accessibly summarized in John L. Cotter and J. Paul Hudson *New Discoveries at Jamestown* (Washington, D.C., 1957). Even more useful to this account has been J. Paul Hudson's full manuscript study of Jamestown and the extraordinary maps and elevations he has prepared as part of that study. I am also indebted to this author for his invaluable personal comments on the Jamestown site. Grateful acknowledgments are also due to James R. Sullivan and to his staff at the Colonial National Historical Park for access to maps and reports dating from the 1905 work of Samuel H. Younge (see his *The Site of Old "James Towne"* [Richmond, 1907]) and to the Report of Charles E. Hatch, Jr., as well as for directing me to the sites described therein. None of these generous scholars bears any responsibility for what they may consider an audacious abuse of their work.

Certainly, they offered no opposition to the Berkeleyan sloops' progress.[71]

As the dying southwesterly wind blew these sloops northwest over the slack tide and along Jamestown's shore, their crews could see, but fortunately they could not smell, the foul and acrid smoke that rose from the kilns, brewhouses, tanneries, and smithies of Jamestown's industrial area. It lay inland, north and downwind of the New Town, and it extended west past the Old Town as well, separating both these residential areas from the main body of the long and narrow "pitch and tar swamp." Beyond the swamp was a broad ridge, topped by scattered houses and farms. These were served by the "frigate landing" on the Back Creek. The creek's four-foot bar restricted traffic to James River "frigates"—long, open, oared boats.

The sloop crews paid little attention to the industrial area or to the island beyond it, for as evening fell and the breeze with it the little vessels had nearly reached Jamestown's westernmost point. They were directly opposite the batteries of the "Brick Fort," sited in a vale just east of that point. Thence, three months earlier to the day, the guns had fired on Nathaniel Bacon's sloop, starting Virginia's revolution.

The brick fort was sited where its guns could sweep the ship channel as it swings north to touch Jamestown Island, a swing that had fixed the site of Virginia's capital and only town. The brick crescent of the fort, its river front 10 feet high and 10 feet thick, had been completed just two years previously. Inland and to the northeast of the brick fort, beyond Jamestown's waterfront wharves, warehouses, and taverns, lumberyards and ship stocks, the Berkeleyan crews could see long brick row houses topped with high slate roofs. These were the hated houses financed by the "great quantities of tobacco that was leavied upon the poor people." Therein upcountry assemblymen had rented rooms at what everyone agreed were "exorbitant rates." These the burgesses charged to constituents, along with their tavern bills. The angry electors referred to "James Citty, [as] a place of vast expense & extortion." The result was an ultimately fatal hatred for the capital town, and a revulsion towards its officialdom which had helped to incite Bacon's Revolution. Now the crews of the Berkeleyan sloops scanned the shore for signs of rebel troops.[72]

There had been five hundred revolutionaries in the Jamestown garrison when its mounted scouts first reported Berkeley's fleet. Some of the

71. Colonial National Historical Park Archeological Survey, Jamestown. "Considerations upon the present troubles in Virginia," C.O. 1/36, 113.
72. The Royal Commissioners, "A True Narrative," in Andrews, ed., *Narratives*, 135. Isle of Wight Grievances, C.O. 1/39, 223, 224. Surrey County Grievances (2nd version), *ibid.*, 209.

garrison fled from the very news, "our numbers being trebeled in the opinion of the Enemie," Sir William wrote. More resolute rebels, under the command of Captain Thomas Hansford, held their ground until the Berkeleyan sloops were anchored opposite the town and their captains sent ashore Sir William's summons to surrender. Doubtless this summons was backed by reports of the strength of the loyalist ships anchored just downstream, waiting for the morning tide to carry them up to Jamestown. The rebel garrison knew the force of the four ships that had been the Baconian navy only ten days before. They had armed the *Rebecca* themselves with guns from the brick fort. The rebels knew that, in the morning, those guns would command the isthmus and so block their only escape from Jamestown. Thus, although Hansford's men rejected the pardon Berkeley offered them, they also fled from Jamestown during the night of 7 September 1676. Most of the men dispersed to their homes but Hansford rode away upcountry to report to General Bacon the return of Governor Berkeley.[73]

Before dawn, word reached Berkeley's sloops that the Baconians were gone. With first light, the little vessels (they drew less than five feet of water) were warped alongside the Jamestown bulkhead and the Eastern Shore mercenaries stepped ashore. Some manned the brick fort. More thronged eastward into the market square. They broke down the doors of the half-timber shops in search of the wine and brandy stored in their cellars. They smashed the shutters of the wooden stalls and stole the food they found there. Charity dictates the hope that some of the mercenaries continued across the market square to give thanks at the Brick Church for their unopposed landing, and for the riches of Jamestown. The massive church tower stood—it still stands—guard over an ancient cemetery and it marks the southeast corner of what was then the market square. Next to the church, on the east side of the square, stood Richard Lawrence's house, its hutch of gold and silver plate a lodestone to the loyalist looters.

Others of Berkeley's men moved northwest, across "the Vale" in which the brick fort stood, to the row of brick buildings which marked the western edge of old Jamestown. Its two stories topped by a great roof, the row was at least 200 feet long in 1676. The northernmost building of this brick row was the statehouse. Its ground floor contained the chamber of the council and general court and the office of the assembly clerk. The burgesses' chamber and the office of the secretary of the colony were upstairs in the statehouse. Three houses at the south end of the row belonged to the councilor and colonel Philip Ludwell. Two other housing units provided occasional quarters for the governor and for his intimates. Apart from his share in the statehouse complex, Sir William Berkeley owned at least three brick and two wooden houses in Jamestown. Town houses were also favorite investments of Berkeley's old friends and colleagues, the royal governors of Tangier, Portsmouth, and New York. All the governors found house property a tax-supported and tax-sheltered investment which also manifested their obedience to royal orders for town development. The cost of Jamestown's development had angered many of the Virginians who now followed Bacon, and who now cut off Sir William Berkeley from Green Spring even though his mansion, the greatest house in the colony, was but three miles west of Jamestown.

Sir William followed his men ashore, taking a boat from the *Rebecca* to land at his capital on the morning of 8 September 1676. Stepping ashore, the governor knelt to give thanks for his safe return. Then he and his aides walked up "the Great Road" past the statehouse and continued a quarter of a mile to "Block House Hill." On this modest elevation stood the wooden fort which overlooked the isthmus. Below the blockhouse, on the western slope, the governor ordered a line of entrenchments dug across the isthmus. This was a fairly easy task, for the soil was sandy and the isthmus was "less than a flight shot" (100 yards) across from the tide line of the James to that of the Back Creek. This trench the governor had backed with palisades and had a battery built at its midpoint. Then, for a week, safely walled in from the revolutionary countryside, the men of the Eastern Shore, recruited by Berkeley's promise of plunder, looted and drank their way through Jamestown.

Sir William's hired hands were in no shape to fight when a few of the enemy at last arrived. At sunset on 13 September 1676, just 136 revolutionary soldiers ended their exhausting day's march of more than 30 miles at the mainland end of the Jamestown Isthmus. The rebels' trumpets and their cavalry's caracoles proclaimed their arrival, but loyalist patrols had already told Governor Berkeley of Bacon's remarkable recovery and undiminished popularity.

Abandoned by Brent's northerners after an unproductive campaign, desperate for a success against Indians, Bacon and the forces of the upper James and of Gloucester County had plunged into the Dragon Swamp in pursuit of the Pamunkey. These were the central tribe of what survived of the Powhatan Confederacy, the linchpin of Berkeley's Indian alliance system. When the expedition at last emerged from the swamp with their Pamunkey prisoners many of the exhausted Baconians dispersed. Then, Captain Hansford, with some of the fugitives from the Jamestown garrison, found General Bacon and his bodyguard. They instantly marched on the capital. En route, their parade of Pamunkey prisoners and plunder attracted some two hundred volunteers from New Kent County and the Chickahominy settlements. They followed Nathaniel Bacon and his bodyguard towards Jamestown.

Although they were outnumbered four to one by the governor's garrison, the revolutionary vanguard drove the loyalist pickets off the isthmus. During the night, they dug their own ditch across it, mostly with their bare hands. At dawn on 14 September 1676, by way of further defiance, some of Bacon's men ran up to the new palisade on Block House Hill, pointed their muskets between the planks, and shot up the governor's guards. Then the upcountry volunteers came in. More militia were drafted: "Bacon sent six troopers . . . with a commission" and a simple choice to the homes of several local captains. Reinforced, the besiegers deepened their "pittifull trench." They tossed brush and timber fascines onto the slowly growing bank. These were useless against the loyalist cannon, however, and Berkeley's gunners now opened fire both from the palisade battery and from the armed ships anchored in Sandy Bay. The rebels were driven back onto the mainland. They reoccupied their trench at sunset on the 14th, just in time to repulse the loyalist sloops that had come up to land men on the rebel flank. The Baconians even captured one grounded vessel after its crew fled from the rebel musketry.[74]

Although the ships' guns and the sloops' crews had not been able to break the Baconian siege of Jamestown, they controlled the James River. Backed by the big ships, loyalist sloops carried raiders to isolated plantations on the north bank of the James. From these the Berkeleyans took provisions, plunder, and prisoners. Early in the morning of 15 September 1676, Berkeley had one of these prisoners, Captain William Cookson, hanged as a traitor at Jamestown. Later on that day, the governor condemned two more revolutionaries to death, one for prying into Berkeleyan secrets and promoting Bacon's cause, the second for social-climbing. His "name was Digby, who from a Servant was preferr'd to the honorable Title of Captain; in which he remain'd till the severe hand of Justice cut off his ambition with his life." Soldier, citizen, climber, the three men executed on 15 September 1676 personified the revolutionary aspirations which excited the loyalists' social fears.[75]

The Berkeleyans revealed their physical fears the next day: they misdelivered their long-expected sortie from Jamestown. Servants and conscripts were forced to the front. Their masters and officers led from behind. Crowded together, the rear ranks sheltering themselves behind the front ones, the Berkeleyans advanced against the Baconian line. When the front ranks fell, however, the rear ones ran: "these 7 or (as they say) 800 of Accomackions who (like scholars going to schoole) went out

74. "The Case of Mr. Richard Clarke," C.O. 1/40, 6. [Lee,] "Bacon's and Ingram's Rebellion," in Andrews, ed., *Narratives*, 69.

75. "More News from Virginia . . . With An Account Of thirteen Persons that have been tryed and Executed for their Rebellion there" [London, 1677], in Finestone, ed., *Bacon's Rebellion*, 27.

with heavie hearts but returned home with light heeles." They left on the field their colors, drums, weapons, wounded, and dead to be collected by the rebels.[76]

To protect their scavenging and re-entrenchment, the victorious revolutionaries added unchivalrous insult to physical injury. They pushed forward a screen of female loyalist prisoners. Even as the loyalists raided upstream, the revolutionaries had raided upcountry, seizing the wives and maidservants of loyalists. Now these women were made to stand in the rain before the Baconian lines, the loyal councilors' wives made prominent among them by their dress. "These ladyes white Aprons" shielded the Baconian plunderers and their rising earthworks from the demoralized loyalists.[77]

Early the next morning, 17 September 1676, the psychologically astute revolutionaries paraded prisoners of another sort. Captured Indians were put up on the entrenchments. They rallied the racist countryside to Bacon's cause and reminded Berkeley's garrison that they endangered their lives for an Indian-lover. Protected by their captives, the Baconians completed a battery. On 18 September 1676, its cannon began to fire on the loyalist ships and to bombard the statehouse. Berkeley's ships had to move downriver. The men of the Eastern Shore were afraid they would be abandoned, and their leaders' councils were shattered by cannonballs crashing through the statehouse walls.

Berkeleyan morale was the only casualty of the revolutionaries' cannonade, but they kept it up despite an unseasonable and incessant rain. The rain was said to be the work of vengeful Indian werowances. It had fallen on Bacon's camps throughout his Indian campaign although surrounding regions remained dry. Now the rain followed Bacon's men on to the Jamestown Isthmus. This month of wet living brought on Bacon's fatal illness, and all the besiegers suffered with him. Yet the governor's garrison, inside Jamestown's walls and under its roofs, sheltered and dry, were nevertheless so humiliated by their failed bombardment and cowardly sortie, so intimidated by revolutionary assaults on their morale, so lacking in loyalty to the old order of governor and grandees, so convinced that the revolutionaries had taken an oath to give no quarter to loyalists, and

. . . soe great was the Cowardize and Baseness of the Generality of Sir William Berkeley's Party (being most of them men intent onely upon plunder or compell'd and hired into his service) that of all, at last there were onely some 20 Gentlemen willing to stand by

76. [Lee,] "Bacon's and Ingram's Rebellion," in Andrews, ed., Narratives, 68, 70.
77. An. Cotton, "Our Late Troubles In Virginia," in Force, ed., Tracts, I, 8.

him, the rest (whome hopes or promise of Plunder brought thither)
being now in hast to be gone to secure what they had gott; soe that
Sir Wm Berkeley himselfe who undoubtedly would rather have
dyed on the place than thus deserted it . . . was at last overper-
suaded, nay hurryed away against his owne will and forced to
leave the Towne to the mercy of the enemy.[78]

"Soe fearful of Discovery" were the loyalists that, during the night of
19 September 1676, they ferried the plunder of the capital downriver to
their ships, weighed anchor on the ebbtide, and drifted away from Jamestown in the dark, anchoring again only when they were safely out of
cannon shot and so out of reach of the shipless revolutionaries.

Before dawn on 20 September 1676, led by Nathaniel Bacon, "General
by Consent of the People," the revolutionaries once again crowded into
the colonial capital. This time, although their own leaders owned both
mansions and taverns, the revolutionaries had no mercy on Jamestown.
Berkeley's occupation had taught the Baconians that, without ships, they
could not long hold the capital. Indeed, there was immediate danger that
the Army of Virginia might be trapped on Jamestown Island. The Berkeleyan ships were still anchored downstream, and one thousand loyalists
were said to be marching on Jamestown from the northern counties. They
could not hold the colonial capital, the symbol and instrument of authority, but neither could the revolutionaries leave it to their enemies. Therefore, General Bacon, "soldier like considering of what importance a Place
of that Refuge might again bee to the governor and his Party, instantly
resolves to lay it level with the ground."

After dark on 20 September 1676, Bacon and his men "sett fire to
Towne, church and state house." The general of the revolution himself
put the torch to Virginia's mother church, the sacred support of royal
authority. His leading political aides, Lawrence and Drummond, fired
their own houses as well as those of the Berkeleyan grandees. "Ye Rebell
Lawrence" not only burned William Sherwood's house, for one, he destroyed in it property worth more than £1,000 (a modest enough revenge
on the grandee who had escaped to call down royal repression on Virginia's revolution). Humbler rebels rejoiced as they burned the homes
and the offices of their oppressors "Saying, The Rogues should harbour
no more there." Governor Berkeley's five houses, worth, with their contents, £6,000 sterling, twenty gentlemen's mansions, and other symbols of
authority—church, statehouse, magazine, office building—all were gutted. The public records were saved by Drummond from the ruin of the

78. The Royal Commissioners, "A True Narrative," in Andrews, ed., *Narratives*, 135.

secretary's office, however, for land patents were the charters of Virginia prosperity. He who held them held power. The future of the revolution lay in the paper Drummond packed away in his saddlebags on the night of 20 September 1676, and which he carried with him until he was killed. But the major buildings of Jamestown's capitol district went up in flames. Its monuments of oppression, most notoriously the costly public housing, were destroyed.[79]

The bulk of Jamestown's wooden warehouses, stores, and taverns (including one with a cellar full of 8,000 gallons of Alderman Jeffrey Jeffreys' best Fayal wine, which, amazingly, neither rebels nor loyalists had drunk) either were consumed by the Baconian bonfire or had already been so badly battered by the Accomac mercenaries as not to seem worth the rebels' burning. Before dawn, 21 September 1676, property worth more than £45,000 sterling was destroyed. Not a habitable house was left in Old Jamestown. Governor Berkeley, his grandees, and his men, "who had so lately deserted it, as they rid a little below in the River in the Ships and Sloops (to their shame and regret) beheld by night the Flames of the Towne, which they, so basely forsaking, had made a sacrifice to ruine."[80]

A way of life, autonomous, colonial, autarchical, traditional, was sacrificed in the fires of Jamestown. The town itself, the assembly system that had been housed in its taverns and row houses, the conciliar government seated in the statehouse, the capital of a colony dependent on England only economically, a life redolent of the more backward shires of England before the mother country's own civil war and revolution, all burned and passed away on 20 September 1676. Now the horrors of Leviathan's century had crossed the Atlantic to Virginia, destroying, transforming, modernizing. The siege of the Old Dominion's capital—in which revolutionaries exposed gentlewomen and threatened race war, in which reaction so overwhelmed Sir William Berkeley, that personification of the old order, that he killed prisoners of war for their political opinions and social ambitions—had broken the bonds of wrath. Now Virginia's civil warriors reduced every civil limit and social tie to the level of the burned-out town. From the perspective offered by the ruins of the past, the revolutionaries reconsidered Virginia's relation to traditional society, and to England.

79. [Lee,] "Bacon's and Ingram's Rebellion," in Andrews, ed., *Narratives*, 71. M[athew], "Bacon's Rebellion," in *ibid.*, 35.
80. "Personal Grievances By Petition of Mr Jno Page on behalf of Jno Jeffreys," Commissioners to Coventry, 14 February 1676/7, Pepys 2582. The Royal Commissioners, "A True Narrative," in Andrews, ed., *Narratives,* 136. The southeasternmost end of the New Town, the farmsteads on the ridges east of Orchard Run, the industrial section, all escaped the flames of revolution. The brick and earth of the forts defied them.

Independence

Traditional society's foundation was unfree human labor, and the leaders of both sides in the revolutionary struggle offered freedom to the servants and slaves of their opponents. Their object was not to extend liberty but to attack property. In men's labor "the wealth of this Country doth consist," and a change of labor, from tillage to fighting, not immediate emancipation, was offered laborers. They were freed from their former masters on condition that they take up arms against them. To emancipate and enlist servants and slaves was unprecedented in the Virginia of 1676. Nothing like it recurred until 1776, when the royal governor of Virginia declared the slaves of rebel planters free and from them formed a "black regiment." In 1676, however, it was the rebels who freed the slaves. Former slaves became the staunchest soldiers of the revolution.[81]

Arming laborers against their masters inverted society, destroyed civil order, and was logically followed by Berkeley's declaration of martial law. Bacon had won the slaves to his revolutionary standard but Berkeley countered with the court-martial and the noose. By the end of October 1676, he had summarily condemned and hanged eleven rebel leaders. Uncounted others Sir William condemned to the slow deaths of imprisonment in log-built corn cribs or in the foul wet holds of ships.

When Berkeley ripped the mask of law and lenience from the face of royal government, he reminded Englishmen in Virginia of republican alternatives. Since republican rule had been overthrown in 1660, commonwealth plots had shaken the crown at home every six years. Their echoes had been twice heard in Virginia. In 1676, royalists everywhere in the empire feared renewed republican risings, for neither English nationality nor English empire had then the power they acquired in America after and because of 1676. For most colonists in that fatal year, the focus of authority and the locus of patriotism was the community, not the colony —much less the empire. Most American governments looked inward to their constituent counties, towns, or parishes, rather than overseas to a distant king, an inchoate nation, a nascent empire.

81. Proclamation, 27 October 1676, C.O. 1/38, 10. Lancaster County Proposals, [14 March 1676,] C.O. 1/39, 217. [Lee,] "Bacon's and Ingram's Rebellion," in Andrews, ed., *Narratives*, 65–66.

Autonomy and locality have always been acknowledged to be New England's norms, but they were general colonial characteristics prior to 1676, despite the best imperial efforts of the governors-general in the strategic West Indian and New York colonies and despite the loyal protestations of colonial agents at Whitehall. It was but one step from practical autonomy to institutional independence. The agents of the Virginia Assembly at the court of Charles II pointed out that "the New Englanders imagine great felicity in their form of government, civil and ecclesiastic, under which they are trained up to disobedience to the Crown and Church of England" but the Virginians insisted, somewhat unconvincingly, that they did not wish to imitate the independence of their northern neighbors and so to "enjoy all the liberties and privileges as the New Englanders do." Nonetheless, the Virginians asked the king for a charter confirming the autonomy of their assembly and their colony vis-à-vis both the crown of England and the commons of Virginia.[82]

Although he and his followers felt themselves victimized by the autonomous assembly elite, the leader of the Virginia commons was as bound by provincial attitudes as were his enemies. As a Henrico County planter, Nathaniel Bacon was concerned primarily with exterminating Indians. Secondarily he had sought county "liberties" (i.e., "freedoms") from the Berkeleyan grandees. Only after the Berkeleyans were driven across Chesapeake Bay did the Baconians begin to seek provincial "priviledges" (i.e., "exemptions") from English mercantile regulation and economic exploitation. Only after they had conquered the counties and the colony did the rebels face the selfish strength of the mercantile system. So, at last, Bacon and his advisers envisioned Chesapeake independence from England.

The county rising had already turned into a regional revolt when, in the waning days of September 1676, the Baconians marched from the ruins of Jamestown to Sir William Berkeley's rich, defensible plantation, Green Spring, there to consider the road towards independence. That a provincial revolution was under way, Bacon reiterated first by looting Green Spring and then by proclaiming its owner, the king's governor, "a Traytor and most pernitious Enemy to the Public." It was a logical step to move from the confiscation of the landed property of the governor and of all the leading loyalists, and the condemnation of the political power they had premised on Berkeley's royal commission, to the conquest of the king's dominion. As an enemy of the revolution put it, Bacon sought to "insnare" the allegiance of the people by "Laying before them the

82. The "Notes, explanatory" of the Virginia agents are printed in Burk, *Virginia*, II, Appendix, liii.

Plunder of the best part of the Country and the Vain hopes of taking the Country wholly out of his Maties hands into their owne."[83]

Even the least venturesome Baconians agreed that they must now replace the traitor Sir William Berkeley as governor. Their candidate was Sir Henry Chicheley. He had four advantages to those who would settle for a change of rulers rather than a change of systems: he was deputy governor and lieutenant general of Virginia already; he was a weak character; he was in a Baconian jail; and William Drummond, the revolution's historical researcher, had found ample precedent in Virginia's turbulent past for the ouster of royal governors and their replacement by figureheads taken from the colony's executive ranks. Those moderates who would change executives were warned of the consequences of success by those who wanted only to reform the Berkeleyan regime: "Should we overcome the governor we must expect a greater power from England, that would be our ruin."

To these fears of royal coercion, and to arguments for mere reform or for a change of executives, three revolutionary rejoinders were made. First, the bulk of both the officers and the people of Virginia were rebels already. By taking Bacon's Oath, Virginians had sworn to resist the authority of the king. They were pledged "to stand or fall in Defense of him [General Bacon] and the country" even against the "Forces of his Majesty." This pledge was, as Governor Berkeley said, "treason by the very words of the act."[84]

Second, said the revolutionaries, the king and his forces were not the most powerful European presence in Virginia, and so they were not the best Old World protectors of New World planters. The Dutch had demonstrated their naval command of the Chesapeake both in 1667 and 1673. The Dutch, so the revolutionaries thought, would arm and protect them in order to secure the tobacco trade and break the English economic monopoly proclaimed by the Navigation Acts. The Dutch had supported the Barbadians against English hegemony in 1652–54. They had freed the New Yorkers from English exploitation in 1673–74. Dutch merchants were still, and would long remain, the preferred trading partners of many Virginians. Surely they would assist Virginians to escape London's hated hold. The ability of the Dutch and the debility of the English seemed the more apparent to the Green Spring conferees because the armed forces of the English king were divided between the rival claimants to his throne.

In their third major argument for independence, the Virginia revolu-

---

83. P. Ludwell to H. Coventry, 14 April 1677, C.O. 1/40, 54.
84. Bacon's conversation with Coode, 2 September 1676, deposed 30 January 1676/7, Coventry Ms. 77, 347–48; also in C.O. 5/1371, 119–23.

tionaries pointed to the contest between the captain-general of the royal army—the king's illegitimate son, the Protestant duke of Monmouth— and the commander of the navy in the empire, the king's brother and heir, the Catholic duke of York. The enmities of Monmouth and York, of opponents and proponents of royal absolutism, of Protestants and Catholics seemed to Virginia's revolutionaries certain to weaken any reaction against their revolt and likely to presage renewed civil war in the British Isles. Such a war would once again, as its predecessor had in the decade of the 1640s, free Virginians, and all colonists, from imperial authority. After Sarah Drummond, termagant wife of the revolutionary leader, reviewed these portents of political and military turmoil in England for the Green Spring debaters, she bent down, plucked a jackstraw, snapped it in two, and declared, "I fear the power of England no more than a broken straw." "We shall," she assured the council of the revolution, "do well enough" independent of England.[85]

Chesapeake Confederation

ALBEMARLE

Determined on independence from England, the Green Spring debaters next asked what other colonies might join Virginia. The revolutionaries sought the alliance of the Massachusetts commonwealth and received unofficial aid at least from that colony's coastwise traders, as well as an official promise of shelter from royal reprisals for refugee revolutionaries. Closer to home, General Bacon was "confident of it, that it is the mind of this Country, and of Maryland, & of Carolina alsoe to cast off theire Governrs." Delegates from both these colonies were at the Green Spring meeting. The Carolinians were from the Albemarle Sound and Roanoke River regions, bordering on Virginia. Bacon's adviser William Drummond had been their governor. He still held land in Albemarle and was well regarded there. His successors, however, and the aristocratic English proprietors whom they represented, had been negligent

85. N.B. the parallel argument of the New Englanders, that royal and metropolitian authority were both negated because the duke of York and his followers had begun a civil war with the support of the city of London (Edward Randolph, "a Short Narrative," 28 September 1676, C.O. 1/37, 191).

and were despised. "The Governours of Carolina had taken noe notice of the people, nor the people of them a long time," Nathaniel Bacon observed, and, he concluded, "the people are resolved to owne their Government noe farther." [86]

The people of Albemarle and Roanoke were mostly migrants from Virginia and, like most Virginians, they were hostile to Sir William Berkeley. Berkeley was doubly disliked as the American agent of the Carolina proprietors and as a proprietor himself. The people of Albemarle also resented, to the point of armed resistance, the English plantations duty of 1673. The isolated people of the autonomous Albemarle found allies along both their outlets to the world. One of these was the shallows of inlet and sound through which the trading ketches of New England came to Albemarle. The skippers of these vessels, if they did not actually incite revolution in 1676, certainly armed and supported it along the Roanoke River in Albemarle (as they did along the James River in Virginia). The overland trail from Albemarle ran north to the James River through the Baconian center of Nansemond County. In September 1676, friends of Virginia's revolution came overland from Albemarle to Green Spring to join the Baconian counsels. In January following, Virginia revolutionaries by the hundred took the trail south into Albemarle. As General Bacon planned at the Green Spring meetings, the Albemarle region would be the refuge of the revolutionaries. "If wee cannot prevaile by our armes at least to make our conditions for peace or obtaine the priviledge to elect our owne Governors [for this was the minimum program of the Baconians] wee may retire to Roanoke," General Bacon said to the Chesapeake colonists. From bases along the Roanoke, Bacon's revolutionaries continued to assault royal authority in Virginia's Southside counties, and to obviate proprietary prerogatives in Albemarle, at least through 1680. Bacon had been prescient when, in September 1676, "he nominated Carolina for the watchword" of the Chesapeake revolution. [87]

MARYLAND

A Baconian revolution which, at its minimum, attacked all Indians, plundered provincial grandees, and promised popular governors, also attracted Maryland's racist, poor, oppressed planters. The Maryland "incendiaries" who attended the revolutionary, intercolonial council at Green Spring in September 1676 were the survivors of the men who in August had called "the common people" to arms and been met by force. "Since Generall Davis and Pate were hanged the Route hath been much

---

86. Bacon to Coode, 2 September 1676, Coventry Ms. 77, 348.
87. Coventry Ms. 77, 348.

amas[d] and apaled," Maryland's deputy governor, Thomas Notley, wrote, "though never Body was more repleat with Malignancy and knavery then our people were in August last, and they wanted but a monstrous head to their monstrous body."[88]

The "monstrous body" of the Marylanders found a voice if not a head in the "Complaint from Heaven with a Huy & Crye and Petition out of Virginia and Maryland." It repeated, in the accents of Maryland, the Virginia and Albemarle attack on taxation, exploitation, and misgovernment by autonomous provincial grandees, proprietors, and governors. Written by Protestants in a colony controlled by Catholics, the "Huy & Crye" added the indelible dye of religious hatred to the revolutionary waters of the Chesapeake. As the Virginians had noted at Green Spring, anti-Catholic fears had crested again in England as recently as 1673, and they still preoccupied the imperial council of the crown in 1676, but little fresh incitement was required to stir Maryland Protestants' passions. These hardly abated between the religious war of 1655 and the Protestant coup of 1689. When it moved from religion to politics, however, the "Complaint from Heaven" showed that, unlike the majority of either the Berkeleyans or the Baconians in Virginia, Marylanders who disliked the provincial status quo of 1676 believed that imperial dominion could regulate grandees, protect Protestantism, and unite the English colonies against the empires of the Iroquois and the French.[89]

Although they concluded their petition with an appeal to ideals of empire, the Marylanders of 1676 personalized the causes of the Chesapeake revolution and located them on the region's inland frontiers:

> Now mark the late Tragedy: Old Governor Barkly, Altered by marrying a young wyff, from his wonted publicq good, to a covetous fools-age, relished Indians presents, with som that hath a like feelinge, so wel, that many Christians Blood is pukkuted up, with other mischievs, in so much that his lady tould that it would bee the overthrow of the Country.

Berkeley, Baltimore, and their clients had allied themselves with the Peoples of the Fall Line to collect furs. All became embroiled with a rising western power, the "Seneca" nations of the Longhouse League. In 1675, the war between the Seneca and Maryland's allies, the Susque-

---

88. Notley to Baltimore, 22 January 1676/7, C.O. 1/39, 21, printed in William Hand Browne, ed., Archives of Maryland, V (Baltimore, 1887), 152–54.

89. "Complaint from Heaven with a Huy & Crye and Petition out of Virginia and Maryland," C.O. 1/36, 213–18; printed in Browne, ed., Archives of Maryland, V, 134–52. On the privy council and religion in the empire see Book II, pp. 189–93.

hanna nation and the Conoy confederacy, had recoiled on the frontiers of English expansion. In Virginia, that war destroyed "above 5 or 600 men, weemen, and children," the "Huy & Crye" reported, "untill Sqr. Bacon, moved with the peoples and his owne loss, repulsed the Indians." "The Berklieu and Baltemore Partys" then betrayed General Bacon and his army to the Indians and outlawed the survivors. In Maryland, they imprisoned Major General Trueman, commander of the anti-Indian forces, "to stop his mouth and prevent his complaining to England. O Treachery plainly discovered out of the Cabinet of Popish Maryland, wch opened further out starts a Number of Grievances."[90]

Thus the Catholic cabinet of Maryland were held responsible by Protestant protesters for "the late murthers by the Susquehannock in Virginia and Maryland." The Maryland elite, like the grandees of Virginia, so their enemies wrote, had preferred fur trade to frontier defense. The Baltimoreans were also blamed for the "Seneca" raids, because they had refused to make the treaty with the League of the Iroquois suggested by the governor of New York. From the war that their greed and provincialism had thus provoked, the Maryland elite now profited by their confiscation of soldiers' plunder, by their exchange of Indian prisoners for Barbadian blacks, by their taxes for magazines of weapons and supplies which, when opened for the 1676 wars, were found to be empty. To offset their own thefts, the provincial elite requisitioned "the inhabitants powder and shot, guns, pistolls, shoes, stockins, and clothes." Their "Provision taken by force and vyolence" was less of a popular grievance than the elite's impressment of the small planters themselves to serve in the militia. There they were forced to pay their officers' costs, as well as their own.

Elite aggrandizement, not public defense, was their rulers' aim. So much was proved to the dissidents of 1676 by the proprietary cavalry's raids on the Delaware settlements claimed by Maryland. Troops who were not made available to fight Indians were ordered to plunder and burn European settlements in 1671, 1672, 1673, and again in 1676. Typical of the Baltimorean behavior had been the work of one Captain Howell, who, "with a troop of Souldiers," rode into Whorekill, as its settlers said, demanded its submission to Maryland, promised "we will protect you . . . and did eat and Drinke with us eighteen Dayes and then set our Housing on fire upon Christmas Eave." To ensure that they burned the villagers out entirely, "the Souldgers . . . took Wheat sheaves & carried [them] up [to] the Chambers & sett them on Fier."[91]

90. "Complaint from Heaven," C.O. 1/36, 213; printed in Browne, ed., *Archives*, V, 134.
91. Depositions of Halmanis Wiltbaink, John Roades, Wm. Clark, Edward Southrin, 5 May 1673, in Leon de Valinger, ed., "The Burning Of The Whorekill, 1673," *Pennsylvania Magazine of History and Biography* 74 (1950): 479, 482.

The 1676 petitioners blamed the proprietary party's military misman-agement, forcible requisitioning, and violent aggression on popery and autonomy combined. Allegiance sworn to the Calvert, Catholic, proprie-tor of Maryland not only violated the treaty by which the Protestant party had returned Maryland to the Calverts and the Catholics in 1658, it also excluded royal rule from Maryland "as if the king's Majesty in England hath nothing to doe there, which is wunderfull strange, considering New Yorke and all other Provinces in America, honour the King's most excel-lent Majesty, with the Emperial Armes and suppremacy of England."[92]

Cut off from royal justice, subjected to proprietorial misrule, the Maryland petitioners of 1676 looked to the provincial assembly for re-lief. They found it closed to popular protests by executive mechanisms like those used by the Berkeleyans to discipline the Virginia Assembly: executive selection of candidates; executive entertainment of delegates; executive patronage to legislators; executive dictation of legislation; ex-ecutive "frowns and threatenings"; and executive vetoes. The dissidents were not surprised to find that "provintiall and privat councellors and Colonels and Cheef Officers" were the enemies of equity and of empire, for they were the chosen "Champions, with the Attournys[,] to judge, advise and maintaine the Lord proprietary's devises," but the petitioners were appalled to find that the elected "Assembly men betray yr trust to your Country for a Collonels or Captains name and office, or peculiar favour, to the oppression and ruyn of many of the King's poore subjects."

Uncontrolled by the crown, unchecked by the commons, the provin-cial elite could tax at will. That taxation was the great grievance of com-monwealthsmen all around the Chesapeake. In Maryland as in Virginia, not only were military head taxes misapplied and elite requisitions extor-tionate, but provincial revenues also benefited the few rather than re-lieved the many. The 2-shilling tax on each hogshead of tobacco exported was, by the commons of both colonies, supposed to be applied to the costs of administration and defense so as to lessen county levies. Instead, it was allocated by the Chesapeake grandees to themselves, not devoted to "the people's common good and the publick wellfare of the Country." A tax on Dutch-shipped exports was likewise misapplied, the petitioners of 1676 complained. To these export taxes were added internal taxes for gifts to provincial favorites, fines, fees, escheats, quitrents, port duties, license costs, "and wee must bear the burthen of Oppression and Taxa-tion in all other respects whatsoever besides." Even the proprietor's dep-uty governor, Thomas Notley, admitted in 1676 that "the last publique leavy being 297 [pounds of tobacco] per poll and the great leavy the year before, hath given occassion for malignant spirits to mutter." Those spirits included the petitioners of 1676, who claimed that the provincial head tax alone consumed "the fourth parts of poore peoples livelyhood and yearly produce out of their labour."[93]

The sum of military mismanagement, proprietary autonomy, and extortionate taxation was the grandees' oppression of the commons "so that there is little difference between them and bondslaves that work for 3 days for themselves and 3 days to maintaine others." To proprietary oppression, add the petty exploiters—retailers, innkeepers, lawyers, under-officers—"which feed upon the people (as the wolves upon the sheepe)"—and the result was that one hard winter, one epidemic of disease, one Indian raid meant that the poor planter lost all he had and "must shuffle and cut amongst the great ones to begin againe."[94]

Maryland, like Virginia and all the American colonies of 1676, was prey to both social and economic underdevelopment. So its people were especially vulnerable to individual selfishness and oligarchical oppression. As the Marylanders put it, "the poore Country is robbed, cheated by the superiors and inferiours, every one serving their owne turne, without any true feare and worship of God, which denotes that the Country is but in a feeble minority." Now, in 1676, the Maryland petitioners wrote, the people had risen against the symbols of their society's immaturity, the oppressive grandees and the dangerous Indians. This was "a miserable extremity the poore inhabitants are and see themselves involved [in,] viz. with oppression and warr from within and Hazard of life and Estate by Indians from without and at hom." The Indians murdered the frontiersmen working in their fields but "the Grandees about St. Marys and the midle of the Country mean while beeing securely guarded by the outside plantations and able gangs or garris[on]ed, knows nothing of it, nor will beleeve, and therefore upon the people's great complaint, all the assistance that came from owr Governor was of late a proclamation which comanded that 10 men of the neighbourhood should resort together into one plantation and fortify themselves, but if above 10 . . . should be punished as rebells and mutineers." Here, in one long sentence, was the popular dilemma of 1676. Neither the Baltimorean elite nor the Berkeleyan grandees believed that the frontiersmen were being attacked. Therefore they construed unauthorized acts of self-defense to be rebellion. But by outlawing supposed rebels, the Chesapeake oligarchs created real revolutionaries.

This oligarchical reaction the Baconians saw as a conspiracy to preserve the fur trade at the cost of frontiersmen's lives and to create rebels

93. *Ibid.*, in Browne, ed., *Archives of Maryland*, V, 141, and see note 88, above.
94. "Complaint from Heaven," in Browne, ed., *Archives of Maryland*, V, 144.

whose property could be confiscated. The Maryland dissidents added that the reactions of the elite were parts of an international popish plot to "overturne the Protestants." In terrorized terms, which anticipated the English hysteria of the "Popish Plot" and reflected London's anti-Catholic, anti-French agitation of 1676, Maryland's Protestant protesters asserted that the Catholics of England and Rome, Maryland and France had united to incite colonial civil war and that they would murder the Protestant survivors. "Thus have they prevailed with the Virginians to have their best common wealths men out of the way by advysing Sir Will Barkly to doe as they did with Davis." Those who had hanged Maryland's commonwealthsmen claimed that they thus "kept Maryland in Awe from a raysing," but, writing to London for aid against the papist and proprietary elite, the Protestant petitioners insisted that "thy did not expect thyr redress by the sword but from owr souveraigne Lord the King, and parliament out of England."[95]

REFORM AND EMPIRE

The Maryland petitioners of 1676 addressed themselves to three elements of English empire. Two, the crown and the merchants, the Marylanders considered major forces in the developing empire of 1676. Third, minor in the Marylanders' view, was the parliament. (The Marylanders would have made good followers of the earl of Danby, monarchist nationalist and lord treasurer, on whom see Book II.) They recognized that "Owr greate Kinge and souveraigne Lord" headed the empire. They, "his humble and loyall subjects inhabited in the American parts," labored in the wilderness "to make it a continent for the enlargement of your Majesty's emperial Crowne and Dignity." More particularly, the Marylanders observed that the "emperial Crowne" received a substantial income from the customs duties it collected on "the fruit of owr labours and industry." In return for enlarging the empire and enriching the crown, they called upon the king for justice and protection. Only perfunctorily, vaguely, did the Marylanders ask the "great noble and prudent parliament" to consider their plight. Finally, at length, and with a sound sense of the logic of mercantilism, the Marylanders of 1676 addressed themselves to the mayor, corporation, and merchants of London, and to merchants "elsewhere in England, whoes off spring wee are, and to whom owr labour and industry affords in exchange for the merchandize many a thousand of thousands of returnes, and employment for a great number of ships and men, which will increase by God's permission as wee increas and decreas

95. *Ibid.*, 145, 146. Notley to Baltimore, 22 January 1676/7, C.O. 1/39, 21.

iff wee decreas: Assist, praye and intercede for us and owr posterity because owr mouths are lokt up and [we are] threatened with destruction iff wee stirr."

Conscious of the chief constituents of empire, the Marylanders of 1676 proposed an imperial reorganization of American government responsive both to the recent strengthening of royal government and to metropolitan merchant initiatives. Both absolutism and capitalism had influenced politically alert Marylanders. Indeed, in every colony during 1676, receptiveness to the rising empire was not just deepened by oligarchical misgovernment and stimulated by Indian conflicts, it was also enhanced by capitalist stirrings, all of which led to popular agitation. Therefore, during the ensuing half-century, Anglo-American relations were transformed along the lines laid down in Maryland's "Huy & Crye."

First, the Maryland petitioners asked that "owr souveraigne Lord and Emperiall Majesty" take the government of Maryland out of the proprietor's hands and into his own, appointing a Protestant as his "Vice Roye or Governor Generallissimo." Second, the 1676 petitioners asked the king to establish as the law of Maryland English custom, royal justice, and parliamentary statute, and they asked to be allowed to appeal from the courts of the colony to the king himself. Third, the Marylanders asked that the crown secure to them a local legislature, chosen and deliberating freely so that it could act "for the comon Generall good for the people and the Country," and, most important, provide for "Protestant Ministers and free schooles and glebe lands." Fourth, the petitioners proposed that all proprietorial revenues be assigned by the king "for maintaining the Governor and other supports of the government and publick uses (viz.) building of forts to defend the Country: guarrisons and the little necessities for the common welfare." Finally, the petitioners moved from requesting that Maryland's government be royalized to asking that all English America be subjected to an imperial government.[96]

FRENCH, INDIANS, AND YORKISTS

The Maryland petitioners asked the king to commission an American viceroy to encounter the interlocking ambitions of the Amerindian, Anglo-American, and French-Canadian empires. The Maryland dissidents were convinced that they were now exposed to international dangers which demanded imperial defenses. The penetration of the Maryland (and Virginia) frontiers by the "Seneca," accompanied by the French, announced a profound change in red-white relations. The war in

96. "Complaint from Heaven," C.O. 1/36, 217v; printed in Browne, ed., *Archives of Maryland*, V, 135.

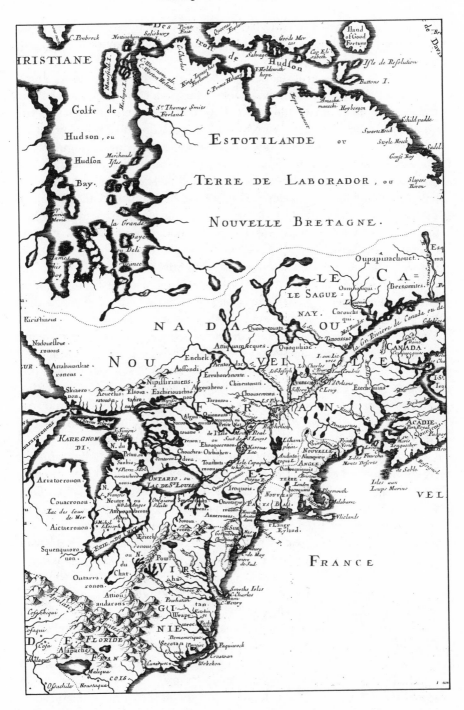

*Le Canada, ou Nouvelle France, &c. . . . Par N. Sanson d'Abbeville Geographe or-
dinaire du Roy. A Paris. Chez Pierre Mariette Rue S. Iacque a l'Esperance Avecq
Privilege du Roy, pour vingt Ans. 1656.*

the west convinced the Maryland petitioners that they faced strategic problems with which papists, proprietaries, and provincial oligarchs could not deal fairly or effectively.

It was to the governor-general of New York, therefore, that the anti-proprietary Marylanders of 1676 looked for protection from French and Indians. Commander of the one colony that bordered both on the Iroquoian heartland and on the French province, Edmund Andros provided Maryland's petitioners with an attractive contrast to their proprietor as Maryland's agent to the Iroquois. Andros was a soldier of the king and not a trader in furs. Distinguished for his Protestantism and his service with the Dutch army, Andros was free from the Roman Catholicism and Francophilia which Protestant, provincial Marylanders feared in their proprietors. Major Andros was an established diplomatic and military intermediary with the Iroquois, not a Calvert come-lately trying to ingratiate his trades-goods salesmen with prospective customers. The proprietor was considered "guilty of the Mischief done by the Sinnico [Cinneque = Seneca] Indian, that com now every yeare down and robb the Country, by not havinge sent and joyned with the Governor of New York, to enter into a league with them, as hee was advised divers yeares agoe, but refused and neglected it." But Andros had assisted the injured Marylanders anyway, for with the Iroquois raiders "severall French cam down in Indian apparell amongst them . . . amongst other plunter they carried away the records which was of late redeemed by Governor Andros and returned from Albany" (presumably during his September 1676 conference with the Iroquois, for which see Book III, Part 3).

To forestall the fatal alliance of the French, the Catholics, and the Iroquois, the Maryland petitioners recommended a fundamental, continental reform: an imperial consolidation of "these severall distinct Governments" of the English in America. In 1676, as the Marylanders complained, every English colony on the mainland save New York was relatively autonomous from England. Each colony vaunted a "self ownd supremacy." Each, literally, fought for its own interests even with its English neighbors. To "reconcile" the competing interests of the colonies, to achieve "concord and amity instead of enmity with one another," and so to resist the French, win over the Iroquois, and reduce the oligarchs, the Marylanders again proposed that the king commission "a Vice Roye or Governor Generallissimo" to command all the colonies.

Presumably, the petitioners of 1676 had Governor-General Andros in mind, for such was the role he won for himself in creating the Anglo-Iroquoian alliance and securing the domestic peace of the duke of York's dominions during this "time of troubles." Certainly the Marylanders had anticipated by a decade Sir Edmund Andros' governor-generalship of the Dominion of New England. They were almost eighty years ahead of their time in advocating the appointment of a royal commander-in-chief for North America. The Marylanders concluded this act of homage to the imperial executive, their plea to metropolitan London, and their bill of indictment against provincial oligarchs, with a prayer to God to "bless and preserve owr glorious Majesty and Souveraigne Lord Charles the II. King of England, Scotland, France and Ireland, and all the English Provinces in America. Defender of the Faith. With his illustrious and puisant parliament in the Twenty and Aight year of his Majesty's Imperiall Dominion Ano: 1676." [97]

Bacon's Revolution

As the Maryland petitioners sought royal government for their province and an imperial union of the continental colonies, they were appalled at the Baconian preparations to resist royal troops and they decried the Baconian focus on the Chesapeake. The Marylanders insisted that the region's problems, whether economic or military, required both imperial and intercolonial solutions. The Maryland dissidents were unsure if they should join the Virginia revolutionaries even to oppose their shared enemies, the Berkeleyan and Baltimorean oligarchs. Defeat would expose them to punishment as traitors to the crown (not just protesters against a proprietor) while victory would only obtain an insupportable, isolated independence. The strategic differences between the Chesapeake dissidents, and thus the objectives of Bacon's Revolution, were the subjects of the Green Spring debates of September 1676 which followed the burning of Jamestown.

Regrettably, the most important evidence regarding those debates is also the most suspect. In January 1676/7, John Coode or Good of Maryland detailed the conversations he had held with Nathaniel Bacon "on or about" 2 September 1676. Coode knew that Sir William Berkeley would hang him if he did not confirm the worst that could be alleged of the Baconians—that is, that they intended "taking the country wholly out of his Majesty's hands into their own." Deputy Governor Notley would hang Coode if he did not deny the existence in Maryland of the revolution he authenticated in Virginia. Coode made the right answers. He

---

97. *Ibid.*, 148, 149, C.O. 1/36, 217. For the Virginia reports on French arms, see S.P. 29/385, 18; S.P. 29/386, 224. On Andros' imperial achievements, see Book III.

blamed Bacon and his revolutionaries and exculpated himself and his
Maryland associates, and so lived to lead them in the Maryland coup of
1689. Still, many of Coode's answers are supported by the events of the
fall and winter of 1676. It seems, therefore, that Coode fairly described
his discussion with Bacon about the external aspects of the Virginians'
revolution against English authority. Moreover, the strategy, the tactics,
and the diplomacy of the revolution, as Bacon allegedly described them
to Coode, were applied not only in the fighting and bargaining of the six
months which followed September 1676, but also in every campaign
fought and every alliance projected by Virginians during the next two
centuries.[98]

Bacon began his conference with Coode by stating that Berkeley had
"sent to the King for two thousand red coats." But, Bacon asked, "may
not 500 Virginians beat them, wee having the same advantages against
them, which the Indians have against us." His Virginians, General Bacon
said, knew the ground better than the English and were "as good or better
shots than they." So the colonists could draw the English invaders into
wooded country and ambush them. In the woods, even the redcoats'
discipline would be a disadvantage. Decimated and demoralized, the
soldiers could not catch the rebels and would have to occupy Virginia.
"The Country or clime not agreeing with their constitutions," all the English would sicken and many of them would die. The survivors would
withdraw, Bacon expected, leaving Virginia to the government of his
seasoned revolutionary army. "Have not many princes lost their dominions so?" asked General Bacon.[99]

Wearing out England's will to hold down the colony would not free
Virginia from dependence on the trans-Atlantic economy. Even the sanguine leader of Virginia's revolution admitted as much to his Maryland
counterpart. Nathaniel Bacon insisted, however, that the Virginians could
soon achieve self-sufficiency in all save munitions. For these they could
trade tobacco to England's rivals. "I believe," said General Bacon, that
"the King of France, or the States of Holland would either of them entertain a trade with us."[100]

Plans to purchase French or Dutch arms with Virginia tobacco were
but one of the extraordinary resemblances between the revolutionary
strategy of 1676 and that of 1776. Bacon put forward a three-part program
in the Green Spring meeting of September 1676: the overthrow of royal
government in Virginia (and of proprietary governments in Carolina and

98. Thomas Ludwell to Arlington [?], quoted by Philip Alexander Bruce, *Institutional
History of Virginia in the Seventeenth Century* (New York, 1910), II, 282. Bacon to Coode,
2 September 1676, Coventry Ms. 77, 347–48; also in *C.S.P.C. 1677–1680*, no. 27.
99. Bacon to Coode, 2 September 1676, Coventry Ms. 77, 347.
100. *Ibid.*, 348.

Maryland); the defiance of the Navigation Acts, followed by the purchase of foreign assistance with Virginia tobacco; and the union of the Chesapeake colonies in revolution, both external and internal. Remarkably similar resolutions were passed by Virginians, meeting in revolutionary convention not ten miles from Green Spring, on 15 May 1776. Once again, after the lapse of the century, Virginians effectively declared royal government ended in the colony, proclaimed the colony's ports open to the ships of the world, welcomed foreign support (again from France and Holland), and supported a union of American colonies to revolt against England. In part by following the sort of military tactics proposed by Bacon and even more by imposing domestic political forms almost identical to those Bacon and his supporters applied in 1676, the Virginians of 1776 won their independence from England in just over seven years of fighting. In seven months the Virginians of 1676 lost to England both their previous autonomy and their proposed independence.

Coode predicted this defeat to Bacon. So doing, he implied the differences that produced the opposed outcomes of 1676 and 1776. First, Coode felt that as few as "500 Redcoats may either Subject or Ruine Virginia," much less the two thousand Bacon expected. The revolutionaries of 1676 could not guard Virginia's water frontiers from the royal navy and its merchant auxiliary. Therefore, royal troops could land unopposed. Once ashore, they would not need to fight Bacon's army to reduce the rebellion. In 1676 the vast majority of Virginia plantations were as yet in Tidewater. English raiders, Coode predicted, "firing our houses, and fences, destroying our Stocks," would soon starve Virginians, and Marylanders, into submission without the risk of battle or the need for occupation. Indeed, Coode pointed out, the imperial forces did not need to land at all to coerce the Chesapeake colonies. A simple naval blockade would take but little longer than amphibious raids to subdue the region. Even if they did not support the royal forces to win their protection from the civil war and Indian war they now suffered, the people would surrender to end a naval blockade. "You may be sure," Coode warned Bacon, that the people who had hastened to support the outlawed hero, his Indian-fighters, and his political reformers, against Berkeley, his Indian traders, and his oligarchical cronies, "when they came to feele the miserable want of food & raiment, will be in a greater hurry to leave you then they were to run after you." [101]

Not just crown coercion and English commerce but material calculation and class allegiance also dictated loyalism in 1676. Most Virginians were recent emigrants from England. Their hopes for the future as well as their present profits were rooted in the parent country. As Coode said

101. *Ibid.*, 346–47.

to Bacon, "here are many people in Virginia that receive considerable benefitts comforts & advantages, by Parents, Friends & Correspondents in England, and many expect Patrimonys and Inheritances, which they will by noe means decline" by committing treason against the king. Besides, Coode calculated, the entirety of Virginia's elite, and their dependents, would ultimately turn against the revolution and support English invaders if the dissidents denounced the crown. Loss of royal government would deprive both physical property and social status in Virginia of their ultimate, imperial, security. Against alienated grandees and their armed households, General Bacon's tactics of terrain and disease would not work. "They and all theyr followers are Seasoned," Coode said, and "they you may be sure will joyne with the Red Coats." Bacon's reply was ominous: "But there shall none of them be."

Killing off the county elites and the provincial grandees—for that is what Bacon apparently proposed—even if it were possible physically, was impossible politically. Resistance to redcoats would be but an attack on strangers, albeit in royal service, and many Virginians did swear to fight the king's men, but to kill county officials was to destroy neighbors and to liquidate county governments and militias, the agencies most important to the security of every man who was not an African slave, a bond servant, or the most oppressed of farmers. And in the event, few besides servants, slaves, and some Southsiders would press revolution to a killing conclusion in 1676.

Coode warned Bacon that he and his republican advisers had mistaken the racial and military sources of revolt for the social and political causes of revolution. "I conceive that yr followers do not think themselves ingaged against the King's Authority," said Coode, "but against the Indians." "But I think otherwise," said Bacon. He knew that the colonists hated their oppressors: governors, councilors, and their favorites. So Bacon assumed that the people would see, as he did, that to end provincial tyranny they must destroy royal authority. A thousand Baconians did see the functional connection between their local oppressors and the distant king in whose name they abused the people, but for most Virginians of 1676 resistance to oligarchs was not revolt against the king.

The identity of the revolutionary programs of 1676 and 1776 nonetheless demonstrates that the logic of Atlantic empires, and so the dynamic of anti-imperial revolution, was established a hundred years before the American Revolution. Driven to republican conclusions by that anti-imperial logic, and by a domestic class war—an "internal revolution"— the Baconians chose revolution against royal government, not unreasonably, but a century too soon. Having chosen, they could not turn back. "I am in over shoes, I will be in over boots," Drummond had said at the

June Assembly. At Green Spring in September, Bacon was told by C͟
that he "must fly, or hang for it." Before accepting Coode's conclus͟
Bacon and his followers resolved to admit, to implement, and to figh͟ ͧ͟͞
their revolution.[102]

Civil War

REBEL POSITIONS

B y 20 October 1676, Bacon's forces had taken control of the valleys of
both the James and the York. Because the former river was the old
artery of Virginia development and the latter one the new, the revolutionaries now controlled more than two-thirds of English Virginia. They had
moved their headquarters from Sir William Berkeley's looted mansion on
the James, to West Point, the strategic center of the colony, where the
York River divides into the Pamunkey and the Mattaponi. Thence the
leaders of the revolution dictated a civil and military system for all of
mainland Virginia. Its nexuses were the delegates to the Middle Plantation Convention. They had "there receaved the oath" to support Bacon's
government against all enemies: English; Indian; Virginian. Now, as "Bacon's Representatives," these political agents of the revolution of 1676,
acting either *per se* or as county officials, administered the oath to their
subordinates. The ganglia of the Baconian system were the revolutionary
committees for property sequestration, army administration, and regional
government, the last being headed by General Bacon's lords lieutenant.
These committees copied the parliamentary committees and county associations of the 1640s (a form of the latter having been recently revived
in Virginia to fund the hated forts) and anticipated the revolutionary
committees and districts of the 1770s. The three revolutions—English,
Virginian, American—perforce adopted a system of executive committees, military commandants, and regional governments, because each
emergency exposed the inadequacy of household executives and traditional county governments to the political and logistical needs of civil
war.[103]

---

102. *Ibid.*, 348.
103. Isle of Wight Grievances, C.O. 1/39, 227, 228. See notes 57 and 113. Edward Hill's
Defence, C.O. 1/40, 153, 154.

No sooner were the Baconian administrative committees, political representatives, regional governments, county civil and military officers, even customs collectors, installed, than the illness Nathaniel Bacon had contracted in wet forest camps, in the Dragon Swamp, and in the rain-scoured trenches of Jamestown cast him down. On 26 October 1676, "much dissatisfied in minde inquiring ever and anon after the arrival of the Friggats and Forces from England, and asking if his Guards were strong about the House," General Bacon died. The revolution of 1676 did not die with him.[104]

The main body of the Army of Virginia did disperse in the month after Bacon's death, but its cadres did not leave the revolution. Rather, they retired into winter quarters, as all seventeenth-century armies did. Bacon's own bodyguard and the revolutionary garrisons along the York came under the immediate command of Lawrence (Joseph) Ingram. Proclaimed "General" by the troops, Ingram also succeeded in persuading many of Bacon's "representatives," "captains," and "justices" to accept his commissions, if only because, in the absence of Sir William Berkeley and his officers, once again in exile on the Eastern Shore, the revolutionary government was the sole apparent alternative to anarchy in Virginia. Given the political supremacy of the revolution despite Bacon's death, its social and military aspects marched towards tragic conclusions.

General Ingram's own military command included both Bacon's last quarters, Major Thomas Pate's plantation on Portopotank Creek in Gloucester County, and West Point itself. From the Point, units of the people's army had moved both downriver and overland to capture the leading loyalists still at large on the mainland—Wormeleys, Wests, and Whittakers, Lewises, Whiteheads, Gwyns, Roysters, Cameses, Deacons, and Burnhams—and to garrison their plantations, strategically sited on both banks of Virginia's greatest rivers, the York and the James.[105]

On the north bank of the York, downstream from West Point, the rebels were in force at Tindall's Point (Gloucester). There Captain William Byrd's Baconian quarters were at the plantation of Colonel Augustine Warner. Nearby in Gloucester County were rebel posts at William Howard's plantation (under the command of his son-in-law John Harris), and the garrisons of those veteran Baconians Major Thomas Cheezeman and Captain Thomas Wilford. The latter, "though he was but a little man, yet he had a greate hearte," a cavalier family, and long experience of Indian languages and trade. Wilford had been with Bacon since his first

104. M[athew], "Bacon's Rebellion," in Andrews, ed., *Narratives,* 28. The Royal Commissioners, "A True Narrative," in *ibid.,* 130.
105. As usual, [Lee,] "Bacon's and Ingram's Rebellion," *ibid.,* 78, has the most amusing account, but for details of the Bacon-Ingram infrastructure, see the depositions of Richard Clarke (revolutionary) and Edward Hill (Berkeleyan), C.O. 1/40, 6, 152–53.

campaign against the Ocaneechi and was, with Bacon, one of the first three rebel leaders outlawed by Berkeley, on 10 May 1676.[106]

On the south bank of the York, two miles below West Point, was the "Brick House." There a Baconian garrison protected the political chiefs of the revolution: William Drummond, the Scot who had commanded in Albemarle, and Richard Lawrence, who, like Drummond, held those "country" opinions that would soon be labeled "whig." "The Country was oppress'd," Lawrence said, by "the frowardness avarice and french Despotick Methods of the Governor." Lawrence himself, the Oxford-educated burgess for Jamestown, was as radical racially as he was politically: he had a black mistress with whom, contemporaries complained, he had the outrageous bad taste to be in love, "as though Venus was chiefly to be worshiped in the Image of a Negro." Integrationist views were especially appropriate in a revolution whose staunchest military supporters were African slaves.[107]

Down the south shore of the York from the revolution's political head-quarters at the Brick House, the next large rebel garrison was posted at King's Creek, on the plantation of the loyalist councilor Nathaniel Bacon the elder, cousin of the late rebel. Here, with forty men, lay Major Thomas Whalley, a name notable in revolution alike in the old England and the new, and, so the loyalists said, "a stout ignorant fellow (as most of the rest)" of the rebels were. Closest to the sea of the York garrisons, and so the post of greatest danger, was the headquarters of Captain Thomas Hansford, former Baconian commandant of Jamestown and "one of the chieftest Champions of the Rebells Side." He held (as best he could, having already lost a finger in single combat with a loyalist captain, William Diggs) the home of Colonel George Reade, the site of Yorktown, a place of crucial importance in both Virginian revolutions, 1676 and 1776.[108]

A dozen miles southwest across the Peninsula from Hansford's garrison lay the ruined capital of Jamestown, no longer dominating Virginia's greatest thoroughfare, the James River. Already the "Middle Plantation," center of the 1634 palisade across the Peninsula, had usurped James-town's position as a place of arms. It had provided the rebel forces with a commanding campsite and convention center. The Middle Plantation would also be chosen as the headquarters, arsenal, and central camp of the thirteen hundred redcoats who were assembling at that very moment, in the last days of October 1676, at the Tower of London, drilling before

106. [Lee,] "Bacon's and Ingram's Rebellion," in Andrews, ed., *Narratives*, 81. Proclamation "By his Maties Governr. & Capt. Genll. of Virginia," 10 May 1676, C.O. 1/37, 2.

107. M[athew], "Bacon's Rebellion," in Andrews, ed., *Narratives*, 40. [Lee,] "Bacon's and Ingram's Rebellion," *ibid.*, 96.

108. *Ibid.*, 86.

they boarded the dozen ships of the royal naval squadron which would
bring them out to subdue Virginia to the crown's imperial will. The
political focus of the James River had shifted from Jamestown to Green
Spring, the great plantation and mansion recently given to Berkeley by
his subservient "Long Assembly." For five months after the destruction
of Jamestown, Green Spring was held for the revolution by Captain
Drew. Near the head of navigation on Powhatan Creek, three miles from
the James River to the west and from Jamestown to the south, Green
Spring boasted defensible high ground. It was quickly fortified by the
Baconians with earthworks and batteries. These were garrisoned by a
determined guard of one hundred men. Invulnerable to the loyalist riverine raiders, Green Spring was the secure center from which the revolutionaries commanded the north bank of the James.

South of that river, the predominant political factors were small planters, their easy communication with the Albemarle, and three active Baconian garrison governments: Colonel Groves' headquarters in Isle of
Wight County; Captains Crews' and Gatlin's post in Nansemond County;
and, most important, Major William Rookins' command at Arthur Allen's
mansion in Surrey County, known to this day as "Bacon's Castle."

At the end of October 1676, the revolutionaries dominated mainland
Virginia south of the Rappahannock River. They also had substantial
garrisons in Rappahannock County and outposts in the Northern Neck as
far as the Potomac River, most notably under Joseph Hardidge and on
the Washington plantation in Westmoreland, and under Tomson and Rice
in Northumberland. The revolution grew more powerful as it spread
south, reaching far into the Albemarle region of Carolina. By Sir William
Berkeley's own estimate, of fifteen thousand men in Virginia, not five
hundred were loyal to his government, but there was a strategy that
would make five hundred loyalists enough to fight a civil war.

COUNTER-REVOLUTIONARY RESOURCES

Three facts favored the seemingly beaten loyalists. First, it was true, as
the Berkeleyan agents in London insisted in the fall of 1676, that many of
the Baconians acted on their "opinion that they doe yor. Maty and all the
country service against the Indians." Without a winter campaign against
the natives, these volunteers would stay home. During the winter, as the
royal resolution to suppress what Whitehall saw as rebellion became
known in Virginia, many of the Indian-fighters would join "the English
party."

Second, the winter and want that drove the bulk of the Baconians to
their homes also compelled both the homeless (runaway servants and
slaves, and Baconian refugees from Jamestown) and the principled revo-

lutionaries into relatively small and isolated garrisons. In these winter quarters, the Baconians waited for spring to renew their war against the Indians and their revolution against the old order. Save for West Point, where eight hundred men were under arms, none of these posts held many more than two hundred men. Most of them were one-fifth or one-sixth of that size (and there were about a hundred occupied houses each harboring from a dozen to forty men, nominally rebels, certainly opportunists). The smallest revolutionary garrisons were those nearest the Chesapeake. This was doubly dangerous because in 1676, as a century later, loyalism was a coastal phenomenon.

The maritime locus of loyalism responded to the third and the decisive fact which favored the old regime: Admiral Neptune, as well as General Winter, opposed the revolution. To begin with, the English captains of the tobacco ships were loyalists, even royalists. The one exception in twenty to this fact was William Carver, and he had been hanged in Accomac. The loyal captains commanded hardened crews and powerful ships. With varying help from the Berkeleyans, the merchant seamen and their ships would win Virginia's civil war.

That war was fought along two avenues during the fall and winter of 1676: the James and the York, their tributaries and their banks. Each riverine campaign was decided by the arrival of an armed English ship commanded by a determined captain who was both a tough fighter and a calculating diplomat, and who had previously served royal government in Virginia waters. The *Young Prince* of London, Robert Morris commander, anchored in the James River on 19 September 1676. The *Concord* of London, Thomas Grantham commander, sailed up the York River on 21 November 1676. No more momentous arrivals occurred anywhere in English America during that fateful year.

JAMES RIVER WAR

Captain Morris' log, "A Journal of ye Time ye Ship Young Prince was in ye Kings Seruis In James River," survives to chart the hitherto unstudied James River campaign. Led by the *Young Prince*, that campaign opened on 20 September 1676, the day after the Berkeleyans abandoned Jamestown. It closed shortly after their reoccupation of the ruined capital on 23 January 1676/7. The amphibious war on the James River, together with the fighting on the York (concluded by Captain Thomas Grantham), reclaimed the heart of Virginia for the loyalists and so, for a century after 1676, for England.[109]

109. "A Journal of ye Time ye Ship Young Prince was in ye Kings Seruis In James River," C.O. 1/37, 181–86, and her crew list in *ibid.*, 187, calendared in *C.S.P.C. 1675–1676*, nos. 1035,

On the afternoon of 19 September 1676, Robert Morris conned the
Young Prince of London (267 tons burden, twenty men in crew) around
Castle Point and into the anchorage at Kecoughtan (Point Comfort). There
lay the ship *Richard and Elizabeth*. Her master reported to Captain Morris that "ye country ware al up in armes." The captains agreed to take
their ships up to Jamestown to support the governor against the rebels.
Perhaps Morris' instantly loyal response was predictable. He had carried
dispatches home from Sir William Berkeley the previous spring. They
had reported that the Indian war had spread south from New England
into Virginia and had been badly managed by the Northern Neck militia
but that Berkeley would try to limit the damage by his control of the arms
trade, the tributary tribes, and the assembly's defense policy. Prior service to the governor and knowledge of the emergency which led to the
revolt against his government presumably predisposed Captain Morris to
back Governor Berkeley. In any case, the *Young Prince* and the *Richard
and Elizabeth* weighed anchor on the morning of the 20th and reached
upriver to join Sir William Berkeley. They only made Newport News
before the wind backed into the north, and the ships anchored in Hampton Roads, sheltering from what even Captain Morris called "very bad
weather," the weather which soaked the revolutionaries' entrenchments
and which would kill their commander and drive his men into winter
quarters. As the ships lay off Newport News, a sloop bound downstream
reported that "ye Governor had quitted Jamestown & was coming down
with his men ye Shipping & ye Sloops." [110]

Unable to take their ships upriver to join the Berkeleyan evacuation,
the English captains sent their ships' boats towards Mulberry Island to
contact the governor. They returned to report that the rebels had burned
Jamestown. Then, on 22 September, Captain Morris wrote that "we received a Command from ye Governor ye Country al flying before him."
Obediently, the *Young Prince* and the *Richard and Elizabeth* detained
fugitive vessels bound for Jamaica (seeking to reverse the usual pattern,
whereby that island's political refugees fled to Virginia). Over the next
few days, the English captains developed the naval tactics of the coming
civil war. Their ships' cannon fire forced fleeing vessels to heave to. They
were approached by sloops crewed by English sailors from the parent

---

1036. Navy officers' report on the petition of Captain Robert Morrice, 22 October 1677, ADM,
1/3548, 247. Sir Thomas Grantham, Kt., *An Historical Account Of Some Memorable Actions,
Particularly in Virginia; Also Against the Admiral of Algier, and in the East Indies: Per-
form'd for the Service of his Prince and Country* (London 1711, 1716; Richmond, ed. R. A.
Brock, 1882), copy courtesy of Duke University Library.
110. *Young Prince* log, 19, 20 September 1676, C.O. 1/37, 181.

ships and boarded, usually by a company of twenty to forty militiamen, impressed for one-month terms (and sometimes led) by Berkeley's officers. The boarders searched the stopped ships for rebels and their goods, both of which were removed to the English ships for safekeeping. The combined forces, commanded by the English ship captains—sheltered below the ships' decks, backed by the ships' guns, armed with firelocks and swords from the ships' armories, and fed with the ships' provisions —were the only organized loyalist fighters in the autumn and winter of 1676.

This naval campaign took strategic shape on the afternoon of 27 September 1676, just a week after the evacuation and destruction of Jamestown, when Sir William Berkeley presided over a council of English ship captains and loyal militia officers at Newport News. The governor doubtless recalled that, in 1652, the commonwealth government had compelled his surrender by a blockade of the James and the York. Now he proposed to reverse the situation. To defeat the commonwealthsmen of 1676, Berkeley organized two tiny squadrons. Each was aimed at one of Virginia's two great rivers and each was supplied from an outlying part of the colony still controlled by loyalists. The ships under the command of Captain Thomas Gardiner (who had captured Bacon and his sloop before the June Assembly met and who had been imprisoned by burgess order until Berkeley retook the capital in September) were to convey the governor, his remaining followers, and their sloops, across the Chesapeake to a refuge in Accomac. Thence they would attack rebel posts on the banks of the York River. The second squadron, commanded by "Admiral" Morris, was to draw upon the loyalists of Lower Norfolk County, Virginia's southeasternmost territory, for the marines, the shipwrights, and the naval stores they needed to operate on the lower reaches of the James River.

Even as the loyalists conferred aboard Captain Larrimore's ship, the *Rebecca*, they were attacked by the rebels. A sloop, commanded by a kinsman of that Digby whom Berkeley had executed at Jamestown, carrying troops commanded by Bacon's chief bodyguard, Baxter, had shadowed Larrimore's *Rebecca* downriver from Jamestown. Now, reaching into Newport News, Digby's sloop "shot Severall Guns against the Governor & against the King's Flag aboard Larrimore." Then the attackers tacked away and carried the flooding evening tide upriver. Governor Berkeley ordered a pursuit. In a dying breeze, ships' boats under oars pursued the Baconian sloop into the night. Soon the loyalists saw the guard fires of the rebel force, which was advancing down the Peninsula from Jamestown. At dawn, the boats' crews spotted the rebel sloop well inshore. They heard the usual insulting shout of "Rogues!" and their boats were fired on by the Baconians ashore. The loyalists retreated until they could be supported by the cannon of the *Rebecca*, which had come upriver on the morning flood. The loyalist boats then landed their militia downstream of the advancing rebels so that they could plunder the countryside as they marched ahead of the Baconians to Newport News. Raid and pursuit, landing and plundering, skirmishes between loyalist marines and rebel guards—sometimes involving hundreds of men—this was the pattern established now, at the end of September 1676. It continued through the fall and winter at every break in the unusually bad weather which further cursed a sad season in Virginia. In such a waterborne and weatherbeaten campaign, the loyalist ships, each of them "a Receptacle for ye Loyall Party and a Gaole for ye late Rebells," were the only advantage—indeed, the only hope—of the "English Party," the enemies of Virginia's revolution.[111]

On 1 October 1676, the *Young Prince* and the *Richard and Elizabeth*, "employed in his Maties Service att Virginia," sailed south across the James from Kecoughtan to the mouth of the Elizabeth River. There these ships, the nucleus of the loyalists' southern squadron, anchored and sent a boat ashore with a message from Sir William Berkeley to Colonel Mason of the Lower Norfolk militia. It noted Robert Morris' "appointment of Admirall" and ordered the colonel to assist him. It was not clear whether Colonel Mason could obey. His countrymen were divided in their loyalty. The men of Lower Norfolk resented the decay of the coastal forts, they objected to the cost of the assembly's English agency, and they disapproved of selling arms to Indians. All these evils they blamed on the Berkeleyans. As old-settlement easterners, however, they were in every sense close to England and they disapproved of the new men and frontiersmen who led the Baconians. And the men of Lower Norfolk were as much seamen as planters. Although they objected to English legal restraints on their trade, armed English ships now lay in their harbor, seizing the small craft—carriers of almost all Virginia's traffic—which plied these, the busiest waters in the Chesapeake. The English admiral, Robert Morris, allowed the boats of declared loyalists to go about their business, but those filled with runaway servants trying to reach the rebels with the weapons and clothes they had stolen from their masters were recaptured, sailed back to their owners, and their crews were either returned to servitude or held by their captors for present forced labor and

111. *Ibid.*, 22, 28 September 1676. Edward Hill's Defence, C.O. 1/40, 158. "Characters of ye Severall Comdrs of Ships," Pepys 2582. The Royal Commissioners, "A Review Breviary and Conclusion," also in Pepys 2582, is printed in Burk, *Virginia*, II, in which see 251 and also 241–42, 245, 248–49, 251. The commissioners' assessment is in their letter to Secretary Williamson, 27 March 1677, C.O. 1/39, 180.

future sale. With the penalties of disloyalty so apparent before them in their own Elizabeth River, the men of Lower Norfolk obeyed Sir William Berkeley's commands to their colonel.[112]

On 3 October 1676, Colonel Mason sailed out to the English ships in a sloop together with his officers and forty impressed militiamen. Given this landing force, and the further local support it prefaced, Admiral Morris' little fleet now checked two Baconian advances towards Lower Norfolk. One was a venture in political economy across the James River. The other was a campaign of invasions and propaganda overland from the west.

Newport News had fallen to the rebels when Berkeley and the loyalist squadrons sailed. It came under the command of Captain Thomas Hansford (whose headquarters were across the Peninsula, at Reade's plantation on the York River) and was the seat of the revolutionary committee for the lower Peninsula. They now sent their customs officer, one Mr. Greene, across the James in a sloop under a flag of truce to negotiate with Admiral Morris and Captain Prynne. Hostages were exchanged. Then the Baconian officer explained to the two English merchant captains the revolutionary government's proposed economic system. A port of entry, customs clearance, passports for trade with the Baconian counties, all were offered to Morris and Prynne. On 4 October 1676, after a night of drinking and discussion, the English captains replied to these overtures that "it was not safe to trade with Rebels." As soon as Morris and Prynne recovered their hostages, they underlined their rejection of the revolution by firing on the rebel sloop. Then they ordered their ships' boats and militiamen away to capture Greene and his vessel. Before the boats could get alongside the sloop, however, a hard northerly breeze sprang up. In these conditions—a new breeze in sheltered water—the more weatherly sloop had every advantage over both the oared boats and the square-rigged ships. "She got off & went to Hampton River in the Night," Morris reported, and Greene reported his failure to Hansford.[113]

Economic appeals having failed to attract the London skippers, the Baconians tried militarily backed political ones. Under Captain James Crews, they had "marched a hundred miles out of theire owne County," the Baconian base of Charles City, eastward into Lower Norfolk County. They occupied the county up to the West Branch of the Elizabeth River. There, the rebels began to outfit sloops for the invasion of the eastern

112. "Characters of ye Severall Comdrs of Ships," Lower Norfolk County Grievances, Pepys 2582. Navy officers' report, ADM 1/3548, 267.
113. *Young Prince* log, 4 October 1676, C.O. 1/37, 181.

parishes of Lower Norfolk. Thence, on 6 October 1676, they sent on board
the *Young Prince* Nathaniel Bacon's revolutionary Declaration. The Declaration's complaints of provincial taxation, political favoritism, defense-
less frontiers, and monopolistic fur trade did not speak to the interests of
either English skippers or their crews, but Bacon's laments about the
absence of port towns, the lack of trade encouragement, and the weakness
of coastal defense were more to the mercantile point. The Southside
revolutionaries, however, had long preferred outport, Irish, New English,
and Dutch traders to Londoners. Now they had resisted London politically as well. The Baconians thus hardly seemed to such London-based
royalists as Morris and Prynne the right men to remedy the defects of
Anglo-Virginian commerce and defense. The rebels' concluding complaint, that Sir William Berkeley had abdicated his government by aban-
doning his command, cut no ice with captains who had found the
governor in action, concerted strategy with him, accepted his military
commissions and orders, and who now maintained a regular, almost daily
communication across the Bay with Berkeley. Those of "his wicked and
Pernicious Counsellours and Confederates" whose arrest Bacon demanded and whose estates his troops plundered, were the leaders of the
merchant-planter oligarchy. Their crops had been marketed and their
stores were stocked by such London ships as the *Young Prince* and the
Richard and Elizabeth.[114]

Admittedly London's dominance of Virginia's trade was not yet so
complete as the civil war of 1676 would make it. Some of the planters
proscribed by Bacon—both the older sorts of Berkeleyans and Sir William himself—had consigned cargoes to Bristol (and sometimes to Plymouth, not to mention the unmentionable Dutch ports). English port
rivalries had long underlain peacetime political partisanships. Even during the civil war of 1676, some English outport captains traded with the
rebels. Others, Bristolmen, refused to join the Londoners in their attacks
on the Baconians. But the Londoners commanded the biggest and best-
armed ships in Virginia waters in 1676, and, as metropolitans as well as
monarchists, they were determined to repress a provincial revolt. As more
ships made the Capes of the Chesapeake during the early winter, the
Londoners persuaded skippers from almost every English port trading to
Virginia to join the fleets that the London captains led against the Virginia
revolution. These metropolitan merchant seamen further demonstrated
their economic nationalism, and their anti-provincialism, by capturing the

114. "To the right honble Herbert Jeffreyes Esqr. Governr. & Capt. Genll. of Virginia . . .
Edward Hill . . . humbly answereth," C.O. 1/40, 153. "The Declaration of the People Against
Sr Wm Berkeley & Present Governors of Virginia," Blathwayt Papers, Williamsburg, 13, no.
1; also in *C.S.P.C. 1675–1676,* no. 1010.

Irish ships and the New England ketches by whose trade "the Rebels are encourag'd and enabled to persist and continue in Rebellion." [115]

These imperial and metropolitan motives, political and economic, led Admiral Morris' little squadron not only to reject Bacon's Declaration but also to take action against the rebel force that had sent it out to them. Morris' fleet and Mason's militia first threatened Captain Crews' concentration on the Elizabeth River. Then they followed the retreating rebels westward, sailing up the south shore of the James to a new base in the broad bay of the Nansemond River. From this western border of the county the English ships and sloops both protected Lower Norfolk from the rebels and cut their communications and harassed their garrisons. After capturing Baconian sloops and agitators, Admiral Morris sent in the sloop *Ann*, Captain Harrison, and twenty-three men, supported by the guns of the *Young Prince*, to beat up the rebel coast guards in Nansemond County. Each action contracted the rebellion, recruited more loyalist militiamen and their sloops. "Man o'war" sloops and soldiers extended the ships' dominance of the James River up its southern tributaries and onto their rebel-held banks.[116]

AMPHIBIOUS CAMPAIGN

Admiral Morris' sloops also skirmished with rebel vessels based in the Hampton River, across the James from the loyalists' main anchorage in the mouth of the Elizabeth River. Whenever Morris' scout boats discovered that the Baconian sloops were away from Hampton Roads, the admiral sent his own armed sloops with militia landing parties across the river to raid the rebel-held plantations of the Elizabeth City region. More than once, however, the loyalist raiders were beaten off by the Baconian guards. Morris was disgusted at what he termed the cowardice of the Lower Norfolk militia, and his squadron failed to secure a beachhead on the north bank of the James River. Morris did manage to take two steps which led to an advance up the south bank. First his cruisers isolated the rebels on the south side of the James from the northern centers of revolution by capturing their boats and crews. Then Morris responded to the Norfolk militia commanders' request that he discipline their men: he tortured "rebellious" soldiers on shipboard. Adding to a more disciplined militia some leaders from among his own obedient men or from the officers of other English ships, Morris produced a landing force not easily

---

115. Berkeley's proclamation against trade with the rebels, 25 December 1676, in Grantham, *Historical Account*, 14–16. *Young Prince* log, 9 November, 5, 12 December 1676, C.O. 1/37, 183, 184. Captain's log, *Bristol*, ADM 51/134, III, 17 May 1677.
116. *Young Prince* log, 14, 20 October, 19 December 1676, C.O. 1/37, 183, 185.

repulsed by rebel garrisons even in a war that grew more bitter, not less, after the death of the first rebel general, Nathaniel Bacon.[117]

The week which ended with Bacon's burial on 26 October 1676 had been one of clear, cold, and blowing weather on the James River. For five days, Admiral Morris' fleet lay at anchor off Kecoughtan, recovering raiders from Elizabeth City County. The fatal day itself came in "raine & fogey ye winde little & westerley & vered to So. raney misty weather." The next day, the loyalist fleet recrossed the James and anchored in the Elizabeth River. On the following day, its captains called on Sheriff Fucher to impress twenty men, with their axes and saws, to cut wood "for ye Service." With wood from the Southside and with the help of the carpenters and smiths of this ancient shipbuilding region, the seamen repaired the hard-used sloops. They complained all the while of the snow and cold but they were heartened by the first, albeit premature, reports that a royal expedition was at sea, sailing to assist them against the rebels.

Presumably, reports of the punitive expedition's preparations reached the rebels as well as the royalists. Certainly, Bacon's death, winter's arrival, sloop war against the garrisoned plantations, the Morris squadron's control of the lower James River all discouraged some rebel leaders on the Southside. So Sir William Berkeley authorized Admiral Morris to pardon those Baconian leaders who would desert the revolution. On 1 November 1676, Captain Gatlin, the rebel commander of Nansemond County, offered to negotiate with Admiral Morris. On 6 November, Morris sailed the *Young Prince,* in company with two other English ships and Colonel Charles Moryson's sloop, out towards the mouth of the Elizabeth River to Craney Island (the un-named promontory on the Thornton map, now almost obliterated by the vast Disposal Area), the rendezvous with Gatlin. En route, Morris' squadron met a sloop inbound from Accomac carrying the governor's specific promise to pardon Gatlin. Berkeley improved on the occasion by enclosing a proclamation urging the people of Nansemond to return to their allegiance to him as the king's governor.

This they were unlikely to do. Nansemond was a basically Baconian county. Its people were hostile to the western forts, to their planter-contractors, to their high cost, and to their military uselessness. They had protested against every one of the assembly's taxes and gifts. Thus aggrieved, the people of Nansemond were "impudent and mutinous" supporters of the "June Laws," which had reformed county government and authorized the genocidal "war with all Nations and families of ye Indians whatsoever without favoringe any" which the Nansemond men had long demanded. Some of them had enlisted in Bacon's army. Many more supported his cause, being "resolved to defend themselves" against In-

117. *Ibid.,* 26–28 October, 1 November, C.O. 1/37, 182, 183.

dians, taxers, and oppressors, and to obey the terms of Bacon's Oath until the king himself redressed their grievances.[118]

Nonetheless, Admiral Morris sent Berkeley's proclamation ashore to be published in Nansemond. He added one of his own to the people of Isle of Wight County. Then he suspended his fleet's raids on the two counties. But the same yawl boats and wherries that took loyalist negotiators ashore sustained the Southside blockade. The boats of the fleet also carried raiders to attack isolated plantations, both on the creek banks of Surrey County (upstream and west of Morris' diplomatic targets) and on the waterways of Lower Norfolk County (to the east and downstream of Craney Island). These raiders returned to the fleet with prisoners as well as with plunder. Those Southsiders who were merely suspected of being revolutionaries were subjected to loyalist persuasion on board Morris' ships. "Principal rebels," however, he sent by sloop to Accomac and the governor's prison ships, the *Adam & Eve* and the *Rebecca*. Eleven of them never returned.[119]

Under such pressures from the loyalist fleet, on 19 November 1676 rebel leaders from Surrey and Lower Norfolk counties joined the negotiations on board the *Young Prince*, off Craney Island. Three days later, Captain John Consett arrived at the Craney Island anchorage. In command of the ship *Mary of London*, Consett was "a very active resolute person," a hard case even among the tough captains whose early-autumn sailings from England now brought them into the James River to add substantially to the strength of the loyalist armada. On the last day of November, the *Young Prince* led elements of this fleet in towards the shore of Nansemond County. "Captain Gatlin came on board," Morris wrote in his ship's log, "where we concluded a peace & he returned to his alegence & took ye oath" of fidelity to the governor and the king. This order of allegiance (which placed Sir William Berkeley before King Charles II) was as bitterly resented by surrendering Nansemond people as it was eloquent of Berkeleyan priorities. With Gatlin gone and "wearied out for want of provisions," however, much of Nansemond County was now surrendered by the rebels to Admiral Morris and his subordinates.[120]

This county's riverside parishes became the bases from which loyalists marched against the still-defiant inland and upland farmers. With friendly Albemarle open at their backs, the backcountry Baconians of the

118. Nancymond First Grievances, and the commissioners' answers, Pepys 2582.
119. *Young Prince* log, 18 November 1676, 19 January 1677, C.O. 1/37, 183, 185. Navy officers' report, 22 October 1677, ADM 1/3548, 271.
120. "Herbert Jeffreys and ffrancis Morryson to Mr. Watkins, Swanns Point April 9th 1677," Pepys 2582. *Young Prince* log, 20 November 1676, C.O. 1/37, 184. Nancymond First Grievances, C.O. 1/39, 247; also in Pepys 2582.

Southside would never surrender, but they might be cowed. Colonel Joseph Bridger, proscribed by Bacon as a traitor to the revolution, reviled by the people of the Southside as their greatest oppressor and one who converted their taxes "to his own private Interest," now returned to the region from his exile in Maryland. He found his wealth in livestock looted. Impoverished and angry, Colonel Bridger took command of the growing numbers of loyalist militia. In December 1676 they were transported by the ships of Admiral Morris' fleet and led by their captains and crews in attacks on upriver Baconian garrisons. These raids combined plunder with politics, revenge with counter-revolution.[121]

Launched from a squadron that now numbered six ships, each paired with an armed sloop and reinforced by a company of loyalist militia, the numerous James River raids frequently produced fifteen casualties a side. The post-revolution canard that Berkeley's twenty-three official, admitted, and listed executions were the sum of Virginia's civil-war losses not only omits some six hundred to a thousand deaths at the hands of the natives and ignores aboriginal losses altogether, it also neglects the uncountable, but heavy costs of domestic fighting. Memories of that fighting lived on for a hundred years in Virginia. In 1776 recollections of the previous revolution still had the power to kindle popular hatred of formerly Berkeleyan families—the Lees, for example—in the Old Dominion. The provincial elite, ashamed of the revolution which had indicted their rule, humiliated by the exile and expropriation which had punished their misgovernment, chagrined that their restoration to power was largely accomplished by English seamen and finally assured by English troops, wrote few details of the civil war of 1676 into Virginia's records and left less inspiration to provincial historians to recount it. So it is that only the memorials of concerned and grateful imperial administrators report the sustained combat of 1676, a combat which flared up all along the James River, from the broad reaches off Norfolk up to the sinuous "Curles" of Henrico.

In its December 1676 sweep up the south shore of the James, Admiral Morris' fleet captured Baconian officials, interloping traders, and rebel coast guards. Behind the naval vanguard, Colonel Bridger's militia, horse and foot, moved westward both by river and overland. At first they advanced by negotiating with the rebels of Isle of Wight County; then they used force. On Christmas Day 1676, "that grand Rebell Groves" challenged the English captains. They replied in a landing at Warraqueoc ("Wariequeke" or "Burwell's") Bay. The rebels ran from the sailors' first

121. Isle of Wight Grievances, C.O. 1/39, 223.

fire and left to the landing party the colors of the revolution, drums, and stores of ammunition. Forty of the squadron's men pursued the rebels inland. They caught them at sunset. In the confused fighting that followed, Captain Consett met Groves and "with his own hand . . . shot him dead." The landing party retired with their prisoners to the ships for the night but they returned to the scene of the action the next day, plundered the plantation headquarters of the revolution in Isle of Wight County, and, after further fighting, brought back thirteen additional prisoners.[122]

The English captains then summoned the remaining Baconians of Isle of Wight County to surrender. The county had been a center of revolution and would be the first county to justify its revolt to the king's commissioners. To their hatred of taxes for frontier forts useless against Indians, expensive to the common people, and profitable to the planter-projectors, the Isle of Wight people added resentment of Sir William Berkeley's Gloucester muster, seeing it aimed at the fifty-seven Wight militiamen who had obeyed the act of assembly and joined Bacon against the Indians. The subsequent flight of the governor "and great men as they call ym" to Accomac and Maryland and England left the Isle of Wight "Under Bacon's Power and Command." Now English ships had brought the "great men" back from exile and the English seamen had killed or captured the leaders of the revolution in Isle of Wight and, as it seemed, in the Southside. At least in the opinion of the royal commissioners who investigated the civil war, the killing of Groves and the capture or dispersal of the guards at his headquarters by the ship captains' forces was the crucial event "whereby ye whole Southern Shore of James River was reduced to its former obedience." [123]

Fighting nonetheless continued in the interior of both Nansemond and Surrey counties. The remaining rebel resistance centered on the fine brick house of Major Arthur Allen, "Bacon's Castle," near Chipokes Creek ("Upper Chipo" on the Thornton map), Surrey County. Since July 1676, Major Allen had been in exile and his plantation had been garrisoned by "a considerable force" under Major William Rookins. On 28 December 1676, the sloops of Admiral Morris' squadron, under the command of Captain Nicholas Prynne of the *Richard and Elizabeth*, sailed, rowed, and finally poled their way up Chipokes Creek. Landing from the sloops, their crews marched on "Bacon's Castle." The garrison fled before them, and Rookins—who had been trying for some time to secure terms

122. The Royal Commissioners, "A Review Breviary and Conclusion," Pepys 2582; printed in Burk, *Virginia*, II, 253. *Young Prince* log, 25, 26 December 1676, C.O. 1/37, 185.
123. Isle of Wight Grievances and commissioners' answers, Pepys 2582. Upper Parish of Isle of Wight, C.O. 1/39, 230. "Characters of ye Severall Comdrs of Ships," Pepys 2582.

of surrender from the admiral—was captured and held pending Sir William Berkeley's (fatal) pleasure.[124]

REBEL ATTACKS, LOYALIST REVENGES

By 1 January 1676/7, the combined forces of the squadron under Morris and the downcountry militia under Bridger had carried the bulk of the rebel posts in Nansemond and Surrey counties, but their latest conquest in the latter county was immediately besieged by four hundred counterattacking rebels. On 4 January, three ships, a ketch (a New Englander seized for trading with the rebels), and three sloops ferried a relief force upriver from Nansemond. Sixty of Colonel Bridger's horsemen kept pace along the shore. On 6 January the combined forces reached the besieged fort, drove off the rebels, and concluded that Surrey seemed pacified. Admiral Morris determined to turn the squadron's attention north, across the James, encouraged by the news, which arrived at 3:00 a.m. on 7 January, of Henrico County's "Riseing for ye king."

On 9 January 1676/7, Bacon's first follower, Captain William Byrd of Henrico, redeemed his rebellion. He joined Admiral Morris, Colonel Bridger, and their "guard" to capture his erstwhile colleague: "about 9 o'clock we apprehended Mr. Drummond." The former governor of Albemarle, one of the chief Virginian revolutionaries, was found "wandering in a swamp." He had lost contact with the other surviving Baconian leaders as they fled westward during a snowstorm. Morris decided to take Drummond across the Peninsula to Berkeley, then at King's Creek. Drummond was chained overnight on an English ship in the York River. The next day, 15 January 1676/7, he was marched in the cold and in irons, without a cloak, to the Middle Plantation. There, after a half-hour "trial" before Sir William Berkeley, Drummond was hanged.[125]

On that day, the Surrey fort was again attacked by rebels, under the command of Colonel William West. Morris sailed back across the James River to lead a relief party to the fort. He landed from the *Young Prince*, mounted eighty men on horseback, equipped ninety more as infantry, and at noon on 16 January 1676/7, captured Colonel West and dispersed his men. The next day, Morris joined Bridger. Their combined forces marched down into Nansemond "to secure yt County & to confirm ym in

---

124. Thomas Tileson Waterman and John A. Barrows, *Domestic Architecture of Tidewater Virginia* (New York, 1932, 1969), 20-27. Lyon G. Tyler, *The Cradle of the Republic* (Richmond, Va., 1906), 205. *The William and Mary Quarterly*, 1st ser., 5 (1897): 189. *Young Prince* log, 27–28 December 1676, C.O. 1/37, 185.

125. *Young Prince* log, 7, 14 January 1676/7, C.O. 1/37, 185v. [Lee,] "Bacon's and Ingram's Rebellion," in Andrews, ed., *Narratives*, 98. According to Edward Hill, there was still a rebel garrison of forty men at Cocke's plantation (C.O. 1/40, 153).

their truth." On the 18th they seized more rebel leaders, and on 19 January 1676/7, "we went to ye Governor & carried him 15 or 16 principal Rebells."[126]

Morris then returned to the James River to recover a sloop he had earlier lost to the Baconians, "but she was al plundered & spoyled," a token of past fighting and present bitterness. On 23 January 1676/7, Admiral Morris brought his fleet into the Jamestown anchorage. On 24 January, in the ruins of the capitol, Robert Morris watched his prisoners tried before Sir William Berkeley. James Crews, John Digby, William Rookins, William West, and John Turner, the Southside leaders of the revolution, all were condemned to death. Berkeley ordered the first two hanged above Bacon's siege works outside Jamestown. Rookins died in the prison. From it West and Turner escaped to join that legion of Baconians never afterwards known by the names which had meant revolution in the Virginia of 1676.

The executions at Jamestown were the gruesome signals that Sir William Berkeley had returned to power. The "revolution" now completed its cycle. To pacify the region where the revolt had begun, Morris conned his ships west, up the James River, to secure the submission of Charles City County. By 26 January 1676/7, the loyalist fleet was anchored at Swineyards, just below William Byrd's Westover plantation and across the James River from "Jordan's Journey." This was the point on which the frontiersmen of Charles City and Henrico had rallied in April 1676 to contrive a defense against the Indians. There they had heard that their pleas had been rebuffed by Berkeley. There Crews and Byrd had brought to them Nathaniel Bacon to be their leader. There had begun the Virginia revolution. There it was ended by the captain and crew of the *Young Prince*.[127]

On 27 January 1676/7, Captain Robert Morris entered in the log of the *Young Prince* that there was "this day fair wether ye wind at NW & I went to visset ye Govenor at Green Spring." Sir William Berkeley was home at last, in the greatest house and "the strongest place in the Country." It had been surrendered to him on 22 January 1676/7 by that flour miller turned rebel captain, Drew. It seemed that the old order had been restored and that the Berkeleyans could ignore the clement counsels of the English ship captains who had returned them to power.

Captain Morris pointed out to the reinstated Green Spring group that he, not they, had brought the Southside—and Charles City County as

126. *Young Prince* log, 16, 18, 19, 22–24 January 1676/7, C.O. 1/37, 185–86. See Isle of Wight's petition regarding William West, C.O. 1/39, 232. (The sixty-five attestations and twenty-six signatures are about average for rebel petitions in their ratio of illiterates to literates. This ratio, and the number of petitioners, were both higher than the Berkeleyan averages.)

127. Tyler, *Cradle*, 214, 222–23. *Young Prince* log, 25–26 January 1677, C.O. 1/37, 186.

well—back to their allegiance, not just by force, but also by a liberal use of the pardoning power given him by Sir William Berkeley. This, he said, was required both by a fair-minded assessment of the circumstances that had driven many of the "better sort" of Southsiders into revolution and by the practical impossibility of reducing every one of their plantations by force. These "rebels," so Morris said, were men whose plantations were "open to the River & so lyable to be plundered by many that lay privately lurking & sculking to plunder," men licensed to loot by the fact of revolution. It was to protect their property that the James River planters had accepted General Ingram's revolutionary commissions, and they exercised the authority they thus acquired to gather their neighbors together for mutual protection during "the war of each against all" which had overspread Virginia in the winter of 1676. Small and defensive, but numerous, these garrisons were best dispersed by pardoning their commanders. So Admiral Morris said. So he had done.

Sir William Berkeley disagreed. Now that he had been relieved of his Eastern Shore exile and returned to Green Spring, the governor told Admiral Morris (and Colonel Bridger) that, despite his earlier orders, "it was not in their commission to pardon such notorious villaines & traytors." Instead, Berkeley ordered one of his enforcers, Colonel Edward Hill, to seize the persons, accounts, and estates of the planters pardoned by Morris.

Robert Morris was as good as his word, however, even if Sir William Berkeley was not. For example, he sent a warning of Berkeley's intentions to Thomas Blaydon, a pardoned planter who, as a factor for London merchants, had long been known to Morris. Blaydon got aboard the *Young Prince* with his accounts (book debts being a major item in every sizable Virginia estate) before night fell and Hill and his horsemen reached the Blaydon plantation. Colonel Hill was rowed out to the *Young Prince* in pursuit of Blaydon. Hill's brandished pistols and shouted threats, however, did not persuade the ship's crew to abandon the planter who had placed himself in their captain's custody and who Captain Morris guaranteed would be made available for any legal proceeding.

Berkeley never proceeded legally against Blaydon. First, he and his henchmen wanted their victims' loot even more than they did their lives. Second, royal representatives soon arrived to deny the Berkeleyans their intended revenge. Meanwhile, Blaydon was cooped up in the great cabin of the *Young Prince*, so Hill's troopers "re-equiped" themselves from the planter's store, seized every piece of his paper they could find, and abused his wife (admittedly, this was the standard practice of both sides in both the civil war and in the repression which followed, at least according to the enemies of each; invariably, the wives in question were pregnant, making the alleged abuse even more reprehensible). Certainly, if any large percentage of the official accounts of Berkeleyan license and looting in 1676 are believed, the last thread of the cavalier myth of seventeenth-century Virginia will have been broken. No sooner were the Blaydons plundered, however, than the royal army and navy arrived in overwhelming strength. Soon the king's officers began to enforce a royal pardon in favor of Virginia's revolutionaries and against Berkeley's terrorists. The king's commissioners determined, as Colonel Hill complained, to "have his Matys Loyall Subjects called to a Severe acct for the Least Slip they have made amiss in Executing the Governor's Commands. . . ." In the process they confirmed the peace which the English sea captains had done so much to win, whether by puissance or pardon, and permitted them to return at last to the trade which had brought them to Virginia in the first place. Admiral Morris' last entry in the log of the *Young Prince* while she "was in ye Kings Seruis In James River" was dated 29 January 1676/7. It needs no gloss. "The cundre being reduced so went about our owne business as pr ye Govenor Poclamatons."[128]

ROYAL CONCLUSIONS

That very afternoon, the king's ship *Bristol*, captain Sir John Berry, anchored well offshore, "in 7 fathom water" in Hampton Roads (just outside a line drawn between Point Comfort and Newport News). The *Bristol* was the flagship and the first arrival of the royal squadron of six men-of-war and eight transports which together brought to Virginia more than a thousand redcoats, their officers, staff, and supernumeraries to the number of three hundred, and the royal commissioners appointed to repress the rebellion and redress its causes.

The royal commissioners were quick to do what the Berkeleyans never would: they gave full credit to the merchant captains for their repression of the revolution. Robert Morris' case they thought particularly hard, "this worthy person having lost to a considerable sume himselfe, but much more to his owners by this Rebellion; Besides his Ship hath not only beene a Receptacle to the Loyall Partie, but to the Rebells a prison." Both loyalists and revolutionaries, in the *Young Prince* and in all the merchant ships that fought Virginia's civil war on the James and on the York, "devoured their Sea-Provisions, wch should carry them home to England." The captains and crews had "noe Regard or recompense given them therefore" by the restored regime, and Sir William Berkeley, who owed the English captains his restoration to the government, did not even assist them to obtain cargoes, "the Governour not soe much as promoting them in their freight homewards bound." "In fine," as the

128. *Young Prince* log, 25–29 January 1677, C.O. 1/37, 186. Edward Hill's answer, *ibid.,* 156. Waterman and Barrows, *Domestic Architecture,* 10–17.

royal commissioners concluded in their official history of the revolution
of 1676, "what signall services were done as to the suppressing this Rebellion must bee justly laid to the incessant toyle, Courage & good success of those few Sea Captains, Morris, Consett, Grantham, Prynne, &
Gardiner, who meritt this due Commendation &c. the more because the
Country have been ungrateful to them in not mentioning them." [129]

Captain Morris' business was complete, his cargo loaded, by 5 April
1677. When he sailed in "very faire weather ye wind Easterly, abt 4 oclock
in the afternoon" of 12 April 1677, from the scene of his winter's fighting,
he carried with him aboard the *Young Prince* the dispatches in which the
royal commissioners again reported that "hee and two or three more
Masters of Ships have beene more serviceable to his Matie and this
Country than all those together, who vaunt themselves soe much of their
Courage and call themselves the Loyall Party." Of course, the Berkeleyans could not adopt this view (nor have their historians been able to do
so since), for it was on the Berkeleyans' assertion that they had restored
order in Virginia that their "Loyall Party" based its claim to go on misgoverning the colony without interference from England. On the other
hand, just as the crown commissioners knew that the captains, not the
Berkeleyans, had put down the revolt, so they came to believe that continued Berkeleyan misrule would incite another rising.[130]

Doubly convinced of oligarchic incapacity, either to fight or to govern,
the officers of the crown imposed direct royal government on Virginia,
backing it on occasion with military force. Thus they displaced the Berkeleyan regime as well as repressing the Baconian revolutionaries by sub-
stituting royal military occupation for English naval patrols. In February
1676/7, for example, Captain Meoles (Miles) and his company of the royal
Guards succeeded Captain Morris and the *Young Prince* as the English
presence on the upper James River. Two bids for Virginian independence therefore failed in 1676. The autonomy of the Berkeleyan regime
had left it free to provoke the revolution, which, in turn, justified the
crown's termination of the oligarchical rule of the old assembly system.
The radical effort of the Baconians to secure independence had failed
because of colonial underdevelopment, but had nevertheless provoked
royal reform of Virginia's government. Ironically, the failed revolutionary
effort combined with obvious oligarchical excess to excite an unprece-

129. Captain's log, *Bristol*, ADM 51/134, Part III. Jeffreys, Moryson and Berry to Williamson,
27 March 1677, C.O. 1/39, 180. Berry and Moryson to Coventry, 5 April 1677, Pepys 2582.
Jeffreys and Moryson to Watkins, 9 April 1677, *ibid.* N.B., however, that while "the Country,"
—i.e., the assembly—arrogated all credit for the counter-revolution to Berkeley and company, they did promise the sea captains cash rewards (C.O. 1/39, 102v).
130. Captain's log, *Bristol*, Thursday, 12 April 1677, ADM 51/134, Part III. Berry and Moryson to Coventry, 5 April 1677, Pepys 2582. Burgess order for address to the king, C.O.
1/39, 94.

dented imperial presence in Virginia. Subsequent sympathizers with either Berkeley or Bacon have ignored such stories as that of the *Young Prince,* for it testifies to the fighting abilities of English seamen and to the crucial importance of English ships, and it explains the English control of Virginia.

The sea captains of 1676, although they have never received their due at the hands of Virginians, were immediately rewarded by their king. Charles II praised the sea captains' services before his privy council and granted the James River commanders—Morris, Prynne, and Consett—double the expenses they claimed to have incurred "during their time in the king's service." The king also paid the shipowners 33 percent over the normal freight for his use of their ships. He granted £200 to Captain Thomas Grantham, whose actions on the York River will be recounted. Grantham's colleague in the York campaign, Captain Thomas Gardiner, received from the crown £567 for the use of his ship and his provisions, and from King Charles £50 additional as a personal reward. Captain Larrimore of the *Rebecca* received in excess of £522.5.9 for freight, provisions, weapons, and loyalty. By the king's command, all of these captains not already so enrolled had their names placed at the head of the list from which the king commissioned the officers of his navy. For King Charles correctly expected that he and his empire would need again, and soon, the services of these tough, loyal, and experienced captains, their determined crews and sturdy ships, all so distinguished in 1676.[131]

The York River Campaign

LOYALIST LOOTERS

The loyal captains' successful military and diplomatic campaign on the James River inspired a shorter and less sanguinary but more

131. *C.S.P.C. 1677–1680,* nos. 764, 888, 939, 940. The Royal Commissioners, "A Review Breviary and Conclusion," Pepys 2582, printed in Burk, *Virginia,* II, 253. For payments of £2,665.10.9 by the crown as freight for the merchant ships used as men-of-war in Virginia, see Privy Council Register 2/66, 137; P.C. 2/67, 136; P.C. 2/68, 109, 144; and ADM 1/3548, 267–71. For subsequent service, see the career of Grantham. En route to Virginia in 1678, the *Concord* defeated an Algerine raider of twice her force. After being knighted by the king aboard his new ship, the *Charles the Second,* of 618 tons, 64 guns, and 300 crew, Sir Thomas suppressed the Kegwin Revolution at Bombay in 1684 and was honored on his return by James II. He was a household officer both to William III and to Queen Anne.

profitable and politically significant set of raids and negotiations on the York. This river was the highway to the new, rich estates of London merchandisers turned Virginia courtiers. They had achieved plantation pre-eminence during the commonwealth and protectorate regimes of the 1650s. They had consolidated their political positions in the era of continued assembly authority in the 1660s. They had apparently co-opted the aging governor in the early 1670s. The younger and more militant members of this "Loyall Party" soon tired of their Eastern Shore exile. Their urge to attack the revolutionaries who held their property grew as they learned of Admiral Morris' advance up the James River, the death of Nathaniel Bacon, and the dispersal of the rebels into winter quarters. Pulled across the Bay by favorable events, the Berkeleyans were also pushed by an anxious governor.

Sir William Berkeley was desperate to recover at least the semblance of command on the mainland before English troops arrived. Otherwise, as they conquered the province the royal forces, in the usual mode of garrison government, would install their own officers and nominees in both civil and military, county and provincial offices. Imperialists would displace localists, whether Baconian revolutionaries or Berkeleyan émigrés. Berkeley's letters show that he knew himself to be disgraced in English eyes by his failure to protect his province against the natives or to repress the revolt incited by this failure. His agents made it clear to the governor that only his recovery of political power prior to the arrival of the royal forces could preserve his "Grand Assembly's" autonomy. So warned, Sir William felt that he "had a long time bin shut up in the Arke." On 7 November 1676, he sent out "a winged messenger" to see if the tide of rebellion was receding from the York.[132]

That messenger was Major Robert Beverley of Gloucester. His wings were the sails of four sloops. Beverley had been "bred a vulgar seaman" and he displayed that ruthless vigor that made English sailors feared fighters, whether for their crown or themselves. Major Beverley and his sloopmen turned pirates as early as 20 October 1676. "A small party of forty, or less," they had sailed from Accomac, landed in Gloucester, kidnapped Sandes Knowles (a nonpolitical planter), robbed his house, stolen his laborers ("3 Negroes and 5 English servants"), food stores, and 2 shallops, and retreated with their loot to Accomac. There Knowles was imprisoned for three months without being charged with any crime, then bailed, and finally, on 15 March 1676/7, pardoned by Berkeley on condition that he cede all his plundered property to Beverley and his men. Now, on Sir William's orders, Beverley and his privateers once more

132. C.O. 1/39, 94. [Lee,] "Bacon's and Ingram's Rebellion," in Andrews, ed., *Narratives*, 79, 80.

THE METES AND BOUNDS OF
BACON'S REVOLUTION

ILLUSTRATIONS FOR BOOK ONE

To the left of the stairs descending into the formal dining room at Berkeley Castle hangs Sir Peter Lely's portrait of *Sir William Berkeley, Brother to John the first Lord Berkeley of Stratton.* Presumably, the portrait was painted during Sir William's visit to England, June 1661–August 1662. In the spring of his return, Berkeley's play of 1638, *The Lost Lady,* enjoyed a revival at the Theatre Royal. Samuel Pepys saw it there twice. He liked it better the second time, despite being "spat backwards upon" by a lady. Besides his play, another episode of Sir William Berkeley's cavalier past was recalled in the cavalry action painted in the background of his portrait, beyond the baton of his command—a memorial, it seems, to his part in the western campaign of 1644.

During his year at home, Sir William used up much of his cavalier credit, renewed by the play, the portrait, and the political campaign at court of which they were elements, by attacking London's mercantilists. To the mind of a Somerset gentleman who was a correspondent of Bristol merchants and a master of tenant farmers in Virginia, the mercantilist dogma was a metropolitan, centralizing, oligarchical legacy of the inverted values of the interregnum. Bad enough in England, it was perversely destructive of Virginia's planters. "We cannot but resent that forty thousand people should be impoverished to enrich little more than forty merchants," Sir William wrote in the pamphlet he published in 1662. Metropolitan exploitation sapped royal military capacity in America by discouraging small planters and tenants. "The more men, the less need of soldiers," Sir William explained, exhibiting an aristocratic preference for peasant rather than professional troops. And, he wrote, mercantilism made for a short-sighted English emphasis on the exotic West Indies: "like flowers, they were quickly at their full growth and perfection, and a Nil ultra is fixt on them." The continental colonies, Englands overseas, were the multipliers, the authenticators of the old England in which Sir William had grown up to be knighted in 1639, an England unaffected by "the worst of men, Cromwell." The king had only to ship an investigator to America to discover "what a growing Empire he has here in which all the Plantations in the West Indies begin to centre. . . ."

Ships were the sinews of Stuart empire, the determinants of Bacon's Revolution. The oil painting of *The Charles Galley* by the elder Willem van de Velde and his son's pencil-and-wash sketch of *ye James galy frigate 1676* represent the vessels that most concerned the king, the duke, and the cabinet during 1676, and which marked an advance in English naval architecture by Sir Anthony Deane. The "galley" type (full-rigged, fine-lined, armed on the upper deck only, carrying about thirty guns on about 500 tons), when it took the form of such large merchant ships as Thomas Grantham's *Concord* of London, became the "defensible ships" which were pre-eminent in England's distant trades (and in those of the Dutch) for half a century after the *Concord* established her dominance in 1676. Ludolf Bakhuyzen's triple portrait (the three vessels to the right in the illustration), dated 1676, shows a civilian ship armed, rigged, and built (especially as regards wales, galleries, and afterdecks) on a model very similar to the *Concord* and to the galley-frigates of 1676.

On 6 February 1675/6, King Charles proposed the design of a ship for Mediterranean convoy duty to his admiralty commissioners and naval officers. This design (actually by Sir Anthony Deane, probably from a French model) had unusually fine lines, being intended to row as well as to sail—that is, to combine the roles "of both a frigate and a galley." The main deck was kept clear of armament so that oarsmen might work from it. King Charles pursued the building of this ship with an avidity unusual even in such a naval enthusiast, an interest equaled only by that of his brother, James duke of York, lord high admiral. The royal brothers quickly decided to build two of the new vessels, each of thirty-two guns and with thirty-six oars, and gave the ships their own names.

Deane himself contracted for the first vessel, the *James* as she became, and she was built at Alderman Johnson's Blackwell yard. When the king determined to have a slightly longer edition (114 feet in the keel and 492 tons displacement, as contrasted to the *James*' 104 feet and 436 tons), he assured his anxious lord treasurer that, if the ship were built in the royal yard at Woolwich of timber already in store, she would be less expensive than her sister. In fact, the hull of what became the *Charles* cost £5,435, as opposed to the *James*' first cost of £3,247. The royal naval enthusiasts then insisted on lead sheathing below the waterline and carved and gilt carpentry above it, as well as great haste. The costs had run far over estimates by the time the king and the duke raced their yachts down the Thames to christen the *Charles*. This was early in October 1676, at the height of the Virginia crisis. The financial burden of that crisis, when combined with additional costs such as those of the royal naval experiments, broke the lord treasurer's plan for the crown's fiscal, and so its political, independence of the parliament.

The new galley-frigates compounded their political costs because the Thames watermen needed "for the use of the oar" in the *Charles* and the *James* were impressed by royal warrant, on his majesty's own order, after much debate in the privy council, without reference to the extant act of parliament. King Charles and his admiral, Duke James, insisted that such coercive power was inherent in the military prerogative of the crown, a function of the royal duty to secure physically the nation and its trade. The imperial ethos was multiply manifest in the galley-frigates of 1676, and in their like-modeled merchant sisters as well.

Sir William Berkeley

The Charles Galley

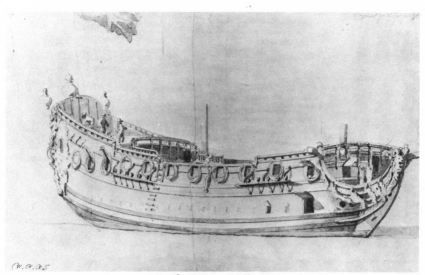

The James Galley

Marina in Burrasca

Green Spring

Bacon's Castle

Sir William Berkeley's Green Spring was the source of even more political and military controversy than were the galley-frigates of 1676. Its very architectural history is disputed. Venerable authorities have termed the Green Spring mansion of 1676 "the first great house of the American colonies." An eminent modern scholar insists, however, that in 1676 Green Spring was still "a typical small English brick country house of the period," and that not until towards the end of the century did it become the massive, arcaded, double-atticed, many-cellared structure pictured here.

The evidence—even aside from the public uses to which Green Spring was put in 1676—favors the former view. A 1683 survey of the governor-general's Green Spring tenancies includes a sketch of the building as it is seen here in a watercolor drawing by the first architect of the new nation, Benjamin Henry Latrobe, executed in 1797. It may well be that the second-floor window to the right contained in its casement the famous "broken quarrel of the glass" through which Lady Berkeley "peeped . . . to see how the show looked" when the Berkeleyan hangman disgracefully drove the royal commissioners' coach away. Also appropriate to Green Spring's civil-war heritage is that the only surviving seventeenth-century building on the estate is the jail.

The occupation of Green Spring, "the strongest place in the Country," by Nathaniel Bacon, on 8 August 1676, marked the moment when rebellion became revolution in the Peninsula. Its surrender, by a flour miller turned revolutionary, to Sir William Berkeley, on 22 January 1676/7, secured the land base of the loyalist revenge. Likewise, William Rookins' seizure of Major Arthur Allen's tall brick seat on the banks of the upper Chipokes Creek, Surrey County, "the sole high-Jacobean house in America," signaled Baconian supremacy south of the James River. The successful assault on "Bacon's Castle" —as the house has since been known—by a landing force from a royalist squadron, 28 December 1676, was *initium finis* for the revolution in the Southside. Captain Rookins died in the Green Spring jail.

His erstwhile headquarters appears here to the left of a pedestrian eighteenth-century addition. Bacon's Castle, its great twisted chimney stacks, powerfully curved gables, and high-roofed entry tower commanded the flat Surrey farmlands in the revolution of 1676. They do so still, in part because Rookins' discipline, or the native respect of his garrison for quality, preserved even the carved timber ceilings and the fine ornamental brickwork of Bacon's Castle as "an incomprable picture of seventeenth-century America."

The portrait of Sir William Berkeley (1606–1677) is reproduced with the consent of the Trustee of the will of the eighth earl of Berkeley, deceased. I am indebted to Wilcomb E. Washburn of the Smithsonian Institution and Gwen Duffey of the University of North Carolina Press for the photograph, which was first reproduced in Dr. Washburn's *The Governor and the Rebel* (Chapel Hill, 1957). Quotations above are from Robert Latham and William Matthews, eds., *The Diary of Samuel Pepys, II, 1661* (Berkeley and Los Angeles, 1970), 18, 25; Sir William Berkeley, "A Discourse & View of Virginia," and his letter of 30 March 1663, Egerton Ms. 2395, fols. 354–59, 364, British Library.

The Van de Velde studies of the *Charles* and the *James* are reproduced by permission of the Trustees of the National Maritime Museum, Greenwich, and the G. Brogi photograph of the Bakhuyzen painting in the Pitti Palace is reproduced by permission of Alinari/Art Resource, Inc. The ship contracts and royal orders quoted in the text are from ADM 2/1, 202; ADM 3/276, 13, 23, 31, 93, 108, 111, 114, 116, 123, 128, 135, 147, 149; and PC 2/65, 368, British Public Record Office.

The Latrobe watercolor of Green Spring appears by courtesy of the Jamestown-Yorktown Foundation, John B. Nicholson, III, Director. Comments on Berkeley's mansion are drawn from "The History of Bacon and Ingram's Rebellion," in Charles M. Andrews, ed., *Narratives of the Insurrections, 1675–1690* (New York, 1915, 1967), 95; Thomas Tileston Waterman and John A. Barrows, *Domestic Colonial Architecture of Tidewater Virginia* (New York, 1932, 1969), 11; Ivor Noel Hume, *Here Lies Virginia* (New York, 1983), 139, 143.
    "Bacon's Castle" is represented by a woodcut from *Frank Leslie's Illustrated Weekly*, and additional comments are from Thomas Tileston Waterman, *The Mansions of Virginia* (Chapel Hill, 1945), 21–25, and from Waterman and Barrows, *Domestic Colonial Architecture*, 20–27.

sailed their sloops, 30 miles diagonally across the Bay from the North-ampton shore to the mouth of the York River. They proceeded upriver after dark on 7 November.[133]

Before dawn, they landed at the York Narrows (Yorktown), surprised the sleeping rebel guards, broke into Colonel Reade's mansion, and cap-tured the rebel captain Thomas Hansford, asleep in bed (he was so soundly asleep, it is said, because he had spent the previous evening paying "his oblations in the Temple of Venus"). Beverley's crews also captured twenty of Hansford's men (whether they were also asleep, and why, is not recorded), plundered the plantation, marched their prisoners to the sloops, cast off, and rode the ebb tide downriver, ahead of all pursuit.[134]

For a day and a night, Beverley's sloops drifted on the Bay. Finally, a strong northwest wind came up with the sun on 10 November 1676. It blew captors and captives to Northampton. Three days later, Sir William Berkeley arraigned Captain Thomas Hansford, rebel commander-in-chief of four counties and president of the Baconian committee of sequestra-tions. Hansford pled that "he had never taken up arms, but for the de-struction of the Indians, who had murthered so many Christians." That plea failing, Hansford asked to be "shot like a Souldier, and not hang'd like a Dog." Berkeley immediately had him hanged, "the first Virginian borne that dyed upon a paire of Gallows." Admiral Morris had the news within the day (so quick was loyalist communication with the James River squadron). He sent it on to Captain Gatlin as a warning and as an encouragement to his surrender.

Even before Hansford was hanged, his captors were under sail once more. Beverley and his sloops recrossed the Chesapeake early on 11 November 1676, carrying with them a fair wind and the governor's orders to "Captain Saml. Groome and every commander, master, merchant, or supercargoe belonging to any shipp already arrived or which shall arrive into Virginia" to give Major Beverley every assistance by sea or by land. The Berkeleyans hoped to emulate on the York River Admiral Morris' successes on the James. Not waiting for help, however, Beverley brought his sloops to the land in his home county, Gloucester. There the loyalists surprised the rebel post commanded by Major Cheezeman and Captain Wilford. The little captain fought hard and lost an eye. He dismissed the loss, saying that when Beverley took him back to Accomac, "though he had been starke blinde, yet the Governour would . . . afford him a guide . . . to the gallows." Wilford was right. His colleague, Major Cheezeman,

133. On Beverley's breeding, see *Narratives*, 79, 80. For the Knowles raid, see "By Petition of Sandes Knowles," Pepys 2582; Henning, [ed.,] *Statutes*, II, 552–53, III, 567; An. Cotton, "Our Late Troubles," in Force, ed., *Tracts*, I, 9.

134. [Lee,] "Bacon's and Ingram's Rebellion," in Andrews, ed., *Narratives*, 80.

had an attorney of sorts to defend him from the like fate. Having somehow gotten to her husband's court-martial, Mrs. Cheezeman told the governor that it was she who had persuaded her husband to join Bacon, and she who should be punished. Sir William called her "W[hore]" and condemned her husband. Major Cheezeman died in an Accomac jail, perhaps from torture, before he could be hanged, but the vengeful old governor found other fruit for the gallowstree. He had Captain George Farloe executed despite the captain's plea that he (like Hansford) had merely obeyed the governor's own commission to Bacon and the assembly act (also signed by Berkeley) when he joined the army assembled against the Indians. He was followed to the gallows by the rebel agitator and propagandist John Johnson.[135]

Sir William Berkeley, puffed up by his bullying presidency of courts-martial and excited by the executions of his enemies, was vulnerable once more to the overpersuasions of Major Beverley. The major repeated his "Gloucester Petition" assurances that his countrymen only waited for loyal leadership to enlist in a counter-revolutionary army. Anyhow, both Berkeley and Beverley saw fat pigeons to pluck in Gloucester. The major aimed at the rebels' "winter-quarters at the house of one Mr. William Howard's in Gloster county." The governor had his avaricious eye on Mrs. Sarah Grindon, she of the sharp, seditious tongue and the rich, absent husband. Berkeley and Beverley loaded 150 Accomac mercenaries (all that they could raise after the fiasco at Jamestown) into four English ships and three Virginia sloops and sailed across the Bay for the York River, probably on 16 November 1676.[136]

As usual, Major Beverley attacked before dawn. Once again, he found the rebels asleep. Having made the garrison of Howard's plantation his prisoners, Beverley ordered both house and store looted. His men even cleaned out Mrs. Howard's dress closet. That Howard was an old man and a loyalist and that his estate was already much damaged by his uninvited rebel guests did not deter Major Beverley from completing his ruin. After all, Howard's son-in-law, John Harris, had commanded the rebel garrison. More to the point, Beverley and his men had become buccaneers.

These looters, the palace guard of the "Loyall Party," henceforward sought to sustain, not to end, a profitable war against the rebels. They defined "rebels" very broadly. As Gloucestermen victimized by the loyalists complained, "all yt were not with ye Governor, but staid at

135. *Ibid.*, 81–82. Berkeley to Groome et al., 3 November 1676, Henning, [ed.,] *Statutes*, III, 567–68.
136. "By Petition of Wm Howard," Pepys 2582. [Sherwood,] "Virginias Deploured Condition," *Mass. Hist. Soc. Collections*, 4th ser., IX (1841), 173–74. Gloucester petition, *ibid.*, 182–83. Moryson to T. Ludwell, London, 28 November 1677, printed in Burk, *Virginia*, II, 268.

home att their own plantations to be secure & quiett were accounted Rebels. . . ." The result, as the royal commissioners observed, was that the governor's favorite ("My Dearest, Most Honoured Major Beverley," Berkeley called him) was "very active & Serviceable in surprisinge and beattinge up Quarters & small Guards," but he also "gott by those un-happy troubles in Plunderings (without distinction) of honest mens Es-tates from others." Afterwards, Beverley "had ye Confidence to saye . . . he had not plundered enough; soe yt ye Rebellion ended too soon for his Purpose."

But Berkeley, Beverley, and their "Loyall Party" did not end the revolution themselves and they did all that they could to keep those who did end it, whether English captains or royal commissioners, from ever ending "Loyall Party" looting. As Berkeley's favorite, Beverley would urge him to deny the rebels all benefit of the king's pardon. Beverley thus set Berkeley against his successor, the royal commissioner, colonel and governor Herbert Jeffreys. Beverley was not only "ye evill Instru-ment yt fomented ye Ill humours between ye two Governors then on ye Place, and was a great occasion of their Clashinge and difference," but also, as clerk of the Berkeleyan assembly, Beverley drafted bills which legislated enormous exceptions to the king's pardon and imposed endless fines on thousands of former "rebels." [137]

SIR WILLIAM'S EXCUSES

As his precedent for endless plundering, Sir William Berkeley cited his experience of the English civil wars. He recalled that when he had fol-lowed King Charles I "in the pursuit of Essex" the king had ordered his soldiers to seize the goods of his enemies. Berkeley also remembered that the king's soldiers did not discriminate politically when they plun-dered. "I was by when Sir Richard Grenvill took the house of my Lord Roberts [Robartes], and out of it at least two thousand pounds sterling in Plate, very Rich hangings and much household stuff." Yet, Berkeley ar-gued, Robartes was so far from being a rebel that he was made lord privy seal at the king's restoration. [138]

Even by Sir William Berkeley's cavalier standards, however, his his-torical rationale for robbery was sophistical. When, on 12 August 1644, he

137. [Lee,] "Bacon's and Ingram's Rebellion," in Andrews, ed., *Narratives*, 84. "Gloster County Grievances," no. 6, Pepys 2582. Berkeley to "My Dearest, Most Honoured Major Beverley," Friday, 29 November 1676, printed in Henning, [ed.,] *Statutes*, III, 568. "A List of ye Names of those Worthy Persons . . . ," no. 16, Pepys 2582. Act V of February 1676/7, printed in Henning, [ed.,] *Statutes*, II, 381–86.
138. Berkeley to Moryson, "From my Bed expecting my Feavour" [11 February 1676/7], Pepys 2582. See also Berkeley to the commissioners, 7 March 1676/7, *ibid.*

had joined the other Gloucestershire royalists under Sir Richard Grenville's command in the seizure and sack of Lord Robartes' house at Lan-
hydrock, Cornwall, Robartes was a leading officer of the parliamentary
army under the earl of Essex. Robartes had persuaded Essex to march
west into Cornwall in part to secure his house and its treasury. The
building itself was a strategic objective because it commanded the Res-
pryn Bridge across the Fowey River. Its capture from Essex' parliamentarians by Grenville's royalists closed the semicircle by which Grenville's
force trapped Essex' army against the coast and, on 2 September 1644,
compelled its surrender. Berkeley's assumption, that those turns of fortune over the next sixteen years which ultimately brought Lord Robartes
into the household of Charles II in 1661 excused Sir William's sacking of
loyalist households, in the moment of their loyalism, in 1676, in Virginia,
shows how deviously Berkeley's mind worked and suggests why twenty-
nine in thirty of his subjects distrusted him. On the other hand, the
old governor's excuses for expropriation also show how long-lived and
influential were the men and memories of the English civil war,
even in America. From personal experience and living memory, the Virginians of 1676 knew what a civil war was and knew that theirs was such
a war.

Contemporary criticism, however, was not addressed as much to the
loyalists' living off the land during the civil war in 1676 as it was to
the fact that, when the fighting was over, Berkeley went on plundering
the planters and stuffing his spoils into the ships of the York River squadron. As prisoners were taken out of the hold of Captain Martin's bark to
be hanged, their places were taken by hogsheads of sweet-scented tobacco, confiscated by Berkeley's order and consigned to his account. With
Major Beverley's help, and that of the "Loyall Party," the outraged old
governor determined "thoroughly to heale himselfe before hee car'd to
staunch the bleeding gashes of this woefully lacerated country."[139]

GLOUCESTER FEUDS AND EXILES

While his colleagues in the old order revenged themselves and refilled
their pockets ashore in Gloucester, Colonel Philip Ludwell represented
the Berkeleyans on the York River. As provincial customs collector on the
York, "which I held by Sr. Wm. Berkeley's commission," Ludwell had
learned the waters of the river and earned the hatred of the Baconians.
When the revolutionaries occupied the riverine estates, they not only
rustled Ludwell's livestock and spoiled his home, they also stripped his

139. Commissioners to Williamson, 27 March 1677, *ibid.*

office of the title deeds, mortgage papers, and account books which were
the instruments of his exploitation of such weaklings as the widow Bland.
When, in mid-November 1676, the loyalists returned to the river, Ludwell
looked for revenge. Finding it, he, like every other loyalist leader,
claimed almost exclusive credit for repressing the rebels. "I was the
prime cause of taking away and securing four of the enemy's sloops,"
Ludwell declared, "which were all the vessels they had but one small
ship, which we had also secured, had she not been removed two days
before" the attackers arrived from Accomac.[140]

Yet the "we" who, apparently, had won back the river from the rebels,
included many more men than Philip Ludwell, each of whom was as
important to the loyalist victory, albeit lost to loyalist recollection (and so
to Virginia's history), afterwards. Captains Thomas Gardiner, Hubert Farrill, and Samuel Groome commanded the all-important ships of the York
squadron, and it included two "barks," vessels equally useful and inele-
gant. Housed in the utilitarian barks, backed by the English ships' batteries, and transported by the Virginian sloops, the loyalist soldiers under
Ludwell either captured four sloops or forced the Baconian crews to
beach and burn them in the last days of November 1676. The only rebel
ship on the York fled upstream to the protection of the garrison at West
Point.

That garrison was immediately threatened by Major Beverley's Accomac mercenaries and by Gloucester County militia raised by Major
Lawrence Smith. In May 1676, this royalist veteran of the English civil
wars had ridden north from Gloucester to organize the defense of Cittenbourne parish in Rappahannock County "to our no little satisfaction," the
frontiersmen wrote. Long famous as "a most Loyal Subject to his Prince,"
the major had also been Governor Berkeley's chief defender in Jamestown during the June Assembly. Subsequently, Smith was seized in Rappahannock and imprisoned by Bacon (being replaced as frontier
commander in that embattled county by Bacon's captain, the equally
popular Simon Miller). Major Smith's popularity now recruited Gloucester militiamen for Berkeley's army. So did the threat of Major Beverley's
raids, the loyalist squadron's command of the York, and the monarchist
preaching of a vigorous priest of the Church of England, Mr. John
Clough. Protector, privateer, seaman, and preacher, these Berkeleyan
leaders personified the strengths of loyalism which again summoned the
Gloucester militia to arms.[141]

140. "The humble answer of Philip Ludwell," 28 March 1678, in Burk, *Virginia*, II, 272.
141. [Sherwood,] "Virginias Deploured Condition," *Mass. Hist. Soc. Collections*, 4th ser.,
IX, 173. "Inhabitants of ye Uppr prsh. of Cittenbourne in ye County of Rappahannacke" to
the commissioners, C.O. 1/39, 200.

The Gloucester militia were the most numerous county force in the colony. Substantial numbers of them now obeyed Sir William Berkeley's orders to muster at Pate's plantation, the scene of Nathaniel Bacon's death. From this muster, Major Smith led some of the Gloucester men into Middlesex County, but briefly, for they fled from the first charge of Gregory Walkett's Baconian cavalry. In the meantime, the Baconian garrison of West Point marched on Pate's plantation, led by General Ingram. The revolutionaries demanded the surrender of all the Gloucester militia remaining at Pate's only to find that Major Smith's forces, fleeing from Middlesex, had come up behind them, but none of the loyalists would attack Ingram's troops. Rather, they stood "still like a Company of Sheep, with the knife at their throats, and never so much as offered to Bleat." Smith, Beverley, and other Berkeleyan officers fled the scene on horseback, but six hundred militia surrendered to Ingram's rebel garrison. For the third time, a loyalist land assault on the revolutionaries had failed. Again, the Gloucester militia had abandoned the Berkeleyans. And now, towards the middle of November 1676, for the first time, a loyalist raid from the York River was smashed.[142]

Captain Hubert Farrill, one of the captors of Nathaniel Bacon the rebel in June 1676, led the November attack against the rebel garrison in the home of the loyalist councilor Nathaniel Bacon the elder, on the south shore of the York at King's Creek. The assignment was dangerous, for the redoubtable rebel Gregory Walkett commanded the Baconian garrison. Nevertheless, Colonel Bacon himself volunteered to guide the raiders to his house, and Philip Ludwell was also present. In fact, every fit loyalist from the fleet crossed the river in small boats from the loyalist fleet's main anchorage at Tindall's (Gloucester) Point for the usual predawn attack. For once, however, an alert sentry alarmed the garrison. Walkett and his men sallied out from Bacon's mansion and broke the loyalists in the darkness. Some they killed, others they captured, and they pursued the survivors to their boats. Captain Farrill had been the first to fall.

In the fallen captain's pocket was found his commission from Sir William Berkeley. Blood-soaked, it was carried through the York River counties by Walkett's troopers, an ensign of the counter-revolution's failure on land, an encouragement, if they needed any, for the rebel horsemen to plunder whatever plantation they came upon at mealtimes. Most of these revolutionaries were escaped servants and slaves, and their attitude towards Virginia's men of property was shown when they visited Mr. Charles Roane's estate: "he had his dwelling house and other houses burnt downe to ye ground; and most of his goods and provisions destroy'd

---

142. [Lee,] "Bacon's and Ingram's Rebellion," in Andrews, *Narratives*, 89. An. Cotton, "Our Late Troubles," in Force, ed., *Tracts*, I, 9.

or carryed awaye by a Party of Rebells commanded by Gregory Walklatt after Bacon's Death."[143]

Obviously, Bacon's death had not killed Virginia's revolution. Its leaders were too many, its class hatreds were too deep, and the personal and principled passions of the "century of revolution" were too profound to be so easily suppressed. Faced by determined revolutionaries in November 1676, Sir William Berkeley had not been able to capitalize on the English seamen's command of the York. He could not bring his counter-revolution ashore. After the loyalist defeat at King's Creek the governor sailed back to exile in Accomac. He left Beverley, Ludwell, and their men aboard the English ships to blockade the narrows of the York River.

Meanwhile, on the James River, Admiral Morris' negotiations for the surrender of Captain Gatlin and the least-committed of the Southside rebels were suspended. With the failure of the York campaign, Morris had to try to intercept every ship entering the Capes of the Chesapeake —and the tobacco fleet numbered some eighty vessels—lest they either be captured by the Baconians or be tempted to trade with them. Those vessels which Morris could enlist in his squadron he did. Others he directed to the northern Virginia rivers, and to Maryland, to trade beyond the reach of the Baconian garrisons. Then November weather idled even Morris' fleet. At this loyalist low point, on 21 November 1676, Captain Thomas Grantham brought his ship, the *Concord* of London, into the York River. He reported that he found "the Country in Rebellion, and the Governor fled to Accomac."[144]

THE *CONCORD*

Grantham's Education

The *Concord* had sailed from the Thames in the last days of September 1676, just before English authorities ordered an embargo placed on all ships bound for Virginia lest they be seized and added to the rebel fleet. Whitehall soon learned not only that Grantham had sailed ahead of the embargo in the *Concord* but also that the situation into which they sailed was desperate. On 12 October, Captain Evelyn made port to confirm the news of Sir William Berkeley's flight (by water, to the Potomac River, Evelyn said) after the Gloucester Petition episode. Bacon had seized the government of Virginia, Evelyn added, and Brent's cavalry were riding north, first to catch the governor and then to carry the rebellion into

143. "A List of ye Names of those Worthy Persons," no. 31, Pepys 2582.
144. Grantham's dispatch, 21 November 1676 ["I then arrived"], Coventry Ms. 77, 301–2. See also T. Ludwell [to Coventry], 13 October 1676, *ibid.*, 254. See also ADM 1/5138, 512; S.P. 29/393, 157.

Maryland. The *Concord's* arrival in the Chesapeake, the cabinet was told, would bring the rebellion to a crisis just as surely as would the appearance of a distinguished royal-naval officer and one of his majesty's ships of war, for Grantham was as loyal and his ship as powerful. The cabinet anticipated that Grantham and the *Concord* would attack the rebels. In a fit of despair, Bacon and his lieutenants would thereupon devastate the whole Chesapeake region, or so the cabinet feared, and the rebels would load Larrimore's *Rebecca* and any other ships they had captured with the spoils of the loyalist estates, and flee from America before the *Concord*. To deal with the anarchy that would ensue, the cabinet ordered the Scots Guards aboard royal frigates to follow Grantham and the *Concord* out to Virginia.

The cabinet was correct in only one of its assumptions: the *Concord* and her captain did determine Virginia's civil war. So they demonstrated the dominance of the English marine in the Old Dominion and in the new empire. The ship herself was as imposing as she was important. Of 500 tons burden, the *Concord* carried thirty-two guns. She was thus among the largest and most warlike of Northern European merchant vessels just as they became supreme on the world's ocean and while they still were the indispensable auxiliaries of national navies. Indeed, given the shortage of cruisers and destroyers in the later Stuart navies, the larger merchantmen were the usual naval instruments of English imperialism.

For years before 1676, Captain Thomas Grantham's ships had served the crown in Virginia. In the spring of 1672, for example, Grantham had returned from the York River and told both the king and the committee on plantations that Virginia lacked arms, ammunition, and orders from England for the colony's defense both against the Dutch, with whom England was at war, and against the Indians, who had attacked the English empire's frontier on the Rappahannock River. To remedy these defects, Grantham volunteered his services to the king. When, in the autumn of 1672, the captain sailed from London bound for the James River in the ship *Edward and Jane* (of 240 tons and a crew of twelve) he carried letters of recommendation and protection from the duke of York, lord high admiral, in whose guard Grantham was. On the captain's arrival in the colony, the governor of Virginia "appointed him Admirall" of the Virginia tobacco fleet. Sir William Berkeley may not have relied just on the duke of York's endorsement of Grantham for the governor probably knew the captain's father, killed at Oxford in 1645 while fighting for the king. In April 1673, Admiral Grantham collected a convoy of twenty-five ships which was to sail home in June.[145]

If Grantham had sailed on schedule, he and his convoy would have

---

145. Grantham, *An Historical Account*, 59. *V.M.H.B.* 20 (1913): 23–24, 27.

barely escaped the attack of the Dutch fleet under Cornelius Evertsen, Jr., but the Virginia fleet was delayed because a royal frigate, commanded by Captain Cottrell and sent out to help escort the tobacco ships home, did not make the James River until 20 June. She could not replenish her firewood, water, and provisions before 15 July, her captain said. In the meantime, the convoy anchored in the James was informed of the dilatory loading of eight Maryland ships big enough to join it, of two other ships trading towards the head of the Bay, of five ships making cargoes in the Rappahannock, and of seven ships from the York River. They all would try to reach the rendezvous by 15 July, Grantham was told. On 12 July, nearly forty vessels were in sight of the James River anchorage when eight sizable Flushingers and Hollanders, carrying up to forty-four guns apiece, sailed into Hampton Roads and attacked the tobacco fleet. For four hours, against odds of four to one, the two royal frigates, commanded by Cottrell and by Captain David Gardner, fought off the Dutch. When his consort was disabled, Captain Gardner attacked the leading Dutch vessels. He "tackt alone upon them with Exterordnary Courage, and for at least one houre fought them all." The royal frigates' brave actions gave most of the tobacco fleet time to carry the flood tide up the James River. Some of the merchant ships sheltered under the guns of Nansemond Fort. Others fled farther upstream to Sandy Bay, beyond the guns of Jamestown. The Dutch were left tidebound, downstream of the English refugees. Only the eleven tobacco ships, which went aground, either in the early stages of the battle or in their subsequent flight, were captured and burned by the Dutch. Even the battered English frigates escaped into the Elizabeth River for repairs. Certainly Grantham escaped, and subsequently he saw his remaining charges, some three-fourths of the James River convoy, safely into Plymouth, Bristol, and London during October 1673, to the enormous relief of royal officialdom, anxious for customs income and mercantile solvency.[146]

In January 1673/4, Captain Grantham was commissioned by the king to command the *Barnaby* (which returned to Virginia in 1676 as a royal troop transport). Acting on orders from the duke of York (despite the Test Act, which prevented Catholics from holding English office, the papist duke continued to be admiral of the empire outside England) and in regular correspondence with the duke's secretary, Sir John Werden, Grantham organized and led the London tobacco fleet out to Virginia early in 1674. Among his favored passengers in the *Barnaby*'s great cabin was Lawrence (Joseph) Ingram. While he wintered in Jamestown, Grantham spent much time with the hospitable Richard Lawrence in that merchant's richly furnished home on Jamestown's market square. In

146. *V.M.H.B.* 20 (1913): 134–40, 243, 248–49. *The William and Mary Quarterly*, 1st ser., 9 (1901): 83–131. C.O. 1/38, 31, 79.

September 1674, Grantham convoyed home the London, Bristol, and Plymouth ships. He also brought to the king and council recommendations from the governor and council of Virginia (based on Grantham's own soundings and advice) for the defense of the James River. Royal ships and munitions, it was hoped, would prevent a recurrence of the Dutch raid, a crisis that had exposed Virginia's military weakness and emphasized the colony's social disintegration.

Unpreparedness and disunity were already being exposed and exaggerated by Indian raids when Grantham sailed from Virginia early in March 1676. He made Deal at the end of April, one of thirty ships to ride the spring westerlies home from Virginia since January. Their masters reported ever-widening Indian raids, hundreds of English casualties, crop failures, epidemic disease, growing taxation (assessed in tobacco). They predicted a tobacco shortage in London and civil unrest in Virginia. These predictions were confirmed by the news from July's arrivals: Indian war and excessive taxation had produced frontier devastation and a mutiny against the governor. These catastrophes were sure to affect the tobacco available from his usual James River sources, Grantham was warned. He sailed anyway, just as conclusive word of Virginia's civil war arrived with Captain Windsor of the *Sampson*, on 25 September 1676. So Grantham may not have known that the military failures he had so long deplored in Virginia had at last led to revolution.[147]

It was revolution nonetheless that Captain Thomas Grantham found when he reached Virginia in the *Concord*, 21 November 1676, and he was ideally qualified to break the stalemate in its York River theatre. On the one hand, Grantham was a king's officer, a master of Virginia's waters and an expert on their defenses, a birthright royalist in high favor with the duke of York and the admiralty at home, and respected by the defeated governor and his few, loyal councilors now exiled anew in Accomac. On the other hand, Grantham was a prominent tobacco trader, intimately acquainted with these rich and recent emigrants who headed the revolutionaries holding the valley of the York, General Ingram and Richard Lawrence in particular. The *Concord*, Grantham's powerful vessel with the peaceful name, was the instrument both of power politics and mercantile conciliation, the manifestation of her cosmopolitan captain's personal eminence and of imperial England's material might.

Grantham's Ship

The *Concord*, at 500 tons Thames measurement, a length on the keel of more than 100 feet and on deck of 130 feet, a beam in excess of 30 feet

147. See especially S.P. 29/385, 213. For a fuller discussion of the London reports, see Book II, pp. 200 ff.

and a depth of 16 feet in the hold, was two or three times as big as most Virginia tobacco ships in 1676 (they averaged only about 140 tons and very seldom exceeded 300 tons). To imposing size the *Concord* added an extraordinary armament, lavish decoration, and a fully developed rig. She was thus a forceful example of one of the most beautiful and impressive ages of sail. The *Concord's* thirty-two carriage guns equaled the fire-power of the royal naval vessels of her tonnage launched in 1676. Like these warships, the *Charles Galley* and the *James Galley,* the *Concord* carried most of her battery on her upper deck. A dozen iron guns to each broadside were mounted on wheeled wooden carriages and pointed through square ports in her bulwarks. The port sills rested on the upper-most wale of the heavy planking which gave the *Concord* much of her longitudinal strength and which protected her hull from piers. In addition to her broadside batteries, the *Concord* boasted bow chasers. Poked through the bulkhead of the *Concord,* the bow chasers' ports opened on either side of the ship's steeply steeved bowsprit.

The bowsprit dominated the *Concord* forward. It was held down against the pull of the foremast stays and fastened to the ship's bows by rope gammoning. The heel of this heavy spar was actually buried deep in the ship between powerful knightheads (to which the anchor cables were belayed) but it was visually upheld by the beakhead. Ascendant from the rams of old, the beakhead curved upwards from the stem of the *Concord* towards the bowsprit, supported by railings run out from either side of the ship's bows. These beakhead rails were pierced and carved and balustered (both for decorative effect and to serve the crew as toilet seats). The elaborate beakhead eventuated in a great, gilded figurehead: a rearing, rampant, crowned English lion. Above the royal lion's crown passed the bowsprit, rising at an angle of 45 degrees for a length of 25 feet. Below the bowsprit hung the spritsail yard (Captain Grantham relied on that spritsail for forward leverage, both to help steer the *Concord* and to balance her high deck works aft). From the cap of the bowsprit a jackstaff rose at right angles to the *Concord's* waterline. Some 12 feet tall, this jackstaff supported both a sprit topsail yard and a great jack, the ensign that reiterated the *Concord's* royal English allegiance.

The next spar aft of the bowsprit in the *Concord* was her foremast. It ran down through the decks of the ship, first through the upper deck (which here was the floor or sole of the forecastle, in which forty or more sailors, the cook, and a few petty officers lived, and in which food was cooked in an open fireplace during good weather or at anchor). The foremast ran on down through the cargo hold and the main deck, through the lower hold and lower deck, and through the orlop deck to a massive step on the keel, the *Concord's* backbone. This forward lowermast, wedged at its heel to the step and braced by partners as it rose through each deck, had tied to its upper section (by caps, trestletrees, and shrouds) a topmast. The fore topmast in turn lofted a royal mast. Each of the foremast's three sections—lower, top, and topgallant—was crossed by a yard. From each yard hung a sail—forecourse, topsail, topgallant. The feet of the tops'l and the t'gallant were stretched to the yards below them. The foot of the course was extended across or along the deck of the *Concord* by sheets and bowlines. The whole mast complex was braced fore and aft by stays. It was supported to either side by shrouds. These shrouds ran down from the mast to massive shelves and chainplates outboard of the ship's rails.

The great rope-bound canvas sails were lashed to their yards, the yards were hauled aloft by halyards and lifts and held there in jeers or slings, and the sails were trimmed by braces reeved to the yardarms and by sheets shackled to the clews of the sail. The size of the sails was altered by reefing the head of the sail to its yard, by brailing up courses, and by partially lowering topsails. In Van de Velde's portrait of the *Charles Galley,* the mizzen is brailed up, the main royal or t'gallant and the foretops'l are half-lowered, and there are two rows of reef points visible across the head of the main tops'l. In restricted waters, such as Virginia's rivers, most ship maneuvering was done under the fore and main tops'ls. These were huge sails in this era before tops'ls were divided for ease of handling, and they were set high enough to catch the breeze above banks and trees. Stays'ls, set on the stays between the ship's masts, were just beginning to migrate from sloops to ships in 1676. When adopted, they increased the ship's fore-and-aft sail area, its weatherliness, and its maneuverability.

As the mention of multiple masts and of a main tops'l has suggested, the mainmast was simply the foremast enlarged and stepped aft of the middle of the ship. The third, aftermost, and smallest of the *Concord's* three masts was the mizzenmast. Its lower section upheld a relic of an earlier, Mediterranean, age of sailing ships: a lateen sail. The long lateen yard, wearing an almost triangular sail, was slung from the mizzen cap and pointed sharply forward and down towards the deck on the starboard side of the mizzenmast. It was the *Concord's* largest fore-and-aft, steering, sail. Above it, the *Concord's* mizzenmast crossed a single yard from which hung a loose-footed topsail.

Each of the ship's three masts was capped by a flagstaff. Each staff was proportioned to the size of its spar, but every flagstaff was a young spar in itself. From these huge staffs the *Concord* flew long pennants and gigantic flags: St. George's Cross at the fore; the Arms of England at the main; a distinguishing pennant at the mizzen. To these emblems of identity were added the jack hoisted forward and an enormous English ensign flown from a tall staff at the aftermost rail. It was an age of banners and their boasts: personal pride; political patriotism.

Aft from the foremast stretched the waistdeck of the *Concord*. This section of the ship's upper deck was bounded fore and aft by the bulkheads of the ship's accommodations—the men housed in the forecastle forward of the waist, the officers quartered in the cabins aft of it. The waist was lined to port and starboard by the rows of cannon whose barrels pierced its bulwarks. The waist was divided along its centerline by hatches which gave access to the cargo holds belowdecks, but under way they were covered with the ship's boats, resting on booms or spare spars and alive with chickens and pigs. At the after end of the waist, the massive mainmast emerged, flanked by the barrels and bars of the ship's pumps. From the mainmast, running rigging—sheets and braces, halyards and lifts—ran down to pin rails around the mast and along the waist's bulwarks. The waist ended at the break of the *Concord*'s halfdeck. The break was formed by a bulkhead that ran across the ship. This bulkhead stood on the upper deck and supported a half-deck. It was pierced by doors that led from the waist into the *Concord*'s wardroom and cabins. There were quartered Captain Grantham, his two mates, the ship's surgeon, perhaps the boatswain and the carpenter, probably the supercargo, certainly any wealthy passengers. Up the *Concord*'s halfdeck bulkhead ran the broad ladders, almost stairways, that led to the half-deck. On that deck, high above the turmoil of the waist (or even higher, if the *Concord* had an old-fashioned quarterdeck aft of and above the half-deck) the officer on watch had his station.

When the ship was under way, the watchkeeping officer shouted steering orders down through gratings to the helmsman, who stood belowdecks at the whipstaff. In heavy weather, the officer also directed crewmen pulling at tiller tackles. The rudder thus controlled by staff, tiller, and tackles was relatively small in area and limited in radius, so that much steering had to be by sail trim, especially of the sprits'l and lateen. Just as important as rudder or sails to the *Concord*'s steering was the form of her hull below the water. The *Concord*'s "cod's head and mackrel's tail" shape made the long, tapering, after sections of the ship a great steering skeg. From the end of that skeg a small rudder exerted a large leverage because of the flow of water flooding past it, directed by the *Concord*'s narrowing hull.

Standing high above the water, on the half-deck or quarter-deck gratings, the officer on watch could see on either hand the roofs of quarter galleries. These elaborately carved semi-circular galleries ran down the quarters of the *Concord* aft. The galleries' carved supporting brackets were pegged to the ship's topsides, where they met her stern. The glazed windows of the quarter galleries' upper story gave light to the cabins of the officers and passengers. The galleries' lower stories enclosed heads from which the decently private defecation of the *Concord's* officers offended only the round tuck of the ship's stern, this last a construction that distinguished the English vessels of 1676 from their European sisters.

The *Concord's* transom stern-works were cantilevered out above the tuck on carved brackets, fierce with lions or lithe with mermaids. Across the stern, a row of nine windows, with carved surrounds, opened into Captain Grantham's cabin and the wardroom. Below, opening onto the maindeck, were square ports for cannon, the *Concord's* stern chasers. High above both the ports and the windows of the ship's stern rose the taffrail. Its solid height above the highest deck protected the officers on watch from the wind blowing from astern. The outer face of the taffrail was splendidly carved with the Arms of England, supported by the lion and the unicorn, further, eloquent, testimonies to the imperial loyalty of Grantham and the crew of his *Concord*. Atop the taffrail stood three great glazed lanterns. By their light, ships sailing in company with the *Concord* kept station, astern of their flagship after dark.

Such a flagship embodied the highest technology of her age. She and her sisters were forceful expressions of England's emerging commercial and imperial stature. Ships such as the *Concord,* and those vessels which her firepower commanded in Virginia, were the lifelines that linked the scattered and endangered colonists with "home," the world of their birth, the source of vital supplies, across the Atlantic. Small wonder that both the rebels watching from King's Creek and the loyalists stationed across the river at Tindall's Point considered the arrival of the *Concord* in York Narrows on 21 November 1676 momentous. The leaders of both revolution and counter-revolution immediately contacted her captain, hoping to make Thomas Grantham and the *Concord* the makeweights of Virginia's civil war.

Grantham's Negotiation

Richard Lawrence wrote to Captain Grantham that the people had risen to defend themselves against the Indians, whom the governor would not oppose, and to resist the tyranny of the corrupt oligarchs, who were the governor's favorites. The governor had recognized that he was the people's greatest grievance, Lawrence wrote, and had announced his own resignation. A struggle for control of Virginia had followed between the governor's corrupt cronies and the injured, angered people. In this continuing contest, Lawrence insisted, the English captains should at worst be neutral. Failing that, the people would burn the tobacco crop. (This was no idle threat: an earlier fire had raised the value of later crops, put shippers in an immediate bind, and cost the crown customs revenue. Subsequently the Plant Cutting of 1682 would be based on the same politico-economic principle.)

Captain Grantham's reply to Lawrence's letter was just that of Captain Morris to Hansford's emissary two months before: he would have no truck with rebels against royal authority; he would support the king's governor. If the ships sailed home empty, Grantham explained, the king would be furious at the loss of the £140,000 he expected from his customs duties on tobacco. His anger would be multiplied by that of merchants resentful at their lost trade. Together, the crown and the commercial men would guarantee the punishment of everyone who nourished the troubles of Virginia. Therefore, Grantham was certain (as he told the revolutionaries) that very shortly Sir William Berkeley would be reinstructed and reinforced from England.

Having thus warned the rebels, Grantham sent a boat to Sir William Berkeley, exiled in Accomac. The governor himself hurried back across the Bay and up the York to meet Captain Grantham. Aboard the *Concord*, Berkeley listened with resignation to the captain's argument that the time had come for compromise. Grantham sought, he said, "to persuade the Governor to Meekness and the People to Submission." With the former, Grantham succeeded because Berkeley was bowed by defeat and by illness. At times he was "soe sick ... of my feavour" that he could not write. Moreover, both the governor and the rebels had been impressed by the loyal vigor of the English captains, and had been warned of the imminent arrival of an expedition from England. All these factors were evident already in Berkeley's approval of Morris' negotiation with Gatlin aboard the *Young Prince* on the James River. Berkeley now gave similar permission to Grantham and the *Concord* to pacify the rebels on the York —if Grantham dared, for an earlier arrival "deerst not goe on shore." [148]

Grantham confidently sailed the *Concord* up to West Point, landed, and rode a few miles to Pate's plantation, winter headquarters of the revolutionary forces. "There I mett with about Eight hundred of them in Armes," under General Ingram's command, Grantham reported. He told the revolutionaries that the king had heard their complaints of oppression and misgovernment. His sacred majesty had therefore appointed commissioners, who were on their way to Virginia under royal orders to collect, review, and redress his Virginia subjects' grievances. On the other hand, Grantham said to the general staff of the revolution, the king had responded to their attack on his governor by dispatching a fleet of warships

148. Grantham, *Historical Account*, 17, 18, 19. Dispatch by Grantham in Coventry Ms. 77, 301–2. Berkeley to the commissioners, 6 February 1676/7, Pepys 2582. The Royal Commissioners, "A Review Breviary and Conclusion," in *ibid.*; printed in Burk, *Virginia*, II, 252. R. Watts to Sec. Williamson, Deal, 6 May 1677, S.P. 29/393, 157, (121), (Part II, 30).

under the famous Sir John Berry, loaded with hardened Scots professional troops commanded by a veteran of garrison service in Ireland. Berry's squadron, Grantham said, was already at sea. He advised the Baconians to come to terms with the governor before the redcoats landed, for a country still in rebellion must expect to be conquered. Scots soldiers' killing and raping, looting and burning, reconquering Virginia on the awful model field-tested in Ireland, would make Virginia's present civil war seem trivial. Even now, Grantham pointed out, the rebel leaders had only to ride down to the river to see the *Concord,* herself anchored evidence of English might. General Ingram and his staff replied to the captain of the *Concord* that if he would guarantee their safety and arrange for their troops to be present, they would meet with Sir William Berkeley.[149]

Grantham took the terms of the Baconian proposal aboard the *Concord,* sailed down the James River and across the Bay to Accomac, obtained Berkeley's consent to his plans, and returned to the James, all by 30 November. Then, less than ten days after the *Concord* had first anchored in the river, "the Chiefe Officers and Army" of the revolution marched down the north bank of the James River to Tindall's Point, "where the Governor had a view of them from the Ship he was in." Grantham offered himself as a hostage for General Ingram's safe return and went ashore, sending out the rebel general to meet the royal governor on board the *Concord.* There they formally signed and sealed the preliminary articles of the treaty that Grantham had written "for a Cessation of Armes till his Maties ships arrived." [150]

West Point

Whatever the willingness of the opposed commanders to stop Virginia's civil war, their men were fighting again within three days of the *Concord* cessation. With a new authorization from Sir William Berkeley and a picked crew from the *Concord,* Captain Grantham set sail in a sloop for West Point to try to save his peace. Not for naught had he spent winters in Virginia boozing and bargaining with the planters. "Above 70£ sterling in Brandy & other strong liquors" were swallowed by the rebels "before I made them sensible of their Errors," Grantham wrote. During the night of 16 December 1676, General "Ingraham and some of the Chiefe Officers made a surrender of West Point to me." Together with West Point, the rebels' general staff surrendered to Grantham four cannon (which the

149. Grantham's dispatch, Coventry Ms. 77, 301. See also Watts to Williamson, 6 May 1677, S.P. 29/393, no. 121, calendared in Davenport, comp., *Bacon's Rebellion,* 213.
150. Grantham's dispatch, Coventry Ms. 77, 301. [Lee,] "Bacon's and Ingram's Rebellion," in Andrews, ed., *Narratives,* 94.

captain hastily had his crew dismount), three hundred soldiers of their bodyguard, and their small arms, flags, and drums, the instruments and emblems of the revolutionary army. Captain Grantham sent the disarmed soldiers off to drink a barrel of his brandy at General Ingram's house, promising to join them later, give them pardons for their former treason, and take from them oaths for their future obedience.[151]

Meanwhile, Grantham rode three miles to the former home of the loyalist exile Colonel John West. It was now the "Chiefe Garrison and Magazine" of the revolution. There the captain faced "about four hundred English and Negroes in Armes." They were furious at their general's surrender of West Point, his betrayal of the revolution to Captain Grantham. "Some were for shooting me," Grantham recalled, "others for cutting me in pieces." Once again the captain assured a rebel audience that the king had ordered a thorough hearing of their grievances and a complete reform of royal government in Virginia. Some rebels had more than political reform at stake: Grantham promised to confirm the personal freedom of the escaped servants and slaves now in the rebel ranks. They had made up two-thirds of the Baconian field army (as distinct from its county garrisons) ever since the burning of Jamestown confirmed the revolutionary nature of Virginia's civil war. Most of Bacon's staunchest soldiers had fought not for Virginia's freedom from English oppression but for their own freedom from Virginian masters. Therefore, Captain Grantham "did ingage to the Negroes and Servants that they were all pardoned and freed from their Slavery." [152]

Grantham's "fair promises and Rundletts of Brandy," together with formal "Noates under my hand," reassured the rebel soldiers "that what I did was by the Order of his Matie and the Governr." The bulk of the Baconian troops cantoned around West Point concluded that the civil war was over. During the night of 16/17 December 1676, most of them slipped away to begin new, anonymous, American lives. They were followed into anonymity by hundreds of other rebel soldiers as news of the West Point surrenders spread to the Baconian winter quarters. For a month afterwards, the snowy woods of Virginia's coldest winter in decades were tracked by disbanded revolutionaries, bound for sanctuaries as near as Albemarle and as far as Boston. An army composed of emigrants and deportees, of servants and of slaves, all mobile men, found "our wilderness," as a rueful loyalist observed, a road to freedom, "since the greatest part of our rude multitude have served an apprenticeship to the Art of

151. Grantham's dispatch (Coventry Ms. 77, 301) gives 2 January 1676/7 as the date of the West Point surrender, whereas the Royal Commissioners date it 16 December 1676. ([Lee,] "Bacon's and Ingram's Rebellion," in Andrews, ed., *Narratives*, 92.)
152. "Characters of ye Severall Comdrs of Ships," Pepys 2582. Grantham's dispatch, Coventry Ms. 77, 301. [Lee,] "Bacon's and Ingram's Rebellion," in Andrews, ed., *Narratives*, 94.

Escape." They left behind them, at West's plantation alone, five hundred muskets, powder in barrels, half a ton of bullets, and three more cannon (again Grantham had his men immediately dismount the only weapons which might damage the *Concord*). At dawn, Captain Grantham and his men selected "several Chests of Merchants Goods and some gold and silver Plate" for themselves from the rebels' loot, and then boarded their sloop. With them sailed the general staff of the revolutionary army: "Ingram their Genll. Colonl. Langston, Collnl. Miller, Capt. Lostage, Capt. Bryan." [153]

Not all of the West Pointers had disbanded or surrendered themselves. So Captain Grantham discovered when he found himself "in Jeopardy of being killed by the Negroes slaves who were disaffected with ye said Treaty being in distrust of their hoped for liberty and would not quietly laye downe their armes being about 100 in number, but threatened to kill Capt. Grantham att ye Generll Surrender then made by ye Rest of their Armes, Colours, Ammunition &c." Grantham quickly exempted the one hundred from the terms of the West Point surrender and announced that they were free to join any of the remaining rebel garrisons. These "Eighty Negroes and Twenty English which would not deliver their arms" decided to cross the York and march down its south bank to join the Brick House garrison and the political leaders of the revolution, Lawrence, Drummond, and company, who had their headquarters there. The one hundred crowded into a sloop, only to discover that it had no sail. Kindly Captain Grantham offered them a tow. On a long line, well astern of Grantham's sloop, the last of the West Point rebels set out down the river. After some miles, and more and more loudly, they demanded that Grantham land them on the south shore. He shouted back that they were not yet at the Brick House. It soon came in sight, but offshore of the rebel stronghold there lay a fourteen-gun ship of the loyalists' blockading squadron. Captain Grantham sailed his sloop, and her tow, between the ship and the shore. He anchored the sloop, rowed to the ship, had her guns trained on the rebels' sloop, and informed them that if they did not immediately hand over their weapons, "the Mouthes of the great guns were against them and I would sink and destroy them all." The "Negroes & Servants" cursed the captain but they surrendered their arms, their sloop was towed down to the *Concord* at Tindall's Point, and the rebels were chained in her hold "till," as Grantham smugly wrote, "I delivered them all to their Masters." [154]

153. Nicholas Spencer to Philip Calvert, Nomoni, 22 June 1677, C.O. 1/40, 249. Grantham's dispatch, Coventry Ms. 77, 301. The Royal Commissioners, "A true and faithful Account," 24 July 1677, Pepys 2582.
154. The Royal Commissioners, "A true and faithful Account," 24 July 1677, Pepys 2582. "Characters of ye Severall Comdrs," *ibid*. Grantham's dispatch, Coventry Ms. 77, 301.

Unlike the rebellious laborers, however, their commanders had seized the moment of Grantham's mercy. To them he kept his word. He delivered the military commanders of the revolution to Governor Berkeley, "telling him I had promised them pardon, which he immediately confirmed." The captain also kept his promise to the three hundred men he had left drinking at General Ingram's headquarters. He sailed back up the river, landed, went to the rebels' camp, and persuaded them to march down to Tindall's Point. On the shore, while Sir William Berkeley watched from the safety of a ship, Captain Grantham administered to the last of the West Point troops the oath he had composed to secure their obedience and to separate them from the political heads of the revolution, their soldiers, and other Baconians still out in rebellion: "I A.B. do willingly and heartily declare that I know, and in my Conscience believe, *Richard Lawrence*, and many others with him, to be in open Rebellion against the King's most Sacred Majesty, and against the Right Honourable the Governor of *Virginia*, and the good established Laws and Peace of this Colony of Virginia."

The last of the West Pointers renounced the revolution and denounced their former comrades. They pledged their lives and property that they would obey the governor and his appointees and support them against all those who still resisted their authority. Captain Grantham then accepted the former rebels' "Armes, Drums, and Colors." With these ex-Baconians he "drank his Maties health, and the Govrs, in Brandy, with three Shouts, in the Governor's sight and soe dismissed them." Once the West Point garrison surrendered, dispersed, were imprisoned, or chose new sides, "the rest of the small Garrisons hearing their magazine was surrendered and their Gen.ll come in they immediately dispersed and went to their homes." [155]

Grantham's Achievement

Two subjects too little studied appear in Captain Grantham's remarkable series of West Point negotiations, maneuvers, and triumphs. The first is the sustained search for freedom by Virginia's servants and slaves which had supported the revolution of 1676 in Virginia. The second subject is the decisiveness of Grantham's diplomacy. "With good Caution faithful Conduct great Experience and Eminent Danger of his life," the crown's commissioners concluded, the captain of the *Concord* had "effected with happy Success" the surrender of the "then chief Rendezvous and Magazine of the Rebells" at West Point. So he made a major contribution to "the Resettlement of the Peace of that his Majesties Collony of Virginia."

---

155. Grantham, *Historical Account,* 23. Grantham's dispatch, Coventry Ms. 77, 302.

In the judgment of the royal commissioners, confirmed by the king, his council, and English legal opinion, the series of surrenders secured by Captain Grantham at West Point ended the civil war in Virginia.[156]

That Captain Morris' squadron continued to fight against the rebels south of the James River for several weeks after the surrenders at West Point suggests that the royal conclusion was a bit sanguine. So too do Captain Grantham's continued efforts at pacification on the south shore of the York. The revolutionary ideologues and their guards at the Brick House were a political menace. The Baconian garrison at King's Creek, under Gregory Walkett, was a military one. To the latter, Grantham paid another of his festive visits, and to liquor he added the most generous promises. Grantham said that the governor would not only pardon Walkett and his lieutenants but would even let them keep their "Indian plunder." It was Grantham's diplomacy, even more than the promises he extracted from Berkeley, however, that won over Walkett and his troopers (as they had Ingram and his army), and they did more than give up the revolution. For the next five weeks, Walkett's troopers pursued "Arnold, Lawrence, and other Rebells which did not surrender." When Grantham sailed from Virginia in the *Concord* at the end of 1676, a leading loyalist privately observed that the captain had been "infinitely Serviceable to the reducing of the Country from ruin of ye insulting rabble: for itt is ye Judmt of Many that unless he had interposed the whole Country had been laid in Ashes." [157]

Berkeley's Revenge

This judgment was justified by Berkeley's behavior once Captain Grantham had pacified the rebel garrisons along the York and Captain Morris had cleared them from the banks of the James. Now that the seafarers had won the civil war, the governor felt free to break the promises by which they had ended it. First Berkeley re-enslaved the laborers to whom Grantham had promised freedom: "the Sarvants and Slaves was

156. "Characters of ye Severall Comdrs," Pepys 2582. See also [Lee,] "Bacon's and Ingram's Rebellion," in Andrews, ed., *Narratives*, 93. This opinion was shared by Grantham himself (S.P. 29/393, 157).
157. The Royal Commissioners, "A Review Breviary and Conclusion," Pepys 2582; printed in Burk, *Virginia*, II, 256–57, 272–73. C.O. 1/40, 36–37. Sherwood to Williamson, James River, Virginia, 29 March 1677, C.O. 1/39, 186.

sent hom to there Masters." Ostensibly this renewed servitude was (at least in the servants' case) only to last until the governor could sign the men's discharges. Instead, as soon as he could assemble the "Loyall Party" as a legislature, Berkeley passed a law providing that servants absent in rebellion were to be punished as runaways. That is, they were to serve double the time they had been away from their work. Then they might be prosecuted for any clothes, food, weapons, or other things they had taken away with them. Since servants owned no property with which to make restitution, they would be condemned to a further term of service, i.e., serial slavery. Next the governor dealt with the freemen whom Captain Grantham had led down from West Point. Sir William ordered some of them chained as prisoners in the hold of Captain Martin's ship, his headquarters on the York. Others, less able to pay ransoms or more enthusiastic about their renewed allegiance, were enlisted as soldiers. These enlistments were further evidence that Grantham, as authorized by Berkeley, had promised all the West Pointers either freedom or employment.

After he dishonored most of the promises made in his name to the soldiers of Bacon's Revolution, Berkeley took his vengeance on their leaders. He began a new series of "court martials" "on board capt. Jno. Martins shipp in Yorke River, January 11th 1676–7." Safe off Tindall's Point, Sir William Berkeley's court was composed of a dozen of his officers, Ludwell, Beverley, and Smith, the loyalist leaders of the York campaign, prominent among them. They quickly condemned four Baconian prisoners. Their circumstances bespoke the roots of Virginia's revolution, both in England's recent past and in the jealousies of the new society.

One of Berkeley's victims was Captain Thomas Young. He had served under General Monck during the interregnum. This alone was sufficient to condemn him in Berkeley's eyes, even though Monck himself had become the king's captain general. Young's particular crime was that he had obeyed Councilor and Colonel Thomas Ballard's orders to impress supplies and men for Bacon's army. Berkeley had forgiven Ballard—his "Mary Magdalene," the governor called his repentant (and rich) client— and Ballard sat on the court that condemned Young to death for obeying his orders. Equal justice was not a Berkeleyan hallmark. So much Henry Page's case also showed. A carpenter, Page had been Berkeley's own servant before the revolution, "butt now for his violence used against ye Loyall party made a Collonell." The Berkeleyans punished Page for his social presumption. The presumption of Thomas Hall, the third victim, was political. For several years before 1676, Hall had angered Berkeley by "a more than ordinary prying in the secrets of State affairs." Hall gave the Berkeleyans the excuse they needed to stop his investigation when, as a county clerk, obedient to the June Laws, he wrote orders for the raising of Bacon's army. Thus it appeared, in the words of Berkeley's court-martial, "by divers writings under his own hand that he hath been a most notorious actor, ayder, and assistor in the rebellion." Hall pleaded guilty, asked for mercy, and was condemned. James Wilson was quickly judged, for he had killed a member of the "Loyall Party"—no matter if it were in battle. These four convicts were rowed across the river and strung up at the elder Bacon's house. Again, as in Accomac, Berkeley's aging energies were excited by abusing prisoners and watching them die, "which he found had don him a grat deale of good." [158]

Revivified and emboldened by the execution of his enemies, Sir William dared leave the shelter of the English ships; that is, "the Governor began to be weary of the Water: and findeing that he be[g]an to gather Strength," Sir William decided "to go a shore" on the mainland of Virginia for the first time since he had fled from Jamestown in September. At Colonel Bacon's house, the governor heard his host's complaints that the rebel Whalley and the garrison had fled, not trusting Sir William's promised pardon. Unfortunately, they had taken £2,000 worth of Colonel Bacon's merchandise with them. On the other hand, it was to Bacon's house, on 14 January 1676/7, that Captain Robert Morris of the *Young Prince* brought sixteen leading Southside rebels as prisoners to Sir William Berkeley and reported that his fleet had cleared the James of rebel resistance.

It was apparent that "the wheele hath turned again." So that astute and ruthless ruler Deputy Governor William Notley of Maryland observed of Virginia on 22 January 1676/7. "About 18 or 20 days since," he wrote, "there hath occurred the greatest Revolution in the Virginia affairs, that can possibly be imagined." The surrender of "Ingram the Titular Generall, who succeeded Bacon, and his Lieutent Generall Waklett, and our Noble Captaine als Coll. Bremington, and all their men" had restored Sir William Berkeley to power.[159]

Nonetheless, Notley doubted that Berkeley would be able to hold his command for long. When warm weather returned to the Chesapeake it would hatch "an other swarme" of rebels "yt may have venemous stings as the late Traytors had." A royal fleet to awe the multitude and royal officers "to settle affairs in Virginia in better order, than I imagine those that are now in Power there can doe" were required to prevent renewed revolution. Because the old order in Virginia was so utterly discredited and so bitterly hated, Notley wrote, "there must be an alteration though not of ye Government yet in the Government, New men must be putt in Power, the old ones will never agree with ye common people." If the

158. [Lee,] "Bacon's and Ingram's Rebellion," in Andrews, ed., *Narratives*, 95, 97.
159. Th. Notley [to Baltimore], 22 January 1676[/7], C.O. 1/39, 20–21; printed in Browne, ed., *Maryland Archives*, V, 153, 154.

Berkeleyans were not replaced "his Matie in my opinion will never find a well settled Government in that Colony."

Yet, at the end of January 1676/7, it seemed to Governor Notley that political reform was impossible and revived revolution unavoidable because "no Kings Shipps nor other Shipps are arrived from London" to bring royal orders or officers. Notley feared that Berkeley would ask for none, and yet without royal remedies the causes of revolt would continue unchecked: misgovernment, high taxes, Indian raids. Caught in the continuing crossfires of the great Susquehanna-Seneca conflict, thirty-five English settlers had been killed in Virginia during the first two weeks of January 1676/7 alone. Added to the many more than five hundred Virginians slaughtered in the previous twelve months, these latest losses made the 1676/7 war the costliest yet in Virginia. More colonists would be killed, Notley noted, if Berkeley's government did not quickly make a general peace with the natives. This Berkeley and his cronies—preoccupied with vengeance and extortion—refused to do. By neglecting to make peace with the Indians, Notley thought, the Berkeleyans ensured renewed rebellion among the Virginians, for it was Indian war that sparked "mutiny" against taxes that bought no security. Nevertheless, the Berkeleyans refused either to organize defense or to end the war. And they intended to continue their heavy levies. Repeated military failure and renewed high taxation, Notley predicted, would give "the Bell weathers" of the revolution still at large an opportunity to reincite "the common people [who] will never be brought to understand the just reason of a publique charge," much less to accept unjust ones.

In January of 1676/7, it was apparent that, because the Berkeleyans would not make peace with the Indians, pardon the rebels, or lower taxes, the Virginia revolutionaries would renew their war on the government in the spring. All these Chesapeake calculations were suddenly upset by the arrival of royal commissioners, with crown commands, a squadron of the king's navy, and a regiment of his troops. On 29 January 1676/7, they began to impose imperial government on Virginia.

The *Bristol* Conference

1 6 7 6 still had almost two months to run by the English calendar when, at two o'clock on the afternoon of Monday, 29 January, after a "tedious" ten-week passage from Portsmouth, the royal frigate *Bristol* anchored in the James River. Her captain, Sir John Berry, soon learned that Sir William Berkeley had just returned to Green Spring and at eight that evening he sent his lieutenant to Berkeley with a startling letter. Writing in the names of himself and his fellow officers commissioned under the great seal of England "for settling the Grievances and Other Affairs of Virginia," Berry reported that he had on board the *Bristol* seventy soldiers who were ready to sail upriver to form Berkeley's bodyguard. These men alone were the largest force of regulars to visit Virginia in a generation, but Berry further reported that the other ships of his squadron—four men-of-war, two fireships, and eight transports—were carrying to Virginia "a Compleate Regiment of a thousand men under the Command of Colonell Herbert Jeffreyes." This regiment was fully equipped and provisioned and, as Berry told Berkeley, brought with it additional stores of war "for your Assistance in carrying on the Warr against the King's Enemies and Suppressing the Present Rebellion." [160]

Sir John Berry had brought out from England the military means to repress all resistance, red or white, to royal government in Virginia, but he had also brought orders that denied Sir William Berkeley control not just of the royal forces but of the government as well. Besides pointing out that the royal regiment was to be commanded by Colonel Jeffreys, Berry informed Berkeley that he himself had royal orders to supersede Berkeley in command of all merchant ships and seamen in Virginia waters. Berry then invited Berkeley to meet the commissioners aboard the *Bristol*, there to receive from them the king's orders for changes in the government. Backed as it was by overwhelming military force, this was an irresistible invitation, even without the compulsion of its shocking enclosure.

With his own letter to Sir William Berkeley, Berry enclosed one from Secretary of State Coventry, "read and approved by his Majesty, Nov. 14, 1676," in which Berkeley was told that the king "hath given a Commission to Col. Jeffries to act in your Stead under the title of Lieutenant Governor, which Letter and Commission will be delivered and shewed you by Colonel Jeffries himself upon which his Majestie expects your return hither, and that he should from that time act in your Stead." [161]

Two days later, the lieutenant of the *Bristol* returned with the lame-duck governor. Berkeley boarded the *Bristol* to receive his marching orders from two of the royal commissioners, Sir John Berry and his privi-

160. Captain's log, *Bristol*, ADM 51/134, Part III. Berry to Berkeley, 29 January 1676/7, Pepys 2582; also C.O. 5/1371, 14–15. See also Berry's orders, 15, 20 November 1676, ADM 2/1738, 61–63, 69v–70v. The two fireships may not have completed the voyage to Virginia. The other men-of-war were the *Bristol* (4th rate), the *Dartmouth* and the *Rose* (5th rates), and the *Deptford*, ketch.
161. Coventry to Berkeley, 15 November 1676, Letters of the Secretary of State to Colonial Governors, Additional Manuscripts 25120, f. 94, British Library (hereafter cited as Add. Ms. 25120, 94); also in C.O. 389/6, 177-78.

leged passenger, Colonel Francis Moryson, formerly a client of Berkeley's and once governor of Virginia in his absence. The third commissioner, Colonel Jeffreys, the royal letter for Berkeley's recall, and the main body of the expedition had not yet arrived. Even in their absence, Berkeley faced a loss of personal authority and the imposition of state power in its place. The royal "Proclamations, Broad Seals, Instructions and other Papers" now presented to Berkeley by the commissioners ordered the old governor to conform to the bureaucratic and political requirements of the modernized English state. This state had not existed when, in 1641, on the eve of the civil wars and revolution which cast the British kingdoms into the maw of the Leviathan, Berkeley had begun his first term in command of Virginia. Out of war and revolution first the national state had emerged in England. Then the imperial state had engorged all Britain, then Barbados, Jamaica, Tangier, New York. It had at last arrived in Virginia, despite Sir William Berkeley's long resistance. Since "the 20th of June 1671," as the king's privy councilors complained, Sir William Berkeley had neglected the paperwork of modern government pressed on his regime from England. Now the royal commissioners informed Sir William that he was to account in writing to the plantations committee of the king's privy council (only one of whose members he knew personally) for his every act under the royal instructions of 1661, and for those of his subordinates as well.

Berkeley was bewildered both by his sudden subordination to an imperial system and by its implied censure of his administration. The royal commissioners assured him, however, that, as ordered by the plantations committee, they would help him with the paperwork. This was no trouble, the commissioners said, for they were under orders to write a parallel review of Berkeley's own behavior as governor and to assist him in implementing his new orders from the king. These orders were inimical not only to Berkeleyan rule but also to American independence.[162]

Berkeley was told to dismantle the assembly system of oligarchical rule that he had built up over the past thirty-five years. This system had made the government of Virginia by "the Grand Assembly" of governor, council, and burgesses practically independent of the English state. To reduce "the arrogancy of the assembly," the king commanded the dissolution of the June Assembly (a prerogative Berkeley had hitherto reserved to himself, but which he had used only once since 1660). The king (not the governor) ordered a new assembly convened. It was to be elected on a parliamentary franchise, as prescribed by the king. It was to meet

162. Privy-council committee for "the care and management of things relating to his [majesty's] Plantations" to Sir William Berkeley, 14 April 1676, C.O. 1/36, 80. Berry and Moryson to Williamson, 2 February 1676/7, C.O. 1/39, 52.

for sessions limited by the king to fourteen days. And the king insisted that the assembly members were to receive reduced allowances. All of these limitations, the king's commissioners told the old governor, would reduce both the assembly's fiscal burden on the colonists and its political independence of the king. To this latter end, the king had now exercised his legislative veto for the first time in America: Charles II had voided all the Virginia laws of 1676.[163]

As for the forthcoming assembly sessions, the commissioners informed Berkeley that he was expected to help them implement royal orders concerning its legislation. First, the new assembly, with the governor at its head, should admit its responsibility for Virginia's rebellion against royal authority. Only then, the royal commissioners told Sir William, could he and his legislators receive the royal pardon for the treasons of 1676. Sir William Berkeley could not conceive that he was a rebel, but the king's commissioners reminded him that he had signed Bacon's commission and those of his lieutenants and so was implicated in their rebellions, just as much as were the clerks he had executed. Most Virginians were at least as guilty of treason as their governor, but only Bacon was excluded from the royal pardon. The indignant governor denounced the inclusiveness of the king's mercy. The royal commissioners gave him five hundred printed copies of the pardon proclamation nonetheless and told Berkeley to send a copy immediately to every county court, thereby announcing the advent of royal government.

The printed proclamations offered the royal pardon to all, beginning with the justices who received and distributed them, who would take the oaths of civil allegiance and religious supremacy to the king "as a test of their future Obedience and Loyaltie." As well as imposing imperial allegiance, the king's proclamation promised the end of assembly tyranny. First, it reported that the king had "already given particular instructions to his Governor, to reduce the salaries of the Members of the Assembly." Second, the colonists were told that the king had vetoed "the Grand Assembly's Acts." Third, the king proclaimed his continuing concern for his abused subjects by declaring that his commissioners would collect the grievances of the people and recommend their royal "relief & redress."[164]

Undertaking to remedy the errors of assembly government reported to him by the people, the king promised a continued crown presence in

---

163. "Interlocutory Heads of such matters in conference with Sr Wm Berkeley Knight . . . ," 2 February 1676/7, Pepys 2582. See also C.O. 5/1371, 16–18.

164. Moryson to Blathwayt, 25 October 1678, *V.M.H.B.* 24 (1916): 78. Privy-council committee to commissioners for Virginia, C.O. 1/37, 205. "By the King: A PROCLAMATION For the Suppressing a Rebellion lately Raised within the Plantation of Virginia," 27 October 1676, C.O. 1/38, 10.

the colony. He had already identified the assembly's primary error and issued orders that the governor and the assembly proceed immediately to undo it. Because it had been race war that incited domestic rebellion and so endangered that prime prop of imperial government, the king's customs on Virginia's tobacco, the assembly's first obligation was to support the crown's commissioners in making peace with the Indians. Its second task was to provide both for those commissioners and for the armed forces which would back them and secure the peace. The astonished governor—"who protested to" Sir John Berry "yt he had neither house nor home for himself"—was told that he and his assembly must find a mansion for the commissioners' residence; landing craft, barracks, magazines, and provisions for a thousand redcoats and three hundred additional officers, engineers, gunners, storekeepers, and volunteers; and food, firewood, and drinking water for the crews of the dozen or more royal ships. Garrison government had reached Virginia.

At this, Sir William Berkeley, "who did believe a single Frigate, or two, would have been sufficient on this occasion (and professing never soe much as to have desir'd soldiers)" was "much amus'd," i.e. stupefied. Without either royal aid or orders, he had, as he saw it, won his own way back to power and to his ruined plantation. He had been there less than a week when the *Bristol* arrived with news that he was to be recalled and that, in the meantime, he was to facilitate a royal counter-revolution as politically destructive to his regime as Bacon's Revolution had been. That is, the crown ordered Berkeley to destroy the autonomous oligarchical assembly system he had constructed since 1641 and to impose in its place a monarchical, military, and bureaucratic government. Nothing less was intended than that Berkeley's colony be converted into an imperial province.

It was, to the classically educated governor, as if a Greek system of city-states and kinship colonies had suddenly been transformed into a Roman Empire of ruling metropolis and garrisoned provinces. Subjected to such shocks as these, Sir William Berkeley suddenly became deaf and collapsed with a fever in the midst of the *Bristol* conference. He was taken ashore to Kecoughtan on 3 February. The next day, as soon as Sir John Berry had taken command of Berkeley's flagship, the *Rebecca*, and the *Adam & Eve* (with Giles Bland, "one of Bacon's Genls," chained in her hold), he sent the old governor up to Jamestown in the *Bristol*'s barge. Once he got home to Green Spring, Sir William Berkeley took to his bed for a week, quite unable to write, at least to the king's commissioners.[165]

---

165. Berry and Moryson to Williamson, 2 February 1676/7, C.O. 1/39, 52. On "amus'd," see William Little et al., comps., *The Shorter Oxford English Dictionary on Historical Principles* (Oxford, 1964). Captain's log, *Bristol*, ADM 51/134, Part III.

Resistance and Revenge

B efore he was overcome by political shock, old age, and malarial climate, Sir William had impressed three points on the royal commissioners. These would complicate, delay, and embitter the transfer of power from the old colonial order to the new imperial one.

First, Berkeley pointed out, the rebellion was repressed, at least until warm weather came. "The Rebell Bacon is dead, his Accomplices dispers'd, some of the Ringleaders taken, tryed, and sentanced by a Councell of War, and about twentie of them lately Executed." Berkeley insisted, moreover, that "No one (under God)" had been "a more eminent or active Instrument in Suppressing this Rebellion, and Quieting the divisions and distractions among the People," than he himself.

Second, having, as he claimed, won the war, Berkeley demanded control of the peace: with the Indians, with some of whose local tribes his emissaries had begun negotiations or from whom they had taken hostages; with the rebels, to none of whom he issued the king's proclamation of pardon, but many of whom he now jailed at his plantation; with the people, whose grievances he at last ordered assessed by his local justices (with predictable lack of results). In all these matters, Berkeley insisted on working through the unreformed assembly, which he had already summoned to meet him at Green Spring.

Third, all of the parties to the rebellion—Indians, Baconians, taxpayers—Berkeley proposed to mulct, through the agency of his assembly, to make up his own losses. These, he estimated to the commissioners, were no less than £8,000 sterling "in houses Goods, Plantation Servants, and Cattle." Four hundred head of cattle, together with "as many sheep, three score horses and near a thousand pounds worth of wheat Barly Oates and Indian Corne," Berkeley claimed had been taken from him by the rebels. More than that, Berkeley lamented the loss of his five houses in Jamestown, "wch cost me very neare three thousand pounds and as much in goods and household stuff." He had come home at last to find his Green Spring mansion ruined "wch will cost me one thousand pounds to repaire." Now it seemed that he was to be replaced by Colonel Jeffreys before the tobacco fleet cleared port—and it was tobacco customs which paid the governor's salary. All in all, Berkeley bitterly remarked, out of what had been the greatest fortune in continental America, "my Poore wife and I shall not have enough to bring our selves into England."

Thus Sir William's resistance to royal reform and his obsession with personal vengeance were now compounded by his desperate desire to hold office long enough to collect his salary, to wring £8,000 from the rebels for himself, and to get something for his followers as well. "The Governour" made it clear above all else to the commissioners at their very first meeting that he was "very much concerned about the Distribution of the Forfeited Estates and Possessions of such as have been concerned in this Rebellion, which he would have to be disposed and given in Restitution to the Loyall Partie that have been loosers by it." Berkeley's unassuageable thirst for rebel estates would finally force the royal commissioners unceremoniously to remove an unwilling Sir William Berkeley from office as the greatest enemy of political pacification and governmental reform.[166]

Berkeley made it his only request to the crown commissioners that they endorse this expropriation. Although they did not yet know that those "concerned in this Rebellion," all of whom Berkeley wanted to mulct, amounted to twenty-nine of every thirty men in Virginia, the commissioners declined to authorize his spoilation. They said the issue was "a thing quite without our instructions." For some time yet, however, Berry and Moryson hoped that the royal instructions and their advice would be implemented by a cooperative governor. They did not know that Berkeley's thirst for revenge and recompense would lead the governor to defy all the king's orders for reform, to resist every one of the commissioners' efforts at pacification, and instead to erect a reign of terror and extortion, "which rather shews his Politique selfish partiality than equitable Prudence and Commisseration. . . ."

After two months the royal commissioners had to explain their initial error in assuming Berkeley's obedience to the king, his assistance to themselves, his mercy to his people, and his truthfulness to anyone: "if wee have been mistaken & deceived in our former Character of Sir William Berkeley, it may be imputed to our too easy Credulity at first being over-persuaded by his own Protestations and calling God to Witnesse and us to be strict Inquisitors of his Actions, when there was noe Body by who could contradict him."[167]

---

166. Berkeley to Coventry, 9 February 1676/7, Coventry Ms. 77, 384. The Royal Commissioners to the secretaries of state, HMS *Bristol*, 2 February 1676/7, Pepys 2582.

167. Berry and Moryson to Williamson "From on Board His Maties Shipp Bristoll," 2 February 1676/7, C.O. 1/39, 52. The Royal Commissioners to Coventry, 5 or 13 April 1677, Pepys 2582. The Royal Commissioners to Williamson, 27 March 1677, C.O. 1/39, 80. The Royal Commissioners to Coventry, 27 March 1677, Pepys 2582. Other copies in C.O. 5/1371, 69–77, 79–83.

COMMISSIONERS' CRITICISMS

Berkeley awakened the commissioners to his "Politique selfish partiality" by his reaction to their first dispatch to him from the *Bristol*. In it they insisted that he immediately issue the royal proclamation "acquainting the Trembling countrye with His Matyes Gracious Pardon." Berkeley refused. Instead, he falsely claimed that the king's pardoning power was "by him to me given" in the royal proclamation. So Sir William justified his issuance, in place of the royal pardon, of another of the indemnities he had periodically put forward during the war. This one exempted forty-one persons by name and it implied that Berkeley would also deny the king's pardon to all active rebels, all prisoners, all bailed persons, all fugitives, and to all who had administered Bacon's Oath. The governor further declared that the indemnity he offered did not extend to the property of any person he deemed a rebel.[168]

With pardon thus converted into an instrument of punishment, Sir William could abandon the law martial. The crown commissioners had told the governor that his drum-head courts-martial were illegal in peacetime (and they dated the peace from Captain Grantham's West Point treaties). The commissioners demanded that any further treason trials be conducted by the court of oyer and terminer. For this the commissioners had brought the king's commission. Of that court they were named judges, together with Berkeley and his senior councilors. Berkeley and his associates therefore began to prosecute their chief enemies before this new court. Given its unvarying verdict—guilty—combined with Berkeley's self-proclaimed ability to withhold the royal pardon, Major Beverley's bandits, and other units of the governor's guards, were armed to extort money and tobacco, livestock and land from the lesser foes of the old regime, all of whom surrendered their property rather than face certain condemnation. Once stripped, many were banished by Berkeley from Virginia.

After ten days of this activity—that is, by 6 February 1676/7, the royal commissioners realized that the governor at Green Spring was not the cowed and cooperative man he had seemed to be on board the *Bristol*. The commissioners, therefore, issued their own "Declaration to his Maties Loving Subjects of Virginia." It invited the colonists to state their grievances about "the State of the Gouermt in generall, and in particular the persons of any of his Majtys Ministers or Officers." This declaration

168. Berry and Moryson to Watkins, 2 February 1676/7. Berkeley's proclamation ("By his Most Sacred Majests: Governor and Capt. Gen!! of Virginia"), 10 February 1676/7, C.O. 1/39, 55, 64. Note the weakness of Berkeley's signature. The king's printed proclamation is in C.O. 1/38, 4–10.

elicited some twenty times as many complaints as Berkeley's earlier proclamation (an effort to head off the commissioners' collection of popular
grievances by authorizing his county justices to certify whatever they
thought grievous to the county's burgesses for the assembly's attention).
That the Virginians, by twenty to one, preferred to ask the crown commissioners for royal redress rather than to apply to Sir William Berkeley,
his justices, and their assembly testified to the popular support
for imperial as opposed to oligarchical rule, a potential exploited by royal
governors-general periodically for the next eighty years.

Nansemond County's declaration made especially apparent the popular basis of this shift of authority from oligarchy to monarchy. "Wee owe
our allegiance to none but our dread Soveraigne Lord the King," wrote
the men of Nansemond, "yet we are sworne [as the condition of their
surrender to Admiral Morris] to assist Sir Will. Berkeley let him doe what
he pleaseth." Now, however, the Nansemond petitioners could protest
against the Berkeleyan oppressions for "His most Gracious Matie hath
sent three Commissioners to us (whome God Preserve) who will by their
loving declaration plead our cause . . . which hath now given us power to
open our lips." "Wee really think," the men of Nansemond wrote, that
the royal commissioners were "the perfect Safeguard of this Collony &
his Maty Prerogative, for had they not come it would have been claimed
& obtained by the Heathen," Berkeley's bad strategy being compounded
in its ill effect by his oppression of Virginia's fighting men.[169]

Fearful of such statements, the Berkeleyans provided a fresh example
of the manipulative and dishonest behavior by which they had provoked
the revolution they could not pacify. Berkeley sent to his sheriffs a pre-
prepared "grievance" to be adopted by every county court and submitted
to the Green Spring assembly as the only "grievance" of the people of
each county. Berkeley had his minions declare "that their only grievance
was that his majestys Honble Govr Sr Wm Berkeley who soe long soe
peasibly Governd this Country for his Matie and Soe much Indulged the
good & welfare thereof . . . should be not only soe undutifully but cruelly
and barbarously dealt with by the ambitious, envious, malicious, and
ignorant rebels." His councilors then declared, on Berkeley's behalf,
"that the Ground of this Rebellion, have not proceeded from any Reall
fault in ye Government." To suppress contrary evidence, Berkeley's
hand-picked assembly further declared that all "popular" (i.e., not prepared by Berkeley) grievances were "libellious, Scandalous, and Rebel-

169. Berry and Moryson to Watkins and Werden, 10 February 1676/7, Pepys 2582. Nancymond First Grievances, C.O. 1/39, 247. Remonstrance of the Inhabitants of Nansemond,
ibid., 255, 256.

lious" and ordered that all their authors should be "sent for and punished." [170]

Despite the Berkeleyans' worst efforts to anticipate, co-opt, and suppress the county grievances called for by the crown commissioners, by 10 February 1676/7, these statements (and those of many aggrieved individuals) had reached the commissioners' headquarters in such volume as to convince them that Bacon's Revolution had been incited by Berkeleyan oppression, had been supported by most Virginians, and was being kept alive by Berkeley's revenge. In light of "the Governors owne Report, that of above fifteen thousand [Virginia men] there that there are not five hundred untainted," it seemed to the commissioners insane of the Berkeleyans to insist not only that the leading rebels must be executed but also that all their followers must either compound for their estates (i.e., pay off the "Loyall Party") or be declared traitors. Yet, the commissioners concluded, so long as Sir William refused to issue the royal pardon or to honor the royal promise of political reform based on the redress of popular grievances, and so long as his career of revenge—"his (alreadie) Hanging and intending to Hang upon this Rebellion, more than ever Suffer'd Death for the Horrid Murder of that late Glorious Martyr of Blessed Memorie," King Charles I—was unchecked, so long the people of Virginia would remain unpacified. [171]

The Virginians were, as the royal commissioners observed, "soe sullen and obstinate" that if domestic peace were not quickly secured, the rich colonists would flee from the Berkeleyan terror, leaving the colony pauperized and without leadership. Unable to escape the Berkeleyan confiscations of their staple crop, the poorer Virginians would "make corn instead of Tobacco . . . careless of what becomes of their own Estates or the King's Customes." If, before pacification and reform were achieved, foreign war recurred with natives, neighbors, or Europeans, the commissioners predicted that the Virginians would revive their plans to win their independence from England. Scourged by a war against which the old regime would offer no protection while still being terrorized by that old order, the Virginians would be "a People Soe ill Qualified as to their Obedience and incouraged at soe remote a Distance from England to cast off the Yoke and Subjugate themselves to a Forreine Power" that they would be lost to the English empire. The king's commissioners agreed with Nathaniel Bacon's strategic estimates. That is, they doubted that the

170. Berkeley to the sheriff of Northumberland, 3 February 1676, C.O. 1/39, 256. Remonstrance of Upper Parish of Isle of Wight County, *ibid.*, 230. P. Ludwell to Coventry, 14 April 1677, C.O. 1/40, 54. Henning, [ed.,] *Statutes*, II, 366–80, 383, 395. "A warrant signed by Sr Wm Berkeley," 3 February 1676[/7], Pepys 2582.
171. Berry and Moryson to secretaries of state, 10 February 1676/7, C.O. 1/39, 66. The Royal Commissioners to Coventry, 5 or 13 April 1677, Pepys 2582.

empire could recover Virginia once its revolutionaries received foreign aid. And they agreed with Bacon's estimate that it was prohibitively expensive to keep a garrison large enough to compel obedience continually in the colony. If rebellions recurred, the commissioners warned the crown "how greate the Difficulty, how heavy the charge & Burden will then prove to reduce them backe to their Allegiance, or continue Forces here to constrain and awe soe stubborn a People to the Obedience of His Maties Royall Power and Government, the Great Charge his Matie is now att too plainly demonstrates." Fear of renewed war, revolution, and the resulting loss of Virginia to a rival empire convinced the crown's commissioners that Berkeleyan misrule and revenge must be stopped, that royal protection and government must be put in their place, and that thereby the mass of Virginians must be convinced it was in their interest to remain productive members of England's empire.[172]

THE *ROSE*'S PASSENGERS

On Friday, 11 February 1676/7, the day after the royal commissioners wrote this decisive dispatch home, the royal frigate *Rose* made Newport News with three of the troop ships in convoy. Aboard them were not only hundreds of soldiers, but new leaders for each side in the Virginian phase of the contest between the old Stuart order and the new Stuart state. Sir John Berry went out in his barge to meet Colonel Herbert Jeffreys, the king's lieutenant governor and commander-in-chief. Jeffreys, a veteran civil warrior and political policeman, personified the professional servants of the new state. From 1642 until 1648, he had fought for King Charles I in England's civil wars—that is, for the nation against the revolt of its provinces. In French exile, he served on the military staff of Charles I's second son, James duke of York, a lieutenant general of the royal forces in their repression of the Fronde, another provincial revolt. In Flanders, Jeffreys helped form the Guards of Charles II. After the Restoration, Jeffreys repressed the political enemies of the crown while in command of Guards garrison companies in Portsmouth, York, and London. Commissioned colonel of the royal regiment raised for Virginia and appointed the king's lieutenant governor there, Jeffreys was also named one of the three royal commissioners of investigation. That Colonel Jeffreys was the brother of the greatest of the court-connected London tobacco monopolists, Alderman Jeffrey Jeffreys, only emphasized his distance from those outport-traders the Berkeleyans, the old governor chief among them.

The bitterest of the Berkeleyans, Frances Culpeper Stephens Berkeley (soon to be Mrs. Philip Ludwell), arrived aboard the *Rose*. She em-

172. Berry and Moryson to Watkins, 10 February 1676/7, Pepys 2582.

bodied the contemporary observation that "where the women engage, there is no bounds to wrath." Cousin of Thomas lord Culpeper, proprietor of the Northern Neck; widow of Governor Stephens of Albemarle; and wife of a Carolina proprietor (Sir William Berkeley), Frances lady Berkeley personified that proprietary mode of colonial organization, which was now giving way to less personal and more bureaucratic imperial institutions. The Culpepers' proprietary patents for Virginia made Lady Berkeley's ambitions suspect to all those of the ruling class who did not share in them. Naturally, she was also an object of hatred to those taxed to pay off the patentees.[173]

Less abstractly, Lady Berkeley's demands for pelf, position, and sexual service from Sir William were popularly alleged to have reduced him to the irascible, greedy, debilitated and neglected condition in which he provoked Bacon's Revolution. Lady Berkeley personally helped incite the struggle by reviling the New Kent volunteers in April 1676 when they came to Green Spring to ask for a commission to counter Indian raids. Hated, she had sought safety aboard Captain Evelyn's *Rebecca* in June 1676. With her to London went dispatches from the governor and from the man who was to become her next husband, Philip Ludwell, Berkeley's councilor and the Culpepers' land agent in the Northern Neck and in Albemarle. These dispatches excited the royal orders to recall the governor and reform the government of Virginia. While in London, Lady Berkeley acknowledged the king's "absolute commands" for Sir William Berkeley's recall. She arrived in Virginia, however, prepared to resist both her husband's removal and every other measure of royal government. First she aided and then she succeeded her sick husband as the leader of the irreconcilables. She found Sir William in Green Spring in bed, "expecting my Feavour" and impotent. On the day after Lady Berkeley's homecoming, Sir William wrote to their old friend, "dear Coll. Moryson," that "My Wife, who lay by mee last Night, presents her service to you, God helpe us, nothing but vocall Kindness pas'd betweene us." [174]

For a moment after ships' boats brought Lady Berkeley and Colonel Jeffreys up the James River, "vocal Kindness" between the old governor and the new seemed to be the order of the day. On Monday morning, 12 February 1676/7, the colonel crossed the river from the commissioners' headquarters at Swan's Point and rode across "ground couer'd ore with deepe Snow and Ice" to view the military quarters being built on 200 acres at the Middle Plantation. From the Middle Plantation, Jeffreys went

173. Robert Southwell to the duke of Ormonde, s.v. 13 July 1678, in Historical Manuscripts Commission, *Calendar of the Manuscripts of the Marquess of Ormonde, K.P., Preserved at Kilkenney Castle* (London, 1895–99, 1902–20).

174. Covering letter and petition to the king from Fr. Berkeley, Deal, 30 November 1676, Coventry Ms. 77, 307, 308. Berkeley to Moryson, 11 February 1676/7, Pepys 2582.

on to Green Spring. There he delivered to Sir William Berkeley the royal orders for Berkeley's immediate recall. Sir William replied "to the Rt. Honble Herbert Jeffreys, Esqr. his Matie Lieut Govern," that he would sail for England "with all the hast the miserable Condition of my affaires will permit me, and shall gladly obey his sacred Maty gracious direction of leaving the Government in my absence in a Person's hands of so worthy a Character." [175]

Berkeley's phrase "in my absence" expressed his adamant argument that he was only ordered home to report and that he had not been dismissed from office. As soon as Colonel Jeffreys had finished reading his commission aloud to the assemblage at Green Spring, the act by which an officer assumed a command, "it was Put by Sr. Wm Berkeley to his Councell, whether hee was immediately to resigne up the Gouerment to Col. Jeffreys or Noe." The council voted "noe," on the grounds that "(by the word *Conveniency*)" Berkeley was free to determine his own departure date, from Virginia and from power. When King Charles learned from his commissioners that it was "the word *Conveniency* upon which Sir Wm Berkeley Clung, taking the latitude of that word to serve his owne turne, private interest, and advantage," his majesty was, as he wrote Berkeley, "not a little surprised to understand that you make difficulty to yield obedience to our commands, being so clear and plain that we thought no man could have raised any dispute about them." The king ordered Sir William Berkeley to leave Virginia on the next ship, "without further delay or excuse," and told Colonel Jeffreys to put him on it, by force if necessary.

Jeffreys had acted against Berkeley even before the royal orders reached him, having waited to oust the old governor only until he saw the outcome of the "long-winded assembly sitting" at his arrival. When that assembly confirmed Berkeley's resistance to royal orders and Berkeleyan revenge on the rebellious people, Colonel Jeffreys, encouraged by the "generall hopes he will soone take ye government upon him" and outraged by the criminal activities of the Berkeleyans, removed his predecessor from command.[176]

175. Berkeley to Jeffreys, 12 February 1676[/7], C.O. 1/39, 71–72. Jeffreys to Coventry, 14 February 1676/7, Coventry Ms. 77, 403.
176. Memoranda dated 12, 13 February 1676/7, Pepys 2582; also in C.O. 5/1371, 46, 47. Commissioners to Coventry, 14 February 1676/7, C.O. 5/1371, 49–51. Charles II to Berkeley, 13 May 1677, C.O. 389/6, 198–99 and ff. Thomas J. Wertenbaker, *Virginia Under the Stuarts 1607–1688* (New York, 1958), 210. *C.S.P.C. 1677–1680*, no. 239. Sherwood to Williamson, 29 March 1677, C.O. 1/39, 186. The crown's intentions further appear in a certificate that, on 18 November 1676, before the privy council, Colonel Jeffreys had taken the oaths of allegiance and supremacy, and to enforce the acts of trade, all of which oaths were "required from him as Governour of his Maties Plantation of Virginia" (C.O. 1/38, 141). See also Secretary Coventry's letterbook, C.O. 389/6, esp. 58, 95; and ADM 2/1738, 72.

Lady Berkeley and the Green Spring councilors incited Sir William's insubordination and his abuses by repeatedly reminding him that he had scores to settle, on his behalf and theirs, with the rebels. When the crown commissioners condemned his confiscation of "rebel" estates, Berkeley first falsely said that he had "seized no Toll or Goods, but in the height of the Warr." Then he defiantly, and revealingly, added that, despite the commissioners' censures, he would nonetheless "doe it hereafter, for from divers honest men I heare, that those that are Criminally Obnoxious, dayly and houerly conveigh away their Goods and Cattle." This was precisely the decapitalization of the colony which the king's cabinet and the royal commissioners had feared. The commissioners sent Colonel Jeffreys' chief of staff, Captain John Tongue, to say again to Berkeley that they have a "Concernment in the People's Grievances, which makes us hereby acquaint you with our Contrariety to such Proceedings, wherein we conceive you have neither Law, Right, nor His Majestys Royall Will to support you." [177]

Yet Sir William remained the fountainhead of the post-revolutionary repression, as he had been of the pre-revolutionary oppression. It was the governor who gave the orders, and even signed the warrants, by which his loyal party partisans ("some particular Persons neare about the Governor") seized the livestock of the poor, the merchandise of the well-to-do, and everyone's best, sweet-scented, tobacco.

Take the case of Thomas Glover. He had been "pressed by [Captain William] Hartwell to serve under Bacon; and was encouraged to goe by Mr. [Thomas] Ballard [successively Berkeley's councilor, Bacon's backer, and Berkeley's "Mary Magdalene"] who told him Bacon's Commission was freely granted &c." At the close of the revolution, in January 1676/7, Hartwell (now captain of Berkeley's bodyguard) imprisoned Glover on warrants from Berkeley and Ballard. Glover was jailed at Green Spring for five weeks. Finally, "Col. Ballard said to me You have a young horse . . . you must give that horse to the Governor and you may bee cleered." Glover obeyed, and he was but one of many.[178]

Servants and slaves, tobacco and corn, pork, bacon, and butter, livestock, shoes, shingles, bedding, cloth, "his cloathes from his back," promises of labor made by those who had nothing else to give the governor and his minions—these were the prices paid for their lives by the men impressed into Bacon's army to those who had first ordered their service and now punished them for giving it. These Berkeleyans, "Our Gran-

177. Berkeley to Moryson, received 11 February 1676/7, Pepys 2582. Commissioners to Berkeley, 13 February 1676/7, ibid. Berkeley ordered seizure, 24 January, and was obeyed 30 January 1676[/7] (C.O. 1/39, 24).
178. Thomas Glover to the Royal Commissioners, C.O. 1/40, 12. Depositions re Hartwell, ibid., 2–5, 7–10, 13–14, 26–31.

dees," the "great men of Virginia," in the last months of 1676/7 rode once again on the rough roads that had brought them to wealth and power early in the preceding generation, and which had provoked revolution at its end. The greatest of these grandees was Sir William Berkeley, who "did say that [if I] would give ten thousand pounds of Pork, he would save my life." [179]

Some of Berkeley's victims were too poor to pay ransoms in fat pork. Their losses were terribly personal. "Edward Lloyd a Mulatto" was imprisoned for three weeks by Hartwell at Berkeley's Green Spring plantation. During that time, Berkeley's guards looted Lloyd's house. The governor's raiders "soe afrighted ye poor petrs wife being great with Child, by pulling the Cloathes off her back, that she presently fell into Labour & in a most sad and Deplorable condition, dyed." Although they had stripped his home and his wife, the Berkeleyans never filed a charge against Edward Lloyd. They held him, however, until he promised to give his next crop of tobacco—he had nothing else left to give—to "ye Capt. of ye Guard," Hartwell.[180]

Other victims were well-to-do. Their losses were the capital of the colony. "Ffower English Servants Seaven Negro slaves six hhds tobacco, and all the Petrs household goods, bedding linen & other Estate amounting to at least £400 Sterling" were Richard Clerke's ransom. Some of what they thus looted and extorted, the Berkeleyan thugs kept for "theire owne uses." Some they brought to the tables, stables, and storerooms of Green Spring, thus "converting it to the King's use," Sir William said. The very best tobacco Berkeley's bandits packed aboard the *Rebecca* of Captain Larrimore in hogsheads branded "WB." By terror, plunder, and personal aggrandizement, "WB" thus prepared to influence the legislators whom he would summon to Green Spring to enact an even wider and yet more lucrative revenge on the revolutionaries.[181]

179. "Sa. Wiseman's memorandum," 19 May 1677, C.O. 1/40, 31. "Personell Grievances agt. William Hartwell," Pepys 2582. Deposition of William Hoare, C.O. 1/40, 17.

180. Edward Lloyd's deposition, Pepys 2582; also in C.O. 1/40, 26. "An Act Disabling Edward Hill and John Sith to beare office," [25] June 1676, in Henning, [ed.,] *Statutes*, II, 364. Articles against Hill and his reply, [May 1677,] C.O. 1/40, 145–238. These sources list the Berkeleyan rank and file, record their status as servants, overseers, and the like to the "Loyall Party" leaders, and present the leaders' plea that their looting was "by the Governors order." See, for examples, C.O. 1/40, 10, 46.

181. Berkeley to the commissioners, 27 March 1677, Pepys 2582. By Petition of Richard Clarke [quotation corrected from C.O. 1/40, 5], *ibid.* Berkeley to Moryson, [11 February 1676/7,] *ibid.* Commissioners to Berkeley, 13 February 1676/7, *ibid.* Gloucester Grievances, C.O. 1/39, 243. See also Berkeley to Coventry, 2 February 1676/7, Coventry Ms. 77, 355.

GREEN SPRING

Sir William called the burgesses to gather "At A Grand Assembly," on 20
February 1676/7. The selection—not election—of assemblymen was in
the hands of loyalist sheriffs. The burgesses they returned were Berkeley's "Owne Creatures & Chose by his appointments." He expected them
to restore the assembly system which had been overthrown by Bacon's
Revolution and was now condemned by the king. Berkeley also insisted
that the assemblymen authorize the "Loyall Party's" revenge on the revolutionaries and on all their popular sympathizers—i.e., most Virginians
—thus dishonoring his own promises and the king's pardon. Berkeley's
vengeful and disobedient intentions—"counsell from your own or other
bodys passion or resentment," Secretary Coventry called them—were
only reinforced when bad weather, as usual, "kept backe" burgesses from
the northern rivers or across Chesapeake Bay. "To my great Charge and
Trouble," as he loudly complained, Sir William Berkeley played host to
the gathering burgesses-select. Their week at Green Spring implicated
and intimidated the burgesses for they were fed from confiscated "rebel"
provisions and they were surrounded by almost two hundred armed men
of the "Loyall Party" (not counting the militiamen drafted to be an
outguard for the governor, but whom Major Beverley used for rough
labor).[182]

The burgesses-select were further impressed, as Berkeley said, because "I keepe at least Thirty Prisoners in my house and maintaine a
Guard of Fifty to secure them." The would-be legislators observed the
"Vehemency of the Cold, the extremity of hunger, trouble & lothesome-
nesse of Vermin" in the Green Spring jails. They witnessed the always
fatal trials of some of these prisoners before the court of oyer and terminer. They watched prisoner after prisoner attempt to escape by paying
the "compositions," "fines," and "forfeitures" assessed by the old governor and his "Loyall Party." The loyalists urged the assemblymen to go
on to realize fully the grandees' greedy premise (which had led them to
incite rebellion in the first place) that "rebel estates will make loyal
inheritances." The loyalists, "Rapacious" and "Implacable," boasted to
the burgesses-select of their party's prowess and of their security because
of the royal forces' presence. As the crown commissioners commented,
the assembly—governor, council, and burgesses—which finally began its
sessions at Berkeley's Green Spring mansion on 27 February 1676/7—
took "a larger freedome & priviledge under the Protection of these our

182. Sherwood to Williamson, 13 April 1677, C.O. 1/40, 51. Sir Henry Coventry to Sir William
Berkeley Whitehall, 15 May 1677, C.O. 389/6, 95. Berkeley to the commissioners, 13 February
1676/7, Pepys 2582; also in C.O. 5/1371, 45. Gloucester Grievances, C.O. 1/39, 243.

[the commissioners'] Forces, which perhaps alone prevents the breaking forth of a fresh flame of Mutiny," than they could otherwise have done. The legislators were further excited to excess by the lash of Sir William Berkeley, who "keepes such a Brow upon his Councill and the Assembly that whatever hee approves, or dislikes, proposes, or persuades is onely done and comply'd with." [183]

Naturally, the first act of the Green Spring Assembly was to approve a "Testimoniall" which praised Sir William's government from 1652 onwards, which denied that either he or his appointees had ever been corrupt or unjust, which asserted that it was by his "greate prudence" that the rebellion was repressed before the arrival of the royal forces, which asked the king to continue Berkeley as governor for life, and which ordered that he be paid a year's salary and allowances out of the agency tax receipts. This order probably had been written at Green Spring before the assembly met. Indeed, all of the assembly's acts were probably pre-prepared at the governor's table. It was thus in every sense a packed house at Green Spring which received at its first formal session an unprecedented letter of address from the crown's commissioners. [184]

This address was the first equivalent of the king's speech from the throne that Virginian legislators had ever heard. Its message was most unwelcome. The first royal wish, the colonial legislators were told, was that they achieve "the name and memorable Reputation of the *healing* Assembly." Their great care should be "to stanch and heale the fresh and bleeding Woundes these unnatural Warrs and Rebellions have caused among you." Insofar as laws could do, the assembly was to alleviate "the present distemper'd Condicion & constitution of the generall Body of the People." Of course, the imperial executives remarked, laws could not do much. Therefore, the great grievances which had caused the rebellion should be reported on by the assembly to the crown commissioners for their submission "to his most gracious Majestie, who out of his Royal Pitie and Compassion has been pleased to Promise you a fitt and speedie Redress thereof, as to his Royal Wisdome shall seeme meete." [185]

For some grievances, the royal commissioners told the Green Spring assembly, the king had already prescribed cures. Therefore he had ordered the assembly to support, by law and with appropriation, the "Peace with the Frontier Indians" which was to be negotiated by the governor

183. Berkeley to the commissioners, 13 February 1676/7, Pepys 2582. Commissioners to Watkins, 27 March 1677, C.O. 1/39, 182. Deposition of John Johnson, C.O. 1/40, 23. Commissioners to Coventry, 13 April 1677, Pepys 2852.

184. "Testimoniall," C.O. 1/39, 97. "Summes of Money . . . ordered to be pd out of the Publique Monies in England," C.O. 1/40, 46. See also note 186, below.

185. Orders of the House of Burgesses, 20 February 1677, "Copia. Test. Robert Beverley," C.O. 1/39, 97. "A Letter to the Grand Assembly," 27 February 1676/7, Pepys 2582; also in C.O. 5/1371, 53–61.

and the commissioners. Diplomatically, the commissioners mentioned as
a model the 1649 treaty of Sir William Berkeley "(here Present)" which
distinguished between friendly and hostile natives. Native allies were
still, the commissioners insisted, "our best Guards to secure us on the
Frontiers from . . . those other more Barbarous Indians of the Continent
who never can be brought to keepe a Peace with us." The revolution had
broken down this vital distinction. It must be restored, to recover the
confidence and alliance of the buffer and tributary tribes. This was the
first step towards protecting the frontiersmen from the Indians and hence
the colony from the frontiersmen. For it was the "dailie Murders & Depredations" of the natives that kept frontiersmen fearful and their rebellion
simmering.

Before they could deal with Indian troubles, domestic causes of rebellion must also be allayed. No alliance with or defense against the
natives could be accomplished, the royal commissioners observed, so
long as, "like men devoyd of reason Religion, Loyaltie, or Humanitie,
wee were murdering, Burning, Plundering and Ruining one another
without remorse or Consideration." Repression must be stopped and reform begun, both by the assembly. Their previous oppression and obduracy, the unbelieving assemblymen were told, was the most important
cause of "the late Wicked & Ruinous Rebellion among you." Therefore,
the king required them to reform themselves. The first thing they must
do was to cut their salaries to the point where their own taxes balanced
them. So they would reduce the pressure of taxes on a poor people. To
accomplish this, the commissioners said, not only lower per-diem rates
but also shorter assembly sessions were essential. One session of fourteen
days, not more often than every two years, at which members would be
paid only for days in attendance, not for travel, and not for the liquor
drunk at committee meetings, secretaries, or exorbitant hotel bills, would
eliminate the people's greatest grievance: the high cost of assemblies.

The commissioners backed their pacific address with military menace. If the assembly obeyed the king's commands concerning diplomacy,
pacification, and itself, and thereby assisted "the Peace and Resettlement
of this Distracted Country," the royal commissioners suggested that they
"may putt a timely stopp to his Majesties Resolves of sending a far greater
force." Not only might "a *healing* Assembly" forestall the imposition of a
greater royal garrison on Virginia, but a truly subservient assembly might
also obtain the recall of the present expedition. If the commissioners
could report to the king the assembly's "readie Conformity and Dutifull
Obedience," this could "alone Prevaile for the Recalling Home the soldiers that are now here." That even the land forces were not wholly
recalled for seven years was due to assembly recalcitrance as much as to
continued threats from redmen and rebels.

Because none of the assemblymen, whether Berkeleyans or moderates, were able to accept any responsibility for the revolution, they did not see any need to respond to royal commands for reform. Instead of recognizing their own liability for civil unrest, the Green Spring Assembly officially insisted that the "foundation and increase of the late horrid Rebellion" lay in the "distempered humour predominant in the Common people (the usuall Causes of mutiny and Insurrections)." Popular hatred of their betters, so the Green Spring analysis of revolution went, had been encouraged by ambitious outsiders, mostly newcomers to Virginia. They had urged the people "to pry into the secrets of the grand assembly of the Country," even to attempt to influence public policy. This popular urge to meddle in assembly business, encouraged by the newcomers' charges of assembly corruption, was further "heightened by an Intervening accident (viz) the first Incursions of the Indians upon the head of Rappahannock River." This "accident" let the dissidents and outsiders charge that the colony's defenses were down because the assemblymen had spent the defense taxes on themselves. Worse than past corruption, in the dissidents' view, had been present neglect: frontier devastation "caused great murmurings because so speedy a revenge was not taken for it" as the populace desired. Hostile to the assembly system of government and terrified by unprecedented Iroquoian attacks, "the precipitous giddy multitude" was ripe for Bacon's influence.[186]

"Himself of ruined fortune," Bacon was "ambitious and desiring noveltys." The worst of these novelties, so the Green Spring apologists told their imperial audience, were Bacon's "designs to Allienate this Country from his Majestyes Royall dominion, and traitorously subject it to forreigners." This plan, so said his enemies, Bacon's deathbed confession proved. But the revolutionary leader had domestic aims as well. The Green Spring Assembly had no doubt that, under Bacon's instigation, an "internal" as well as an "external" revolution had been fought out in Virginia during 1676: "he insinuates into and possesses the people with lyberty and free[dom] . . . from Bondage," the horrified representatives of the ruling class remembered. Worse than liberty, they said, was the equality which Bacon had promised to the common Virginians: "he would make the meanest of them equall with, or in better condition than those that Ruled over them." And Bacon had kept both his promises: liberty and equality. Declaring the assembly oligarchs "traytors against the people,"

---

186. P. Ludwell to Coventry, 14 April 1677, Coventry Ms. 78, 40. Green Spring Assembly Orders, 20 February [1676/7], "Copia. Test. Robert Beverley," C.O. 1/39, 93. The date of this order, one week prior to the actual meeting of the assembly, suggests the prior composition of the Green Spring legislation by Beverley and the Berkeleyans. *N.B.* some of Beverley's minuscule text may be incompletely transcribed here. See also C.O. 1/39, 94; C.O. 5/1371, 61–62.

the general of the revolution "Confiscates theire Estates and distributes [them] to his followers, sett prisoners for debt and otherwise at lyberty and declares freedom to all servants that belonged to any Loyall persons, and lists them as his Choice and Standing Army and forces many to follow him in Armes, threatening theire Ruine if they Refused." That a political, social, economic, and military revolution had happened in Virginia in 1676 its victims were in no doubt. That they had suffered through as brief but as thoroughgoing a revolution as their century, "the century of revolution," had to offer amply explains the inability of the Green Spring assemblymen, the restored reactionaries of the *ancien régime,* to accommodate themselves either to popular need or to royal reform. Victimized by Bacon's popular revolution, they were vulnerable to an imperial counter-revolution.

Rejecting popular revolution but fearful of royal absolutism, the Green Spring Assembly long refused that admission of colonial guilt which was the prerequisite for the royal pardon. They even resisted any expression of gratitude for the royal clemency. They did not, so they thought, require any forgiveness themselves and they wished to deny it to their enemies. The assembly were equally unwilling to recognize either of the duke of York's interventions in Anglo-Virginian affairs. To admit that the duke had eliminated the proprietary grants at no cost to Virginia would force the assembly to account for the agency-tax money. Its collection had helped ignite the revolution even when it had some apparent legitimacy, but it was now being shared out by the assembly elite, just as the rebels had predicted it would be. The duke's denial of a charter to the Virginia Assembly could not be recognized without compelling the Virginia elite to face their constitutional dependence on the imperial crown.

Even when the crown's commissioners, each of whom considered himself a servant of the royal duke, finally bullied the assembly into accepting as its own the apologies and acknowledgments to the king and the duke which were prepared for the legislators by the commissioners' secretary, Samuel Wiseman, the assembly amended the document to reassert their claims to autonomous authority. The legislators insisted that the "Loyall Party's" unaided (as they described it) suppression of the rebels had vindicated their request for a royal charter confirming the assembly's political privileges. More, these putative loyalists wrote that their victory in the revolution of 1676 justified their request that the king extend their authority to proprietary Maryland and rebellious Albemarle. Unrepentant and aggressive, the Berkeleyans assembled at Green Spring had taken no cautionary lessons from the success of Bacon's Revolution, and they still aspired to oligarchical autonomy despite the presence of a royal regiment, naval squadron, and crown commissioners.

REDCOATED REPRESSION

The irrationality of autonomy was apparent not only in clear warnings that the royal duke wished to hear no more of charters for Virginia's Grand Assembly and that the king himself thought the assemblymen guilty of treason, or in the powerful prerogative presence of their armed forces, but also in continued revolution. Despite the surrenders negotiated by Captain Grantham at West Point, the royal commissioners reported, Virginians were still obsessed with the knowledge that Richard Lawrence, "a Colonell & Grand accomplice of Bacon's, a most stubborne resolved and desperate Rebell (with others fitt to head a new Faction) is yett out." So were those of the Southside Baconians who, captured by Admiral Morris, had escaped from the Green Spring jail after being condemned to death by Berkeley's court-martial. Several hundred men of Bacon's army were also known to be at large, most of them ranged along Virginia's southern border. Despite the continued menace of both revolutionary commanders and soldiers, the loyal party kept revolutionary sentiment alive in the mass of the colonists by continued and renewed oppressions and by their utter unwillingness to make any reform in government, economy, or society. The result, as the crown commissioners wrote, was that "the Commons of Virginia," in February and March of 1676/7, were as apt to "Emmire themselves as deepe in Rebellion as ever they did in Bacon's time." [187]

Yet, for a time, sustained civil unrest actually encouraged loyalist intransigence, for it compelled the redcoats to back the Berkeleyans. The royal expedition's first responsibility was to put down the Baconian Revolution and to restore the king's peace. Only secondly were the forces of the crown expected to impose political reform and to redress popular grievances. Determined to restore the majesty of authority, and vice versa, the crown commissioners wanted the gubernatorial power to be reestablished before Berkeley left Virginia. Therefore, they assiduously avoided public criticism of the old governor, "having all along endeavoured only to keep off from him the Character & Odium of the persecuting Sir William Berkeley." The crown commissioners screened the old governor despite his obvious determination to obstruct the transfer of power—that is, "to lay down the Government here with as much Confusion and disorder as possibly he could." For two months, notwithstanding his vindictiveness and obstructionism, the crown commissioners and the royal forces supported Berkeley simply in order to restore "the King's

187. Commissioners to Coventry, 27 March 1677, Pepys 2582. "Thomas Notley Esqr Lieutenant General of the Province of Maryland to Charles Lord Baltimore, proprietor of ye same," 22 May [1677], C.O. 1/40, 186.

owne Honour," which included "the Honour & Power of a Governor" ruling by royal commission.[188]

The royalists continued their support for Berkeley even though he fomented popular fears of the very king and regiment who kept him in office. Playing on the widespread expectations that the monarch's men would be let loose to live off rebels' lands, Berkeley asserted (or so the royal army officers wrote) that the king "has plac'd us here on free Quarters," although "in truth" it was Berkeley himself who planned "to seize and plunder" the people. It was the easier for Berkeley to excite opposition to the royal army and its officer-statesmen because redcoats were in fact quartered in the most rebellious Virginia counties and because they did support the authority of those county commanders who asked the royal military staff for help.

Colonel Jeffreys himself ordered companies of his regiment across the James River to garrison the Southside counties where the Baconians were still organized and active, Nansemond in particular, and to patrol the border crossings to the rebel refuge in Albemarle. He also sent a unit up the York River to quell the Baconians of New Kent County. At first, Colonel Jeffreys sent only munitions to help restore authority in the northern counties of Virginia. Northern Neck militia commanders asked for and received 150 carbines and ten barrels of powder to arm their select militia as bodyguards and as frontier patrols. Munitions and militia proving insufficient, however, Colonel Jeffreys dispatched a hundred of his men to support the northern leaders and to protect the frontier plantations. The colonel also ordered 6 tons of shot issued from the *Deptford's* stores. With this ammunition (for example, the eight barrels issued to "one Coll Claiborne of New Kent") burgesses armed their supporters county by county. In support of authority, detachments of regular troops also marched along the Peninsula from their cantonment at the Middle Plantation. One company held Kecoughtan, the former Baconian port of entry. Two hundred soldiers posted at the Falls of the James did double duty against both rebellious frontiersmen and the proximate provocation of their rebellion, "forreign Indians."[189]

188. Commissioners to Watkins, Swans Point, 4 May 1677, C.O. 1/40, 131.
189. Commissioners to Watkins, 6 May 1677, C.O. 1/43, 131. Jeffreys to Coventry, 11 June 1677, Coventry Ms. 78, 64–65. See also: orders of the house of burgesses, 20 February 1676/7, C.O. 1/39, 92; Captain's log, *Bristol*, 22 February 1676/7, 16 July 1677, ADM 51/134, Part III.

Oyer and Terminer

Jeffreys did more to punish rebellion and restore authority than merely arm the local leaders (selected, presumably for their imperial potential, by Colonel Moryson) or garrison the key counties of the revolution. For a month, from mid-February until mid-March 1676/7, Colonel Jeffreys and his colleagues of the crown commission sat with Sir William Berkeley and some of his councilors on the court of oyer and terminer to try those of the captured Baconian commanders whom Berkeley had not already killed. In doing this, the crown commissioners' intent was "to convince this Country that wee are come to condemne and Punish, and not to Countenance or bolster out their Rebellions."[190]

The commissioners joined the governor in this judicial brutality because they shared seventeenth-century authoritarians' genuine horror at Virginia's example of the rebellion endemic in their age. The ensuing executions, the crown's commissioners agreed, were political admonitions "least upon any dislikes of a future Governr. ye people may believe they have no more to do but to mutiny and be rid of him." It was to protect future imperial authority and "to possess the People of this Colony . . . of his Majestyes Severity and Justice" that the crown commissioners joined Berkeley and company on the bench at Green Spring "both at the Tryall and Condemnation of Seven or Eight of the most notorious Criminalls." Three of these cases were of special concern to the commissioners. Each of them evidenced the interaction of the warlike past, veteran personalities, and political principles in the troubled Anglo-American world of 1676.[191]

ARNOLD'S ATROCITY

Anthony Arnold would have been hanged by much milder-mannered royalists than Berkeley, Jeffreys, and Moryson, all former civil warriors

---

190. Commissioners to Coventry, 27 March 1677, Pepys 2582; also in C.O. 5/1371, 69–77.
191. Commissioners to Williamson, 27 March 1677, C.O. 1/39, 180. Colonel Jeffreys' memorandum, Coventry Ms. 77, 421. The Royal Commissioners, "A true and faithful Account . . . ," 24 July 1677, Pepys 2582. Berry's and Moryson's report, 20 July 1677, *ibid.* "A Commission of Oyer & Terminer for ye Plantacon of Virginia," 6 November 29 Charles II [1676], *ibid.* Commissioners to Coventry, 27 March 1677, Pepys 2582. "Proposals most humbly offered to his most Sacred Matie by Tho Ludwell & Robt Smith" (C.O. 1/38, 35) anticipate most of the Berkeleyan program of resistance, alike to royal force and to the rebellion of the "meanest people."

and exiles, and Sir John Berry, the son of a priest of the Church of England deprived of his parish by revolutionaries, risen in royal service from
poverty and prison to military fame and the favor of that most absolute
prince, James duke of York. The royal judges were appalled by Arnold,
this "horrible resolv'd Rebell and Traytor." He had not just led Baconian
troops; he had forcibly championed in Virginia Hobbesean and republican doctrines. Arnold had not only declared "that hee had no Kindnesse
for Kings, and that they had Noe Right but what they gott by Conquest
and the Sword," he had added "that hee that could by power of the sword
deprive them thereof had as good & just a Title to it, as the King himselfe:
and that if the King should Deny to doe him right (or what in himself
hee thought such) hee would make noe more to sheath his sword in His
heart or Bowells than in his owne mortall Enemyes." The judges all
agreed that Arnold must die for these "Treasonable words," as well as
for his actual rebellion, and that his exemplary execution should take
place in his home county. They regretted, in Arnold's case more than in
most, that the lamentable lack of skilled executioners in Virginia prevented them from having him hanged, drawn, and quartered. They
agreed to do the next-worst thing. The judges ordered Arnold to be
suspended from the gallows in chains, there to die slowly and decay
noisomely, an awful example in dying and death to the leveling
revolutionaries and anti-monarchical republicans whom he had led
in life.[192]

The unique harmony that Berkeley and the commissioners exhibited
in Arnold's trial and condemnation was marred by one minor, but illuminating, disagreement. The governor insisted in Arnold's case, as in
most others, that Colonel Jeffreys provide an escort of regular troops to
march the condemned man down to his county from Green Spring and to
guard against local rescuers. The royal commissioners refused, "that the
Country might have no cause to think or say that wee were affraid of any
Rescue or Tumults." This the Berkeleyans did fear, and with reason.
Further revolt seemed the only protection for the mass of Virginians
implicated in the revolution, for Sir William believed that any "leniency
would lead to a fresh Rebellion." Therefore, he was "for filling the Gaol
up faster than we could empty it," as the commissioners complained,
until every opponent of his regime was either executed or expropriated.
The crown commissioners, however, insisted that six exemplary executions would suffice to sanction order. They tested their assumption by
that many unguarded executions in the counties. Each was a "Tryall of

192. Commissioners to Watkins, 27 March 1677, C.O. 1/39, 180v; C.O. 5/1371, 87–91. See also
postscript in Coventry Ms. 78, 20.

the Temper of the People, which proved very peaceable and submissive." [193]

BLAND'S BLAME

Now that order was re-established, only one of Sir William's prisoners still seemed culpable to the commissioners. Giles Bland was the customs officer whose reports of Berkeleyan misgovernment and extortion (circulated at Whitehall by his father, the eminent free-trader John Bland, and his father-in-law, the influential Cromwellian and Restoration colonial adviser and bureaucrat, Thomas Povey) had led the crown to pardon the Virginians, to reshape their government, and to recall Sir William Berkeley. Yet the sea captains' reports from Virginia, received with Bland's critiques, made it clear he had become a leader in the revolution he described. Bland's opposition condemned himself as much as it did Berkeley in English eyes. Bland's influence, however, was admitted even by his worst enemies. When the discredited governor received the king's orders releasing him from the burden of command, and when the royal commissioners censured his oppressions and his assembly's obduracy, Berkeley remarked that "we very wel know from whome this kindnesse and severity proceeds and the causes of both." After five and a half months chained in the hold of the *Rebecca*, Giles Bland was dragged ashore to face the judges at Green Spring. That the judges included Berkeley and both of the Ludwells—all three looters of the Bland estates and angry victims of both his critical reports to London and his rebellion in Virginia—and the crown commissioners, prejudiced against him, made Bland's condemnation almost certain.[194]

Yet Bland opened his defense by producing a copy of Sir William Berkeley's latest instructions from the king, read it to the court, and pled that the royal pardon mentioned therein applied to himself. All the judges were embarrassed. The crown commissioners asked where Bland had gotten Berkeley's private instructions. "Calling God to Witnesse that hee had never lett them goe out of his own hands or Traunke," Sir William said that Bland must have received a copy through Thomas Povey. Why, then, the commissioners wanted to know, was Bland's copy signed by Robert Beverley, the governor's favorite and the clerk of the assembly? The commissioners suddenly realized that the governor had publicized,

193. Commissioners to Williamson, 27 March 1677, Pepys 2582; also in C.O. 1/39, 180. Commissioners to Watkins, 27 March 1677, C.O. 1/39, 182.
194. Berkeley to Coventry, 9 February 1676/7, Coventry Ms. 77, 382. Bland's estate was mulcted by order of the Green Spring Assembly, 20 February 1676/7 (C.O. 1/39, 95) to pay the costs of his imprisonment on board Captain Thomas Gardiner's ship.

even to his prisoners, his discretionary powers, the royal prerogative delegated to the governor by the king. To make himself great and his victims subservient, Berkeley had criminally exposed the royal instructions, revealing to Virginians that the policy of the crown varied with the degree of popular resistance to it. This seemed to the commissioners "especially pernicious to his Majesty's Interest at this tyme to have the Comon Rabble and dissaffected party observe." It was never clearer than in the opening scenes of Giles Bland's trial that "his Majesty's Interest" was of no concern to Sir William Berkeley and his partisans, except insofar as it strengthened their campaign of revenge and plunder.[195]

The royal commissioners were doubly embarrassed because although they opposed most Berkeleyan revenge, they had to deny Bland the benefit of that royal pardon which they intended to enforce in favor of all future defendants. Imperial political pressures compelled the crown commissioners to condemn Bland (although they hoped that his execution could be stayed). "By God, Bacon and Bland must die," the duke of York had allegedly told them. Certainly, the commissioners were quick to report Bacon's death and Bland's forthcoming trial and ensuing condemnation to their princely patron. The duke's fatal demand had one root in the notoriety of Bland's leadership of the revolution. He and Bacon were the only leaders named in the dispatches which reached England before the royal expedition sailed. The reaction this caused appeared in John Bland's plea to the king to suspend judgment against his only son until the royal commissioners reported. The second root of the duke's prejudgment of Giles Bland may have been his father's ill-case with the imperialists—that is, the Yorkists.[196]

Just as the duke's men made the suppression of the Virginia rising and the execution of its known leaders—Bacon and Giles Bland—their particular responsibility, so they had earlier and often quarreled with John Bland about imperial discipline. In 1667, as the first mayor of England's North African outpost, Tangier, Bland made countrified demands for civil rights, corporate privilege, and local tax control that became an imperial *cause célèbre*. His opponent was Colonel Henry Norwood, then the deputy governor of Tangier, formerly a royalist exile, treasurer of

195. Commissioners to Coventry, 27 March 1677, Pepys 2582.
196. "Wee will not omitt to lett His R Highness know that the Governor intends to try Bland ... by a Jury & c. after the manner of the Lawes of England, those already executed having been tryed and sentenced by a Councell of Warr" (Berry and Moryson to the duke of York's secretary, 2 February 1676/7, Pepys 2582). Stephen Saunders Webb, " 'Brave Men and Servants to His Royal Highness': The Household of James Stuart in the Evolution of English Imperialism," *Perspectives in American History* 8 (1974): 53n.

Virginia throughout this period, a "cousin" of Sir William Berkeley and, in 1676, a Yorkist courtier as member of parliament from Gloucester who advised the crown about its colony. Equally offended by Bland's civilian and corporate stance had been the Tangier Board, headed by the duke of York. Moreover, Bland, through his son's marriage, was tied to Thomas Povey, who was playing loose if not fast with the Tangier accounts. Both the elder Bland and Thomas Povey were involved in attempts to establish the primacy of peace and commerce with Spain, to free Virginia tobacco trade from the control of such court-connected monopolists as Jeffrey Jeffreys, and so to establish the imperial policies and personnel associated with the earl of Arlington. All these objectives were anathema to Yorkists. The association of the elder Bland, Thomas Povey, and the younger Bland with one another and with Bacon's Revolution was manifested on 28 August 1676. Then there arrived, presumably from Giles Bland, "for Thomas Povey, Esqr. at his house in Lincolns Inn Fields" the Baconian circular of 8 July and a request, which John Bland and Thomas Povey honored, to lobby against royal reprisals. That the younger Bland's policies were not entirely his father's—Giles Bland was a civilian and an enemy of the Berkeley connection, to be sure, but he was also a customs man and an imperialist of Danbyite stripe—did not save him from hostile prejudgment by the Yorkists in England in 1676. Both reputation and prejudgment influenced the crown's commissioners (as well as the Berkeleyans) against Bland in Virginia.[197]

The royal commissioners saw no choice but to join the Berkeleyans in condemning Bland for his share in the revolution, despite his well-informed plea for a share in the royal pardon. Since his royal office and his prominent family had persuaded even Sir William Berkeley to let Bland survive more than five months in custody, however, it seemed he might yet hope to escape on appeal. Back went Bland to the hold of the *Rebecca*. He lay there for a month, under sentence of death, until, on the third day of the new year, 27 March 1677, he became the last of Berkeley's victims. "Mr. Bland was executed this day in the Afternoone at James Town," the crown commissioners reported. As if to exculpate themselves and blame Berkeley for Bland's execution, they added that the imminence of Bland's death "was more than himselfe or any Body but the

197. Giles Bland to Thomas Povey, 8 July 1676, C.O. 1/37, 84. Thomas Bacon attempted to prevent this prejudgment by forwarding to the king the June Assembly's letter of 25 June 1676 "as tending to his [Nathaniel Bacon's] vindication or at least extenuation" (C.O. 1/37, 31). For the printed "Remonstrance of John Bland in Behalf of the Inhabitants & Planters in Virginia & Maryland" against the monopolistic London merchants, see C.O. 1/36, 142 ff. See the privy-council discussion of Norwood's and Bland's Virginia assessments in Book II, especially pp. 202–5.

Governor knew till this day came, for hanging here goes by chance & destiny." [198]

JONES' LOYALTY

By the time Bland's death surprised the royal commissioners they had long since determined to end judicial executions and so stop the Berkeleyan extortion. First the commissioners refused to countenance any further trials by their presence. This decision was set off by Berkeley's prosecution of Robert Jones. "Bearing in his body many marks of a Loyall Souldier and Subject to the late Kinge of blessed Memory," Charles I, Jones had been captured after being wounded during the English Civil War, transported to Virginia, and sold into servitude. He survived his service and settled, finally, on the upper James River, On that embattled frontier in the spring of 1676, the old veteran was stirred first by Indian raids and then by the Baconian charges that Berkeley and his Indian-trading clique were responsible for them. Commanding a company of Indian-fighters in what became the army of the revolution, Jones did not surrender to Berkeley until 3 February 1676/7, and then only on the governor's promise of indemnity. It was a worthless promise, of course, and Jones had no significant property with which to plead for his pardon with the governor. His upcountry officer friends were all as guilty of treason as Jones himself. So Berkeley and company condemned him to die for his undoubted part in Bacon's Revolution.[199]

Learning this, Captain William Byrd and other Baconian officers sailed down the James from Henrico to Swan's Point (retracing Nathaniel Bacon's route of 6 June 1676) to ask the royal commissioners, resident at Colonel Swan's, to save the life of Robert Jones. That the former rebels came to the crown commissioners to ask for an exercise of imperial authority and that the commissioners responded favorably was a first step in the process whereby the royal officials recognized the aspirant newcomers to Virginia, the leaders of the revolution, as part of the province's new ruling class. So, from the colony's seventeenth-century rebels the crown created the province's eighteenth-century aristocrats.

When they accepted Byrd's plea for Jones, the commissioners were moved, not just by prospects of provincial empire-building, but also by their own royalist records. These inclined them to be merciful to another

198. Commissioners to Watkins, 27 March 1677, postscript, C.O. 1/39, 183: also in Coventry Ms. 78, 20.
199. "Coll Morrison to ye Lady Berkeley," 25 March 1677, Pepys 2582. Judgment, 15 March 1676/7, in Henning, [ed.,] Statutes, II, 550. Petition of Robt Jones, Charles City County, to the king, C.O. 1/45, 113r. "Motion of Col. Morrison & Sir John Berry," 18 March [1676/7], Pepys 2582.

old soldier of the king. The crown commissioners were also troubled by the prejudicial conduct of the Berkeleyan judges. The commissioners had observed "some of ye Loyall party yt satt on ye bench with us att ye Trials to be so fierce in impeaching accusinge revileing ye prisoners at ye Barr wth yt inveteracy as if they had been ye worst of witnesses rather yn Justices of ye Commission, both accusinge & condemning at ye same time." Colonel Moryson, the crown commissioners' legal expert, had early gone on record as being opposed to any overt challenges by the commissioners to Berkeley's role as chief judge. Nevertheless he undertook to write to his old friend Frances lady Berkeley in Jones' behalf.[200]

The colonel told the lady that he trusted "yt yor own Merciful and tender Bosome will move you to interceed with ye Governor in behalfe of this poore Unfortunate Wretch." Lady Berkeley's reply was a bitter one. "If I am at all acquainted with my hart," she wrote, "I should wth more easiness of mind have worne ye Canvase Linnen ye Rebells said they would make me glad of, yn have had this fatall occasion for my interceedinge for mercy." Since it was Colonel Moryson who had asked for Jones' pardon, however, the governor would consent, "Mercy beinge as Inherent in him as itt is in Sr. yor most Humble Servant ff Berkeley." Afraid that this was so, Colonel Jeffreys, "as commander in chief of his Matys forces," reinforced Moryson's plea. Jeffreys "desired" Major Robert Beverley, Sir William Berkeley's military aide, to "move ye Governor" towards mercy for Jones. Finally, Sir John Berry took a hand. Because he commanded the squadron, Sir John was seen by every assemblyman not obsessed with Berkeleyan localism as the greatest check on the soldiers, whether rebels or redcoats, and everyone knew that Berry was now the master of Virginia's trade. When he put his name at the head of an address from the commissioners which asked the assembly to call on Berkeley to end all treason trials and executions, they immediately made it their "vote and Addresse to the Governor to forbeare." Not only was Robert Jones saved from Berkeleyan vengeance, but Sir William Berkeley's hold on the Green Spring Assembly was broken.[201]

The royal commissioners immediately, publicly, and formally challenged the governor's abuse of the courts. In the oyer-and-terminer session of 15 March 1676/7, each of the commissioners in turn stood up to denounce an aspect of the day's proceedings. Then they issued a joint statement that Berkeley had no authority to try or sentence anyone for rebellion. Instead, as they insisted before a roomful of prisoners, the

200. The Royal Commissioners, "A true and faithful Account . . . ," 28 July 1677, Pepys 2582.
201. Swans Point, 25 March 1677, Pepys 2582; also in C.O. 5/1371, 92–93. "ff Berkeley" reply, 25 March 1677, Pepys 2582; also in C.O. 5/1371, 93–94. Commissioners' memorandum, 18 March 1676/7, Pepys 2582. Commissioners to Williamson, 27 March 1677, Pepys 2582; also in C.O. 1/39, 180.

king's pardon was fully in effect. The commissioners recorded their for-mal judgment that all Berkeleyan confiscations made since the surrender at West Point were unlawful. They called to the bar the former Baconian commanders of West Point and of the York River garrisons. These officers had been arrested by Berkeley, contrary to the surrender agreements. Now he had demanded that their estates be forfeited to him for their treason. Encouraged by the crown commissioners, the ex–Baconian com-manders pled the king's pardon.

"Hereupon," the clerk of the court records, "a fierce debate arise in open Court, first moved by ye Governor, conceminge Restitution of ye Estates of those persons and other offenders of ye like Nature, which the Governor would have all Seized and forfeited." Despite the governor's furious objections, the commissioners discharged the five men at the bar —Ingram, Scarborough, Seaton, Whalley, and Knowles—and declared that the royal pardon was universal and that it extended to the property as well as to the lives of all Virginians who pledged their allegiance to the crown. The crown commissioners announced that they had already appointed their own investigators and accountants—all ranking Virginia militia officers—to describe to the king every confiscation made since the West Point surrender. They declared that Sir William Berkeley was per-sonally liable to be sued for all and every such seizure at the initiative of either the king or any one of his aggrieved subjects.[202]

A Statute of Remembrance

The commissioners' condemnations of Berkeley's judicial abuses on 15 March 1676/7 dictated their reaction to the legislation announced by the Green Spring Assembly when it was adjourned six days later. The assemblymen argued that it was Sir William Berkeley's legal prerogative, combined with his position as presiding officer of the assembly, that permitted him and them to make exceptions to the king's pardon. The assembly further identified the old governor with their defiance of crown commands and royal intentions when they assigned to Sir William the largest share of the money previously raised to finance the agents' in-tended purchase of Virginia from the proprietors. When the duke of York

---

202. Wiseman's memorandum (as clerk of the court), 15 March 1676/7, Pepys 2582. Commis-sioners to Coventry, 27 March 1677, *ibid.*

secured the king's commands for the free surrender of the proprietary patents, he had assumed, and the crown commissioners had therefore promised the colonists, that these moneys would be returned to Virginia to lighten the local tax burden. Instead, the Green Spring Assembly now divided these tax receipts among the loyalists. Then the costs of the ineffective forts, the failed Indian war, and the bitter civil war were assessed as new levies at 400 pounds of tobacco per poll, the largest tax in Virginia's history. Finally, the assembly declared that "all people ought to Acquiese with that Levies that are made by the Grand Assembly, and whosoever shall oppose them in hostile manner [are] to be deemed Rebells and [to be] prosecuted accordingly." [203]

Far from "healing" the wounds of war and revolution, the Berkeleyans were determined to deepen and perpetuate them, not only by increased taxation but also by describing those who declined to pay these taxes as "delinquents." Once the assemblymen had accepted the royal pardon for themselves, they went on to define delinquency so broadly as to criminate most other Virginians. "Delinquents," declared the Green Spring Assembly, included Bacon and nineteen persons condemned by Berkeley's court-martial (all of whom were also now attainted of treason by the assembly—an exclusive authority of the English parliament—and their estates declared forfeit, a consequence of court-martial inadmissible under English law); all the rebel leaders who had escaped from the Brick House; nine persons executed by Berkeley since 22 January 1676/7; twenty-two captured rebel officers and all of their troops; a deserter from Beverley's colors; the Baconian propagandists Sarah Grindon and Edward Phelps; all persons banished by the governor to date, and all those who deserved to be banished for their part in the rebellion; all the commanders at West Point and King's Creek; all persons who "displundered any loyall person," or who were present at such plundering, or who commanded any troops who plundered; and all "servants" (i.e., bondsmen) who had joined the revolution. All these classes of "delinquent" persons were by an act of the Green Spring Assembly declared incapable of benefit from the king's pardon. [204]

The assembly then condemned fourteen additional Baconian commanders and the men of their garrisons either to beg for their lives publicly, on their knees, with the hangman's noose around their necks, or else to pay heavy fines and be banished from Virginia. The assembly went on to make elaborate provision for a few "loyall persons" to recover the "horses, sloopes, boates, armes, servants, slaves, and other goods"

---

203. "Publique Charge," C.O. 1/39, 101–2. Committee reports of the burgesses, *ibid.*, 99.
204. These acts appear *in extenso* in C.O. 1/39, 71–81; they are abstracted in *ibid.*, 82–85; and partial printed texts are in Henning, [ed.,] *Statutes*, II, 366–86, 395.

they had lost "during the tyme of the late horrid rebellion," or else to recover the value of their claims, and of all other debts owed them by rebels, from the estates of those whom the assembly had exempted from pardon.

After they had condemned, pauperized, or humiliated as many of the rebels as possible, the Green Spring Assembly decided to "blow on the Coale of strife and discord afresh" by forbidding the leaders of the revolution either to enter or to re-enter legitimate politics. The Berkeleyans enacted a loyalist monopoly of office by declaring "that all persons who have assumed any title or command in this late most horrid rebellion . . . or [were] eminent in giving councell . . . aiding or encouraging the said rebellion . . . are hereby made for ever incapable of beareing any office, civill or military, within this colony." The Berkeleyans knew that the basis of politics is opinion, so they went on to censure the expression of revolutionary opinions and to prohibit all attacks on colonial authority, verbal or armed. Anyone who condoned the rebels or defended the rebellion was to be whipped, fined, or prosecuted for treason, "and whereas it hath been frequent for rude and ill disposed persons to contemne and revile authority and magistrates as well as [by] words as in actions," all those who criticized the governor, councilors, justices of the peace, or field officers of the militia were to be whipped and fined. If more than five armed persons assembled without order, they were to be deemed guilty of riot and mutiny.[205]

As Colonel Jeffreys observed, the convention at Green Spring had determinedly and repeatedly defied the royal commands to pacify Virginia. Far from being a "healing Assembly," they "had made a Statute of Remembrance; to last and intail trouble from one Generation to another." By doing so, the assembly demonstrated its unfitness to reconcile or to rule Virginians and it reinforced the royal determination to reduce the autonomous Virginia Assembly to the level of a corporation council.[206]

Royal Reaction, Popular Reform

The crown's commissioners directed that determination. They called for an immediate royal veto of the punitive acts of the Green Spring

205. Commissioners to Watkins, 27 March 1677, C.O. 1/39, 182.
206. Jeffreys to Coventry, 4 May 1677, Coventry Ms. 78, 44b.

Assembly. In their place, the commissioners suggested that royally drafted acts of pardon and oblivion should be sent over for forced passage by a reconstituted assembly. As the royal commissioners wrote home, "Nothing but a generall Penall Act of oblivion can serve to make up these Breaches, and reconcile the Rancors and bitter Animosities among them, the seeds for future Discontents and disturbances." The king must instantly order Sir William Berkeley removed from Virginia and from the presidency of the assembly. The royal investigators wrote that "wee thinke it impossible . . . that ever things should be put into that Peaceable posture and happy composure desired and by us endeavoured while Sr. Wm. B. continues Gouernour upon the Place." His cronies, especially those who had first forced Virginians to follow Bacon and then joined the Berkeleyan terror, must be stricken from the council, for "those who stile themselves the Loyall Party are the onely cheife Disturbers and Obstructors of the Peace and Settlement of this calamitous County." The commissioners concluded that the king must replace the Berkeleyan "Loyall Party" in provincial offices with men who would do his bidding.[207]

Once the leadership of the assembly was transformed by royal replacements, its initiative reduced by royal bills, and its authority limited by royal vetoes, the commissioners insisted that the crown should complete the remodeling of the provincial legislature, and reform county governments as well, by a purge of the county elites (who manned the assembly's lower house). The colonial military appointments made illegally by Sir William Berkeley after Colonel Jeffreys' arrival must be denounced by the captain general of the empire, the duke of Monmouth. Further, the crown must confirm the wholesale changes in the county militias which Colonel Jeffreys had proposed. Finally, Berkeley's extortionate military finance, fraudulent fortification, and inequitable enlistments, which had enriched the old assembly elite and excited the rebellion of Virginia's fighting men, must be reformed. The crown's commissioners called for a royally approved, locally equitable, militarily effective defense system which would recruit, promote, and support a fresh generation of militia commanders, officers loyal to the new provincial and imperial government.

That new, royalized, government's agenda, the crown commissioners observed, had already been set by the popular testimony they had collected. When the royal commissioners wrote their preliminary reports and recommendations to the crown in the last days of 1676, they already

---

207. Commissioners to Williamson, 27 March 1677, Pepys 2582. See also commissioners to Watkins, 27 March 1677, C.O. 1/39, 182; Berkeley to Coventry, 27 March 1677, C.O. 5/1371, 87–91; commissioners to Williamson, 27 March 1677, Pepys 2582.

had in hand grievances from eleven counties. These were the initial responses to the commissioners' call for popular statements of the causes of the revolt against the old regime. They provide a unique analysis of what seventeenth-century Englishmen in America wanted from colonial governments, what the autonomous old order had failed to give them, and what they now hoped for from the imperial crown.

Six of these first eleven county statements denounced the basic tobacco tax. It was unaccounted for, they said, and so it was presumably misemployed. Most of these county complaints went on to indict the fort levies as useless: what had not been poured into mud walls had been diverted to develop new plantations for the fort contractors. Besides the "forts," almost everything to do with Indian policy angered Virginians. Neither the savages nor those who traded with them had been sufficiently controlled. Far worse was the Berkeley government's "slow prosecution of the Indian War." The counties also denounced failures in Anglo-Virginian relations. In particular, the tax levied to pay off the English proprietors (the petitioners did not yet know it had been misappropriated by the loyalists) was a double grievance, first unexplained and then ineffective. Complaints about taxes and defense inspired the petitioners' unanimous insistence that the assembly, which overtaxed, underdefended, and misrepresented Virginians, should meet less often, be bound by English law, and lower its members' salaries and expenses.[208]

The remainder of these eleven county grievances denounced Berkeleyan officers' exactions and discriminations in the counties, by taxation, on the land, and since the revolution. The colonial commons demanded that the fees of Berkeley's county sheriffs and justices be reduced and their terms be limited to one year; that the governor and his councilors pay the poll tax on their laborers, as everyone else did; that the Indian prisoners the Berkeleyans held be sold for public profit; that the weapons the "Loyall Party" had seized be restored to their owners; and, most fundamentally, that the grandees' great landholdings be taxed—indeed, that all lands be taxed—in proportion to estate size.

Land taxes, the crown commissioners themselves "as much wished as [they were] desired" by the popular petitioners. Therefore, although a general and equitable land levy was at present impractical, the commissioners recommended to the king that at the least he should order taxes imposed on all landholdings in excess of 1,000 acres. This would, the royal investigators hoped, discourage that engrossment of land which impeded village growth, impaired military mobilization, diluted frontier

208. See especially James City County Grievance, no. 4, and commissioners' reply, Pepys 2582.

defense, and discouraged freehold farming. Compact colonialization and family farms, the crown commissioners believed, were the foundations of a militarily strong and socially stable province. The growing rate of tenancy in Virginia, the commissioners concluded, was a cause of both military weakness and social unrest. New immigrants "think it hard to be a Tennant upon a Continent."[209]

The land reforms proposed by the people and endorsed by the commissioners, "being never to be admitted or liked of by those great engrossers of land there, if done it must be effected by his Maties immediat Commands," the royal investigators wrote. Likewise, every reform of the old order would require direct royal intervention through the imperial agents who were imposed by force on Virginia in 1676. For example, the regulation of the terms of fees of local officers, the crown commissioners said, could not be accomplished by the old elite but would be enacted by "the new Governor," Colonel Jeffreys. So too it was Jeffreys who restored or replaced the people's weapons, for the royal commissioners agreed with the county petitioners that the people must be armed to protect themselves from raiders by land and sea; to kill game, which was their only fresh meat during most of the year; and "to destroy Wolves and vermine which infest ye Plantacions."

Not only on the land and in the counties, but even as to the assembly itself, the crown commissioners promised the aggrieved colonists that the king would command what they proposed: that the assembly would meet less frequently; that "ye manner of their proceedings [would be, as it was subsequently] prescribed by his Matie to be as near as maybe to ye laws of England"; and the commissioners told the county petitioners that the salaries of the assemblymen had already been "reduced . . . according to his gratious Majtys Royall Instructions laid on us."

The royal investigators also agreed with the dissident Virginians' complaint that the Berkeleyan regime had failed to defend them either from Native Americans or from English proprietors. Like every authority of their age, they agreed that protection by the government was the prerequisite for the obedience of the people. The commissioners promised the colonists that the king's governor, Colonel Jeffreys, would protect them in Virginia. They pointed out that the king himself had protected their interests in England by commanding (through his brother, the duke) the free surrender of the Virginia proprietary patents. To finance their protection, however, the commissioners warned the colonists that they must pay the tax levies, for these were "ye only support of the Government." The royal officials did promise, though, to provide the Virginians full

209. James City County Grievance, no. 10, and commissioners' reply, *ibid.*

value and accurate accounting for their taxes, according to their petitions and by the king's command.[210]

These promises of imperial action and internal reform, made by the crown commissioners in reply to popular grievances, alarmed and infuriated the Berkeleyans. They recognized, as Burke would after them, that "the court (working with the mob) may assume as uncontrolled a power in this country" as any absolute monarch was then doing in Europe. Though they were initially balked by the Berkeleyans, the royal commissioners soon pacified Virginia by a combination of military force, royal forgiveness, and popular politics. First, by force applied against both domestic dissidents and Indian enemies (including half a dozen exemplary executions), the crown's officers had physically imposed royal rule. Then the commissioners insisted on the universality of the royal pardon. Finally, by their collection of both county and individual grievances against the old regime and by their systematic cultivation of revolutionary leaders (and of others outside the Berkeleyan clique), the king's men had built political bases for imperial rule both in public opinion and in a new class of rulers, responsive to royal orders. Now the crown commissioners wrote to their ministerial correspondents that the imperial executive must continue its direct government of Virginia, both to undo the Berkeleyan acts opposed to pacification and political change and to break up the assembly system of Berkeleyan oligarchy which equated its own self-interest with this destructive and disobedient legislation. The Berkeleyans' "Green Spring Faction" saw in the absolutist interactions of popular grievance and royal redress their own condemnation, the exculpation of the rebels, and the end of their autonomous, practically independent, government in Virginia.[211]

Autonomy's End

The oligarchs of the old order had resisted the imperial presence and provincial pacification by their vindictiveness in the law courts, by their disobedience in the legislative assembly, by their reappointment to

210. James City County Grievances, nos. 10 (the complaint of six counties), 5, 6, 7, and commissioners' replies, *ibid.*
211. Committee reports of the House of Burgesses, "ratified by the Assembly," February 1676/7, C.O. 1/39, 98–100.

civil and military office, in colony and county, of the enemies of both the rebellious people and of the royal commissioners. As the winter of 1676 melted into the spring of 1677, however, the leading Berkeleyans found they could not act effectively outside of Green Spring: they dared not ride abroad among a hostile population to enforce their orders or collect their rents.

As Councilor Spencer put it, "the putrid humors of our unruly inhabitants are not so allayed, but that they do frequently vent themselves by unsavoury bitches, and was they not awed by the over ruling hand of Majitie would soon express themselves by violent acts." But majesty's overruling hand was the royal army, and redcoats seemed to Green Spring almost worse than "unruly inhabitants." In the spring of 1676/7, the royal troops suggested that Sir William Berkeley ought to be hanged and his councilors be damned for resisting royal orders. The Berkeleyans turned to the royal navy to defend them against both a rebellious populace and redcoated soldiers.[212]

Therefore they were without recourse when Colonel Jeffreys and his fellow commissioners Colonel Moryson and Admiral Berry, backed by their armed forces, naval as well as military, deposed Sir William Berkeley, dismissed his councilors (Ludwell and Ballard first among them), and demoted, disbarred, and disqualified Robert Beverley. Succeeding Sir William Berkeley as governor, Colonel Jeffreys appointed London loyalists and former Baconians to take the places of Berkeley's ousted associates. The old governor found himself once again unwillingly bound for exile aboard that vehicle of his varied fortunes, Captain Larrimore's *Rebecca*. On Saturday, 5 May 1677, she carried Sir William down the James River, past the bonfires on the banks which celebrated his departure, and that of the old order, from Virginia. Sir William Berkeley took with him to an unlamented end the misgovernment of an autonomous colony—independent from England in all save the name. After 1676, for a century to come, Virginia would remain what it now became, an obedient province of England's empire.

212. Nicholas Spencer to Lord Baltimore, "Potomecke River in Virginia," 24 May 1677, C.O. 1/40, 188.

SOME SUGGESTED READING
FOR BOOK ONE

Modern work on the social context of *The Chesapeake in the Seventeenth Century* (Chapel Hill, 1979), with special attention to the pattern-setting studies of Maryland's social history by "the Hall of Records gang," is reviewed in the well-organized historiographic essay by Thad W. Tate. It is hoped, however, that the present essay will do something to counter Tate's contention that the Chesapeake was "uninviting terrain" for ideology and politics, and needs must be abandoned to the counters and calculators.

Several of the essays (edited by Thad W. Tate and David L. Ammerman) which follow Tate's review are leading examples of "the new social history." They may in time achieve the status of minor classics, which already adheres to several studies in a volume which, like *The Chesapeake*, was the product of an Institute of Early American History and Culture conference, James Morton Smith, ed., *Seventeenth Century America* (Chapel Hill, 1969). Of these outstanding essays, the most important to *1676* is Bernard Bailyn's "Politics and Social Structure in Virginia," certainly the most influential article ever written about the subject.

The fullest effort to meld the political and social histories of the Old Dominion is Edmund S. Morgan's *American Slavery American Freedom* (note 3, page 16). Preceding Morgan's illuminating work, and of fundamental importance for an appreciation of the Virginia county, is the work of the late and much-lamented Wesley Frank Craven, *The Southern Colonies in the Seventeenth Century* (Baton Rouge, 1949). On "the time of troubles," see Craven's splendidly synthetic study, *The Colonies in Transition 1660–1713* (New York, 1968). Still indispensable to the understanding of Anglo-American institutions are the first three volumes of Charles M. Andrews, *The Colonial Period of American History* (New Haven, 1934–37).

Much more modest studies than these have nonetheless been especially useful to this work in providing portraits of the first colonial capital. In addition to the works cited in note 70 of Book I, see also Tyler, *The Cradle of the Republic*, Henry Chandlee Forman, *Jamestown and St. Mary's: Buried Cities of Romance* (Baltimore, 1938), and Carl Bridenbaugh, *Jamestown 1544–1649* (New York, 1980).

The fundamental political and social study of *Virginia Under The Stuarts* (Princeton, 1914) remains Thomas J. Wertenbaker's. It has been reprinted with two companion volumes (of 1910 and 1922) in *The Shaping of Colonial Virginia* (New York, 1958) (see note 176, page 139). And I must repeat that Wertenbaker's *Torchbearer of the Revolution* (note 19, page 28) has scholarly and literary merits neglected by critics of its admittedly excessive rhetoric. The ultimate rebuttal of Wertenbaker's work on Bacon is Wilcomb E. Washburn's *The Governor and the Rebel* (Chapel Hill, 1957), a learned yet powerful panegyric on Sir William Berkeley. On the other hand, Wertenbaker's work has been carried forward by Richard L. Morton's *Colonial Virginia* (Chapel Hill, 1960) and added to by Jane D. Carson, *Bacon's Rebellion, 1676–1976* (Jamestown, 1976).

Wertenbaker's work remains distinguished by its clear and direct derivation from the documentary sources. Among present-day students, Warren M. Billings' dissertation, " 'Virginias Deploured Condition,' 1660–1676: The Coming of Bacon's Rebellion" (Northern Illinois University, 1968), and his documentary collection, *The Old Dominion in the Seventeenth Century: A Documentary History of Virginia, 1606–1689* (Chapel Hill, 1975), notably sustain the Wertenbaker tradition while extending it to consider servants (on which see, besides essays in the two collections cited above, Abbot Emerson Smith, *Colonists in Bondage* [Chapel Hill, 1968]) and Indians, both subjects somewhat neglected by the master.

As for the Indians of the Chesapeake in 1676, apart from Robert Beverley's sensitive, near-contemporary account in *The History and Present State of Virginia* (London, 1705, 1722; ed. Louis B. Wright, Chapel Hill, 1945) and Nancy Lurie's article on "Indian Culture Adjustment" in Smith, ed., *Seventeenth Century America*, reliance must be placed on the admirable essays in Bruce Trigger, ed., *Northeast*, volume 15 of the *Handbook of North American Indians*, William C. Sturdevant, ed. (Washington, 1978).

On the imposition of imperial government on Virginia and its domestication there in the seven years following Bacon's Revolution of 1676 (and subsequently in Maryland and the Carolinas), see my *The Governors-General: The English Army and the Definition of the Empire, 1569–1681* (Chapel Hill, 1979) and my articles, reprinted from the *William and Mary Quarterly*, in the standard collections edited by James Kirby Martin, *Interpreting Colonial America* (New York, 1978), and Stanley N. Katz and John M. Murrin, *Colonial America Essays in Politics and Social Development* (New York, 1983).

Book Two

THE WORLD
VIEWED FROM
WHITEHALL

Introduction

The institution of the king-in-council was the center of the English empire. Yet its imperial procedures, processes, and policies seldom have been studied, and then only in the limited contexts of the council's committee (actually committees) for "trade and plantations," and the privy council's appellate function. The imperial role of the English executive during the formative period of American politics has hardly been studied in the past generation. Yet, in that generation, the disappearance of English empire and the accession of its former American provinces to world power ought to have refreshed, if not transformed, consideration of every aspect of Anglo-American empire. Of special interest is the adaptation of insular institutions and ideas to a changing imperial environment, for this occurred in 1676 and has happened again three centuries afterwards. An assessment of 1676 implies answers to such questions as how domestic politics become imperial ideologies, how national self-interest is rationalized for overseas application, whether the state's legal control of and increasing involvement with international corporations and trade competition militates against the survival of local liberties and the achievement of equal economic access.

Put differently, 1676 raised issues that have been perennial ever since. What are the necessary consequences of an alliance between finance capital and political authority? Does government become an interlocking directorate of wealth and power? Can self-government coexist with empire in any of its provinces or protectorates, domestic or foreign? To these questions, a generation of historians born and educated in the nineteenth century, writing prior to the Second World War, necessarily gave localist, libertarian, legislative, and legalistic answers. Hitherto unchallenged, but often repeated, these paradigms of Anglo-American history seem to accord ill with the experience of imperial America.

A powerful present thus conspires with neglected sources and subjects to produce this attempt to trace some of the institutional and ideological alterations in the Anglo-America of 1676. The American crises of that year, summarized as Bacon's Revolution in the Chesapeake and King Philip's War in New England, revealed the military debility of the colonial regimes and so exposed them politically. Offering protection, either directly to Virginia or through the agency of New York to New England, the imperial government centered in the king-in-council felt able to insist on American obedience.

To secure its political prerogative in America, to provincialize the hitherto autonomous colonies, the crown modernized its administrative methods in Virginia and reconfirmed its economic bargain with the tobacco colonies. That is, the king-in-council ordered garrison government imposed upon the Old Dominion and it forcibly enforced the American tobacco monopoly against English producers. During 1676 the crown also reconsidered the anomaly of New England's independence and free trade in a monarchical and monopolistic empire and encouraged royal agents to set about the external confinement and the internal subversion of the puritan commonwealths. In 1676, the duke of York's lieutenant, Edmund Andros, and Andros' allies the Iroquois, made permanent the limits of New England that were scorched on the land by the Algonquin Indians while Edward Randolph reinfected the "sterile ward" of God's commonwealth in Massachusetts with the courtly, cosmopolitan, commercial germs of empire.

To this infection—centralizing, metropolitan, and capitalistic as it was —a "country" resistance, social and political, flourished and grew apace in the Anglo-American provinces. They were separated from England physically but not politically by the Atlantic. Perhaps a majority of "the middling sort" throughout the empire supported the country's contradictory combination of political nostalgia and reform, economic reaction and ambition, religious piety and anti-clericalism. Nonetheless, the musket marriage of the crown with the city, of monarchy with metropolis, of imperialism with capitalism proved too strong for the hysterical autarchs of Anglo-America in 1676.

This outcome apparently surprises present-day observers—at least they have been reluctant to write about it—because the country party has seemed to intervening generations to have built the future we embraced. The country nurtured support for the rule of legislature and law. It did so by developing a free press to incite public discussion and to inform public opinion against the court: absolute, Anglo-Catholic, military, monopolistic. And the influence of the informal institutions of the country in 1676 in arousing opposition to imperial authority was evident across the Atlantic. The newsletters and coffeehouses of London were the capital's counterparts of the news wives and inns of Jamestown, the political precursors of the Boston press and its smoke-filled taverns. The agencies and attitudes of the country were coordinated and inspired by the greatest politician of his age, save for the king himself, the earl of Shaftesbury, "inventor" of the modern political party, author of the Popish Plot, orchestrator of the Exclusion Crisis.

Yet Shaftesbury and his associates were successfully purged from the privy council. The influence of the authoritarians, militarists, and monarchists—Lauderdale for Scotland, Ormonde for Ireland, Danby for England, York for the empire overseas, and the king himself overall—triumphed in the provinces, in the parliament, and (given fortunate neutrality and diligent diplomacy) in the circum-Atlantic theatres of imperial rivalry. Cavalry, commissioners, clergy were the provincial agents of the military police, the developing bureaucracy, the Erastian church of the imperial monarchy of 1676. In the "new-model" government ordered by the duke of York for Virginia, in the orders-in-council of 1676, contemporaries foresaw not only the end of autonomy in the Old Dominion but also the disenfranchisement of Anglo-American oligarchy, the defeat of country ideology, the degradation of legislative government everywhere in the empire. Neither the designs of the court nor the fears of the country would be fully realized. During 1676, however, the monarchists did advance the transformation of the traditional privy council. From being the agenda committee of the aristocracy it metamorphosed into a departmentalized, administrative, imperial government. That government was in unprecedentedly firm control of the metropolis and of British and American provinces at the end of 1676.

The institutional adaptation and ideological assertion which advanced the privy council's ongoing alterations of its domestic, household responsibilities into imperial, bureaucratic institutions may be traced in the council's manuscript register. This record has been associated here with the scattered manuscript minutes of its major committees and with files of the state papers "domestic" both in print and in manuscript. From these has been reconstructed a narrative of the council's imperial concerns and actions, its executive actors and operations, in January of 1676. This narrative supplies the context for consideration of two momentous meetings, on 10 March and 19 April 1676, in which the apparently scattered, nearly worldwide, concerns of the courtiers coalesced into an imperial policy. In these meetings, the government of "Greater Britain"—

Scotland and Ireland, the Channel Islands and Tangier, the West Indies and America—was identified with policies monarchist and military, maritime and mercantile.

Once the pragmatic responses of the privy council to the background events of 1676 had amalgamated into imperial policies, these policies dictated the council's subsequent reactions to the evolving crises in the Chesapeake and New England. "Virginia's frolick" incited imperial responses both to the reformist rhetoric of Giles Bland and to the antiquated autonomy of Sir William Berkeley. Challenges to outmoded authority in Virginia led the duke of York to dictate the introduction of the garrison and government of the metropolis into the Old Dominion. In the North, the military failure of the New England colonies persuaded the privy council to authorize political interventions and press campaigns which had equally transforming effects on the puritan commonwealths.

The reduction of New England required a realignment of English attitudes. This in turn required an exercise of the primitive press and developing public opinion of the metropolis. The reporting of the New England war offers an interesting revelation of the American coverage of English newsletters and their supplements. Reactions to that reporting suggest something of the nurturing of a nascent public opinion in the London coffeehouses, more about the privy council's management of information. The result was that shifting of establishment attitudes towards the puritan colonies which underlay the privy council's determination to end their autonomy. The press had demonstrated the inability of the puritan regimes in America to protect the king's subjects from the onslaught of the Peoples of the Fall Line. That very attack made New England's resistance to royal authority less powerful than had been expected.

Imperial intervention was further encouraged by the bifurcated estimate of the New Englanders in old England's press. The press encouraged a public admiration for the beleaguered English settlers and fed English fascination with the exotic warfare by accounts of the American frontier (nothing like it had been read about in London since the Cromwellian reconquest of Ireland). But this praise for the hard-pressed planters re-emphasized courtly and metropolitan contempt for the military inadequacy of their colonial governments, especially the predominant puritan corporation, the Massachusetts Bay Company. The resulting imperial impetus to English intervention produced, first, the elimination of the puritan commonwealths by the short-lived Dominion of New England and then the permanent anglicization of New England society and culture. The unlikely instruments of both processes were introduced to metropolitan opinion by the press in 1676 (and are the subjects of Book

III): Edmund Andros, governor-general of the ducal dominions called "New York," and his Iroquoian allies, called "the Mohawk."

Andros and the Iroquois, the king and his council, all expressed a jaundiced view of New England's territorial ambitions, its mealy-mouthed leaders, and its oligarchical institutions. Such views are again fashionable, as they are periodically (if only out of reaction to New England's self-satisfied and insular historiography). I must therefore take the liberty of saying that the hostile expressions in this Book are my sources', not my own. I do admit substantial sympathy for criticisms of the moral blindness, racial bigotry, and military imbecility of the Connecticut and Massachusetts colonies (as will be voiced by their injured and/or outraged neighbors, red and white, south and west, in the course of Book III). Nonetheless, New England's agony, the bitter, burning light of seventeen lost towns, the destruction of the southern Algonquin, the crumbling and disappearance of the edge of the English world viewed from Whitehall, reminds me that my own people were killed in Swansea and Rehobeth, that they were killers at Turners Falls. I mourn the loss of life, liberty, and utopia in the New England of 1676.

Domestic Imperialists

The domestic records of the English executive in 1676 reveal a paradoxical view of the world as it was seen from that royal rabbit warren, the palace complex of "Whitehall." In a geographic sense, nothing could have been less domestic than the world view recorded in the register of the privy council, in the journals of its committees, and in the state papers domestic. By sea, this world encompassed two-thirds of both hemispheres. In the north, the English leaders looked eastward from Hudson's Bay to the Barents Sea (and during 1676 they tried to see beyond Nova Zemla to Tartary and Japan). In the south, the English executive also looked east, from the Straits of Magellan via the Cape of Good Hope to Bombay, Ceylon, and the East Indies. But in startling contrast to its wide global outlook, Whitehall's world view was determinedly domestic as it applied to institutions and to politics.

When Whitehall's denizens dealt with this wide world in 1676, they were determined to dominate, to exercise a Roman *imperium*, but their mechanisms of empire, whether governmental, commercial, or religious,

A New Mapp of the World According to Mr. Edward Wright Commonly called Mercator's Projection. By John Thornton at the signe of England Scotland & Ireland in the Minories London.

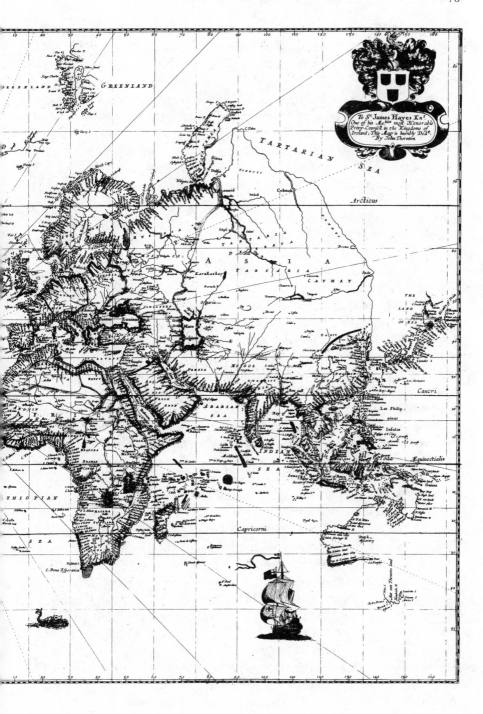

were simply English. In a single century after 1676, the English executive made its empire predominant in the Atlantic world and made its influence felt around the globe, but the social and political ideas of the imperial executive remained those of the English ruling class. The domestic dynamics of that class, the contests and accommodations of landlords with merchants, of rentiers with capitalists, of churchmen with dissenters, of court with country, were the constructs of the English empire just as they were of the kingdom of England. This insular fact became the foundation of an empire in 1676. It rapidly displaced the early colonies' diversity and divergence from English norms. These norms soon prevailed and then predominated for a century in what became "Anglo-America." Finally, the domesticity of the world as viewed from Whitehall explains the disintegration of the English empire in 1776: an empire wholly constructed on English political models and entirely attuned to alterations in England's ruling class could have no sympathy for provincialism, especially when it was touted as purity.

Politically speaking, the English empire, seen from Whitehall between 1676 and 1776, was the relationship of a single metropolis to its dependencies. In both the domestic kingdom and the imperial realm, this relationship was pre-eminently shaped by the ways in which the metropolitans of London and of Whitehall, of the city and of the court, apprehended the lesser cities, the county towns and the rural counties or, as they were called and esteemed by their people, whether in Northumberland (England) or Gloucester (Virginia), "Countries." All these localities were at odds politically with the metropolis, for the English provinces and their capitals preserved from a decentralized and antenational past and conveyed to their American counterparts attitudes and institutions autonomous if not independent of royal authority. With the local elites embodied in city corporations and county commissions, the king and council had traditionally negotiated the degrees of provincial compliance with metropolitan, monarchical, commands. In the ideal politics of this antique, "country," order, the king-in-council was itself but the greatest of county commissions, the agenda committee of the aristocracy, through which was governed both England and its expanding roster of dependencies. And the country view was political fact in most of those dependencies, prior to 1676.

Yet for a century before that date, with ever-rising authority and force, the bases of direct government, monarchical, national, professional, had been ever more apparent and influential. At the national capital, at Whitehall, at "the court," the rise of the executive appeared in the transformation of household and privy council into bureaucratic departments: treasury, admiralty, state, and, most recently and most imperially, war,

trade, and plantations. In "the country," the provincial elites of the port
towns, or regional capitals, and of the dominant estates, loathed the increasing activity of the royal customs and excise, the royal army and navy,
the king's rebuilding of coastal fortresses and his regarrisoning of city
citadels. The bases of direct, metropolitan, courtly government, and the
resentment of them by the country oligarchies, were alike in England
and its dependencies. And of both the realm and the dominions, the king-
in-council, the fountainhead of authority both traditional and modern,
decentralized and direct, country and court, saw itself as the collective
executive. Ireland and the Channel Islands, Virginia and Tangier, Jamaica and Barbados, were ruled much as England itself by the king-in-
council and their committees.

From England's ancient kingdom and its worldwide realm, as viewed
from Whitehall, only Scotland stood apart institutionally. Uniquely in the
English realm of 1676, Scotland preserved all the forms and dignities of
an independent kingdom: king, privy council, army, administration,
church. Yet Scotland's apparent independence was a transparent mask
for her substantial subjection to the purposes of England's most authoritarian and imperialistic ministers of state. Their inclusion in the Scots
privy council in 1674 merely manifested in the northern kingdom's executive body the dominion of the English monarchy. This dominion was
already apparent in the Scots parliament through the lords of the articles
while both the Scots executive and legislature were dictated to by the
king's secretary of state for Scotland and high commissioner to the Scots
parliament, the duke of Lauderdale, whose brutality (but not his scholarship) appears in his miniature by Cooper.

That the fiction of Scottish independence merely masked the kingdom's forceful functions and subordinate status in England's empire appeared in the English parliament's attack on the Scottish secretary. As an
English privy councilor, so his country critics said, Lauderdale had publicly hoped that the Scots Presbyterians would revolt so that he could
bring over the Irish papists to cut their throats. Worse, from Westminster's
viewpoint, it was Lauderdale who had secured the act of the Scots parliament which authorized the king to march the northern kingdom's militia
south into England "for any service whereby his Majesty's Honor, Authority, or Greatness may be concerned." King Charles replied to the
English parliament's criticism by giving Lauderdale the high honor of
bearing the sword of state before the king when he walked into Westminster Hall to prorogue the parliament. The prorogation lasted, as it
happened, for the unprecedented period of fifteen months. That the year
1676 saw the crown's authority established in the realm—and so in the
dominions as well—was due even more to the elimination of parliamen-

tary opposition in the kingdom of England than it was to the subservience of the kingdom of Scotland.[1]

The *Register of the Privy Council of Scotland* for 1676 is thus a record of instant obedience to incessant commands for the reorganization of the king's forces in Scotland and for the repression of the religious opposition to the episcopal polity of the crown. This tyranny found a few echoes in the English privy council's records. When the earl of Kincardine ventured to come into court to protest the persecution of the Scots, he was dismissed from the royal councils in both kingdoms. Other pejorative references to Scots subjects in the English privy-council records sketch Scotland's peculiarly subordinate place in the English empire of 1676: economic exclusion from the English common market under the acts of trade and navigation; religious imposition of English episcopacy on the Scots church. So complete was the subjection of Scotland to the service of the crown that it seemed to the English privy council preferable to preserve its nominal independence than to pursue further negotiations to unite the British kingdoms.[2]

Like Scotland's institutions, apparently anomalous to English empire but actually its servants, were the great trading corporations. Chartered by the crown, governed by privy councilors, and financed by the court's city bankers, these corporations carried Whitehall's writ out to the coasts of Newfoundland and Hudson's Bay, the Levant and the Baltic, Africa and India. These corporations' executive administration, territorial holdings, and economic investments were regular features of the privy council's agenda, essential components of the world viewed from Whitehall.

MINISTERS OF COUNCIL, CABINET, AND RUELLE

Constitutionally, the world-encompassing work of the imperial executive was supervised in its entirety, and some of it was actually accomplished, by the collectivity of the king-in-council. By 1676, however, the growth of both council numbers and of executive business had demanded the delegation and departmentalization of what was still, in constitutional

1. F. H. Blackburne Daniell, ed., *Calendar of State Papers, Domestic Series, March 1st 1675, To February 29th, 1676* (London, 1907) (hereafter cited as *C.S.P.D.* 1675–1676), 23 November 1675, 413–14. Notes on the debate in the commons, 13 January 1673, Add. Ms. 61486, 159v, British Library.

2. P. Hume Brown, ed., *Register of the Privy Council of Scotland*, 3rd ser., vols. IV, V (Edinburgh, 1911, 1912). Register of the Privy Council of England, vol. 12 (1 October 1675–27 April 1677), Public Record Office, London (hereafter cited as P.C. 2/65), 335. Gilbert Burnet, *Bishop Burnet's History of his own time*, ed. Martin J. Routh (Oxford, 1823), II, 58. W. C. Mackenzie, *The Life and Times of John Maitland Duke of Lauderdale* (London, 1923), 385–95. The cabinet's discussions of the union may be conveniently followed in the foreign committee minutes, S.P. 104/176, 75v, 157, 176.

theory and country ideology, the business of the whole privy council. The monarchists' practical need had coincided with their autocratic intention: in 1676 the most sensitive, controversial, and significant issues of politics were concluded in small, sometimes secretive, subsets of the larger council.

King Charles' own decisions were very often taken in his private closet or in the salon of his chief mistress. This salon was the council chamber of the king's "female ministry." Though Charles II had "ministers of the Council, Ministers of the Cabinet and Ministers of the Ruelle [the bedroom], the Ruelle was often the last appeal," for it was an appeal to the raw sensuality of the man unmasked in Lely's sketch portrait of King Charles in 1676. The "Ministers of the Cabinet" were those members of the privy council appointed to the committee for foreign affairs. This committee was commissioned to discuss diplomacy in secret. In fact, its members were the arbiters of domestic and imperial issues as well. The "foreign committee"—that is, the cabinet council—was often associated with, even indistinguishable from, the committee of the privy council commissioned to conduct the affairs of the admiralty.[3]

Here, although supposedly denied office as a Roman Catholic by the Test Act of 1673, the king's brother and heir, the duke of York, was still active. Beyond his work in the admiralty and, later in 1676 especially, in the "foreign committee"—where he led the subcommittee "to see ye forms of Government in ye Severall Plantations" and to attack proprietary autonomy—the duke dealt with the affairs of realm and kingdom in his household council, a sort of "shadow cabinet." And he still sat publicly at the head of the boards of royal agencies and corporations whose cabinet spokesman he remained. He appears in Lely's unfinished, unvarnished, study of his character as the forceful and determined, haughty and stubborn, even stupid man he was. Yet James Stuart was perhaps the bravest of English kings, certainly the best administrator, for a sovereign, since Elizabeth.[4]

The third person in the government was the lord high treasurer, the earl of Danby. He directed the fiscal affairs of the empire, not only in the

3. [George Savile marquis of] Halifax, *Complete Works*, ed. J. P. Kenyon (Baltimore, 1679), 256. Ruelle: "a bedroom where ladies of fashion in the seventeenth and eighteenth centuries, especially in France, held a morning reception of persons of distinction; hence a reception of this kind 1676" (C. T. Onions et al., eds., *The Shorter Oxford English Dictionary* [Oxford, 1964], 1764). More accurately, the ruelle appears to have been the railing surrounding a bed of state.

4. On York's presence, see for example Williamson's note in *C.S.P.D. 1675–1676*, 480. It was a matter for comment on the rare occasions when "the D not there" (see the secretary of state's entry book, S.P. 29/366, 37, and the minutes of the foreign committee, S.P. 104/179, 4v). His championing of the Royal African Company in the "Foreigne Comittee," and the general reconsideration of imperial government, are in *ibid.*, 151–52.

cabinet and its committees, but also from his offices in the Cockpit at Whitehall. There the treasurer sat for public business (half-days on Wednesday and Friday). At Wallingford House, the lord treasurer heard private petitions (half-days Tuesday and Thursday). The vanity, ambition, and assurance of this north-countryman, an hereditary champion of the prerogative in the provinces, are effectively expressed in the formal study of Danby in his garter robes, done (by Lely's studio) on the occasion of his feast and installation at Windsor in April 1676.

Even when the privy council itself adjourned and the court went on holiday with the king to Windsor or to Newmarket, the imperial triumvirs of 1676, the king, the duke, and the treasurer, often meeting as the foreign committee, made practical dispositions and, on occasion, determined broad policies, for England and its empire. Together with the duke of Lauderdale, that "serpent among the eels," the triumvirs also dominated —indeed, they often substituted for—the privy council of Scotland, directing the course of that kingdom towards the authoritarian, military, and episcopal administrations, which were the official objects of royal government everywhere in the British kingdoms and in the realm overseas. Troops of horse, commissioners of customs, bishops of the church: these were the characteristic instruments of the triumvirate of 1676, the arbiters of English empire.[5]

Most, though not all, of the imperial triumvirs' decisions were eventually reflected in the proceedings of the privy council. Not only did the council thus retain its constitutional, clearinghouse function, but its lesser committees also accomplished a great part of the business of royal government. This was especially so in the imperial realm, through the council committees for trade and for plantations. Since 1660, in fact, the imperial responsibilities of the privy council had increased in direct proportion to the decline of its interest in and influence over English local government. This shift reflected the transformation of England from a self-absorbed kingdom to a world empire, trading and territorial. And the committee system of the privy council provided the mechanics whereby this insular institution became an imperial executive. In 1676 the busiest committees of the privy council were those for trade, especially as it was affected by European diplomacy, and for foreign plantations, that is, for the government of the colonies and outposts of the empire. The records of the privy council of England and its committees therefore afford the fullest view of the world seen from Whitehall in 1676, of the official

5. By a warrant of 12 July 1676, the chancellor, the treasurer, the duke of Ormonde, and the secretary of state attending the king were to be privy councilors of Scotland, at whose head sat the duke of York (*C.S.P.D. 1675–1676*, 223). See also *ibid.*, 135–36, 222–23, 445, 448, 461–62, 475, 476, 516. On Lauderdale see W. E. Middleton Knowles, ed. & tr., *Lorenzo Magalotti at the Court of Charles II His Relazione d'Inghilterra of 1668* (Waterloo, 1980), 55.

concerns of the rulers of a new empire, of the public policies of "Greater Britain."[6]

The privy council entered upon its deliberations in 1676 with a crowded board, most of it rather ineffectual. As was customary after the Christmas holidays and during the winter season in the metropolis, the nineteen active privy councilors were joined for formal meetings of the entire council by many of the twenty-one more casual councilors. The latter were not "men of business." They were seldom asked to sit on the privy council's standing committees for navigation, plantation, Ireland, or admiralty. Of course they were never invited to join the committee for foreign affairs. Officially, this committee, the cabinet council, included, besides the triumvirs, the chancellor (Heneage lord Finch), the duke of Ormonde (lord steward of the household), the duke of Lauderdale (as secretary of state for Scotland), the lord chamberlain (the earl of Arlington), and the two English secretaries of state, the principal or "southern" secretary (Sir Henry Coventry) and the junior or "northern" secretary (Sir Joseph Williamson, he of the indecipherable handwriting, a defect disastrous in a secretary). Despite their official membership, the secretaries of state were often excluded from sensitive political discussions, but of such things ordinary privy councilors knew only what they picked up in Whitehall gallery gossip or in the coffeehouses.[7]

The insiders of 1676, the lords of the cabinet council, the king's "ministers," dominated the proceedings of the privy council itself and of its several committees. Without the king's presence and participation, nothing of moment was done in the cabinet and little at the admiralty during the early months of 1676, for Charles II had personally taken up the leadership in both these cabinet committees which his brother had perforce abandoned when he assumed the command by sea and land against Holland in the spring of 1672 and which, following the Test Act and his remarriage, he did not resume until the Virginia crisis in the summer of 1676 coincided with the king's distraction by Hortense Mancini duchesse

6. This and the subsequent paragraphs are developed from the Privy Council Register, 1 October 1675–27 April 1677, Public Record Office (P.C. 2/65), to which reference may be made by seeking the dates given in the text. The manuscript has not been printed. It is at Chancery Lane, where, when last I used it, the rain came through the roof of the Round Room onto the page. Fortunately, the clerks of the council used good ink. See also the council's committee records, listed in notes 7 and 67 below.
7. The discussions of the committee for foreign affairs are recorded in a variety of scattered sources, some printed, such as Williamson's notes in the *C.S.P.D.*, most in manuscript. Of these, the most useful have been vol. 77 of Secretary Coventry's Manuscript at Longleat (hereafter cited as Coventry Ms. 77); "A Journal of the Meetings of the Lords of ye Admiralty from the 1st January 1675/6" (ADM 3/276, Public Record Office); the Foreign Committee's Entry Books (Secretary Williamson's Journals, S.P. 104/176–80, Public Record Office). See also note 61 of Book II, below. On being "a man of business," see S.P. 29/386, 21. The next step was "to become somebody of consideration."

de Mazarin, in the ruelle and by his diplomatic negotiations at Nimeguen. Even before his resumption of command, the intervention of the duke at either the cabinet or the admiralty marked moments of unusual imperial importance. Only less important to committee work than the royal brothers was the earl of Danby. Without the treasurer, the admiralty and the plantations committees conducted only routine business.

Other ministers' special spheres were more limited. Ormonde was always consulted in Irish affairs, and in 1676 he was returned to dominion over England's greatest province. Likewise Lauderdale forwarded, where he did not direct, the king's commands for Scotland. Arlington still claimed special consideration (although he was less and less often accorded it) in England's relations, diplomatic and economic, with the United Provinces and with Spain, and through them with the West Indies. The king and the duke reserved to themselves the all-important questions of French fiscal subsidies and military support for their monarchy and their religion, albeit with the occasional, unwilling, assistance of the treasurer. Secretary Coventry, though no "minister" in the political sense, preserved from his years as the junior secretary interests and information which made him the cabinet's chosen operative for crucial American affairs. In short, the leading lords formed a steering committee of the council's sub-groups. The ministers' advantages of information, authority, and access to the king marked these six statesmen as first among the nominally equal members of the privy council.

THE COUNCIL AND THE EMPIRE

In January 1676, many of the particularly pressing issues before the privy council and its ministerial steersmen reflected the recent war with the Dutch for ships and bases, trade and empire, and the resulting crises of English government finance and of the commercial economy of England and its dependencies. Therefore the privy council was determined to reinforce the exclusion of the Dutch from trade with England's colonies. It gave short shrift to Barbadian petitions against the English monopoly. Responsible for carrying out the peace treaty, the privy council supervised the English settlers' evacuation of Surinam (exchanged with the Dutch for New York) and their reception in Jamaica. New York, privy councilors felt, was the instrument required to curb the independence of New England, now weakened by an Indian war which was the talk of London in the first week of 1676. The manifestation of puritan independence most harmful to the empire was its free trade. Fear of extending such trade by granting corporate privileges, like those of the New England colonies, to Virginia had led some privy councilors to resist the granting of a royal charter of incorporation to that colony's assembly. The

agents of the Virginia Assembly, however, had convinced the majority of
the crown's councilors that the colonial assembly's aim in seeking incorporation was simply to buy out private proprietors and so to unify and
strengthen what was, in name at least, a royal government in Virginia.
Then, on 3 January 1676, the privy council read of the outbreak of that
Indian war in the Old Dominion which cost Virginia its charter because
it led first to revolution in the colony and then to its forcible royalization.

In January 1676, the privy council was also busied providing for the
subsistence of the 3,258 sailors of the royal navy. Every aspect of empire
depended upon the ship, the technological basis of European expansion,
and on the ships' ever-more-experienced sailors. The merchant navy,
vastly enlarged by captures from the Dutch, presented the privy council
with complex problems concerning the passes by which English ship
ownership was attested internationally. These passes were supposed to
secure merchantmen from seizure by the agents of rival empires, France
and Spain, and by the heathen corsairs of the Barbary States. With all of
these maritime powers, fresh naval treaties were in negotiation under the
aegis of the king-in-council. The lords listened to dozens of tales of
French brutality at sea and injustice at law. These did much to confirm
the conviction of most privy councilors (acquired during the ongoing
negotiations at Nimeguen for a general European peace) that France had
replaced both Spain and the Netherlands as the greatest enemy of English empire by sea as well as by land, in commerce as well as in colonization, in Europe as well as in the wider world viewed from Whitehall.

The British territory of England's empire most exposed to French
aggression was Ireland. That kingdom's guards and garrisons were being
rearmed, its finances reorganized, its government reshaped under the
direction of the English privy council and on the basis of the board's
reaction to the bitter debate between Ireland's former and its present
governors-general. The great struggle of the duke of Ormonde with the
earl of Ranelagh was ostensibly financial, but the duke conducted his
defense in terms of "the duty of a chief Governour of Ireland." Those
terms were illustrative of viceregal responsibilities in every province of
England's empire.[8]

The primary problems of provincial government in Ireland were conspiracy and rebellion, Ormonde observed. This meant that the payment
of the garrison was the first fiscal duty of the governor-general. That
obligation could not be met, Ormonde implied, as long as the king himself diverted the Irish revenue to the rebuilding of his great castle at

8. P.C. 2/65, 220–26. For detailed citations to garrison-government practices and principles
in Ireland under Ormonde, see my *The Governors-General: The English Army and the
Definition of the Empire, 1569–1681* (Chapel Hill, 1979), especially 43–48.

Windsor and the bedecking of his mistresses at court. Further, as Ormonde said—and his words were echoed by every English proconsul in 1676—it was impossible for him to regulate the revenue as long as collection and audit were in the hands of officers appointed in England and exempt from his control. The revenue itself was much reduced by the English acts of trade which excluded Ireland (as they had Scotland) from the trade with England's American possessions. Unless the English king and parliament adopted less selfish and exploitative attitudes towards Ireland, Ormonde concluded, not even his political success in securing a permanent revenue from the provincial parliament would make Ireland physically and politically secure, much less make it a prosperous part of England's empire. King Charles felt compelled to admit, in full council, the justice of Ormonde's arguments but he resented (all the more because they were true) the duke's implied criticisms of himself. For the rest of 1676, the king was cold to his greatest subject. At last he proved himself in some measure worthy of his "imperial crown" by recognizing both Ormonde's unequaled loyalty and unexampled ability. King Charles recommissioned the duke as governor-general of England's greatest colony and he retained Ormonde in the Irish command for the remainder of his reign.

"COFFEE AND COMMONWEALTH"

The Irish question, like every other imperial issue, was debated as fully in the coffeehouses of London as in the council chamber at Whitehall. And the public opinion of the capital, brewed in the coffeehouses, was often as important to the outcome of imperial debates as was the opinion of privy councilors. But theirs was a world view that admitted no public share in public business. That public opinion in London was critical of the king's government was equally abhorrent. That coffeehouses were the breeding grounds of critical opinion made them the targets of the first privy-council proclamation of 1676. "The Character of a Coffee-House" clarified the causes of the crown's antipathy:

> Coffee and Commonwealth begin
> Both with one letter, both came in
> Together for a Reformation
> To make's a free and Sober Nation.[9]

9. "The Character of a Coffee-House" (1665), printed in Aytoun Ellis, *The Penny Universities: A History of the Coffee-Houses* (London, 1956), 260. The official attitude is trenchantly put in a letter to Secretary Williamson, 10 November 1673, on the coffeehouse commentary about Mary of Modenta: "every carman and porter is now a statesman, and indeed the coffee-houses are good for nothing else. It was not thus when we drank nothing but sack

A public opinion theoretically inadmissible by a divine-right government and, puritan and parliamentary as it was, a public opinion ideologically abhorrent to the Anglican authoritarians of the king's government
was nevertheless very influential, even in the privy council itself. Londoners constituted one-tenth of the entire English population. Their militia outnumbered the royal army. They were the masters of most of the
nation's finance capital and the managers of its worldwide trade. They
built and owned the bulk of its merchant marine. London's opinion could
not be ignored by a government the personal weaknesses of whose head
were the talk of Garraway's Coffee House.

There, the great men of the Exchange came across the Cornhill to
strike deals and start rumors, to trade in the furs of the Hudson's Bay
Company and to criticize "the new Queen of the Amazons." This was the
duchess of Mazarin, whose addition to the royal harem was already a
matter of vast expense. The coffeehouse opinion was that "the nation,
already too sensible of the amorous excesses of their Prince, may be more
inflamed by such an accession of great expense that way." [10]

After all, as they said at the Palgrave's Head (the lawyers' house
without Temple Bar, named after the Protestant champion, Frederick of
Bohemia, the husband of the "winter queen," Elizabeth Stuart), to pay
for "that new pretender," Mazarin, Tangier would be sold to the French
king (as Dunkirk had been). "All the foreign plantations" would follow
the North African outpost into the empire of Louis XIV. So the London
bankers would be broken again, as they had been by the crown's refusal
to pay its debts in 1672, and the lord treasurer—head of the cavalier party,
symbol of fiscal responsibility, national self-respect, and resistance to
France—would be discredited. The proposed doubling of the royal
guards would, so it was said in London's coffeehouses, hardly suffice to
save a king who had alienated the best friends of English monarchy and
empire in order to purchase a used French whore.

The earl of Shaftesbury, leader of the parliamentary opposition, told
his city audience at John's Coffee House (in Smithen's Alley, a noted
venue of quack remedies) that he had himself invested £20,000 in those
plantations which might at any moment be sold to the French to pay for
the mistress Louis XIV had provided King Charles. (Such proto-whig
agitations, having been launched on seas of London coffee, crossed the
Atlantic to become rife in the West Indian colonies in 1676.) His property,
said Shaftesbury, like that of his fellow city residents, was at the mercy

---

and claret, or English beer and ale. These sober clubs produce nothing but scandalous and
censorious discourses, and at these nobody is spared." William D. Christie, ed., *Letters
Addressed from London to Sir Joseph Williamson* (Camden Society, n.s., VIII–IX, London,
1874), II, 68.
10. *C.S.P.D.* 1675–1676, 432–33.

of a government at once profligate and arbitrary, partly papist and mostly francophile. Against such misgovernment the earl contended in pamphlets that his partisans passed out over the coffee cups. These were printed and propagated by Benjamin Harris, who escaped the royalist reaction by settling his press and coffeepots in Boston. There his ideologically loaded *The Protestant Tutor* became the famous *New England Primer,* his Shaftesburian newsletter became *Public Occurrences,* the first American newspaper. Harris also printed the laws of Massachusetts "so that the people may be informed thereof." The burden of his 1676 pamphlets for Shaftesbury was that only the parliament of England could stand against the "arbitrary" administration of the triumvirs. The fifteen-year-old cavalier parliament, now bought up for the king by the treasurer, should be dissolved. A new representation of the people could then be elected. A new parliament would save property, protestantism, and political liberty, the proper constituents of English empire, from the strength of King Louis and the weakness of King Charles, from the religion of the duke and the corruption of the treasurer. Such was the republican refrain sung in the coffeehouses of the imperial metropolis:

> All monarchs I hate, and the thrones that they sit on,
> From the hector of France to the cully of Britain.

The chief of the coffeehouse poets struck even more particularly at the imperial family. He asked, "but canst thou divine when things will be mended?" He replied, "When the reign of the line of the Stuarts is ended." [11]

Coffee and commonwealth could not coexist with church and king. With a view to stamping out these coffeehouse "seminaries of sedition," there had been printed in the last *London Gazette* of the old year the proclamation of the king and council "for the Suppression of Coffee-Houses." Part of its rationale was social: coffee-drinking distracted "Tradesmen and others" from their "Lawfull Callings." But the proclamation's primary argument was political: the coffeehouses promoted "The Defamation of His Majesties Government and . . . the Disturbance of the Peace and Quiet of the Realm." By 10 January 1676 these noxious nuisances were to close forever. [12]

---

11. *C.S.P.D. 1675–1676,* 563. John Wilmot, earl of Rochester, "A Satyr on Charles II," in *The Complete Poems,* ed. David M. Vieth (New Haven, 1968), 61. Andrew Marvell, "A Dialogue Between the Two Horses" (1676), George de F. Lord, ed., *Poems on Affairs of State Augustan Satirical Verse, 1660–1714* (New Haven, 1963), I, 282. Bryant Lillywhite, *London Coffee Houses* (London, 1963), no. 635, 546. Isaiah Thomas, *The History of Printing in America* (New York, 1970), 88–89.

12. *The London Gazette,* no. 1055 (27–30 December 1675). Citations to the *Gazette,* its manuscript verse headings, and its appended pamphlets are from *The Third Volume of*

The popular reaction was almost as violent as the coffee-drinking versifiers had predicted it would be:

> When they take from the people the freedom of words,
> They teach them the sooner to fall to their swords.

The privy council found itself subjected to the same sort of abuse as its royal master had been. A "seditious and traiterous libel presented to the Board by Mr. Secretary Williamson" compared the king's councilors to his spaniels:

> His very dogs at Council Board
> Sits grave and wise as any lord.

The comparison might be just but it was unquestionably invidious. The privy council determined, on 7 January 1676, to prosecute "sundry false, infamous and scandalous libels," designed to "stirr up and dispose the mindes of his Maties Subjects to Sedition and Rebellion." This selective prosecution, however, was designed to cover the ministry's retreat on the main issue, the closing of the coffeehouses, for it now seemed that "a convulsion and discontent would surely follow" an actual closure of what were the newsrooms, the economic exchanges, "the penny universities," of the city's middling sort of people. The privy councilors therefore concluded that the licensing laws were intended to collect taxes, not control opinion. To do that, the privy council now required the coffee dispensers to post bond to permit no libels to be spread in their premises. Then the council "permitted" the coffeehouses to remain open for five months on condition of good behavior. The gazetteer versified the official view of this compromise:

> Rods lie in piss, take heed if you be wise,
> Authors and Printers of Seditious Lies.
> The Coffee-man may yet 5 months abide;
> Meanwhile his Good behaviour tyde.

But the commonwealth wits did not confuse discretion with defeat:

> Let the City drink Coffee and quietly groan;
> They that conquer'd the father won't be slaves to the son.[13]

Gazetts, With Severall Narratives, Relations, And Other Papers, relating to Intelligence of Affairs both at Home and Abroad. From July 22 1673 till June 5 1676 (London, 1673–76) and from The Fourth Volume of Gazetts . . . From June 5 1676 till December 2 1678 (London, 1676, 1677, 1678), both in the British Library.
13. Marvell, "Dialogue," Poems on Affairs of State, I, 283. C.S.P.D. 1676–1677, 97–98. P.C. 2/65, 65, 85–87, 93. The London Gazette, no. 1059 (10–13 January 1675[/6]). Like all effective

IMPERIAL ECONOMY

The privy council took up a number of other imperial problems in January 1676. Some were long neglected, others new, but all were the subject of much complaint from the city. At long last, the privy council took measures to strengthen the English colony on St. Christopher—and so the rest of the Leeward Islands settlements of the English (under their governor-general, that admirable old Irish soldier, the lieutenant colonel of the first Barbados Regiment, Sir William Stapleton)—against their French and Indian neighbors and enemies. Next, the privy council protested the failure of the Dutch to honor the recent peace treaty in places as far apart as Hamburg (where English ships had been burnt) and Surinam (where Jewish colonists had been deprived of their slaves). To deal with these imperial issues, the privy council, in the month of January 1676 alone, acted through the king's courts, the royal navy, the English ambassadors, the governors-general, and its own committees. It ordered action against French and Spanish privateers in the Channel and in the West Indies. It investigated the relations of the Royal African Company with Suffolk cloth manufacturers and with Jamaican interlopers. It sought to protect the possessions of the Hudson's Bay Company from French Canadians. It demanded the punishment of the murderer of an English subject in Lisbon. It insisted on the rights of Scots aliens to work in the London labor force. The privy council examined the misapplications (in Ireland, that is) of the Irish revenue.[14]

Having conducted a *tour d'horizon* of imperial problems, the privy councilors concluded their work for the first month of 1676 by adopting the great fiscal reform program of the lord treasurer, England's first national and imperial budget. The treasurer sought to make royal finances planned, balanced, and bureaucratic rather than haphazard, indebted, and personal. Success would render the crown financially self-sufficient, at least in peacetime, and so make the monarchy independent of the need for parliamentary subsidies for the ordinary course of government busi-

---

libels, the one about King Charles' spaniels and his councilors had some relation to truth. The king's dogs did come to council. Indeed, they came to his bedchamber. There, as the fastidious Mr. Evelyn tells us, Charles "suffered the bitches to puppy and give suck, which rendered it very offensive, and indeed made the whole court nasty and stinking." But the king was comforted by his pets, who, in return for passing attention and table scraps, gave him unfailing company and unswerving loyalty. And, unlike the king's councilors, his dogs never bit the hand that fed them. Unapt though it might be, the spaniel smile stuck to the councilors for years after 1676: "At council Board / Where every lord / Is led like a dog in a string" (1684) (*Poems on Affairs of State*, III, 479). On the salvation of the coffeehouses, see *Examen*, by Sir Roger North, quoted in Edward Forbes Robinson, *The Early History of Coffee Houses in England* (London, 1893), 167.

14. P.C. 2/65, 86–116, 123.

ness. Fiscal independence of parliament meant executive freedom from the complaints of its members, the only legitimate critics of the crown.

To accomplish these ends, the treasurer presented the privy council with a 1676 budget that halved royal pensions, salaries, and fees; provided for payment of debts in course, of public debts before private ones; and established a priority of payments: £1,000,000 for national debt service (by a factor of three the greatest cost of government in 1676); £300,000 for the navy; £212,000 for the guards and garrisons; £110,000 for pensions (of which much the largest were the queen's and the duke's); £57,200 for Tangier; £52,247 for the royal household and £36,000 for the king's privy purse; and full salaries for those essential public officials the judges and the tax collectors. Separate establishments were also put forward by the treasurer for the Leeward Islands and for Jamaica.

Yet the treasurer's plan was premised on peace, and in Virginia there was war and revolution. The war in Virginia—Bacon's Revolution—cost the crown a large part of its £100,000 annual revenue from taxes on Virginia tobacco. To repress the revolution cost in excess of another £100,000. Further, losses perhaps as great as £40,000 were incurred because of tobacco production in Maryland lost to the Indian war. In 1676 war and revolution in the Chesapeake cost the imperial crown more than its entire army did in England. So the lord treasurer's prescient plan for financial restraint and political power failed. Such was the unity of Anglo-American politics that the cost of repressing revolution in Virginia checked absolutism in England. Before the year was out, the king had to convene the parliament and ask it for aid.[15]

PURGES, PAPISTS, PROTESTANTS

While the privy council reordered the governments, reviewed the problems, and reformulated the finance of the empire in January 1676, its own ranks were cleared of the most principled opponents of the triumvirs. On 7 January, the king struck the name of the earl of Halifax from the register of the council. The earl had offended the duke of York, heir to the throne, by the fervor of his parliamentary use of that eastern compliment, "O King, live forever!" The treasurer never forgot the laugh that went up in the privy council when Halifax observed that the treasurer's rejection of a bribe had not been so stern as to forbid reapplication. It was, Halifax said, as "if a man should ask the use of another man's wife" and be refused "with great civility." As for King Charles, although he was, by all accounts, "the easiest king and best-bred man alive," and although it is

15. *Ibid.*, 111–14.

rumored that he enjoyed Halifax's company in private, his majesty was publicly offended by the earl's self-satisfied morality, vaunted political moderation, and articulate contempt for greedy courtiers, even for a king who seemed constant in nothing save the service of his own contentment. Whenever the court wished to show the country that it could command the services of the ablest and most upright statesmen, however, Halifax would be called back to the privy council. He was thus to make his mark in imperial circles by defending the rebalanced constitutions of Jamaica and Virginia in 1680, and by opposing the imposition of arbitrary government on New England in 1684. In 1676, however, the moderation of the great "trimmer" of the ship of state was not allowed to interfere with the crown's decisive assault on American independence.[16]

With Halifax was dismissed Lord Holles, the senior Presbyterian peer and the host of the opposition statesmen in London. The best remembered of these is the earl of Shaftesbury, the president of the former council of trade and plantations (whose business had been officially resumed by the privy council in 1675, and by January 1676 was actually being addressed). When he was dismissed from the privy council, Halifax fell ill, Holles retired from public life, but the sick little earl of Shaftesbury remained in the city, drinking coffee and directing the opposition to the court.

To him, King Charles sent his secretary of state, that very active if somewhat insipid privy councilor, Sir Joseph Williamson, to say that his majesty was aware of the earl's political activity in the city and felt that Shaftesbury would be wise to retire to his Dorset estates. The earl replied that the king's informants must be mistaken for he never meddled in politics, the exclusive sphere of the king's government (outside of parliament), except occasionally in jest. It was, the earl said, his plantations investments and his trading-company business that kept him in town. Surely the king did not expect him to neglect his own property, nor would the monarch restrict his subject's liberty to attend to his fiscal affairs.

To his allies in the city and his cronies in John's Coffee House, the earl was more forthright. He did not believe that there were six privy councilors who dared sign the warrant for his arrest. In fact, there seem not to have been more than two, for, despite the urgings of the king and the treasurer, Williamson refused to write such a warrant. London letters announced the victory of liberty, property, and the privileges of peers, in the usual, entirely personal, terms of the period: "Lord Shaftesbury was forbidden the Town last week, but does not obey." Contemporaries understood this to mean that the leader of the opposition remained at

16. Burnet, *History*, II, 103. Helen C. Foxcroft, *The Life and Letters of Sir George Savile, Bt., first marquis of Halifax, with a new edition of his works* (London, 1898), I, 104, 123.

large and at work against the court. So he did for a year, until a parliamentary misstep put him in the Tower and the king took his revenge for the insult of 1676. Did the earl find the tower miasmal and so ask for his release? "If my Lord thinks this an ill aire, ye king will think of some other Prison in a better air." [17]

Lesser coffeehouse wits, pamphleteers, and rumormongers were not spared the hostile attentions of the government. Their general argument was that there was a conspiracy against liberty, property, and religion by the courtiers, the Catholics, and the French. Conspiracy's tools were political oppression, religious persecution, and a standing army. This conspiracy theory took on extreme forms during 1676, forms that were adopted, if not invented, by Shaftesbury and the opposition in England to excite the campaign against the court, forms that are remembered as "the Popish Plot"—the recurrent nightmare of the English in the seventeenth century—forms that encouraged opposition to the crown across the empire.

The most extreme form of the evolving plot story held that the duke of York had killed or was about to kill the king and flee to France to obtain the help of the French army in a new English civil war. This was the story that gained credence in the colonies in 1676 and encouraged both the independent New Englanders and the Baconian revolutionaries of Virginia. More true and more comic, but not very flattering to the king's majesty, was the report that the royal drab (read "duchess") least in favor with the concupiscent King Charles had taken the royal exchequer with her to France. This report acutely anticipated the change in Charles II's chief mistresses. Barbara Villiers, duchess of Cleveland, displaced by Mazarin in King Charles' affections (and financially despoiled, if not physically exhausted, by John Churchill), left Whitehall for Paris in April 1676. She took with her the remains of a royal fortune. And all these rumors also reflected the absolutist and, in the case of the king and the duke, the Catholic and the French aspirations of the imperial executive.[18]

As popish absolutism was the opposition's phobia, so protestant dissent was the crown's. In the view not just of the king and the duke, but also of the lord treasurer's anglican partisans, the dissenters' conventicles were even more dangerous than the coffeehouses, for criticism of the crown at the conventicles was rooted in religious belief, that of the coffeehouses only in their customers' caffeinated consciousness. On 18 Feb-

---

17. *C.S.P.D. 1675–1676*, 559–61, 563. Sir J. Lowther to Daniel Flemming, 22 February 1675 [/6], in Historical Manuscripts Commission, *12th Report, Appendix, Part VII, the Manuscripts of S. H. Le Fleming, Esq.* (London, 1890), 125. K. H. D. Haley, *The First Earl of Shaftesbury* (Oxford, 1968), 403–6. Williamson's minute in the foreign committee, 3 August 1677, S.P. 104/179, 146.

18. In addition to the citations in note 17, above, see P.C. 2/65, 285.

ruary 1676, therefore, the privy council summoned to Whitehall all the officers of the city corporation and all of the justices of the peace for the counties of London and Middlesex to receive orders for "the Suppressing of Conventicles." Their previous negligence in repressing religious dissent, the councilors told the citizens, demonstrated "little affection to the Government of the Church of England, which his Majesty is pleased to maintain and Support." [19]

The persecution of protestants, pursued as it was not just in London but nationwide, and against individual ministers as well as against public meetings, was seen in the empire as it was at home to be the precursor of popery rather than the defense of anglicanism. These former fears were dramatically confirmed at Easter 1676 when the duke of York refused even to attend the services of the Church of England. And James refused to give his permission for his daughter's confirmation in the established church. Yet, directed by the committee for foreign affairs, the privy council ostensibly exercised an even-handed enmity against all the enemies of the national church. As well as attacking protestant conventicles, it insisted upon "hindering the growth of Popery" and so closed to Englishmen the chapels of the Catholic diplomats and the queen, arrested the publishers of Catholic books, and confiscated their stock.[20]

Domestic divisions in the kingdom made religious uniformity impossible overseas. Yet, during 1676, Lord Treasurer Danby tried to extend the doctrines of church and king from England to its empire. In the privy council, the symbol of this policy was the bishop of London. Henry Compton, a cavalryman turned cleric, was "a property to Lord Danby and was turned by him as he pleased." He was named to the privy council. Compton's taking the Presbyterian lord Holles' seat could not have been improved upon as a symbol of his patron's religious politics. Then Compton's diocesan jurisdiction was extended by the council, first to Tangier and afterwards to every other colony. The bishop found, however, that only in Virginia and Barbados had the anglican aspects of the Restoration prevailed. Every other colony retained the religious coloration of its colonization or of its conquest as part of "ye Dominions of his Maty of Great Britain." Thus Catholicism was powerful in Maryland and in Tangier, and popery also held a place in the duke's province, New York. Puritanism still prevailed—more in attitude than institutionally—in Cromwell's conquest, Jamaica. Of course the Congregational dictatorship character-

19. P.C. 2/65, 122–23, 393.
20. Newsletters, 22 February, 7 March 1675[/6], in *Manuscripts of Le Fleming*, 125. P.C. 2/65, 333, 336. The cabinet's instruction on these measures—which also pointed to another rampant racial, religious, and military English phobia by excluding Irish officers from Whitehall—dated 2 July 1676, are in S.P. 104/179, 45v; S.P. 29/366, 104; *C.S.P.D. 1676–1677*, 201.

ized the New English commonwealths: Massachusetts, Plymouth, and Connecticut.[21]

The established Church of England occasionally fulfilled its Erastian mission in Barbados and in Virginia. Its militant ministers demonstrated their loyalty to the king's sacred majesty at the head of royalist forces in the civil wars of 1652 and 1676. Elsewhere, however, the Church of England's legal monopoly of religion and its divine-right royalism, challenged from both extremes as these ideals were even in the metropolis, had small prospect of success in the larger English world viewed from Whitehall. The Church of England could never become the church of England's empire. That the treasurer, at the head of the party of church and king, devoutly desired an anglican empire only serves to show, once again, how great was the gap that divided him from the Stuart princes, the king and the duke. The sovereign and his heir, by policy if not by conviction, were religious tolerationists even more in the empire than in England. In the colonies, the royal brothers were free from the predominance of the church, and they wielded overseas an authority far less fettered than it was in England. The duke and the king therefore ordered their viceroys to tolerate all religions privately practiced and peaceably conducted. Under the later Stuarts, "Greater Britain" became truly tolerant. Great Britain did not.

THE CROWN AND THE CORPORATION

Their religious differences did not deeply divide the triumvirs in 1676 or much affect the work of their privy council, because corporate self-government, far more than religious dissent, seemed to challenge the monarchical monopoly of politics. To counter self-government in London, Virginia, or "Boston" (the privy council's politically limiting, corporate label for the Massachusetts Bay Company), early in the year 1676 orders-in-council imposed on corporate officers oaths of allegiance, and enjoined political obedience on all officials. These oaths and admonitions were followed everywhere in the empire by the reduction of corporate privilege, beginning, on the last day of May 1676, with the privy council's decision to suspend its approval of Virginia's charter. In June, the privileges of London's citizens were brought to the unfavorable attention of the privy council by the speech of Francis Jenks, a linen salesman from Cornhill.

Speaking to the common hall, the assembly of the city's freemen and the wellhead of English popular politics, Jenks recalled the horrific fire of London and he reminded his fellow citizens that a series of enor-

21. *Manuscripts of Le Fleming*, 123, 155, 357. Burnet, *History*, II, 90–91.

mously destructive and apparently mysterious fires had recently swept not only London's Southwark section but several provincial towns as well. Now, "all the Citys Burroughs, Towns Corporations and places of principal trade throughout the whole kingdom are perpetually in danger, so that no rational . . . man amongst us can promise himself, his wife, his children, or estate, one night's security. . . ." Everyone but the government seemed to know, Jenks said, that these incendiaries were French papist terrorists, "wicked, hellish, instruments hired to fire our houses." Jenks went on to say, to the applause of the Londoners, that it was French restrictions on English imports, French dumping of textiles in England, French conquest of the trading cities of the Spanish Netherlands, of the United Provinces, and of Germany, and French capture of English merchant vessels, that had together destroyed English trade and so injured every citizen of the English metropolis. "Their privateers daily take our Merchant's ships, plunder others, strip, imprison and torment our seamen to the great discouragement of our *English navigation* and almost ruin of the Merchant," Jenks added, and he said that these grievances too the government had not even addressed, much less redressed. "Worse than all the rest" was the danger within the English government itself. The life of the king was menaced and the survival of the protestant religion was threatened by the presence of a popish heir, a bigoted absolutist, backed by France, and by Rome.[22]

French and Catholic aggression against English property and their infiltration of the king's government, Jenks concluded, meant that only a dissolution of the treasurer's corrupt and long-standing parliament and a fresh election of the representative of the nation could save the lives, properties, and privileges of Englishmen, in both the city and the country, from the conspiracy to "make us a province, and tributary to France, and subdue the Nation by a French army, or to the papal authority." Therefore, Jenks said, the common hall must demand that the city petition the king for a dissolution of the old parliament and the election of a new one. This fear of Franco-Catholic conspiracy, and this prescription of a popular parliament to combat it, advocated in London in 1676, was

---

22. P.C. 65/243. Entries Relating to Virginia, vol. 2, Colonial Office, Class 5, vol. 1355, Public Record Office (hereafter cited as C.O. 5/1355), 17b; *C.S.P.D. 1676–1677*, 449, 450, 476. For printing "An Account of the Proceedings at Guild Hall, London, at the Folke-Moot, or Common Hall, the 24th of June 1676," the privy council ordered the printer's press broken and the printer himself prosecuted for seditious libel "with the utmost severity of Law" (P.C. 2/65, 300). Mayor of Lancaster to mayor of Kendall, 13 June 1676, newsletter, 27 June 1676, in *Manuscripts of Le Fleming*, 127. "Jenk's Speech spoken in a Common Hall, the 24th of June 1679" (date *sic* for publication of 1676 speech on expiration of the licensing act in December 1679) in *Tracts*, I, 1, 33, British Library. Coincidentally, the Southwark fire, the conspiracy rumors, and "New England the Depty Govr Letter" were discussed together by the cabinet on 18 June 1676 (S.P. 29/366, 99; also in *C.S.P.D. 1675–1677*, 165).

accepted in Jamestown and St. Mary's, New York and Port Royal. It became the common cause of the royal government's opponents everywhere in the empire.[23]

Royal government everywhere reacted against such agitators. As Bacon was arrested in Virginia, so Jenks was jailed in London. The warrant was signed by no fewer than twenty privy councilors. Yet the royal council met mercantile opposition in London as its counterpart had in Virginia's capital. London merchants, equally rich and dissaffected (the metropolitan equivalents of Bacon's backers, Jamestown's Richard Lawrence and William Drummond), directed Jenks' successful appeal to the ancient law, that of Richard II and of Edward III, against the present prerogative of Charles II. To support the ancient law and modern liberty, the elder Nathaniel Bacon's parliamentary discourse was reprinted in London in 1676. And the London merchants posted Jenks' bail and held him up to his fellow citizens in the urban centers of public opinion as the champion of English liberty, protestant religion, private property, and free parliaments.

This popular agitation was part of a coordinated protest both in the English and in the overseas provinces of the empire. It predicted, it even defined, the crises of Popish Plot and Exclusion. In 1676, however, popular agitation was repressed by the normally prevalent powers of the imperial government: the monarchy's monopoly of professional military force, built up over the preceding decade in British guards and garrisons, now extended in America; the crown's increased control of corporations, first in England, then elsewhere in the empire.

In London, the king personally lobbied the aldermen (a much more courtly group than the citizens of common hall and common council) to secure the election of a biddable lord mayor. The king also nominated a more pliable recorder. When King Charles condescended to dine with the city fathers, they moderated their protests. To do otherwise, as one of them said, would be as if they had invited his majesty to share a roast with them and then beaten him with the spit. Regaled and reinforced in the metropolis (and having launched the Virginia expedition and remodeled that dominion's government), King Charles left Whitehall for Newmarket and the races on 3 October 1676. But the king took no chances with the temper of the city, the decisive fact in the politics of empire. He commissioned that constant loyalist (and assiduous privy councilor) the earl of Craven "to Command in Chief during Our absence all such Troops [elements of four Guards regiments] . . . which Wee have found necessary to leave behind for the Securing the peace and quiet of the City, and

---

23. Shaftesbury's comment on conspiracy, made on the occasion of Danby's proposed Test, is in Burnet, *History*, II, 76.

the Suppressing Tumultuous Meetings and Disorders . . . and in case of Resistance, where the Civil powers shall not be sufficient . . . to execute the same by Killing, slaying. . . ."[24]

To make the civil power more biddable, if not more sufficient, when the king returned from the races he dictated a proclamation of his privy council that compelled every city officer not only to swear allegiance to him as king and to pledge obedience to him as head of the Church of England, but also to renounce the doctrine of taking arms against the king's person under cover of his authority and to denounce the design of the Solemn League and Covenant to make Great Britain Presbyterian. Next the court disqualified several of its opponents as candidates in the election for the common council. The oligarchs of the opposition expressed their anger over electoral restrictions in language very like that used to describe the Berkeleyan barons disqualified by Colonel Jeffreys. Both sets of would-be oligarchs used the common country form put forward by Shaftesbury in opposition to Danby's proposed loyalty test: "it was a disinheriting men of the major part of their birthright, to do anything that would shut them out from their votes in electing," and electing whom they pleased, to public assemblies.[25]

Commanding allegiance and restricting election, the court did in London in December what in October it had ordered done in Virginia. The results were the reverse of the royal intention. Discrimination in London led to the loss of a loan for the king. Repression in Virginia cost the crown £100,000. The fiscal crisis that followed—oddly combined with the treasurer's assurance that, despite the crown's cash crisis, he had bought a balance of the commons' votes in support of increased royal revenues— led to the order of the king-in-council, dated 15 December 1676, that the parliament meet on 15 February 1676/7.

THE RIGHT USE OF PARLIAMENTS

In the interim, each of the triumvirs of 1676 sought parliamentary support from his particular constituents by addressing their special concerns. So doing, they rehearsed the public issues of the nascent empire. The lord treasurer promised the city bankers fair interest on the national debt. He

24. C.S.P.D. 1676–1677, 388–89. S.P. 44/29, 171.
25. P.C. 2/65, 393. C.S.P.D. 1676–1677, 475. Burnet, History, II, 74, to which compare the Berkeleyan protests in Coventry Ms. 78, 134, 135, 168–70, and, more particularly, lord Culpeper's remarks in behalf of the deprived Virginia councilors, that the royal restriction on their election "barred the free Liberty of choosing whom they think can best represent them" (Culpeper to William Blathwayt, Blathwayt Papers, XXVII, 2, Colonial Williamsburg, Inc.). Further discussion of this issue appears in Webb, The Governors-General, especially 365, 401.

THE FACES OF POWER, 1676:
KING, CABINET, CAVALIERS
ILLUSTRATIONS FOR BOOK TWO

"The King of England would be ugly if he were a private gentleman, but because he is the King he manages to pass as a well-made man." This 1676 portrait, after Lely, of King Charles II (1630–1685) shows the swarthy, black-haired, big-nosed, deeply lined monarch. He habitually wore a curly black wig which, as he complained, cast him as a villain (the king was most annoyed by the theatrical convention that invariably put heroes in light-colored wigs, such as his younger brother wore). Yet "a certain smiling look coming from the width of his mouth so greatly clears and softens the roughness of his features that he pleaseth rather than terrifies."

Quick, witty, intelligent, blessed with a prodigious memory, a gifted amateur of warship design and of fortification, King Charles was the greatest politician of his century. When excited, as he was by the prospect of French funds early in 1676 or by the potential loss of Virginia tobacco revenues at the end of the year, the king could do everything expected of an absolute monarch: "none of his Council could reason more closely upon matters of State, and he would often by fits outdo his ministers in application and diligence." Nonetheless, King Charles let "the love of Ease exercise an entire Sovereignty in his thoughts." While his loathing of strife and strenuosity was the key to Charles II's political success—"a Specifick to preserve us in Peace for his Own Time"—his laziness and hatred of business meant that forward policies, in the empire especially, were the work of his ministers. The result, their apparent "Superiority," was because the king "chose rather to be eclipsed than to be troubled."

Yet the king, dependent as he was on them, "lived with his Ministers as he did with his Mistresses: he used them but he was not in love with them." Chief among Charles II's ministers was his brother, James duke of York (1633–1701). As this unfinished sketch of the duke in 1676 (by Lely) suggests, James Stuart was as fair as Charles was dark. As aquiline as the king was bulbous, the duke impressed observers with "a certain fierceness that substitutes the idea of a severe prince for the air of a fine gentleman," so much the mark of the king. James was as courageous and famous a commander on the battlefield as Charles was an active and excited lover in the bedroom. (Even there the king's "tenderness" contrasted with the duke's "vicious brutality.") The duke was an active, attentive, assiduous administrator, whose subordinates gave good service (by and large) in return for sure rewards (or as sure as princes provide). The king was notoriously averse to business and was as ill served as serving (with exceptions mainly noted here). To all appearances, then, James was far more the king than his brother, especially in 1676. King Charles' natural jealousy and dislike of the duke was multiplied by his contempt for James' bigotry, inflexibility, credulity, and irrationality. Charles II would have applied to himself and enjoined on his brother Shelburne's saying: "indolence, when it is not the result of weakness or vice is a very great virtue."

For all their contrasting characters, appearance, and abilities, the royal brothers agreed about the essentials of imperial politics. They were not just monarchists, but absolutists, allied secretly (most recently in February 1676) with their cousin Louis XIV of France, and publicly sympathetic with the sovereign pretensions of their nephew, William of Orange. Nonetheless, the Stuarts competed for influence and income overseas with both France and the Netherlands. The apparent paradox of simultaneous monarchical alliances and national rivalries was easily encompassed by these sovereigns. They did not measure their personal and princely requisites by political and national needs. "Charles Stuart could be bribed against the King" was an observation of more than venial applicability. All these princes were personally sovereign, preferring to rule at home, as in their empires, by edict and armies rather than by laws and legislatures. Nonetheless, tradition and taxation bound them all, in varying degrees, to civilian politicians and representative parliaments. Monarchical dependence upon imperial incomes, most marked in England, further compelled a certain princely attention to national interests. Here they were closely allied to princely prerogatives. In the case of provinces especially, and in 1676 in particular, the interests of the rulers and their realm were one.

Therefore, the king and the duke acted on an imperial program through a ministerial intermediary, a nationalist politician, the earl of Danby. The lord treasurer was set the impossible task of making absolutism not just popular (that he could have done if he had been permitted to attack France; instead he had to witness the king's and duke's renewal of their clientage to their cousin Louis) but profitable and parliamentary as well. The empire—its customs income, its political opportunities, its national aggrandizement—offered Danby opportunities to reconcile absolutism with nationalism, align the prerogative with patriotism, and finance monarchy without parliament. Danby, in keeping with the peculiar wisdom of his nation, "chose rather to make the War in another Country, then to keep all well at home." Such were the stakes which meant that the crisis of 1676 in America paradoxically cost both crown and colonies their independence: the crown from the parliament, the colonies from the crown.

Danby, "that great false jewel," was execrated by the parliamentary opposition "for taking pains and telling lies" for the crown, but he was well rewarded by the king. Sour grapes impelled Halifax to observe that King Charles "seldom gave profusely, but where he expected some unreasonable thing, good rewards were material evidences against those who received them." Danby (1631–1712) ap-

King Charles II

James, duke of York

Thomas, earl of Danby

John, duke of Lauderdale

Prince Rupert

William, earl of Craven

pears here, painted by Lely's studio, in the garments of royal
gratitude, the garter robes he first donned for his installation at Windsor in April 1676. He exhibits at length the extraordinarily attenuated
appearance of which the enemies of his wholesale purchase of parliamentarians made such fun:

> He is as stiff as any stake,
> And leaner, Dick, than any rake;
> Envy is not so pale.
> And though by selling of us all
> He wrought himself into Whitehall,
> Looks like a bird of jail.

If Danby looked odd, Lauderdale was grotesque. It is not surpris-
ing that so few pictures of the man survive. This brilliant miniature
by Cooper shows the duke a dozen years prior to 1676. It seems,
however, to accord with the description of Lauderdale (1616–1682)
by Bishop Burnet, who knew the tyrant of Scotland intimately and
for many years. Burnet's contrast of Lauderdale's physical grossness
with his intellectual acuity bears repeating. "He made a very ill
appearance," writes the bishop of the duke. "He was very big. His
hair was red, hanging oddly about him. His tongue was too big for
his mouth, which made him bedew all that he talked to, and his
whole manner was rough and boisterous, and very unfit for a court.
He was very learned, not only in Latin, in which he was a master,
but in Greek and Hebrew. He had read a great deal in divinity, and
almost all the historians, ancient and modern; so that he had great
materials."

Lauderdale had acquired these great materials in a hard school:
the ten years he spent in prison after he was captured fighting for
Charles II at the battle of Worcester. From him, Lauderdale's loyalty
never wavered. By him, the duke's rewards were ample. For him,
the secretary of state for Scotland kept that kingdom subdued by
unremitting, ever-increasing, more and more domesticated military
force. Finally, age forced him to resign and to retire to the spas and
to his London mansion, Ham House, which preserves to this day the
decoration he gave it in 1676, the year in which Lauderdale was the
only minister, apart from the duke of York, whom the king trusted
with the French treaty. A brilliant buffoon, Lauderdale was hated by
many and loved by none and he returned their sentiments. Burnet
expressed an opinion universal (outside the cabinet council) when
he called Lauderdale "the coldest friend and the violentest enemy I
ever knew."

Coldness was no part of the character of the cavalier Prince Rupert (1619–1682), count Palatine, duke of Bavaria and of Cumberland,
and (as he is here portrayed by the studio of Lely, c. 1670) knight of
the garter. He was, as this official portrait may not entirely suggest,
"tall in stature, slight and slender of figure, has a noble appearance
but is not handsome, his face being long, gaunt, dark, and disfigured
by the smallpox."

Prince Rupert's career on the battlefield, where, among many other accomplishments, he was arguably the most brilliant commander in the first English civil war; in colonization, where, closest to 1676, he founded the Hudson's Bay Company; in the navy, where he commanded at sea and at the admiralty during the Dutch wars; in the laboratory, where in mathematics, metallurgy, and mezzotinto engraving Rupert was a virtuoso—all made the prince something of a hero to a younger generation of cavalier officers, the more so as his antipathy to the French as England's failed allies and his supplanting of the Catholic duke as admiral made him attractive to men of "country" sympathies.

In 1676, as its constable, the prince was supervising the reconstruction of Windsor Castle—"it was the only palace easy to fortify"—and his apartments there were (as their replacements remain) an eye-opening armory, a place of pilgrimage for such second-generation cavaliers as Major Edmund Andros.

The diminutive earl of Craven was a miniature of the Palatine prince. Craven's portrait is ascribed to Prince Rupert's sister, Louise, and is dated 1647, fifteen years after Craven (1606–1697) had entered the Palatine service. In that service, Craven had shared every turn of military fortune with Prince Rupert. To it he would welcome Edmund Andros. Like his prince and his protégé, Craven came to England at the restoration of the Stuart sovereigns and, also like them, on the death of Elizabeth of Bohemia in 1662 he transferred his services to her nephews, Charles and James. Under King Charles, in 1676, the earl was lord lieutenant of Middlesex and Sussex, lieutenant general, colonel of the Coldstream Guards, commissioner for Tangier, and proprietor of Carolina. To the Stuarts, Craven was loyal to the end, becoming Rupert's executor and guardian of his daughter in 1682. Finally, on the evening of 27 December 1688, in personal command of the Coldstream Guards then on duty in the capital, the earl refused to admit the Dutch troops to St. James or Whitehall. Personally ordered to dismiss the Guards by the defeated king, James II, Craven retired from public life, but he lived on until his ninety-first year. A year later, in 1698, Sir Edmund Andros retired from Virginia. The cavalier era of imperial command had ended.

These portraits are reproduced by permission of the National Portrait Gallery, London. The quoted comments about their subjects are largely from the earl of Halifax's "Character of King Charles II"; Lorenzo Magalotti's *Relazione d'Inghilterra*, trans. W. E. Middleton Knowles; and Bishop Burnet's *History of My Own Time*, ed. Osmund Airy, all cited in the text. Additional comments are taken from the delightful collection of characters assembled by Andrew Browning, ed., *English Historical Documents 1660–1714* (New York, 1953), 900; George de F. Lord *et al.*, eds., *Poems on Affairs of State: I. 1660–1678* (New Haven, 1963), 254; Antonia Fraser, *Royal Charles* (New York, 1979), 328; and Sir Lewis Namier, *England in the Age of the American Revolution* (London, 1963), 36.

assured country members "that the King to his knowledge had no design but to preserve the religion and government as established by lawe." The duke of York rallied old Clarendonians, new imperialists, and would-be authoritarians to oppose any parliamentary limitation on his succession to the throne. More positively, he asked the elements of his "interest" to promote a parliamentary grant of money for the royal navy. The royal duke also added Ireland to Virginia on the list of dominions for whose grievances he publicly promised redress. King Charles himself took time to tell worried commoners that "it is said . . . that I intend to govern by an army and by arbitrary power, to lay aside Parlaments, and to raise money by other ways. But every man, nay thos that say it most, knows it is false." Such agitators, said the king, were either rabid commonwealths-men seeking revolution or squeaky wheels wanting grease. Each of the triumvirs used these closet conversations with the commons to sound the depth of the popular demand for a war with France, the duke to resist it, the king to exploit it, and the treasurer to build upon it the national, even imperial, triumph of a well-armed, well-financed, and popular monarchy.[26]

To the disgust of the privy council, these closetings were soon the talk of the coffeehouses. Their proprietors' licenses were extended (on 17 January 1676/7) only on condition that parliament not be discussed on their premises. This privy-council limitation was not merely futile, it was defeated by the government itself. On 19 February 1676/7 crowds of coffee consumers considered *The London Gazette*'s own edition of "His Majesties Gracious Speech, Together with the Lord Chancellors To Both Houses of Parliament." These speeches opened the parliamentary session and vividly sketched the courtly lineaments of Anglo-American politics in 1676.[27]

King Charles called on the legislators to resume "the right use of Parliaments." Parliament, he said, should honor the bargain by which, in

26. P.C. 2/65, 417, 422, 461. Newsletter, 13 February 1676[/7], in *Manuscripts of Le Fleming*, 132. *C.S.P.D. 1676–1677*, 541–42. James J. Cartwright, ed., *The Memoirs of Sir John Reresby . . . 1634–1689* (London, 1875), 106–8. Andrew Browning, ed., *The Memoirs of Sir John Reresby . . . 1634–1689* (Glasgow, 1936), 110–12. Whatever the king's intent, the treasurer pointed out that once an army was raised it could be used to coerce parliament (Andrew Browning, *Thomas Osborne, earl of Danby and duke of Leeds, 1632–1712* [Glasgow, 1944–51], II, 68). And Danby's disclaimer—that "to his knowledge" the king intended no attack on the constitution—was significant, given the existence of the Treaty of Dover. By it, King Charles promised to undo both parliamentary government and the anglican monopoly with the aid of Louis XIV's army and subsidy.

27. *The London Gazette*, no. 1174 (15–19 February 1676[/7]), appendix. The skillful editing of the *Gazette* appears in its masterly compression of the king's speech (for which see *A Collection of the Parliamentary Debates In England From the Year M, DC, LXVIII To The Present Time* [Dublin, London, 1741], I, 188–94) and in its association with responses to the speech from across the empire.

return for his preservation of the protestant religion in the shape of the Church of England and for his protection of his subjects' property and liberty, parliament granted him the monetary means to these governmental ends. In particular, the king required funds to repair and enlarge the navy and an extension of the excise to support his government. As the work of his privy council had been designed to demonstrate, these parliamentary grants would underwrite such unquestioned royal responsibilities as the restoration of the king's peace and imperial commerce in Virginia and the protection of English merchant shipping from French privateers and Barbary pirates. Those perverse legislators who would obstruct these proper uses of parliament, by fomenting quarrels between the houses so that the government's business could not be done, who would stint supplies to the crown by exciting jealousies in the people about the king's intentions, those were the real enemies of parliaments, not, said Charles II, himself.

The chancellor amplified his master's message and specified its political meaning. In a world at war, he emphasized, England was at peace, in church and state, at home and abroad. Domestic peace dominated the chancellor's speech to the legislature, for about his majesty's foreign affairs the parliament (theoretically) could have nothing to do. The chancellor complained, therefore, of the domestic enemies of the king's peace. These men recalled past political passions and rejected the royal pardon for old offenses against royal government. The king had granted oblivion in England, the chancellor observed (just as the king was pardoning repentant rebels in Virginia even as the chancellor spoke). Yet malignant men would now reincite civil war by reviving invidious political discriminations. "Away with those ill-meant Distinctions between the Court and the Country, between the Natural and the Politique Capacity" of the king, cried the chancellor: "Nothing Deserves the Name of Peace, but Unity."

The king's plea for parliamentary propriety and the chancellor's call for political peace (together with the duke's organization and the treasurer's bribes) met with remarkable success in the spring of 1676/7. The king got his grants and the opposition got jailed. Shaftesbury and his noble coadjutors sought to make the parliamentary session seem illegal, and so to render the court's corruption ineffective, by securing a resolution that parliament was dissolved by the long prorogation. Appealing to "the statutes of 4th and 36th of Edward III" cited in Jenks' speech in June 1676, the opposition leadership demanded dissolution and asked the king "immediately to call New Parliament." So doing, the opponents of the court challenged the present parliament's sense of self-preservation. The demand for dissolution also threatened parliament's determination to act against France by rebuilding the navy. Pressing against these sentiments, the opposition lords were sent to the Tower. The king himself, having gotten his grants, dismissed the parliament. He took the occasion of an address from the commons (that he act to save the Netherlands from the French) as an invasion of his own prerogative in foreign affairs and so he prorogued the parliament at the end of May 1677. But by the end of this parliamentary session, it appeared that 1676 had witnessed the triumph of the crown throughout the empire.[28]

To a pacified metropolis and an enriched royal exchequer came the loyal tributes of distant provinces to commemorate the king's birthday and the monarchy's restoration. The coffeehouse audiences heard reports from Edinburgh of popular celebrations of the royal anniversary and the king's peace, "whilst the rest of the World lies bathed in blood, and distracted by a thousand confusions." The East India Company reported its commercial and territorial gains for the empire of Charles II and he responded by knighting the company's Bantam agent. From Virginia, *The London Gazette* had already printed Admiral Sir John Berry's dispatches of March 1676/7, with a poetic précis:

> Virginia sees our Fleet, our Fleet sees that
> Those half-Sunk Tumults may soon lie flat.

Now the Virginia Coffee House rejoiced in Colonel Jeffreys' reports, on the occasion of "His Majesties most happy Birth and Restoration," of rebellion repressed and natives pacified:

> Virginia's frolick ends, those Troubles cease
> Her hairbrain'ed Tumults now conclude in peace.
> The Savage Natives too at last grow tame:
> New Amity puts out that Indian flame.[29]

"Virginia's Frolick"

Lelse

ondon read of the outbreak of Virginia's "Indian flame" in the first *Gazette* of the new year, 1675/6. In the same week, the crisis of New

28. Newsletter of 17 February 1676[/7], in *Manuscripts of Le Fleming*, 132–33. Haley, *Shaftesbury*, 412–22. Yet "the coffee houses still maintained the point" (North, *Examen*, quoted in Robinson, *Coffee-Houses*, 169n).
29. Manuscript verse glosses of accounts in *The London Gazette*, no. 1190 (12–16 April), and no. 1221 (30 July–2 August 1677).

England's war with the Algonquins was the talk of privy council and coffeehouses alike, as were Barbados' hurricane and slave revolt. It was as the privy councilors prepared to renew the English empire's struggle with the French (and Indians) in the Leeward Islands (and in Hudson's Bay) and with the Moors in Tangier, that it learned, with the rest of the metropolis, that the natives had risen in Virginia. "More Devils yet?" the *Gazette* asked, "is Hell broke loose below? / Virginia plagu'd with cross-grained Indians too?"[30]

The *Gazette* story, as usual, was based upon a more detailed report acquired from merchant sea captains by a seaport correspondent of the junior secretary of state. The secretary's office released some of the story through the printed *Gazette,* more through handwritten newsletters, and all of it to the interested privy councilors. They found such informal reports unsatisfactory and complained to Virginia's governor, Sir William Berkeley, that they had had no official account of his government since 1671. That Berkeley was unwilling to meet the growing concern of the privy council in imperial affairs, and that the council's information on the colonial emergency came not from the governor but from Williamson's correspondents, from the Virginia agents, or from dissident royal officials in Virginia, went far to explain the privy council's judgments, first, that Sir William was not up to the increasing demands of the imperial government, and second, that he was to some extent to blame for the debacle in the Old Dominion.

Three months passed before, on 14 April 1676, ships making port in Plymouth from Virginia reported to the secretary of state that Colonel Washington had attacked the Susquehanna fort. The upshot of that botched attack was related at court the next day: "the Indians had been too hard for the English killing near 200 of them with a loss of 30 of theirs." Acting on this report, the agents of the Virginia Assembly came to the privy council. The agents asked the councilors to encourage the colonists to defend Virginia against the Indians, by ordering the chancellor to pass under the great seal of England the charter of assembly privileges and anti-proprietary measures which the colonial agents had negotiated with the privy council during the preceding year.[31]

The agents' request provoked the full privy council to a noteworthy debate on imperial policy in its Virginia context. The debate demonstrated how thoroughly the Virginia agents themselves had absorbed the prerogative tone of the privy council that helped end American indepen-

30. Manuscript verse head for an account in *The London Gazette,* no. 1058 (6–10 January 1675[/6]); P.C. 2/65, 87–89. For the assemblage of and reactions to this account, see *C.S.P.D. 1675–1676,* 490; Colonial Office, General File, vol. 36, Public Record Office (hereafter cited as C.O. 1/36), 80.

31. S.P. 29/380, 242. *C.S.P.D. 1676–1677,* 73, 74, 80.

dence in 1676. Responding to the challenge of the lord chancellor, the Virginia agents insisted that their assembly would never use the privileges they asked from the crown to "Justle with the Royal Prerogative." They only sought to incorporate the governor, council, and burgesses so that they could buy out the private proprietors to whom the king had granted much of Virginia's soil and government (an imperial example of Halifax's complaint that "Charles Stuart would be bribed aginst the King"). By incorporation "(a word wee are by noe means in love with)," the Virginians said that they did not intend to acquire the self-government beloved of English municipalities and New England colonies, but, rather, to secure land titles and so to reduce unrest within and against the king's government in Virginia and to encourage the colonists to defend the king's territory and their own from the natives. The whole aim of the proposed charter, the assembly agents argued, was to guarantee that "Virginia shall have noe other dependance, but only upon the Crowne of England" and so, by being obedient to the crown, earn its protection.[32]

The colonial representatives responded to council queries with a self-contradictory set of disclaimers and demands. These political contradictions were produced by the Anglo-American paradox of 1676: a novel need for physical protection and governmental legitimacy bred new promises of economic and political obedience to the crown, but a long tradition of practical independence stimulated calls for continued autonomy from England. Promising obedience, the Virginia agents told the privy councilors that, by the proposed charter, "we doe not intend or hope for any unlimited power to be granted us, or such as may lessen his Maties Authority in that Countrey." Nor, said the agents of the colonial ruling class, would their peers "presume to nominate to his Matie a Governr and Councell or refuse any that he shall please to send us." Nonetheless, they added elements of autonomy, asking that the king order his viceroy to reside in the colony and that he commission as his governor-general's deputy a Virginia councilor and landowner. Appointing resident governors-general and local deputies was already imperial practice and, as the colonial agents told privy councilors disturbed by Sir William Berkeley's silence, charter provisions about the executive were only to ensure that "His Matie may have the better account of his Countrey . . . and that his subjects may not be left (in case of the Govrs absence) to strangers."

In contrast to these submissions to imperial authority, however, the Virginians of 1676 also made the demand fundamental to the reacquisition

32. For the debate of 19 April 1676, see P.C. 2/65, 187; W. L. Grant and James Munro, eds., *Acts of the Privy Council of England, Colonial Series*, vol. I, A.D. 1613–1680 [hereafter cited as *A.P.C.C.*] (Hereford, 1908), no. 1074; C.O. 1/36, 84; and, most important, the memorandum in Coventry Ms. 77, 46 ff.

of American independence in 1776. They asked for chartered assurances from the crown that there would be "Noe taxe of Imposition layd on the people of Virginia, but . . . by the Grand Assembly." Yet this was a limited claim. It only reserved local taxation to the local representatives, for the Virginia agents in this debate repeatedly pledged colonial observation of the acts of trade and the colonists promised payment to the crown of the duties authorized by acts of parliament. Still, the association of taxation with representation in a local legislature was fundamental to present colonial autonomy and future American independence, and it was justified on grounds that nullified any imperial right to rule, that is, that "both the Acquisition and defence of this countrey hath been . . . at the countries charge." Besides, the assembly agents said, the cost of the colony's government was also met by local taxes.

The agents argued, nonetheless, that the assembly's request to be recognized by the crown as the colony's self-sufficient, authoritative, and omni-competent legislature, was designed only to increase the authority of assembly acts within the colony, not to reduce royal suzerainty over Virginia. The veto of Virginia statutes by the king-in-council, as well as by the king's governor-general in the colony, was admitted by the colonial agents. Assessing the balance between autonomy and obedience which the royal charter would mandate for Virginia, the agents insisted that the proposed government was "in a humble subordination representing and agreeing to the English monarchy." The king-in-council thereupon ordered the lord chancellor to pass the Virginia charter.

BLAND'S BUSINESS

The privy council's consideration of the Virginia charter was but one of the issues of the great imperial debate of 19 April 1676. Also on that day the full council conducted a lengthy review of the Guernsey garrison's contempt for civil authority "under pretence they are Soulders & noe ways Subjects to the Civill Jurisdictions." (After recalling the errant garrison commander, the island's deputy governor, to a hearing at Whitehall, the council decided, as it nearly always did in these cases, that the king's officer had been unduly provoked by upstart civilians.) The privy council also debated the future of Newfoundland—whether as a settled colony under a military governor or as a seasonal fishing station under a naval commandant. The councilors also discussed the relation of the island to the fisheries which rivaled England's there, those of the aggressive French and of the unscrupulous New Englanders. It was logical for the privy council to travel from the problems of the trans-Atlantic fisheries to the issues of international privateering and of the ship's passes which the council conceived of as the legal means of combating the corsairs. This maritime discussion in turn led to the revocation of mayoral authority to issue passes, beginning with that of London's lord mayor, a characteristic council decision against urban autonomy and in favor of royal centralization and imperial bureaucracy. At the end of a very long day in council, the clerks neglected to enter the order to incorporate the Virginia Assembly. It was a slip made ominous for American independence by a petty bit of business at the very next meeting of the privy council.

On 22 April 1676, the privy council read and referred to its committee for foreign plantations the petition of Sarah Bland, mother of Giles Bland, royal customs collector in Virginia. Apparently innocuous, the petition presented a sanitized version of Giles Bland's quarrel with Philip Ludwell, the Virginia Assembly's protest that Bland had nailed Ludwell's dishonored gage to their front door, and the governor and council's order for an unexampled fine against Bland, remission of which by the king-in-council was petitioned for by Mrs. Bland.

It was the character of the players that gave this minor melodrama its imperial interest. The Blands were well connected. Giles' father had been mayor of Tangier. The family were related to Thomas Povey and his kinsmen, leading advisers to the imperial executive since commonwealth times, and functioned with them in imperial affairs. Mediterranean merchants of substance, the Blands were also London landlords from whom the admiralty committee of the privy council rented office space. Additionally, the family were large-scale investors in Virginia, and their connections with the lord treasurer were such that Giles, the Blands' representative in the colony, had been commissioned collector of royal customs. The Ludwell of whom the Blands now complained was the brother of the Virginia Assembly agent in London, the colony's secretary, Thomas Ludwell. Much of his case for the proposed Virginia charter was that the government it would incorporate "by 50 years experience hath been found most easy to the people and advantageous to the crown." But the Blands now alleged that the old regime's governor, council, and assembly, whom the charter would invest with privileges, had collaborated to obstruct the royal customs collector in the enforcement of the acts of trade, exactly as the lord chancellor had predicted autonomous Virginians would.[33]

The privy councilors were annoyed by the demeaning slanging of Giles Bland and the Berkeleyans—"pittyfull fellow, puppy, and Son of Whore," "mechanic fellow, puppy, and a coward," were the libelous labels pinned on the principals. Their lordships were also bothered that

---

33. The petition is in C.O. 1/36, 86, and the order-in-council upon it is in C.O. 5/1355, 19. Ludwell's contention is in Coventry Ms. 77, 48. On the Virginia events here referred to, see Book I, above.

Giles Bland seemed to be carrying on his father's habit of quarreling with cavalier governors. Bland's reports were referred to his father's antagonist from their Tangier service, Treasurer Norwood, by Secretary Williamson (together with a request for Norwood's comparisons of the original Virginia Company charter with the agents' draft).

Colonel Norwood was seriously ill and his reply was delayed for many weeks, but when it came it unexpectedly confirmed Bland's criticism of Berkeley's administration, and it summarized London's information about the causes of revolt in Virginia. High taxes, misappropriated, for unbuilt coastal forts, for apparently ineffectual agents in England, and "2 millions tobacco raised for building of forts at the heads of the rivers upon great men's new plantations and settlements"—these were the public issues, Norwood wrote. The great incitement to current unrest, however, was the Berkeleyans' misgovernment. Norwood reported "the great Injuries that is done in Courts by the Insinuation of some that make advantages by the governor's passion age or weakness." The old governor's evil councilors were also responsible for the assembly's errors, Norwood said, for they controlled its committees, legislation, and ordinances. But Berkeley himself had diverted the king's supply of munitions for Virginia defense to its Indian enemies by means of his favored traders, Norwood concluded, and as the colony's commander, Sir William was responsible for that "which hath been the main cause of those tumults the not tymely Suppressing the Incursions of these formidable savages whereby many men were Cut of and several plantations deserted."[34]

In the harsh light of the reports that Norwood summarized, the privy councilors began to believe that there might be colonial maladministration as well as Indian enmity to deal with in Virginia. This was but one step from relating the two things as cause and effect. And Virginia's troubles, civil or military, political or racial, could not be ignored by the king-in-council, for they threatened the receipts from the tax on tobacco. Slippage here would undermine the treasurer's great plan of budget, retrenchment, payments in course and of interest on the national debt. Virginia's troubles could cripple the capacity of the crown to govern without parliament.

The alarm of the imperial executive was amplified by the news received from the merchant ships that made English ports from Virginia on 23 May 1676. Their captains reported that "the tyranny of the natives exceeds that of the rebellion of Ireland, if possible, roasting men and

34. C.O. 5/1355, 22–23. Norwood's report is in C.O. 1/21, 156–58, misdated as "17 July 67" (sic for "76"). The error is repeated in C.P.S.C. 1661–1668, no. 1532, and so in Webb, The Governors-General, 341 and note 21.

causing their neighbors to eat them." The words "natives," "Ireland," and "rebellion" were associated in the minds of every politically sentient Englishman with the Irish uprising of 1641 and with its disastrous economic and political consequences for England. And terrible reports from New England—"that the people there are very much skirt on by the natives and dare not go a mile out of ye Town, that all provision and other things are 6 times the value they were a yeare agoe"—continued to come in. In 1676 as in 1641, native atrocities in the realm overseas threatened the peace of the kingdom itself. The relations of the American provinces of the realm to the central administration of the kingdom thus required full-scale reconsideration. It began with Virginia. On the last day of May 1676, the king-in-council ordered the chancellor "to Stop the Grant of Virginia," and the committee for foreign plantations began the reassessment of the relation of the colony to the kingdom that was to end for a century Virginia's practical independence from England, and which carried down with the Old Dominion into dependence on the imperial crown of England many another hitherto self-governing colony.[35]

BERKELEY'S CATASTROPHE

On 8 June 1676, now that it was too late to save his own reputation and authority and his assembly's charter and autonomy, Sir William Berkeley's letter of 1 April at last reached Whitehall from Virginia. In it, he stressed the interdependence of American and West Indian war, economics, and politics in ways which, added to the reports of other officers on the same events, increased imperial pressures for English intervention in American government.[36]

The basic cause of the war which had begun in New England and spread to Virginia, Sir William wrote, was that the English colonists had seized more native land than they could defend from its former owners. The natives had no choice but to attack the invaders, Berkeley explained, "for the Indians complained that [the English] had left them no land to support and insure their wives and children from famine." The native counterattack "destroyed divers towns in New England," Sir William told his metropolitan audience (which, although he seemed not to know it, had been reading blow-by-blow accounts of the fighting in New England).

But Berkeley's estimate of the cost of the war to the northern colonists was higher, and perhaps it was more accurate, than that of the New

---

35. *C.S.P.D. 1676–1677*, 122. P.C. 2/65, 243. C.O. 5/1355, 17b. S.P. 29/380, 69, 274.
36. Berkeley's dispatch is in C.O. 1/36, 65 ff., and *C.S.P.C. 1675–1676*, no. 858.

England reporters. The natives, he wrote, have "killed more than a thousand fighting men, seldom were worsted in any encounter, and have made the New England men desert about a hundred miles of ground they had divers years seated and built towns on." The governor anticipated, quite accurately, that the New Englanders "will not recover these twenty years what they have lost." Their imperial trading position was also gutted, "for they have lost all their beaver trade, half their fishing, and have nothing to carry to Barbados" directly and nothing to trade for the Virginia tobacco and provisions which they had also exchanged for Barbadian sugar. Not mentioning that the loss of the New England trade had hit hard at his own government's smaller planters, Berkeley concluded with an antique irrelevancy (of the pejorative kind so disliked by King Charles, and that can only have enhanced the idea that Sir William, and the system of colonial autonomy he represented, had outlived their time). If it were not that the New Englanders were regicides, Sir William wrote, he could find it in his heart to pity them. In 1676, it was no longer fundamental to royal estimates of the New England colonial governments that they sheltered King Charles I's murderers. What was more important to the privy council's imperial assessment was that those autonomous enclaves of dissenters had provoked an Indian war which killed the king's subjects and ruined the trade of the realm.

Sir William Berkeley's analysis of intercolonial catastrophe was extended by the governor-general of Barbados, Sir Jonathan Atkins. He portrayed a pervasive crisis of England's American colonies in 1676, a crisis accelerated in the case of Barbados by crop losses in the recent hurricane and by labor losses from the Barbadian slave revolt. The gutters of Bridgetown had run with the blood of beheaded blacks and the island air was polluted with the stench of burned bodies. Worse yet, Atkins argued, was the recently reinforced monopoly of the metropolis over the colony's staple crop, sugar. As it had just bound by new oaths the American governors-general to enforce strictly the 1673 act of trade and its predecessors, the privy council not only rejected but also resented Atkins' argument. And the council was even more offended that the governor-general had connived at complaints by the Barbados Assembly against the acts of trade and the Royal African Company, "when on the contrary, it was ye duty of Yor Maties Governor to have supprest any such address from the Inhabitants." The "right use of parliaments," it seemed, no more extended to criticism of the crown in the colonies than it did in the kingdom. Still, the privy councilors were equally, and more constructively, concerned that Atkins had confirmed Berkeley's allegation of a continental conspiracy of the natives against the colonists. "And it is almost incredible what intelligence distant Indians hold with one the other," Virginia's governor exclaimed. Certainly they were the equal of the colonists' communications, and Indian divisions were no deeper than those of the English.[37]

That the settlers were divided within the colonies as well as between them, threatened to make a desperate situation disastrous, despite Sir William Berkeley's (quickly discredited) assertion that his government had "now such a strength on the frontiers of all our plantations that we cannot fear the natives if they were five times the number." That Sir William's assurance was mistaken became apparent to the privy council when, on 13 June 1676, Secretary Williamson read the report Giles Bland had written only a month earlier in Virginia. Bland appealed directly to the crown and to its unified, imperial, concerns about "any of his Maties: Governments, and the Interests of State at home and abroad." The king and council must act immediately on behalf of the English subjects in Virginia, Bland wrote, if they hoped to save the £100,000 tobacco excise. Revenue, subjects, state—all were endangered, Bland warned the crown, by the militarily ineffective, politically disgraced, and fiscally corrupt government of Sir William Berkeley and his associates, and by the colonists' violent rising against both the Indian enemy and the Berkeleyan regime.[38]

PRIVY COUNCIL COERCION

The next day, the privy council responded to the Virginia crises, first by reinforcing the colony's imperial economic advantage, its monopoly of the English market. In an order initially signed by the leading royal ministers of 1676—the chancellor, Finch; the treasurer, Danby; the Scots and Irish chiefs, Lauderdale and Ormonde; and by the earl of Arlington, the leading Anglo-American minister of the previous decade—the privy council called for the destruction of all the tobacco which had been planted in England "to the great prejudice of the Navigation of this Kingdom, Hinderance of his Maties foreign Plantations and customs & loss of the trade." Royal customs officers and the king's cavalry, assisted by the entire local executive of England's counties and corporations—sheriffs, militia lieutenants, justices of the peace, mayors, bailiffs, and constables —were to destroy tobacco on the eve of its harvest in half a dozen different English counties.[39]

37. For Atkins' comments of 3/13 April 1676, see C.O. 1/36, 70; C.S.P.C. 1675–1676, no. 862. See also C.S.P.C. 1675–1676, nos. 714, 911. The privy councilors' criticism of Atkins is in C.O. 1/38, 66. Berkeley's conspiracy theory is in C.O. 1/36, 66.
38. Berkeley to Coventry, April 1676, C.O. 1/36, 66. Bland's letter to Williamson is dated from Jamestown, 28 April 1676, and endorsed "Rec. June 1676" (C.O. 1/36, 109). C.S.P.C. 1675–1676, no. 905.
39. P.C. 2/65, 256, 257. A.P.C.C., no. 1085.

In the same meeting, the privy council ordered royal government in Virginia physically reinforced. Sir William Berkeley had written (never suggesting that the crown could or ought to assist the colony or its governor, a noteworthy evidence of Virginia's utter separation from both imperial assistance and authority) that the Indians could be defeated "if we can get our merchants to trust us with some considerable quantity of Powder." Rearmed since the Restoration, the crown could do infinitely more than merchants about munitions, and without cost to the colony. The privy council ordered the royal ordnance office to prepare for shipment to Virginia a thousand muskets, seven hundred carbines, five hundred hand grenades, and gunpowder and ball in proportion, all to be paid for by the lord treasurer.

At first, the uncertain dimensions of the Indian war and of civil unrest in Virginia made it unclear how best to send the royal munitions to the embattled colony. On 26 June, however—the same day that Jenks was arrested for his attack on the government and that the crown responded to that attack by opening its investigation of urban arson—the imperial cabinet decided to intervene directly in Virginia's civil war, as well as to ensure the defeat of the natives. Meeting at Mr. Secretary Coventry's, the cabinet council declared that the king had decided to dispatch a warship "to Virginia soe soon as he shall have any further Intelligence concerning ye State of ye Disorders." Samuel Pepys, secretary of the navy, was ordered to select ships fit for the voyage. On 1 July 1676, another step was taken in these proceedings, a step most menacing to American independence. The admiralty committee of the privy council ordered the navy board to outfit a warship to transport elements of the royal army to Virginia.[40]

The "further Intelligence" for which the cabinet waited reached Westminster during the first ten days of July 1676. Through Secretary Williamson's port agents, ships' captains returning from the Chesapeake now not only amplified previous reports of the Potomac River fighting with the natives, they also narrated the spread of civil disturbances in Virginia. A resistance to the assembly's war taxes, followed by squabbles between frontier and coastal counties over the burden of defense, had finally produced open fighting between rebel forces under Nathaniel Bacon and Governor Berkeley's defenders. And the merchantmen's captains added that the like causes had provoked skirmishes between the proprietary party in Maryland and that colony's popular military leader, General Trueman.[41]

The royal reaction was immediate and forceful, both political and

40. C.O. 1/37, 206. C.O. 5/1355, 23–24. C.S.P.D. 1676–1677, 185. ADM 3/276, 70, 72.
41. C.S.P.D. 1676–1677, 204, 216.

military. On 10 July 1676, Secretary Coventry wrote at the king's command to "Sr William Bartly," acknowledging the governor's brief note of 1 April about the beginnings of the Indian war. But, Coventry went on, other letters and reports had described a civil war as well as an Indian one. The king thought that Berkeley's English enemies were more dangerous than the natives, Coventry wrote. So his majesty had resolved to send the governor three hundred troops, paid on the English establishment. He would have sent more, but the Virginia agents protested that Berkeley's government could not feed them. The agents had also told the cabinet council of "the defect of Sr. W. Berkeley his Authority in Point of Warre." So the ministers had agreed to send Sir William the king's commission as general so that he could repress rebels and Indians (something less, perhaps, than the captain general's commission which was now a standard authority of royal governors-general commanding provinces). Before the king's letter or his commission could be sent to Virginia, however, yet more alarming news suggested that additional imperial force would be required to pacify, and royalize, Virginia, despite the continued objections of the assembly's agents.[42]

BERKELEY RECALLED; YORK ASCENDANT

Sir William Berkeley broke five years of silence about Virginia's government with a dramatic dispatch dated 3 June 1676. He revealed a rebellion. He asked to be recalled. "Sr," wrote the governor to Secretary Coventry, "I am so over weaned with riding into al parts of the Country to stop this Violent Rebellion *that I am not able to support my selfe at this Age six months longer and therefore on my knees I beg his sacred majesty would send a more Vigorous Gouvenor.*" This pathetic plea was accompanied by the old governor's insistence that the rebellion was against "the whole assembly" in Virginia, not just himself. No sooner had the cabinet council read the aged executive's *cri de coeur* than they received the governor's report of 1 July to the assembly agents on the progress of political revolution and the deepening of social war in Virginia.[43]

Sir William listed the dreadful sequence of his colony's collapse: the agency tax; the Susquehanna siege; the fort fiasco; the frontier rising, first

---

42. Coventry's letter of the 10th is in his letterbook, Additional Manuscripts 25120, 88, British Library (hereafter cited as Add. Ms. 25120). The cabinet minutes are in Coventry Ms. 77, 150. See also *C.S.P.D. 1676–1677*, 224.

43. Berkeley's letter [to Coventry] is in Coventry Ms. 77, ca. 115 (italics in original), and his report [to Ludwell] is in *ibid.*, 143–46. Berkeley had not heretofore informed any of the imperial executive about the growing political unrest in Virginia, but had written to Thomas Ludwell, the assembly agent, on 1 April 1676, about the "mutinies" of the two previous years.

against the Indians, then against the government; the Baconian electoral campaign against "al leavies and forts and Assemblies not chosen by the People." All this, wrote Governor Berkeley, had culminated in the political revolution of the June Assembly. That Bacon there extorted from the governor a commission as general evidenced, as Sir William Berkeley himself lamented, his inability to govern a people of whom "six parts of seaven at least are Poore Endebted Discontented and Armed." The armed underclass was frantic with fears of a continental conspiracy of the Indians against the English. At the same time the ruling class was weakened by the age, absenteeism, and factionalism of the governor's council. Only royal force could restore the king's peace. So Berkeley begged that "the next Governor may come in a frigate."

Sir William wrote that he would have expanded upon the uses of force in the colony (judging from his use of subsequent royal reinforcements, what he had in mind was plunder and vengeance) but he feared that his letter would be seized by the customs collector, Giles Bland, and revealed to the rebels. Indeed, said Sir William, in the authentic accents of outraged autonomy, he would resign the government—"as God is my Witnesse I would not willingly keepe it one hour longer"—even if his only problems were Commissioner Bland's enforcement of the parliament's acts of trade and the privy council's passport regulations, "for Armed with my Lord High Treasurer's Authority never man did such things extra judicially and Extra officially as he does and I have beene severely checkt out of England lately for not obeying and seconding his Actions."

Berkeley's dispatches had revealed to the king-in-council that their authority was in danger on three fronts in Virginia: from the native rebellion; from the colonists' revolution; and from the Berkeleyans' autonomy. The victory of any one of these enemies of English empire would destroy the treasurer's grand plan to build royal authority on a basis of the excise on provincial products. So great was the danger of the Chesapeake revolution to empire and authority that the leading imperialist, James duke of York, now publicly resumed his place in the cabinet, in defiance of the Test Act of 1673.

Such was the threat of the intercolonial crisis, not only to the king's empire and authority but also to James' prospects as their heir, that the royal duke now became pre-eminent in the cabinet—the privy council committees for the admiralty and for foreign affairs—as he had not been since April 1672. Otherwise, not only might Virginia be lost to provincial revolution, but James' rival for the imperial throne itself, Charles II's bastard the duke of Monmouth, captain general of England, would seize the military patronage and the political prestige accruing to an imperial prince who chastised the enemies of empire and regained provinces. So much Monmouth attempted in the abortive Algerine expedition of 1676 and accomplished in the 1679 repression of rebel Scots. Therefore, the duke of York, and his clients in the admiralty, the army, and the secretariat, dictated the orders, instructions, and commissions, designated the military and political officers, readied the expeditionary ships and regiments to recapture and royalize Virginia, and, it was hoped, New England also. It was the duke of York who forced the earl of Arlington and Lord Culpeper to surrender their proprietary claims on Virginia. These claims were doubly objectionable to the imperialists as the roots of political unrest among the colonists and as the bases of private governments within the king's realm. It was the duke of York who declared Sir William Berkeley unfit to rule for the king in Virginia and ordered his removal from the office he finally refused to resign. It was the duke of York who told his clients, Colonel Herbert Jeffreys and Admiral Sir John Berry, that "Bacon and Bland must die."

On 20 August 1676, the latest dispatches from Virginia were read to the cabinet. Williamson's cryptic references—to "the ship," to "men," to the Virginia agents' opposition to coercion and to their reluctant agreement that commissioners must be dispatched "at least to know ye truth" —marked the direction of the decisions to be made by James duke of York.

On 22 August 1676, the king was absent from the cabinet council. The duke took the chair. For the next three months, he directed the Virginia operations of the crown. In this meeting, fundamental to the future not just of Virginia but of the entire empire, the ministers of the king—the duke, the treasurer, Ormonde, Arlington, and Coventry—decided "1. Sr. W. Berkeley to be recalled." They did notice the old governor's request for relief and honored it by "giving him leave to come for England &c." The ministers also said that Sir William should be assured of "the King's gracious Acceptance & Esteeme of his long & faithful Service &c." Simply put, however, they had recalled Berkeley. Their major concern was now to meet the crises he could not and to try to install in Virginia a royal regime that could both prevent their recurrence and respond to the king's commands.[44]

The cabinet listed the colony's problems, the crown's concerns: the civil "disorders," the Indian war, the failure of the governor and council to protect the country against either of these outbreaks despite the king's "repeated Commands" to take defensive measures and despite "the Summes raised by the Country" for military purposes. The cabinet

44. Williamson's cabinet notes of 20, 27 August 1676 are in S.P. 104/179, 61, 64. The cabinet ("present His Royal Highness [York], the Lord Treasurer, the Duke of Ormond, Sir W. [illiamson]") composed its "Virginia Despatch" on 22 August 1676 (Coventry Ms. 77, 187–91).

readily agreed that the first requisite of a reformed, royalized, government was that the king commission a regular army officer as commander-in-chief of the colony. This military governor was to have full powers to supersede Berkeley's commission to Bacon as general, seize the cashiered officer, and execute him under martial law, if the political state of the province would permit it, or else to send him to England. Within the week, by 27 August 1676, Major Thomas Fairfax had been nominated as the royal commander in Virginia and Sir John Berry was selected to lead his convoy.

Once the new commander-in-chief had repressed the rebellion with the help of the navy, he was to obey the dictates of modern government by systematically collecting information about recent events in Virginia. From these data the new chief executive was to decide how to pacify the province himself, and he was to derive a set of policy recommendations for the crown: "what is necessary to be done in all kinds for restoring things to their first Peace & Settlement." Data and suggestions were to be sent to the cabinet so that the crown could make informed decisions about its province. One decision the cabinet made immediately: it would pass its own version of the Virginia charter—promising direct royal government, negating the assembly's argument for incorporation by accepting the duke's offer to vacate the Virginia proprietorships.

The assembly agents recognized that the duke of York had taken charge. Henceforward they directed their petitions about Virginia to him. But their petition to the duke to order Sir William Berkeley, and so his party, their principals, restored to power before he had the governor recalled and had the government reformed was rejected by the cabinet early in September 1676. Instead the cabinet formalized the reform process by commissioning royal investigators and by ordering that, from the moment of the commissioners' arrival, Sir William "enter not into the exercise of the Government." The duke declared that Berkeley was "totally unsuitable for the execution of so weighty a charge as the management of the king's affairs." The cabinet issued his unconditional recall, required his immediate departure from Virginia, replaced him with an officer commissioned (and supplied with the requisite force) to govern by martial law.[45]

The governor-general was to be both superior to and free from the provincial council, as Sir William Berkeley had not been. The king's council in Virginia was now to be directly appointed from Whitehall. The themes of executive authority and direct government were reiterated in

45. In addition to the sources cited in note 44, see "Instructions Given at the Come. for Forrain Affairs Sepr. 1st 76. Concerning Virginia," Coventry Ms. 77, 195; Webb, *The Governors-General*, especially 347, note 31.

the governor-general's orders for the assembly. The burgesses·of its lower house were to be elected on an English franchise. The governor-general, royal council, and reformed burgesses were to constitute a provincial legislature. Most important acts were to be introduced by the governor-general, or dictated by the privy council in England, and the resulting acts reviewed, revised if necessary, or rejected by the king-in-council. The same agency both authorized and would accept appeals to itself from the provincial courts. The bulk of these reforms were written into the governor-general's commission and instructions. As read and approved by the king-in-council, these royal directives now became in fact what royal prescriptions had been in theory for fifty years, the crown's constitution for Virginia. These orders-in-council of 1676 were the model— formalized in 1681—that underlay the constitution of every English colony which became a British province during the coming century.

"IMMEDIATE DEPENDENCY UPON THE CROWNE OF ENGLAND"

Royal government by commission and instruction left small place for the Virginia charter, intended as it had been to incorporate and perpetuate the old assembly system. Instead, the cabinet council—especially the duke, the treasurer, and the steward (Ormonde, the constitution of whose Irish province provided the model for Virginia's royalization)—made the charter into a declaration "that all the subjects of us, our heirs and successors . . . inhabiting within our colony and plantation of Virginia, shall have their immediate dependency upon the Crowne of England, under the Rule and Government of such Governor or Governors as We Our Heirs and Successors shall from time to time appoint in that behalfe, and upon no other person or persons whatsoever." Neither colonial council nor private proprietor was henceforth to control the king's government of Virginia. The crown confirmed the title to Virginia's soil in its present possessors, whether the sovereign or his subjects. The measure of justice between them was declared to be the laws of England, as applied by the governor-general and his crown-appointed council. The Old Dominion was declared to be "an extension" of England. A clearer declaration of the onset of empire, of the end of Virginia's practical independence from the crown, could not have been conceived.[46]

The agents of the old, colonial, assembly might have objected more strenuously to their principals' loss of autonomy but, at the crucial mo-

---

46. The revised charter text is in C.O. 389/6, 64–65, and in William Waller Henning, [ed.,] *The Statutes at Large; Being a Collection of All the Laws of Virginia* . . . (New York, 1823; Charlottesville, 1969), II, 532–33.

ment, 3 September 1676, there arrived at Whitehall the Virginia dispatches of 25–28 June. Written at the close of the June Assembly, these papers included eloquent testimonies to Sir William Berkeley's loss of authority: his forced exoneration of Nathaniel Bacon and his commission to Bacon as general. These dispatches also included a letter from William Sherwood, that criminal turned attorney, to his victim turned patron, Secretary Williamson. Sherwood told the secretary that Virginia had been devastated "by the common Enimy ye: Indians, & farr more by ye rebellion and outrages of the common people." Only "the kings Maties expeciall care of us," Sherwood declared, could save the colony from these doubled disasters.[47]

Reading these reports, the privy councilors concluded that the crown must take physical and political command of the colony or lose it, either to the Indian enemy or to the English rebels. On 20 September 1676, the cabinet brought to the privy council its program simultaneously to pacify Virginia and convert it from an American colony to an English province. Therefore, the king's pardon to penitent rebels and reformed assemblymen was balanced by the crown's commission of oyer and terminer to royal officers for the trial of the obdurate. In parallel fashion, the royal orders to Sir William Berkeley (to put down the rebellion with the aid of the king's forces) were balanced by instructions to the crown's commissioners to reform Berkeley's government so that in future it would respond to both provincial needs and to the king's commands. Likewise the privy council backed judicial and political measures of provincial reform by authorizing the ordnance expenditures, drafts, and recruitment for the expeditionary force which would take control of the colony for the crown. Once the entire privy council approved these ministerial measures to establish England's empire in Virginia, the further instruction, organization, and dispatch of the punitive expedition passed back into the hands of the privy council's executive committees—the foreign committee and the admiralty—and to the crown offices of treasury, ordnance, wardrobe, and war, and out of the political paths of privy-council debate, assembly agents' influence, and coffeehouse comments.[48]

The crown did all that it could to ensure that the politically ominous rebellion against royal authority in Virginia did not become a matter of public debate in England. The official *London Gazette* printed nothing on the Virginia situation. English republicans, however, took advantage of the Virginia revolution to reprint the work of its leader's kinsman and

47. The chief of these dispatches are in C.O. 1/37, 33–40. See also *The Virginia Magazine of History and Biography* I (1893): 167 (hereafter cited as *V.H.M.B.*).
48. P.C. 2/65, 346. *A.P.C.C.*, no. 1094. C.O. 1/37, 190. See also C.O. 389/6, 78v, 84v–85, 88. Within a few days of this privy council meeting, Edward Randolph reported delivering the king's letter to the Boston magistrates (C.O. 1/37, 191).

namesake. The Cromwellian councilor Nathaniel Bacon's work, *An His-torical Discourse of the Uniformity of the Government of England*, sup-ported the most subversive doctrines of 1676, whether Francis Jenks' assertions of parliamentary self-sufficiency or the younger Nathaniel Ba-con's revolutionary insistence upon the legislative and popular bases of military authority. *An Historical Discourse* was a most eloquent, and apparently learned, exposition of the subject's rights under the ancient law of England. It denied the crown's prerogatives as a military mon-archy. The privy council ordered the arrest of the printers and pub-lishers of Bacon's *Discourse*. They fled into exile abroad and the book was seized and burned by executive agents, the "messengers" of the king-in-council.[49]

Despite crown censorship and official silence, the ruling classes in city and country, and the London coffeehouse cliques as well, were con-stantly alerted to the widening Indian war, the developing revolution in Virginia's politics, and the deepening distress of its economy, by the reports of merchant captains to the crown's secretary and by the newslet-ter summaries of those reports written by the secretary's clerks (or by their illegal competitors). On 25 September 1676, two ships reaching Fal-mouth in flight from Virginia with but partial cargoes reported that the upcountry English had been driven from their plantations by the Indians, that "the Governor Bartley and the Council is dispersed, and the said Governor fled from his house for safety; it is said the cause was for laying great taxes upon the comon people; soe they have made choice of Esquire Bacon to be their Comdr. in chiefe, who is at the head of 15 M men." Of course "these disturbances" had cut the potential tobacco crop severely, the captains observed, so that this year's scanty shipments would be smaller still in the coming season. These reports were expanded on, and corrected, in the newsletters posted from Secretary Williamson's office on 3 October. "Bacon at the head of twelve or fourteen hundred men plays the absolute master," the newswriters informed provincial magis-trates. The deputy governor and the principal planters had been im-prisoned by the rebels. Sir William Berkeley had fled from Virginia to Nevis. Therefore, the newsletters announced, the privy council had pro-claimed an embargo on all shipping bound for Virginia in order to cut the rebels off from English supplies.[50]

In its usual, contradictory way, the crown thus gave out through one

---

49. *An Historical Discourse of the Uniformity of the Government of England . . . With a preface being a Vindication of the Ancient way of Parliaments in England* was originally published in two parts, 1647 and 1651. The "Advertisement to ye edition of 1688/9" contains a useful publishing and political history of the work.

50. Tho. Holden to Williamson, 25 [September] 76, S.P. 29/385, 213. *C.S.P.D. 1676–1677*, 337. Newsletter of 3 October 1676, in *Manuscripts of Le Fleming*, 129. ADM 1/5138, 512.

agency the information about provincial revolution that it repressed elsewhere. Some of that newsletter information was politically sensitive and
wholly unauthorized. To their Virginia news, for example, the 3 October
1676 newsletters not only added reports of French and Dutch fighting
over the Newfoundland fisheries, they also revealed that a naval expedition was designed against the Algerines in which the duke of Monmouth
was to command (offsetting the duke of York's prestigious involvement
in the Virginia expedition). Undersecretary Yard was severely censured
for revealing cabinet deliberations not yet reported even to the privy
council. Saying that he had not imagined that something so openly talked
of after chapel on Sunday "was a secret that ought not to be divulged,"
the undersecretary insisted nonetheless that he had not supplied this
information to the coffeehouses (where its discussion may have persuaded the government to abandon the Algerine expedition for want of
secrecy). In fact, London lawyers lobbying at Whitehall had also picked
up this report (and others too, presumably) in the galleries. Of course the
embargo proclamation soon alerted every port in England to the serious-
ness of the Virginia situation. Then as now, information restriction by the
executive was designed primarily to prevent public interference in politics, for intragovernmental secrecy was hardly even attempted. And, as
usual, all that censorship achieved was to advertise the censors' insecurity.[51]

"MR. NATHANIEL BACON PLAYS REX"

The cabinet council was increasingly sensitive and insecure about Virginia for, during the weekend prior to its 1 October 1676 meeting, its
members read transcripts of the revolutionary resolves of the Middle
Plantation Convention, of Bacon's manifesto, and of Bland's circular. On
1 October, the cabinet ordered Sir William Berkeley's immediate recall,
and his replacement by Guards Captain Herbert Jeffreys, the expansion
of the expeditionary naval squadron from two men-of-war to six, plus
troop transports for a doubled infantry force and a headquarters and ordnance staff of 130 officers. One thousand redcoats were drafted or recruited into five companies marching under the colors of their parent
regiments: the crowned lion, the crowned oak, and the St. George's Cross
of the Guards; the cipher of James duke of York (for his Admiralty Regiment); and the blue, green, and white of the Holland Regiment. Of this
big battalion Colonel Jeffreys took command. His commission gave him

---

51. R. Yard to Williamson, 12 October 1676, S.P. 29/386, 32. *C.S.P.D. 1676–1677*, 356–57, 360,
368. ADM 3/276, 119. J. G. Muddiman, *The King's Journalist 1659–1689* . . . (London, 1923),
206.

the martial-law authority of a captain general over both redcoats and colonists. In this commission, the crucial words "Kill & Slay" ensured Colonel Jeffreys' ultimate authority as the crown's policeman in the province of Virginia, just as they had empowered the earl of Craven to hold the City of London for King Charles.[52]

On 3 October, the cabinet council met again and, impressed with the urgency of the Virginia reports, decided to send Sir John Berry out in the *Bristol* ahead of the fleet, with fifty Guardsmen as marines and with small arms for the loyalists in Virginia. Berry himself was called into the cabinet chamber and told to hire troop transports for a thousand men from London's river. Meanwhile Mr. Pepys was to make inquiries of the outports for more ships, and Colonel Jeffreys was to recruit the five hundred additional soldiers to be added to the men drafted from the Guards and garrisons. That afternoon, the whole privy council approved the necessary commissions.

As the expedition assembled, the king, duke, and court went to the autumn races, but imperial business went with them. Before he went to bed on his first night at Newmarket, the king signed commissions for all the regimental and staff officers of the Virginia Regiment. The next morning the cabinet met at Newmarket, its theme set by Arlington: "I am heartily sorrie for the sad news from Virginia[:] if the reduction of that colonie must be made by money, the mischief is doubled upon us." Led by the lord treasurer, the king's ministers nonetheless approved the Virginia Regiment's annual establishment for pay, passage, food, medicine, and bedding, a total of £16,139. The treasurer found ready money in the exchequer for most of this cost but, as he told the cabinet, the balance of the expeditionary expenditures would have to await the return of the fleet with its customs-producing tobacco cargoes. For the treasurer had previously paid the costs of recruiting, of new uniforms and extra greatcoats for the notoriously hard Virginia winter (the "Little Ice Age" was at its coldest in 1676), of a fund for contingencies, of four months' advance (!) pay for the redcoats and six months' pay and provisions for the crews of the naval vessels. The expenditure of £11,178.3.6 in cash, plus the regiment's costs, used up the crown's ready reserve. The rest of the reconquest of Virginia had to be accomplished on credit. That credit was

---

52. S.P. 29/366, 119 (1 October 1676). *C.S.P.D. 1676–1677*, 347. The decision may have been made on 28 or 29 September. See Webb, *The Governors-General*, 354, n. 44; C.O. 5/1355, 28b. See also C.O. 5/1355, 207–11, 219; S.P. 44/29, 186; S.P. 104/177, 66. The cabinet decided that each company, double the usual hundred men, was to have a captain, first lieutenant, and ensign (promoted second lieutenant for the expedition) from its parent regiment, plus a newly commissioned ensign and six sergeants (instead of the usual three). For these and other military measures taken to meet the perils of a society in which Williamson, for one, believed "slaves are 8 times as many as the masters," see S.P. 29/366, 119. See also C.O. 389/6, 55; C.O. 1/37, 207–11, 219.

readily forthcoming, despite the reluctance of the London merchant community to make unrestricted loans to the crown in the previous summer, suggests that the imperial metropolis fully shared in the royal determination to recapture Virginia. The symbiosis of market with monarchy, of rising capitalism with the imperial crown, was clearly expressed in 1676.[53]

To the horror of the bureaucrats left behind in London, the private newsletters of 4 October 1676 had published all the details, not just of the growing Virginia revolution but of the intended royal repression as well. The publicists wrote about "Mr. Nathaniel Bacon who is at ye head of 1000 men, yt ye generality of ye people if not joining with him, yett favouring his pretences, playes Rex there, yt he had imprisoned Sr Henry Chichely ye Depty Governor and several of ye most considerable Planters, yt Sr. William Berkeley, ye Governor to avoyd ye like or worse treatment had . . . to retire to Nevis upon wch ye King hath resolved to send thither forthwith a 1000 men to quell these Mutineers," and that an embargo was laid in English and Irish ports "to ye end those people may be deprived of ye Necessaries they receive from hence." By 9 October, as Secretary Pepys complained, these reports were "publically exposed at Elford's Coffee House, London."[54]

Bored by Newmarket, the king returned to London in mid-October to find that Captain Evelyn's ship had just come in with dispatches from Virginia dated 10 August 1676. Evelyn himself reported "that Bacon and his associates have taken 2 English ships, and that he himselfe was forced to make his Escape having no more than half his Loading on bord. He further says that the Rebels increase in their number & have put the whole Country in confusion." The privy council immediately proclaimed a £300 reward for the capture of Nathaniel Bacon, but it rejected the typically Berkeleyan suggestion made by two of the Virginia agents, Secretary Thomas Ludwell and Major General Robert Smith, that the Indians be incited to pursue their great enemy, the rebel Bacon. Nothing could have been better calculated to confirm either the people's regard for their hero, the Indian-fighter, or to authenticate their assumptions of the Berkeleyan government's connivance with the native enemy.[55]

The Indian rising in Virginia, so all accounts agreed, was rooted in New England. Provoked by the greed of the puritans for native land, the native rebellion had exposed the military imbecility and political independence of the colonial commonwealths. It was natural, therefore, that

53. Commissions dated at Newmarket, 4–8 October 1676, S.P. 44/29, 173–84. Establishment, 7 October, S.P. 29/386, 8. P.C. 2/65, 373. A.P.C.C., no. 1101, ii. S.P. 29/385, 276. Coventry Ms. 77, 256.

54. S.P. 29/386, 329, 333.

55. S.P. 29/386, 160. C.S.P.D. 1676–1677, 369, 371. Coventry Ms. 77, 254. Privy Council Register for 25 October 1676, P.C. 2/65, 359. A.P.C.C., no. 1097.

on 20 October 1676, the cabinet council should have discussed the possibility of sending some of the royal commissioners on from a pacified and royalized Virginia to "visit" New England. The commissioners were to sail in the *Bristol* to Boston, together with an impressive Guards escort. Such discussions ended suddenly with the next news from Virginia.[56]

On 14 November 1676, Berkeley's capture of Bland was reported to the cabinet council. It might seem that Berkeley's success should have reduced royal anxiety about Virginia. Yet the reverse was the case. King Charles reacted violently to the news, as if by leaving the king's forces out of the rebellion's repression and so by reducing the royal justification for reform in Virginia Sir William's victory endangered the crown's plans to recall the governor and royalize the colony. The resulting cabinet minute records the royal reaction: "Upon his Maty speaking with one Capt. Smith, a master of a merct vessell just come in from Virginia giving an acct of Blands being taken Prisnr. and Sir William Berkeley's being possessed of the Shipp there, It was Resolved that Sr. Jno Berry and Col. Morrison [the Virginia agent turned royal investigator] should be hastened away before the rest of the Forces, and that they should be out of Towne before tomorrow morning."[57]

Since the *Bristol* was already anchored at Spithead, and had been since 27 August in accord with the earlier orders for its advanced departure, the king's order for her immediate sailing was readily obeyed. On the 16th of November, Berry and Morrison were out of London; on the 17th they reached Portsmouth and found royal money, commissions, and instructions awaiting them. On the 18th, "Early in ye morninge," the crew of the *Bristol* "haled home or fore top saile sheets and hove a peake," and on the 19th, the wind turning northeasterly, the *Bristol* "sailed fro Spitthead Bound to Virginia." So urgent and so repeated were the king's commands that the entire Virginia fleet sailed for the Old Dominion on Tuesday, 5 December 1676. A week after that, the newsletters reported Bacon's burning of Jamestown. Still, the cabinet council was confident that the royal forces would repress the rebels. As soon as the cabinet received Sir John Berry's report that he had left soundings en route to the Chesapeake, it had moved the privy council to order the admiralty to lift the embargo on vessels bound for Virginia.

The release of the Virginia tobacco fleet—the ships of which were, on second thought, ordered to report to Sir John Berry on arriving in the James River and to obey his orders "for HM Service and the Good of

56. "Friday Octr 20th 76 Com. Forr. Affaires/Virginia," Coventry Ms. 77, 260.
57. ADM 3/276, 146. This news was public by 20 November (newsletter, in *Manuscripts of Le Fleming*, 129–30). Captain's log, *Bristol*, ADM 51/134, Part III. Instructions to Berry, 15 November 1676. ADM 2/1738, 69v–70v. Newsletter, 12 December 1676, in *Manuscripts of Le Fleming*, 130. ADM 3/276, 152. P.C. 2/65, 393.

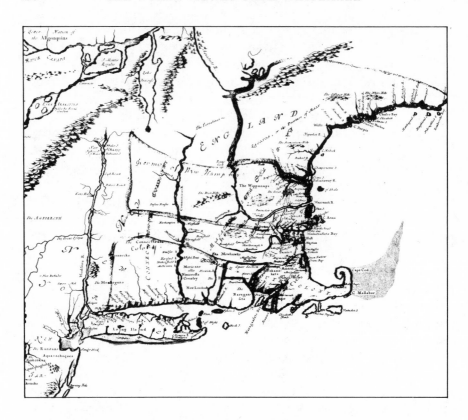

A Map of New England New Yorke New Iersey Mary-Land & Virginia Sould by Robert Morden at ye Atlas in Corn-hill neer ye Royal Exchange and by William Berry at ye Globe between York House & ye New Exchange in ye Strande London.

the Trade"—was ostensibly a royal response to the humble petition of the London merchants. On the same day, however, the privy council ordered the Corporation Act enforced against the officers of the City of London. The restoration of commerce, the regulation of the city, and the royalization of the colony were of equal importance to the assertion of English empire in 1676. Stabilizing Anglo-American society, the empire of England ended for a century the independence of its trans-Atlantic provinces.[58]

58. P.C. 2/65, 395. A.P.C.C., no. 1103. S.P. 29/366, 130.

"This Favourable Conjuncture":
An Imperial View of
King Philip's War

"PROVOKING EVILS"

L ondon coffee consumers were as well informed about the origins and progress of the Algonquin uprising in New England as they were tardily and incompletely told of Virginia's Indian and civil wars. Even *The London Gazette* reported regularly and extensively on the war in New England. Its stories, like the dispatches to Secretary Williamson which they reflected, displayed divided attitudes towards the northern colonies and their colonists.

In imperial eyes, the avowedly republican commonwealths of New England all were compounded into "the magistrates of Boston in New England." These petty, puritan, corporate functionaries, so the London press told its English readers, had stolen native land, botched colonial defense, and refused aid from imperial possessions lest it compromise their own independence. To the greed, inefficiency, and defiance of "the Bostoners," the English press contrasted the tribulations and triumphs of "the English," the dramatically embattled, sometimes heroic, ultimately triumphant colonists. Clearly such colonists, preserving the English, Christian, imperial prowess of Cromwell's time, should be reincorporated into the empire of Charles II. But their magistrates, antiquated, ineffective, and isolated, should be replaced by the anglophile, mercantile, and cosmopolitan critics of the Boston regime.

These critics wrote most of the dozen pamphlets which, in addition to the newssheets, detailed for English audiences King Philip's assaults on the puritans. All but one of the half-dozen of these pamphlets, which were issued as supplements to the official *Gazette,* were critical of the Boston regime. The odd man out was Increase Mather, but his rebuttal of the earlier reporters' allegations—"worse than mistakes," Mather called their statements—only confirmed their contentions that puritan exclusivity, greed, and self-righteousness had provoked the war, and that Massachusetts' autarchy had prolonged it.[59]

59. Printed as an appendix to *The London Gazette,* no. 1156 (14–16 December 1676), was "A brief History Of the War ... From June 24, 1675 ... to August 12, 1676 ... By Increase

When Mather wrote that the war was a divine punishment for New England's failure to convert the heathen and for its "provoking evils" of increased worldliness (i.e., cultural and commercial accommodation to Restoration England), he was recognized as an old-fashioned, isolationist, saint by every English reader. When he then alleged that "the Heathen People amongst whom we live, and whose Land the Lord God of our Fathers hath given to us for a Rightful Possession, have . . . been Plotting mischievious Devices against that part of the English Israel," he spoke in the authentic accents of God-given and exclusive puritan independence, aggression, and a greed both hypocritical and disloyal. If anyone other than the natives owned the land, in English opinion that person was the king. That, by their defenders' own testimony, the puritans had admitted, even boasted of their abuse of both native proprietors and royal right only re-emphasized the opinion of nearly every commentator in England that the Bostoners had arrogantly begun the war and unnecessarily widened it throughout New England to dispossess the Indians illegally and so to broaden the territorial base of Massachusetts' independence from England.

All the earlier *Gazette* pamphlets were hostile to "the magistrates of Boston," or at least to their conduct of the war. All stressed the enormous, almost crippling, physical cost of the war to New England and its peoples, both red and white. All criticized the colonial governments' near-fatal independence from the rest of the empire, especially by repeating that the war was won for the English colonists, against the will of the New England authorities, by the Mohawk Iroquois in alliance with the ducal government of New York. These criticisms, and others produced by the crown's own agents in New England, both immediately before and during 1676, led the king-in-council to conclude that they should do in New England as they were doing in old England—that is, transform puritan corporations into royal governments.[60]

As 1676 came on, therefore, Massachusetts was endangered by English political as well as Algonquin military attacks. Asked by the privy council how much sovereignty the crown had conceded to Massachusetts under the 1629 charter, and how valid the procedures voiding that charter in 1637 had been, the attorney general had admitted that the concessions had been substantial and that the revocation was not in due form, but he opened up the possibility of a royal remedy by suggesting that the

---

Mather . . . (London, Printed for Richard Chiswell according to the original copy printed in New England, 1676, Licensed 2 December 1676 by Roger L'Estrange)."

60. Charles H. Lincoln, ed., *Narratives of the Indian Wars 1675–1699* (New York, 1913, 1966), 21–22. Cabinet dictation of *Gazette* coverage is noted in S.P. 104/177, 31v.

bay corporation's bylaws were invalid unless reviewed by the king-in-council, which of course they had not been.[61]

Others aggrieved by the Massachusetts corporation took advantage of the crown's critical attention to the colony's excessive autonomy to enter their own claims against the dissenters' state. Indeed, these claimants provided the privy council with most of its ammunition for the first stage of the royal assault on the puritan government. Their chiefs were the inheritors of the New Hampshire jurisdictions swallowed up by Massachusetts. Significantly, although it tried to avoid the appearance of pre-judgment against the puritans, the privy council nonetheless linked its consideration of the appeal of Robert Mason and Ferdinando Gorges to the council's own advocacy of enhanced enforcement of the acts of trade and navigation by recommissioned royal governors-general. The association of the imperial landlord with disputed land titles was an extraordinarily corrosive solvent of colonial autonomy everywhere in America. The linkage of the crown's political command with state direction of commerce also animated the privy council's antipathy to New England independence. Much more, then, than the old grievances of private proprietors was behind the 22 December 1675 order of the king-in-council to the bay company's officers to send over agents empowered to answer for their corporation before the council. So "the king may put an end to this matter which hath soe long depended for judgement before him." [62]

The king and council were concerned about Massachusetts' autonomy not only because of the pecuniary complaints of deprived proprietary landlords, angry English merchants, and defrauded royal customs officials, but also because of Massachusetts' affronts to empire. The royal prerogative and statute law, the established church and political morality, national patriotism and imperial defense, all of the crown's concern "for the good safety and protection of the whole Country" was offended and obstructed by Massachusetts' independence. To the hostile testimony of the only royal official who had spent any appreciable time in the bay commonwealth in recent years, Captain John Wynbourne of the royal navy, all the angry Englishmen appealed against Massachusetts' arrogant independence.

61. The most comprehensive review of the commercial and diplomatic context in which privy councilors placed the Massachusetts claim to continued independence is Secretary Williamson's notebook for the period 1673–77 (S.P. 29/366), partly deciphered in *C.S.P.C. 1675–1676*, no. 405. See also Williamson's records of the cabinet ("Foreigne Comittee") actions (primarily in relation to his "northern" province), S.P. 104/178 ("Williamson's Journal," 20 March 1675/6–22 May 1679), and S.P. 104/179 (clerk's minutes for the foreign committee, 6 January 1675/6 to 18 November 1677), as well as those listed in note 7 to Book II, above.

62. P.C. 2/65, 77–78. *C.S.P.C. 1675–1676*, no. 747.

"A FREE STATE"

Assigned to the North American station during the recent war with the Dutch, Captain Wynbourne had brought his majesty's ship the *Garland* (a fifth-rate of Cromwellian construction, 260 tons, 85–110 men, and 28–38 guns) into Boston to refit and reprovision late in 1673. He remained there for three months. As the first royal officer resident in Boston since the crown commissioners of 1664, the captain of the *Garland* had been much resorted to by the enemies of the puritan corporation. His report on New England politics, present and prospective, was immediately digested by Secretary Williamson and was read into the record of the privy council's committee for foreign plantations on 2 December 1675. It provided the premises of privy-council deliberations regarding Massachusetts and its confederates during 1676.[63]

From his vantage point in Boston harbor, the captain had observed the colony's illegal, direct, trade with Europe in staple crops and manufactured goods. During his stay, ships "dayly arrived from Spain ffrance Holland & Canareys" with the commodities that the Bostoners exchanged for the enumerated crops of English colonists. Wynbourne perforce protested this violation of the acts of trade "to the Magistrates of Boston." They replied that "they were his Majestys Vice Admirals in these Seas and that they would doe that which seemed good to them."

Rebuffed in trade regulation, Captain Wynbourne next tested the patriotism of the puritan corporation. He suggested to "the Magistrates of the Corporation" that they enlist soldiers and seamen, and collect provisions and ships, to assist him in recapturing New York from the Dutch. Only if the prospective conquest became part of Massachusetts would the magistrates agree. Otherwise, they said, they would much prefer to have the Dutch control the colony than the king and his brother. Their officer, Colonel Lovelace, if restored as the governor of New York, "might prove a worse neighbor" to independent New England than had England's enemy, the Dutch. Captain Wynbourne naturally concluded that the Massachusetts magistrates considered their colony to be "a free State

63. Captain Wynbourne's report (as paraphrased by John Mason, claimant against Massachusetts for title to New Hampshire) is in C.O. 1/35, 269–70. Mason's history of the Massachusetts charter, which prefaces the manuscript, is largely omitted from the calendar of the document (*C.P.S.C. 1675–1676*, no. 721), but Wynbourne's report is given almost verbatim. For a large-scale anticipation of Wynbourne's report, and a remarkably prescient prediction of the future of English empire in New England (if something like King Philip's War had not intervened, this commentator held that New England would have declared its independence by 1691), see the journal of admiral the earl of Sandwich for 2 July 1671, in F. R. Harris, *The Life of Edward Montague, K.G., First Earl of Sandwich* (London, 1912), II, appendix K.

and not at all to be interested or concerned in the differences or wars which his Maty may have with other Nations."

If the leaders of the commonwealth would not actively aid the king, perhaps they would passively assist the war effort. Captain Wynbourne asked the Massachusetts magistrates to order some of the English seamen who had taken refuge in Boston from the royal navy's press gangs in London to be turned over to him for service. In reply, the magistrates told the mob about the captain's request and so incited the first impressment riot in America. Attacked in the street, the wounded Wynbourne was saved from death only by the timely arrival of the *Garland*'s well-armed crew. Despite the captain's formal complaint against his attackers, the corporate government refused to try them, and "no other punishment was inflicted upon that rabble then one nights imprisonment of some twenty persons."

In contrast to the fraud, disloyalty, misgovernment, independence, and homicidal abusiveness of the officers of the bay company, Captain Wynbourne found that the people were "generally for a submission to his Matys Government." Indeed, they were disappointed that it had been so long delayed. To encourage the king to send them a governor-general some dissident magistrates "and principle of the Merchants" promised not only to obey but even to save the king the cost of governing them. They told the captain that, "if his Maty would send a person of honor to be their Vice Roy or Lord Lieftn," they would not only submit to his government, they would also build him a palace and pay his salary. This proposal was not personal flattery. The loyalists made that clear to the commoner who commanded the *Garland* by stressing that "by no means they would not have any mean person to be sent over as Governor in Chief over the whole Country."

The captain was not stopped by this display of prejudice against "tarpaulins" from exposing the fatal peculiarities of puritan politics. As a royal professional officer he dutifully detailed the religious quarrels, the legal and political deficiencies, and the regional jealousies which, by weakening the Massachusetts hegemony, reinforced the potential for imperial government in New England. The religious bases of royalism were apparent, Wynbourne wrote, both in the hostility of many persons to congregational orthodoxy and in the anglican devotion of "those of the better sort." They were "for the Church of England and have the Comon prayer book in their houses and will not have their children baptised after any other forme." Legally, it was clear to the captain that the corporation's laws were both arbitrary and at variance with those of England, to which every government in the empire was expected to conform. Politically, although it appeared that these laws were passed by popularly elected magistrates, Captain Wynbourne pointed out that the annual elections were conducted "in such a manner as the people have not any voice." Not only did the corporation fail to represent the people, it also antagonized its neighbors. Massachusetts' political predominance over "other provinces by force and fraud," Captain Wynbourne observed, made all New England anxious for "a general Settlement and uniting of all the Colonys under his Mats government."

An imperial dominion of New England would do more than serve the English subjects settled there, it would materially assist the defense and expansion of the English empire in America. Certainly direct government would strengthen the royal navy as an instrument of that empire. The region's ships and seamen, naval stores and provisions meant that "there is noe place in his Mats Dominions in America can contribute soe much to the suppressing or overcoming of any enemies in those parts as New England." Moreover, the English navy itself could be as commodiously and cheaply supplied with ship's timber from New England's coastal forests as from those of Norway, with obvious advantages to imperial self-sufficiency.

Not just the empire and its subjects, but the native inhabitants as well would be benefited by royal government, Captain Wynbourne concluded, if only because the horrid hypocrisy of a government that was founded to Christianize the natives but which instead debauched and exploited them would be brought to an end with the demise of the puritan commonwealth. The captain insisted that "the chief if not the only cause of the Indians making war upon the English in New England is occasioned by the tyrannical Government of Massachusetts." An awful example was the corporation's construction of a castle on an island in Boston harbor by the forced labor of hundreds of Indians. For violations of its law against native drunkenness, the corporation's courts condemned the Indians to labor. Then the captives were given liquor just before the expiration of their sentences and were recommitted to Castle Island, "which barbarous usage made not only those poor sufferers but the other Indians to vow revenge."

Captain Wynbourne's own revenge was his indictment of the Massachusetts Bay Company's officers as illegal traders, disloyal subjects, usurping governors, tyrannical rulers, and religious dictators, abusers of both their English and their native neighbors, violators of the laws of England and contemnors of the king's prerogative. Alternatively, the captain applauded New England's imperial potential: the patriotism of the populace; the promised obedience and tribute of the mercantile upper class; the region's military resources. The captain's accusations were the stuff of the crown's successful assault on the independence of puritan Massachusetts. His alternatives to puritan hegemony underlay the erection of an imperial dominion over all of New England.

During 1676, Wynbourne himself became an agent of the privy council as commander of the annual naval convoy for the fishing fleet in Newfoundland. The captain investigated the privy council's understanding that the New Englanders shipped "Brandy & Wyne from the Maderias & rum from home [i.e., New England] to debauch the Fishers" of Newfoundland, to their detriment and to that of the royal customs. The privy councilors' easy assumptions about the unscrupulous and selfish character of the Yankee merchants made the English authorities all the more ready to favor every complaint brought against the New England governments as 1676 began. In addition to proprietary and piscine objections to saintly rule, the duke of York's secretary entered caveats against Connecticut's pretensions to New York territories, and the Dutch ambassador prepared a petition to the privy council "agt those of Boston in New England" for their aggression against the Dutch who were resident in Maine.[64]

"THE BEST LAND IN NEW ENGLAND"

Metropolitan assumptions about the origin of colonial conflict in the aggressiveness of the New England governments were further reinforced, as 1676 began, by the colonists' own reports, printed in the *Gazette*. These dispatches declared that English forces had swept the Mount Hope Peninsula of uncooperative natives and boasted that "the Land we have already gained on the said Promontory, is worth £10,000." The same report nonetheless indicated that the puritan commonwealths, for all their roundhead reputation, might not be able to contain the native hostility they had incited. It admitted that the Indians had escaped from the English sweep and had fled westward, where "we fear they may greatly annoy our Plantations." That fear grew quickly, as London readers learned from the pamphlet appended to the first *Gazette* of the new year. Even as King Philip fled, he had convinced other tribes that unless they united against the aggressive English, his people's fate would soon be theirs: "if they did not Joyn together, they should lose their Lives and Lands."[65]

64. Wynbourne's Newfoundland assignment appears in P.C. 2/65, 185; *C.S.P.C. 1675–1676*, nos. 882, 1169, 1175. The continuing influence of his report is evidenced in *ibid.*, no. 889. On New England and the fisheries, see P.C. 2/65, 185. For the caveats and complaints against New England, see *ibid.*, 77–78, and the Journal of the Foreigne Comittee, 22 January/1 February 1675/6, S.P. 104/179, 9, where the cabinet decided to bring the Dutch complaint to the full privy council.

65. *The London Gazette*, no. 1017 (16–19 August 1675). No. A1051 of the *Gazette*, "The Present State of New England with Respect of the *Indian* War . . . 20th June–16th November 1675. Faithfully Composed by a Merchant of *Boston*," was printed in Lincoln, ed., *Narratives*, 24–50 (see especially 26).

As the number of native enemies grew, initial English successes in seizing Mount Hope, "judged to be the best Land in New England," were succeeded by the first firings of the New England frontier villages. The success began with Plymouth's ouster of Philip from Mount Hope. Massachusetts boasted of the awful accomplishments of Captain Samuel Mosely, an old Cromwellian "Privateer at Jamaica, an excellent Souldier." Mosely terrified the natives with the ferocity of more than a hundred of his buccaneers and their slave-hunting dogs (one wonders what they all had been doing in puritan Boston). His wig, taken off in the heat of combat, also seemed exceedingly unfair to a scalp-hunting enemy. Mosely's men captured 223 Indians. They were shipped from Boston to be sold into slavery at Cadiz and, for a time during 1676, these unfortunate Algonquins became galley slaves in the English oared ships at Tangier. But native counterattacks quickly cost the English all of three frontier villages and most of two others.[66]

Soon the spreading conflict became a race war. At least the English thought it so. They complained in Massachusetts, as they would in Virginia, that "they cannot know a Heathen from a Christian [Indian] by his Visage or Appareal." The natives' tactic of ambush made their inscrutable physiognomy all the more menacing. Unable to distinguish native friends from Indian enemies, the English took actions that made the former into the latter. Even from Christian converts, the colonists took hostages. Then, still fearful, the colonists crowded these Christian converts into concentration camps. Finally, they attacked every Indian found outside the camps. What had been the uprising of a few tribes now became the revolt of an entire people. The numerous Nipmuck nation announced their accession to King Philip's cause by killing Captain Edward Hutchinson, just forty years to the day (so the *Gazette* appendix said) since his famous mother, Anne, had been axed by Indians. Then the Nipmuck besieged Brookfield.

Still, there was balm in Gilead: the reverend Increase Mather reassured his Boston parishioners that no town with a regular church congregation had been attacked. Boston obviously required reassurance: merely on a false alarm, twelve hundred men turned out in two hours. Everyone admitted that their speed owed more to panic than to preparedness. From this force, relief was twice sent to beleaguered Deerfield, and twice ambushed. As a result, Londoners were enabled to peruse the antique lan-

---

66. "The Present State" says Mosely had twelve men, but, as A. J. F. Van Laer, ed. and trans., *Minutes of the Court of Albany, Rensselaerwyck and Schenectady* (Albany, 1928), II, 177, 181, makes clear, the buccaneer's force was far larger. On 29 April 1676, the admiralty ordered that the (New England) "Indian Slaves" supplied by Captain Spragg of the *Sampson* merchantman be returned to him at Cadiz from his majesty's galley at Tangier (ADM 3/276, 50).

guage and logic of the fast-day resolve of the governor and council of the Massachusetts Bay Company. The puritan penitents attributed the Indian war, "in this good Land, which the Lord hath given us," to divine wrath at the "ill Entertainment of the Ministry of the precious Gospel of Peace; Leaving our first-Love, dealing falsely in the Covenant of the Lord our God: The Apostacy of many from the Truth unto Heresies, and pernicious Errours; Great Formality, inordinate Affection and sinful Conformity to this present evil vain World."[67]

Worldly Londoners may not have understood the underlying message of this lament—that is, that "these accusations refer to neglect at Plymouth to provide for the adequate support of the established [i.e., Congregational] ministry and to the growth of the Baptists, Episcopalians, and Friends, as well as to the lukewarmness of church members." But Restoration readers recognized the dated diction of the saints. Soon they were told of its ineffectiveness against the subsequent native attacks on Springfield, their devastation of what had been the richest plantations of New England, and their threat to every inland settlement of Massachusetts. There was but one victory to report. That the first battle of Hadley was won by the profane privateer Samuel Mosely did nothing to redeem the military reputation of the Bostonians (which had long been a deterrent to crown interference in New England). Nonetheless the bay corporation, Londoners learned in January 1676, was about to widen the war by attacking the greatest nation of southern New England, the Narragansett, supposedly on suspicion of their disloyalty to Massachusetts but actually, as some suspected, to pre-empt other colonies' claims to Narragansett land. Indeed, the official incitement to Massachusetts' war on the Narragansetts, according to the "Merchant of Boston" who wrote "The Present State of New England with Respect of the *Indian* War . . ." was the failure of the Narragansetts to surrender Weetamoo, the famous "Squaw Sachem," widow of Philip's brother, Alexander, "which if she be taken by the *English*, her Lands will more than pay all the Charge we have been at in this unhappy War."

LEVERETT'S COMMAND IN IMPERIAL CONTEXTS

At this momentous moment, potentially so prosperous to the puritan corporation, the *Gazette* pamphlet closed. Fortunately for London's information about the war in New England, however, an old Cromwellian

---

67."The Present State," *The London Gazette*, A1051, 18; Lincoln, ed., *Narratives*, 48. The fast-day proclamation quoted in the text is found in Lincoln, ed., *Narratives*, 45–46, and the exegesis on 46, note 1. On the exaggerated estimate of the puritan militias (shattered by the revelations of Philip's war) see Sandwich: "They have 50,000 trained bands well armed and disciplined" (Harris, *Sandwich*, II, 338).

cavalry captain, John Leverett, now the elected governor of the Massachusetts corporation, provided telling and terrible detail of what became
not puritan profit but the loss of an imperial frontier.

In a long letter to Secretary Williamson, Leverett explained why his
government could not act on the rather minor property matters previously
referred to the Massachusetts magistrates by the king-in-council (Leverett
had yet to receive the royal order to send agents to Whitehall). The
veteran soldier's explanation was a description of the winter war which
had cost New England seven towns south of the Kennebec and the whole
county of York (i.e., Maine) north of that river. The governor's narrative
was written with a lucidity creditable to Oliverian military professional-
ism.

The natives, Leverett wrote, had laid waste the English settlements
along a 300-mile crescent. From the war's first scenes at Plymouth's
Mount Hope west and north to the Connecticut River, thence north and
east to the Kennebec and beyond, the swath of savagery smoldered. The
Indians, Leverett estimated, had killed three hundred English militiamen as they ravaged the entire length of the New England frontier. Yet
Leverett hoped that an army of the New England confederacy, led by
Governor Winslow of Plymouth, would destroy the refuge of King Philip's noncombatants and the source of his supplies by attacking the Narragansett nation in their winter camp.[68]

News of the battle reached Whitehall on 1 February 1675/6, from the
same shipping that brought Leverett's letter. The gazetteer versified a
victory report:

> New-English in fierce fight with Savage Foes
> Kill them 500 and 200 lose.
> Since first that war began, the Smartest Fray.
> The Indians run, the English get the day.

The London Gazette of 4 February added that Major Winslow's fourteen
hundred men had met three thousand natives. They had fought face to
face until the natives' munitions gave out. Then the Indians broke and
ran. They were pursued for sixteen miles through the snow by the victorious English. The victors also burned the native fortress and three
hundred huts before they retreated from the onset of night and cold.[69]

On 6 February 1675/6, the cabinet council met and, in time taken from
untangling the protocol complexities of the Nimeguen negotiations for a

68. Leverett's letter to Williamson, 18 December 1675, "Rec. 1 February 1675/6," is in C.O.
1/35, 288, and C.S.P.C. 1675–1676, no. 745.
69. The London Gazette, no. 1066. See also S.P. 29/366, 46.

general European peace, and England's relations with Holland and Hamburg, the cabinet considered both Leverett's letter and the news of Winslow's victory. The ministers agreed that Secretary Williamson ought "not to lose this favourable conjuncture." To what this cryptic injunction might refer appeared in part during the privy-council deliberations of late February and early March 1675/6. On 24 February, some of the councilors met at the lord chancellor's. He was hot against the Virginia charter as providing the sort of corporate privileges so abused by the New Englanders in their evasion of the acts of trade. Naturally, the councilors' discussion moved on to New England's usurpation of the staple trades of the English plantations, to the potential role of these staples—tobacco, sugar, and indigo—in rebalancing the European trade now dominated by the combined development of French cloth manufactures and French absorption of Spain's American income. These February discussions influenced parts of the important imperial resolutions of the privy council on 10 March 1675/6, especially in cases where the council's general policies regarding the plantation trades and ships' passes were applied to New England.[70]

The agenda for the 10 March privy-council meeting was enormous. It opened with the committee for trade's report on ships' passes for Russia and the Baltic States, a relatively minor matter the reading of which gave latecomers—who, as usual, included the busy treasurer—time to take their seats. Then the lord treasurer presented his budget for Ireland. First he provided for the royal bureaucracy: law courts, customs collectors, church, exchequer operation. All told the Irish civil list was £45,906.01.01. This was exceeded threefold by the Irish military establishment. The pay of the officers general (headed by "the Lord Lieutenant and Governor General of Ireland") and their headquarters staff; of the ordnance officers and gunners on the staffs of Ireland's four military provinces and fifteen fortified towns; and of the army, composed of Guards regiments of horse and foot and seventy-four garrison companies—that is, the cost of Ireland's military government, police, and security—was £146,260.19.8. After some debate about the accuracy of the figures and the likelihood of the budget's being observed, the privy council accepted this, the greatest of the empire's provincial budgets. It accurately reflected military primacy in imperial administration.

The privy council then considered the Gambia Company's African liabilities, and it condemned the port administration by the civil government of Guernsey. Next, a group of leading ministers took a moment to sign the politically symbolic but pecuniarily pitiful pension recommen-

70. Williamson noted "Leverett's lre to me of 18 Dec:" and determined "not to lose this favourable conjuncture" in his statement to the cabinet about "New England" on 6 February 1675/6 (S.P. 104/179, 11). The relevant printed minutes of the committee for foreign affairs are in C.S.P.D. 1675–1676, 544, 574. See also P.C. 2/65, 139; S.P. 29/366, 46.

dations for royalist civil-war veterans. The privy council then reviewed and approved its committees' new rules for ships' passes, in accord with the recent treaties between his majesty of Great Britain and the states of Holland, Algiers, Tunis, and Tripoli. The imperial assumption of the privy council's passport program was that England's neutral status in the European war should advance her commercial penetration of Mediterranean markets and her acquisitions of Atlantic trades and territories. Unfortunately, both France and Spain, while claiming to respect English rights, used privateers and proconsuls to capture and condemn English prizes.[71]

The *Society* of Boston, laden with New English provisions on the account of a London merchant, bound for Jamaica, was seized by a French privateer and stripped by order of the governor of Tortuga. The privy council's protest to the French court was neglected (presumably for a price from the privateer's owner) by the corrupt assistant to the English ambassador. (The ambassador was lord Berkeley, Sir William's brother. His involvement in this sort of incident did not enhance the family's standing at Whitehall. Like his brother, lord Berkeley was soon recalled.)

The effort to eliminate technical excuses for confiscation of English ships by reforming the passport process could serve political and administrative purposes of the imperial executive as well. To centralize the administration of trade and shipping in the capital would reduce the importance of the outports, pleasing the London clients of the crown. The same process would increase the authority of the royal admiralty and customs while reducing that of corporate officers. On 10 March 1675/6, therefore, the privy council accepted the complete reorganization of the system of ships' passes for vessels sailing not only from England, but also from "Scotland, Ireland, Tangier, and other his Matys Plantations, the Islands of Jersey and Guernsey, and ye East and West Indies." In all these possessions, the crown's proconsuls were to administer new forms of bonds, oaths, certificates, and testimonials that the documented ships belonged to inhabitants "in the Dominions of his Maty of Great Britain."[72]

The centralization, bureaucratization, and royalization of maritime registrations throughout the empire made Massachusetts' autonomy appear increasingly anomalous. The privy council took disapproving notice of Governor Leverett's ships' passes. While they prepared instructions for an investigator to be sent directly to the colony, the council also

---

71. P.C. 2/65, 140–59. The case of the *Society* appears in *ibid.*, 310.

72. These regulations, prepared by the privy-council committee for trade dominated by Danby, are in ADM 3/276, 8 ff., and the privy-council discussion is in P.C. 2/65, 151–58.

ordered immediate action taken against ships trading staple crops from the plantations to the Channel Islands, contrary to the acts of trade. This order's particular incitement was the *Speedwell* of (New) Plymouth. She had been an active trader in tobacco and news throughout the crisis of the Indian war in New England. Now, on 10 March 1675/6, the *Speedwell*, having attracted the hostile attentions of the king himself for her impudent violation of the acts, appears to have been condemned for illegally trading tobacco. So she became a vehicle that widened the view of the world seen from Whitehall.

IMPERIAL RECONNAISSANCES, EAST AND WEST

On 11 March, the king met with those of his privy councilors appointed to administer the admiralty. His majesty announced that, pursuant to his conversation with the explorer Captain John Wood (of Straits of Magellan fame), he would provide a ship to Tartary, Japan, and the East Indies. The duke of York's syndicate would provide a trading cargo for Wood to carry out to the Far East via the Northeast Passage. On 18 March 1675/6, his majesty's ship the *Speedwell* (either the fifth-rate of 1655 or the confiscated New England ketch) was made available to Captain Wood. By 27 March, the duke had decided to provide a second vessel to be taken into the royal navy for the voyage. On 26 April, Samuel Pepys reported that the "North-East Passage business" was well advanced. Backed by the presence of the duke at the admiralty board, Pepys offered the *Prosperous Pink* to be chartered by the navy from her owners (the Yorkist syndicate, of which both Pepys and Williamson were members). Pepys nominated her officers to be commissioned into the navy by the king. The pink and her crew were duly commissioned to accompany the *Speedwell* on her voyage to open up a new route to the Far East.[73]

Four months later to the day, Sir John Berry reported the *Bristol* ready to sail for Virginia and Captain John Wood told the council of the loss of the *Speedwell* on the coast of Nova Zemla. All during June 1676 they had sailed east among the ice floes of the Barents Sea. They ran by dead reckoning along the 70th parallel, in the haze of the northern summer and in a higher latitude than ever Englishmen had sailed those seas. But there was "noe sun, moone or stars to be seen though all the while daylight." On 29 June 1676, after a month's sailing in the northern mists, the *Speedwell* struck a cape of the great island of Nova Zemla. Her crew were cast

---

73. ADM 3/276, 31, 33.

away on the snow-covered coast. The *Prosperous Pink* had sailed by her sister in the mist (presumably she was still standing south towards "Waigat's Strait," for which see the Wright/Thornton map, pages 174–75). She was ten days beating back to the castaways, but she rescued all save two of the *Speedwell's* crew and brought them safely home to report the farthest penetration to date of the northeast by an English vessel. King Charles read Captain Wood's journal "with great satisfaction," rewarded him with the salvage he had recovered from the *Speedwell,* ordered the expedition's crews fully paid, and turned to consider the results of another imperial initiative taken on 10 March 1675/6.[74]

On that day, the king-in-council had dictated the royal letter which marked the beginning of the end of the Massachusetts Bay Company. In the king's name, Secretary Coventry protested "to the Govr and Magistrates of Our Towne of Boston in New England" against "the Violence and strong hand of Our Subjects the People of Boston, and others of the Massachusetts Colony," which kept the proprietors of New Hampshire lands from their property. Not wishing to condemn the bay corporation unheard, the secretary wrote, the king required them to send agents fully empowered to answer for Massachusetts before him in council. To this text, approved by the privy council, Secretary Coventry added, by the king's special command, a clause requiring the letter to be read aloud in a full and public council, and in the presence of the king's messenger Edward Randolph. Randolph, the Boston officials were told, was authorized by the king to report upon their response to the letter and upon the proceedings of Massachusetts.[75]

The objects of Randolph's report were the subjects of imperial politics, as it was conceived of at Whitehall in 1676. On 10 March, the plantations committee of the privy council, under instructions from the cabinet that the whole investigative process was "well to be thought on," directed Edward Randolph to describe the locus of political power in Massachusetts, its corporation, churches, and college. He was to secure copies of the local laws in force that were contrary to those of England. The agent was to ascertain the religions, professions, and social classes of the colonists and to assess their military capacity. He was to chart the boundaries

---

74. ADM 3/276, 100, 115. Newsletter, 22 August 1676, in *Manuscripts of Le Fleming,* 128.
75. C.O. 1/36, 59. Sir Henry Coventry, secretary of state since 8 July 1672 and principal secretary since 11 September 1674, presumably acquired a personal sense of the political isolation of the puritan leaders when he read Randolph's report that Governor Leverett, looking at the signature of the royal letter, "asked me who that Mr. Coventry was" (Randolph to the king, 20 September 1676, in *Edward Randolph: Including His Letters and Official Papers . . . 1676–1703,* ed. R. N. Toppan and A. T. S. Goodrick [Boston, 1898], II, 216–17).

claimed by the colony and (so) to identify the cause of the war with the Indians. Randolph was to record the colony's commerce, legal and illegal, and to analyze the sources and amount of its public revenue. He was to describe the present state of Boston and the relations of Massachusetts with other colonies.[76]

In the answers to these inquiries lay the physical possibility of English intervention in Massachusetts and the legal materials for a revocation of the bay company charter, but, imperially, the privy council's most suggestive inquiry to Randolph was "how they [the inhabitants of Massachusetts] generally stand affected to ye Government of England, which persons are the most Popular, and at present in the Magistracy, or like to be soe at the Next Election." In the answer to this query was the stuff of the colonial political revolution which could, and after 1684 did, make independent Massachusetts into an imperial province. The king-in-council expected to convince the anglophile portions of the colonial ruling class that their own political authority, even their physical survival, depended upon their adoption of the English institutions, civil and military, to be imposed upon New England by a royal governor-general and his conciliar administration. Both viceroy and council were already, in 1676, projected for New England by the king-in-council. Indeed, many of the privy councilors did not want to wait either for Randolph's replies or for the Massachusetts agents to arrive before acting against the independence of the bay commonwealth. They were persuaded to delay, however, by the lessons of 1637 and 1664 that English orders not backed by physical force would be spurned by the saints, by the injustice of condemning the corporation unheard, and by the press of imperial business before the council on 10 March 1675/6. "But they do agree that this is the Conjuncture to do some thing Effectual for the better Regulation of that Government, or else all hopes of it may be hereafter lost."[77]

The councilors' agent, Edward Randolph, confirmed their worst fears of Massachusetts' present independence in his dispatch of 17 June 1676. Randolph wrote that he had confronted Governor Leverett with the presence of European ships in Boston harbor, "contrary to the late Acts of Parliament for encouraging Navigation and trade." The governor of the bay corporation "freely declared to me that the Laws made by Our King and Parlmt obligeth them in nothing but what consists with the Interest of New England." If English law had little place in the puritan republic, royal prerogative had none at all. According to Leverett, the king had

76. See C.O. 1/36, 62–63. Toppan and Goodrick, eds., *Edward Randolph*, II, 196, date this 20 March. The cabinet discussion, as Williamson recorded it, was on 21 March, and the king's letter was to be dated 24 March 1675/6 (S.P. 104/178, 2).

77. C.O. 1/36, 62v. A.P.C.C., no. 1050. Toppan and Goodrick, eds., *Randolph*, II, 196.

neither legal jurisdiction nor military authority in Massachusetts, much less religious supremacy.[78]

Yet Randolph discovered much less capacity for resistance to empire and much more desire for accommodation among Massachusetts' neighbors than in the bay colony itself. Even including Massachusetts, the New England militias had turned out many fewer men than the court had expected. Apart from those led by Governor Winslow of Plymouth, they had proved largely ineffective in the field. Between Winslow's colony and the bay corporation, moreover, there was little love lost. Indeed, wrote Randolph, every one of her neighbors feared aggressive Massachusetts. Therefore they "would readily and willingly submitt to your Majesties pleasure and commands in the disposal and settlement of the civill government." The worst terms the rest of the New Englanders could expect from the crown would be far better than the imprisonment and spoliation Massachusetts had visited upon Rhode Islanders or on the men of Maine. Therefore, the royal agent alleged, "the loyal colonies of New Plymouth, Connecticut, New Hampshire and Maine . . . are very desirous of submitting to a general governour to be established by his Majestie."

Even in Boston, some few leaders and "the generality of the people complaining of the arbitrary government and oppression on their magistrates . . . doe hope your Majestie will be pleased to free them from this bondage by establishing your own royall authority among them and govern them according to your Majesties lawes." It seems that the royal agent had found the constituents of a court party in the puritan country, a party anxious to escape the dictatorship of the regenerate by embracing the rule of a governor-general, a party willing, in the secular climate of the Restoration, to exchange God's commonwealth for the king's empire. Small wonder that Leverett accused Randolph of planning "a mutiny and disturbance in the country and to withdraw the people from their obedience to the magistracy of that country." Even when they condescended to ask Randolph to report favorably of them to the king, the saintly governor and council warned him "that those that blessed them God would blesse, and those that cursed them God would curse." [79]

DEVASTATION AND DEPENDENCE

By the time that this report was delivered and Randolph himself appeared before the privy council on 28 September 1676, the revolution in

---

78. Toppan and Goodrick, eds., *Randolph*, II, 206, 219. C.O. 1/37, 18. The very next day, as it happened, the cabinet considered Leverett's latest letter to Williamson, together with the rash of fires in Southwark, and alarms from Bristol, Dover "&c." (S.P. 104/179, 45v).
79. Toppan and Goodrick, eds., *Randolph*, II, 223, 224, 254.

Virginia had absorbed the imperial attention of the king-in-council. Yet the Virginia expedition itself might be the means by which the northern commonwealthsmen as well as the southern revolutionaries could be reduced to imperial obedience. Randolph's report of 12 October 1676 gave point to this possibility by describing the symbols of Massachusetts' independence from England. "As a marke of sovereignty," he wrote, "they coin mony . . . stamped with these figures, 1652, that year being the era of the commonwealth wherin they erected themselves into a free state." And Randolph took advantage of the availability of a punitive expedition to propose a forceful remedy for puritan pretensions: "that 3 frigats of 40 guns with 3 ketches well manned lying a League or two below Boston . . . would bring them all to his Mat.s own terms and doe more in one Weeks time than all the Ordrs. of King & Councill to them in Seven years." As it happened, Randolph's thinking was shared at Whitehall. On Friday, 20 October 1676, the cabinet council directed Secretary Coventry to write the royal orders that, as soon as Virginia was pacified and imperial authority had replaced both Bacon's rebels and Berkeley's cronies, Sir John Berry's squadron should sail for Boston.[80]

Yet even the most devoted privy-council proponents of direct rule understood that the mundane business of provincial government was primarily an affair of local elites. Berry's fleet could back them, the crown's commissioners could direct them, but "the most popular and well principled men" of New England, as identified by Edward Randolph, must choose to do the crown's business because it enhanced their own stature, increased their colonies' security, and promoted trans-Atlantic trade and commerce. As the vehicle to transfer the allegiance of New England elites from colonial corporations to the imperial crown, it was proposed that the king appoint a regional commission of the peace. Besides the present governor of each colony, the royal commission was to include the militia officers, merchants, and landlords deemed most likely, first, to swear allegiance to King Charles; second, to proclaim Nathaniel Bacon a traitor and stop shipments to his partisans; third, to keep the king's peace in their respective colonies; and, fourth and most important, to execute future orders of the king and council in the hitherto independent colonies. This was, of course, the outline of the forthcoming Dominion of New England council. Many of the future members of that council were on the 1676 list, but it was 1684 before the council was actually constituted "to unhinge the commonwealth" of Massachusetts Bay and, subsequently, to displace the rest of New England's colonial regimes.[81]

80. *Ibid.*, 229, 208. Coventry Ms. 77, 260.
81. Coventry Ms. 77, 295. Toppan and Goodrick, eds., *Randolph*, II, 255. It was soon understood in London that Bacon had applied to the New England governments for assistance

The immediate transformation of the New England corporations from colonies to provinces was prevented by the long delay of the expeditionary fleet in Virginia. The resulting sickness of the sailors left Sir John Berry with hardly enough able-bodied men to weigh his ships' anchors from the bottom of the James River. Whatever his orders or inclination— and he expected further directions from the cabinet to reach him in Virginia—Berry had no choice but to sail straight for England in June of 1677. As for the crown commission of the peace in New England, its immediate purpose was to prevent New England's providing either refuge for or assistance to the Baconian rebels. This purpose was most speedily accomplished, at least in theory, by the peremptory orders against aid to Bacon sent by the crown to every private jurisdiction in North America and enforced, in southern New England, by the duke of York's lieutenant in New York. Essentially, and ironically, however, it was that old cavalier Sir William Berkeley's resistance to royal orders in Virginia that delayed Berry's fleet and so saved the independent republics from imperial rule for another seven years.

That the delay was no longer owed something to the new imperial determination and capacity of the English crown. It owed as much again to the devastation and demoralization of the New England commonwealths in 1676. Not for a century would the per-capita wealth of their colonists recover its pre-1676 level. In the interval, the economy of New England became increasingly integrated with that of old England. At the same time, the territorial expansion of New England was restricted by the very forces that had defeated King Philip and which would define and defend Stuart sovereignty in North America: the royal military executives of the duke's province of New York, and their allies, the Five Nations of the Iroquois. The contrast between puritan aspirations before 1676 and their subsequent circumscription appears in the alterations made in 1681 to the Morden and Berry map of 1676 (page 220).

These factors—devastation, demoralization, dependence—were interrelated as early as 20 February 1675/6 by Richard Wharton, merchant of Boston and one of the cabinet council's nominees for the royal commission of the peace. In a letter read by the privy council, Wharton predicted that famine would follow war in New England: "wee are like to have little leasure this year to sow and less opportunity to reap, the Narragansetts and all the Indians we have ever heard of except the Mohegans and Mohàwks having one way or other declared themselves our enemies." To the Mohegan (whose good relations with the English dated back to the war of 1637) Wharton gave some credit for the assault on the

---

against the royal government and that the laws of the Massachusetts Bay Company offered a refuge to Virginia revolutionaries, just as they had to English regicides (*ibid.*, 233).

Narragansett. Other correspondents reported to the metropolis that the Mohegan had led Captain Mosely's vanguard across the great "swamp" (the word entered the English language in 1676 from these reports) to the native fortress. But the victory won in Rhode Island had been wasted in Boston, Wharton wrote. "Were our great Councillors at home as expeditious and pollitick to supply and command as our Souldiers have been deligent and couragious to fight the Narragansetts had been utterly subdued," rather than merely dispersed to avenge themselves on the English frontier. But the army had been inexplicably recalled, the frontiers were entirely ungarrisoned. Despite two weeks' prior warning, the Boston authorities had left Lancaster unsupported to face a siege. Medfield was burnt even as Wharton wrote home that, "except God give greater wisdome to our Rulers or put it into the King's heart to rule and relieve us, these colonies will soon be ruined" and reduced to submission to any governing power which can protect them: England, as it happened.[82]

Agreeing with Wharton that, of the Massachusetts magistracy, Governor Leverett was "crazy in body and many more soe are in their heads," other reporters took up the tale of King Philip's War where Wharton had left it, among the Mohawk. A Boston letter of 18 May 1676 brought to the privy council of England news from the western frontier village of Hadley, on the Connecticut River, "that the Maquaes [Mohawk] have fallen upon the enemie & slayne 79 of them." (So impressed were the mapmakers of 1676 by the Iroquois' exploits that they wrote "Mohawk" onto Massachusetts.) From the northern frontier beyond the Kennebec came word that "many of the enemy are cutt off by the Maques." In southern New England, it was reported that Mohawk pressure was largely responsible for the starvation that drove Philip's people back into the arms of the English. Secretary Williamson read in mid-October 1676 of "Some [Indians] that ye English killed the wch they ripped open & they had nothing but grasse in their bellyes."[83]

In the same week, however, the privy council was told by Edward Randolph that "the government of Boston" acknowledged only one contribution to the war, and that negative, by Albany (whence Captain An-

82. C.O. 1/36, 40. *The London Gazette*, no. A1091, "A Continuation of the State of New England; Being a Farther Account of the Indian Warr, and of the Engagement Betwixt the Joynt Forces of the United *English* Collonies and the *Indians*, on the 19th of December 1675 . . . Together with an Account of the Intended Rebellion of the *Negroes* in the Barbadoes. Licensed March 27, 1676. Henry Oldenburg," printed in Lincoln, ed., *Narratives*, 53–74. The official report of the deputy governor and council of the Massachusetts Bay Company, 6 April 1676, came to a similar conclusion as to the severity of the war, its destruction of crops and commerce, but the bay officials begged the crown "to believe that the Losses & Sufferings befallen us have not proceeded from want of care in the Government" (C.O. 1/36, 75).
83. C.O. 1/36, 170. S.P. 29/386, 62. *C.S.P.D. 1676–1677*, 371.

thony Brockholes had obeyed Governor-General Andros' orders to set the
Mohawk and their Iroquois brethren onto King Philip and his allies): that
enemy Indians brought ammunition there. As for the governor-
general of the duke's dominions, Edmund Andros, his offer "to have
engaged the Mohawkes and Maquot Indians to have fallen upon the
Sachem Philip and his confederates" had been "slighted" by the government of Boston. The day after Randolph reported this to the privy-council
committee on plantations, the crown censor licensed a pamphlet supplement to *The London Gazette* for 23–26 October 1676 entitled "A New and
Further Narrative of the State of New England." Its author, "N.S." (Nathaniel Saltonstall), carried the story of the war down to 22 July 1676. N.S.
repeated "Boston's" suspicions of "Fort Albany" and its traders, but he
also expanded both upon Boston's rejection of Edmund Andros' Iroquois
allies and on their decisive contribution nonetheless to the defeat of the
Algonquin enemy.[84]

In February of 1675/6, N.S. began, New England had been "almost
destroyed and laid waste" by a savage enemy "well furnished with Arms
and Ammunition (by the base treachery we fear of some of our neighbours)." The dispersal of the Narragansett from their fortress in the preceding December had by February converted Philip's war with
Plymouth into an Algonquin assault on the English everywhere in New
England. In the first two months of 1676 eight towns had been burned, a
garrison wiped out, relief forces ambushed, and twenty-one hundred
armed Algonquin, aided by five hundred "French Indians," and by Philip's own force, had concentrated in a camp near Hoosac, some 40 miles
from Albany. Thence the Algonquin warriors planned to march on Connecticut in the spring and burn their way north to Boston by the fall of
the leaves.

At this terrible juncture, as N.S. wrote to his London audience, "there
was much Discourse and Consultation" about using "the Mohauks" of
New York against the northern invaders and their Algonquin allies. "And
it was certainly reported, that the Governour of New York would, upon
request, and reasonable Proposalls, freely make use of his Interest
amongst that People, (which is very great,) for effecting so good a design."
The Mohegan, major Indian allies of the New Englanders, pressed
the Boston (and Connecticut) magistrates to accept this proposal by
Governor-General Andros, "affirming that the said Mohauks were the
only Persons likely to put an end to the War, by hindering the Enemy
from Planting; and forcing them down upon us." But the alliance of

84. C.O. 1/36, 75. *The London Gazette*, no. A1091, 11. Randolph's reply to the privy-council
inquiries, 12 October 1676, printed in Toppan and Goodrick, eds., *Randolph*, II, 242. *The
London Gazette*, no. A1141 (dated from Boston, 22 July 1676), printed in Lincoln, ed., *Narratives*, 77–99.

Boston with ducal New York and the Iroquoian Mohawk was rejected, as N.S., himself a Boston merchant, told his English audience, "for I know not what good Reasons of Some amongst us," and to general disappointment.[85]

"THE WARR HATH BEEN VERY BLOUDY"

That disappointment deepened with the disasters of April 1676 in southern New England. *The London Gazette* supplement reported that the frontier forces of Massachusetts and Connecticut, based on the town of Marlborough, were unable to catch the native raiders, they "being so light of Foot that they can . . . pass Boggs, rocky Mountains and Thickets, where we could by no Means pursue them." The only answer was to employ native allies—if not the Mohawk, then the Mohegan. With their warrior captives (whose families were held hostage for their good behavior), the Mohegan scoured the Narragansett country, plundering abandoned villages and bringing in stragglers. Yet the refusal of Boston to aid Plymouth kept New England's ablest army in garrison through the spring. Instead it was a mixed force of native allies and Connecticut volunteers who caught and killed Connochet, the chief sachem of the Narragansett and the greatest war leader of the allied Algonquin, on 11 April 1676. In the meantime, however, the Boston militia had been withdrawn from Marlborough. The Algonquin then destroyed the town, save for one garrison house. Its defenders soon marched with a militia company from Dorchester to the relief of Sudbury. The militiamen were ambushed. They fought their way to a knoll, formed a ring, and held out for four hours against great odds. Finally, the Indians resorted to hunting technique. They fired the woods to windward of the English perimeter, burnt the militia off their hilltop, and killed them, almost to a man.[86]

"So insolent were the Indians grown" at this success, N.S. wrote from Boston, "that they sent us Word, to provide Store of good Chear, for they intended to dine with us upon the Election Day," 3 May 1676. So seriously did the Massachusetts council take this threat that they called out the trained band of every remaining town in the colony to muster on the fatal day. The militias were ordered to use martial law to repress the usual election-day parties, and the electors were advised to vote by proxy rather than risk travel.

Yet by election day 1676, the Algonquin began to lose skirmishes in Massachusetts and London read that "the praying Indians as they call

85. See especially "A New and Further Narrative of the State of New England," *The London Gazette*, no. A1141 (23–26 October 1676), 8–9, in Lincoln, ed., *Narratives*, 88–89.
86. See also S.P. 29/385, 115.

them have contributed much to the subdueing & vanquishing of them."
To the south of "Boston Colony" the Mohegan found more and more
stragglers returning to the Narragansett country. In the west, the garrisons
of Hadley and Northampton marched through the night to attack the great
encampment of King Philip and his people at the falls of the Connecticut.
Philip's people were largely noncombatants, but the English were full of
such stories as the one N.S. related to his London audience about "the
two poor Travellers, that had nothing but small sticks to defend themselves with," who were attacked "by a great number of Indian women."
The squaws "beat out their Brains, and cut off their privy Members,
which they carried away with them in Triumph." So the militiamen recognized no innocents among the Indians.

Firing on the sleeping natives at first light, the English were mistaken
for Mohawk. The natives panicked. They were slaughtered by the
hundred. The survivors were driven into the river and over the falls. After
them, the English threw the natives' forges, tools, and stock lead. The
militia were ambushed in their retreat (thirty-eight Hadley and Northampton men were killed by the first volley), and they ran, but the natives,
starving, despoiled, and demoralized, dispersed.

Those who returned to their homelands in the east were soon rounded
up by the English and their native allies, but Philip went west to join the
"Northern Indians." His band again encountered the force that had prevented Philip's people from planting and compelled them to expose
themselves too long at the spring fishing: "the Mohucks marched out
very strong, in a warlike Posture upon them, putting them to Flight. . . ."
The Mohawk victory meant the end of Philip's war. With no retreat left
to them, hundreds of the natives of southern New England "came in and
submitted themselves to the English at Plimouth-Colony; and Philip
himself is run skulking away into some Swamp, with not above ten Men
attending him. . . ." On 12 August 1676, just three weeks after the report
by N.S. was dated and shipped to London, King Philip was run down and
killed by Plymouth volunteers and their native allies on the Mount Hope
peninsula, where the war had begun thirteen months before.

Anticipating "a good Account . . . of that Prime Incendiary," Philip,
N.S. had counted the casualties of the war. They were worse for the
Indians. King Philip had seen his people, the Algonquin of southern New
England, extinguished before his eyes. Six thousand natives, so N.S.
estimated, had been killed or sold into slavery, or captured and reduced
to serfdom, by the English. "Besides vast quanties of their Corn, Houses,
Ammuhition, and other Necessaries," the stuff of Indian independence,
had been consumed by the conquerors. But the material cost to the vic-
tors, if a people so savaged can be called "victors," was also enormous.
Twenty-five English towns had been pillaged. Half of them, at least,

perhaps as many as seventeen towns, were burned to the ground. N.S. could make no count of the number of outlying farms and plantations, the richest acres in New England, which had been damnified or destroyed as agricultural assets.

As no record of the colonists' loss can be compiled, so no account of their century-long effort to recover from the war of 1675/1676 has been written, but, twenty years after that war, New England's leading propagandist admitted that not all of the towns ravaged in 1676 had been reoccupied, much less redeveloped. Per-capita incomes in New England did not recover their 1675 levels until 1775. They did not exceed the pre-1676 norm until after 1815. Admittedly, in the century after 1676 a tenfold increase in population was accommodated, largely within the area pioneered before 1676. These children of the puritans, however, started from scratch, and "scratch" was not what it had been before 1676. A large share of the capital of the puritan fathers, the investments of their all by the colonizing generations of New England, had been consumed in the fires of King Philip's War. A century of dependence on England would be required to recover the physical basis of New England's independence.

"And as to Persons," N.S. wrote, "it is generally thought, that of the English there hath been lost, in all, Men, Women and Children, above Eight hundred, since the war began." Other casualty estimates, ranging up to one adult male in ten of the English population or between eight hundred and a thousand men killed (plus fifteen hundred women and children), were much higher than those of N.S. A typical account, received in the fall of 1676 from the *Rebecca* of New York, reported that although the starving Algonquin were undoubtedly subdued "& become more slaves yn formerly" to the New Englanders, "the warr hath been very Bloudy, there having been 17 townes or Villages destroyed by the Indians & as neare as they can compute it about 2500 men women & children killed. . . ."[87]

The dead left a living legacy of hatred behind them. As the descendants of the survivors of the Indian war of 1676 in Massachusetts and Virginia became the leaders of American opinion, the image of the Indian savage which this year's conflict confirmed became a racist stereotype. N.S. fostered this hatred among the Bostonians, most of whom, like himself, had been safe during the struggle and never saw what he described and they believed. Worse than the number of casualties among the colonists, N.S. wrote, was the barbaric manner of their deaths. The English were "destroyed with exquisite Torments, and most inhumane Barbarities, the Heathen rarely giving Quarter to those that they take, but if they

87. S.P. 29/386, 223, 224.

were Women, they first forced them to satisfy their filthy Lusts and then murdered them; either cutting off the Head, ripping open the Belly, or skulping the Head of Skin and Hair, and hanging them up as Trophies, wearing Men's Fingers as Bracelets about their Necks, and Stripes of their Skins which they dresse for Belts." [88]

And the horror of race war was not yet over in New England. The northern Algonquin, the Abenaki confederacy, having driven out the English, fought the Mohawk Iroquois to a draw. Only the intervention of Edmund Andros' officers and the establishment of the duke of York's new Maine headquarters persuaded the Abenaki to make peace. Faced with few permanent English settlers beyond the Kennebec (and, indeed, few beyond the Piscataqua and Salmon rivers), and backed by the French and their Catholic missionaries, the Abenaki could not be reduced for forty years to come. These years repeatedly tested New England's shrinking autonomy. Repeatedly the puritan provinces were found to be too weak to sustain the independence from old England which peace and distance had supported prior to 1676. More positively, the shrinking moat of the Atlantic, the growing strength of English commerce, crown, and empire, and the alliance of the western imperialists, Yorkist and Iroquois, combined in 1676 to confine, and would soon eliminate, the independence of New England.

88. "A New and Further Narrative," *London Gazette,* no. A1141. Lincoln, ed., *Narratives,* 98–99. The tone of N.S.'s narrative is typical of the contemporary accounts received in London which the present text reflects. The report of Sir William Berkeley (pp. 205–6) approximates the one-in-ten casualty figure. In the wake of this demonstration of the vaunted puritans' actual weakness, the cabinet immediately moved to challenge the legal bases of the Massachusetts Bay Corporation. See the cabinet minute, 7 February 1676/7, S.P. 29/366, 149, 150; also in *C.S.P.D. 1676–1677,* 538–39. Thence it was an easy step for the duke of York to question the "absolutenesse" of proprietorial authority in Maryland and the Carolinas (S.P. 104/179, 152v).

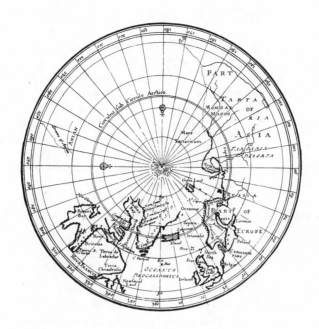

SOME SUGGESTED READING FOR BOOK TWO

The standard bibliographies for the period that centers on 1676 (the Restoration) are May F. Keeler, *Bibliography of British History, Stuart Period, 1603–1714* (Oxford, 1970), and William L. Sachse, *Restoration England, 1660–1689* (Cambridge, 1971).

The most recent, most thoughtful, survey of the period is J. R. Jones, *Court and Country, 1658–1714.* For literary pleasure, as well as for its introduction to the English life of the period, read Thomas Babington Macaulay, *The History of England from the Accession of James II*, C. H. Firth, ed. (London, 1913–15). See also the indispensable review of the period by David Ogg, *England in the Reign of Charles II* (rev. ed., Oxford, 1955, 1956). A well-chosen and well-explained sample of the documents of the period is in Andrew Browning, ed., *English Historical Documents,* VIII (London, 1966).

Two interpretive studies of great power affect this work: J. H. Plumb, *The Growth of Political Stability in England, 1676–1725* (London, 1965), and J. G. A. Pocock, "The Limits and Divisions of British History: In Search of the Unknown Subject," *The American Historical Review* 87 (1982): 311–36.

The backgrounds to Book II are annotated generally in my *The Governors-General,* but several other studies of the particular concerns of this book have been especially useful here. On the conjoint subject of public opinion, published news, and the coffee-houses as generators of the first and consumers of the second, see the studies of the coffeehouses by Ellis, Lillywhite, and Robinson cited above (note 9, page 184; note 11, page 186; note 13, page 187). George Kitchen, *Sir Roger L'Estrange* (London, 1913); Peter Frazer, *The Intelligence of the Secretaries of State, and Their Management of Licensed News 1660–1688* (Cambridge, 1956); and J. G. Muddiman, *The King's Journalist 1659–1689* . . . (London, 1923), also speak to the issue of the legal press.

For the operations of the royal government, one must still begin with E. R. Adair, *The Sources for the History of the Council in the Sixteenth & Seventeenth Centuries* (London, 1924; New York, 1971), which suggests that the study of the privy council has not advanced in recent years. Edward Raymond Turner, *The Privy Council of England in the Seventeenth and Eighteenth Centuries 1603–1784* (Baltimore, 1927); Ralph Bieber, *The Lords of Trade and Plantations, 1675–1696* (Allentown, 1919); and Charles M. Andrews, *British Committees, Commissions and Councils of Trade and Plantations 1622–1675* (Baltimore, 1908), insofar as it deals with council committees, only confirm this feeling of underdevelopment in the study of the empire's central institution. Among the almost equally dated studies of the secretaries of state, Florence M. Grier Evans, *The Principal Secretary of State . . .* (Manchester, 1923), has been most useful.

On the vexed issue of political ideology in England and its empire prior to the Exclusion Crisis, the surveys listed above remain fundamental. Keith Feiling, *History of the Tory Party, 1640–1714* (Oxford, 1924), is the most graceful as well as the most illuminating study of its subject and its time. Two more specialized studies influenced this account: John Miller, *Popery and Politics in England 1660–1688* (Cambridge, 1973), and J. G. A. Pocock, *The Ancient Constitution and the Feudal Law: A Study of English Historical Thought in the Seventeenth Century* (Cambridge, 1957; New York, 1967).

On these ideological issues, as on most other questions, the biographies of statesmen retain a centrality to discourse in this era hardly equaled in other periods. Mackenzie's *Lauderdale* and Harris' *Sandwich* quote documents incorporated in the text (and so appear in note 2, page 178, and note 63, page 224). Even more reliance has been placed on the modern masterwork of the period's political history, Andrew Browning's *Thomas Osborne, earl of Danby and duke of Leeds, 1632–1712* (Glasgow, 1944–51), especially for its discussion of the budget of 1676 in I, 186–87. On this same topic see William A. Shaw's comments in his edition of the *Calendar of Treasury Books*, vol. V, part I, 1676–1679 (London, 1911). A reference is also owed to Stephen B. Baxter, *The Development of the Treasury 1660–1702* (Cambridge, Mass., 1957), on Danby's reforms. The connection between the revolution in Virginia and the failure of Danby's imperial fiscal program is most perceptively discussed by Wilcomb E. Washburn, "The Effect of Bacon's Rebellion on Government in England and Virginia," *United States National Museum Bulletin* 225 (1962), especially 148–49.

Haley's *Shaftesbury* (note 17, page 191) is also eminently useful for the mid-1670s. On Ireland's viceroy, especially suggestive material for this study appears in Thomas Carte, *An history of James duke of Ormonde 1610–1688* (Oxford, 1851), s.v. 1676, and Winifred A. H. C. Gardner [Lady Burghclere], *The Life of James first duke of Ormonde 1610–1688* (London, 1912). Helen C. Foxcroft's *Halifax* (see note 16, page 190) and her condensation of it in *A Character of the Trimmer* (Cambridge, 1946) remain the indispensable studies of that quintessential moderate, but the introduction by J. P. Kenyon to his edition of Halifax's *Works* (Harmondsworth, 1969) adds some necessary acid to the engraving. On the ruelle, Antonia Fraser, *Royal Charles* (New York, 1979), and Allen Andrews, *The Royal Whore Barbara Villiers Countess of Castlemaine* (London, 1971), are engaging, while the sketches by Magalotti are cited in the text (note 5, page 180). Magalotti, like the young Samuel Pepys, describes a more careless court and a more youthful king than appear in 1676, but the flavor of the times is still best tasted in the (at last!) complete edition of Robert Latham and William Matthews of *The Diary of Samuel Pepys* (Los Angeles and London, 1970–83). Samuel A. Bryant, *Samuel Pepys* (Cambridge, 1933–38), informed the northeast-passage account.

The destruction of the puritan frontier seems less horrific to us in a present at once vastly more populous and infinitely more scarred than was 1676, but the standard modern account, Douglas Edward Leach, *Flintlock and Tomahawk: New England in King Philip's War* (New York, 1958, 1966), 242–50, gives a powerful account of the cost of the conflict to the colonies. The revisionist study by Francis Jennings, *The Invasion of America: Indians, Colonialism, and the Cant of Conquest* (Chapel Hill, 1975; New York, 1976), puts "savage war" in the context of its European counterparts, as well as estimating the costs of the "Second Puritan Conquest" (324–25). Most startling are the maps in Lois Kimball Mathews, *The Expansion of New England* (Boston and New York, 1909), which compare the shrunken New England settlements of 1677 with those of 1675 (65–67). For the scale and duration of the devastation, see Jackson Turner Main's meticulous scholarship in "The Distribution of Property in Colonial Connecticut," in *The Human Dimensions of Nation Making*, ed. James Kirby Martin (Madison, 1976), 54–104.

BOOK THREE

THE ANGLO-IROQUOIAN EMPIRE

ILLUSTRISSIMO
PRUDENTISSIMO~
POTENTISSIMOQ₃ PRINCIPI
IACOBO
DUCI EBORACI &c.
Hanc Defcriptionem Noviffimam
IAMAICÆ
Humillime D.D.D. Edw. Slaney.

[I]

"THE PRINCE AND THE ORATOR":
GARACONTIÉ OF ONONDAGA

Introduction

In 1653, the French prepared to evacuate their besieged colony on the St. Lawrence. They could not resist much longer the assaults of the Five Nations of the Longhouse League, the terrorist Iroquois. "They come like foxes through the woods, which afford them concealment and serve them as an impregnable fortress," wrote the Jesuit chronicler of Canada. "They attack like lions and, as their surprises are made when they are least expected, they meet with no resistance. They take flight like birds, disappearing before they have really appeared." No settlement, no farmstead, no traveler or hunter, no one and nothing beyond the walls of Quebec itself was safe from these insatiable warriors, each, as they said of themselves, "a stealthy man who liked to kill." It was, wrote the chronicler, "a kind of miracle that the Iroquois, although able to destroy us so easily, have not yet done so."[1]

Unable to save themselves, the French were saved by the Iroquois.

---

1. Ruben Gold Thwaites, ed., *The Jesuit Relations and Allied Documents Travels and Explorations of the Jesuit Missionaries in New France 1616–1791* (Cleveland, 1896–1901), XLV, 197, 199 (hereafter cited as *Jesuit Relations*). Arthur C. Parker, *The Constitution of the Five Nations*, 17, in William N. Fenton, ed., *Parker on the Iroquois* (Syracuse, 1968).

The motives to a clemency so uncongenial to the Five Nations appear in the public life of an Onondaga Iroquois, Garacontié. He was the chief diplomat of the Five Nations from the moment of the Iroquois' decision to spare New France in 1654 until, during 1675, 1676, and 1677, in the last negotiations of his lifetime, he linked the Five Nations to the English empire in the Covenant Chain. Garacontié's goal was to make actual the Onondaga's titular leadership of the Iroquoian League and to secure the league's control of the Great Valley of the Susquehanna. Achieving his ambition by making peace with the French, achieving alliance with the English, and waging war with the Erie, the Mahican, the Susquehanna, the Shawnee, and the Illinois, "the prince and the Orator" of the Onondaga gave territorial shape and diplomatic meaning to the extraordinary events of 1676. As important to the future of America as either revolution and counter-revolution among the English, or Algonquin and Susquehanna attacks upon the colonists, were Iroquoian victories over all their rivals, red and white. These victories were unexampled since the Iroquois' great half-decade of northern and western conquest of 1649–54, and they would never again be repeated. These victories ranged down the whole length of New England, from the Kennebec River to the Narragansett Bay. All along the Hudson, Susquehanna, and Potomac rivers, and on down the western frontiers of the Chesapeake colonies, the Iroquois raiders triumphed. The ensuing partnership of necessity between beleaguered English imperialists and overextended Iroquoian expansionists—the Covenant Chain agreements of 1675–1676–1677—served both English and Iroquoian ambitions in mid-America for a century to come. Their alliance preserved the Iroquoian sphere until it became successively the empire of the English and the heartland of the Republic. The Onondaga author of the diplomatic revolution of 1676, Garacontié, was seen by his contemporaries as "the most noted man among all the Iroquois." He may claim from us recognition as the greatest American diplomat of the seventeenth century.[2]

Garacontié spoke for the Onondaga, the "name givers" or parliamentarians of the Iroquoian League. The name that he was given was the senatorial "Sagochiendagehté," the title of that lord of the Longhouse League whose position was analogous to today's Thadodaho, the agenda chief and presiding aristocrat of the grand council of the Hodenosaunee. Garacontié's duties as the voice of his nation and the league exposed him to the spiritual and the political beliefs, as well as to the material culture, of the European invaders of those Algonquin lands which lay between the Iroquois and the Atlantic world. The demise of their ancient Algonquin enemies delighted the Iroquois, but removing the middlemen not

2. Thwaites, ed., *Jesuit Relations,* LIV, 112; LV, 55.

only increased Iroquoian access to advanced technology, it also exposed the real people to an alien culture.

As the chief diplomat of his people, Garacontié secured them the military technology and the foreign aid essential to Iroquoian victory over all their Amerindian enemies, but to do so he became the most acculturated sachem of his age. What the anglicization enforced by the English empire was to the American colonists, the acculturation effected by the European invasion was manifold to these Amerindians. Garacontié nevertheless insisted that his literacy in a European language and his life and worship as a Christian—in addition to doing as his peers all did: wearing cloth; wielding a knife; and firing a fusil—did not at all diminish his Onondaga identity or reduce his patriotic effectiveness as the presiding lord of the Lodge Extended Lengthwise. On the contrary, he said that speaking French and worshiping Christ greatly enhanced his ability to win for his nation and the league their age-old objective: control of the great valleys of the Susquehanna and the Delaware.

The Sagochiendagehté's success in securing their south for the Iroquois, and, in so doing, making Iroquoian ceremony the matrix of international diplomacy, authenticated Garacontié's assertion. Garacontié's unmatched career exemplified the adaptive genius which made the Iroquois politically supreme among native nations. The condolence council, its form unchanged for aeons, was the religious ritual which the Five Nations adapted to a variety of modern political necessities, diplomacy among them. It had been evolved among Amerindians to compensate for the crippling products of pervasive death: excessive personal grief and transitory political leadership. Clan associations—moieties—within or among the villages and nations of the Iroquois had found in formal condolence ceremonies a means by which clans bereaved of sachems were comforted and so enabled to raise up successors. Condolence councils were held successively by the elders of each aggrieved entity of the League of the Iroquois: village, nation, confederation. By reducing the costly culture of mourning to affordable dimensions and by providing a legitimate succession to every office, the Iroquois not only achieved unsurpassed economic efficiency and unequaled political stability, but also developed a mechanism of international diplomacy, first among the Five Nations, then with their native neighbors, finally with the European invaders. By the condolence council, aggrieved and accommodating parties were brought together and a certificate of credentials, a prefixed agenda, a process of negotiation, a form of treaty, methods of ratification and renewal all were established. And such was the cultural self-confidence, the military terror, and the geopolitical importance of the Five Nations, that all the Europeans who wished to deal with them adopted the Iroquoian form of diplomacy, the condolence council, the métier of Daniel

Garacontié, rather than imposing European treaty forms, as was elsewhere, universally, the case.

Garacontié's initial diplomatic accomplishment was to close the first
great period of Iroquoian conquest by achieving peace between the Five
Nations and the French and their native allies. This peace Garacontié
personally maintained for the next twenty-three years. During these
years the Five Nations exploited the hunting and commercial opportunities in the north and the west they had won by war since 1649, and
defended themselves against the aggression of the English-backed Susquehanna from the south and the French-supplied Mahican from the east.

The Sagochiendagehté

This period of northern and western pacification and exploitation, and
of eastern and southern defense and reorientation, began in September 1653. Then an unnamed Onondaga promised peace to the French. In
February 1654, an advance party of Onondaga envoys arrived at Montreal
to collect the first dividend of peace, Huron refugees sheltering among
the French after the Iroquoian devastation of their homeland five years
earlier. Many of the Hurons were already at Onondaga, living in all the
lesser ranks of the aristocratic Iroquoian society. Now, in a continuing
competition with their Iroquois confederates, the Onondaga ("the people
of the mountain") were seeking Huron personpower to reconstitute their
war-drained society, to submit to their system of domestic slavery, and to
become victims in dreadful ceremonies of implacable revenge for the
thirty-four Onondaga ambassadors slain by the Huron some years earlier.
To the Huron, the Onondaga boasted that they were protected east and
west by their lodge brothers, in whose company they waged war east to
Maine and west to the Ohio. It was a contemporary commonplace, however, that the Onondaga were primarily oriented north and south towards
trade and diplomacy with the ostensible enemies of their league, the
Huron and the Ottawa to the north, the Susquehanna to the south. The
Onondaga thus offered the Huron refugees the happy chance "to become
friends of the conquerors, and to go to a victorious country and a land of
Peace which was about to wage war at a distance, itself receiving no harm
therefrom." [3]

---

3. *Thwaites, ed., Jesuit Relations*, XLI, 55.

Under ferocious pressure from both the Onondaga and their brethren the Mohawk ("cannibals"), knowing that a decision for either would ensure the enmity of the other and that a decision for neither would bring down the wrath of both, the Huron and their French hosts had promised to consider the Onondaga requests when and if their ambassadors arrived to make peace in the spring of 1654. Early in May, "the people of the mountain" did disembark at Montreal, the prearranged place of the conference. The Onondaga were led by "a Captain who, of all his Nation, bore the most influential Name, Sagochiendagehté." This was the council name of the Onondaga chieftain, Garacontié. He was so called because he spoke in confederate council as the representative of his people, "the gentleman from Onondaga." Pre-eminent in ritual, sachem of the Onondaga Bear Clan, first among the fifty lords of the Iroquois League, Garacontié had no sooner landed at Montreal than he fell, as he thought, into a trap of almost Iroquoian subtlety and vengefulness.[4]

The Onondaga embassy was warmly received and conducted into the French fortress. Once inside the walls, however, they were told that a young French surgeon had just been seized by the Oneida Iroquois. The ambassadors "trembled and turned pale," expecting the French to avenge their loss on the handiest Iroquois. Reassured, Garacontié put his life at stake—literally, and in the unhesitatingly courageous manner by which Onondaga diplomats testified to their own sincerity and to their authority in their nation. To secure the return of the French prisoner, and so to attain peace with the French, Garacontié said, "for his life I will pledge my own; and, if the people of my nation have any respect and love for me, the Frenchman will live, and his life will save mine."[5]

The gift of life was henceforward the greatest of the presents by which, in accordance with condolence-council form, Garacontié would authenticate each clause or "word" of his many agreements with the French. Because they spared the life of the Onondaga ambassador, the French ultimately received eighty-six of their countrymen in return. The first was the captured French surgeon, rescued from the Oneida scaffold as he was being bound for torture. He was presented to the French by Garacontié, the first of twenty presents each confirming a "word" (the rest of the presents were beaded belts or collars of wampum, shell beads, the money of aboriginal America).

Garacontié's first ten presents were to obviate the incident that had embarrassed the embassy, and to insist that the Sagochiendagehté spoke not just for the Onondaga but also for the Seneca (and for their Cayuga

4. *Ibid.*, 69. On the identity and attributes of "the gentleman fron Onondaga," see the note by the Rev. W. M. Beauchamp of Onondaga to *ibid.*, 79.

5. *Ibid.*, 71. For a famous precedent, see *ibid.*, XXXIII, 117–25.

dependents as well), the Oneida, and even on behalf of Mohawk interests, although, as "the name bearers," the Onondaga organizers of the
league, admitted, in this matter of peace with the French and their commercial clients north of Lake Ontario, the Mohawk did not yet know
where their own best interests lay. Still, speaking for the league, as well
as for the Onondaga keepers of its council fire, the Sagochiendagehté was
anxious to remove the rocks, scrape away the shoals, and smooth the
rapids of the river which so powerfully connected the Iroquois with the
French.

Speaking personally, Garacontié asked that a Jesuit be sent to live and
teach in Onondaga. "We shall receive his teachings with love," the Iroquoian lord promised, "and it is our wish to worship him who is the
Master of our Lives." Whether the master of Garacontié's life was to be
Taronhiaouagon and that culture hero's dreamed directions, or Jesus
Christ and the authority of the Scriptures, was a question that took fifteen
years to answer. More materially and immediately, the Sagochiendagehté
assured the French that the Iroquois would, as a matter of policy, no
longer attack them. Since war was their life, however, they had to attack
someone. So "this very summer we shall lead an army" against the Erie.
In the Ohio Valley, "the earth will shake," said the Sagochiendagehté,
but the settlements of the St. Lawrence would be tranquil.[6]

Garacontié promised to preserve this peace personally, "flying" to
Montreal whenever any eruption of youthful hooliganism threatened his
agreement with the French. "My presence will put a stop to all disorders," said the Sagochiendagehté. It appears that he was believed. Both
the eminence of the Onondaga sachem and his personification of the new
peace between the Five Nations and their northern neighbors were recognized by the gift given Garacontié by the allies of the French: the
Tobacco and Ottawa nations. Receiving eight Seneca and five Wolf (Mohawk) captives, Garacontié was personally honored and so publicly reassured in his plan to pacify militarily and exploit economically the
northern frontier of Iroquoia so that the "upper" or western Iroquois
nations (all the Five Nations save the Mohawk) could expand their influence to the south and west. The Sagochiendagehté then concluded the
negotiations of 1654—"covered the council fire," in the terms of the condolence ceremony—with a poetic metaphor for the alliance of French
with Onondaga interests and a prescient plan for open covenants openly
arrived at. "We—the Frenchman and I, the Onontaehronnon—are now
one, our arms are linked together in a bond of love; and he who shall
seek to sever it will be our common foe." The Sagochiendagehté further
promised that "we shall do nothing in secret; the Sun will witness our

6. *Ibid.*, XLI, 75.

actions; and may it cease to shine on him who shall choose the path of darkness."

"The Ground Was Stained with Blood and Murder"

Still on the dark path, the Mohawk were furious at Garacontié's diplomacy. The Onondaga appeal to the Huron refugees; the practical assertion of Onondaga's traditional pre-eminence in the politics of the league; the opening of the trade of Montreal to the western Iroquois (which would evade the Mohawk's abusive monopoly of access to Albany) all threatened the interests of "the keepers of the eastern door" of the longhouse. Worst of all was Onondaga acquisition of French missionaries (hostages of the highest order and distinguished cultural ambassadors), French soldiers (increments to Onondaga security at home and valued military advisers on the war path abroad), French artisans (primarily valued as weapons mechanics and tinsmiths), and French traders (the organizers of an Onondaga entrepôt in the fur trade). Every Frenchman at Onondaga enhanced an Iroquoian sphere of influence independent of the Mohawk. Every Frenchman was an asset in the Onondaga plan of a united Iroquoian policy and polity under Onondaga leadership. This plan, Garacontié's life-work, would realize the Five Nations' hegemony, so long proclaimed by Iroquoian ideology, over all native nations. In the Great League of Peace (and Power), the Mohawk would have to accept Onondaga pre-eminence.

The Sagochiendagehté, the voice of the Onondaga and of the league, had stolen a march on his Mohawk rival, the "Flemish Bastard." When this Mohawk-Dutch chief—Garacontié's counterpart among "the people of the flint"—returned Jesuit hostages to Quebec in July 1654 as his nation's earnest of the peace, he found that "the gentleman from Onondaga" was already paddling home with Father Simon LeMoine. Having lost to Onondaga the Jesuit masterpiece in the great game, the Mohawk voiced the indignation of his nation in the classic metaphor of the confederation, the longhouse. "We, the five Iroquois Nations, compose but one cabin," the Mohawk explained to the French. He admonished them to "enter the cabin by the door" to the east, the Mohawk door, rather than make a burglar's entry at Onondaga "by the roof and through the [smoke hole]. Have you no fear," the Flemish Bastard asked the French, "that the smoke may blind you and that you may fall from the top to the bottom," lacking Mohawk ground "on which to plant your feet?"[7]

Having warned the French of their misguided approach to the Five Nations, the Flemish Bastard pursued the Onondaga party upriver to take LeMoine from them and carry him off to an uncertain existence among "the people of the flint." The Onondaga had too much of a lead. On 4 August 1654, Father Simon LeMoine, the French ambassador and Jesuit missionary, recruited by the Sagochiendagehté, was welcomed by that statesman's nephew, 4 leagues from the great village "Onnontagé" ("on the mountain"). LeMoine climbed in festive procession up the long south slope of "Indian Hill," through miles of cornfields, towards the headquarters of Iroquoia and, as it became in Garacontié's lifetime, the capital of mideastern North America. An embanked and palisaded town of more than one hundred longhouses, plus corn cribs and vegetable stores innumerable, Onnontagé was guarded east and west by two tributaries of the Limestone Creek. On the ridge between their ravines, some 1,000 to 1,600 feet wide, the village ran nearly a mile from the southern approach to a sharp drop-off. Fifty feet down this precipitous slope the flatland ran away to the north, full of the graves of a people whose life expectancy was less than thirty years, two-thirds of whose beloved children died "before they have the use of reason," and whose fundamental culture—in nothing more than in the condolence council, which was the pattern of Iroquoian diplomacy—was designed to adjust to a single, overwhelming, omnipresent fact: death. Simon LeMoine, like every Jesuit missionary to the Iroquois, made his way to the league's capital baptizing ranks of dying children.[8]

Joyful himself at reaping this harvest for heaven, LeMoine was received with equal joy by the Onondaga as the emissary of peace. His host, Garacontié, reported that the warriors of Onondaga had confirmed the peace with the French, encouraged thereto by ambassadors and wampum from the Seneca and the Cayuga nations, that the Oneida had expressed relief at remission of their quarrel with the French, and that even the Mohawk had had to follow their united brethren into that settlement with the French which, as Garacontié told LeMoine, had long been his

7. Thwaites, ed., *Jesuit Relations*, XLI, 87, 89.
8. *Ibid.*, XLIX, 107. On Indian Hill, see: the personal observations, dated 1677, of Wentworth Greenhalgh, in John Romelyn Brodhead, ed., *Documents Relative to the Colonial History of the State of New York* . . . (Albany, 1853), III, 251 (hereafter cited as *N.Y.C.D.*); the topographical description of Joshua V. H. Clark, *Onondaga* . . . (Syracuse, 1849), II, 255; the discussion of the settlement's archeology by James A. Tuck, *Onondaga Iroquois Prehistory* . . . (Syracuse, 1971), 177–86, as modified by James A. Bradley, The Onondaga Iroquois: 1500–1655 . . . (unpublished Ph.D. dissertation, Syracuse University, 1979), 412. I am grateful to Dr. Bradley for guiding me over the site.

ambition. The Jesuit, said his host, "was to be of good cheer, since I bore with me the welfare of all the land." [9]

Joy instantly gave way to alarm and fury when Erie raiders killed three Onondaga hunters within a day's walk from Onnontagé. LeMoine thus acquired some insight into Garacontié's martial motives for peace with the French. Less than a week later, the councilors of the four western nations, plus a fortuitous Mohawk visitor, assembled at Onnontagé. LeMoine adopted the protocol of the condolence council and, echoing Garacontié's presentation at Montreal, urged the warriors to avenge their losses on the Erie, leaving the northern native nations free to trade.

This ratification of the 1654 treaty was concluded for the Longhouse League by "the Onnontaerhonnon Captain," presumably Garacontié. "Five whole Nations address thee through my mouth," he said. "I have in my heart the sentiments of all the Iroquois Nations, and my tongue is faithful to my heart." Four "words" the spokesman of the Onondaga and the league sent to Onnontio, the governor-general of the French: (1) The Iroquois would receive from the Jesuits news of "the master of our lives." (2) Onondaga was the capital of the confederacy, the site of all peace parleys ("*pour parlers pour la Paix*"). (3) A French settlement should be built on the shores of the Iroquois' great lake: "place yourselves in the heart of the country, since you are to possess our hearts" (and satisfy half of the Onondaga ambition for a north-south commercial and cultural corridor centered at Onnontagé). (4) The leagued nations would fight new wars, leaving the French in peace.[10]

As always, Garacontié was as good as his word. For twenty-three years of unceasing application, amid the snares of intra-confederate conflict, enemy ambush, and warrior bloodlust, he kept the Five Nations' peace with the French largely intact. For his kinsmen, Garacontié had secured not just peace but material support from the one European power that could destroy them. For the French, the reverse was true. Their appreciation of Garacontié was well put by his Jesuit eulogist: "he was the first who induced his Countrymen to make peace with us; . . . and who, since that time, has Preserved it to us by his authority and Counsels, always turning elsewhere the weapons of the Iroquois. . . . If war has not again broken out, with the baleful and terrible consequences which it brings in its train, it is mainly to him that we are under that obligation." Few statesmen can claim as much.[11]

The Mohawk were the great enemies of the peace of 1654. Their prior pre-eminence in the Iroquoian League's politics and economy depended

9. Thwaites, ed., *Jesuit Relations*, XLI, 101.
10. *Ibid.*, 116, 117.
11. *Ibid.*, XLI, 23.

upon their control of their kinsmen's access to Albany and its European technology. The Onondaga-inspired connections with Montreal and Quebec bypassed that control. In the years immediately after the peace a stream of French coins flowed into Onondaga, displacing Dutch bale seals as commercial indicators at Onnontagé. The Mohawk "were bent on thwarting this design" of the Onondaga. So "the two sides fought with each other until the ground was stained with blood and murder." Not only the Iroquoian principals in this contest, but also their kinsmen, allies, embassies, and finally the French themselves were put at risk by the rivalry of Onondaga with Mohawk, of the people of the mountain with the people of the flint.[12]

Of course and as always, then and henceforward, the Onondaga themselves were divided. For the inescapable concomitant of Garacontié's policy of peace and trade with the French was the corruption of traditional Iroquoian society by Christianity. The ambassadors of that peace, the culturally subversive Jesuit missionaries, were also the doctrinal comforters of the Huron underclass, almost wholly Christian. In the eyes of their Iroquoian commercial rivals, the priests were also the "chief clerks of the [French] fur trade." In every role, the missionaries were agents of acculturation, dividers of a society hitherto marvelously integrated. And the Jesuits were proponents of peace not just with the alien French but also with their Indian allies, with whom no properly feudal Iroquois could ever be reconciled for long.[13]

Only Garacontié's irrefutable arguments, that the Five Nations could not conduct a four-front war and that peace with the French offered military advantages to the Iroquois against all their native enemies, had brought warriors and traditionalists to an uneasy acceptance of the peace of 1654. But every victory over enemies west or east became another argument for ending the unnatural peace to the north. Only the generation-long war with the Susquehanna to the south compelled even the upper Iroquois to keep the peace with France, and it did not long survive their final victory over the great southern foe.

The symbol of the peace, the focus of every jealousy, the target of Mohawk hatred, was the new French settlement on the north shore of the Onondaga lake. On the bluff above Ganuntaha—"material for council fire"—on the traditional site of the founding council of the Five Nations, rose the mission settlement of Ste. Marie. In September 1655, just thirteen months after the grand council's ratification of the peace with New

12. *Ibid.*, XLIV, 149.
13. On the Jesuits as "chief clerks," see George T. Hunt, *The Wars of the Iroquois* (Madison, 1960), 71.

France, sixty Frenchmen had accepted Garacontié's invitation and were palisaded in Onondaga.[14]

To Mohawk raids on Onondaga communications to the east and north and to the assaults of the Mohawk's "nephews," the Oneida, on the French and their native allies along the St. Lawrence was now added the ultimate challenge to the Onondaga sponsorship of the peace. The Mohawk demanded that the grand council approve the assassination of every Frenchman at Onondaga. They threatened to kill every sachem who opposed these murders. When, in the summer of 1657, the final victory over the Erie was achieved, Seneca and Cayuga warriors began to join in the raids on the outskirts of Montreal. Garacontié himself has been accused of contributing to the collapse of the peace. It is said that he began the August 1657 massacre of the Huron group his party was escorting to Onondaga when one of their women rejected him.

"Subtle, adroit, arrogant knaves," the Jesuits labeled their Onondaga adversaries. But the capture of eleven Onondaga at Montreal brought Garacontié back to that city on 16 September 1657. He delivered twenty-six "words" in behalf of the four western nations, reporting that they would now dispatch their warriors westward, beyond the country conquered from the Erie, against the "Fire Nation." He returned French prisoners (whom he had ransomed from the Iroquoian raiders) to exchange for his Onondaga "nephews." Garacontié received no ostensible satisfaction, but on 19 October his nephews "escaped," and new peace negotiations seemed possible. The Mohawk put a stop to this by taking more Frenchmen captive. In retaliation, on 1 November, the French imprisoned every available Iroquois in Canada. The Mohawk carried their case against the French back to the grand council at Onondaga in February 1658. Threatening to kill every Onondaga who dared to defend the French, the Mohawk won council consent to permit the kinsmen of the Iroquois imprisoned in New France to murder the Frenchmen who were snowbound at Ste. Marie.[15]

Garacontié could not resist the anti-French resolution, but he advised delay until the absent warriors returned to Onnontagé from war and the hunt. Meanwhile, at the risk of his life, Garacontié warned the French of their danger and advised their escape. There followed the famous "eat-all" feast, given by the French to their delighted captors on 20 March 1658. At 11:00 p.m., the hosts abandoned their stupefied, misled, and bemused guests. The epic flight of the French over the ice of Ganuntaha

14. On Ganuntaha (and for most of the classic observations on Iroquoian life) see Louis Henry Morgan, *League of the Ho-de-no-sau-nee or Iroquois* (Rochester, 1851; facsimile ed., New York, 1962), 471.
15. Thwaites, ed., *Jesuit Relations*, XLIV, 149.

and down the frigid waters of the St. Lawrence in prefabricated bateaux ended in safety at Montreal on 23 April 1658. Not until Garacontié's death was his authorship of the French flight revealed, so he survived his betrayal of the Mohawk and his subversion of the grand council's resolve. Garacontié's survival, and that of the sixty Frenchmen he saved, meant that the possibility of peace still existed despite the "jealousy almost verging on fury" of the Mohawk for the Onondaga's French connection.[16]

"The Father of the French"

In the three years following the French escape from Onondaga the semi-hostile balance between New France and the Five Nations was sustained. The kinsmen of the Iroquois held prisoner in Canada prevented an all-out attack on the French. Yet the vengefulness of the escaped Onondaga, the enmity of the Mohawk, and the Oneida resumption of the Ottawa war all led to Iroquoian raids on both the French and their Indian allies. Garacontié nonetheless sent word, via an Oneida spokesman, that he had preserved the French residence, and he invited Father LeMoine to return to Onondaga. This he did in the summer of 1661.

By then the losses of the four western nations of the Iroquois to the formidable Susquehanna necessitated their renewed alliance with the French. For their part, the French had made the easy choice between antagonizing one nation, the Mohawk, by reoccupying the Onondaga outpost, or offending the remaining four nations by refusing to settle an embassy at the confederate capital. Even the murderous Mohawk, although they continued to harass Onondaga's communications with Montreal, were preoccupied with a series of losing struggles with eastern enemies: the Abenaki confederacy in the Kennebec country; the Sokoki of the upper Connecticut tributaries; and, most menacing, the Mahican of the Hudson Valley itself.

The military crises of the Iroquoian confederates dictated not only the revival of Garacontié's peace with New France, but also his domestic political triumph. Simon LeMoine observed that, when Garacontié came out an unprecedented distance from Onnontagé to welcome him, the senior sachem was accompanied by the other elders and was backed by a tumultuous popular welcome. The village was "almost hidden from my

16. *Ibid.*, XLIII, 129.

view," the missionary ambassador wrote, "so covered with people were the palisades, cabins, and trees." Within the festive capital of Iroquoia, "my host, Garacontié, prouder than I of this splendid reception, wished to conciliate the men of his Nation, who might have felt jealous at having no share in procuring this new peace." So the sage sachem lodged Le-Moine not in the longhouse of the Bear clan, but elsewhere in Onnontagé —sharing with his peers the honor of being hospitable to this visitor of distinction. In his reception of LeMoine, Garacontié moved beyond hospitality to devotion. He had prepared a chapel in his own longhouse for the Christians of Onondaga, both the missionary-ambassador himself and the convert captives of the ten defeated nations then enslaved in the Iroquoian capital. Other chiefs might have LeMoine's sleeping body in their house but Garacontié, always ahead in the diplomatic game, would possess the soul of the Jesuit beneath the totem of the Bear.[17]

The eminence of the astute Onondaga appeared anew when the sachems of the Five Nations met in grand council at Onnontagé in midsummer 1661 and there ratified his peace with the French. To the first question put them by the French ambassador—would they confirm the peace between Onnontio and the Sagochiendagehté, the heads of the French and of the Five Nations?—the assembled elders gave the ritual assent, *"Hai!"* Then they picked up (that is, they accepted) the present by which LeMoine pledged his sincerity. So too to his second question —would the Five Nations exchange prisoners with the French?—the third—would mutual killings be forgotten and revenge renounced for the casualties of the St. Lawrence raids?—and the fourth—would the Seneca join the Onondaga in a new embassy to Canada to carry out these agreements?—the elders answered *"Hai!"* and they accepted all of LeMoine's presents. In a fifth "word" the French ambassador warned the Mohawk that their efforts to have him assassinated would force the French to take nondiplomatic means to secure Mohawk adherence to the peace.

For days following the French ambassador's speech the lords of the leagued peoples smoked their clan effigy pipes and reviewed their nations' liabilities and options. To the south, so strong were the Susquehanna attackers that the Seneca had had to provide an escort of six hundred warriors to fight their fur train through to Albany; the unobstructed water route to French firearms and stewpots should be tried. To the east, the Abenaki had murdered the Five Nations' ambassador; he must be avenged. To the west, the Shawnee seemed a good source of slaves; but they were many hundreds of miles off, and the warriors who attacked them would be absent from the defense of Iroquoia for two years, as the men who fought the Ox nation (Sioux) had been. North of

17. Thwaites, ed., *Jesuit Relations*, XLVII, 75.

the Iroquois lake, there were old enemies—the Tobacco nation (Petun) and the Nez Percé—to be dispersed from their desirable hunting territories. New foes, the Ojibwa in particular, should be reduced so that the Iroquois could tap the trade of the Hudson's Bay watershed. All of this was to be accomplished by a people ravaged by the smallpox they had picked up during a failed siege of the Susquehanna capital. Garacontié was right, then, the Iroquoian lords concluded. Every nation's interests required peace with the French. Now the *royaner*, the lords of the long-house, admired Garacontié's wisdom in ransoming twenty Frenchmen from the fires of the Mohawk. They could be exchanged for the Five Nations' warriors slowly dying in French prisons. And Garacontié's invitation to "the black gown," Simon LeMoine, had brought to Onnontagé not only a French ambassador of peace, but one who would also make a splendid hostage himself for the safe return of his Onondaga counterpart. LeMoine was recalled to the council fire and told, to his delight, that half of the French prisoners would be sent to Montreal with Garacontié himself, "the Chief of the Embassy" to Onnontio. To his undisguised horror, however, LeMoine was also informed that he himself would be held at Onnontagé with the moiety of his captive countrymen *"pour des raisons d'Estat."* [18]

These reasons of state Garacontié announced when, early in August 1661, he arrived at Montreal after two troubling checks. First he had suffered a "sudden illness" when he met thirty Onondaga bedecked with French scalps, led by his great rival Otreouati dressed in the cassock of a murdered priest. After finally concluding that the life of the priest he had left behind him was sufficient surety for his own despite Otreouati's outrage, Garacontié went on, only to encounter a war party of Oneida bound for the St. Lawrence. These he deflected. Proceeding past these typical obstacles to Iroquoian diplomacy, Garacontié made "a splendid display of thirteen fine presents" at Montreal. Four of these presents authenticated especially important words. The first accompanied the release of the nine Frenchmen Garacontié had brought with him from Onnontagé to the negotiations and promised that he would return with the rest of the hostages in the spring. A second present refreshed the peace between the upper Iroquois and the French, the Mohawk having declared themselves "absolutely determined upon war, and resolved to conquer or perish." The third present invited the Jesuits to the villages of the Onondaga, Cayuga, and Seneca. The final present accompanied a word which measured both the scale of Iroquoian arrogance and the range of Garacontié's diplomacy. It proposed that the French settle them-

18. *Ibid.*, 80, 81.

selves and their religion in Iroquoia so as to "unite anew, in a genuine alliance, France and America." [19]

The French were unsure what to make of Garacontié's eloquence. He was, after all, the voice of Onondaga, and, in the official French estimation, duplicity was as much a national characteristic of the Onondaga as ferocity was of the Mohawk. Yet the returned prisoners were full of praise for Garacontié, his boundless hospitality, his facilitation of their Christian observances, his ransoming of them from the fires of the Mohawk. Then the people of Montreal declared their judgment of the sachem's sincerity: by them he was "called the father of the French." The little children of the frontier town, one by one and to Garacontié's evident enchantment, filled his canoe with handfuls of meal or ears of corn. As the Iroquoian envoy embarked, every musket and cannon in Montreal was fired in salute. The popular judgment was not misplaced. On his return home, Garacontié recalled LeMoine from the Cayuga exile whence he had fled from the insults of the drunken pagans of "the pot-house of Onnontaghé" and regaled the starving missionary with "a truly delicious dish" of fresh squash. To encourage respect for the French ambassador, Garacontié displayed to the Onondaga the wonderful wampum the French had sent. Finally, in August 1662, "this generous Savage and protector of the French" saw to it that twenty Onondaga boatmen conveyed both Le-Moine and his ten fellow French hostages safely to Montreal. [20]

C anoo. fiue Navicula
e corticibus arborum

Navis ex arboris trunco
igne excavata

"Within Two-Finger-Breadths of Total Destruction"

Garacontié overcame terrible difficulties to preserve the peace with the French during the decade after 1664, for in that span the formerly all-conquering Iroquois came "within two-finger-breadths of total destruction." Only the French alliance preserved them. Indeed, Garacontié himself was nearly lost in May 1664, when his party of thirty Onondaga was ambushed and defeated, some killed and all dispersed by a hundred Ottawa and Montagnais in the rapids above Montreal. In this disaster

19. *Ibid.*, 101, 103.
20. *Ibid.*, 101, 103, 189.

were lost Garacontié's presents for peace, a "prodigious collection of porcelain [i.e., beadwork or wampum], which is the gold of the country." With it, everyone feared, was lost the peace itself. "For the Iroquois would cease to be Iroquois if they did not make every effort to avenge the deaths of these Ambassadors" at the hands of the allies of the French.[21]

Yet vengeance might be, for once, an unaffordable luxury. It would further undermine Garacontié's credibility, and he was the personification of a peace which the Five Nations had to have. Garacontié's inability to restrain wayward warriors, vengeful chiefs, and pagan sachems had led the French to conclude that much of his peaceful rhetoric was specious, "that the Iroquois is of a crafty disposition, adroit, dissembling, and haughty, and that he will never descend so low as to be the first to ask peace from us, unless he has a great scheme in his head or is driven to it for some very pressing reason." Of course, Garacontié did have "a great scheme in his head," a scheme for Onondaga and Iroquoian aggrandizement to the south and penetration to the north, and the Five Nations had "very pressing" reasons indeed for seeking peace from the French.[22]

Famine and disease were widespread among the Iroquois. Each of the three senior nations had also suffered particular disasters. The Mohawk beat off a Mahican assault on their eastern frontier village only to be defeated, together with their allies from as far west as Onondaga, when the Iroquoian counterattack reached the Mahican stronghold. The upper Iroquois sent an army to besiege the Susquehanna citadel. It came back sick and, as some accounts have it, minus twenty-five Iroquois chiefs. Acting as ambassadors, they were seized and were burned to death on scaffolds elevated above the Susquehanna walls. All their helpless compatriots witnessed the Susquehanna defiance of the Five Nations. Then the Algonquin attack on Garacontié's embassy embarrassed the Onondaga. Worst of all was the arrival, between May and October 1665, of twelve hundred French veteran troops, the regular regiment of "Carignan-Salières." They fortified the Richelieu River route to Iroquoia, preparatory to carrying out Louis XIV's orders "totally to exterminate" the Five Nations.[23]

Even after learning of this impending disaster from Dutch traders and French captives, Garacontié could not get back to Montreal until December 1665. As an introduction to the recently arrived lieutenant general of

21. Thwaites, ed., *Jesuit Relations*, XLVIII, 235; XLIX, 145, 147.
22. *Ibid.*, XLIX, 137, 139.
23. See "Exterminating the Andastoguetz," below, pp. 290–95, and the Instructions of Louis XIV to Jean Talon, 27 March 1665, in *N.Y.C.D.*, IX, 25. On the regiment and its campaigns against the Mohawk, see Francis Parkman, *The Old Regime in Canada* (Boston, 1907), I, 241–60, 265–67.

French America, the marquis de Tracy, Garacontié brought with him another freed French captive, Charles LeMoine, brother of the late Jesuit father. Asking for his exchange for a captured Onondaga, Garacontié pointed out that he had restored Sieur LeMoine "in health, without even one of his nails being torn off or any part of his body being burnt." He insisted that this extraordinary forbearance testified to his care of French prisoners in Iroquoia. Moreover, Garacontié said, the Onondaga, and the Cayuga and Seneca for whom he also spoke, were willing to forgive the injuries done them by the French (such as their acceptance of diplomatic presents and words without replying to either) and even by the allies of the French (Garacontié mentioned especially the attack on his embassy).

In exchange, Garacontié said, the French must honor the existing treaty themselves with those of the nations that observed it; the French must make it possible for Iroquoian warriors to accept their elders' commitments to the peace by restraining the attacks of their Huron allies on Iroquoian hunters; and the French must give directly to "Captain Garacontié" the Iroquois he named who had been captured by the Mahican allies of the French, and a Huron squaw belonging to a family in Onondaga. Only thus, Garacontié said, would he be able "to convince his nation of the good faith of the said French and the gratitude they evince for the care he has taken to preserve their brothers."

In return for the gift of life, that greatest commodity of Iroquoian diplomatic exchange, Garacontié pledged that not only the three upper nations of the Iroquois but the Oneida also would cease merely to "cling to the hem of the French coat" as they had done heretofore, and instead would clasp the French "around the waist." And Garacontié did his best to save his Mohawk brothers as well from the impending French invasion. He insisted (not very believably, one fears) that the Mohawk had not heard either of the arrival of the French troops or of their orders to destroy the Five Nations. This was why they had not joined his embassy. Therefore Garacontié asked that the French attack, which was now limited to the Mohawk, be suspended even against these last hostiles until he could reach them. Garacontié promised that if, after he had spoken to the Mohawk, they failed to join the Franco-Iroquoian peace, the other four nations would "abandon the Mohawk to the French."[24]

The Mohawk proved obdurate, despite Garacontié's eloquence. On 9 March 1666, Daniel de Rémy, the Sieur de Courcelles, governor of New France, began his march to the Mohawk country. His expedition, six hundred strong, stumbled on unaccustomed snowshoes to the outskirts of Schenectady—it had missed the Mohawk villages entirely, and was

24. Explanation of the Eleven Presents of the Iroquois Ambassadors, 1 December 1665, N.Y.C.D., IX, 37–38.

cut up by Mohawk raiders in its retreat. Still, even the effort at invasion impressed everyone but the Mohawk, who still refused the entreaties from Onondaga that they join the peace. In October 1666, Lieutenant General Tracy himself marched into Mohawk country with a thousand men and burnt the Mohawk towns. It is said that when the brethren of the Mohawk heard that they were starving as a result of the French destruction of their stored corn, they uttered the Onondaga equivalent of "tough."[25]

The contrast of the homeless, hungry Mohawk with the prestigious, relatively prosperous, Onondaga was instructive to all the Five Nations. Even at Onondaga, however, there was only one of the precious priests, talismans of peace with the French, Father Julien Garnier. To keep him at Onondaga, Garacontié first built the father a chapel. Then, acting on the invitation Garnier had brought him from Onnontio, Garacontié traveled to Quebec to acquire for Garnier the French associates he demanded. He took with him the four clan chiefs of the dominant moiety at Onnontagé. For years they had been the "braces" of the Onondaga-French alliance. Now the sachems' prestige was the greater among their nation, both because the terrible defeat of the Onondaga army deep in the Susquehanna Valley had strengthened the peace party these royaner represented, and because the Mahican-French alliance to the east had enabled the Mahican to move men west of Albany once again, making the western Iroquois' trade there more precarious and the French trade (for which Garacontié's peace was a prerequisite) more essential.

Garacontié was well equipped for this round of diplomacy. Not only was his influence great at home, but his reputation as the champion of the French alliance had also gone before him to Montreal. There Garacontié was an object of friendly curiosity to the governor, Courcelles, and to the intendant, Jean Talon, even before his arrival. Before them in council, on 20 August 1667, Garacontié reviewed the reversal in the power balance between the French and the Five Nations during the dozen years since he had first headed the Onondaga embassy. Then, he recalled, the Iroquois were dominant and he had given the gift of life to twenty-six Frenchmen. Now, he admitted, the French were so powerful as to give the gift of life to all the Five Nations. None of them, he said, could have resisted the French army that had marched into Iroquoia the previous year. Yet the French had humbled only the Mohawk and so forced them, in June 1667, to join the peace of which Garacontié had been so long the champion.

He had the more praise for the restraint of the mighty French monarchy, Garacontié said, because he understood (from Albany) that it was

25. Hunt, Wars of the Iroquois, 140.

not forced to forbearance. On the contrary, French victories in the Netherlands would both release resources to strengthen Canada and its garrison and weaken the Dutch ability to supply Albany and so the Iroquois (as they continued to do for half a century after the English conquest of the New Netherlands, and despite French wars and English laws). The might of the French, said Garacontié, made him all the more grateful for their expressions of sympathy for Iroquoian losses to the Susquehanna. Now the French could afford to make that sympathy tangible, and further extend their influence among the Five Nations, not only by sending more missionaries but also by posting *"chasseurs"*—alpine soldiers—as military advisers to the Onondaga and by restraining the Mahican from attacks on Iroquois communications.

Courcelles accepted every one of Garacontié's requests. He sent two Jesuits back to Onondaga with its sachems and dispatched two priests to the Cayuga refuge from the Susquehanna (at the Bay of Quinté, on the north shore of the Iroquois lake). The governor also promised the Iroquoian delegation that he would "send young men into thy settlements, to engage with thee in the common defence." (Henceforward, there were random reports of as many as fifty French soldiers in Onondaga from time to time and of French military advisers with the western Iroquois' war parties in backcountry Maryland and Virginia.) Courcelles even promised to restrain the Mahican, always providing that Garacontié controlled his warlike "nephews." [26]

Such control could never be complete, given the individualistic, even anarchical attributes of Iroquoian warfare, but by the close of Garacontié's embassy of August 1667, the French menace had been converted into French support, the native allies of the French to the north and east of Iroquoia were discouraged in their attacks on the Five Nations' hunters and traders, and the league itself had, virtually for the first time, achieved a united foreign policy which permitted them to concentrate their formidable energies against the ultimate enemy, the Susquehanna. The Five Nations had stepped back from the brink of destruction into a union of counsels which at last made their confederation as effective in foreign as in domestic affairs. The architect of that union was Garacontié.

26. Thwaites, ed., *Jesuit Relations*, LI, 249.

"Famous Garakontié Longs for Baptism"

The centerpiece of the union was the Five Nations' peace with the French. That peace in turn depended upon the unusually affable and trusting relationship Garacontié had established with the new generation of French provincial executives, military and civil, secular and religious. Inevitably, in an age of state religions, personal and political trust implied religious alliance. Diplomatically compelled towards sympathy with Catholicism, Garacontié also found that its emissaries were powerful political tools with which to consolidate his influence in his nation and in the league. The Jesuit missionaries intended to enlarge the kingdom of France as well as that of Christ, but they unintentionally did as much to enhance the sway of the Sagochiendagehté in Onondaga and of the Onondaga in the league.

The brilliant Father Julien Carheil, for example, was literally brought to Onondaga by Garacontié only to be "given to Oiogouen [Cayuga] by Garacontié, the famous captain." Offered to the senior sachem of the Cayuga together with "a present of a porcelain collar to confirm the peace," Carheil's prestigious person bound Cayuga to the French alliance. Conferred by Garacontié (whose right to retain the presents of peace in his own longhouse was an unquestioned ambassadorial prerogative), Carheil and the collar also confirmed the Sagochiendagehté's own authority with the Cayuga and reaffirmed Onondaga's political pre-eminence in the league.[27]

"The gentleman from Onondaga" paid the usual diplomat's price for the foreign alliance he arranged and the domestic prestige he acquired from aliens. Intimate with eminent Frenchmen, he absorbed their culture, compromised his own, and so became suspect to the less cosmopolitan of his own people. The first symptom of Garacontié's apostasy was literacy. In regular written communication with the intendant, Talon, it appears that Garacontié became literate in French. This was a unique accomplishment among the Iroquois of his generation, but far more portentous, politically and personally, was Garacontié's conversion to Catholicism.

For fifteen years, the Sagochiendagehté had eloquently expressed his admiration for the teachings of "the black gowns." Garacontié may have

27. *Ibid.*, LII, 181, 183.

been led to this praise by admiration for the religious devotion and Christian lives of the Huron captives at Onondaga as much as by Onondaga-French diplomatic necessity. He is on record as approving of two of the Huron's Christian characteristics: avoidance of the devastating drunkenness and of the maniacal anger of the pagan warriors. Additionally, the senior sachem's official duties placed him in prolonged contact with the Jesuits resident at Onnontagé. By virtue of their offices, both he and they conceived of themselves as men of peace. To shared idealism was added mutual respect for personal courage, political prowess, and popular command. The Onondaga elder especially esteemed Simon LeMoine, for whom Garacontié had endangered his life and honor in March of 1658.

When, in December 1665, he eulogized Father LeMoine, Garacontié's words reflected his own stature and accomplishment and they anticipated his conversion to the faith so nobly exemplified by the priest, "Ondessonk." Ondessonk, said Garacontié, had repeatedly risked his own life in the fires of the Mohawk to rescue his compatriots from them. Brave himself, Ondessonk had nonetheless been the persuasive ambassador of "peace and tranquility." The powerful statesman was an equally popular leader. The paternal protector was also a true believer. So said his Iroquoian eulogist. "We have seen thee," Garacontié said to the deceased Ondessonk, "on our council-mats deciding questions of peace and war; our [longhouses] were found to be too small when thou didst enter them, and our villages themselves were too cramped when thou wast present —so great was the crowd of people attracted thither by thy words. . . . We weep for thee because, in losing thee, we have lost our Father and Protector. Nevertheless wee will console ourselves with the thought that thou still holdst that relation to us in Heaven, and that thou hast found in that abode the infinite joy whereof thou hast so often told us." Garacontié made sure that he would hear again Ondessonk's welcome message of life eternal. When he restored the mission of Ste. Marie in 1667, it was to a chapel in his own longhouse.[28]

At last, in 1669, the great Onondaga diplomat's long affiliation with the missionary ambassadors of the French led him from pantheism to Christianity. Father Carheil reported from Onondaga "that Famous Garakontié, the most renowned of all the Savage Captains, and the best disposed of all towards the French, longs for Baptism in good earnest." Garacontié had lost his Iroquoian faith. The "master of life" no longer spoke to him in dreams. Garacontié found himself unable to tell his dream-driven people that he had anything but rational reasons for his counsel to them. On hearing this, sachems of rival clans, keepers of the faith, medicine men

28. *Ibid.*, L, 129.

and men of the curing societies, and those whose kinsmen had been injured by the French, all said that Garacontié, having abandoned the traditions of his people, had ceased to be one of them.[29]

They distrusted his Christianity and his policy of peace with the French. Both went against the grain of the Iroquois (or, as they called themselves, the Ongweoweh, "the real people"), for they found "all their pleasure in burning one another, and in strengthening themselves by the ruin of their Neighbors." The Ongweoweh, however, or at least the older and wiser of them, were realists. They recognized that they could not dispense with either Garacontié's policy or its exemplar. The arrival of five additional companies of French regulars at Quebec (and a cargo of 150 women to keep them there after disbandment) was a forceful fact which greatly strengthened Garacontié's authority in the almost continuous negotiations by which he doused the fires begun by "the secret sparks in hearts which breathe only pillage and war," the hearts of "the real people."[30]

Least of all the Ongweoweh did the Mohawk, so injured by the French, find peace with them easy. The Mohawk were distracted from adventures on the St. Lawrence by their war with the Mahican, but this too reminded the Mohawk that these, their most ancient enemies, were newly allied with the Canadians. Still, for a time, the Mahican permitted the Mohawk no other hostile interest. At first light on 18 August 1669, three hundred of their warriors fired through the landward palisades of the Mohawk's eastern frontier settlement, Ganaouagué (on the west bank of the Cayadutta Creek at its junction with the Mohawk River).

After two hours of hard fighting, the Mahican were driven off. The one casualty they could not carry away was quickly butchered for the Mohawk pot. Heartened, the warriors of all three Mohawk towns embarked in canoes to overtake their enemy. They passed the Mahican raiders during the night, then ambushed them in their retreat the next morning, just as they reached the eastern frontier of Mohawk country, a dozen miles west of the Dutch frontier hamlet of Schenectady. The Mohawk killed more than fifty Mahican. Then they sent west to Onondaga for aid. Every Iroquois understood the need to drive back the Mahican. Neither Iroquoian homeland nor Dutch trade would survive a Mahican victory over the Mohawk. Four hundred warriors from the four eastern nations quickly repaid the Mahican visit. As was usually the case in aboriginal warfare, however, the attackers failed to take the enemy town.

When the Iroquoian survivors met at Ganaouagué to mourn their dead

29. *Ibid.,* LII, 181.
30. *Ibid.,* LIII, 35.

in condolence council, the angry Mohawk began to abuse Father Jean
Pierron, a Frenchman and so an ally of the Mahican, a Christian and so
an intruder on their mourning ceremony. The priest escaped to the quarters of the Onondaga visitors and complained to Garacontié. Before the
end of the day, formal Mohawk apologies were given to Father Pierron.
Garacontié had pointed out to his hosts that if the Jesuit carried out his
threat to return to Quebec and there made a bad report of the Mohawk, it
would not only endanger the peace, but would also, as experience ought
to have taught them, bring down on the Mohawk enemies far more formidable than the Mahican. Then, the trails to the east having been
cleared of Mahican by the recent expedition, Garacontié left Ganaouagué
to trade with the Dutch at Albany.

On Garacontié's return, he spoke again to the Mohawk sachems. They
called in the Jesuit. Speaking well-rehearsed lines to Garacontié, the
Mohawk spokesman said that, marvelous though his speech had been,
the Frenchman's sermons were even better. The Mohawk sachem then
astonished the priest by repeating in its entirety Pierron's last sermon
(although, being Iroquois, he had to make improvements on its pallid
European imagery). Then it was Garacontié's turn to play a part in this
farce of appeasement. He rose to protest, in his most indignant tones, the
preference of the Mohawk for a Frenchman's oratory. Besides the damage
done to his personal honor by such an insult, he complained, the preference would cost him much prestige among his own people. "But all at
once, changing the tone of his voice," Garacontié warmly thanked his
brother the Mohawk "for thus despising my voice and preferring to it that
of a man who sacrifices himself for thy salvation, and brings thee the
voice of God. What he has told thee . . . are important truths for thy welfare; they have entered my own heart." [31]

From a sachem of Garacontié's stature, from the Sagochiendagehté
himself, whose "great authority and the reputation for an excellent intelligence that he has acquired for himself among all the Iroquois Nations"
had made him the most powerful and persuasive of councilors, this recommendation of Father Pierron was impressive. Even more so were his
official and personal endorsements of Christianity. Joined with the inescapable fact of French military power, and the menace of their Mahican
allies, Garacontié's set piece began to work a religious revolution among
the Mohawk. Under Father Pierron's devoted teaching, in the next half-
dozen years perhaps half the Mohawk became Christian converts. In
1676, led by a chieftain named Kryn, they began to move by scores to
French mission stations in the St. Lawrence Valley. Given the vaunted

31. *Ibid.*, 233.

military capacity of the keepers of the eastern door of the Iroquoian longhouse, no more strategic shift of residence and religion could be imagined in eastern North America.

"Daniel Garacontié: Captain General"

The disintegration of one of the Five Nations, as Garacontié was to make clear, was much more of a capitulation to his long-standing peace policy and his growing commitment to Christianity than he wanted. His alliance with the French and their religion was always premised upon the physical and moral strength he felt that they would lend to the Iroquois, ravaged as they were by native enemies and Dutch brandy. And his journey to Montreal in September 1669 confirmed the Sagochiendagehté's belief that the Iroquois' native foes could only be overcome if the French were allied to the Five Nations. The French, however, were more insistent than ever that their Ottawa trading partners be included in the peace. Garacontié might have paid less attention to this demand save that the presence of French traders with the Ottawa meant that Iroquois attacks on the Ottawa communications with Montreal endangered the peace with the French as well.

When Garacontié undertook to make this clear to his brethren, he found that the western and eastern nations of the Iroquois had reversed their previous attitudes towards the French and their allies. The Mohawk, formerly the most obdurate enemies of the French, had given way to the reality of French military might and the attractions of their religion. Their neighbors, the Oneida, had been equally determined enemies of the French and of their Ottawa allies. To redirect the Oneida's enmity, Garacontié shared the Onondaga's Susquehanna captives with the Oneida in December 1669. In March 1670, he delivered himself of an unprecedented total of forty-six "words" "to assure the [Oneida] that he will always be at one with them" and to convince them that both the greatest danger and the largest opportunity for all Iroquoia lay among the Susquehanna and their allies and dependents to the south. He invited the Oneida "to light the fire of peace at Montreal" in the coming summer, during the Ottawa's annual trading time. In the meantime, however, six hundred warriors of the upper Iroquois, previously the props of Garacontié's peace policy, sallied north and west to hunt and raid in the trading territories of the Ottawa. A village of Ontouagannah (Shawnee) allies of the Ottawa was destroyed by the Seneca and Cayuga raiders. One hundred women and children were brought back to Iroquoia as prisoners. An Ottawa counterattack destroyed an outlying Seneca village. All that Garacontié could do by way of redeeming the peace was to send wampum belts west with his words. He asked the Seneca and Cayuga to appoint ambassadors to join him, and the representatives of the eastern nations, at Montreal in the summer to make peace with the northerners in the presence of Onnontio.[32]

The "captain general" of the Onondaga was encouraged by the Cayuga response to his efforts to keep their warriors aimed south: either they killed the Susquehanna peace envoy or they permitted the Onondaga to assassinate him. The Seneca did nearly as well by announcing that they would march west against the Fox in the spring of the year. Then the Onondaga warriors came home with nine Susquehanna prisoners from a war which had otherwise been going very badly indeed for every nation except the Mohawk (whose southern concession to Garacontié's united Iroquoian foreign policy was limited to two war parties). These unfortunate Susquehanna were shared by the Onondaga with their neighbors and juniors in the league, the Oneida and the Cayuga. They became slowly burnt offerings to the unification of Iroquoia from east to west and its reorientation from northern to southern expansions, both processes centered on Onondaga and on "the Prince and the Orator," Garacontié.[33]

As he prepared to leave Onondaga for the Canadian peace conference, Garacontié asked the resident Jesuit, Father Pierre Millet, for a letter of recommendation to Onnontio. "It must be acknowledged that he is an incomparable man," Millet wrote of Garacontié, worth "more esteem and consideration than all the others" of his colleagues and contemporaries. "The soul of every good work accomplished here," Garacontié, "upholds the Faith by his personal repute; he maintains the Peace by his authority; he controls the spirits of these Barbarians with a skill and prudence which equals that of the wisest men of Europe. He declares himself so boldly for the glory and interest of France that he can justly be called the Protector of that Crown in this country; he has a zeal for the Faith comparable to that of the first Christians; in short, he knows how to conduct himself in such a way that he always maintains the fame and authority conferred upon him by his Office of Captain-general of this Nation, and uses it only to do good to all the people."[34]

With Father Millet's commendation safely stowed in his beautifully

32. Thwaites, ed., *Jesuit Relations*, LIII, 257.
33. *Ibid.*, LIV, 113.
34. *Ibid.*, 47, 49.

beaded pouch, Garacontié set out for Montreal early in July 1670. He expected to encounter his Iroquoian colleagues en route, but he arrived at Montreal towards the end of the month still alone save for his Onondaga escort. The governor-general of the French was also absent. All but the last band of the northern and western Algonquin—some four hundred strong, in eighty or ninety canoes—had already paddled away upstream. The tortuous logistics of wilderness diplomacy had never been more obstructive to peace, nor the challenge to Garacontié's authority more marked. "Garacontié was at a loss," an observer remarked, for he was without the sachems of the other nations whom league protocol prescribed as his coadjutors.[35]

Yet as events now made clear, after sixteen years as the Sagochiendagehté, as the "Captain of Onnontagué," Garacontié's tireless diplomacy had made the Onondaga in practice what they were in Five Nations theory, "chief of all the Iroquois Nations." Garacontié himself, senior sachem of the Bear Clan, the Onondaga Nation, and the League of the Iroquois, sat in the seat we now think of as that of Atodatho, the convenor of the confederacy. So it was that, at the end of July 1670, Garacontié determined to act alone for all the Iroquois. Onnontio then persuaded each of the Algonquin nations represented at Montreal to send a delegation of twenty to take canoe to Quebec with Garacontié.[36]

At Quebec, Garacontié faced a stiff diplomatic challenge. His response to it transformed both his life and the life of his people. The Ottawa complained to Onnontio that the Seneca had broken the peace by attacking the Ottawa's allies. They demanded that the French governor-general keep his word to punish aggressors against the peace. Courcelles temporized, saying that as he had executed his own nephews—the Frenchmen who had "massacred near Montreal" eight Iroquois earlier in the year and so threatened the peace—so he would hold the Seneca captives now brought to him by the western tribes. He reminded those nations' representatives, however, that their very presence was evidence that the trade provided for by the peace was going forward without interruption.

Garacontié was encouraged by Onnontio's sets of sanctions—forceful on behalf of injured Iroquois, limited on behalf of those they injured— and by the Frenchman's words on behalf of the peace. The Sagochiendagehté now rose to speak for all the Iroquois. In his best diplomatic manner, he argued that the Seneca had neither insulted nor injured the Ottawa when they attacked the Shawnee. That nation had never been

35. *Ibid.*, LIII, 43.
36. *Ibid.*, 41.

taken into the peace by name, Garacontié pointed out, so that an Iro-quoian attack on them violated no prior agreement. So much for fine diplomatic distinctions.

Garacontié had also to reply to the inevitable, impassioned, and, given its authors' fear and hatred of their Iroquoian conquerors, hostile ideological argument of the Huron. The Iroquois, said an aged Huron, ought to realize that neither trade nor territory nor alliance, but, rather, Christianity was the great blessing of the French connection. So the Five Nations should more carefully keep the peace which extended Christianity. Garacontié was not content with demonstrating that the Shawnee, whom the Christian Huron defended, were themselves pagan and so excluded from any Christian peace. He rebutted the Huron's anti-Iroquoian implications with a dramatic personal declaration. "As for the Faith which Onnontio wishes to see spread abroad everywhere," Garacontié said, "I profess it publicly among those of my own Nation, and no longer adhere to any superstition—renouncing Polygamy, the vanity of dreams and all kinds of sins."[37]

The Ottawa were confounded, the Shawnee excluded, the Huron out-flanked, and the French enthralled by Garacontié's declaration. That "that worthy Iroquois Captain—who for sixteen years, has always shown himself the friend and protector of the French in his Country—spoke with so much fire and zeal, in the Council, of the love he had for the Christian Faith," that he carried such an effusive Jesuit recommendation, and that he had been able, all alone, to rejuvenate the peace which he had created and which had saved New France from the wrath of the Five Nations for so many years, all demanded from the French authorities a public recognition, both religious and secular.[38]

François de Montmorency de Laval, bishop of Canada, announced that he would personally baptize and confirm Garacontié. The governor-general stepped forward to give his name, "Daniel," to his Onondaga godson. The daughter of the intendant stood up as Garacontié's god-mother. The ceremony took place "in the principal Church of Canada, the Cathedral of Quebec." There, Daniel Garacontié was honored by the attendance of a horde of Huron, Ottawa, Algonquin, Mahican, even the western Wyandot, and all of the Five Nations save the Cayuga. After the service, Daniel Garacontié walked through the throng of his admirers to the citadel. There the entire garrison was drawn up to do him honor, and all the castle ordnance was manned. Daniel Garacontié received the general salute of every musket and cannon in the French capital. Then he

37. *Ibid.*, 40–49.
38. *Ibid.*, 53.

sat down to the "sumptuous feast" presented to "all the Nations assembled at Quebec" by the governor-general of New France in the name of Daniel Garacontié, as a testimony to his Christian commitment.[39]

Four of these nations were Iroquois. On the traditional beliefs of all five of the leagued nations the conversion of the paramount sachem of the Onondaga and the league would have transforming effects. By 1676, his example had been followed by senior sachems of the other elder brothers of the kinship confederation, the Seneca and the Mohawk nations. The Iroquois had at last encountered ideals they could not assimilate into their traditional culture, either easily or soon. More than two centuries passed before the Iroquois achieved, in the Code of Handsome Lake, a synthesis of surviving tradition with intrusive Christianity. Until that time came, from the moment of Daniel Garacontié's conversion, the Ongweoweh were helplessly infected with an alien ideology so at odds with their own that they became a divided people: Christian and pagan.

Supremely successful as an international and intercultural diplomat, a master of the consensus politics of his people, Daniel Garacontié saw no such division as inevitable. He spent the rest of his life insisting, and trying to demonstrate, that to be a Christian was not incompatible with being an Onondaga. As soon as Garacontié reached Onnontagé he announced his conversion "at a feast attended by the Chief men of his Nation." His speech was a noble summary by one of the *royaner* of the public creed of these Iroquoian lords, a creed now undergirded, as he saw it, by Christian faith and precept.[40]

"You know my brothers," he began, "how I have ever supported the Public interests." He had always, he reminded them, been bold to speak whenever duty demanded. He had repeatedly risked his life and reputation in the national interest *("la conservation de ma patrie")*. He had also met the claims made on the personal generosity of every Iroquoian leader and he had facilitated the public charity enjoined on his people by kinsmanly custom. The poorest of clanspeople, even the despised old widows, he said, would testify that Garacontié had "used my authority" to help them meet the two great calamities of Iroquoian village life: the loss of essential field labor to illness or to death; and the loss of personal possessions and shelter to the fires which so often burnt bark houses (the more often since every vengeful drunk with a torch was excused his arson by his excess). Honor, said Garacontié, had spurred him to oratory and bravery and paternalism, as it did all the good lords of the longhouse. Now, Daniel said, he would be inspired to do his unchanging duty as a

39. *Ibid.*, 57.
40. *Ibid.*, LV, 55.

sachem by the scriptural commands of God, "the sovereign Master of our lives."[41]

God commanded Garacontié to sustain his traditional public duty as an Onondaga sachem, but he ordered Daniel to abandon the life style of an Iroquoian lord. Even among his polygamous peers, Garacontié had been a notorious rake and the master of many concubines. As a Christian, however, he adopted Christian marriage. Long the ritual chief of his nation, Garacontié had inaugurated the great ceremonies in which the will of Taronhiaouagon, the culture hero, "the master of lives," was sought in dreams and his commands divined by the frenzy of dream-guessing and wish fulfillment—the Onnonhuronia—which banished the boredom of February in Onnontagé. Now the converted chief announced that he would not countenance such superstition (and, when February came, he astonished the Onondaga by refusing to open the Onnonhuronia). He declared that divination was not, as was traditionally believed, "the mainspring of our country and our lives," uplifting the one and lengthening the others. "Rather," he said, dream-guessing was "the cause of our ruin and sure only to hasten our destruction" in a modern, rational, cosmopolitan, intercultural world.[42]

Daniel Garacontié's public declaration of Christianity and his denunciation of pagan practice, combined with the instant and profound alteration in his personal behavior, had enormous influence among the Onondaga. From Garacontié's conversion the missionaries dated the flowering of Christianity among "the real people" themselves, not just, as heretofore, among "the captive church" of their Huron dependents. Once again, the masters had adopted the religion of their servants.

His conversion also increased Daniel Garacontié's stature among the Europeans, daily more important to the Iroquois. The French now valued Garacontié's religious example—which they held up to all the aboriginal Americans who attended their annual rendezvous for trade in furs, territory, and influence at Montreal—almost as much as they did the peace which he had so long personified and preserved. And Garacontié's reputation as a diplomat and as a Christian went before him to meet the other European power with which the Iroquois must come to terms. This was not the Netherlands. The Dutch had been content to deal mostly with the Mohawk, usually in commercial terms through the *handlaers* of Albany. Now, however, the English conquered New Amsterdam, and their executives, the vanguard of empire, saw the Iroquois in political and strategic terms, as well as in those of the fur trade.

41. *Ibid.*, 57.
42. *Ibid.*, 57, 61, 63.

"The King of England's Country or Their Plantations"

The first English executive for New York had been its conqueror, Colonel Richard Nicolls. He converted the fact of conquest into the structures of empire in the heartlands of the duke of York's vast new territories. This Nicolls did by creating a sense of common interest among the varied people in the new province: puritan colonists, Dutch traders, Iroquois tribesmen. Of the greatest assistance to Colonel Nicolls in this effort were the two French invasions of the Mohawk "plantations" in the ducal territories of the king's dominions. Terrified by the French attacks of January and October 1666, Nicolls' conquered subjects, Indian clients, and English compatriots all saw the identity "as well of his Maties as of your own true Interest in these times of difficulty with the ambitious French."[43]

The Mohawk survived the second French assault in large part because of Dutch supplies and shelter at Albany during the winter of 1666–67. Albany itself was spared a French garrison only because it already had an English one. Cadres of Nicolls' troops then transformed a third of the Dutch militias into proto-dragoons, and they developed Albany's rear echelon by garrisoning Esopus (Kingston). Their colonel coordinated the defense of the upper Hudson and Connecticut valleys against the French and their Algonquin allies in cooperation with the leaders of the puritan west, Governor John Winthrop and Major John Pynchon. Only "the grandees of Boston are too proud to be dealt with," Governor Nicolls reported to Secretary Arlington, and "comply not with their duty as they ought." The grandees were surly if only because they jealously realized what the conqueror of New York told his king, "how advantageously wee are posted by situation, to bridle his Enemies and secure all his good subjects" (there was no question, then or afterwards, into which category the undutiful Bostonians fell).

Chief among the king's "good subjects," Nicolls insisted, were the Mohawk. In his view the two French invasions of their territory (and England's) had been "fruitless." Thanks to the Mohawk's timely retreat and to the Dutch community and English garrison of Albany, that Iro-

43. Nicolls' correspondence is in C.O. 1/21. For these quotations, see fols. 4, 6v, 7v, 246, 253, 287.

quoian nation which Nicolls' captive turned tutor and partner, Peter Stuy-
vesant ("late Generall of the New Netherlands"), had taught him were
the key to "the Trade for Beaver (the most desirable Comodity for Europe)" had lost but three people to the invasion, all of them too old to flee
the French, and two of whom immolated themselves in the flames of
their longhouses. Moved to negotiate peace by the French invasion, the
Mohawk were nevertheless still a formidable people who could make
their own terms with the French, and make Colonel Nicolls' as well
(especially since the bulk of the Carignan-Salières regiment had sailed
for the West Indies to fight the English).

Sending up a smoke screen of Francophilia, Christianity, and sol-
dierly camaraderie before the eyes of Lieutenant General Tracy, Colonel
Nicolls instructed "the Maquas Sachems" to resist the French. Nicolls'
agents were Captain Jervais Baxter, his Albany commandant; that town's
Dutch commissaries; Arent Van Curler or "Corleaer"; and a phalanx of
Iroquoian emissaries, the most active of whom was "Smits Jan," alias "Le
Bâtard flammard." It was characteristic of Nicolls' astute handling of his
agents that when the Flemish Bastard, like Garacontié, was suspected of
turning Frenchman, Nicolls warned him that "hee hath drawn so much
blood from the french that he cannot be so foolish as to thinke they have
good intentions for him." Simultaneously, however, the colonel reassured
the Albany commissaries that Smits Jan "is reported to love both English
and Dutch."

Through agents and clients so shrewdly balanced, Colonel Nicolls
brought the nascent English empire into the general negotiations for
peace which were organized by Garacontié and the French in the summer of 1667. The Mohawk, Nicolls said, must insist that, for their part, the
French should abandon all their forts on or near Lake Champlain and
forgo all incursions into Iroquoia—that is, into "the King of England's
Country or their Plantations." These counsels were well received by the
Mohawk. So Nicolls wrote further that "because the Maques desire my
advice it is that they make a good peace now with the french, such as
may bring in beaver to Albany, and leave them without feare or jealousy
of the french." To secure this peace, "the Maques should declare to the
french that the King of England is the Great King of all their Country and
parts adjacent and unto him they are Subordinate." Imperial subordination, Nicolls told his new allies, was both "his Maties Interest and your
owne against the Comon Enemy." "The Maquas Sagamores" must understand, Colonel Nicolls concluded, "that it is their Interest to make an
honorable Mention of the King of England, what numbers of English
there are round about . . . and with what friendship the English Dutch
and Maquas live together in all counts except warr with the Christians."

The upshot of these domestic accommodations, this anticipated imperial union of English and Iroquoian forces, and the 1667 negotiation with the French and Indians at Montreal, was the shaping of the Anglo-Iroquoian understanding which, in the wake of Bacon's Revolution, King Philip's War, and French expansion, would blossom into the alliance systems of the Covenant Chain. Not only did the Mohawk now adhere to Garacontié's peace with the French (and his war with the Susquehanna) and so unify Five Nations foreign policy, but they also began their lasting association with the expansion of the English empire, to support their own growing sphere of influence and as the particular Iroquoian partners of the English military executives in ducal New York.

In 1668, Nicolls was succeeded as the duke's lieutenant in New York by Colonel Francis Lovelace. Like Nicolls, Lovelace was a veteran of the civil wars and of French service under the duke of York, but his exile had also included a command in Virginia under Sir William Berkeley. This American service did not make Lovelace the equal of the founder of New York, either as a builder of English institutions or as an ally of the Iroquois. Prodded by Nicolls' old friend, Governor Winthrop of Connecticut, however, Lovelace did realize that the commercial ties of the Iroquois with Albany could be used to incite their interdiction of French influence in the Hudson and Connecticut valleys. He also agreed with the Dutch commissaries of Albany that an agreement with the Iroquois might persuade them to end their attacks on the native peoples closest to the English settlements, attacks disruptive to the frontier economy in which the native neighbors of the English were valued as commercial hunters and casual laborers. To these ends, Lovelace attended a council of Iroquoian chieftains that gathered at Albany in August 1671. He asked them particularly to end their long war with the Mahican, a war which, since their reverses of 1669, the eastern Iroquois had been winning.

Victorious Iroquois were always arrogant ambassadors, and their chief, Garacontié, now proselytized his faith as firmly and eloquently as he represented the diplomatic demands of the Five Nations. "He even went so far," when the Dutch Reformed Church held its Sunday service during the time of the 1671 council, to enter the church and pray, "on both knees in the midst of the conventicle. . . . When the minister bade him withdraw, he replied, in a loud tone of voice: 'Wait, I have not yet finished my prayer. You make it easily seen that you are not Christians, for you do not love prayer.' " Certainly it was dreadfully impolite as well as suicidally impolitic of the Dutch dominie to interrupt an Iroquoian ambassador, but, then, polite attention to anyone was not the hallmark of the Albany church or its ministers, an extremely quarrelsome lot of disputationists.[44]

44. Thwaites, ed., *Jesuit Relations*, LXI, 25.

Governor Lovelace, as was his wont, made a bad situation worse. He abused Garacontié's proud new Catholicism, "asking me why I wear this Crucifix and Rosary at my Neck, making fun of them, and saying they are of no account." The aim of the anti-Catholic Lovelace, like that of all subsequent English executives regardless of religion, was to reduce the political influence of the Jesuits among the Iroquois. It was hard—and for Lovelace, as for the Catholic missionaries themselves, it was impossible—not to identify political influence with religious teaching. But Lovelace should have known better than to ridicule the Sagochiendagehté. He had been told by the Dutch to defer to Garacontié "as to a man of good sense and experience in affairs." Now, deeply offended, Garacontié loudly lectured the luckless Lovelace, contrasting his irreligious attitudes to the piety of Onnontio. Garacontié suggested that Lovelace, a tyro in American diplomacy, would do well to emulate the French governor-general and so secure the blessing of God on his proposed peace treaty.[45]

Having said so much, Garacontié nonetheless led the Iroquois delegations to conclude a peace with the Mahican, not at Lovelace's request but as the best means of clearing the road to Albany's resources of iron-age technology. And the conference exposed Garacontié directly, rather than through Mohawk or Dutch intermediaries, to nascent English imperialism. It would, in a few years' time, help him secure at last that southern sphere of Iroquoian influence which had been the age-long objective of the Onondaga. The diplomacy that legitimated the acquisition of the Susquehanna Valley by the Five Nations would be the final work of the greatest aboriginal statesman of seventeenth-century North America.

"As Clever as a Demon":
Garacontié at Cataracoui

As yet, the European element in a successful Iroquoian drive against the Susquehanna to the south still depended not on godless English imperialism but, rather, on Garacontié's ability to neutralize if not to exploit the French. In 1672, however, both his personal influence and his religious association with the French provincial executive were greatly

45. *Ibid.*, LV, 61, 59.

discounted. Garacontié's godfather, the governor-general, his correspondent, the intendant, and his spiritual director, the bishop, all were recalled to France. One dominant personality replaced them in command of New France, the aggressive, anti-clerical Louis de Buade, comte de Frontenac. With Frontenac came word that the French had again attacked the Netherlands and that the English were once more preying on Dutch shipping, endangering the Iroquois' Albany access to European technology. Since the Old World was forever being called in to redress the balance of the New, these facts put Garacontié at even more of a disadvantage when he led the Five Nations embassy down from Onondaga and across the Iroquois lake to meet Frontenac at the site of a new French fortress. Just as Garacontié was about to set out downriver from Onondaga to the lake, however, word came that the Dutch had recaptured New Amsterdam from the English (the hapless Lovelace being absolutely elsewhere at the time). Garacontié could expect to benefit from Dutch initiatives against the French in the Iroquoian buffer zone between them, as well as from Dutch armaments.

Besides this encouragement to Garacontié's developing balance of the European powers, the fortunes of the Five Nations seemed (the Susquehanna front excepted) to be improving in the summer of 1673. The hunters, traders, and raiders of the upper Iroquois were opening new territories to league influences. North to Hudson's Bay and northwest to Lake Superior, Iroquoian traders and hunters acted in association with the English Hudson's Bay Company under its governor, that imperialist minister the duke of York. And the Iroquois had pushed west to Green Bay, backed by the Albany Dutch. Both advances took place under cover of Garacontié's peace with Onnontio. Also on the northern front, "the black gowns" did all that they could to maintain Garacontié's prestige with the new Canadian administration.

Father Jean de Lamberville wrote from Onondaga that when Garacontié came to confession, "it seems to me that I see one of those Christians of the early Church who maintained their baptismal innocence. . . ." Garacontié himself candidly reported that "he could not find that he had committed any sin." He had kept his promise to the bishop to obey all of God's commandments. He had refused to give dream feasts, the sachem reminded the priest, "then he added, with a smile: 'As to marriage, you know well my wife's ill temper. Had I not been truly a Christian, I would have sent her away long ago.' . . ."[46]

The leaders of the traditional Onondaga, however, had continued to criticize Garacontié's Christianity. They said "that he had become French" and so was untrustworthy. Yet as the years passed after his conversion, Garacontié's very constancy, both to his diplomatic policies and to his Christianity, seemed to most of the Onondaga, and so to the Iroquois generally, evidence of his credibility and sincerity. Garacontié's command of Onondaga's affairs, domestic and foreign, was thus unimpaired by either his Christianity or his Francophilia: "he is the mouthpiece of his Nation, by whom he is highly esteemed. No ceremony takes place without Garacontié speaking; it is He, they say, who knows all the affairs and who is as clever as a demon." When he fell ill in the winter of 1672–73, all jealousies were forgotten. "The Chief men came in a body to thank him for the attention and faithfulness with which he had managed affairs" and to take his directions for the future conduct of Iroquoia. When Garacontié recovered, he found himself universally esteemed by the Onondaga "as the soundest mind and the best councilor they have." In July 1673, he led them across Lake Ontario to meet the new Onnontio.[47]

The Onondaga were of two minds (as usual) about Frontenac's fortress in their country. At the ratification of the great peace in 1654, Garacontié had invited the French to make such a settlement. It would be Onondaga's Albany, available without tribute to the Mohawk, a source of European technology clearly in the Onondaga corridor. Since that time, however, the French had both revealed their limited commercial capacity and demonstrated their militant political ambitions. Meanwhile, the Onondaga had opened a trading relationship with the Ottawa. Only by playing hard upon the ancient enmities of these native nations had the French authorities been able to prevent large-scale exchanges of Dutch merchandise with the Ottawa at Onondaga. Such commerce would at once realize Onondaga ambitions and be the ruin of New France. So commercial as well as military motives drove Frontenac, as soon as the ice broke in the spring of 1673, to send the Sieur de La Salle to Onnontagé to invite the ambassadors of the Five Nations to meet him in midsummer at the Supplican mission to the Cayuga on the Bay of Quinté, there to consult about the erection of a French post on the Iroquois lake. The Onondaga replied that a Cayuga town was no place either for a grand council or for a trading post. Frontenac quickly said that he would alter his course to Cataracoui, the strategic site of a former Onondaga settlement.

On 12 July 1673, Garacontié came ashore at that site (where the Rideau River enters Kingston harbor), leading "more than sixty of the oldest and most influential of the sachims" of the Five Nations, their relatives and retainers. He found a formal military camp already in place on the promontory, a fortress—"Fort Frontenac"—under construction by brigades of Canadian militiamen, and the new Onnontio surrounded by splendidly

47. *Ibid.*, 139.

uniformed guards. (The Iroquois were not very impressed by the governor-general's guards, however, referring to them as "Hedgehogs" —that is, helpless children callously abandoned by shameless parents.)[48]

Ever the diplomat, despite force, fortress, and guards in Onondaga territory, "Garacontié, who has always been the warmest friend of the French, and who ordinarily acted as spokesman," opened the council on behalf of the Five Nations with a graceful expression of the Iroquois' delight at the honor done them by Onnontio's visit to their county. Despite the alarm felt by "some evil disposed spirits" among them at the arrival of the French in force, Garacontié said, the Five Nations had come to meet Onnontio in confidence that his visit was intended to confirm the peace and to protect his children from their enemies. They would, Garacontié promised, surely obey whatever commands Onnontio gave them to these ends. He was, he concluded, "speaking in the name of the Five Nations, as they had only one mind and one thought, in testimony whereof the Captain of each Tribe intended to confirm what he had just stated in the name of the whole." They did so, severally and at length, offering elaborate acknowledgments to Onnontio for altering the place of meeting and confirming their "words" of welcome with full belts of wampum.[49]

Onnontio replied (through the experienced interpreter Charles Le-Moine) in correct Five Nations form. First he addressed the nations in order, beginning with the Onondaga. He praised their (newfound) unity of counsels. He responded paternally to their filial respects (for Garacontié, always seeking a new conference card and for twenty years an official observer of European society, had decided to exploit the Europeans' odd family hierarchy and address Onnontio as "Father"). Frontenac adjured the "ancients" of the Iroquois to receive with respect "the black gowns," to attend to their teachings, and to protect them from the insults of the elders' unruly "nephews." In return, Frontenac promised, he would punish any of his nephews who injured the Iroquois. The governor-general displayed the armaments, cannon included, that he had brought through the rapids of the St. Lawrence and proclaimed himself the arbiter of peace and war on Lake Ontario. He demanded that the lords of the Five Nations make peace with the allies of the French. He asked visiting privileges for the relatives of the Huron held at Onondaga. He announced that the fort the elders saw abuilding would become the commercial center of Iroquoia. He asked them to protect and patronize it, rejecting the merchandise of Albany and the advice of his own disobedient neph-

48. "Journal of Count de Frontenac's Voyage to Lake Ontario in 1673," in *N.Y.C.D.*, IX, 95–114. For these quotes, see 103, 111.
49. *Ibid.*, 103.

ews, the *coureurs de bois* based in Albany (and in Onnontagé). Finally, the new Onnontio, father of the Iroquois, asked that the Five Nations send their children to him to be educated at Quebec.[50]

The next day (the conventional overnight of consensus-building having been used to good advantage) Garacontié and his four senior associates replied in form, a present authenticating each "word." The most telling word was the Cayuga sachem's observation that, somehow, Onnontio had forgotten to tell the Iroquoian ambassadors the prices of the trade goods he proposed to sell to their people at Cataracoui. He admitted that the Iroquois "had heard of the ruin of the Dutch and of the [French] King's conquests in their Country." Naturally, the sachem said, the Iroquois were distressed by the national disgrace of their European friends, and they were impressed by the danger thus posed to their primary suppliers. Certainly they appreciated the commercial advantages that this fact and the new fort on Ontario might give Onnontio's nephews in trade with the Five Nations (the irony of this, since all the principals knew that the Dutch had just recaptured New York, hardly needed emphasis). Still, said the Cayuga sachem, their newly acquired father did not want "roguish children," so he would secure them reasonable prices. The present that authenticated this word merely pointed again to the commercial chink the Cayuga had found in Frontenac's imperial armor: his best prices were twice those of the Dutch. He might bring cannon by the score up the river, but they would do the empire of the French little good unless trade goods followed.[51]

A second sachem made a specific demand for French military aid against the Andastoguetz (the Susquehanna), the last enemy left in what was to become the Iroquoian sphere of influence for a century. The Susquehanna war, so the sachem said, was going very badly for the Five Nations. Well supplied with canoes and men, the enemy could attack the Iroquoian villages at will, but the Susquehanna themselves were too strongly fortified to be attacked in return. Surely "it would be a shame for [Onnontio] to allow his children to be crushed, as they saw themselves about to be."

The Iroquoian ambassadors added that, given French commercial concessions and military aid, they would of course accept Onnontio's orders to let the Huron go where they would, without violence or restraint. They did regret that they could not at present accede to his request for their children. That was a matter for the clans to decide. They were not such neglectful parents as those of Onnontio's "hedgehogs," they said, and besides, he had Iroquoian hostages enough already. The

50. *Ibid.*, 105–9.
51. *Ibid.*, 110.

Iroquoian ambassadors, with Garacontié at their head, had asked much and promised little, despite Frontenac's forceful presence in their country.

Covering the council fire, Onnontio reiterated all of his words and recapitulated the unsettled issues. He admitted that he could say nothing either specific or encouraging about prices, if only because freight costs up the river were as yet unsettled. He promised, however, that since the Iroquois had proclaimed themselves his children he would treat them as Frenchmen in trade. He would decide how to help his Iroquois children against the Susquehanna when they came to Quebec to tell him their resolution about the French education of their children. Weapons and ammunition, coats and food, liquor and tobacco certified Onnontio's words. When the council fire was covered, Onnontio gave a private dinner, personal presents, and tokens for their children to each of the Five Nations' spokesmen, due tributes to their political power and their diplomatic skill.

To Garacontié, Frontenac also gave a letter for Father de Lamberville at Onondaga. In his reply, the missionary reported Garacontié's opinion that both Frontenac's presents and his politeness had genuinely charmed the Iroquois ambassadors. Once he had spoken to the other nations during the winter, Garacontié anticipated that Frontenac would be sent the Iroquoian children for whom he had asked (the Susquehanna war was still going very badly in the south, and the opening of the Iroquois' ultimate war in the west, against the Illinois, only increased the need to win French support). Yet there were other bidders for the alliance of the Iroquois than the politic Frontenac. The new Dutch government of New Amsterdam did send twenty envoys to Iroquoia during the winter to incite the Five Nations against the French.

In these winter negotiations, Garacontié continued to be the presiding sachem of the Five Nations, the exemplary Christian convert, and the champion of peace with the French. It was he who opened the grand council of the Five Nations by narrating the great Iroquoian legend of the world's beginning on the back of the great turtle, but the Christian Garacontié advised the lords of the longhouse that this creation story was but a fable. The master of the lore of his people, Garacontié spoke of the creation of the real people by the master of life, but he added that, rather than their culture hero, "Jesus was the sole master of our lives." The easy identification or substitution of Christ with or for Taronhiaouagon, so common among Iroquois of the 1670s, may have made Garacontié's apostasy more palatable to his peers. Certainly his discounting of Iroquoian belief did not prevent his kinsmen from pursuing his pro-French policy. The Dutch initiatives were rejected, the newly allied Mahican were ordered to stop their trade-disrupting attacks on the Ottawa, and in the

FOUR INDIAN KINGS, THREE
ARMORED ANDROSES, AND NEW YORK

ILLUSTRATIONS FOR BOOK THREE

Of the sachems pictured here, the famous "four Indian kings" who were lionized in London during April 1710, the most senior was barely a contemporary of Daniel Garacontié. Tee Yee Neen Ho Ga Row, "Emperor of the Six Nations," or Hendrick, was born in 1676. His portrait by John Verelst, together with the same artist's studies of his three companions, Sa Ga Yeath Qua Pieth Tow, "King of the Maquas," or Brant; Ho Nee Yeath Taw No Row, "King of the Gene-rethgarich," or John; and Etow Oh Koam, "King of the River Nation," or Nicholas, are the earliest verifiable representations of the Iro-quois, and of a Mahican. Of course, none of the subjects were kings. They were so called as part of a public relations campaign designed to launch the Anglo-Iroquoian conquest of Canada. Three of the "kings" were Mohawk clan sachems: Hendrick and John of the Wolf Clan village of Tinontougen (the object of Edmund Andros' 1675 visit), and Brant of the Bear Clan village, Caughnawaga. The totem of the third Mohawk clan (and of its village, Canajoharie) was the Turtle, also the totem of the Mahican headman, Nicholas. His place with the Mohawk embassy memorializes the consolidation of the Mahican bands with the refugees of King Philip's War, as the "River Indians," under the aegis of Edmund Andros in 1676.

The accoutrements of these sachems are of varied authenticity. All the items of native manufacture depicted here actually survived until very recent times, and several may at present be seen in London. The "kings' " costumes, however, seem to have been run up by a theatrical tailor for the sachems' portraits and stage appearances. Scarlet cloaks were thought appropriate for all four regal figures. Hendrick's suit is the first of the court costumes he acquired in successive visits to London. They became family heirlooms, mementos of English greatness observed, Iroquoian loyalty honored. And the mezzotinto prints of the "kings' " portraits, suitably framed, were brought to New York by General Francis Nicholson "to be hung up in the Onnondage Castle the centre of the 5 Nations where they always meet," and were treasured over time as political icons. So the Communion Service, given "to her Chapel among the Mohawks" by Queen Anne in response to the four kings' request, is still enshrined at Tyendinaga and at Brantford.

The sachems' belts or burden straps, decorated with red, white, and black moosehair and porcupine quills, moccasins with similar decorations, wooden weapons (whose use was demonstrated in the portraits' vignettes), personal tattoos, Brant's tasseled pouch, and, recalling the Covenant Chain itself, Hendrick's broad belt of purple wampum, all represent the Iroquoian culture which predominated in the largest part of the Anglo-Iroquoian condominium after 1676. And the metal weapons—not so much the trade tomahawks, which Verelst and company have made the prevalent symbols of the martial Amerindian, or the presentation falchion slung at Nicholas' belt, but Brant's musket—testify to the technological basis of Iroquoian authority.

Hendrick (1676–1755) premised his career on this symbiosis of Iroquoian ambition and Anglo-Dutch technology. He polished and extended the Covenant Chain whose silver links bound the Five Nations to the empire of the English. He continued to insist, as Carondondawe (Hendrick's predecessor as the sachem of the Mohawk Wolves) had done in 1676, on the special relationship of his people to Corleaer, as the governors-general of New York subsequent to Andros continued to be called by the Iroquois.

Born a Mahican but early adopted by the Mohawk Wolves, Hendrick (Theyanoguin) replicated Garacontié's career of religious, diplomatic, economic, and military leadership. In his teens, he joined the Dutch Reformed Church of Albany. At twenty-one, he traveled to New France during the armed truce that followed the Peace of Ryswick (1697), trying to recall the Mohawk migrants of 1676 from their new Caughnawaga on the St. Lawrence. In 1698, Hendrick successfully opposed the land grab by his Albanian religious mentor the Rev. Godfredius Delius. The English government of New York invalidated Dominie Delius' deed. Thus encouraged in his English allegiance, Hendrick refused to accept the neutrality between New France and the English provinces declared by many of the Iroquois in 1701. Instead Hendrick joined the Iroquois signatories who made over to King William the vast hunting lands that the Five Nations (soon afterwards, Six Nations: the Tuscarora Iroquois joined the league by 1710) had seized from the Huron. This cession was made on the condition that the English crown expel the French from those lands and preserve the rights of the Iroquois in upper Canada "forever and that free of all disturbances." To that end, and in the hope that he could, by expelling the French and the Jesuits, reunite the Iroquois in Canada with their dwindling brethren in Iroquoia, Hendrick spent the rest of his life instigating and commanding Anglo-Iroquoian imperial assaults on Canada.

On the morning of 18 September 1755, at the head of the column marching to the relief of Fort Edward, Hendrick and his Mohawk followers were challenged by their Caughnawaga kinsmen, the first line of the great Franco-Indian ambush. To that challenge—"who goes there?!"—Hendrick replied, "We are the six confederate Indian Nations the Heads & Superiors of all Indn. Nations of the Continent of America," and one of his Mohawk shot the impudent Caughnawaga challenger. An imperial Iroquois to the last, Hendrick did not survive this battle of the kinsmen parted in 1676. All of his companions of 1710 had long predeceased him, without ever establishing greater claims to fame than the mission that produced these portraits.

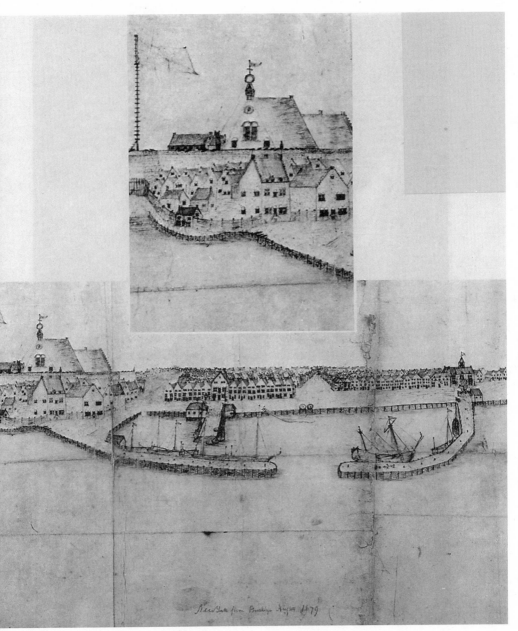

New York from Brooklyn Heights

Sa Ga Yeath Qua Pieth Tow
("Brant")

Tee Yee Neen Ho Ga Row
("Hendrick")

Ho Nee Yeath Taw No Row
("John")

Etow Oh Koam
("Nicholas")

Thomas (or Amias) Andros

Amias (or Edmund) Andros

Sir Edmund Andros

Also superseded by 1755 was much of the view of *New York from Brooklyn Heights 1679* by the Labadist Jasper Danckaerts. It is nonetheless an admirable illustration of the changes wrought in the capital of the duke's dominions in the first five years of the Andros regime. To the left, on the southern tip of Manhattan, the remounted cannon atop the great gray walls of the rebuilt Fort James menace both the East River anchorage and the city, walled off from the foot of the fort by the new palisades. Above the walls of the citadel rise the roofs of the barracks, the "King's Chapel," and the governor's mansion. In a great crescent, from the residence of the former English officer now serving as mayor (at the water end of Whitehall) around to the old City Hall at Coenties Slip, runs the "Great Dock" begun in the spring of 1676 and finished before winter 1679. Its cribs and pilings appear clearly, filled with stone and boasting bollards and anchors, sheltering seven sloops and a small ship, the rebuilt wharf, its customs and weigh houses, and a flotilla of small craft. Inland, the newly paved streets run into the re-surveyed city from the re-bulkheaded riverfront (the house of the unfortunate Cornelius Steenwyck is next to the former Dutch West India Company warehouse, at the head of the wharf). To the right of the view, outside the reinforced city wall, on pilings over the water, marking the outer boundary of the Andros redevelopment, lies the new slaughterhouse begun at the end of 1676/7. Inland of it are the first suburbs of New York on Manhattan, evidences of Andros-induced prosperity in an era of imperial economic decline and American disaster.

Substantial confusion beclouds the exact identities of two of the three armored Androses pictured here. When, in 1912, the two oil portraits came out of the estate of the Carey heirs of Sir Edmund Andros, their owners insisted that the older gentleman was Sir Henry Morgan. Presumably, the old pirate's portrait had entered Andros' collection during that untraceable West Indian governorship in 1672, likewise an article of faith among Andros' heirs. The family supposed the younger sitter to be Prince Rupert, the acknowledged patron of Sir Edmund. The Careys, far from the self-importance and self-confidence so characteristic of their Andros forebears, seem to have been unable to believe that these aristocrats were members of their own family.

Expert opinion soon established both sitters as Androses, however, and added that their portraits had been executed c. 1649 by Pieter Verelst. If this opinion is correct, Amias Andros (1610–1674) was an aged-appearing thirty-nine-year-old. His son Edmund (1637–1714) was certainly a most mature twelve-year-old. Much aging of Androses could be attributed to the hardships of civil war, but recent opinion is that the older subject is Thomas Andros (1561–1637), Amias' father, and that the younger cavalier is Amias himself. No one seems to have any doubt that our third sitter is Sir Edmund. The engraving here reproduced first appeared as the frontispiece of

W. H. Whitmore, ed., *The Andros Tracts* (Boston, 1868), taken "from the original picture in the possession of Amias Charles Andros Esq. of London."

In each of these three Andros images, the similarity of pose emphasizes that of the nose, long under heavy brows. Each sitter exhibits a wide, compressed mouth subduing a modest, but well-defined, chin. In each portrait, the dramatic contrast of starched white linen and lace with serviceable, black, articulated, polished armor bespeaks the gentleman and the soldier combined in the royal administrator. That the Andros inheritance was so fully realized in Sir Edmund's stern, seigneurial, soldierly, statesmanlike command of the duke's dominions seems almost a Darwinian instance of inherited attitudes and abilities. After five generations of service to the crown, however, this branch of the Androses became extinct. Sir Edmund was the last, as well as the most accomplished, of a long line of Andros officers and governors involved in the extension of English empire. They figured in the empire's modern institution, which followed England's loss to France of the last remnant of its European sway (with the fall of Calais, where the first of the Andros line, Captain John, died in 1554). The imperial service of the Androses spanned all the succeeding years down to the achievement of English empire in America and the restoration of England to equality of power with France in the Treaty of Utrecht (the year of Sir Edmund Andros' death, 1714).

Photographs of John Verelst's original oils, commissioned by Queen Anne, were secured from Public Archives Canada (negative numbers C-92420; C-92418; C-92416; C-92414) and are reproduced by the kind permission of the Archives. In this connection also, and for facilitating my examination of the Iroquoian relics of 1710, I am indebted to J. F. C. King, Department of Ethnography, British Museum. To Chief Melville Hill of Tyendinaga, my thanks for showing me Queen Anne's gift of Communion Plate. King Hendrick's last words are recounted by Daniel Claus, Hendrick's pupil in Mohawk, in Claus' *Narrative of his Relations with Sir William Johnson and Experience in the Lake George Flight* (n.p., n.d.), cited by Milton W. Hamilton, *Sir William Johnson* (Port Washington, N.Y., 1976), 160. Other contemporary comment is from Richmond P. Bond, *Queen Anne's American Kings* (Oxford, 1952; New York, 1974), 52; and John Wolfe Lydekker, *The Faithful Mohawks* (London, 1938; Port Washington, N.Y., 1968), 192.

New York from Brooklyn Heights, The Labadist General View of New York, is in the collections of the Long Island Historical Society. It is reproduced by the permission of the Society.

The photographs of the portraits of Amias (?) and Edmund (?) Andros by Pieter Verelst (?) are from Archives of the National Portrait Gallery, London, and are reproduced by permission of the Gallery. I am grateful to S. Wimbush for generously assisting my researches in the Archives. The photograph of the engraving of Sir Edmund Andros is by Al Edison, Syracuse.

spring of 1674 eight hundred Iroquois, with Garacontié at their head, traveled to Montreal. They carried with them eight children selected from leading clans for Onnontio's "education" program. He received them with ill-disguised glee, reporting to the imperial minister, Jean Baptiste Colbert, that the eight young Iroquois "are so many hostages . . . for the peace so necessary for this Colony, and which [the Five Nations] would not dare, henceforward to break."[52]

Yet it is clear that the three easternmost of the Five Nations now had no desire to break the peace with the French, if only because it offered them alternative trade routes and goods and an alternative form of acculturation—religion instead of brandy—to those of the Dutch. For a time longer, the motives yet prevailed which had retained the support of the western Iroquois nations for Garacontié's French peace policy. Less accessible to the Dutch and more exposed to the Susquehanna, the Seneca were willing to accept the Onondaga-sponsored intrusion of the French into western Iroquoia during the continuation of the Susquehanna war. The Seneca "Captain-General of all the Five Nations" (one of the league's two permanent military leaders) actually came back to Cataracoui after the council fire was covered, to negotiate, under Frontenac's patronage, an economic agreement with the tribes on the north shore of Lake Ontario. Fort Frontenac, then, was a convenience, it was placed in Onondaga territory at the invitation of that nation, and it was first built at a moment when the eyes of the western Iroquois were fixed upon the crisis of the Susquehanna war and the onset of the Illinois conflict. The defeat of the Susquehanna, however, coincided with a breathtaking instance of French aggression. In 1676, La Salle rebuilt Frontenac's Ontario fortress in stone. Then, in 1679, he built a trading post at Niagara, just west of Seneca country and right across their great western trail. Only a personal visit from Frontenac briefly delayed the Seneca destruction even of the first of these intrusions, the expulsion of the missionaries, and war with the French based upon a new alliance with the English.[53]

In the midst of the Iroquoian diplomatic revolution of 1676, set between the increasingly pro-French Mohawk and Oneida and the increasingly anti-French Seneca and Cayuga, were the Onondaga and their paramount chief. As usual, war decided their diplomatic dilemma. The impetus of Garacontié's friendship with the French and of the Five Nations' northern peace had been the war with the Susquehanna. If the course of that war changed, so might the whole balance of Iroquoian diplomacy, with a concomitant challenge to its senior statesman. In Onondaga, the talk was of nothing but war. Jean de Lamberville wrote to

52. Thwaites, ed., *Jesuit Relations*, LVIII, 211. *N.Y.C.D.*, IX, 117.
53. *N.Y.C.D.*, IX, 113.

his superior on 18 June 1676 that he would "hear as much about war from this quarter as from Europe. The Minds of our Iroquois are always full of it, and there is no probability that they will cease to kill men (as they say) so long as they find them in the Woods."[54]

Sesquahana fort'
Demolished

"Exterminating the Andastoguetz"

The men whom all of the Five Nations save the Mohawk wished most to kill in 1676 were Susquehanna. Yet it was the Mohawk who had begun the Susquehanna war, the longest, hardest-fought contest in all the century-long Iroquoian career of conquest. And this southern war too, like the strike north against the Huron in 1649, the Mohawk had begun against the will and counsel of the Onondaga. The people of the mountain had for ages past traded goods and culture with their neighbors to the north and south, the Huron and the Susquehanna. The rise of the Dutch trade after 1626, via the Mohawk, had not altered the Onondaga orientation, for the Mohawk so taxed the trade to the east that they soon became "unbearable even to their allies." Between 1652 and 1655 they triggered an endless set of feuds between all the more western of the Five Nations, on the one hand, and, on the other, their Susquehanna suppliers of European goods from the Delaware and Chesapeake ports. Then the Mohawk withdrew from the fighting and split the Delaware and lower Hudson commerce with the Susquehanna (who they now remembered were their kinsmen).[55]

It was left to the little Oneida nation to attack the Piscataqua dependents of the Susquehanna in 1661, and to a force of eight hundred of the upper Iroquois to assault in vain the Susquehanna citadel itself—with its four new Swedish cannon and its fifty Maryland English gunners—in 1663. The Susquehanna counterattack, together with the materiel and diplomatic help they gave to the enemies of the four western nations of the Iroquois, almost destroyed these nations. This counterattack, added to the Mahican and the Sokoki defeats of the Mohawk, nearly eliminated the Five Nations as an aboriginal power. At this moment of disaster, Garacontié was ambushed en route to plead for help from the French.

54. Thwaites, ed., *Jesuit Relations*, LX, 185.
55. *Ibid.*, XXXIII, 123. The archeological evidence for this revision of the standard views of the Onondaga orientation is given at length in Bradley, The Onondaga Iroquois: 1500–1655.

The assistance Garacontié secured did not prevent the Susquehanna from destroying the army of the Onondaga in 1666. In 1667, the Susquehanna allied themselves with the Shawnee and the Erie to attack the Cayuga and the Seneca. The former of these two nations was much the smaller, and the Susquehanna drove them right across the Iroquois lake to the Bay of Quinté. Under Susquehanna attack the Oneida soon followed their brethren north. When the two defeated nations considered peace in 1670, the Onondaga had to kill the Susquehanna ambassador to sustain the war. Then the Onondaga offered to aid the Mohawk against the Sokoki in return for Mohawk re-entry into the Susquehanna struggle. Despite the Mohawk diversions, and by Mohawk admission they did not amount to much, the southern expedition of the Seneca and Cayuga in 1672 was not more successful than the Onondaga assault had been. Sick though he was, Garacontié immediately went down to Montreal to meet with Courcelles in hopes of preventing a second front from being opened against the Iroquois by the French. The year following, he led the league's ambassadors to present the now united Five Nations' case to Frontenac and to plead for French aid against the victorious Susquehanna.

As dependent as the Iroquois were on French (and Dutch) military assistance and supplies, the Susquehanna were equally reliant on support from the English of Maryland (and from the multinational Delaware settlements). In 1673, as Garacontié was soliciting munitions from the French, the Maryland Assembly passed a provincial tax to supply the Susquehanna with gunpowder. Yet, as the repeated Iroquois attacks on the Susquehanna followed their migration down the river that still bears their name, the Indian war began to impinge upon the Maryland settlements. The Iroquoian attacks inspired in the Marylanders, as they did in all other Europeans who learned the hard way about the Iroquois, an ever-more-urgent desire to convert these raiders into traders. The proprietary council of Maryland decided to try to make peace with the "Seneca," as they referred to the four western Iroquois nations, even if it meant alienating their old allies the Susquehanna. It seems that the Maryland authorities urged the Susquehanna to make one more southward move, out of the path of the Five Nations and away from the frontier plantations of the English. Under pressure alike from their allies and their enemies, in February 1675 the Susquehanna moved their headquarters one last time, to the junction of the Piscataqua Creek with the Potomac River.

The change was calamitous for the Susquehanna. First, it deprived them of their Delaware fiefdom (where Maryland too had long sought to govern in association with the Susquehanna). In April 1675, Major Edmund Andros, governor-general of the duke of York's American domains (in succession to Lovelace), having just completed peace treaties with all the coastal tribes from the Hudson to the Delaware, took advantage of the Susquehanna's southward departure to detach their Delaware dependents, the Lenni-Lenape or Delaware nation, and ally them to New York. In October the prescient major observed the rising storm (and forecast the origins of "the Empire State"): he offered to negotiate, on behalf of that pre-eminent imperialist, the duke his master, a grand reorganization of authority in the two great valleys, the Delaware and the Susquehanna. Andros' proposal was premised upon the rising power of the Five Nations and their neighbors of New York, and upon the declining strength of the Susquehanna and their allies, the Chesapeake colonists.

The power balance now shifted dramatically in the direction of Andros and the Iroquois. The Susquehanna ceased to be allies of the Chesapeake English and instead become the deadliest enemies those colonists had faced for fifty years. Indeed, such was the fighting strength and strength of will of the Susquehanna that they were the most awful enemies faced by colonists of the Bay over the ensuing century and a half. By a series of boorish blunders and racist outrages, the frontier militias of Maryland and Virginia, hostile to their own governments and uncaring that they were allied with the Susquehanna, killed outlying Indians of that nation in September 1675. Then the militia besieged the Susquehanna in their new fortress at the first Falls of the Potomac. They massacred the five Susquehanna chiefs who came out to make peace, but the frontiersmen failed to prevent the escape of the entire native garrison and their families in mid-October. The Susquehanna proceeded to take a full and ritual revenge on the backcountry English, killing fifty colonists for every one of their assassinated chiefs and ten English for every other Susquehanna casualty.

Wolves to the English, the Susquehanna were sheep to the ravaging Iroquois. Fled from the last of their famous fortresses and so deprived of their cultural as well as of their military center, dispersed in small bands in the wilderness, the Susquehanna's situation was now like that of the Huron, the Erie, the Petun, and the Neutral Nations, prior victims of the Five Nations. During the bitter winter of 1675–76, and in those that followed it, the Susquehanna were found by the western Iroquois "behind Virginia" and ceased to exist as a people. By consumption, by enslavement, by settlement, by adoption, over the next four years the Susquehanna became Iroquois.[56]

Some of the scattered, surviving Susquehanna began to negotiate terms of amalgamation with the Iroquois, under the aegis of Governor-

56. [M.] Nicolls to Albany Magistrates, 15 January 1677/8, in B. Fernow, ed., *N.Y.C.D.*, XIII, 516. On the Susquehanna demise, see above, Book I, pp. 23–24.

General Andros, as early as February 1676. Later in the month, Andros went north to meet the Iroquois at Albany. To them, he was "Corleaer," the council name (like that of the Sagochiendagehté) given Andros by the Mohawk, an affectionate and functional label commemorating Arent Van Curler, the Albanian who had died in the diplomatic service of the Iroquois in 1669. On his return to New York, Corleaer (Andros) met, in Fort James, delegates from the largest outstanding band of Susquehanna, now encamped along the Delaware. He proposed to them either settlement with the Mohawk or adoption by the Onondaga and Oneida. Those who did not accept these peaceful proposals, passed on from the Iroquois by Corleaer, could expect less favorable terms of incorporation into the Five Nations. The Onondaga and their Oneida "children" were still mopping up Susquehanna irredentists in 1679. As early as August 1676, however, that astute observer Deputy Governor Thomas Notley of Maryland said of the Susquehanna that, "by the means of Collonel Andrews the Governour of New Yorke a peace was made last Summer between them and their old Enemy the Cinigo's [i.e., "Sinnique" or "Seneca," the four western nations of the Iroquois] so that now they are at Ease and out of our reach." [57]

With the Susquehanna to Andros and the Iroquois would go both the Delaware and the Susquehanna valleys. To control the Susquehanna was to command their domain. In August 1676, therefore, the Maryland authorities canvassed with their native allies the idea of making peace with the Susquehanna on the Delaware and of capturing the Susquehanna resettled under Onondaga supervision in the ancient Susquehanna capital at the Great Bend, but the game had already been lost to Andros and the Iroquois. The Maryland plan was abandoned and, in September 1676, Andros warned all of the outlying Susquehanna (and their former English allies) that unless the Susquehanna "came in" to either the Mohawk or the western Iroquois, they would be attacked by them. [58]

In December 1676, those Susquehanna encamped at the trading post of Maryland's chief negotiator, Jacob Young, were attacked by the "Seneca." In mid-March 1676/7, representatives of the western Iroquois, of the Lenni-Lenape (Delaware), and one of Andros' officers met at Shackamaxon (Philadelphia) on the Delaware River to divide the Susquehanna survivors among them. They also substituted the Mohawk, acting for Corleaer and the Five Nations, for the Susquehanna, acting for themselves and for Maryland, as the suzerains of the Delaware nation. These last had already dispatched some of their Susquehanna guests up the

57. Notley and council to Berkeley and council, 6 August 1676, in William Hand Browne, ed., *Archives of Maryland* (Baltimore, 1887–), XV, 122.
58. Andros' instructions to Captain John Collier, commander in Delaware, 23 September 1676, in B. Fernow, ed., *N.Y.C.D.*, XII, 556–57.

river on Andros' orders. On their way home, the "Seneca" conscripted
the Susquehanna warriors from their old capital to help man the attacks
they now planned on the native allies of the French to the north and west
of Iroquoia, and perhaps to assault the French themselves.[59]

In 1676, defeat of the Susquehanna by the Iroquois was a by-product
of the Chesapeake revolution of the English, but it transformed Iroquoian
diplomacy both by achieving an age-old ambition of the Onondaga and
by making English empire a fundamental support of an expanded Iroquoia. Garacontié's generation of peace with the French in the north had
allowed the Onondaga and their brethren to win the great war against the
Susquehanna in the south, given the mistaken attack of the Chesapeake
frontiersmen on that famous people. If the Iroquois themselves were to
avoid the fate of the Susquehanna, however, they must find an agent of
English empire as responsible as Onnontio was for the militant French.
During 1676, the negotiations of Edmund Andros—"Corleaer"—with the
Iroquois, the Susquehanna, their respective dependents, and both the
English and the French provincial regimes, made it clear that such an
English imperial agent had been found.

His Iroquoian counterpart, Garacontié, sought to negotiate with Corleaer a treaty of peace and an agreement about their governments'
spheres of influence in the territories taken from the Susquehanna. This
pact would be equivalent in importance both to Iroquois and Europeans
to that which Garacontié had agreed on with Onnontio twenty-two years
earlier concerning the spoils of the Huron war. Given such a settlement
with the English, the Five Nations would be able to shape their relations
with Europeans upon the balance-of-power principle. So they could end
their dependence upon the French. Writing of the missions to the Iroquois in 1676, the Jesuit Relation put this poor prospect for the French
future quite directly: "since these Barbarians have at last succeeded in
exterminating the Andastoguetz, who had held out against them for over
20 years, they have become so insolent that they talk only of breaking the
missionaries' heads by way of beginning hostilities against New
France."[60]

A different but equally deflating prospect was posed to the older
expansionist and autonomous English colonies which bordered upon the
vast territories that would be dominated by an alliance of the Five Nations with the English empire. The claims of the duke of York on behalf
of the crown, forwarded by Corleaer, and of the Iroquois, urged by Garacontié, together filled a great E-shaped band, with its head upon the coast

59. Notley to Calvert, 22 January 1676, in Browne, ed., *Archives of Maryland*, V, 152–54.
Coursey [to Notley], 22 May 1677, *ibid.*, XV, 246–48.
60. Thwaites, ed., *Jesuit Relations*, LX, 173.

of Maine, its midpoint at New York City, and its foot on the Tennessee River. Within the upper arc of the Yorkist-Iroquoian empire were confined the colonies of New England. Its lower arc bounded the future development of the Chesapeake colonies.

The Chesapeake agents received full and immediate instruction concerning the power of the new masters of their northern and western frontiers. At the end of the Chesapeake revolution in March 1676/7, Maryland's proprietary officials tried to re-establish contact with the Susquehanna and come to terms with the "Sinnique" through the agency of Edmund Andros, in accord with his hitherto neglected proposal of October 1675. The victory of the Iroquois and the popular pressures voiced by the "Hue & Crye" of the Maryland rebels compelled the proprietary regime's approach to Andros. Colonel Henry Coursey, the agent of Maryland (and Virginia), together with Jacob Young, the Susquehanna interpreter, entered Andros' government at Newcastle-on-Delaware just after the conclusion of the Shackamaxon conference. Finding only four low-ranked Susquehanna in the area, and obtaining no cooperation from either Andros' captain or the Lenni-Lenape (now doubly dependent upon Andros and the Mohawk), the agents could not follow their orders to re-establish Maryland's alliance with the Susquehanna and recover proprietary influence along the Delaware and Susquehanna rivers. The Maryland agents perforce proceeded to New York. There, during June 1677, Edmund Andros wrote the negotiating script he permitted them to take to Albany in mid-July to meet the ambassadors of the Iroquois. The chief of these was Garacontié.[61]

The "Death-Song" of Garacontié

The transformation of Iroquoian diplomacy externally, as an English association emerged to offset the French connection, and internally, as the Cayuga and the Seneca assumed the anti-French attitudes formerly taken by the Mohawk and the Oneida, only re-emphasized the diplomatic centrality of the Onondaga and of Garacontié. He remained, as he

---

61. The "Complaint from Heaven with a Hue & Crye and petition out of Virginia and Maryland," in C.O. 1/36, 213–18, and printed in Browne, ed., Archives of Maryland, V, 134–52, is discussed as it relates to the Iroquois and Andros above, in Book I, 3–4, 76–79. The Delaware and New York negotiations are detailed in Book III, Part 3.

had been for twenty-two years, the senior sachem of his clan, his nation, and his confederation. His prestige, and his role in the acculturation of the Onondaga, were both reinforced in the three feasts he offered in the spring of 1676. At the first, he denounced dream-guessing rites and the belief that wish fulfillment prolonged life. At the second feast, he decried the eat-all orgy. In the third, "as he is very aged, he Sang his death-Song."[62]

This lord of the longhouse people presumably began his death song, as he did all of his formal presentations to his people, by rehearsing their political tradition. This ideology of peace and power had inspired and informed his diplomatic career. This vision of a lodge of kinsmen extended lengthwise across aboriginal America had been ritualized and realized where Garacontié stood to sing his death song, at the council fire of the Onondaga nation and the Longhouse League. At this fire, he chanted the Condolence Hymn, a tribute to the constituents of the clan confederation:

> I come again to greet and thank the league;
> I come again to greet and thank the kindred;
> I come again to greet and thank the warriors;
> I come again to greet and thank the women.
> My forefathers—what they established!

The aged lord and his auditors now knew that Garacontié was about to become one of the class of forefathers, the ancestors, the ultimate rank in age-graded Iroquoian society.[63]

After uttering the invocation to the condolence council, the traditional mourning chant of his own people, Garacontié added to his death chant cultural acquisitions from his diplomatic career. He hailed the Christian Master of Life as "the sovereign of our fortunes." On Him, Garacontié said, "not on our dreams depended our life and our death." In the alternating inflections and deep-chested tones of the Iroquoian chant, the venerable sachem greeted the central personalities of his past in the formal fashion of his people, that is, as if the persons addressed were actually present. Among them were the sponsors of his baptism. Garacontié assured them he would die in the faith. He asked them for their prayers. Speaking to them, he renounced all the errors of his pagan period.[64]

62. Thwaites, ed., *Jesuit Relations*, LX, 193.
63. John Bierhorst, ed., *Four Masterworks of American Indian Literature* (New York, 1974), 140–41. Note that this hymn was often chanted apart from the condolence-council ritual, as an invocation.
64. Thwaites, ed., *Jesuit Relations*, LX, 193.

As custom demanded, the death chant of Garacontié was attended to "with admirable attention" by his guests. Subsequently, however, both his political rivals and his religious enemies said that the aged lord's appeal to French personages and his introduction of Christian clauses into his death chant demonstrated that "the faith had upset His Mind." Nonetheless, the senior sachem of the Bear Clan, the Onondaga nation, and the Iroquoian League preserved his political pre-eminence "by his strength of mind." So great in fact were his "Rank and reputation" among the Iroquois that he was no longer named personally. He had become "the Old Man," "the Elder," "the Man of Note." [65]

On 21 July 1677, in the Albany statehouse, "the Man of Note" spoke first for the Onondaga and for the Five Nations in reply to the propositions of Corleaer and Coursey, the governor-general of New York and the ambassador from Virginia and Maryland. Although Garacontié's wonted eloquence is lost in the crude translations from the Onondaga by successive Dutch and English interpreters, there still emerge from the record the structure of the condolence council and the significance of its celebrant. Once again, the Europeans had conformed to the diplomatic conventions of the Iroquois, expressed by Garacontié. This time the Iroquoian treaty form framed a supremely significant agreement. It determined the present disposition and future development of mideastern America—south of the lakes, east of the Illinois, north of the Tennessee —and all the territories dependent upon or related to that American heartland.

As condolence-council protocol required, Garacontié began his presentation of the Five Nations' position by acknowledging Corleaer's call to the council fire. "We are sent for by a Belt of Zewant [wampum] to Speake with his Honr. the Govr. Genll.," he said. This traditional summons had contained Edmund Andros' long-planned agenda for the Iroquoian council. His message had been followed by another belt. By it, Colonel Henry Coursey both presented his credentials as ambassador to the Iroquois from the Chesapeake colonies and their Indian allies, and put forward the proposal he offered anew on 20 July 1677 to open the council at Albany. This was to exchange between the Five Nations and "those liveing among you" (the Susquehanna) on the one hand, and the Chesapeake colonists, their Indian allies and subjects on the other, oblivion for past offenses in return for future peace. [66]

"For the future," Garacontié agreed, neither those for whom he spoke "nor none liveing among us" would attack "the People of Maryland or

65. *Ibid.*, 195.
66. The text as quoted appears in C.O. 1/40, 81v. It is printed, with some variations, in Lawrence H. Leder, ed., "The Livingston Indian Records," *Pennsylvania History* 23 (1956): 43–44, and Browne, ed., *Archives of Maryland*, V, 254–55.

Virginia." The Iroquoian orator frankly admitted "that we have killed of yor. Christians and Indians formerly," but this Garacontié is said to have blamed largely on Colonel Coursey's interpreter, the Susquehanna's associate, "Jacob Young alias my friend." With this wilderness entrepreneur seated across the courtroom from him, Garacontié repeated that "Jacob Young was a great leader and captain" of the Susquehanna against the Iroquois, "whereby the wars have been continued." (Eventually the Iroquois made Young so obnoxious to Maryland that he was tried for treason and saved only by Susquehanna threats to take a chief's revenge for his life.) Despite this record of admitted hostility to the peoples of the Chesapeake and despite Young's repeated provocations of the Iroquois, Garacontié said that those for whom he spoke asked "that all wch is past may be buried in Oblivion," as Colonel Coursey had proposed.

Then, in an apparent *non sequitur* to Coursey's proposals, Garacontié accepted, for all four nations of the upper Iroquois, Corleaer's original proposal. "We," said the senior sachem of the Bear, the Onondaga, and the league, "doe make now an Absolute Covenant of Peace, wch we shall bind with a Chain." What the governor-general of Yorkist America had proposed and what the Sagochiendagehté had accepted, was a continental division of political responsibility, a bipolar definition of an interracial frontier, extending along its eastern border some 700 miles from the St. Lawrence to the Dan. This proposition Andros had developed in discussions with the Iroquois which began in the summer of 1675. It was made possible by the revolutions of 1676. It was now concluded, in July 1677, with Garacontié's proclamation of the Covenant Chain.

This chain linked together the colonies of New England and the Chesapeake through the agency of the governor-general of New York and its associated territories from Maine to Delaware, with the Five Nations, their allies, tributaries, and adoptees, led by lords of the longhouse, of whom Garacontié was the senior and spokesman. The agreement announced and ratified by Garacontié on 21 July 1677 summarized the geopolitical consequences of 1676. It was the most important diplomatic event in North American history. The Covenant Chain ultimately dictated the victory of English language, culture, religion, and economy, over all of England's rivals for American empire. It placed the Iroquois in such a commanding position in aboriginal America that they remain to this day the most influential Native Americans east of the Great Plains.

The Covenant Chain won America for the English because it first served the interests of the Iroquois. For the hundred years of its heyday (the chain continued to be burnished by the Five Nations until at last the English dropped their end in the spring of 1982), the Covenant Chain supported the consolidation and delimited the administration of the vast Iroquoian sphere of influence. That sphere was first the frontier and then the backcountry of colonial America. And it was on Iroquoian lands confiscated from that sphere that the dominant states of nineteenth-century America would be built. The Five Nations, who had survived because of Garacontié's peace with the French, now secured as surrogates of English empire the territories they had won under the protection of his French peace. With the power of the French limited by the lakes, and until the English empire, and its successor states, grew strong enough to act on the legacy of 1676, for one hundred and twenty years, the Five Nations exercised over the great valleys of eastern America the dominance so long envisioned for them by the genius of Garacontié. He had realized the age-old ambition of the Iroquois: to make the League of Peace and Power prevail over all of its native neighbors.

The instrument of Iroquoian ambition was the Covenant Chain. The term "Covenant" is another testimony to the respect commanded by the condolence council. The English recognized the mixed religious and political nature of the Five Nations' diplomatic procedure, so they applied to its treaty product the appropriate label of "Covenant." To the English, this term partook of both the legal and the theological. "Chain" was an equally suitable Iroquoian adoption of an English metaphor. It was needed, the Five Nations' spokesmen felt, to express the specific, limited, directional, and powerful ways in which these new "Covenants" bound them to European polities. For a time, they spoke of "the Rope" which tied them to, for example, the Dutch, for the Iroquois had been impressed by ships' anchor cables. Subsequently, the Mohawk said that they were linked to the Albany Dutch by an iron chain. But in July of 1677, Garacontié defined the "Covenant Chain," and it was a chain of silver.

To set the Five Nations' seal to the Covenant Chain, Garacontié authenticated his "word" of agreement with an expressive present: a wampum belt thirteen rows across. On this mnemonic memorial, the figures of "the real people" were linked, arm by arm, to the chain of the covenant and so bound to the representations of the European signatories of this, the greatest treaty of Anglo-Iroquoian diplomacy. Many other peoples besides the principals were bound by the Covenant Chain. The western Iroquois nations were already peopling the great valley committed to their care by this covenant with the remnants of the native nations they had displaced from their former homelands, now Five Nations' hunting preserves. Susquehanna, Shawnee, Lenape, Illinois, all became buffers for the Iroquoian heartland against the alien—"those who speake strangely"—whether these were Indians to the south and west or Europeans to the east. And each dependent people provided warriors for the wars of the Iroquois, paid tribute to the prestige of the Five Nations annually at Onondaga, and, often, were a source of the slaves who served the Iroquoian aristocracy in house and field.

So fruitful an agreement required an extraordinarily creditable commitment. This Garacontié was in a unique position to supply, as Corleaer recognized. The English imperialist Edmund Andros was infinitely more insightful than his predecessor, the ineffectual Francis Lovelace, so the new governor-general of New York respected the quality of his opposite number among the Iroquois. Garacontié, Corleaer knew, was a diplomat who had negotiated on equal terms with a generation of French proconsuls. Himself a Norman seigneur and a most cosmopolitan figure, Andros appreciated the French literacy of the Sagochiendagehté. And Andros represented a Catholic prince at the Covenant Chain council as well as directing the emissaries of a Catholic proprietor, Calvert of Maryland. Naturally he warmly praised the Catholic constancy of the convert hailed by the Jesuits as "the best of all our Iroquois Christians."[67]

Garacontié was thus assured that he could cite, with favorable effect on Corleaer and on Colonel Coursey, the precedent of his previous peace treaty with the French, and that he could strengthen the force of that example by drawing upon his own Christianity. So Garacontié welded fast the links of the Covenant Chain, and demonstrated his place and that of the Onondaga nation at its center, by pointing out to the Albany negotiators that the Five Nations had fought wars with New France every bit as devastating as those in which they had involved the Chesapeake colonists in 1676, and that they had suffered in return reprisals equal to those inflicted by the Susquehanna. Yet, after all of this carnage in the north, Garacontié said, "a good peace followed." "Soe it is now wth. us," the Sagochiendagehté said to the Albany congress, and he added, in words reminiscent of his rebuke to Lovelace in the same place (but in vastly different circumstances) three years before, "we desire that God Almighty who dwells in heaven may give his blessing" to the peace secured by the Covenant Chain.

Blessed peace demanded due determination to maintain it. To this work Garacontié had given his life, so he asked that, when the inevitable incidents occurred between English and Iroquois or between warriors of the Five Nations and the Indian allies or dependents of the English, negotiations and reparations might be the result, that "we might give one another satisfaction and not immediately fall in war." In sealing this word with a present, Garacontié extended to those linked by the Covenant Chain the fundamental function of the Longhouse League, for the league

67. Thwaites, ed., *Jesuit Relations*, LXI, 31, 33.

had been founded as the mechanism whereby reparations were substituted for revenge among allied nations.

A long lifetime of diplomatic experience had educated Garacontié to the problems of making peace effective over a vast area of haphazard communications. He warned Colonel Coursey, therefore, that "there are of our four Castles of the Sinniques" (i.e., the Oneida, Onondaga, Cayuga, and Seneca) war parties still out "fighting against the Susquehannocks." The Maryland authorities were to warn their native clients not to endanger the new peace either by sheltering fugitive Susquehanna or by refusing to feed their pursuers: "friends eat out of the same bowl." This word as well, the Sagochiendagehté, "the gentleman from Onondaga," ratified with a present. Then Garacontié was seated, his last and greatest diplomatic act accomplished.

Such public diplomacy, then as now, was but the interim, summary report of the ongoing negotiating process, the private conversation of ambassadors or, as the evocative Iroquoian phrase put it, "talk in the bushes." The bushes in this case were Colonel Coursey's lodgings in Albany. There Jacob Young, whom Garacontié had so slanged in public, gave the Onondaga sachem words and wampum to promise that the Chesapeake delegates would do the right thing next spring. They would come overland, direct to Onondaga, to the council fire of the Longhouse League, bypassing the Albany statehouse and both Governor-General Andros and his Mohawk cronies. At Onondaga, the Marylanders would negotiate about the great valley and its future directly with its new masters. In October 1679, the Onondaga were still waiting for the Marylanders to honor their promise. For many months of that year, the Onondaga sachems refused to meet the agents of Virginia at Albany, hoping that they could yet secure the legacy of Garacontié, undisputed control of their ancient southern vector.[68]

"Onnê Ouagicheria"

B ut Garacontié did not wait with his brethren, and the aims of Onondaga were to be, at best, incompletely realized, for Garacontié had

---

68. On "talk in the bushes," and the protocol of Iroquoian treaty-making generally, with particular emphasis on the eighteenth century, see the standard work by Francis Jennings et al., eds., *The History and Culture of Iroquois Diplomacy: An Interdisciplinary Guide to the Treaties of the Six Nations and Their League* (Syracuse, forthcoming).

received something else besides words and wampum at Albany. A draught of wine was given the aged lord, perhaps at Colonel Coursey's, perhaps from the hand of Jacob Young "alias my friend." Whatever the quality of the draught, Garacontié had known only brandy as an intoxicant. He had drunk not at all since his conversion to Christianity seven years before. Taken unawares, for one night he became that thing he most abhorred, a drunken Indian. Humiliated, he went home to Onondaga in August 1677. There he made a public confession of his sin, his only sin in seven years. Six weeks later he was dead.

It seemed as if Garacontié's pagan critics had been correct. Having accepted that extra-human baptismal contract with the Deity, Garacontié, they had said, "would die at the first sin that he should commit." So he had done, vomiting up his life with his offense, unable to receive the Eucharist he desired. He asked other sachems at his farewell feast to voice his counsels to his people: keep peace with the French to the north; make war with the Shawnee to the west; and seize the future for the Iroquois in the Ohio Valley, now that the Susquehanna were defeated and their valley won for Onondaga. And "he Entreated them all to become Christians, and quit their superstitions, as he had done." [69]

His farewell feast was over. Garacontié had watched his last guest leave the longhouse. He said, "*Onnê ouagicheria*"—"See, I am dying"— and collapsed in the arms of Father de Lamberville. Garacontié's head was placed in the lap of his brother, who was to take up the name, character, and policies of "Garacontié," and the old lord died. He was immediately buried, in European fashion, in a coffin the planks of which he had provided himself. In keeping with his last wish, a high cross was erected over Garacontié's grave to testify to his people that their senior sachem had been, still was, a Christian.

69. Thwaites, ed., *Jesuit Relations*, LVII, 139; LXI, 27.

[II]

EDMUND ANDROS,
ENGLISH IMPERIALIST

Introduction

"He has no easy game to play yt comes after Sr Ed. Andros," wrote William Penn, "for tho he was not without objection he certainly did great things more than both his predecessors" as chief executive of the duke of York's dominions: the universally admired conqueror of Dutch New Amsterdam and founder of English New York, Colonel Richard Nicolls; and the uniformly denigrated Colonel Francis Lovelace, the commander in whose absence New York was lost to the Dutch. Reclaiming the province, Major Andros not only picked up the administrative, military, and economic pieces dropped by Lovelace, Andros also—in just the first two years of his epochal term in command of New York—converted a market town into a provincial metropolis, and established the physical and political presence of the imperial crown in mid-America, reclaiming Long Island from Connecticut, resisting Massachusetts' pressure on the upper Hudson, the "North River." Along the province's "South River," the Delaware, Andros built the society we know as the state of Delaware, providing its three seminal settlements with military and civil government, physical security, and economic organization. On both rivers, and along the sound as well, Andros won the confidence, even the affection, of the aboriginal inhabitants. Consolidating European societies and conciliating Amerindian entities, Andros protected the peoples of the duke's dominion from the great Algonquin uprising of 1675–76, the greatest Indian assault in American history, an outburst that seared and set back for more than a generation every other set of settlements north of the Albemarle Sound. Small wonder that the pacifist, libertarian Quaker William Penn so highly estimated the soldierly, authoritarian, anglican Edmund Andros, offered him much of Delaware as his personal fief, and tried to secure his executive services to administer the Pennsylvania which had come to exist and which continued to prosper as a result of Edmund Andros' activities as James Stuart's lieutenant.

Extraordinary accomplishment requires especial opportunities. Major Andros was assigned to direct traffic at the crossroads of 1676, the strategically located string of territories in which English imperialism and Iroquoian ambition became symbiotic partners. Both Amerindian and European societies within the territories called "New York" were at their most malleable when Andros arrived. Each reflected changing and linked balances of power. The last battles of the Peoples of the Fall Line increased the population, prosperity, and political power of King Charles' subjects in New York, red and white alike. These same struggles drastically diminished the resources of all of New York's previously predominant neighbors, from the Susquehanna Indians to the Ottawa, and from the Chesapeake Bay colonies to those east of the Connecticut River. Like England's empire, New York's sphere benefited enormously from being itself at peace in a world at war. Although the favorable geopolitical environment of Andros' administration was the indispensable underpinning of his accomplishment, exploitation of this environment required an aggressively capable, socially and politically self-assured, militarily and administratively experienced man. For almost all of the thirty-seven years prior to his New York commission, Edmund Andros had been in training for an imperial command.

Andros was born a monarchist and courtier, for his father was an officer of Charles I's household. Inheritor of the ancient seigneury of Sausmarez, Andros was inherently aristocratic as well. His family's feudal base in Guernsey also introduced him to the needs of colonial economies and the petty dynamics of provincial politics. Both civil war and social revolution quickly destroyed the Andros family's courtly, comfortable, provincially prestigious position. Eighteen years of parliamentary revolt, commonwealth revolution, protectorate dictatorship, made Edmund Andros' upbringing an unhappy epic of flight, fight, and uncertainty in all save allegiance to the Stuart sovereigns. A life at war, formalized by an army education, created a combative authoritarian, a cavalry commander, a soldierly scion of an entirely military family. That it was in the Netherlands and at the Bohemian court that the clan Andros found household service and military employment meant that the Dutch church, language, and the Stuart princes of Orange and of Bohemia all became as much parts of Edmund Andros' experience as England, Guernsey, and Whitehall ever were. Andros' acquisitions as an exile made him the most effective "English" administrator of New York—most of the population there was Dutch—in the seventeenth century (and only General Robert Hunter equaled Andros' executive accomplishment in New York during the eighteenth century).

The English army supplied Andros (as it did Hunter and nearly nine-tenths of all imperial executives of America during the seventy-four years of their consecutive service in colonial command) with a camaraderie which produced constellations of imperial administrators; with combat experience which instilled ruthless realism in its veterans; with practice as political police, both metropolitan and provincial, within England and without, which taught that "force gives the law to law"; with experience of deprivation in distant commands, which bred self-reliant resourcefulness in provincial acquisition (and administration), regardless of local legislative opposition, English parliamentary parsimony or regulation, or royal neglect; with the command responsibilities for military subordinates and a protectiveness towards civilian populations, which were rewarded with loyalty, even popularity.

Commissioned major of the first American regiment of the English army, that Barbados infantry whose officers became the dominant cadre of island administration in the imperial era which followed their West Indian service, Andros' first imperial command was based in Barbados, and he saw service throughout its Leeward Island dependencies. The courtly manners and martial ability which always won Andros executive recognition made the major a favorite of the Willoughbys of Parham, governors and generals in the West Indies. On their staffs, Andros participated in the provincial interplay of command and commerce, law and necessity, England and its colonies.

Then, stationed in Nevis, an isolated, impoverished, and exposed island garrison, Andros experienced the problems of new and precarious societies in the Americas. Militarily, the "French and Indians" were as much menaces of Caribbean settlers as of continental ones. Andros fought the French and helped to form an alliance with the Indians. The Barbados Regiment backed negotiation of the treaty with the Caribs, which was the precedent of Major Andros' pacification agreements with the Algonquin of the American coast and so was the first step towards his vastly consequential diplomacy with the Iroquois.

Impressed with the importance of Indians to empire, Major Andros came home to his old London lodgings with the earl of Craven in Drury

Lane. Thence he acted in the interwar years in regimental reconstruction, marine salvage, marriage negotiations (both his own and those of the duke of York), and lobbying at Whitehall for his Barbados, Guernsey, and military clients, until two crises—one national, the other personal—completed Andros' apprenticeship to empire.

The national crisis was the third and last Dutch war. Andros' cadre infantry companies became the Barbados Regiment of Dragoons, mounted police who symbolized the political power of permanent, professional armies, pre-eminently that of the king of France. Major Andros found himself, his regiment, the army of which it was a part, his colonel, Prince Rupert, and his patron, the duke of York, all involved in the "standing army" controversy, the nub of Anglo-American politics in the ensuing, imperial era.

In the context of the war, the issues of absolutism and empire, military and geopolitical, came expressly to include the lost colony of New York. Its strategic position vis-à-vis the tobacco colonies to the south, the republican states to the north, the French competitors for the fur trade and territory to the west, and the sugar colonies of the Caribbean, was now realized by English imperial authorities in terms as redolent of 1776 as of 1676.

In the context of an Atlantic imperial dynamic which prevailed unchanged for a hundred years, Major Andros was commissioned by the king and the duke to capitalize upon the freshly perceived provincial potential of New York when it was surrendered by the Dutch. Before he sailed for America, however, Andros had to capture and crystallize the Guernsey inheritance, personal and political, opened to him by the death of his father. To secure his succession as bailiff of Guernsey, Edmund Andros had officially confirmed his father's informal reorientation of the office: the former head of autonomous island institutions had become the crown's civil executive in England's dependency. While Edmund Andros instigated the acts of the privy council which made the administrators of Guernsey royal appointees and imperial executives, and while he introduced the law of England into the courts of the island, the bailiff did not abandon Guernsey's conciliar, representative, and customary politics. The "Royal Court" or council, and the "States" or assembly of Guernsey, as well as the particular customs of its people, economic as well as political, all provided their bailiff with patterns for provincial institutions and measures of essential deviation from both mercantile norms and English attitudes. His Guernsey inheritance proved to be both precedential and practical when Edmund Andros constructed new societies in America.

Inheritance and Exile

1637 – 1661

In London as in Onondaga, most children died young. Two children, their namesakes, had already been lost to Amias Andros, master of the ceremonies to King Charles I, and Elizabeth Stone, his wife, when, in April 1637, Amias' father, Thomas, seigneur of Sausmarez in the island of Guernsey, died at the age of sixty-six in his manor house. Thomas Andros had been the third generation of his family to serve an English monarch as governor or lieutenant governor of the famous fortress island, England's channel frontier with France. Now Amias Andros was heir to the seigneury and the fourth generation of his family to serve the English crown. When he found that his wife was four months pregnant, Andros was filled with the hopes of an aristocratic man in a dynastic age. He therefore arranged one of those celebrations of honor and loyalty which, combined with force, governed England and its empire.

On the morning of 6 June 1637, as King Charles I passed in procession through Whitehall to chapel, he paused in the presence chamber and sat down in the chair of state beneath the canopy of the lions and lilies. "The sword of state borne before him by the Earl of Northumberland, and the great lords and officers of state attending," King Charles raised his sceptered hand. The royal bodyguard formed two ranks from the door of the presence chamber to the foot of the throne. Between these ranks came Amias Andros, flanked by the earl of Arundel, the earl marshal, and by the earl of Pembroke, the lord chamberlain. Andros bowed thrice to the king as the duke of Normandy, whose last possession was the Channel Islands. He laid down before his liege lord the symbols of his seigneury, his cloak and his sword. Then he knelt before the royal duke in the posture of prayer. With his hands clasped in those of his lord, Amias Andros pledged his homage: "Sire. Je demeure vostre homme à vous porter foy et hommage contre tous." Accepting this vow, the duke of Normandy confirmed his vassal's rights and possessions. He appareled with the regalia of his fief the former Amias Andros, now "the seigneur De Sammares (by which Name he was henceforth to be called), quitting his ordinary appellation of Andros." After receiving "the honor of a kisse from his majestie," the seigneur retired to his place in the royal procession and resumed his life of service to the Stuart sovereigns. Himself fully fulfilling his promise to be the king's liege man, the seigneur of

Sausmarez would be succeeded in his title and his loyalty by his son Edmund, born in London, 6 December 1637.[1]

Five years later, the filigree façade of the Caroline court was shredded by civil war. The seigneur of Sausmarez and his family were besieged in Castle Cornet, the citadel of Guernsey. Their island enemies were presbyterians, inheritors of Guernsey's Reformation past as a refuge for French Huguenots and a target of English reformers. The presbyterians now became parliamentarians to defend local autonomy from Erastian religion and imperial monarchy. Autonomy achieved, the anarchistic islanders fought among themselves. The "better sort" divided into a bailiff's faction (mostly parliamentarian, entirely presbyterian supporters of the island's civil executive) and a jurats' faction (mostly royalist, occasionally anglican adherents of the Guernsey council). The "poorer sort" of islanders sought political power for their parish representatives in the "States," the island assembly.

The royalists who had taken refuge in the castle entered this domestic political quarrel in October 1643. They lured the three dissident, parliamentarian, jurats onto what these "rebels" thought was a safe ship, then forced them from it into Castle Cornet. As the jurats came into the castle courtyard, the seigneur of Sausmarez read them the royal warrant for their execution. Half an hour before they were to be hanged, on 3 December 1643, the prisoners finished weaving ropes from old gun match and cut through the floor of their dungeon. They lowered themselves into the storeroom below, forced its door, and rappelled down the two western walls of Castle Cornet. Fortunately for them the tide was not just out but at low water springs, so the prisoners ran dry-shod around the foot of the castle walls towards the town. The sentries posted on Cornet's landward side saw the escapees and sounded the alarm. The ready-loaded castle cannon vomited grapeshot at the fugitives. Miraculously, they escaped into the town, but their danger was not over. The seigneur of Sausmarez took the occasion of every royalist raid to try to recapture the rebel jurats and he obstructed every potential royal pardon to them. Moreover, the jurats had escaped execution only to be immersed in another sort of horror.

Eight thousand people were crammed onto Guernsey, an island only 26 miles in circumference. They formed one of the densest populations in Europe. Guernsey had not been self-sufficient for centuries. Instead, its enterprising people traded fish from Newfoundland, tobacco from Virginia, and sugar from Barbados for wool from England and food from

---

1. Ferdinand Brock Tupper, *The History of Guernsey and Its Bailiwick* (Guernsey, 1876), 233. The account by Sir John Finett is in Jonathan Duncan, *The History of Guernsey . . .* (London, 1841), 89.

France. The wool was knit and woven in the only island industry. Now royalist privateers based in Jersey damaged, almost eliminated, island trade. Castle Cornet commanded the island's only harbor, Peter Port. The looms and knitteries of the town had to be abandoned under the bombardment of "more than thirty thousand cannon shot fired on the town" from the castle batteries. For the rest of the civil war, the islanders paid for local self-government with semistarvation.[2]

The defenders of Castle Cornet were sustained by the roving seigneur de Sausmarez' shipments of supplies from Jersey and St. Malo to his comrades in the castle. The besiegers built batteries to try to sink the supply boats. Soon Sausmarez' duty became the most dangerous service done by or for the garrison. There was some compensation for the daring seigneur. In times away from the castle he not only bought supplies, but also exercised a royal commission for the regulation of privateers. In both February and August of 1645 the seigneur, "who hath been in the castle ever since the rebellion," "who hath suffered for the king's cause," and "whose hart is entirely his," was touted as governor both by Colonel Carteret of Jersey and by the troops of the Castle Cornet garrison. They repeated the old Guernsey observation that, since the island was England's frontier with France, its commander must be a soldier of proven skill and enterprise. Such the seigneur of Sausmarez had shown himself to be, but in a losing cause.

As the situation of the royalists grew hopeless, "Good Mrs. Samares," the seigneur's lady, tried to escape to St. Malo. Her ship was stopped by parliamentary cruisers and she was delivered to her enemies on the island of Guernsey. Somehow, at the end of October 1645, "Mrs. Elizabeth Andrews, Samares," escaped from "the ill usage of her enemies" to Jersey. There she took shelter with her husband's Carteret kin. She wrote to the king's governor in Castle Cornet, begging him to release Sausmarez from his duty there so that they could reunite their family and recoup their exhausted finances. She was told to "have patience and not expect your husband yet." Edmund Andros' part in his parents' years of fight, flight, and deprivation can only be imagined, but the result—a reserved, ruthless, militant monarchist—would make his own record in the foreign exile which was the lot of defeated loyalists.[3]

The chief of these was Prince Charles himself, Charles I's heir. He and his court escaped from their last English base, the "refractory town" of Barnstaple, to the island of Jersey in mid-April 1646. Sausmarez im-

---

2. Tupper, *Guernsey*, 251–55, 282. See Stephen Saunders Webb, *The Governors-General: The English Army and the Definition of the Empire* (Chapel Hill, 1979), 31–32, 37. The diary of Peter Le Roy, 19 December 1651, is quoted in Ferdinand Brock Tupper, *Chronicles of Castle Cornet . . .* (Guernsey, 1851), 304.

3. Tupper, *Chronicles*, 71–72, 99–100, 101, 115–16, 173–74.

mediately asked the prince's permission to join his court. In his reply, Prince Charles praised the seigneur's "affection to the service of our royal father and your sufferings for that service in the island of Guernsey and . . . in the castle there." He promised "to remember the same to your advantage." The politics of the Restoration would be a monument to the prince's capacity to keep such promises to the men who had fought for his father and who shared his own exile, clan Andros not least among them. For the moment, however, Prince Charles ordered the seigneur to remain in Castle Cornet to encourage "the officers and soldiers to a cheerful performance of their duty," and to report any way in which the prince, by force or favor, might recover the island for its sovereign.[4]

The sovereign was martyred on 30 January 1649. One of the first regal acts of his successor was to commission the seigneur of Sausmarez "Bayly of our Island of Guernsey." This grant of civil authority was silly enough when it was made, for the new king commanded only Castle Cornet. It soon became an altogether empty honor. After Charles II was defeated at the battle of Worcester, 3 September 1651, the forces of the commonwealth were free to mop up the royalist enclaves at the extremities of the English empire: Barbados and Virginia in America; Jersey and Guernsey in Europe. On 22 October 1651, Castle Elizabeth on Jersey was evacuated. Castle Cornet surrendered, after a siege of nearly nine years, on 15 December. It had been the last place in England's European empire to hold out for the Stuarts. Both Channel Island garrisons were allowed to follow their royal master into exile on the continent or to sail for that royalist refuge so well known to tobacco-trading Channel Islanders, Virginia, the last American outpost of the imperial monarchy. The royalists paroled from the Channel Islands who chose Virginia, Philip Ludwell and Francis Lovelace among them, became Sir William Berkeley's courtiers. They never lost the habit, so appropriate to exiles, of pledging loyalty to the king but looking out for themselves. Quite another attitude to both monarchy and morality was open to the Andros family, for they were sure of a royal welcome at The Hague.[5]

There, at the court of Elizabeth Stuart queen of Bohemia, Edmund Andros' uncle Sir Robert Stone was the cupbearer. Edmund's uncle Joshua Andros had been killed in 1618, fighting for Queen Elizabeth and the protestant cause in the Palatine. Edmund's uncle John was killed in 1641 while serving the Stuarts as master of artillery to Prince Maurice, one of Queen Elizabeth's martial sons (the audience of Amias Andros'

4. Charles P. to Mr Andros, de Samares, Jersey, 4 May 1646, in *ibid.*, 179.
5. Patent dated at Perth, from Guille manuscripts, in Edith F. Carey, "Amias Andros and Sir Edmund His Son," *Transactions of the Guernsey Society of Natural Science and Local Research*, VII (1913–16): 43. For Ludwell, see Book I, and for Lovelace, Book III, Part 1, above.

pleas for help in Guernsey), who was soon lost at sea in the West Indies. (The commander of that expedition, one of two survivors from the royal flagship, was another of Queen Elizabeth's sons, Prince Rupert, afterwards Edmund Andros' commander.) Only his uncle Charles, just nine years Edmund's senior and subsequently his coadjutor for decades in the government of Guernsey, was not part of the Palatine ménage at The Hague. Wounded five times in the English civil wars, Charles Andros had joined the royal officers under the command of another of Edmund Andros' subsequent commanders, James duke of York, in the French army.

Arms are the profession of exiles. By April of 1656 "Mun" Andros himself was apprenticed to his uncle Sir Robert, a famous captain of horse. From him, Edmund Andros learned the business of commanding heavy cavalry, the most aristocratic of military formations. His father, the seigneur, captained another troop of cuirassiers. Both units were under contract to the Dutch and under the command of that stalwart soldier Prince Henry of Nassau. They were directed by him to the defense of his Danish allies against the attack of the veteran Swedes of Charles X's army. Young Andros served two bitter winter campaigns fighting in Denmark, 1655–56 and 1657–58. He witnessed, if he did not exacerbate, the devastation of the peasant population. He fought at the siege of Copenhagen. He shared in the final victory over the Swedes at Funen. All these actions only reiterated the lessons Andros had learned in Guernsey's civil war. A prince's first duty is to protect his people. Short-sighted and selfish, they will evade military service themselves and also resist his every requisition for their defense. Therefore, the populace must be guarded by the prince's army and can only be governed by its well-born, battle-hardened, officers. Edmund Andros acquired not only these soldierly ideals in his years of exile but the languages in which to express them. To his father's French and his mother's English, Andros added his uncle's Dutch, and he even learned enough of the language of his Swedish opponents to qualify as an English envoy to their court in later life.

Such were young Andros' family's fidelity, his own martial merits, and his courtly bearing and accomplishments that, on his return from Denmark, Queen Elizabeth named him a gentleman of her household. There he became an intimate servant of the Stuarts at The Hague. He waited not only on Elizabeth of Bohemia, the "queen of hearts," but also on her nephews King Charles II of England and the young prince of Orange, who, upon becoming king of England himself thirty years afterwards, made a point of assuring Sir Edmund Andros that he remembered him well from their shared youth at The Hague. More immediately, Edmund Andros' commander was Queen Elizabeth's champion, the veteran subordinate of Maurice of Nassau and Gustavus Adolphus in the Thirty

Years' War and the last defender of James II of England, William earl of Craven. From 1658 on, that brave little man was Edmund Andros' unfailing friend and patron. The support of an earl as wealthy as he was courageous was to prove no **mean sustenance** to Andros' career in the service of the Stuarts.[6]

English Guardsman and Barbadian Major

1661–1668

In May 1660, Edmund Andros helped escort his mistress and her nephew William to their parting meal with King Charles and his brother the duke aboard the newly named *Sovereign*. Then the royal brothers sailed for England and to the restoration of their family to its imperial throne. Next, Andros saw off his parents as they sailed to recover their seigneury in Guernsey. Edmund Andros, however, remained for a year at The Hague, until Queen Elizabeth moved to London. There her household took up residence in the earl of Craven's mansion, in the midst of its famous gardens at the end of the elm-lined Drury Lane, Edmund Andros' London home for decades to come. There the queen of Bohemia died on 13 February 1662. No sooner were her obsequies concluded than, on 1 May 1662, her late gentleman Edmund Andros was commissioned as an ensign in the king's First (the Grenadier) Guards. "The Regt. of Guards," as it then was, were the king's household troops, quartered in "the imperial metropolis of his empire." They were the restored monarchy's first resource "in defence of the Crown and in support of law and order," at home as well as in the extension of royal rule overseas. The senior formation in the imperial army, the Guards constituted a "regimental connection" of obvious and abiding importance to its officers' paramilitary careers in the politics and administration of the English empire. The foremost defenders of king and country, the officers of the Guards were the primary cadre of imperial administrators.[7]

6. On the Palatine court, see Keith Feiling, *A History of the Tory Party, 1640–1714* (London, 1924), 61.
7. Andros' commission is dated 4 June 1661, but its place in S.P. 44/3, 6, places it in 1662. Sir F. W. Hamilton, *The Origin and History of the First or Grenadier Guards . . .* (London, 1874), I, x, 55; Webb, *Governors-General*, 4, 468, 486.

In the crisis of the Derwentdale plot of 1663, the battalion of the Guards in which Andros served policed the capital. The second battalion, newly returned from garrison duty in the Dunkirk and the Channel Islands, occupied the former Cromwellian strongholds in England for the crown. In October 1663, Ensign Andros' political police activity won expert approval from such a notable political prisoner as Colonel Thomas Hutchinson, when he arranged his interrogation at Whitehall and then conducted him back to the Tower with the assistance of a squad of Guardsmen. After the king's declaration of war on the Dutch, 22 February 1665, public revulsion at war losses and the activities of Dutch agents encouraged English republicans and religious fanatics to assault the monarchy with the aid, as they hoped, of an invasion force from the protestant republic. Most exposed to this triple danger was the Isle of Wight. There Thomas lord Culpeper (afterwards Virginia's viceroy and Sir Edmund Andros' predecessor in that post) was the king's governor. In September 1665, Ensign Edmund Andros was dispatched with a hundred Guardsmen to help Culpeper defend the island against the Dutch and the dissenters, both political and religious. The dissidents rioted, the militia mutinied, and Andros' Guards jailed their leaders "in a noisome dungeon in Carisbrooke castle, to their great grief and discouragement." [8]

After their tour of duty in the Isle of Wight, Andros' company of the Guards escorted the king to the meeting of the parliament at Oxford. It helped to garrison Andros' own island, Guernsey. It fought fires and republicans in London. Meanwhile, the war worsened in ways that first propelled Edmund Andros towards privateering and then launched his colonial career. In January 1666, both the French and the Danes joined the Dutch in war with England. Before the end of February, Ensign Edmund Andros had fitted out a privateer in Guernsey. Its attacks on Dutch tobacco ships and French coasters violated the island's traditional neutrality but, as "Mun's" friend, partner, and fellow Guards officer, the king's commander in Guernsey, Colonel Jonathan Atkins, wrote to Andros' father, "I am for ruining the enemy, let us fare as we can." [9]

In a like spirit, the French and the Dutch made the maritime bases of England's empire—its shipping and its colonies—their primary targets. The West Indies were the focus of seventeenth-century European imperialism. There the war began with a surprise assault by the French on the English section of St. Christopher, the chief of the Leeward Islands. Then Antigua and Montserrat were captured by the French. The very center of

8. Richard Worsley, *The History of the Isle of Wight* (London, 1971), 136–37. F. H. Blackburne Daniell, *Calendar of State Papers, Domestic Series, of the Reign of Charles II* (London, 1860–1938; Nendeln, Lichtenstein, 1968) *1665–1666* (hereafter cited as *C.S.P.D. 1665–1666*), 350. Webb, *Governors-General*, 105.
9. 23 February 1666, in Tupper, *Guernsey*, 367.

the English sugar trade, Barbados, was threatened. The loss of trade, taxes, and territory—"the sweet negotiation of sugar"—could not be borne if the English empire was to remain in the war.

King Charles therefore ordered the lord high admiral, James duke of York, to send out Captain John Berry and a squadron of five men-of-war to the Caribbee Isles, to be followed by Sir John Harman with eight more warships. "By soe considerable a force our good subjects in these parts may be defended," and the king also hoped to see "our Enemys driven out of those Our Territories which they have usurped." To provide infantry for this imperial expedition, on 11 February 1667 the king commissioned officers to raise "the Barbados Regiment of Foot." The colonel was Sir Tobias Bridge. Formerly a Cromwellian major general and a member of the protectorate's "committee for managing his Highnesses affairs in Jamaica & the West Indies," since the Restoration Bridge had become the hero of Tangier's defense against the Moors and the recipient from Charles II of one of the first English military medals. The lieutenant colonel of the Barbados Regiment was William Stapleton. This admirable Anglo-Irish soldier of fortune, who had long served in France, was to make the recovery and reconstruction, the government and defense of the Leeward Islands his life-work. The major of this, the first American regiment of the royal army, was Edmund Andros.[10]

While his family and friends feared for his life amid the notorious disease and ferocious fighting of the Caribbean, all agreed, as Colonel Atkins put it, that "since he must go I am glad he goes in so honorable a place as Major." And indeed, to leap from ensign to major was a promotion almost unprecedented. Majors were the administrative heads, "the eyes, hands, and feet" of every regiment, "the greatest Affairs of the Regiment being carried forth by the Major." Andros' elevation in duty, from quelling Quakers on the Isle of Wight to fighting the French (and Indians) in the West Indies, was itself as astonishing as his rise in rank. Both promotions were portentous, for it was as the major of three Barbados regiments, from 1667 to 1678, that Edmund Andros achieved Anglo-American rank and reputation, and his new duties taught him the limits and directions of Atlantic empire.[11]

Only a month after being commissioned, Major Andros sailed "suddenly" from Portsmouth with the six overstrength companies of the Barbados Regiment, some eight hundred English and Irish soldiers. With them sailed the new governor-general of the Caribbee Isles, William lord Willoughby of Parham. The ships also carried great quantities of royal

10. S.P. 44/24, 35. C.O. 1/21, 35. Egerton Ms. 2395, 123, British Library.
11. Major Richard Elton, The Compleat body of the Art Military . . . (London, 1650, 1659), 179–80. Atkins to A. Andros, Castle Cornet, 23 February 1666, printed in Tupper, Guernsey, 367.

munitions for the use of the island militias. After a voyage of six weeks, on 23 April 1667, the fleet anchored off what was afterwards known as "Bridgetown," Barbados. The islanders were just ten days away from being "all ´. . . together by the eares"—that is, from renewing their own civil war of royalists against republicans, of proprietary and anti-proprietary partisans, of authoritarians and "Magna Carta men." Divided, obviously open to invasion, Barbados clearly could no longer succor her Leeward Island dependencies.[12]

Do the Barbadians credit. Between April 1666 and March 1667, they had invested the equivalent of £40,000 in the defense of the Leeward Islands, "for which the Nation is greatly oblidged" to them. Their last resources were the men and provisions with which the Barbadians had loaded six merchant auxiliaries. They sailed down to the defense of Nevis early in March 1666/7, under the command of Captain John Berry in the king's ship *Coronation,* convoyed by the three other royal warships which came out to Barbados with the *Coronation* (and two munition ships). On 10 May, Berry proved himself "an Expert Seaman and a Dareing bold Commander." The ten ships under his command defeated the twenty men-of-war and ten auxiliaries of the Franco-Dutch invasion fleet as it approached Nevis. Then Berry's ships chased the would-be invaders back to their base in St. Kitts. Captain Berry's victory in Nevis Roads underlay his promotion to admiral's rank when he led out the expedition of 1676 to Virginia. More immediately, it not only saved Nevis from the French and the Dutch, it also emboldened the English to put two-thirds of the effective men of the newly arrived Barbados Regiment—all who could be spared from policing Barbados itself—on board the king's ship *Jersey* (commanded, of course, by a Carteret) and on the *East India Merchant* to spearhead the recapture of St. Kitts.

Thirty-two hundred men were mustered at Nevis on 2 June 1667 for the invasion. Two botched landings had thoroughly alerted the French defenders, led by a "veteran regiment from Picardy." The companies of the Barbados Regiment finally got ashore at the delta of the Pelham (or "Pelan") River, at 8:00 a.m. on 8 June. "And now began the tragedy."[13]

Only three routes led off the beach and up the steep bluff to the island interior. Two of these routes were narrow ravines that angled up the bluff,

12. Vincent T. Harlow, *A History of Barbados 1625–1685* (London, 1926; New York, 1969), 181. William lord Willoughby to the king, 7 May 1667, C.O. 1/21, 80. William lord Willoughby's account for 23 April 1667–13 July 1668, C.O. 1/22, 39.

13. *Calendar of State Papers, Colonial Series* (London, 1860–) *1661–1668* (hereafter cited as *C.S.P.C. 1661–1668*), no. 1477, 1484, 1488, 1773, and see 1524, 1880. The narrative of John Scott, in "Tracts on the E. and W. Indies," Sloane Ms. 5662, 56v British Library and in C.O. 1/21, 139. Newsletters in S.P. 29/231. Some accounts say that (all) six companies of the regiment were dispatched on the St. Kitts expedition, but it is clear that additional companies were raised locally for the regiment in Barbados and perhaps in Nevis.

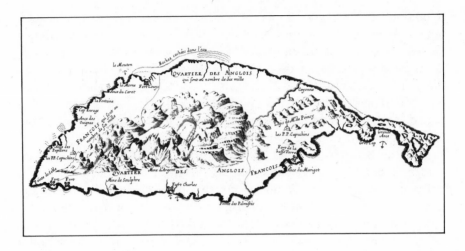

Carte de Lisle de Sainct Christophle Scituée a 17 Degrez 30 Minutes de Lat. Septentrionale. A Paris chez Pierre Mariette, rue S. Iacques a l'Esperance. Auec Priuilege du Roy.

one to the right and the other from the center of the regiment's beachhead. The dry bed of the Pelham River formed the left flank of the Barbados position and was the third access to the island plateau. After a national quarrel, Lieutenant Colonel Stapleton quickly led his company of Irish recruits up the central ravine but "the ground broke and slid under them." Before Stapleton's men could struggle to the top of the bluff, the French commander and six horsemen of his escort blocked the head of the ravine. As French reinforcements came up, Stapleton's soldiers were fired on from three sides. He himself was wounded in hand-to-hand combat as he fought to save his company color from capture. Wrapped in the flag he fought for, Stapleton was carried down the ravine by his retreating troops. They took shelter under the bluff.[14]

Then it was the turn of an English company. They tried the river bed. It was obstructed by boulders and defended by 120 men of the Regiment of Picardy. Beaten back, the English were followed onto the beach by the French. A formal exchange of volleys ended when the French commander saw that the English were in a helpless position. To save lives, he withdrew his men to defensive positions atop the bluff. The last hope of the Barbados Regiment was a push up the ravine to their right, but it was "d'un tres difficile acces," it was defended by four French companies

14. "Major Scott's Relation," in W. Noel Sainsbury et al., eds., *C.S.P.C. 1661–1668*, no. 1574. As a fugitive from New York, Scott presumably gave Andros his first view of that colony. Henry Willoughby to William lord Willoughby, 15 June 1667, *ibid.*, no. 1498.

from Navarre, and, "by means of Capt. Berry breaking his cable and falling leward," the planned naval bombardment of the French position failed. Another ship was brought on station but by then "our men were before at club end of their muskets for that pass: where many fell." After two and a half hours of fighting in this last pass, the Barbados Regiment was beaten back to the beach.[15]

Reinforced by the militias of three islands, the French soldiers began to roll boulders off the top of the bluff onto the survivors of the Barbados Regiment who were lying at its base. All of the regiment's officers had been wounded. No help arrived from the fleet offshore. Its bombardment of the French proved ineffectual, "The bravery of the boats" coming into beach nonetheless got off many men of the second wave and a few of the advance guard, "the forlorne," of the Barbados Regiment before the boats were driven off by French musketry. Isolated, after seven hours of fighting, with 150 of their number dead, the two hundred survivors of the Barbados Regiment still on the beach finally surrendered. The incomplete list of the captured English and Irish officers does not tell us whether Major Andros was among "ces braves Officers Anglois ont cette glorie dans leur malheur, qu'ils se font batus en gens d'honneur & de couer."[16]

To the horror of the English recruits, all of the Irish and those of the regiment's English officers who were veterans of European campaigns immediately began to fraternize with the French regulars. All joined in honoring the Barbados Regiment's dead. Shortly, forty surviving prisoners were exchanged for Frenchmen recently captured by Captain Berry at Antigua, but the rest were held until peace was proclaimed, in November. They then returned, after "induring great hardship for a Season," stripped and starving, to the Barbados Regiment.[17]

It was in little better case, "our Soldrs generally very beare and naked in reference to Cloathes, and the officers exceeding necessitous," their colonel reported. In letters to the king and to the captain general, the officers of the Barbados Regiment filled in the details of the hard service which had reduced them to this decaying condition. After the assault on St. Christopher with its crippling casualties, the two whole companies had been hurried down from Barbados to Nevis on board the ships of Sir John Harman's fleet. They had made Barbados on the very morning of the St. Christopher fiasco, just too late to make that operation a success.

---

15. Henry Willoughby to William lord Willoughby, 15 June 1667, C.O. 1/21, 102.

16. R. P. du Tertre, *Histoire Générale des Antillés Habité par les Francais* (Paris, 1667–71), IV, 261, 266, 273. Partial lists of officer casualties appear in C.O. 1/21, 132, 140. Subsequently, Scott reported 506 English killed, 218 wounded, 140 captured. French casualties were about 470 (*ibid.*, 155).

17. The officers to the king, 27 May 1668, C.O. 1/22, 190.

Despite the fleet's arrival in Nevis with the regular companies on board, however, the council of war concluded that the French on St. Kitts, blooded, inspired, and newly dug in, could not be dislodged. The fleet sailed away in a cruise of conquest that carried it all the way to Surinam, but the Barbados Regiment was left to hold Nevis, the key to the English Leewards.[18]

"Wee cannot but acknowledge the great kindness wee received from the Governor and Inhabitants of Nevis," the regimental officers wrote to the captain general (by the hand of Major Andros). The islanders were impoverished by war and hurricane, but they did everything possible to support the regiment that protected them from the French. Still, they were "noe wayes able to afford any other than a very slender accomoda-con." Even that required the governor of Nevis to trade with the Dutch, despite the acts of trade (as Major Andros would have to do to supply his forces in New York), and to requisition both the provisions William Dyre shipped in from America and the ketch that carried them (by way of recompense, the king would commission Dyre customs collector under Andros in New York). The sad result was that, although the soldiers praised the planters' efforts and the planters formally thanked the regiment both for its defense of the island and for its disciplined restraint in dealing with the inhabitants, the soldiers were poorly fed and housed, and neither clothed nor paid.[19]

When peace lifted the menace of French invasion from Nevis and restored its prisoners to the Barbados Regiment, the reunited corps (save for thirty-seven men too weak to travel) took ship to "reduce" the Caribs of St. Lucia and St. Vincent. As Lord Willoughby wrote of the regiment's service, "I had means by their Countenance to establish so firme a Peace with the Indians (the common disturbers of new Settlers), that the People, being freed from their usuall danger, will (I doubt not) flourish & advance his Matys Dominions." Not only were Major Andros and his comrades taught the positive connection between Indian pacification and provincial development, they also observed the fundamental military importance of native fighters to the outcomes of European rivalries. It was "the Indians, to whose assistance they [the French] are indebted for the greatest Matters they performed against us." Major Andros would apply this West Indian lesson to winning the American continent from the French through the agency of the Iroquois.[20]

The contract of Anglo-Indian cooperation, whether to protect English settlement or to offend French empire, was the treaty, for, as Andros

18. *Ibid.*, 189.
19. *Ibid.*, 190. C.O. 1/23, 108. C.O. 389/5, 45.
20. C.O. 1/21, 192, 193v.

learned in the Leeward Islands, warlike natives could be influenced but not compelled by European arms (a lesson he preached in vain to obdurate and racist American colonists). "Wee finding an impossibility of reducing them by force," the Barbados officers reported, their regiment nonetheless supplied the necessary incentive for the Carib captains to sign an agreement with the king's governor, Lord Willoughby. It embodied the standard terms: the Indians acknowledged themselves to be the subjects of the king of England; they made his enemies and his friends theirs also; they accepted free trade and admitted free communication with the English colonists; they promised to return all the English settlers, servants, and slaves whom they had captured, and to extradite any future fugitives from the English islands.

With these fundamental lessons in the military and diplomatic importance of the Indians in mind, Major Andros and the other officers of the Barbados Regiment led their companies on a tour of the Leeward Island colonies "to confirme the secure and orderly settlement of his Matys subjects." That is, the regiment authenticated pledges of protection made by the king's viceroy and it enforced obedience to him in a hitherto loosely associated set of quite autonomous settlements (Major Andros would make just such a tour in the duke of York's American territories as soon as his military command of them was assured). Then the regiment returned to their quarters in the homes of the Barbadians, "whoe we find altogether unwilling to receive us." Landing on Barbados late in April 1668, the military commander of the colony, Colonel Bridge, "found very great difficulty to persuade the Country to receive the Soldiers on any Terms." "At length the Assembly ordered quarters for the Soldiers," but they refused "to take the least notice of any of the officers." [21]

The "Barbarians" could hardly be blamed for not wanting to quarter the royal regiment in their houses and feed them their provisions. The island capital had been largely destroyed by fire and by the ensuing explosion of the powder magazine. The cost of the war in direct taxes and in the loss of manpower and food had reduced the islanders to near-famine. Only the timely arrival of supplies from New England and New York saved the sugar-growing colonists from disaster. The royal navy's enforcement of the hated and hurtful English trade monopoly and the Royal African Company's monopoly of the slave trade only made it more difficult for the islanders to support the king's regiment, even if they had approved of its backing for Lord Willoughby's authority.

Of course the governor-general praised the Barbados Regiment as incomparably superior to the militia in combating the French, the Dutch,

21. C.O. 1/22, 129, 96, 192, 190; Sr Tobias Bridge to the captain general the duke of Albemarle, April 1668, *ibid.*, no. 78.

the Indians. Even in its depleted state, undermanned, unclothed, unpaid, the viceroy wrote that the Barbados Regiment "doth awe both French and Indians more . . . than all the other forces in our Islands." And the regiment enhanced the discipline of the militias. "Their example of good Conduct" will "make the Planter become formidable to the Enemy." As important as their cadre function in colonial defense was the regiment's political function in repressing Barbados' own dissidents. To disappoint "theire hopes of being a Republique," it was essential that the king's government command "a certain strength of veterane souldiers to keep up his [majesty's] Interest." The viceroy asked the king to make the regiment the island's permanent garrison.[22]

In sixteen months of fighting and police work in the Lesser Antilles, Major Andros and his colleagues had become a regimental connection of almost legionary influence in the province they defended and garrisoned. Like the commanders of the regiment of Carignan-Salières in Quebec and along the Richelieu River, the officers of the Barbados Regiment became formative figures in the settlements of a debated frontier. Colonel Bridge went on to conquer Tobago and to preside in the council of Barbados. Captain Lieutenant John Painter was Bridge's associate in island politics. Lieutenant Colonel Stapleton was successively governor of several of the Leeward Islands before he became the first, and best, governor-general of the Leeward Islands federation. Captains Cotter and Morley became the deputy governors of Montserrat and of Antigua, respectively, and Lieutenant St. John was secretary of the council in the latter island. Ensign Abednego Matthews became deputy governor of St. Kitts and founded a double dynasty in the officer corps of the English army and the governments of the Leeward Islands.

It was Major Andros, however, who was able to give the greatest scope to the lessons he had learned in the West Indies. There he had received an intensive education in imperial governance. He had heard the complaints of the Barbadian planters against the acts of trade. He had observed the islanders' reliance on an Atlantic range of resources: American provisions; Irish and Scots servants; Dutch capital, markets, and technical advice; English arms and authority. He had championed royal authority in the factional politics of island cavaliers and roundheads, monarchists and republicans. He had witnessed that assertion of local autonomy which led the Barbados Assembly—six years ahead of its Virginia counterpart—to seek incorporation from the crown and to lobby for "a planter governor" (with the help of Ferdinando Gorges, of all people). On the other hand, Major Andros had enjoyed mutually supportive relations with the people of Nevis and seen their governor prefer military

22. *Ibid.*, 192, 193v. C.O. 1/21, 336 v.

security to both parliamentary prescriptions and private property. He had suffered from the rivalries of the three British peoples and yet led them against the French, the Dutch, and the Caribs. He had learned the vital importance of the Indians to American settlement and imperial war, and observed that diplomacy was more efficacious than force in allying them to English empire. He had listened to Jamaicans, New Yorkers, New Englanders, and Surinamese describe the peculiarities of their provinces. He had fought by sea and land, with mixed forces, regular and militia, military and naval. At the orders of the king, the governor-general, and his colonels, Major Andros had applied armed force both to protect an imperial province and to assert there the authority of the crown and its officers.[23]

The officer corps of the Barbados Regiment had become a body of imperial executives, but their companies were as unaffordable to the king as they were, in peacetime, unwelcome to the colonists. The soldiers could be quartered on the hostile inhabitants, but the Barbados Regiment had received only one month's pay from the king in the past year, even though they were constituted collectors of the royal revenue in Barbados. In July 1668, therefore, the fleet that carried home the island assembly's protests against English exploitation and coercion also conveyed the complaining officer-delegates of that instrument of English authority, the Barbados Regiment. Major Edmund Andros for the English, and Captain James Cotter for the Irish, were to represent their comrades' sorry state to the king, the captain general, the secretaries of state, and the privy council.

Solicitor, Surveyor, and Dragoon

1668–1674

Major Andros' American accomplishments and imperial attitudes became apparent to the royal authorities in the nearly three years of negotiations he conducted on behalf of "his Superiors & Regiment." From his arrival in England in August 1668 until the privy seal was passed for the payment of the Barbados Regiment on 31 May 1671, Andros repeatedly testified to his unit's service, usefulness, and difficulties in Barbados and its dependencies. He procured and shipped out the regiment's

23. Harlow, *Barbados*, 196 n. 1. Willoughby's Account, C.O. 1/23, 40.

new uniforms (perhaps the first tropical kit issued to a royal English regiment). He secured orders for fellow officers on leave. He became a familiar figure to members of the privy council's committees for trade and for plantations, to the treasury commissioners, and to the army secretariat. The major was marked at court as something of a diplomat as well. He was assigned to welcome and escort the visiting prince of Tuscany, Cosimo de' Medici, in February 1669. It was a frustrating assignment, for what with shifting winds and the convoy's "a turning and stopping tides," no sooner did Major Andros prepare the prince's lodgings and arrange salutes at Plymouth than Medici was reported bound for Cornwall.[24]

Still, Andros emerged from all these episodes with credit, so much so that on 24 September, Lieutenant General Henry Willoughby—under whose command Andros had served in the Leeward Islands—nominated the major as governor of all the Leeward Island colonies. Writing to Thomas Povey for secretary lord Arlington's attention, Willoughby observed that, the English portion of St. Christopher having been restored by the French, the crown now had a base from which to provide for the "care and protection" of English settlers in the Lesser Antilles in a much-enhanced fashion. The cabinet had agreed that "there must be a Governor such as Ld. Willoughby shall recommend to his Maty," and Henry Willoughby wrote, "I can name a person . . . very agreeable to the King & Councell & it is Major Andrews Maior to Sr Tobias Bridges Regimt."[25]

Major Andros did not take up this Caribbean government. Instead Sir Charles Wheeler disgraced himself as the first, if not quite the worst, governor-general of the Leeward Islands. He was succeeded by Lieutenant Colonel Stapleton, who was on the spot as deputy governor of Montserrat. In the meantime, however, Major Andros enhanced his agreeableness to King Charles and his council by a venture into marine salvage. This episode was profitable to Andros and his sovereign alike. It was also remarkably useful training for the masterwork of Andros' first American command, construction of the mole at New York. Back in August 1665, "being extraordinarily pressed for the raising a present sume of money" to meet the cost of wartime secret service against the Dutch, King Charles had shipped Cornish tin to Ostend. Unfortunately, one of the tin ships had sunk, fully loaded, in Ostend harbor. In August 1669, Major Andros was commissioned to supervise the salvage of the royal metal.

24. Petition of 23 July 1669, Blathwayt Papers, B.A. no. 10, Huntington Library. S.P. 29/255, no. 162, 14 February 1669. Andros to Williamson, 19 March 1669, S.P. 29/257, no. 129, C.S.P.D. 1668–1669, 239. S.P. 104/176, 139.
25. Minute of the foreign committee, 25 July 1669, S.P. 104/176, 184. H. Willoughby to Mr. Povey, 24 September 1670, Egerton Ms. 2395, fol. 470.

Naturally, the Dutch made trouble: no one likes to finance enemy espionage. Diplomatic interventions in Amsterdam were required by Andros' old acquaintances Sir George Downing and Sir William Temple. Then the Spanish governor, mayor, and port officials of Ostend had to be "considered" and "gratified" in order to procure the necessary permits and political assistance. Major Andros even got special permission to give the governor's wife a (rather unromantic) present of two tin ingots. Once diving actually began, Andros had to keep the divers to their dangerous work in the shifting sands, sue failed diving contractors for malfeasance, and hire new ones. As the tin was brought up, Andros warehoused the king's share, offered it for bids in London, Amsterdam, Antwerp, and Bruges, and shipped the amounts contracted for, returning remittances to the treasury. Finally, on 26 March 1670, Major Andros received the royal thanks and a grant for £250. He took a long holiday in Holland.[26]

By now, Edmund Andros was the London agent for a variety of family members and military colleagues in far-flung outposts of the empire. He used his official connections with the treasury to obtain wool licenses for Guernsey knitters, to win customs concessions for Barbadian sugar shippers, to wangle favorable reviews for his lucrative regimental clothing contracts, and to get his own arrears of pay as major actually issued (some less-well-connected officers of the Barbados Regiment had not yet been paid off in 1682). The key to the major's success was the cabinet order of 10 September 1670 that the treasury lords accept Major Andros' musters and arrange a schedule of payments. In 1671 and 1672, this powerfully introduced, fiscally astute, and active-service army officer was consulted by the treasury concerning issues of military finance ranging from the application of the Barbados revenues down to the "pinchgut money" which the governor of Dover had withheld from his garrison's food allowance.[27]

During 1671, that governor and other officers commanding the port towns from Plymouth eastward had reported to the war office the arrival of job lots of English soldiers from Barbados. These men had taken up the royal promise of paid passage home that had been made to them by no fewer than three governors-general when they disbanded the Barbados Regiment early in June 1671. All of the soldiers' applications, and those of three captains as well, were referred to Major Andros. By mid-September 1671, more than two hundred men had come home, enough for Andros to reconstitute four companies of the regiment. Part of the

26. Additional Manuscripts 28076, fol. 3, British Library. S.P. 44/17, 122–24. William A. Shaw, ed., *Calendar of Treasury Books, 1669–1672* (London, 1908), vol. III, 287, 302.
27. The cabinet order is in S.P. 104/176, 253–53v. See also Shaw, ed., *Treasury Books*, 1032.

build-up for the impending Dutch war, the revival of the Barbados Regiment was also said by the king to be a "particular mark of our acceptance of the good service performed by the said regiment" in the Caribbean. London correspondents quickly told their Guernsey gossips of Edmund Andros' good fortune. As "Major & Captain of the Barbados Regiment newly establisht here upon the Kings pay as his other Regiments are," Andros "hath 13s a day allowed to him." More than that, it was rumored that Major Andros had been tipped for "an extraordinary employment."[28]

In November, that extraordinary step occurred. Major Andros was ordered to mount his four companies for service under Prince Rupert, the great royalist cavalry captain, the soldierly son of Elizabeth of Bohemia. During the winter, eight additional troops were raised in Northamptonshire and Warwickshire to complete an entire mounted regiment. Major Andros and the other officers of the old Barbados companies acquired the increased pay and prestige of cavalry commanders on the cheap. They had only to purchase horses, not also to raise recruits at the rate of forty per captain, twenty per lieutenant, ten per cornet, and five per sergeant, "with all imaginable dilligence," in order to receive their commissions or appointments.[29]

While the regiment was being raised, its major left his command to undertake some delicate diplomacy for James duke of York. Widowed in March 1671, James soon dispatched envoys to examine every eligible princess in Europe. To Sweden, in October and December 1671, the duke sent Major Andros, himself just at the conclusion of a successful courtship, an officer with Swedish experience, and a firm protestant as well as an accomplished courtier. Guernseymen, following Andros' career with their habitual avidity, soon read that "at Court" it was widely reported that Major Andros "hath speded well & performed his business very well, what it is is not clearly knowne, only some conjecture that it is about the Marriadge of His Royal Highness the Duke of Yorke, with the Princess of Holstein, a neare relation of the King of Sweden's." Unfortunately for James' political reputation—given his countrymen's growing fear of France and their unabated hatred of Catholicism—the duke ultimately married the French-sponsored, papally blessed (and altogether beautiful) Mary of Modena. The royal duke had nonetheless formed a high opinion of his envoy to Sweden, Major Andros. Henceforth, he considered him one of his household and preferred Andros to posts of ever-increasing importance.[30]

A new war gave Major Andros additional executive experience. On 12

28. S.P. 44/35A, 28–29. James Havilland to Christopher lord Hatton, 11 September 1671, Add. Ms. 29553, 307.

29. S.P. 44/35A, 37b.

30. Havilland to Hatton, [1 December 1671,] Add. Ms. 29553, 331v.

March 1672, Sir Robert Holmes, "bashaw" of the Isle of Wight (in succession to Lord Culpeper) and "the cursed beginner of the two Dutch wars," opened hostilities, as he had in 1664, this time with an attack upon the Dutch convoy inbound from Smyrna. On 17 March, King Charles declared war on the Dutch republic. On 30 March, the officers of the Barbados Regiment of Dragoons received their commissions. It continued to be noteworthy in military and Guernsey circles "that Prince Rupert is raising a regiment" and that "Andrews," that is "Samueres his sonne," would be its major. The new unit was the subject of both professional and political interest because dragoons—mounted infantry—were a new type of military formation, primarily used as military police and subject to a deserved notoriety because of the "dragonades" of Louis XIV's troops against French Protestants. Novel sorts of soldiers, the Barbados Dragoons were also technologically innovative, as befitted a command of their inventive colonel, whose hands "are always scratched and calloused by the continual use of the file, chisel, and adze." Prince Rupert's dragoons were the first unit in the English army to be equipped with "the great knife," the bayonet.[31]

Once the eight new troops were formed up and the whole regiment was uniformed in blue, their major led them to Yarmouth in April 1672. There Major Andros took command of the garrison and supervised the fortification of the town while his dragoons policed both the town and the camp of the eight thousand men assembling for the invasion of the Netherlands. The major shouldered substantial administrative burdens, for his colonel, Prince Rupert, retained his titular command of Windsor Castle and was soon engrossed in his work as "general at sea," especially since, as of 2 May 1672, he took the duke of York's place as both naval and military chief of the cabinet council (the duke having gone to sea in command of the combined English and French battle fleets). The dragoons' lieutenant colonel, Edmund Andros' old company commander in the Guards, Sir John Talbot, remained on duty in the capital and in James Stuart's household. Such was Major Andros' independence of command at Yarmouth that he not only developed it as a garrison town but also began to recruit the subalterns who would form his American staff. In the dragoons these included his youngest brother, George, future commander of Maine, and Anthony Brockholes, a gentleman formerly of the duke of York's own troop of the Horse Guards, who would be Major Andros' first lieutenant and deputy governor in New York and afterwards

31. Sir Charles Littleton, formerly deputy governor of Jamaica, presently colonel of the duke of York's Admiralty Regiment and governor of Sheerness, to Hatton, March 1672, Add. Ms. 29577, 109b–10. S.P. 104/177, 9v–10. W. E. Middleton Knowles, ed., *Lorenzo Magalotti at the Court of Charles II His Relazione d'Inghilterra of 1668* (Waterloo, 1980), 58.

commander of a garrison company in the Dominion of New England under Governor-General Sir Edmund Andros.[32]

To Edmund Andros the particular importance of his promotion to major of dragoons was that he now had the rank and resources to ask for the hand of Marie Craven, the niece of the earl. Since he had moved in as one of the queen of Bohemia's household in 1662, Andros had made the earl of Craven's home his London address. It requires little imagination to appreciate the attraction that the wide-eyed, straight-mouthed, aquiline-nosed, curly-headed soldier with the courtly manners and aristocratic address had for a well-born but modestly dowered thirty-seven-year-old spinster. Marie Craven was two years older than that family familiar, "Mun" Andros. Both of them were long past the usual age of marriage (twenty-three for women, twenty-seven for men). Now they took their chance. In February 1672, while the Blue Dragoons were still in winter quarters, the major and Marie were married.

The old earl gave them his blessing and 48,000 worthless acres in Carolina. These were organized in four unsurveyed wilderness "baronies." They underlay a laughable title of Carolina nobility, complete with an odd coat of arms. Neither the Androses nor their heirs (for they had no children) ever got the slightest benefit from the easy generosity of Craven the Carolina proprietor. Still, the earl was also a privy councilor, soon to be named to its powerful plantations committee, and he was colonel of the Coldstream Guards. A man of overformal manner, made somewhat ludicrous by his small stature, Craven was nevertheless a powerful patron who cared for few people. Among them was Edmund Andros. Major Andros' career had acquired its ultimate prop. And he had found someone to love. The only tender emotion ever recorded of this hard man was when Lady Andros, exhausted by an Atlantic crossing and the Boston winter, caught pneumonia and died on 24 January 1687. Sir Edmund, governor-general of the Dominion of New England, was prostrated by his "great sorrow for the losse of his good lady." When, twenty-five years afterwards, his will was executed, it provided that the night obsequies he had held for Marie Craven should be repeated for himself.[33]

The new Dutch war offered the newly married Major Andros no chance to add to his reputation. Although he led his dragoons to one rumored invasion site after another, the Dutch did not land. On the other hand, the English army of invasion, of which his regiment of 960 men was a part, often went to sea but never got ashore in the Netherlands.

32. S.P. 44/35A, 57. On Rupert's presidency, see S.P. 104/177, 29 ff., where cabinet dictation of the *Gazette* also appears.
33. R. N. Toppan and A. T. S. Goodrick, eds., *Edward Randolph Including His Letters and Official Papers 1676–1703* (Boston, 1898), IV, 197.

Despite the desperate battles of Sole Bay, the Schoneveld, and of Kijk-dum, all of them arguably English victories (in the last of them Andros' colonel, Prince Rupert, commanded in place of James duke of York), the Dutch retained a fleet-in-being to prevent the English army from landing. Yet, in each summer of the war, the English army of invasion reassembled. Every summer, fears of its domestic political potential grew in proportion to the army's size at home and its unemployment abroad.

In June 1673, a summer in which Major Andros appeared actively in the records of English military command, the politics of the empire took on the militantly partisan tones it was to retain for the next thirty years. The members of the council for foreign plantations, for example, led by their president, the earl of Shaftesbury, "all went after dinner to see the formal and formidable Camp on Black-heath." Some of them thought it really had been "raised to invade Holland" but others "suspected for another designe &c." To them, in the "dark hovering of that Army, so long a *Black-Heath* might not improbably [be] seen the gatherings of a Storm to fall upon London." [34]

In October the parliament was convened, against the better judgment of the king. In November they refused to vote supplies for the army. Instead members attacked the idea of a standing army, deplored its being quartered on the civilian population, denounced martial law, and decried army amorality. Who of the king's ministers, the speaker of the commons demanded, had advised "governing by an army"? Secretary Arlington's reply was not reassuring: he was, he said, "not so vain as to think this great nation can be awed by 20,000 men." The commons critics of the military replied that sixteen hundred men in London would suffice. As indeed they had. Since he was an avowed militarist, absolutist, and Catholic, the duke's marriage to a Catholic client of France was also attacked. So was the new lord treasurer, the earl of Danby. As a result the king prorogued parliament, dismissed Shaftesbury, and sent his council for foreign plantations after him. In their places, the prerogative politics and personalities who shaped 1676 were installed. When parliament reassembled in January 1675 it attacked with increasing virulence the army "as a number of men unlawfully assembled," denounced its garrisons in Scotland and Ireland, decried its emplacement in the royally rebuilt and reoccupied citadels of England, and protested the presence of the king's household troops in London as "guards, or standing armies, . . . only in use where princes govern more by fear, than by love; as in *France*, where

34. Esmond S. DeBeer, ed., *The Diary of John Evelyn* (Oxford, 1955), 12 June 1673. Andrew Marvell, "An Account of the Growth of Popery," in *Poems on Affairs of State Augustan Satirical Verse, 1660–1714*, ed. George de F. Lord (New Haven, 1963), I, 46.

the government is arbitrary." Thus assaulted, fiscally unsupported, Charles II withdrew from the war. So he won far more than fighting could ever have gained him: an American empire.[35]

The peace of Westminster, signed on 9 February 1674, gave the English empire four years of neutrality while war in Europe continued to distract and enfeeble England's rivals. These years, centering on 1676, were crucial to the contest of Atlantic empires. During them, the restored monarchy achieved political and military predominance on the American continent. In 1676 especially, the "imperial crown of England" overcame colonial autonomy, European rivalry, Algonquin hostility. This, the imperial achievement of 1676, was based in the vast and central province of New York. Stretching from Maine to Maryland—albeit with bumptious interruptions in New England—New York encompassed the heartlands of eastern America. It was recovered from the Dutch by treaty in February. In March it was once again conferred by the king on his brother, and the duke commissioned Major Edmund Andros "lieutenant and governor-general of all his royal highnesses territories in America."[36]

Bailiff of Guernsey and
Seigneur de Sausmarez

The newsletters of 24 March 1674 reported that "Major Andros is appointed Governor of New York, which by the articles of peace is to be restored to us. He goes by the first opportunity." It was many months before that opportunity arrived. In the interim, policies were defined, commissions and instructions written, a garrison and staff recruited, munitions and equipment procured, old accounts settled, the Barbados Regiment provided for, and, most important to Edmund Andros, his Guernsey inheritance was preserved from hostile islanders and political rivals by being made part of the imperial prerogative of Charles II.[37]

35. *C.S.P.D.* 1673–1675, 103–6. *A Collection of the Parliamentary Debates in England from the Year M, DC, LXVIII to the Present Time* (Dublin, London, 1741), I, 63–64.

36. David Ogg, *England in the Reign of Charles II* (Oxford, 1956), I, 387–88. John Romelyn Brodhead, *History of the State of New York* (New York, 1871), II, 314 ff. C.O. 5/1112, 3. Brodhead, ed., *Documents Relative to the Colonial History of the State of New York* (Albany, 1853), III, 215 (hereafter cited as *N.Y.C.D.*).

37. Historical Manuscript Commission, ed., *12th Report, Appendix, Part VII, the Manuscripts of S. H. Le Fleming, Esq.* (London, 1890), 180.

Just four days after his son was named to the New York command, Amias Andros, seigneur de Sausmarez, bailiff of Guernsey, master of the ceremonies to the king, hereditary cupbearer to the duke of Normandy in his island fief, castellan of Jerbourg, died, "at 10 o'clock as he sat in his chair in his study." Instantly his enemies organized to oppose his son's succession as bailiff. As early as 23 November 1673, however, the Androses had obtained an order of the king-in-council that greatly increased the authority of the bailiff whenever that post should change hands. Then, in January 1674, father and son passed through the offices (in the record time of just five days) the king's grant to Edmund Andros of the office of bailiff, in reversion to his father and for life.[38]

The governor's partisans on Guernsey insisted nonetheless that by his patent "all that belong's to the King's right and goeth under the King's name, is granted to the Governor." They added that the governor's local knowledge would produce apt appointees to provincial office and that the governor's authority depended on his control of such patronage. Arguing that, therefore, he should nominate the new bailiff to the king, the governor of Guernsey, Lord Hatton, expressed the arguments of the older, courtier, class of governors everywhere in the empire. The imperial reply was written by Sir Heneage Finch, the lord keeper and for decades to come a firm supporter of imperial authority and of Edmund Andros. Together, the lord keeper and the cupbearer argued so effectively against island autonomy and gubernatorial independence that Lord Hatton's opposition to Andros' appointment "was resented by ye king & all ye grandees." On 22 April 1674, the governor was given strict orders by the king-in-council not to "disturb the said Major Edmund Andros in the admission to and the execution of his office of Bailiff in the said island of Guernsey."[39]

This was the crown's centralizing tone, its direct government of imperial dependencies, so offensive to Berkeley in Virginia and to Atkins in Barbados in 1676. King Charles declared that, henceforward, he would not only name the bailiff of "the Royal Court" in Guernsey but also, to make the court truly royal, appoint its prosecutor and comptroller, and the dean of the church as well. Guernseymen of autonomous and republican tendencies reacted in the same terms as their colonial counterparts. Andros' appointment and the centralization of patronage, they said, were "don by Despotical Power & Government." Then came news that the king's bailiff was a truly imperial executive: that he was also the king's officer in Ireland—where the old infantry companies of the Barbados

38. Guernsey jurats to Lord Hatton, 29 March 1674, Add. Ms. 29554, 261. Order-in-council, *C.S.P.D. 1673–1675*, 95.

39. William de Beauvoir to Hatton, 8 June 1674, Add. Ms. 29554, 324, and see 334, 358, 376. Ferdinand Brock Tupper, *The History of Guernsey and Its Bailiwick* (Guernsey, 1876), 374.

Regiment had been transferred—and the duke's governor at New York. "The whole discourse of this place is of the great favour young Andrews has att Court and the great expectation of his being here." Expectations expanded as Guernseymen realized that, in the person of their new bailiff, their government had been incorporated into the new imperial regime.[40]

What this meant for Guernsey appeared when Major Andros came ashore on Monday morning, 29 June 1674. He produced the royal warrant for his reversion to the office of bailiff "to the immense satisfaction of all their [the Androses'] party, and the others seeming rejoicing." Indeed, the captain of the garrison said of these Guernseymen, "there are none of them but are better acquainted with dissimulation than with honesty." Dissimulation dissolved at the weekend. On 4 July 1674, the new bailiff convened the royal court. He demanded that its jurats enroll among the island ordinances the order of the privy council redefining the office of bailiff. This order-in-council so demeaned the legislative and judicial power of the elected jurats and so enhanced the authority of the king's bailiff that, as the dissident jurats said, "if he goes out to make water we must attend him." Such was the bailiff's new "power & exaltation" that he could now choose to apply English custom instead of Norman law or Guernsey practice in any particular court case. He alone sentenced the guilty. The defenders of local law and magistracy complained that "the King's Subjects here who ought by all our Laws, Charters, Priviledges, to be Judged and punished by the King's Royal Court alone, are left to the arbitrary judgement & punishment of a single man alone."[41]

The Guernsey opponents of arbitrary, English, executive government protested volubly, as the enemies of Andros and empire would always do on these occasions. They insisted, in the usual provincial manner, that the king would never have so reduced their privileges unless he was misadvised. They therefore demanded a delay in the registration of the royal order reducing local autonomy until the king could be informed (by them, of course) of the actual state of local affairs. King Charles, however, had found in Major Andros a soldierly executive who knew the royal will and applied it absolutely. Andros cut short the speeches of the opposition leader, demanding that he "say in a few words whether it [the royal order] should be registered or not." Andros dismissed pleas for "freedom of expression." He called for a vote. He and his father had done their work well, so the bailiff knew that there was a majority in the royal court, a majority not just in favor of his position but actually composed of his

---

40. Add. Ms. 29554, 358. Captain Stock (captain of the Guernsey garrision, formerly captain and commissary of the New York garrison; colonial adviser to Lord Baltimore regarding the Delaware settlements) to Hatton, 1 June 1674, *ibid.*, 346.

41. Beauvoir to Hatton, 7, 27 July 1674, *ibid.*, 364, 376, 377.

family. The order of the king-in-council was duly registered as the law of Guernsey.[42]

The next day, Sunday, 5 July, Bailiff Andros took Communion in the Church of England, swore the oaths of allegiance and supremacy, and subscribed the (anti-Catholic) test. The new bailiff then named his uncle Charles Andros to be his lieutenant, as he had been the old seigneur's. Despairing of any further obstruction to the Andros succession, the opposition oligarchs concluded that, as long as Edmund Andros retained the royal favor, "neither Governor nor Jurats will be anything, the baily will be the center of all honour & authority here." In fact, they said, he "shall be Governor and Court." It was to be thirty years before Sir Edmund Andros fulfilled this prediction. In 1704 he would be commissioned lieutenant governor of Guernsey while still bailiff. In the intervening generation, however, he was all that the enemies of royal prerogative and English empire feared, in every colony from Maine through Virginia. The center of their fears was a more-than-royal province, New York. On Thursday, 10 July 1674, the bailiff of Guernsey sailed from his ancestral island to begin in the duke's dominion a career of thirty-seven years as a governor-general in England's empire.[43]

New York Repossessed

W hat Edmund Andros had learned and become in the era of civil war and restoration in Guernsey government and society, he applied to the government of New York, the key to English empire in America. Only after they had lost New York to the Dutch (because the cabinet could not find the ships and troops they required to match the Dutch raiders, whose expedition the cabinet anxiously followed almost from its inception), only in the matured, interconnected, geopolitical view of the world as it became visible to Whitehall in the mid-1670s in the wake of the third Dutch war, and only in the context of the revival of English revolutionary politics—only then did the Stuart imperialists appreciate the lost outpost of empire. It was small in European population. It was impoverished economically. New York's undisputed importance thus testified to the strategic irrelevance of great numbers or wealth and demon-

42. *Ibid.*, 376.
43. Beauvoir to Hatton, 7, 27 July, 14 August 1674, *ibid.*, 364, 388, 376–78, 364b.

strated the importance of determined individuals and geographic place during the formative period of Anglo-American society.

The council for foreign plantations collected the consensus of colonial and commercial, political and military opinion about New York in November 1673. In words that formed the basis of English strategy for more than a century to come, the council concluded "1st That New York being a very good & ye only fortified Harbor in all ye Northern Plantacons of America" would control the Capes of Virginia and the Chesapeake Bay. Whoever held New York could reiterate the recent Dutch raid on the tobacco fleet, the colonial councilors observed, with all of the losses that disaster dictated to English trade, royal revenue, and colonial tranquillity, prosperity, even population. "The inhabitants there by their scattered way of living and want of fortresses in a Country that hath so many great and open rivers" could never resist seaborne raids and must, as they did in 1676, either flee from or submit to seapower, especially if it was sustained from a base at New York.[44]

In their second anticipation of the geopolitics of revolutionary America (whether that of 1676 or of 1776), the king's colonial councilors observed that New York's northern neighbors in autonomous New England, although they were not so vulnerable to Dutch forces (or others) by sea as were the Chesapeake colonies, were even more susceptible to the lures of Netherlands economics and politics. "Ye Inhabitants of New England, being more intent upon ye advancement of their own private trade, then ye publique Interest of yor Maties crowne and Governmt.," said the councilors, will trade with the Dutch in New York. Given New England predominance in the coastwise and West Indian trades of America, and the low price and high quality of Dutch manufactures, Dutch–New England commerce would destroy England's economic monopoly of its American colonies. Worse, the economic collaboration of the New England commonwealths with the Dutch republic would constitute the economic basis of a diplomatic, even military alliance between the states of the Netherlands and those of New England. This would be fatal to the English empire in America, "if not terrible to England itself."

The loss of strategic New York entailed more immediate dangers to England's West Indian colonies. Soldiers such as Edmund Andros reported that the sugar islands depended on provisions from the North American plantations. Of these, "noe small quantities came from New York itself" and the rest from New England. If New York were not recovered, the plantations councilors concluded, all the Caribbean possessions of England would "either be reduced to extremity; or else all that

44. N.Y.C.D., III, 211. C.O. 1/30, 195–203.

Trade come into New Englandmen's hands . . . which would be of as ill consequence."[45]

Before the council's plans to recapture New York could be effected, the Treaty of Westminster restored the strategic colony to the English crown. On 30 March 1674, therefore, the king wrote to the States-General of the Netherlands asking them "to despatch . . . the Necessary instructions to your Governor or Commandant of the place called New York in the West Indies to surrender it to Sieur Edmond Andros." On 30 May, the day after Charles II had regranted the province to his brother, the king reinforced "Sieur Edmond's" command by commissioning him captain of a "Company of Foot to be in garrison in New York in America." On 1 July, "having conceived a good opinion of the integrity, prudence, ability and fitness of MAJOR EDMUND ANDROS," the duke of York constituted him his "Lieut and Governour." On 7 August, Charles II accepted Andros' homage as the "Seigneur de Sausmares" in the same feudal form as his father's submission to Charles I.[46] The royal duke then gave the seigneur his lieutenant final instructions. Fortunately they were, for the most part, a grant of that discretion which was essential if so obedient a soldier as Major Andros was to act as an opportunistic and constructive executive. The duke also helped Andros pay for his outfit, financed the garrison company's clothing and supplies, provided his lieutenant with transportation (two warships, whose crew and provisions cost the duke £2,200), and authorized his annual gubernatorial salary of £400 and his pay as captain of the garrison, £145.12 per annum. (In addition, and also by favor of the duke of York, Andros drew £227 as major and captain of the Barbados Regiment in Ireland.) These were large sums in an age of annual wages averaging £5 a year, and Andros was expected to multiply his £772.12 in salaries many times over by "gifts" and "gratuities," fees and presents. Edmund Andros was bound, recompensed, and (as he told his Guernsey compatriots on 17 August 1674) "commanded by his Maties' and Royal Highness' Service to New York in America."[47]

Major Andros sailed for New York in his majesty's ship the *Diamond*, one of the survivors of the commonwealth fleet, which still composed half of the smaller rates in the royal navy. At 548 tons and with 42 guns, however small she was in European naval terms, the *Diamond* would be

45. *N.Y.C.D.*, III, 212.
46. *Ibid.*, II, 544. The colony was to be surrendered "with all its dependencies, arms, artillery, ammunition and material of war" (Hugh Hastings, ed., *Ecclestical Records: State of New York* [Albany, 1901–16], I, 644). C.O. 5/1111, 9–16; C.O. 5/1112, 2, 3; S.P. 44/35A, 88; *N.Y.C.D.*, III, 215; *C.S.P.D. 1673–1675*, 326.
47. E. Andros Directions for the Government of Guernsey, in Carey, "Andros," *Transactions of the Guernsey Society*, VII (1913–16): 52–53.

an impressive aid to Andros' authority in New York, where the average ship was less than a fifth of her size. She was a sound ship as well as sizable, for she survived the revolution of 1689 and was still on the navy list of that year, then aged thirty-eight. There had been no planned obsolescence in the ships built by Phineas Pett in the Deptford Navy Yard.

Still, the *Diamond* must have been a crowded vessel en route to New York. She was laden with Andros' staff: thirteen infantry officers; five gunners; a surgeon; a chaplain; a storekeeper; and a customs collector. The governor's lady, his steward, and their servants were also on board, together with the proprietary governor of New Jersey (Andros' Jersey cousin Philip Carteret) and Captain John Manning, who was returning to the site of his surrender of Fort James to face court-martial. (Colonel Lovelace, absent in Connecticut at the moment of Manning's disgrace, was now dying in the Tower of London, having been cashiered for his failure as a soldier and incarcerated for mismanaging the finances of New York. Moreover, Major Andros had been ordered to confiscate Lovelace's estate in New York as recompense for the £7,000 the duke said he was owed by the unfortunate ex-officer.) Also on board was Captain Silvester Salisbury, the old English soldier and Long Island settler who was to become Governor-General Andros' most reliable subordinate. In company with the *Diamond*, the *Castle* carried out some of the one hundred garrison soldiers, several factors, four English merchants now entering the New York market, and "a number of New Colonists." The *Castle* is usually called a "frigate" in the sources but was probably a fireship brought into the navy in 1671/2. She displaced 329 tons and mounted 8 guns. With the exception of the spare governor, the guilty captain, and the new merchants, this crowd was pretty much the standard personnel of a garrison staff in England. They were now transported across the Atlantic to reimpose garrison government in New York.[48]

However crowded they were, the governor-general and all of his companions remained cooped up on board after their trans-Atlantic voyage to New York. The *Diamond* and the *Castle* lay in tantalizing sight of the country town on the East River for just over a week after they anchored under the lee of Staten Island. From 22 to 31 October the Dutch city fathers and their retiring governor negotiated the terms of their surrender with the incoming English executive. Major Andros was anxious beyond expression to get possession of the fort. It was the key to the city, the province, and, as it happened, to the future of mid-America. So, sometimes disingenuously, he agreed to every Dutch proposition regarding their property rights, including those they had established by ousting the

48. Brodhead, *New York*, II, 269. See also S.P. 104/176, 135v.

English colonists during the occupation. He promised that no Dutchman would be impressed into military service (although it turned out that he and they had different views of what "impressment" meant). He pledged complete freedom of worship to members of the Dutch Reformed Church (which freedom, he observed, was mandated by the duke's instructions). What Major Andros could not promise, much though he wanted to, was free trade between New York and the Netherlands. This was forbidden both by act of parliament and, much more important to Major Andros, by the duke's orders. At the end of eight days of negotiation, the Dutch governor-general surrendered the famous fort as it stood, looming hugely, stone-walled, high-roofed, over the little town, commanding the anchorage in the East River where the captains of the *Diamond* and the *Castle* were anxious to shelter their ships from the storms of autumn.[49]

Construction and Conciliation

A s if to make amends to Major Andros for the protracted negotiations, Anthony Colve, the Dutch governor, left to his successor his coach and team. The new governor-general was gracious in his acceptance but he found the almost useless vehicle (New York had but one short paved street) small recompense for the ruin the Dutch had made inside "Fort James." Within the great stone square, its curtain walls 30 feet high and 200 feet long between the corner bastions, lay a classic provincial headquarters: governor's residence, chapel, barracks, guardhouse, officers' quarters, storehouse, and magazine (also, unwisely, used as a jail). It was a wreck.

"Soldiers, his owne Servts and Negroes," Andros set to work (for which he paid them the going wage) to make good the vandalism of the departing Dutch garrison. First they repaired and then they built anew a magazine for the six hundred stand of good arms the duke sent from England. The garrison then remounted forty-six cannon and replanked the gun platforms. Next, they replaced the palisade on the lip of the moat, reroofed the governor's house and rebuilt its stairs, patched up their barracks, and constructed a new hospital, officers' quarters, and secretary's office. They filled the storehouses and built a new kitchen and dining hall. In the spring of 1675, when the warships sailed home, the

49. S.P. 104/176, 140. See Book III, Part 1, n. 43, above.

governor-general moved into Fort James. Henceforward it was his habitual workplace and conference center. He never left it without placing a trusted subordinate in command and alerting the garrison. He had learned Lovelace's lesson: "If I should surrender without the Duke's order," Andros said, "it is as much as my head is worth."[50]

Outside the walls of Fort James, but within the city walls (Wall Street), stood some four hundred buildings. They housed a population of fifteen hundred or two thousand of New York's twelve thousand Europeans. (That is, the town was the size of Garacontié's Onondaga and the colony's non-native population was about equal to that of the Five Nations—a comparison that speaks volumes about the logic of Andros' egalitarian treatment of the Iroquois.) Nearly four-fifths of the city population were Dutch, although eighteen languages are said to have been spoken in the cosmopolitan settlement. The polyglot population was concentrated in the streets which ran from the landward side of Fort James parallel to the East River and as far north as Smee Street (William Street). Thence the town center extended inland, around the great canal, the Heere Gracht, which ran in from the river to the foot of Prince (Broad) Street.

Of all these city folk, but four were rich (that is, worth more than 45,000 florins in the 1674 assessment). Of these four "men of abilities and integrity," the sort of local worthies whom Andros was instructed to consult, three became his allies. The fourth was Cornelius Steenwyck, the handsome and arrogant mayor during the Colve administration. Steenwyck had led the burgher delegation to the *Diamond* to demand privileges from Andros. Prominent among those privileges was "that they may be excused from impressment, if not wholly at least against their own Nation." Andros, whose Dutch was fluent, knew full well that the burghers, inspired by the departing governor, sought complete exemption from any future defense of New York against the Dutch. Andros had said to Steenwyck and his associates that he had "neither Orders Nor directions for any pressing whatever." All the major meant, as the duke of York's secretary later told an angry Dutch ambassador, was that the governor-general would not draft—i.e., "impress"—anyone into the royal army or navy. No other exemption was implied. On 16 March 1674/5, with the fort repaired and the warships still present, the governor-general took advantage of this moment of maximum military strength to impose on the populace of New York the oaths of allegiance to King Charles and of fidelity to the duke of York. The former of these oaths pledged physical support for the king against "all his enemies." Cornelius Steenwyck felt

50. *N.Y.C.D.*, III, 307, 311. Brodhead, *New York*, II, 305.

betrayed by Edmund Andros. Steenwyck organized other patriotic Dutchmen to help him resist the oath of allegiance.[51]

"Governor Andros not only illy received, but peremptorily rejected" their petition against the oath. He denounced Steenwyck and his associates as "disturbers of the king's peace." He had them marched off to jail in Fort James. They protested to the States-General of the Netherlands that their rights under both the general peace treaty and the New York surrender agreement had been violated. The states complained to both the king and the duke in London, but no relief was granted. Governor-General Andros' first court of assizes, where he presided, bailiff-like, condemned all the protesters as rebels and confiscated their entire estates. Their property, minus fines and costs, was restored only when they took the oath and promised to remain, with their goods, in New York (a restriction completely at odds with both the peace treaty and the surrender agreement). Not only were the dissident burghers humbled, their leader, Steenwyck, was excluded from public life under Andros. Despite all his fine words—previous to the surrender—about equal justice to the Dutch and due observation of the peace treaty, the duke of York told his American lieutenant that he "was very well satisfied with your care and prudence in quelling and composing those disorders with soe much calmness." He ordered Major Andros, "upon all occasions to keepe ye people in due obedience and subjection, and all inclinations towards mutiny severley supprest."[52]

On the other hand, the governor-general was told to pardon the penitent and to encourage the obedient. Among these were the other three Dutchmen of wealth: Frederick Philipse (who by 1676, under Andros' patronage, displaced Steenwyck as New York's wealthiest man), Nicholas de Meyer, and that old soldier who had realized the dream of every ranker and turned brewmaster, Olof Stevense Van Courtlandt. They had taken the uncompromising measure of the governor-general at the outset. They did not object to impressment. They took every oath offered them. Within two years they became Edmund Andros' business partners. They were appointed by him first as aldermen, then as mayors, and finally as councilors. The major encouraged the obedient. They supported him. Such was the stuff of every successful imperial government.

Among the nine men of moderate means (10,000–12,000 florins) seven were politically active merchants. Andros did as well in his recruiting

51. The duke to Andros, 19 February 1674, in Hastings, ed., *Ecclestical Records*, I, 641–43, and see 662. The duke to Andros, 1 July 1674, *N.Y.C.D.*, III, 218.
52. Cornelius Magistris [Steenwyck] to the States-General, in Hastings, ed., *Ecclestical Records*, I, 671. Sir John Werden to Andros, St. James, 15 September 1675, *N.Y.C.D.*, III, 233.

among the merchants as he did among the men of wealth. The governor-general encountered only one obstructionist, a former soldier of the Dutch West India Company who had married money, become a militia captain and a leader in the Albany Indian trade, and who remained a Dutch patriot and a religious fanatic, Jacob Leisler. The remaining six merchants of means were stalwarts of Andros' administration. They included Gabriel Minvielle, Johannes de Peyster, Jan [James] Lawrence, and Nicholas Bayard (who served in Andros' governments for fifteen years to come).

Small wonder the leading Dutchmen of New York City quickly collaborated with Edmund Andros. First, he gave them no choice. Then he built them a city, laying the foundations of a more salubrious as well as a more prosperous future while every other colony north of the Carolinas fell into the horrors of the great Algonquin risings of 1675–76.

In just two years, Edmund Andros applied his experiences in London and Yarmouth, Ostend and Bridgetown, to the remodeling of New York. He made it a place as functionally urban and commercially prosperous as it was already militarily defensible and politically subdued. He began by ordering a housing census taken. Then he forced the owners of unbuilt lots either to build or to sell out. Andros ordered the construction of a new mercantile exchange and covered market, the first of their kinds in the continental colonies. He had public warehouses and a customs house erected, the latter on the rebuilt East River pier. To cleanse the town, the governor-general ordered the shambles and the tanneries moved beyond the city wall (along which he had five new stone bastions constructed to cover its flanks and gates), and he had New York's first public "conveniences" constructed. He insisted that the smelly Heere Gracht in Broad Street, and its branches, be filled in, leveled, and paved, producing New York's second, third, and fourth paved streets.

The governor-general's concluding, greatest, and most long-lived civic improvement occupied his spare moments for several years. He designed, contracted for, and personally, daily, supervised the construction of the most important structure, save for the citadel, built in New York for fifty years on either side of 1676, the great semicircular dock, mole, or breakwater that protected the newly rebuilt East River pier, bulkheaded shore, and reconstructed slips along New York's East River front from Whitehall to the City Hall. Sheltered from storm, tide, and ice floes, lying within and alongside stone-filled timber cribs, the sloops which linked the provincial metropolis to its outposts from the Kennebec to the Delaware, the sloops which traded wheat and timber to the West Indies for rum, sugar, and slaves, and the lighters which served the oceangoing ships anchored in the East River, all could safely lie and lade. So assisted, during Edmund Andros' administration New York's "Navigation increased att least tenn tymes to what it was" and so produced customs revenue enough to pay the cash costs of every improvement to fort, town, and riverfront.[53]

To facilitate, regulate, and legitimate this growing trade, the governor-general decreed comprehensive economic regulations, equally resented and successful. Merchantable grain, the settled province's major product, was no longer to be distilled. Instead, it was to be traded to the West Indies for (highly taxed) rum in fat times and peacetimes and stored for food in lean times and wartimes. Processed grain, whether baked or bolted, bread or flour, was to be inspected and labeled before export or sale (this was another of the regulations afterwards termed Andros' "tyranny"). Before the end of his New York administration, Andros had restricted to the city all grinding, processing, and packing of wheat products for export. Thus he facilitated inspection and taxation, employment and exchange, and strengthened the economy of the metropolis, as the imperial duke had directed. From the duke, Andros secured remission of the tax on salt, encouraging the barreled-meat and preserved-fish trades. As the good servant of his master the duke, who was governor of the Royal Fisheries Company, Edmund Andros developed the fisheries of the Bay and the Sound by organizing New York's first commercial corporation. (Predictably, the duke was delighted at his lieutenant's enterprise, seeing for his province as for the empire as a whole that ocean fishery was the "most likely thing to produce wealth and power at sea.") Andros also regulated timber milling to improve the New York product. He arranged for the inspection as well as the taxation of the tens of thousands of fur pelts shipped annually from New York. The city was also strengthened by being made, for most purposes, the sole port of entry for the province, New Jersey and Delaware included. The governor-general then concluded his comprehensive program for the economic development of the province around metropolitan centers and regulated trades, designed to foster the province's population and power by developing a merchant class—the heart of the seventeenth-century economy.[54]

53. See Jasper Danckaerts' sketch in the illustrations and read Andros' reply to queries, 31 December 1681, *N.Y.C.D.*, III, 313.
54. *Ibid.*, 234.

The Government of the
Duke's Dominions

THE GENERAL COURT

A ndros' instrument for regulation, taxation, and legislation was the court of assizes. The governor-general would have preferred an elected assembly on the model of the Guernsey States. There he could have traded with the provincial elite—grievance resolution for legislation. Assemblymen would spread the political basis of the government throughout the duke's dominions and provide the executive with agents of his authority in every community. In January 1676, however, the duke of York, so abused by parliament at home and so alarmed by the excesses of American assemblies, Virginia's among the rest, refused to accept Andros' request for an elected legislature unless the duke was assured in advance of substantial revenues and political restraint, "nothing being more knowne then the Aptness of such Bodyes, to assume to themselves many Priviledges, wch prove destructive to . . . the Peace of ye Governmt. . . . Neither doe I see any use of them wch is not as well provided for; whilst you and your Councell govern according to ye Laws Establisht (thereby preserving every man's property inviolate) and whilst all things that need redresse may be sure of finding it, either at ye Quarter Sessions or by other Legall and Ordinary wayes, or at last by appeale to myself." [55]

The duke here seemed to eliminate all thought of an elected legislature for New York. Yet, in an earlier letter on the subject, the duke had pointed out to Andros that the annual court of assizes could redress grievances—if necessary by passing ordinances—as well as any assembly, for in the court "the same persons (as Justices) are usually present, who in all probability would be theire Representatives, if another constitution were allowed." With as much ducal allowance as this, Edmund Andros felt authorized to adopt for New York the model of Guernsey's Royal Court: a system whereby closed elections selected local representatives to sit in a senatorial body both legislative and judicial. [56]

55. The duke to Andros, Whitehall, 28 January 1675/6, C.O. 5/1112, 20v; printed in *N.Y.C.D.*, III, 235. See also the duke to Andros, 6 April 1675, *N.Y.C.D.*, III, 231, which Andros received before he convened his first assizes in October.
56. The duke to Andros, 6 April 1675, C.O. 5/1112, 17v.

The governor-general ordered each of the courts through which he governed the duke's dominions—ultimately seven in New York proper, three on the Delaware River, and one each from the Vineyard, Nantucket, and Maine—to elect two of their justices as members of the body that the governor-general came to refer to as the general court in its legislative capacity, and the court of assizes in its judicial capacity. The court met annually in October at Fort James. Reinforced by the presence of the governor-general, his executive council, and the mayor of New York, the court acted in the several fashions familiar to Andros from the Royal Court of Guernsey. He presided over and directed the court in much the same terms, both legislative and judicial, as he, and his father before him, had as bailiff in Guernsey.

The court responded generously to the governor-general's proposals. It approved numerous taxes in cash and kind (for others to pay, in typical legislative fashion). The mole alone required twenty-four thousand cartloads of stone, paid for by a special assessment on the city. It consumed miles of timber for cribs and pilings, timber requisitioned from the forests of Long Island. It used up the (unpaid) labor of the city militia, conscripted company by company in every temperate month for years on end. Palisades and masonry for the endless work on Fort James (the refortification of 1676 alone consumed 100,591 stockades, each 12 feet by 4 inches) also were requisitioned. The new public buildings called for additional legislative orders and taxes, either by the general court or by the city corporation. (And the improvements that Andros instigated on so large a scale in New York City, he also ordered in the district capitals of the duke's dominions, Albany [New York], Newcastle [on Delaware], and Pemaquid [Maine], through the appropriate district courts and on proportionately smaller scales.) Finally, the soldiers had to be fed, the new bureaucracy of city surveyor, customshouse weighers, viewers, inspectors, and the like had to have their salaries authorized and their fees set, all by orders of the general court.

The governor-general took his cuts too, authorized or surreptitious. At least his enemies alleged that "in the years 1675, 76, & 77 the customes ammounted . . . to £14700 & odd pounds," twice what Andros' accounts admitted to. But the laborer was worthy of his hire. Edmund Andros found New York a village. He left it a city. Of course, much credit was owed the international situation. The growth and improvement of New York was a wonderful example of the vast and irrevocable benefits reaped by the English empire during the four years when England was at peace and her rivals were at war. Yet in every other English colony, from the Carolinas northward, the immeasurable disasters of the great Algonquin wars set colonial development back by more than thirty years. New York alone was spared. New York alone had Andros.[57]

ANDROS VERSUS THE YANKEES

The disparate populations of the duke's dominions took various times to appreciate the fairness and effectiveness of Edmund Andros' imperial order. None took longer than the Connecticut Yankees of eastern Long Island. Andros began his administration of the three towns settled on Long Island from Connecticut, as he did everywhere except in the city, by reappointing Lovelace's officials. In the two Hamptons and Southold, however, the regime they displaced was Connecticut's, not that of the Dutch conquerors of 1673. Dutch efforts to impose administrators on the eastern towns had been beaten off—in comic, casualty-less "battles"— with the aid of officers and men sent across the Sound by Connecticut Colony. Protection always entails obedience. Connecticut appointed magistrates in the three towns. They refused to accede to Andros' orders of 4 November 1674 for their replacement. With characteristic legalism, the Connecticut officials on Long Island held that Andros could not command for the king and duke territory never conquered by the Dutch and so not reclaimed from them by the peace treaty. The royal claim to their obedience had been lost, the Long Island officials said, "when his Royal Highnesse Lieutenant [Lovelace] had left us without either Aide, or Councell, Starre or Compasse."[58]

Andros had one answer to political resistance: obey or be "declared rebels and proceeded against accordingly." He commissioned Captain Salisbury as high sheriff of Long Island to serve summonses on the recalcitrant magistrates. To separate them from those Long Islanders who were willing to be loyal subjects of duke and king, Andros had Salisbury offer the oaths of allegiance, reinstate the duke's laws, and organize new elections for local officers in every town and precinct that would accept them. Then the governor-general wrote a polite but uncompromising letter to the governor of Connecticut Colony. Andros expressed his confidence that Governor Winthrop would not "obstruct his [majesty's] Prerogative Royall and his Royall Highnesse Right" on Long Island. John Winthrop was politically astute (and physically ill). He had observed the rising tide of royal authority and he knew that, although the duke's legal claims to Long Island were as weak as most colonial claims, ducal officers had actually governed the Long Island towns for a decade before the Dutch reconquest. So the governor sent his son (who ultimately became

57. John Lewin's report, 24 May 1680, N.Y.C.D., III, 306.
58. John Mulford, John Howell, John Young to Andros, 18 November 1674, ibid., XIV, 681.

major general of the New England militia under Sir Edmund Andros) to welcome Major Andros to New York and to disabuse the islanders of their belief that Connecticut would help them to resist the duke as they had the Dutch, equally alien though Dutch and English seemed to the puritan townsmen.[59]

Once diplomacy had removed Connecticut from the contest, Andros applied force to the island obstructionists. He led fifty mounted and armed retainers (not for nothing had the governor-general been a major of dragoons) the length of Long Island. Andros' troops stood guard as the militias of each town were re-formed by Captain Salisbury. Then the last three local leaders who had held out against Andros' administration were arrested, carted off to Fort James, jailed, tried for sedition. They were sentenced to public humiliation. The two less culpable were tied to the whipping post on market day, with appropriate signs hung round their necks. The third and most stubborn townsman, John Burroughs, was stripped, whipped, and jailed.

The duke of York declared his special pleasure at his lieutenant's "conduct in reduceing to obedience those 3 factious towns at ye East end of Long Island." In a wise and conciliatory tone not usually associated with James Stuart, however, the duke also admonished Andros "to take care to see ym by degrees soe settled with the rest under yor governmt yt ye people may be wtout apprehensions of any injustice towards ym and yourself secure in their willing compliance to ye laws established." The duke's politically balanced counsels were law to his governor-general. So, in December 1674, the Long Islanders formally bade farewell to Connecticut's jurisdiction. It has never been resumed. The islanders observed that a governor-general who could do them so much present harm could do them an equal amount of good in the future. As the events of 1675 and 1676 would demonstrate, this was as prescient a forecast as it was a prudent conclusion.[60]

By March 1675, the governor-general felt that his internal control of New York and of its immediate dependencies on Long Island and up the Hudson River was such that he could impose the oaths of allegiance on all the subjects of the king and duke, compel all vessels trading with them to clear customs in New York City, and begin to assert the imperial sway of the Stuart sovereigns over "other his majestys and royal highnesses territories in America." By April, Andros had eliminated the authority of aggressive Massachusetts on Martha's Vineyard (where Andros' advent had been longed for "as in time of great drouth, for the latter

59. Andros to Winthrop, 4 December 1674. *Ibid.*, III, 682. Winthrop to Andros, *Collections of the Massachusetts Historical Society*, 5th ser., 7 (1882): 164–66.
60. *N.Y.C.D.*, III, 231.

rain") and on Nantucket (where Andros' appearance was hailed "as the rising of the sun after a dark and stormy night"). As yet, however, he could do nothing to undo Massachusetts' hold on the duke's Pemaquid Province (Maine), or its claims to trade and territory in the Albany region.[61]

Andros' victory over Connecticut in their contest for control of the disputed Long Island towns suggested that her pretensions to the duke's domains were more easily contravened than Massachusetts'. Moreover, Connecticut's issuance of land patents in what was clearly New York's territory (according to Connecticut's own agreement of 1664 with Governor Nicolls and the royal commissioners, under which the New York–Connecticut line was to run north from Mamaroneck on the Sound, parallel to and 20 miles east of the Hudson River) was just the sort of illegal aggression that excited Edmund Andros. He called Connecticut's bet and doubled the stakes. On 1 May 1675, the governor and general court of Connecticut read Andros' letter calling on them to surrender their present possession of a part of the duke's patent, for it encompassed "all ye land from ye West Side of Connecticut river to ye East side of Delaware Bay." Andros announced that he had been commissioned by the king and the duke to provide "effectual care for the future defence & protection" of their subjects within the duke's dominions, and to act for their "benefitt and prosperity." Therefore he asked "(and will not doubt, from so worthy an assembly)" that the Connecticut General Court transfer to him, "in his Royal Highnesse behalfe, that part of his Territories as yet under yor Jurisdiction"—that is, all of the colony west of the Connecticut River.[62]

THE DUCHY ON THE DELAWARE

Without waiting for Connecticut's reply to this demand for most of its territory and population, the governor-general crossed to New Jersey, via Staten Island, on 3 May 1675. He spent the night with his cousin Philip Carteret. Carteret's government of New Jersey was not authorized by the duke of York's grant of the soil of that colony to Sir George Carteret, but Sir George's command of Jersey in the civil war had established him as the ancient ally of the Andros clan. For Sir George the duke also had "much esteeme and regard," dating from the time when he, like the Androses, had taken refuge from republicans and regicides on Carteret's Jersey. The duke's secretary therefore instructed Andros that "at present

61. Brodhead, New York, II, 278.
62. Andros' commission, 1 July 1674, N.Y.C.D., III, 215. Andros to the governor and council of Connecticut, 1 May 1675, N.Y.C.D., XIV, 689. J. Hammond Trumbull, ed., The Public Records of Connecticut from 1675 to 1678 (Hartford, 1852), 569–70.

in respect to Sir George we suffer things all we may not to disturbe his choller." Still, Andros was warned that "the duke was not at all inclined to lett goe any part of his prerogative" in New Jersey. He expected his lieutenant to assert his political authority in that part of his province in due time: should Sir George Carteret's "foot chance to slip, those who succeed him must be content with less civility yn we show him." For the moment, however, Philip Carteret's administration was undisturbed by Edmund Andros. Indeed, he was a valued member of the governor-general's executive council. For his part, Carteret administered New Jersey as a dependency of New York. Incoming settlers took out land patents from Andros at Fort James. Ships bound to and from New Jersey cleared customs at Andros' new customs house on the East River pier. So it was that, in May 1675, the duke's lieutenant felt free to borrow thirty horses from Governor Carteret and they rode off together, accompanied by Captain Salisbury, Aldermen Minvielle and Cornell, Secretary Nicolls, a group of debt-collecting New York merchants (trade followed the flag rather closely), and the governor-general's guard, to establish ducal dominion on both banks of the Delaware, according to the now standard Andros model.[63]

On the west bank, the duke's claim by conquest from the Dutch in 1664 was challenged by the Maryland proprietary government. The Calvert government's brutal raids on the Delaware settlements that denied its jurisdiction had continued into Lovelace's time. As late as 1676, a proprietary posse felt free to pursue the rebel leaders Pate and Davis to Newcastle and carry them off to be hanged. Just two days after his arrival in New York, however, Major Andros had written the Maryland leaders to say that he would exercise the duke of York's authority in the settlements on the Delaware and would extend royal protection to them. At Upland, Newcastle, and Whorekill, Andros said, he would "prevent or redress any kind of injuryes." Now, in May 1675, he set out to give those settlements the social organization—executive and ministry, militia and courts—by which the Delaware peoples were for the first time relieved of that awful insecurity which had hitherto been their bane. Obeying the duke's imperial orders, the governor-general provided for the king's subjects in "New York and its dependencies . . . protection and benefit, for ye encouragement of Planters and Plantations and ye improvement of trade and commerce, and for ye preservation of religion justice and equity. . . ."[64]

"Protection" was first in the governor-general's priorities. As soon as

63. Werden to Andros, 31 August 1676, *N.Y.C.D.*, III, 240.
64. Andros to the governor of Maryland, 3 November 1674, *ibid.*, XII, 513–14. Andros' commission, *ibid.*, III, 216; also in C.O. 5/1112, 3–4. The Delaware settlements appear on the Thornton/Greene Map. For the Maryland raids on these hamlets, see Book I, p. 72.

he reached the capital of the "South River," Newcastle-on-Delaware, Andros ordered the recovery and remounting of castaway cannon in two batteries, one to cover the anchorage there and another to command the river itself where it narrowed. Then the governor-general consulted with the sheriff, Captain Edmund Cantwell. They produced a list of potential militia officers and, on 14 May 1675, "Edmond Andros Esq. Seigneur of Sausmarez Lieut. and Governor Generall under his Royall Highnesse James Duke of York and Albany etc. of all his Territories in America" issued standard military commissions to the officers of a full company of militia at Newcastle and to the officers of other, smaller, units at six other Delaware settlements.[65]

"Planters and Plantations" were the primary objects of protection, for their preservation was the essential objective of pioneer societies. "People are the wealth of Plantations." So much Major Andros had learned in the Lesser Antilles. From the moment he reached the Delaware River, the governor-general was besieged by petitioners for land patents, large and small. Ordered by the duke to "give all manner of encouragement to planters of all Nations to come and settle under yor Government," Andros was free to set what specific terms he would for land grants. His terms were those of governors-general throughout the empire in his generation. Like them, Andros thought close settlement in family farms, self-defensible and self-sufficient, desirable both militarily and socially. He adopted a headright system: 60 acres for every head of family; 50 acres for each of his dependents; 50 acres to each servant on completion of his indentures. These grants were to be held in fee simple on condition of actual improvement, the payment of local taxes, and the return of a nominal quitrent to the duke. Certification of improvement and tax payment was made by the newly named surveyor, Sheriff Cantwell. Registration of survey in the central records was made by Secretary Nicolls. All old grants were to be resurveyed, recorded, and patented to produce what became a novel and a major achievement of every Andros administration, a uniform system of land titles.[66]

Andros anticipated that the chief product of the new plantations, in addition to people, would be grain. So his general court on the Delaware issued orders for the repair or construction of grist mills and set a schedule of tolls. As in the North River colony, the governor-general required the district court to forbid the distillation of salable grain, for it was, as he said, the food of the Barbados (and Boston) trade in peace, the stuff of survival in war.

65. Charles T. Gehring, ed. and trans., *New York Historical Manuscripts: Dutch*, XX–XXI (Baltimore, 1977), 63. *N.Y.C.D.*, XII, 520.
66. Egerton Ms. 2395, 158. *N.Y.C.D.*, III, 216.

Planters, plantations, production along the Delaware existed at the sufferance of the aboriginal owners of the land. The natives had been restless of late, killing the occasional traveler in revenge for the abuses of passing fur traders. Because their territory lay athwart his overland connections with both parts of New Jersey and with the path to the settlements on the Delaware, the governor-general had quickly come to terms with the sachems of the Navasink nation, a Munsee-speaking band of "the Delaware Indians," usually associated with a tribal territory in the Sandy Hook Highlands. The nearer neighbors of the Delaware settlers were Unami-speaking Delawares of the lower valley. These were the "Lenni-Lenape" or, as they said, "the original real people." Pressed hard by the European settlers downriver of their tribal center on the east bank of the Delaware, and by the Susquehanna upriver, the Lenni-Lenape had achieved remarkable political consolidation under the sachem Renowewan of Sawkin. To negotiate with Renowewan and his associates was the first business Edmund Andros assigned his newly organized Delaware government.[67]

In the discussions of 13 May 1675, Edmund Andros capitalized on his West Indian experience and first displayed what became his habitual and highly successful policies and attitudes towards the native nations. First, he took the initiative. He called a strategic people's sachems to council. There, he declared "his desire to continue in friendship with them." He announced "his readiness to protect them" from Europeans and natives alike. He thanked the native negotiators for their attendance with the courtly courtesy he always exhibited to men of authority. This, as Frontenac's success with the Iroquois had shown, eastern natives valued as highly as European aristocrats did. As their conventions required, the Lenni-Lenape reciprocated, appreciating Andros' offers, returning his acknowledgments, accepting his apparent respect.[68]

Then Andros established the psychological superiority that served him instead of physical force in his diplomacy with the natives. They were "told that it is not that the Governor wants their helpe," although he counted himself sure of the pledged friendship of the Lenni-Lenape. "If the other Indians will be bad," Andros said that he needed no assistance, but could "deale well enough with them." Although he was under no necessity to do so, the governor-general nonetheless expressed himself as being "willing to be kind to those that will live quietly and well," regardless of their nationality or any previous enmity of theirs towards

---

67. Andros to Cantwell, 23 April 1675, N.Y.C.D., XII, 519. Andros also renewed the peace with the Navasink's cousins, the Esopus (Mahican), and refreshed the Mohawk peace, in the spring of 1675.

68. Gehring, ed. and trans., N.Y. Hist. Ms. Dutch, 71–72. A variant translation appears in N.Y.C.D., XII, 523–34.

the English. "They believe so," said the spokesmen of the original real people. So Andros put to them his usual bargain with the coastal peoples: if they would be peaceable, and spare not only the Christians but their livestock as well (their pigs rooted in the Indians' unfenced cornfields, nut pastures, and vegetable gardens) the governor-general would assure the natives justice, both personal and economic, in the provincial courts.

Renowewan rose, declared his acceptance of Andros' offer, and sealed the agreement with wampum, a massive belt fifteen strands wide and the length of his body. "His heart," said Renowewan as he held up the wampum, would be "so long and so good to the Governor-general and the Christians, and should never forget the Governor-general." Andros accepted Renowewan's pledge. In return he presented coats and cloth to the native dignitaries. Then, to show the Lenni-Lenape that his justice could be relied upon, he convened the first general court held on the Delaware.

With due formality, the court took their places. The governor-general sat in his chair of state. On his right were Governor Carteret, Captain Salisbury, and the two New York aldermen. Then the governor-general read aloud his commission from the duke. The sheriff and those of the fifteen new magistrates appointed for the three districts who were in attendance read their commissions from the governor-general. He administered to them their oaths to the duke, to the king, and to the duty of their office. Then the justices were seated on the governor-general's left. The crier called the court into session. The clerk took the roll. A jury was selected.

Fully constituted, the General Court of the Delaware was presented with the indictment of James Sandyman, prisoner at the bar, for manslaughter in the fatal ejectment from his tavern of the Indian Peeques. Since 27 March, Andros had demanded prosecution of this case "effectively without delay though not demanded by the Indyans." Only the governor-general's personal presence, however, now compelled the colonists to offer the Indians even the semblance of justice. Andros asked Renowewan and all his party to hear and, if they wished, to testify in the Sandyman case. A leading Lenni-Lenape did speak against Sandyman. The defendant, however, found other Indians to testify for him. The governor-general, bailiff-like, charged the jury, and he explained the law to the Indians in court. The jury retired, and returned some hours later with a verdict of "not guilty." [69]

The forms of justice had been fulfilled but the governor-general

69. Andros to Cantwell, 12 March 1675, *N.Y.C.D.*, XII, 518. Gehring, ed. and trans., *N.Y. Hist. Ms. Dutch*, 67, and see 74.

doubted that actual justice had been done. On his way home from the Delaware, he held a special court at Upland. After it, Andros stripped Sandyman of his militia captaincy, fined him for keeping a disorderly house, and, responding to the invariable request of native leaders, forbade retail sales of liquor to Indians. Andros had, as he wrote to Charles Calvert, "been the more hastened to this place by ye neighbouring Indyans rudeness with the Christians," but "all which I hope is now remedied." So it was. The fast friendship of the governor-general of New York and the presiding sachem of the Lenni-Lenape was a crucial contribution to their continued, shared, peaceable possession of the Delaware Valley, despite the brutal advances of Maryland's grandees (whom Andros warned off once again when he reported this settlement) and the retreat of the Susquehanna into what they still considered their dependency. So much would become apparent during Andros' negotiations of 1676 with Maryland and with the Lenni-Lenape over the disposition of the dispersed Susquehanna and the canceling of their claim to suzerainty on the Delaware.[70]

While the jury was out in the Sandyman case, the general court began to issue the orders by which the governor-general implemented his instructions from the duke, and obeyed his own constructive instincts, to improve trade and commerce, and to preserve religion, justice, and equity among the people of the Delaware Valley. Trade disputes—bad bills, bad bargains, bad debts, bad decisions by local officials—all were redressed by the court during its two-day session. Wills were reviewed, estates divided. (Was the "Jacob Young" who declined to appear to answer his mother-in-law's suit "Jacob my friend," the ally of the Susquehanna and the nemesis of Garacontié?) Commerce required communications. The Andros court acted to develop a riverside road linking the three towns, diked and bridged as necessary to avoid the dangerous woods. A ferry was established at the falls. Despite upriver complaints, Andros insisted on enacting exclusive privileges for Newcastle as a port of entry. Only thus could a local administrative and economic center be developed and customs revenue collected to finance the new regional government.[71]

Religion, regular and otherwise, also concerned Andros' general court at Newcastle. After much discussion of ministers and parishes, the court authorized a fourth church to serve the growing population of the valley. The district court at Upland was "empowered"—in words which described the hierarchy of civil government Andros had now established in the Delaware region—"to raise a tax for its building, and to agree upon a

---

70. Andros to Charles Calvert, 5 May 1675, *N.Y.C.D.*, XII, 528.
71. Gehring, ed. and trans., *N.Y. Hist. Ms. Dutch*, 74–77.

competent Maintenance for their Minister, of all which they are to give an account to the next General Court, and they to the Governor for his Approbation."[72]

In four days on the Delaware, Edmund Andros had constituted and exercised a government, civil, military, and religious, which soon produced three counties and then became the State of Delaware. He had secured for his master territories on the west bank far beyond anything the duke's patent specified. Yet, fresh among the "many troubles" that the locals observed Andros attacking, was command for the duke of the east bank of the river. It had seemed safely within the joint jurisdiction of the Lenni-Lenape and their friend the governor-general. It was clearly in the duke's domain, or so Andros thought. By sales and resales, all illegal and much too complex to narrate here, however, the "New Jersey" land claims of Lord Berkeley, derived from an old grant by the duke, had passed, for £1,000 cash, from the hands of that calculating courtier into those of Major John Fenwick.

Fenwick had been an officer of General Monck's in Scotland. In the citadel of Leith, Major Fenwick was converted to Quakerism by George Fox himself. George Monck's influence as captain general won Fenwick a pardon for his Cromwellian "crimes" from Charles II, but Fox's influence kept Fenwick preaching in the streets. There the king's soldiers beat him up. It seemed wise to leave London for less abusive climes. In November 1675. Fenwick sailed up the Delaware in the *Griffen* with 150 settlers. Landing on the east bank, he demanded that Major Andros recognize him as proprietor and governor of West New Jersey. He ejected planters from lands patented to them by the governor-general. Then he rejected Andros' orders that he come to New York to justify his pretensions and persecutions.

Major Andros had learned how to deal with defiance of his authority, and that of his royal masters, in a school every bit as hard as Major Fenwick's. As the unfortunate pretender protested, "my house was beset, my door broken down, my person seized on in the night time by armed men sent to execute a paper ordered from the Governor of New York, to whom I was sent prisoner in the depth of winter by sea, where he tried me, himself being judge, keeping me imprisoned for the space of two years and three months—albeit that it was not, nor could be proved that I had broken any of the Kings laws." As far as the governor-general was concerned, his authority and the duke's prerogative were the king's laws.[73]

72. Court Orders, 13, 14 May 1675, *ibid.*, no. 4. An uncorrected version is in *N.Y.C.D.*, XII, 576.

73. John E. Pomfret, *The Province of West   '' Jersey 1609–1702* (Princeton, N.J., 1956), 84.

SOUNDINGS

The governor-general left the Delaware determined to sail up to Albany to conclude his "extraordinary" tour "to the sevll parts of ye Governmt" —so like that by which Lord Willoughby had established his authority across the Leeward Islands. When Andros reached New York, however, he found a provocative reply, dated 17 May 1675, to his letter to the Connecticut General Court claiming western Connecticut. On 7 June, Major Andros replied that, since the Connecticut court had appealed to patents, he had the duke of York's new one open before him. It was perfectly clear from that royal grant that the duke's boundary was the Connecticut River. Therefore, Andros wrote, he concluded that the Connecticut authorities had conceded the disputed territory. Acting with his habitual secrecy, by 28 June, the governor-general had prepared proclamations declaring the duke's government in the affected towns and continuing in office all of the town officials who would swear allegiance to the king and fidelity to the duke. Major Andros then prepared a little expedition to sail to Saybrook, at the mouth of the Connecticut River, "Upon the Accot of the Limits expressed in his Maties L[ette]res Patents." [74]

In the meantime, the first fighting of King Philip's War had broken out in Plymouth Colony. The news reached Hartford, the Connecticut capital, on 1 July and was sent west by express to "Governour Andross." He received the messenger in Fort James at 3:00 a.m. on 4 July 1675. "Very much troubled at the Christians' misfortunes, and hard disasters, in those Parts, being so over powered by such heathens," the governor-general convened his council, secured their advice to speed up his previously planned visit, and wrote to the Connecticut authorities that he was prepared to sail with "a fforce to bee ready to take such Resolucons, as may bee fitt for mee, upon this extraordinary occasion, with which I intend (God Willing) to sett out this evening, and to make the best of my way to *Conecticutt* River, his Royall Highnesse Bounds there." [75]

Of course, Major Andros understood that this was not Connecticut's idea of the frontier. He knew "that *Connecticott* doth not expect or desire assistance from us in relacon to the Indyan Disturbance, at this time." His expedition would be seen by the colonists as the power-grab and exploitation of their misfortune that it was. The governor-general's council argued, however, that Connecticut had underestimated the threat from the natives and that the colony really would need, perhaps even want,

---

74. *N.Y.C.D.*, XII, 528. Franklin B. Hough, ed., *A Narrative of the Causes Which Led to Philip's Indian War, of 1675 and 1676 . . . with other Documents* (Albany, 1858), 51.
75. Trumbull, ed., *Records of Connecticut*, 332, 579. *N.Y.C.D.*, XIV, 691.

Andros' expert military assistance. In any case, the council thought that the colony's attitude about boundaries was a threat to the duke's prerogative and should be repressed whatever the occasion. The governor-general, it seemed to his council, had before him in Connecticut a double opportunity to extend protection and to enforce obedience.[76]

Unfortunately for Andros' imperial intentions, Saybrook was the founding fortress of Connecticut. When the sails of Andros' sloops were seen on the horizon early on the morning of 8 July 1675, Saybrook's militant minister called the saints to arms in defense of the godly commonwealth, lest their persons, estates, or consciences "be made a prey unto men." The governor-general was "amazed," or so he said, to see the Saybrook militia drawn up to resist his landing. Even before Andros' emissaries concluded preliminary negotiations with the embattled puritans, their reinforcements arrived from Hartford. There the receipt of Andros' letter of 4 July had excited immediate orders for armed resistance to him and to his pretensions to either jurisdiction or assistance.[77]

Andros took days to accept the impasse. As late as 13 July, "the Govr. Andross still speakes of his purposes of defence and protection of us here against the Indians, and wonders much at our jealous[y] of him." Finally everyone agreed to save face. The governor-general landed and, standing on the beach at Saybrook, proclaimed the duke's right to western Connecticut while the Connecticut militia turned their backs. Then the Connecticut captain, the aptly named Thomas Bull, bellowed Connecticut's protest against Andros' invasion and the duke's pretensions. This protest Andros immediately termed "a slander and so an ill requittal for his kindness" to Connecticut. Then the governor-general was rowed out to his sloop and his little fleet tried to sail away while their guns exchanged (ironic) salutes with the Saybrook fort. But the failing breeze so typical of "the Dead Sea" in summer denied Andros even a dignified exit from the scene of his defeat.[78]

Yet there was a real and growing military emergency to be coped with, the first phases of King Philip's War. Even though Connecticut refused to permit him to fight the war on the mainland—and the disappointed major never forgave them the loss of this grand professional opportunity—he had the duke's people to protect. He did it with an

---

76. Council minute, 4 July 1675, in Hough, ed., *Narrative*, 44. See also Thomas Dongan, "answer to enquiries" [March 1687], *C.S.P.C. 1685–1688*, 334, no. 1160: "I have found some memorandums of Sir Edmund Andros that he actually went out with an armed force to annex Connecticut in 1676, so convinced was he that this was necessary for New York." Only the clause beginning "so convinced" is quoted by Charles M. Andrews, *The Colonial Period of American History* (New Haven, 1937, 1964), III, 103 n. 2.

77. Rev. Th. Buckingham to the Connecticut Council, in Trumbull, ed., *Records of Connecticut*, 585.

78. *Ibid.*, 583–84.

efficiency and success that suggests what the puritans lost when they turned the governor-general away. Basing his flotilla at Southold, Andros dispatched sloops eastward, to New London, with munitions for the use of his friend Major Winthrop. He also sent ammunition to the Vineyard, Nantucket, and Rhode Island (with which colony, victimized as it was by the puritan commonwealths, Andros had the most cordial relations). The governor-general himself then visited all the eastern towns of Long Island before he rode down the island towards New York. He reviewed and encouraged the militia of every island town, disarmed the local Indians, ordered local retreats built for noncombatants. By securing Long Island, Andros not only prevented local native risings, but also cut off the "Genll Intelligence & confederacy between the Indyans even to Delaware Bay" which was feared by the battered New Englanders.[79]

By contrast with New England and every settlement outside of New York and north of Albemarle Sound, Long Island (like every part of Andros' command) was spared the slightest physical harm during the greatest Indian war in American history, the enormous Algonquin uprising of 1675–76. As Long Island and many other instances demonstrated, Andros' unequaled military preparedness played its part in winning his command this happy exemption from disaster. Even more important, however, was the governor-general's inspired Indian diplomacy with every native nation in the duke's dominions, all the way from the Delaware to the Hoosac, even on to the Kennebec. This it was that made New York and its dependencies islands of interracial symbiosis in a sea of red-white strife.

In negotiations as in war, had the puritans been able to admit Andros' abilities, the devastation of King Philip's War might have been prevented. The Rhode Island authorities had met with King Philip just before the outbreak of hostilities. They proposed that the governor-general of New York arbitrate the disputes between Philip's people and the Plymouth colonists. Andros was, the Rhode Islanders told the aggrieved Indians, the representative of the king, the "one supreme to Englishmen." Without the king's command, the Rhode Islanders said, no loyal Englishman would make war, much less, as the disloyal puritan bigots had done, violate "the law of nations and the law of arms" in order to defy their monarch's prerogative and despoil the natives' property. The Rhode Islanders contrasted Edmund Andros to the puritan theocrats, "so blinded by the spirit of persecution" toward both Native Americans and loyal Englishmen. The governor-general, they said, was not just, as a royal officer, the sole legitimate arbiter of peace and war, he had already established an unblemished reputation for fair dealing with the Indians. Tragically, "King Philip's War" was begun by the puritans of Plymouth before Andros' good offices could be called upon. There was now nothing to save New England from the just recompense of its racism.[80]

80. John Easton, "A Relacon of the Indyan Warre, 1675," in Lincoln, ed., *Narratives*, 17.

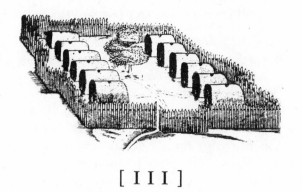

[III]

THE COVENANT CHAIN

Introduction

The forging of the Covenant Chain illustrates the paradox of seventeenth-century America. All of its societies were not only still dependent upon Europe, they were also, increasingly, reliant upon it technologically and politically. So much 1676 had shown to all who doubted, whether Baconian independents or New England republicans. Even while losing their present independence, however, the Americans of 1676 outlined their future freedom through acts of self-determination. In the case of the Covenant Chain, these acts were elaborate and consequential diplomatic agreements, accomplished in peculiarly American forms, shaping the present ownership and government, the future nationality and culture, of the early American heartland.

The independence of Amerindians and Anglo-Americans had declined dramatically in the years between 1654, when Daniel Garacontié and Edmund Andros had entered public life, and 1677, when the Sagochiendagehté died at Onnontagé and the governor-general sailed for London. From the first, Garacontié's diplomatic career was directed by the technological imperative of Amerindian dependence upon European weaponry, tools, and textiles. As the Europeans militarized and centralized their colonial outposts, Garacontié had also to accommodate Iroquois ambitions to the amplified physical and political presence of the French and English empires. Edmund Andros' parallel career was premised upon the rise of England to European military prominence and the consequent expansion of its Atlantic empire. He first encountered Indians and fought the French in defense of England's staple-crop colonies in the West Indies. Then Andros was ordered to garrison and govern conquered New York on behalf of that eminent imperialist the duke of York, and as part of the rising English empire's deprivation of the Dutch. Andros' career was not just a consequence of European imperial rivalries; his instructions were premised upon English recognition that the fledgling province of New York was an apt instrument by which to extend imperial authority on the American continent. Yet Andros quickly saw that his ability to defy the French, coerce New England, subdue the Dutch, and define Delaware all depended upon conciliating the Iroquois, a fact not hitherto appreciated at Whitehall.

Garacontié's reciprocal recognition, that the prosperity, perhaps the survival, of his people required not only an evasion of French power but also an exploitation of the new English resources of New York, represented by "Corleaer" (as the Iroquois henceforward addressed Andros), brought the Anglo-Iroquoian statesmen together. Their first meeting appears to have been at Tinontougen, on the western edge of Mohawk country, in August 1675. There they began to forge the Covenant Chain, a uniquely American agreement but one with unequaled results for the outcomes of European imperial rivalry.

Both the subjects and the methods of Anglo-Iroquoian diplomacy were entirely American, despite the trans-Atlantic imperial dynamic that propelled their principals. The transfer of sovereignty in the Susquehanna and Delaware valleys, from aboriginal suzerains and proprietary claimants to the Five Nations and New York; their joint resolve to resist the encroachment of New France in the Anglo-Iroquoian sphere south of the St. Lawrence and Lake Ontario; their agreement to pacify and preserve the Mahican, as the riverine defenders of the Anglo-Iroquoian heartland—all achieved at Tinontougen in the summer of 1675, prepared the peoples of the Sagochiendagehté and Corleaer to profit from the catastrophes of 1676 and, as it happened, to define the shared domain of the grand council of the Iroquois and the privy council of England for a century to come.

The assault on King Philip and his Quebec-backed allies by the Iroquois, directed and supplied from New York, opened western and northern New England to the Anglo-Iroquoian alliance and filled its ranks with refugees. Imperial opportunities and refugee reinforcements led to a second set of negotiations between Garacontié and Corleaer, this time in English territory, at Albany, in June 1676. The Anglo-Iroquoian principals and their coadjutors assessed the opening to the east: they reviewed

Mahican resettlement; they agreed to absorb the Algonquin refugees; they offered to negotiate with the New England colonies; and they began to look towards a Mohawk-Yorkist condominium in Maine at the expense of the Abenaki enemies of the Iroquois and the puritan opponents of the crown.

The contentious issue of the 1676 council was the future of mid-America. A vast region between the coastal settlements of the English and the Ohio enterprise of the Iroquois, between the southern edge of Iroquoia proper (today's New York–Pennsylvania line approximates this boundary) and a line extending south and west from the head of the Chesapeake towards the Blue Ridge and thence down the Virginia Piedmont to the Catawba, had been opened to the Five Nations by the dispersion and defeat of the Susquehanna. Here and now, all English interests took second place to those of the Iroquois. Buoyed up by the triumphant conclusion of a generation of war with the mighty "roily water people," the four western nations of the Iroquois ("the Seneca," in English terminology) rebuffed Andros' every effort either to make the Susquehanna his tributaries in their old homeland or to absorb them into the Delaware or Mohawk populations under his aegis.

Andros had spent most of 1676, up to the time of the Albany conference in June, negotiating with the potential parties to his proposed protectorate, but the western Iroquois simply rounded up the Susquehanna and took control of their former territory. Rather than risk losing it to Maryland, Andros acquiesced in his allies' accessions. The upshot was that Garacontié used the next available diplomatic opportunity to have every English colony acknowledge the western Iroquois' acquisitions. He did so by making international agreements in the traditional Iroquoian form, the condolence council. He called the resulting treaty complex the "Covenant Chain."

This apogee of Anglo-Iroquoian diplomacy was reached in two stages, one in April and the second in July and August of 1677. In the April negotiations, Corleaer and the Mohawk consolidated their gains to the east in the wake of their victory over King Philip and their humiliation of puritan New England. They met with agents of Massachusetts and Connecticut, of the Mahican and Mohegan, and of those Algonquin refugees from New England afterwards known as the "River Indians." The Anglo-Iroquoian allies promised the New England colonists to defend the northern frontier against the French and their native clients and to attack the Abenaki in Maine. In return, the colonial agents gave goods to the Mohawk, acknowledged Andros' regional sway, and formally admitted the sovereignty of England's king over all his subjects, even in New England. The Algonquin refugees took shelter from both the New Englanders and the Mohawk under Andros' "Tree of Peace." In return for the governor-general's protection, they agreed to patrol the eastern frontier of New York, from the Hoosac down the length of the Hudson, against all incursions, colonial or aboriginal.

Their eastern border secured, Corleaer and the Mohawk met Garacontié and the western Iroquois at Albany during the height of the summer of 1677. In this, the second stage of the Covenant Chain council, the conferees undertook to establish the diplomatic, territorial, geopolitical outcomes of the Susquehanna war and the Chesapeake revolution. This agenda had been generally suggested to the Iroquois by Corleaer in May as a summary of their past two years' discussions. In June, the ambassadors of the Chesapeake colonies and their Indian allies had been allowed by Andros to add specific proposals regarding their relations with the conquerors of the Susquehanna. The governor-general could not control the Iroquois' disposition of the Susquehanna but he could and did control colonial approaches to "his" Iroquois. Representatives of Algonquin peoples dwelling between the Delaware and the Hoosac also attended this diplomatic conference, for it aimed at establishing nothing less than "a universal peace" in Eastern America.

To the English initiatives of Corleaer and the Chesapeake colonists, Garacontié himself responded for the Five Nations and their dependents, the Susquehanna included. He pledged Iroquoian adherence to "an Absolute Covenant of peace" among all the contracting parties. This covenant, Garacontié said, would "Bind with a Chain" the Five Nations to each other and to Corleaer. Through him the chain would connect the Iroquois to the Chesapeake peoples, the River Indians, the New Englanders, and even to "the Great King Charles who liveth over the Great Lake."

Garacontié announced that, in proclaiming the Covenant Chain, he had replicated his great peace with Onnontio and the French, made twenty-three years earlier. Just as the Iroquois' campaign against the French and their Huron allies, the pursuit of the Huron fugitives north and west into the territories of such nations as the Erie, Petun, Tobacco, and Nez-Percé, and the Iroquois' obliteration or disposal of these peoples had passed from conquest to consolidation in 1654, so the subsequent wars of the Iroquois against the Susquehanna to the south, and the Mahican and Sokoki to the east, were transformed from hostility to incorporation as Garacontié forged the Covenant Chain in 1677. Neither peace ended the wars of the Iroquois, but each vastly enhanced their political range, their economic importance, and their territorial sphere. And the Covenant Chain so linked the Iroquois to the English as to determine the future of America.

It was at the invitation of Corleaer that Garacontié had defined the new southern sphere of the Iroquois in condolence-council terms. Edmund Andros' special relationship with the Iroquois was variously defined by the Five Nations. The Mohawk asserted that "the governr. Genll. & We are One." The Seneca declared that the governor-general "We have taken to be our greatest lord." In Five Nations form and in English fact, the governor-general of the duke's dominions became the chief intermediary between the Iroquois and the colonists of every colony, as well as the nominal agent of the Iroquois' Indian allies and dependents from Maine to the Carolinas.

Between these boundaries, the events of 1676 had proven and the Covenant Chain confirmed, that the Anglo-Iroquoian allies were the predominant powers everywhere outside the settled areas of the older colonies. The cooperation of the English imperialists and the Iroquoian nations therefore secured almost a century of primarily peaceful development for mideastern America. The Covenant Chain encircled the great growth area of the American colonies in the coming century, and of their successor states, ultimately pre-eminent in the Union. For two hundred years after 1676, a succession of the most significant American societies were established within the confines marked out by Garacontié, Corleaer, and their associates.

In part, this was so because the English context of American development was redefined as a result not just of the experiences of 1676 but of the reports of that year's imperial initiatives and Iroquoian acts presented to the English privy council by Sir Edmund Andros. Knighted for his success in creating a universal peace and an imperial presence in the wake of widespread war and autarchical assertions, Sir Edmund insisted that the imperial executive must henceforward determine peace and war in America, control negotiations with the Amerindians, and reorganize American institutions according to English norms by uniting the scattered colonies and offering their peoples princely and prerogative alternatives to popular and parochial institutions.

Andros' observations so well summarized the changes in Whitehall's world view wrought by the events of 1676 that his recommendations characterized imperial policy for decades to come, as regards both American colonists and Amerindians. Indeed, the Anglo-Iroquoian alliance Andros had negotiated with Garacontié survived until 1982. English language, institutions, and imperialism as yet prevail in the region of the Covenant Chain.

Corleaer at Tinontougen
(and Albany)

B y 4 August 1675, the dreadful war was irreversibly under way and the governor-general was back in New York, ready to take sloop up the Hudson on his long-intended voyage to all-important negotiations with "the Maques and their Associates" of the Five Nations. On 5 August, Andros left his lieutenant in command of Fort James and sailed upriver. Two days later he was at Esopus (Kingston). There he reconfirmed the peace with the local Mahican band and reviewed the town's militia (stronger than most, given its infusion of soldier-settlers from Colonel Nicolls' garrison). Reaching Albany in mid-August, the governor-general exhibited that insight into the empire and the Indians which distinguished the entirety of his quarter-century in American commands.[1]

He realized, as those far more experienced in the Mohawk-oriented trade of Albany had not done, that not just the Mohawk keepers of its eastern door but, rather, the entire Iroquoian League encompassed the future of English empire in America. The great menace to that future, Andros observed, was the French government's intimidation of the Iroquois and their subversion by the Jesuits. On his arrival in Albany, Major Andros called in Father Bruyas from the Mohawk country and ordered him to avoid politics in his Iroquoian mission. The governor-general also warned his counterpart in New France "not to molest" the Mohawk further and "forthwith to release any hostages" of the Iroquois. Informed by his Caribbean service about the importance of the Indians and the danger of the French to English empire, Major Andros was also instructed by the duke to devote "yor best care and conduct in the well management of an affaire of soe great importance to his service" as keeping the French on their side of the lake and protecting the Mohawk as the managers of the trade of the Five Nations.[2]

It was the trade of Albany, especially the arms trade, which won the

1. Franklin B. Hough, ed., *A Narrative of the Causes Which Led to Philip's Indian War, of 1675 and 1676 . . . with other Documents* (Albany, 1858), 68–69.
2. John Romelyn Brodhead, ed., *Documents Relative to the Colonial History of the State of New York* (Albany, 1853) (hereafter cited as *N.Y.C.D.*), III, 233; XIII, 483.

Iroquois for the English and which underlay the triumph of the Five Nations. Albany, however, was just as dependent on the Iroquois hunters, looters, and traders as they were on the weapons and utensils for which they traded every imaginable kind of fur. New York's chief, almost its sole, returns to England were fifteen kinds of fur. Therefore, the duke's orders to build up "ye Forts of New York and New Albany, upon wch . . . depend ye safety and trade of ye whole country" also compelled his lieutenant to court the Iroquois. To the east of Albany as well, the Iroquois were vital to Andros' command. The executives of New York over many years had found the Five Nations the best, if not the only, means of disciplining the tribes of southern and western New England. To these objectives of New York's Iroquoian association, Andros added those of resisting French influence among the tribesmen of northern New England and of countering the wiles of New England merchants among the Hudson Valley peoples. Determined to defend the upper Hudson from the territorial and mercantile designs of Massachusetts, based on its Springfield outpost, and from those of Connecticut, centered on its emigrants in Northampton, Massachusetts, Andros realized, as he considered the widening context of King Philip's War, that if he could amplify Iroquoian influence on the Algonquin tribes to the east, he could put paid to New England expansion to the west. Andros intended to save Albany, the Iroquois, and the future of mid-America from the puritans as well as from the papists.[3]

Such intentions put the highest priority upon an agreement with the Iroquois. No sooner had Andros landed in Albany than he set out overland to extend personally to the Five Nations the terms of alliance he had already offered the coastal and riverine peoples. He discovered that the Iroquois had imperial ideas of their own. To meet the native dictators of the American future, Edmund Andros had marched west 100 miles through the Mohawk country to "Tiondondoge our third Castle," the Mohawk recalled. And he sent runners 300 miles before him to invite every one of the Five Nations to the council at Tinontougen. There, at the eastern terminus of the Five Nations road between Onondaga and the Mohawk River, the governor-general of New York met in formal council with sachems of the Iroquois.[4]

At Tinontougen, the governor-general "was pleased to accept" from the Five Nations the "council name" of a man "that was of good disposition & esteemed deare amongst us (to witt) The Old Corleaer." At Tinon-

3. *Ibid.*, III, 216. C.O. 5/1112, 5.
4. *N.Y.C.D.*, III, 559.

tougen, the new Corleaer accepted the wampum pledges of the Five
Nations. These renewed "there former Allyance" with the Albanians and
the English and extended it to Corleaer personally. This the Iroquois did
"in an Extraordinary manner," Andros noted, "with reitterated promises
accordingly."[5]

At Tinontougen, Corleaer was impressed not only by these formal
repetitions of mnemonic ritual, but also by the Five Nations' initiatives
regarding joint military efforts with New York against mutual enemies
and their anticipations of increased Iroquoian use of and reliance on the
governor-general's leadership of all the English governments in America.
At Tinontougen, Edmund Andros must have met Daniel Garacontié, for
ever afterwards he asked for him by name when negotiations of note
were intended between the English and the Iroquois. At Tinontougen,
as their subsequent references to these discussions show, the Sagochiendagehté and Corleaer discussed the reduction of the Susquehanna and
the control of their valley by the western Iroquoian nations, the restoration of the kinship relation of the Susquehanna to the Mohawk, and the
protection of the Christian colonists of the Chesapeake during the war
which these "adjustments" would entail. Andros himself undertook to
"order matters accordingly" with the Susquehanna and to alter the Lenni-
Lenape status from tributaries of the Susquehanna to clients of the governor-general, and of his particular associates among the Iroquois, the
Mohawk. Corleaer further agreed to make a final peace between the Five
Nations and the Mahican. They were then relocated during 1675–77 as a
buffer and link between the peoples of New York and the Algonquin of
southern and western New England. In the course of those years, the
Mahican first allied with Philip's forces and then led their survivors, the
"River Indians," into a lasting agreement with Edmund Andros to define
and protect the eastern boundaries of New York. After Tinontougen,
therefore, Corleaer and his Iroquoian brethren were poised to expand
both the English empire and the Five Nations' sphere. They would win
great and mutual gains for their symbiotic sovereignties out of the catastrophe of King Philip's War and the devastation of the Chesapeake Revolution. The Anglo-Iroquoian empire emerged from the American
cataclysms of 1676.[6]

By 24 August, "the Right Honorable Governor General Edmund Andross" was back in Albany. There he presided over the Court of Albany,
Rensselaerwyck and Schenectady. This court, like its counterparts
formed or reformed by Andros in every district of the duke's dominions,
was the governor-general's agency for defining and directing the magis-

5. *Ibid.*, 254.
6. Andros to the governor of Maryland, 21 October 1675, *ibid.*, XIII, 491.

tracy, militia, and ministry. These were the agents, everywhere in the empire, of imperial authority—and, in New York, of Major Andros.[7]

In these sessions of the Albany court, the governor-general issued orders which reshaped the municipality along lines English and military. He instituted the office of constable and ordered its holders to double the watch and to impose the discipline of a garrison on the daily schedules of the inhabitants: reveille, tattoo, gate guards, and patrols became the routine of the town. The governor-general had the local long guns moved to the new fort and mounted on ships' carriages. He had short guns put on field carriages for the use of the town militia. He commanded the repair of the fort's bastions and the city's gates, lest the disasters of New England be visited on Albany.

The best preservative of peace, however, was cautious, fair, and officially supervised dealings with the natives. Andros empowered the Albany commissaries to sit with the commandant as a board of commissioners for Indian affairs. In cooperation with these experienced partners of the Five Nations, the governor-general tried to reduce the traffic of native middlemen, whether Iroquois or Algonquin, with New France. In the interests of making Albany's trade fairer and so more attractive to the Indians, Andros had the court forbid any dealings with the natives, hospitality excepted, "outside the city of Albany." Trade was to take place publicly, under the supervision of the English commandant and the Albany commissaries, lest the Indians be abused, with alcohol or otherwise. Andros sailed from Albany for New York at the end of August. To help hold the town, he left behind him most of his escort. His brother-in-law, Ensign Caesar Knapton, and that vastly experienced sergeant Thomas Sharpe, also remained in Albany to carry out Corleaer's agreements with the Five Nations.[8]

Gunpowder and Geopolitics

The governor-general had made it clear that he expected his officers to meet the rising storm of King Philip's War not, as every other English colony save Rhode Island did, by attacking Indians *per se*, but, rather, by

7. A. J. F. Van Laer, ed. and trans., *Minutes of the Court of Albany, Rensselaerwyck and Schenectady 1675–1680* (Albany, 1928), II, 9.
8. *Ibid.*, 17.

honoring the new pacts of mutual peace and protection which Edmund
Andros had made with every native nation in the duke's dominions from
the Hudson to the Delaware. "Resolved," wrote the clerk of the executive
council at its first meeting after Andros returned from Albany (10 September 1675), "that we ought not to breake with our Indyans upon Acct of ye
Warre between Our Neighbours and their Indyans." Even New England
would be helped, although the puritans never admitted it, by New York's
native alliances. At the least, these kept most of the nations west of the
Hudson and south of the Sound from adding themselves to New England's long list of enemies. Here again, the crucial fact in persuading
smaller septs to honor the peace was Corleaer's alliance with the predominant Iroquois.[9]

The governor-general and council summoned "all the Sachems" of
the Long Island and River peoples to Fort James "to acquaint them with
ye Peace made above at Albany, and to assure [them] that comporting
themselves as they ought, and have done, they shall be protected, and
may live quiet." In a week's time, delegations from these neighboring
bands met the governor-general in the fort "to bid him welcome Home
and promise all Friendship . . . assuring him that their Heads were good"
and exchanging presents with him. Andros got deerskins and hostages.
He gave duffel coats and drams of liquor. Andros also ordered their weapons returned to all the tribes save those tributaries of the Narragansett at
the eastern end of Long Island. Even they were to enjoy "equall Justice,
and (if quiet) Protection as others of ye Government."[10]

The other eastern Long Islanders were the puritan townsmen. They
were horrified at Andros' leniency. They always took their ideas from
Connecticut. There it was gospel that all Indians were enemies and
should be treated as such. The townsmen said that the local tribes were
preparing to massacre them. The governor-general's response was to punish them for rumormongering. He reminded the panicked puritans that
the best way to create enemies where none actually existed was to exhibit
fear and act with hostility.

On the other hand, real dangers had to be guarded against and reasonable precautions taken to reassure the European populace: protection is
the price of obedience. So the governor-general again ordered the watch
doubled in every locality. To impede communication with the Narragansett, he had native canoes confiscated along the Sound and also sent out
an armed sloop on patrol. He ordered exposed settlements along the
Hudson to get in goods and grain from all their outlying farms and to
fortify at least a portion of every village's houses. He sent cannon to

9. Hough, ed., *Narrative*, 71.
10. *Ibid.*, 76.

places willing to build bastions for them. He forbade the sale of gunpowder to any Indian on Long Island or at New York.

On 10 October, Andros learned of the Philippine victories in the upper Connecticut Valley and of Algonquin plans to attack Hartford at midmonth. He hurried off a warning to the Connecticut authorities, and he sent Captain Brockholes up to Albany with reinforcements for the garrison and orders to arm the Iroquois against the possibility of an Algonquin invasion of New York. The governor-general ordered his lieutenant to provide the Five Nations ("the Maques and Sinnekes") with all the munitions they asked for, but no other natives were to be sold powder or lead. As the war spread west through New England in the autumn of 1675, Hadley and Deerfield, Northfield and Springfield were torched. Alarmed at the approach of the conflagration, the governor-general prepared to animate the Iroquois against the rebellious Mahican of the upper Hudson and other local recruits to King Philip's cause.[11]

On 19 October the governor-general learned of the destruction of Springfield. He ordered Captain Brockholes not only to redouble Albany's guards but also to execute Andros' new instructions about the Iroquois: they were to be urged to attack not just King Philip's Hudson recruits but Philip's own armies. Inciting the Iroquois, the Albany captain was to keep up that tone of command which was fundamental to Andros' success with the native nations. It was vital that "the Maques may see tis ffriendship, not Apprehension or Need of them, but for their Good," that led Corleaer to suggest targets of mutual opportunity and to arm them for the attack. "Hearing that they and the Sinnekes are inclinable to a Warre with the Indyans to the East," the governor-general wrote, "twere well the said Maques were rather encouraged than hindred; and you may let them have a free Market for Powder &c. as formerly, continued."[12]

Andros reiterated his orders that no other Indians were to be sold ammunition, save for quarter-pound lots to some newly allied Mahicans personally known to the commandant or the commissaries, and to beaver hunters outbound from trading furs at Albany. Albany merchants nonetheless exchanged powder for plunder with "the Northern Indians," a term applied both to Philip's people and, more accurately, to their Sokoki and Abenaki allies. New England's accusation that their Indian enemies were supplied from Albany was accurate. What cannot be established is whether or not the governor-general of New York knew that it was.[13]

Andros did know that if these allegations of aid given to the heathen against the Christians by persons in his government were believed in

11. *Ibid.*, 91. John Romelyn Brodhead, *History of the State of New York* (New York, 1871), II, 289–90.
12. Hough, ed., *Narrative*, 100.
13. Van Laer, ed. and trans., *Minutes of Albany*, II, 56.

England, they would devastate his reputation. Worse, they "would not only reflect on mee, and all the Magistrates of this Government, but also on his Royal Highnesse, and the King himself, whose Commissions I have." To protect the image of the empire as protective of Englishmen, their settlements and societies, Andros had to rebut the charges.[14]

On 7 December 1675, the charges were printed in Boston. Andros responded by sending special emissaries to the commonwealth capital from New York to protest what he insisted was a libel on his government. When he was home on furlough to receive his knighthood from the king (and cash and commendations from the duke), Sir Edmund Andros protested to the plantations committee of the privy council about this slander. The agents of Massachusetts were summoned to the council board and made to admit that they had no evidence to support any such reports. They declared that, if such trade with the heathen enemy had taken place, it was doubtless done by the soulless Dutch and without the knowledge of the English governor-general. Andros bridled even at this sort of imputation. There were, he had said to the Connecticut magistrates when they made such a charge in the winter of 1675–76, no "Dutch" in New York, "there being none in this government but his Maties subjects, which obeyed all his lawes," without any distinction of race or nationality.[15]

Such a racially blind policy did wonders for domestic peace and social tranquillity in the duke's dominions but, besides their resentment that Andros refused to act according to their racial prejudices against Indians and Dutchmen, the New Englanders resented the very existence of the ducal domain as putting limits to their expansion. They hated the duke's governor-general as the enlarger of these dominions and as the exponent of anglican empire. They resented his commercially successful European subjects. They feared his, as they saw them, treacherous Indian allies and tributaries. The Albany arms trade, the basis of New York prosperity and Iroquoian power, was therefore offensive to New Englanders even when it was not abused to supply their heathen enemies. The puritans then, and their laudators now, could not and cannot believe that, in the first three months of 1676, Edmund Andros rallied the multiracial forces of New York to defeat decisively King Philip and his allies. So doing, the governor-general won the war for New England. At least as important, he secured mid-America for the English empire and the Five Nations.

14. Andros to the governor of Rhode Island, 25 December 1675, in Hough, ed., *Narrative*, 130.
15. Andros to the governor and council of Connecticut, 20 January 1675 [/6], in J. Hammond Trumbull, ed., *The Public Records of Connecticut from 1675 to 1678* (Hartford, 1852), 404.

The Assault on King Philip

In the first week of 1676, the governor-general was alarmed that "the Indyans to the Eastward" had "soe great Success in Plymouth and Massachusetts Colonyes" that they had been able to incite virtually all the New England Indians against the colonists, that they had recruited French-supplied and French-directed "Northern" Indians as well, and that they were now "endeavouring by all Meanes of Command and Profitt to engage the Maques" in the war against New England. Despite Algonquin invitations and Jesuit subversion, however, there "remained firm the Maques and by there Meanes the Sinnekes," Andros wrote. He added that, since the Five Nations' strategic position was unequaled, for "Good or Harme," they could only be dealt with diplomatically, being "too farre and particularly the Sennekes [the western four Iroquois nations], if they fall off to be forced." [16]

Fortunately for the future of English America, Edmund Andros' diplomacy with the all-important Iroquois had not only retained their allegiance, but had also underwritten and organized an offensive against the Algonquins. On the night of 5–6 January 1675/6, Andros received word "that Philip & 4 or 500 North Indians, fighting men, were come within 40 or 50 miles of Albany" to take up winter quarters. The governor-general instantly sent north to Captain Brockholes the orders that determined King Philip's War. In Corleaer's name, the Albany commandant was to send to the Mohawk an offer of shelter for "their old men, wives & children . . . within our Towne & Fortifications" at Albany and to issue from the fort magazines "all necessaries"—weapons, food, and clothing—for their warriors, providing that the Mohawk, and such of their western kinsmen as they could quickly call upon, would attack King Philip's winter camp at Hoosac Falls. Within the month, the Mohawk and their brethren had taken up the governor-general's unprecedented offer. As the Mohawk remembered the decisive moment, "our Govr Genll did Incourage us, & told how his frindes in N. England were involved in a great war wt Indians and that some of yr Enemyes were fledd to hoosack, Incourageing us to goe out against them." [17]

16. Andros to the governor of Maryland, 10 December 1675, in Hough, ed., *Narrative*, 123–24.
17. Trumbull, ed., *Records of Connecticut*, 397; *N.Y.C.D.*, XIII, 509, 528.

On 4 February 1675/6, the governor-general revealed how far the Anglo-Iroquoian plans had advanced by asking the Connecticut authorities if they "would desire & admit our forces, Xtians or Indians, particularly Maquase & Senques, to pursue such enemies, unto any part of yor Colony." In any case Andros warned the puritan oligarchs that their wonted ways with the natives would not do in dealing with the Iroquois. The Connecticut government, Corleaer said, must warn their own forces, and those of Massachusetts in the upper Connecticut Valley, not to offer the least provocation to the "Maquase or Sineques" they would soon encounter. Any affront to the Iroquois would prove of ill consequence, "the Sineques & associates being 3000 or more good fighting men, and to farr to be easily forced. . . ." [18]

The "good fighting men" were now ready to march. On 8 February 1675/6, the Albany commander rushed runners down the Hudson River ice to tell the governor-general that the crisis was at hand. Andros replied urging that every encouragement be given to the Iroquois, every precaution taken to secure Albany, its dependencies and peoples. At this moment, Andros also heard from both the Massachusetts and Connecticut authorities. They repeated their suspicions of him and of his Iroquoian allies, "we haveing had so large experience of sundry other Indians that have long prtended friendship to us & other English, who have in this day of conspiracy proved false." [19]

New Englanders' narrowness had never been worse-timed. As their letters were read at Fort James, Edmund Andros was interrogating English scouts escaped from Philip's army. They reported that 2,100 warriors were encamped along the Hoosac. Most of them were Philip's allies from southern New England, the largest number being Narragansett escaped from the Great Swamp Fight in mid-December. There were "Northern Indians" also, Sokoki and Abenaki. In addition, "5 or 600 French Indians with straws in their Noses" were encamped along the Hoosac, their pouches full of French gunpowder. The local Mahican had welcomed and were provisioning this army of young men who boasted of their plans to level Hatfield, Hartford, and Boston in the spring. [20]

Despite the numbers and equipment of the enemy, the Mohawk and their Iroquoian brethren were prepared to act on Corleaer's invitation. Brockholes wrote from Albany on 12 February 1675/6 that "ye Maques Indyans being moved in a warrlike Manner against ye North Indyans," he had kept Corleaer's part of the bargain and supplied their warriors, sheltered their noncombatants. As the Mohawk themselves said, "we and

18. Trumbull, ed., *Records of Connecticut,* 406.
19. *Ibid.,* 406–7.
20. Examination of Thomas Warner, 25 February 1675[/6], in Hough, ed., *Narrative,* 143–45. For the London reports and reactions regarding this crisis, see Part II, 238–41.

our Govr Genll being as it were one body, [we] went out, upon his desire against them [the Algonquin army], and killed some and Putt ye Rest to ye flight, & soe have Continued in ye warr ever since."[21]

As the governor-in-council considered the Albany dispatches, the ice opened on the Hudson, a month betimes. Andros and his advisers made three momentous decisions. The governor-general would take all the available soldiers and munitions up to Albany in six sloops, "forthwith to settle matters there, it being of very great import." He would not consult Connecticut, Plymouth, or Massachusetts colonies, or permit them to interfere in his Indian diplomacy, alliances, or war, they "not having made us acquainted with their Concernes, and some of them slighted our friendly Tenders." Andros was to act "for the good of this Government." To that end, a new diplomatic front, another potential expansion of the Corleaer-Iroquois condominium, would be opened by negotiation with the "North Indians." These discussions were designed to redeem the upper Hudson and Hoosac regions from the ambitions of Massachusetts and Connecticut, perhaps even to liberate Maine from the puritan usurpers.[22]

On 4 March 1675/6, Edmund Andros landed at Albany "and found att his arrivall aboutt three hundred Maquaas Souldiers in towne, returned ye Evening afore from ye pursuite of Philip and a party of five hundred with him, whome they had beaten, having some prisoners & the crowns, or hayre and skinne of the head, of others they had killed." The Iroquois warriors—for several of the upper nations had joined in the Mohawk attack—reported that the Hoosac camps had been broken up by the Five Nations' assault and that the several New England native nationalities had been dispersed. The Abenaki and Sokoki had fled towards the Canadian refugee camps. Philip's own people had scattered towards the Connecticut River. The first objective of the English and Iroquoian allies was accomplished: their joint territory was cleared of the enemy. Second, the Algonquin capacity to attack the chief New England towns had been eliminated. Third, the allies' influence was now palpable in southern New England. There the terror of the name "Mohawk" lasted for a hundred years in Algonquin minds. There was no further New England effort to infiltrate New York for three-quarters of a century.[23]

The imperial-minded governor-general and his brethren the Mohawk, always the most aggressive of the Iroquois, nonetheless disagreed about the uses to be made of their joint victory. Corleaer tried to stop "the

21. Council minutes, 26 February 1675/6, in Hough, ed., *Narrative*, 147. Testimony of six Mohawk sachems, 1 August 1678, in *N.Y.C.D.*, XIII, 528.

22. *N.Y.C.D.*, XIII, 493–94.

23. "A short Accompt of the Generall Concerns of New Yorke from October 1674 to November 1677," *N.Y.C.D.*, III, 255.

people of the flint" from raiding southern New England. They might well
run afoul of the trigger-happy colonists, whom, as Christians, he was
bound to protect from the very Indians with whom he was leagued.
Besides, Andros had better uses for Philip's people than slow incineration
by the Mohawk. He wanted to settle the remnants of the New England
nations in the Hoosac Valley, securing it for New York and increasing the
population of the duke's dominions.

The governor-general sent Lieutenant Gerrit Teunise out from Albany "to finde out Philip or other North Indians, lately within this Gov-
emt," secure from them any Christian prisoners, and warn them not to
invade New York again. In the spring, however, they would find that he
had "planted a Tree of Peace" for them in the Hoosac Valley. Under its
shade they might live safe from both the Iroquois warriors and the English colonists. Lieutenant Teunise's mission was a great success. He met
with some four hundred warriors from five varied nations in Philip's
camp. From them the lieutenant secured close to one hundred English
captives, an earnest alike of the shortage of provisions among the fugitives and of their interest in Andros' offer. This offer, uncounted hundreds
of southern New England Indians took up during 1676.[24]

As the success of the Teunise mission showed, the Anglo-Iroquoian
attack on Philip's forces in February 1675/6 had been the decisive action
in the war: the Algonquin army never reassembled and its southern components fled from the Iroquois back to the Connecticut Valley and into
the grasp of the colonial troops, red and white, Jamaicans and New Englanders. The remnant of Philip's own force was found on the Connecticut
at Turner's Falls by the Hadley and Northampton militiamen on 18 May
1676. There, as an Indian survivor said, "the shot came in like rain upon
us." The westward recoil of Philip's people was stopped by another Mohawk attack in June. By July 1676, there remained only two choices for
Philip's people, to flee west to the Hudson and see if "the great man's"
offer of safety was genuine, or to slip home to tribal territories. Philip
himself chose the second option. His fate was typical of those who did.
He was hunted down in his ancestral homeland of Mount Hope, where
the war had begun, by a party of Plymouth Indian-hunters, red and white.
King Philip was killed, dismembered, and displayed on 12 August 1676.[25]

The death of Philip, the dispersion of his allies, the domestication of

24. *Ibid.*, XIII, 494. Hough, ed., *Narrative*, 148.

25. Court-martial of Indians charged with complicity in Philip's design, in Hough, ed.,
Narrative, 180–81. Francis Bretton to Sec. Williamson, "9 br ye 9," 1676: "all things are very
quiet at New England, ye Indians being in July discomfited & become more slaves yn
formerly, King Philip & ye Queen taken his head on ye gates of Plimouth, & his quarters on
ye gates of Boston & ye Queen burned . . . ," State Papers Domestic, vol. 386, Public Record
Office (hereafter cited as S.P. 29/386), 223.

so many previously powerful tribes, chief among them the Mahican—so recently terrible to the eastern Iroquois—under Corleaer's tree of peace, and the desolation of New England, together meant an enormous increase in the strength—both relative and absolute—of the Anglo-Iroquoian allies. As the headquarters of the alliance, the governor-general built *"a new stockadod ffort with ffour Bastions, each capable of six gunns, said ffort so seated as to Defend and Command the whole town of Albany." The new fort, as a good citadel should be, was capable both of providing protection to the town population and of compelling their obedience, for the governor-general was a practiced practitioner of garrison government. At the end of March 1676, Major Andros left Fort Albany for Fort James. There, on 4 April, he reported to his council his most recent negotiations with the Mohawk, and with the "North Indians" of King Philip's former army, regarding the residence in Anglo-Iroquoian territory of red refugees from every theatre of the wars of 1676.[26]

Refugees and Resolutions

White refugees overcrowded the coastal enclaves, nowhere more than on Rhode Island. In cordial contact with the Rhode Islanders, themselves racially reasonable and victims of puritan aggression, the governor-general of New York was informed of their refugee problem. Early in May 1676, he sent eastward the same sloops that had taken out the munitions used in the Great Swamp Fight in the previous autumn. This time they were to bring back New England refugees. To them Andros offered land on Long and Staten islands. From them, as from Governor Easton of Rhode Island, Andros learned of the great real-estate prize of King Philip's War, the Narragansett lands. Andros was ultimately responsible for having these lands ("the King's Province") granted to Rhode Island, rather than to any of the grasping puritan commonwealths that had attacked the Narragansett in hopes of expropriating their homeland.[27]

Returning from Rhode Island on 28 May 1676, the captain of the governor-general's own armed sloop reported that "Boston" was trying to

---

26. N.Y.C.D., III, 255; Hough, ed., *Narrative*, 153.
27. Hough, ed., *Narrative*, 161. See Morden and Berry map (p. 220). For a full account of the role of "the King's Province" in Anglo-American politics, I am indebted to Theodore B. Lewis, Massachusetts in Transition . . . 1660–1692 (unpublished manuscript).

outflank every other colony in the scramble for postwar plunder by making treaties with various of the "North Indians." On 30 May 1676, the
governor-in-council, meeting at Fort James, responded to Massachusetts'
rumored initiative by reiterating and extending to the northern Algonquins Andros' earlier offer to their southern relatives. The commander at
Albany was ordered to send "word by some good Mahicander eastward
. . . that all Indyans that will come in and submit, shall be received to live
under the Protection of the Government." The Mahican emissary was to
offer safe-conduct to delegates of undecided Algonquin groups to attend
a general council at Albany with Andros and the Iroquois. In fact, the
governor-general had just taken elements of three southern Connecticut
tribes into lower New York, on their understanding that he would preserve them from the Mohawk as well as from the Connecticut colonists.[28]

The Mohawk war parties, after killing 140 Algonquin along the fall
line of the Connecticut River, reported that the lower reaches of the river
were being deserted as bands availed themselves of Andros' sanctuary.
One of the refugee bands from Connecticut was led by Cospechy, the
famous Springfield Indian sachem. It was with his people, and others of
the southern New England and two Mahican tribes, that the governor-
general traveled out from Albany in May 1676 to the beautiful Hoosac
Valley at Schaghticoke, near the site of Philip's winter camp. These
"River Indians," as the refugees and their Mahican hosts became known,
recalled the event long afterwards. In 1702, they remembered, with precision, that "26 years agoe Sr. Edmund Andross then Governor of this
Province, planted a Tree of welfare at Skachkook and invited us to come
and live there which we very luckily complyed withall, and we have had
the good fortune ever since that wee have encreased that Tree and the
very leaves thereof are grown hard & strong, the Tree itself is grown so
thick of leaves & Bows that the sun can scarce shine throw it, yea the fire
itself cannot consume it. . . ."[29]

The Connecticut authorities were consumed with rage that hundreds
of Algonquin were escaping the execution, enslavement, and expropriation that they, and all their puritan confederates, were meting out to the
"Indyan enemy." As band after band passed west into New York in August 1676, the Connecticut leaders wailed that "a criticall season of advantage" was being wasted. Andros and the Iroquois must "comply with our
reasonable request for . . . the utter extirpation of such as have imbrued
their hands in the blood of so many of his Maties good subjects in the
severall plantations of these United Colonies"—Massachusetts, Connecticut, Plymouth. Andros refused to act, or to ask the Iroquois to do so. In

28. Council minutes, 30 May 1676, in Hough, ed., *Narrative*, 167.
29. *N.Y.C.D.*, IV, 991. See the portrait of their chief, Etow Oh Koam, or Nicholas, following
page 290.

fact, he treated the occasional Mohawk outrage on the refugees as a breach of their alliance with him. He also refused repeated Connecticut requests to permit their own agents either to "excite" the Mohawk or to allow United Colonies soldiers to sail up the Hudson. When malicious young Albanians spread the rumor that the terrible Captain Mosely, with his dogs and buccaneers, was coming from Massachusetts to attack the refugees—causing due panic in "River Indian" camps—Andros' officers had the youths whipped. Baffled, the bloodthirsty puritans moderated their vengeful demands to Andros. If he refused the "destruction of those enemyes that are now in those parts, if not under yor power," he might have his allies do some selective killing: "possibly if but ye chiefe men were cut off by those Indyans [the Iroquois] as it was with the Pequots [in 1637], it may do; wee do not so concern ourselves for others or women or children, they delivering themselves to mercy unto your honor there." [30]

To Andros and the Iroquois, it suddenly seemed, in the early summer of 1676, that they might attract to their shared sphere both northern and southern Algonquin refugees, that, reinforced, they could look westward past Lake Erie and spread their joint influence south to the Chesapeake. Fresh counsel about the vast range of prospects opening to Edmund Andros and his advisers would have to be taken with the sachems of the Iroquois. It was especially important to confer with the Onondaga states-man the breadth and direction of whose vision of the Iroquoian mission was equal to this truly imperial opportunity. On 30 May 1676, after two days of debate, the governor-general and his council resolved that a general conference of the Anglo-Iroquoian allies should be convened to consider the postwar possibilities. A councilor and a captain were ordered up to Albany to "send word to the Maques and Sinnekes" that Corleaer was en route to Albany "and that he desires and orders that some of them will meet him there, and particularly Carriconty." [31]

Daniel Garacontié and Edmund Andros—the Sagochiendagehté and Corleaer, to give their council names—met in council at Albany in June 1676. There they developed the Anglo-Iroquoian agreements of the previous summer's Tinontougen council. During the year between the Tinontougen and Albany councils, in every case save that of the Lenni-Lenape, ancient enmities of one or another of the Five Nations towards the Indian objects of Anglo-Iroquoian diplomacy had impeded plans for widening the allies' sphere of influence. The "Sinnekes" had taken advantage of the Susquehanna dispersion to brutalize that people. The Mo-

30. Connecticut council to Andros, 19, 31 August 1676, in Trumbull, ed., *Records of Connecticut*, 470–71, 478.
31. Hough, ed., *Narrative*, 167; also in *N.Y.C.D.*, XIII, 496–97.

hawk had beaten up the Mahican in their new settlements near Albany. Mixed war parties of the Iroquois had continued to attack the very tribes of southern New England with which Andros wished to establish cordial relations. Yet Corleaer's alliance with the Five Nations themselves had dramatically deepened during 1675–76, and he came to the meeting with Garacontié and his fellow sachems in June 1676 prepared to link their most recent conquests, the Iroquoian victories of 1676, with his own plans for the extension of Stuart sovereignty.

The Susquehanna Solution

In defining their shared interests during the Albany council of June 1676, the Sagochiendagehté made it clear to Corleaer that, however tolerant the Mohawk were towards their "brothers & Children" the Susquehanna, as willing as the Mohawk were to adopt them, and as anxious as Corleaer was to strengthen the Mohawk, the other Iroquois nations would accept nothing but unconditional Susquehanna surrender. Then the western nations would absorb the best of the Susquehanna warriors as the janissaries of the Iroquois. They would oversee the settlement of the remaining Susquehanna in the southern ambit of the Onondaga. The division of opinion between Corleaer and Garacontié about the future of the Susquehanna, the former being very much the Mohawk's man, the latter the leader of the western Iroquois, was so widely apparent that a Marylander remarked on it. The western Iroquois, he said, wanted the Susquehanna "not to hurt them for every one of the fforts strive what they can to get them to themselves and Governor Androes to get them to the Masoques for . . . if they had them they would make war immediately with the ffrench." [32]

Andros had held out as best he could for the Susquehanna and Mohawk interests for he had promised the Susquehanna his protection and in becoming Mohawk they would sharpen his best tool for carrying out the duke's orders to keep the French out of his northern territory (and it was soon to appear to Andros that the Susquehanna might be even more valuable agents of ducal dominion in the south). To add them to the

32. Coursey to Notley, 22 May 1676, William Hand Browne, ed., *Archives of Maryland* (Baltimore, 1887–), V, 247; also in Colonial Office, General, vol. 40, Public Record Office (hereafter cited as C.O. 1/40), 76.

Anglo-Iroquoian sphere, from February 1676, Andros had been in contact with Susquehanna delegates. On 21–22 June 1676, the two days before the governor-general took sloop to Albany and the Iroquoian council, he had met in Fort James with two Susquehanna sachems from the refugees encamped along the Delaware. Andros told Conacheoweedo and Sneedo that he had already discussed their sad situation with their kinsmen the Mohawk, that he had heard nothing but good of the Susquehanna, that he was "sorry from his heart of their trouble, and would willingly help them out." He promised them that, "if they will come & live anywhere within the Government," he would give them shelter, but he warned the Susquehanna that he could do nothing for them outside the boundaries of the duke's dominion. They must accept his control to receive his protection.[33]

Looking ahead, the governor-general told the Susquehanna sachems that in the forthcoming negotiations with the Five Nations, he would "take care the *Maques* & *Sinnekes* should be at peace with them." Continually widening his diplomatic range, Andros also promised the Susquehanna that he would "make peace for them with Virginia & Maryland," thus adding the Old Dominion to the potential constituents of an Anglo-Iroquoian condominium. The Susquehanna sachems replied that they must consult their people before agreeing to a move, but, anticipating acceptance of Andros' proposals—it was an offer too good to refuse—the Susquehanna said that they would return shortly, with the presents appropriate to diplomats, and "they departed well satisfyed." Andros thus went up to the Albany meeting with Garacontié and his fellows of the Five Nations aristocracy with specific proposals for the incorporation of the Susquehanna into the League of the Iroquois and for the incorporation of the Chesapeake colonies into the expanding Anglo-Iroquoian alliance.

Even after Garacontié had insisted on the acquisition of the Susquehanna by the upper Iroquois, his Onondaga first among them, Andros, in September 1676, again encouraged the Susquehanna to join the Mohawk as offering them the best terms. Of all the Five Nations, the Mohawk were most in need of replacements, not just to make up war losses but to fill the social gaps left by the families who had succumbed to the preachments of Father Bruyas and to the sober attractions of the new mission of St. Francis Xavier on the St. Lawrence. These losses alarmed Andros almost as much as they did the Mohawk. The Mohawk middlemen were the chief prop of the Albany community which Andros had just reorganized and rebuilt in the interests of Indian trade and diplomacy. Tradi-

33. "At a Meeting in the Fort of some *Susquehanna* Indyans from Deleware the head of ye Bay & those parts, having beene sent for by the Gv." 2 June 1676, *N.Y.C.D.*, XIII, 497–98.

tional Mohawk interests eastward were closely connected with Andros' defense of New York's New England boundaries and his desire to recover the duke's territories in Maine. A reinforcement of Andros' closest allies, the Mohawk, with the warlike and commercially shrewd Susquehanna, a people formidable to their enemies but friendly to both Corleaer and the Mohawk, seemed to Andros ideal. Such were the Mohawk ideals as well. Both were thwarted by third parties. On the native side, Garacontié and the western nations whose interests he represented would not accept this solution to the Susquehanna problem. On the English side, the proprietary party in Maryland began to explore the possibility of making peace with the Susquehanna independently of either Andros or the Iroquois and of using that peace to re-establish Maryland's presence on the Delaware River at the expense of both Andros and the Iroquois.

On 4 August 1676, the governor-general and his council considered the continuing influx of the Susquehanna to the Delaware, fugitives from the revolutionary militias and Baconian district commanders of Virginia, the aroused frontiersmen of Maryland, and the war parties of the western Iroquois. Such were the numbers, reputation, and sudden accessibility of the Susquehanna that it now occurred to Andros that they might play a part in his imperial plans for an expanding New York independent of the Iroquois. Therefore Andros said that, if the Susquehanna "came in" to camps at the Falls of the Delaware, he would "endeavour to [effect a] composure of all things in Maryland, and [to] perfect a peace with the Maques and Sinneques, after which the said Indyans may return to their land." Thus Andros could win a powerful native ally on the southern ducal frontiers without increasing New York's dependence on the Iroquois. Of course none of the other parties liked Andros' proposal. Even the Susquehanna, in difficulties though they were, tried to play off Maryland and New York to save themselves from subjection to either, or to the Iroquois.[34]

To prevent the loss of the Susquehanna to Maryland, Andros commissioned Captain John Collier as both commandant of the militia and negotiator with the natives on the Delaware. Captain Collier was ordered either to retain the Susquehanna on the Delaware or to persuade them to join Andros or the Mohawk in New York. Rather than permit the Susquehanna to resume an independent existence as the lightning rod of the Chesapeake or let them succumb to Maryland's proffered alliance, however, Andros admitted that he would prefer that they be surrendered to the western Iroquois. At the least, making the Susquehanna Iroquois meant that Corleaer would have indirect influence over their strategic

34. *Ibid.*, XII, 553, 554. Proceedings of the Maryland deputy governor and council, 6 August 1676, in Browne, ed., *Archives of Maryland*, XV, 120–24.

homeland. He admitted as much to Maryland: "I have some Interest with the Maques and Sinniques, which can best deal with them," i.e., the Susquehanna.

So irresistible were the ambitions of the western Iroquois, however, that, at the end of September 1676, Andros had to abandon his plans for a separate southern Susquehanna–New York pact and return to his previous plan to incorporate them and their territory in an expanded Iroquoia. He told the Susquehanna that he could now offer them no option but to join the Five Nations. They might choose to join him and his Mohawk brethren (the Susquehanna did send a sachem's son to look over the Albany area in October 1676), and that freely, "for it is their good hearts, not Riches that I minde or value," the governor-general said. Otherwise the Susquehanna would have to amalgamate with the western Iroquois nations. While he would not force them to join any of the Five Nations—Andros reassured the Susquehanna that "they shall receive no harme from the Governmt"—he warned them that, such was the "Sinnique" determination to reduce the Susquehanna to subservience, he could no longer "undertake to secure them from others where they are," on the Delaware.[35]

In December, the western Iroquois attacked the Susquehanna outliers encamped at Jacob Young's. By the end of January, the deputy governor of Maryland appreciated that peace negotiations had to be held "both with the Sennico and the Susquehannoch, especially with the Sennico if to be obtained, they being the greatest and most considerable Nation, and our league with them will occasion our security from the Delaware or Masquas Indians." If the Susquehanna joined their interest in the Delaware Valley and the Lenni-Lenape with that of the Mohawk, as Major Andros had proposed, the result would be fatal for Maryland's northern and western claims and trade, the Mohawk and Susquehanna "being both Nations the bloodiest people in all these parts of America." On 6 March 1676/7, however, another option appeared to the anxious Marylanders. The Susquehanna themselves asked for peace negotiations with Maryland "and all the English."[36]

These, and the other threads of the coming season of post-revolutionary resolution, were being drawn together by Major Andros. On 12 March, the governor-general and his council recapitulated the results of the war years in the central area of the duke's domain. The refugee Indians, from New England or elsewhere, were to be "incorporated" into resident nations, Iroquoian or Algonquin, a denial of national identity which antici-

35. Andros' commission and instructions for Capt. John Collier, 23 September 1676, *N.Y.C.D.*, XII, 556–57. Andros to deputy governor of Maryland, 25 September 1676, *ibid.*, 558. See also *ibid.*, 572.
36. Notley to Baltimore, 22 January 1676/7, in Browne, ed., *Archives of Maryland*, V, 153.

pated the fate of the Susquehanna. No one—i.e., no New England trader, negotiator, or Indian-killer—was to pass up the Hudson to tribal territories without license from the governor-general. The other meddlesome Europeans, the French and their Jesuits, were also warned off from tampering with New York's growing native populations. The Mohawk had complained "that ye Governr. of Canada doth pretend some Jurisdiction" over them. The governor-in-council "ordered That ye Maques Indyans and Associates on this side ye Lake (having been alwayes under a part of this Governmt) have Nothing to do with ye ffrench." The Albany court was to summon Father Bruyas and the Mohawk sachems into their presence, read them the order-in-council, and (again) tell the Jesuit that the governor-general expected him to govern himself accordingly.[37]

The sap was surely rising, for just two days later, on 14 March 1676/7, the "Seneca," the Lenni-Lenape, and Andros' captain met in Delaware to divide up the Susquehanna sheltering there. On the 18th, the Iroquois headed home with some of the refugees. En route they took thirty of the "chief warriors" of the Susquehanna from their old capital and divided them among the several Iroquois "forts" on 28 March. On the same day, the governor-general recalled the Mohawk from their New England raids until he could refresh the agreements that protected them from insults by the Massachusetts and Connecticut colonists. Looking westward once more, on 6 April Andros reacted to the recent Delaware developments. He reiterated his orders to the Susquehanna that they must come in to the Mohawk "or any other our Indyans," but he said that they were not to remain on the Delaware or with the Lenni-Lenape, for their presence attracted the attentions of both the western Iroquois and the Marylanders, endangering the Delaware settlers, red and white.[38]

"Ye Govr. Genl. Is
Become Our Father"

No sooner had Andros approved the order-in-council for the removal of the Susquehanna to Iroquoia than, on the evening of 6 April 1677,

37. N.Y.C.D., XIII, 503. Van Laer, ed., Minutes of Albany, 211.
38. Coursey to Notley, upon Delaware River, 22 May 1677, C.O. 1/40, 76; printed in Browne, ed., Archives of Maryland, V, 243, 246–48. Ibid., XV, 150, 151. N.Y.C.D., XII, 572.

he set sail for Albany. He arrived there on the 11th for a three-week stay. In the midst of this visit he supervised the first of the famous Covenant Chain negotiations by which the imperial outcomes of the Chesapeake revolutions in the south and west and of King Philip's War in the north and east were written into treaties of Anglo-Iroquoian alliance, an alliance which controlled American development until the next era of revolution, a century in the future.

The first of these climactic New York councils was that of the New Englanders with the Iroquois and Andros. The communications of the agents of Connecticut and Massachusetts with the Iroquoian sachems were regulated by the governor-general, he "being allwayes present, & Manageing the discourse on all hands that they might not prove prejudicall to the Interest of his R[oyal] H[ighness] in this Province." Only in public, only in the Albany statehouse, "and that in ye Govr. Genll. Presence," as the Mohawk themselves admonished the New England agents, could any business be done. It was not the business the New Englanders wanted done. The agents repeatedly asked for the extradition of "enemy Indians" from New York. Andros "obstructed" every request, pointing out that both the "North Indians" and the coastal Algonquin had fled west through Iroquoia as far as the Seneca and were now one with their hosts. The stubborn agents left Andros a list of the most-wanted Indians and threatened him with official action by the colonial assemblies if he refused to surrender them. He was not impressed.[39]

New England's emissaries did secure an Iroquoian promise (soon broken) to spare the Mohegan allies of the New England Confederation. Andros was much in sympathy with this exception to enmity, having already made his own approaches to the Mohegan, as he did to other New England tribes. The "Macques & Sinekes" also agreed to attack the "North Indians" if they ventured out of their Canadian sanctuaries. This too was agreeable to Andros, being as much a protection of New York's peoples as it was of New England's settlements. Additionally, the Iroquois accepted from the New England emissaries a repetition of Andros' charge to attack the Abenaki in Maine. This, the Massachusetts authorities admitted, "we find very difficult by reason of unknown and almost unpassable woods, ryvers . . . greatly obstructing our English soldiers." In return for these agreements, the delegates of the Five Nations collected from the agents (Major John Pynchon for Connecticut and James Richards for Massachusetts) a handsome present, a safe-conduct for the warriors of the Five Nations faring through New England, and a picture

39. Captain Brockholes to Captain Salisbury, 2 August 1678, N.Y.C.D., III, 530. Lawrence H. Leder, ed., "The Livingston Indian Records," Pennsylvania History 23 (1956): 39. "The Maquase Answer," N.Y.C.D., XIII, 529. Trumbull, ed., Records of Connecticut, 492–95.

on paper of a codfish, symbol of the coastal colonies. Such was the Andros-enforced amalgam of ducal, colonial, and Iroquoian interests in this, the first of the Covenant Chain treaties that, at the close of the negotiations, on 26 April 1677, the Mohawk announced that "the Govern Genll & you of New England & we are in one triple Allyance with [one] another." [40]

Also through Edmund Andros' agency, a parallel negotiation was carried on between the New England agents and "the Mohekandrs and other River Indians." In the final agreement, signed in the statehouse at Albany on 24 April, the riverine sachems disingenuously assured the New Englanders that, during "ye late unhappy Warr against the English" of 1675–76, they had "satt still according to ye Command of ye Honble Governr of New Yorke &c." The agents had to accept this assertion at face value and support the subjection the Indians now admitted to in hopes that, at least in the future, the imperial executive would moderate native behavior. Therefore the agents declared that, "being of the same Nation, under ye same Prince, and soe as one with ye sd Governor," they would join him in a league of friendship with the natives, if the Indians would henceforward warn the colonists of impending attacks and refuse to shelter those natives still at war with the colonists. [41]

The Mahican and their associates assured the New England agents that "now of Late years ye Govr. Genl. is become our father." So they were at peace with everyone: the "Christians of the North" (the French); the abominable Mohawk (whom the Mahican never named); as well as with the colonists represented by their old friend "Kinshon." Therefore, the Hudson River bands pledged that "there shall be no shrubs or rubbish grow along ye River." That is, as the Mahican spokesman "read" the wampum, his people would keep the banks of the Hudson, from Albany "even quite down to N. Yorke," clear of the enemies of New England.

In two spring months of 1676/7, in these first two sets of the Covenant Chain treaties which defined the results of 1676, the governor-general of the duke of York's American territories asserted and/or provided for the defense of the ducal boundaries from the Kennebec River to Lake Ontario. By these treaties, the governor-general had established himself and his Iroquoian associates as the primary political powers in all of New England beyond the boundaries of actual settlement. The terms of these treaties also summarized Edmund Andros' understandings and alliances with the various Algonquin nations and bands now "belonging to" his government.

40. Trumbull, ed., Records of Connecticut, 494, 489. N.Y.C.D., XIII, 529.
41. Leder, ed., "Indian Records," Pa. Hist., 23: 39–40. Note that Andros had already employed the "River Indians" to prevent unauthorized (New England) cargoes from sailing upriver (N.Y.C.D., XIII, 502–3).

As the number of these nations grew, Andros refined the administration of Indian affairs. At the conclusion of the first Covenant Chain conference, on 27 April 1677, "the Govr Genll Andross" met with the Albany court and compelled it to authorize a salary for Robert Livingston as secretary of Indian affairs. Andros noted Livingston's labor in translating and recording the recent agreements between the Mohawk, the Mahican, and the River Indians of New York with the various representatives of New France (Father Bruyas), New England, and Uncas' Mohegan. Andros anticipated continued employment for the English empire's first Indian-affairs bureaucrat. Then, "having urgent occasions at Yorke," Andros took sloop for the city.[42]

"Undeceive Lt Genll Andross"

The governor-general's "urgent occasions" were the emissaries of the Chesapeake colonies, and of the Lenni-Lenape, come to negotiate with Andros himself, the western Iroquois, and the Susquehanna. These delegates visited Fort James en route to the second and, in terms of the future of North America, even more important section of the Covenant Chain resolutions of the revolutions of 1676.

While Andros had been in Albany, the Maryland proprietary officers had discovered that, since the Susquehanna peace "Overture" early in March, the nation had "Submitted themselves to and putt themselves undr the protection of the Cinnigos or some other nations of Indians . . . within or neer unto the Territory of his Royall Highness the Duke of Yorke." The "Confederacy" between the Susquehanna and the western Iroquois so menaced Maryland that, on 30 April 1677, the proprietary councilors reluctantly concluded that they had to take up Major Andros' previous offers to mediate between Maryland, the Iroquois, and the Susquehanna. Only thus, it now seemed, could the great war of 1675–76 between the Chesapeake colonists and the Susquehanna, a war which increasingly involved the western Iroquois as well, be ended at last. Only by the governor-general's mediation could Maryland secure "an universall peace betweene us the Susquehannoh Cinnigoes & the rest of the Indians to the Northward, as also between the sd Indians and all the

---

42. Van Laer, ed., *Albany Minutes*, II, 226. Andros to the governor and council of Connecticut, Albany, 16 April 1677, in Trumbull, ed., *Records of Connecticut*, 495.

lowland Indians in league and Amity with us." Thus the Marylanders introduced the Conoy confederates to what would become the Covenant Chain.[43]

To protect their allies and themselves from the Susquehanna and the Seneca, the Maryland authorities authorized a councilor, Colonel Henry Coursey, "to treate with Edmund Andross Esqr Seigneur of Sausmarez Lt: & Governor Genl. under his Royll Highness James Duke of York & Albany &c. of all his Territoryes in America," on behalf of Maryland, Virginia, and Maryland's Indian allies. Through Andros' good offices, Coursey was to negotiate with the "Cinnigo Indians, and ye Susquehan-nohs if yett there be such a Nation." Taking an ample escort with him, Colonel Coursey crossed the troubled border into the duke's Delaware territory. On 15 May 1677, he reached Newcastle. There Coursey found Captain Collier and the Delaware militias out in arms, "uppon their Garde" against another invasion from Maryland.[44]

Being on guard against Maryland aggression was the prevailing concern of Andros and his officers in the negotiations that now began on the Delaware. The governor-general, Colonel Coursey found, was "incensed" that the Maryland authorities had slighted his earlier offers to mediate. The proprietor's people had said "that Maryland would make war or peace att their own pleasure" (just as the New Englanders had), although war and peace were the prerogative of the king and Edmund Andros was the sole royal representative north of the Potomac. Andros was certainly annoyed that the Maryland council had just chosen to oust his settlers and impose their own on 8,000 acres of the disputed lands along the Delaware-Maryland border. Not disposed to do Maryland any favors, Andros held trump in the diplomatic game, for, as Colonel Coursey soon discovered, most of the Susquehanna had been taken from the Delaware to New York by the western Iroquois, and the Seneca acknowledged "the Governor Genll to be our greatest Lord."[45]

Colonel Coursey spent a week at Newcastle. He told Captain Collier that he was en route "to Coll Andros by his meanes to come to a treaty with the Cinnigo Indians at ffort Albany." Actually, Coursey tried to find some way to bypass Edmund Andros and to negotiate directly with the Susquehanna. Together, Captain Collier and "the Emperor of the Delaware," Renowewan, finally convinced the Maryland envoy that the

---

43. Th. Notley's commission to Henry Coursey as "Embassadr. or Envoy," C.O. 1/40, 73; printed in Browne, ed., *Archives of Maryland*, XV, 149–50.

44. Instructions for Coursey, C.O. 1/40, 74; printed in Browne, ed., *Archives of Maryland*, XV, 157. Francis Jennings, "Glory, Death and Transfiguration: The Susquehannock Indians in the Seventeenth Century," *Proceedings of the American Philosophical Society* 112 (1968): 41.

45. C.O. 1/40, 76, 83.

governor-general commanded the diplomatic process. Jacob Young came in to report that the "Seneca" indeed controlled the Susquehanna. Some of them, he said, had "fled to the Senuques" for protection from the Chesapeake colonists and their tidewater Indian allies. Others had been seized, bound, and carried off by combined war parties of the western Iroquois before they could make peace with Maryland. The "Seneca," however, had offered to make peace for the Susquehanna, as well as on their own behalf, at the forthcoming general conference. Perforce, then, Colonel Coursey set off for New York. He took with him all of the Susquehanna still encamped along the Delaware whom Renowewan could collect, "it being Governor Andrews orders to Capt. Collier to send them." The colonel's party was followed by Delaware delegates as well, all being obedient to the summons of Corleaer and the Five Nations to their council fire.[46]

The southern delegations entered Fort James on 6 June 1677. To "undeceive . . . the Honble Lt Genll Andross" about Maryland's purported diplomatic independence and its aggression in Delaware, and to secure his good offices in negotiating with the natives, Colonel Coursey paid Andros £100 sterling. Undeceived indeed, the governor-in-council reviewed and largely rewrote Maryland's draft proposals for a treaty with the Five Nations.[47]

The first issue was that Maryland claimed to represent Virginia. If the Old Dominion were not included in the peace with the Iroquois, southbound war parties would continue to carve up Maryland settlements on their way to Virginia. The Maryland proprietary government would then be criticized at Whitehall, if only because of the collapse of the crown's customs revenue from tobacco consequent on Indian war, but Maryland officials anticipated that they would suffer in the opinion of the English public as well "for having abandoned our Brethren and fellow Subjects."[48]

Such had been the turmoil in Virginia during the spring of 1676/7, however, that the Maryland authorities had not consulted its government about the proposed treaty. As Maryland's executive understood the situation, until Sir William Berkeley was at last deported from Virginia (on 5 May 1677), his hostility to the royal commissioners prevented anything being "done in the Countrey either to secure it from the Barbarous Indians or to settle the peace or constitution of either Genll. or County Courts." Still in power under Berkeley's baneful aegis, "the great men of Virginia" had no "zeale unto his Maties Services." They went on

46. Coursey's instructions, 30 April 1677, *ibid.*, 74; Coursey to [Notley], 22 May 1677, *ibid.*, 76, 77; printed in Browne, ed., *Archives of Maryland*, V, 247.
47. Notley to Coursey, 2 June 1677, in Browne, ed., *Archives of Maryland*, 249.
48. *Ibid.*, 246; also in C.O. 1/40, 74.

"strangely" misgoverning the people and so kept revolution alive on the frontier with the natives, as elsewhere. On 29 May, however, Colonel Herbert Jeffreys, the royal commissioners, and the Virginia Regiment combined to impress both "the great men of Virginia" and the local Indians in the martial ceremony by which they imposed peace on the tribes and celebrated the birth and restoration of King Charles. Soon after this, Colonel Jeffreys led his soldiers upcountry to protect the planters against the "Seneca" raiders.[49]

The counter-revolution in Virginia and Colonel Jeffreys' counterattack against the Seneca compelled the New York negotiators to consider his views. Now that there was a real royal governor-general in Virginia, —a serving officer from Major Andros' own first regiment, the Guards— the major refused to permit Maryland to venture upon "A Treaty with the Heads of the Several Nations" who had the power to make war in the Chesapeake until he was assured by Colonel Jeffreys that the proposed treaty would "not thwart your designs" regarding the natives or damage "His Maties or your own Honors . . . interest." Andros asked that Jeffreys indicate if he wanted "to join with him" in the negotiations or if he had articles to add to the "peace now to be made at ffort Albany with the Susquoesahaimohs Cicinigos and other Northern Indians."[50]

The second contention concerning Maryland's draft treaty resulted from the transformation Andros worked in Maryland's assumptions about the Iroquois. They were "his Indians," the governor-general insisted, and they were bound to him by respectable covenants which they honored, and which acknowledged the sovereignty of the king. As Coursey said to the Iroquois, he had learned from "the Honble Governor Genll. of this place that ye were a people who were always obedient to this Governmt of New York, and that you were faithfull in yor words and promises, which we seldom find in others." Therefore, the Iroquois could not be dealt with apart from New York or in any other terms than Andros—as the representative of the king of England and the duke of York—approved of.[51]

Not only could Maryland's envoy not have free access to the Iroquois, but the governor-general would insist upon a monarchical, imperial, unitary view being expressed in the Maryland proposals, just as he had in those of the New England agents. All the English, Colonel Coursey was made to say, in a third alteration of his proposals, "have but one Soveraign Lord and King over us all." Despite the severality of the colonial governments, "yet as for peace or warr we are all but one people." Such certainly

49. Notley to Baltimore, 22 May 1677, C.O. 1/40, 186.
50. Notley to Jeffreys, 22 June 1677, in Browne, ed., *Archives of Maryland*, V, 250–51.
51. Order-in-council for "Coll. Henry Courcy to be made use of at the Congress the 15. July 1677," *ibid.*, 251–52; also in C.O. 1/40, 79.

was Edmund Andros' conviction, and he forced imperial unity on hitherto autonomous colonies by the diplomacy of the Covenant Chain.

Fourth, the original object of Maryland's attentions, the Susquehanna, was erased from the draft treaty. The parties to the peace were to be New York, the Iroquois nations, and their (unnamed) dependents on the one hand, and, on the other, Virginia, Maryland, and her native dependents, particularly the Piscataway Indians (who soon shifted suzerains, becoming subjects of the Iroquois: such was the consolidating tendency of the Anglo-Iroquoian alliance). A fifth alteration in the draft treaty provided that, if any of the Iroquois violated the agreement, they were to be surrendered on demand, not to the Chesapeake authorities, as Coursey's draft originally provided, but, rather, "to the Honble Governr Genll of New Yorke." A final revision dashed the economic hopes of the Maryland authorities. Nothing of their prewar trade with the Susquehanna, nor any share in New York's trade with their new Iroquoian overlords (modeled on "what articles are made by Coll. Andross"), was permitted by the governor-in-council to be mentioned in Colonel Coursey's official proposals.[52]

"Submitting to Providence"

By mid-June 1677, when the Chesapeake terms had been defined, the governor-in-council of New York agreed to send a wampum "word" west to each of the Five Nations, requesting the presence of their spokesmen to meet Colonel Coursey by mid-July in Albany. There they could coordinate the revised proposals of the Chesapeake ambassador with the previous two years' negotiations between Edmund Andros and Daniel Garacontié. In fact, the Chesapeake propositions were but add-ons to previously scheduled discussions. As early as 2 May 1677, Corleaer had sent English, Dutch, and Iroquoian emissaries westward through the Five Nations to call their sachems to Albany for that remarkable resolution of the events of 1676 which is known as the "Covenant Chain."

This was an ever-changing and widening negotiation. Even Colonel Coursey's message to the Five Nations was further generalized and moderated after the Chesapeake spokesman reached Albany at the end of June. There he witnessed two episodes of Anglo-Iroquoian diplomacy

52. C.O. 1/40, 80, 74.

and war that carried links of the Covenant Chain to the shores of the Atlantic at points as far apart as Narragansett Bay and the Kennebec River.

At the end of May 1677, two hundred "Maques" warriors (whose ranks included some young toughs recruited from "Northern Indians" and some refugee warriors from southern New England as well) encamped outside Albany. They beat up the local Mahican settlers, plundered their villages, and took from them refugee "Indians who were under the protection of the governor." Worse than that, the Iroquois and their new recruits agreed that the Mohegan, bitter enemies of them all but allies of the New Englanders, were an irresistible target. They raided all the way to Narragansett Bay, terrorizing the Indian-shy colonists by their very passage, and by mid-June had brought back to Albany, among other prisoners, Uncas' own son, Owenoco.[53]

Horrified, the Mohawk sachems returned the "River Indian" captives and hurried down to Albany to apologize for these violations of the covenant so recently signed with the New Englanders under Corleaer's direction. They shamefacedly admitted "the bad side of their people who go against their commands." They reminded the Albany authorities, nonetheless, that "we cannot simply turn our backs on our soldiers, for they are our protectors and have to fight for us since we are old people." Still, the sachems said, they had done what they could to redress the injuries done by their warriors, so they begged that their covenants with and through Corleaer not be considered broken. That, they said, would make the Mohawk "the laughing stock of the other Nations." The sachems sent belts of wampum down to New York in hopes "that the governor will not be angry about this." The Mohawk elders knew that the prosperity, if not the survival, of their nation depended upon its association with New York and particularly with Edmund Andros, Anglo-Iroquoian imperialist. "Until now Corleaer has constantly worked with us to our great pleasure, and we hope the same will continue," the sachems concluded.[54]

Andros' response illustrated both the limits and uses of his alliance with the Iroquois. Since reparation had been made by the Mohawk sachems and since his own officers at Albany advised him to accept it, he would accede to the sachems' request. Their soldiers' offenses, he said, would "be cast into the well of forgetfulness." But Corleaer took advantage of the Mohawk's unwonted humility. He told the Albany officers to summon the sachems and "to put them in Mind how I protected them in the time of the warr, & gave their old men, wives & children, admittance within our Towne & Fortifications, & that I doe expect that whosoever

53. *N.Y.C.D.*, XIII, 508; Van Laer, ed., *Minutes of Albany*, II, 245.
54. Leder, ed., "Indian Records," *Pa. Hist.*, 23: 40–42.

doth or shall come in & submitt themselves & live quietly with our Indyans shall be protected from any outrage or force & I shall . . . looke upon any violence . . . as done to my selfe."[55]

Andros had to protect the Algonquin refugees from his own Mohawk allies as well as from angry New Englanders, and now he had to protect the Mohawk themselves from the righteous wrath of the Connecticut authorities. "I am still very sorry & troubled for such actings of ye Indians," Andros wrote (apologies were as alien to him as they were to the Mohawk, but he had to excuse the excesses of those he claimed to command). He insisted, however, that Connecticut should take no advantage of the Mohawk outburst to violate the covenant with the Indians, good faith "being of great import particularly with them." Andros did promise to get Owenoco back from the Mohawk. He made the Mohawk cough up their prize. They did it very reluctantly indeed.[56]

Something constructive had to be done with the warlike energies of the young Iroquois and their new recruits. Andros' answer was Maine. The ultimate weapon of 1676, the Iroquois, had been called up to the service of English settlement in Maine—and on behalf of New York's influence there—in the recent covenant with Connecticut and Massachusetts. Therefore, as Massachusetts put it, "some doings of the Mohawks may rationally be expected there for helpe. . . ." Edmund Andros agreed, although the result he had in mind was the reverse of Massachusetts' intention. Andros had already asked the Mohawk to attack the Abenaki in Maine, and he was about to divert to the Kennebec some Oneida war parties bound for the Chesapeake when, on 1 June, word came out of Boston that the French-supplied Abenaki had driven the English entirely out of Maine. The governor-general thereupon decided to launch his own pre-prepared expedition both to assist his Iroquoian allies against the Abenaki and to reconquer Maine for the duke of York and hold it against the puritans of Massachusetts. On 13 June 1677, Major Andros ordered Captain Brockholes, Ensign Knapton, and Secretary Nicolls to take a hundred troops, a prefabricated fort, cannon, and a year's supplies and sail "Eastward to the Duke's Territories at Pemaquid and adjacent country."[57]

Andros happily acted the major for the Maine expedition. He wrote detailed orders about the siting, construction, and guards of the fort; about gun mounts and stockades; about stores, sloops, and dispatches. All these were to be applied by his officers, both to offer "protection and en-

55. Andros to the Albany magistrates, 12 July 1677, N.Y.C.D., XIII, 509. See also Van Laer, ed., Minutes of Albany, 244–46, for the message as delivered.
56. Andros to the council of Connecticut, 3, 13 July, 28 August 1677; Trumbull, ed., Records of Connecticut, 499, 502.
57. Ibid., 498. N.Y.C.D., III, 248–49.

couragement to any his maties subjects, planters or fishers," and to make
peace with the Indians, in return for their surrender of all Christian
prisoners and fishing vessels. The peace was to include "Massachusetts
and adjacent colonies if they accept itt." Moreover, the duke's officers
were to bring up from Boston and reinstall in authority the magistrates
previously ousted by Massachusetts, with whom the˙governor-general
had been planning since December 1676 to reassert Stuart sovereignty in
Maine. It was hoped that all these endeavors would be supported by the
"Maques." Andros ordered his officers "to receive and use them kindly,
as att Albany, giving them Intelligence particularly of our friends as well
as Enemyes."[58]

Within a month, Andros' officers obtained the return of thirty-five
English prisoners and several fishing ketches captured by the Indians,
and made peace with the Abenaki in Maine, a peace in which the Indians
most reluctantly included Massachusetts. Massachusetts was even more
reluctant than the Abenaki to accept this peace, coming as it did as a gift
from the ducal government now re-ensconced in Maine. Even though
Connecticut refused to assist so flagrant an act of aggrandizement, the
Bay Colony sent its own expedition to Maine on 28 June. It suffered 50-
percent casualties at the hands of the Abenaki in an ambush at Black-
point. The remnants of the force fell back on Pemaquid. There they
threatened Andros' officers, to no avail. Finally, with the worst possible
grace, "submitting (as they said) to Providence," the "Bostoners" accepted Edmund Andros' peace. It "still continues," the governor-general
observed a year afterwards, and "is all the peace (knowne) they have with
the Indyans." So Edmund Andros, and the Iroquois, ended King Philip's
War in New England.[59]

"An Absolute Covenant
of Peace"

At last, on 20 July 1677, the mediation of Edmund Andros, English
imperialist, brought the Chesapeake ambassador before the sachems
of the Five Nations at the Albany statehouse. Colonel Coursey repeated

58. *N.Y.C.D.*, III, 249.
59. *Ibid.*, 256, 265.

his Andros-ized propositions "to ye Maques & Sinneque Indians." He was informed, the envoy said, that the Iroquois "are of this Government" —that is, that they were the subjects of the king of England in the duke of York's province commanded by the seigneur of Sausmarez. He understood that they were "faithfull & constant ffriends to the English under our Great King." As such, he spoke to them on behalf of "all his Maties Subjects of Virginia & Maryland."[60]

"Mistakes," "discontents," and "injuries," Colonel Coursey explained, had come between the Five Nations and the Chesapeake colonists. "Upon the good report" of the Iroquois "by the Honble, the Governor Genll.," however, the past would "be buryed and forgott" by the English of the Chesapeake. In return, the Five Nations, those (the Susquehanna) "living among yu," and persons passing through Iroquoia (which now extended to the border of Maryland) were to refrain from injuring the persons or property of the colonists, the Piscataway "or other our Indians liveing with us." If guilty of such injuries, the Iroquois were to make reparations. Unless there were such injuries, the "Maques & Sinnekes" would be esteemed "our good Neighbours and ffriends." If injured themselves by Chesapeake Indians, the Iroquois should ask the English colonists to "call them to Accot for ye Evil done to yu . . . to propose Satisfaction . . . and Soe to continue the peace." The cause of the colonial conflict with the western Iroquois had been Susquehanna lies, but the Susquehanna existed no longer. "Wee may now live in peace as Brethren Created by the same God." This would be a peace agreed on "as well between all the said Christians as all the said Indians to last as long as the World shall endure."

After the overnight consideration called for by condolence-council protocol, the senior sachem of the senior nation, Garacontié of Onondaga, answered the Chesapeake propositions for all of the Iroquois. Garacontié delivered three "words" of descending importance. In his first word, the Sagochiendagehté said that his people had accepted the wampum of "his Honr the Governr Genll." in May and had hastened their journey to Albany on the strength of the belt sent by Colonel Coursey in June. The Iroquoian spokesman reiterated and then accepted the Chesapeake proposals. He said that his people "doe thank the Gentlemen there that they doe exhort us to the peace, for we are so minded."

A generation of war had eliminated most of the native-born Iroquoian warriors. The ranks of the Five Nations had been refilled with adoptees, most recently the refugees of the wars of 1676, of whom the most impor-

60. "Propositions made to ye Maques & Senneques Indians," C.O. 1/40, 81. A similar account, but without the last proposition, is in Leder, ed. "Indian Records," *Pa. Hist.*, 23: 42–43. A fuller record of what Coursey had intended to say is in C.O. 1/40, 79–80.

tant were the Susquehanna. The process was destroying "the real people" at an accelerating rate, however, and it seemed to Garacontié that the wastage of the Iroquois need not go on. For to Garacontié's great peace with Onnontio, and so with the French, the Five Nations had added an even more supportive covenant with Corleaer. Now, through him, that peace could be extended to all of the English colonies, and to all of their Indian allies and dependents north of the Carolinas. That peace would divide control of eastern America between the agents of the English king and the half-kings of the Iroquois. It would be sustained as it was created, by an Anglo-Iroquoian alliance which made possible a century of peaceful development within its confines. The Anglo-Iroquoian alliance preserved for generations the aboriginal supremacy achieved by the Five Nations in 1676 and, by the security it pledged to the territories it controlled, it was the making of every English colony from Virginia to New York in the century after 1676. It was, therefore, a matter of great moment in Anglo-American history when the sachems of the Five Nations, as Garacontié now announced, chose to make "an Absolute Covenant of peace wch we bind wth a Chain." To weld fast the Covenant Chain, the prince and orator of the Onondaga gave "A Belt of 13 Deepe." [61]

In his second word, Garacontié countered Maryland's suggestion that the Susquehanna, now become Iroquois, had either begun or continued the war. He insisted instead that Maryland's own agent, Jacob Young, was responsible. The Christian Daniel Garacontié then happily expanded upon the blessing that God Almighty would give to the peace, but the diplomat, the Sagochiendagehté, insisted that the reparations agreement proposed by the Chesapeake delegate be extended to bind the colonists as well as their native clients to pay for injuries offered the Iroquois.

In his afterword, the great sachem said that each of the four western Iroquois nations had war parties out to deal with the remaining Susquehanna. He warned Colonel Coursey that peace depended upon Maryland's orders to its Indian associates not to interfere with this last stage in the Iroquoian victory over the Susquehanna and so, with the accomplishment of Garacontié's lifelong ambition, Onondaga control of the Susquehanna Valley.

To extend Iroquoia southward, fighting for control of the former Susquehanna territory, the Oneida had twenty warriors out against the Indian allies of Maryland (and many more Oneida would have gone towards the Chesapeake had not the governor-general diverted them to the Kenne-

---

61. C.O. 1/40, 81v. Leder, ed., "Indian Records," *Pa. Hist.*, 23: 43–44. Browne, ed., *Archives of Maryland*, V, 254–55.

bec). For the Oneida, as they told Colonel Coursey, the peace could not begin until the warriors came home. That the Onondaga had said already. The Oneida speaker, the sachem Swerisee, assured the statehouse audience that "we doe absolutely approve of that which the Onondagaes have now said." Indicating a rank order and a term for it that were both new to Iroquoian domestic usage, Swerisee spoke of the Onondaga as the "fathers" of the Oneida. So he also referred to the Christians of New York. Agreeable imperialists, the Oneida added that they were "willing and ready to obey the Command of the Great King Charles who liveth over the great Lake" when he ordered either peace or war. The Oneida had only plundered those Christians who wounded them, and only killed livestock when hospitality was denied to them. Peace being enjoined on them, however, the Oneida "are now come together to make the Covenant, and doe again absolutely approve of that wch the Onnondages have done." The Oneida, they said, were one with the Onondaga in the condolence-council partnerships. They had listened when Colonel Coursey spoke "to the Onondagaes and when they gave their answer." If the Oneida failed to honor that answer, if they did not respect Garacontié's pledges, they should be scorned as oath-breakers, "but we are not soe minded."[62]

"The Governr. Genll. and
We Are One"

The Mohawk were the odd nation out among the Iroquois. They spent the weekend, not the traditional overnight, considering their answer to Colonel Coursey's Chesapeake propositions and to the extraordinary addition by Garacontié, the "Covenant Chain" statement. As to the former, the Mohawk had little to discuss, for, as a nation, they had been but little involved in the Susquehanna war and not all engaged in the ensuing skirmishes with the Chesapeake Bay colonists and "their" Indians. Discussion was further reduced for the Mohawk did not adhere to the consultative requirements of the condolence-council ritual. The Mohawk alone consulted no other nation in preparing their answer, arrogantly

62. Browne, ed., *Archives of Maryland*, V, 255–56. Also in Leder, ed., "Indian Records," *Pa. Hist.*; 23: 44–45. C.O. 1/40, 82v.

avoiding the exchange of counsel and the achievement of consensus fundamental to the condolence-council process of decision-making. Stressing their autonomy, the Mohawk alone refused to accept Onondaga as the capital of the League of the Iroquois. Adopting Albany instead as the place for the council fire of the Covenant Chain alliance, the Mohawk were able to distance themselves from Onondaga diplomatic dominance without rejecting the multinational alliance proclaimed by Garacontié. In fact, the Mohawk insisted, they and their Corleaer were the central links in the Anglo-Iroquoian chain to which the New Englanders and the Hudson River peoples had already shackled themselves and to which the Mohawk were now quite pleased to add Colonel Coursey's Chesapeake clients. The bulk of Mohawk discourse was designed to deny Onondaga pre-eminence in the Iroquoian league, even though this entailed Mohawk identification with an English imperialist.

The superiority of the Mohawk and their association with Edmund Andros was the theme of the "cheef Sachim of ye Maquase," Carondondawe. His town was "Tionondoge," according to the minutes of the Covenant Chain council—that is, Tinontougen, the westernmost Mohawk "castle," double-palisaded on its bluff, a bowshot across cornfields from the river. Tinontougen had been the site of Corleaer's formative council with the Five Nations, the 1675 meeting which had made 1676 a year of Anglo-Iroquoian triumph. To reaffirm that alliance and to record the results of that triumph, Carondondawe rose to speak before the sachems from every Mohawk castle and some hundreds of his nation.

The Mohawk sachem prefaced a significant statement about the Covenant Chain to his perfunctory acceptance of the Chesapeake proposals. "We are glad," he said to Colonel Coursey, "that the Kings Govrs. of Maryland and Virginia have Sent you hither to speak with the Maquas." They were equally pleased, Carondondawe said, "that the Governo^r. Genll. hath been pleased to appoint this place to Speake with all Nations in peace." For this Carondondawe thanked Corleaer, and for his giving the Chesapeake envoy permission to appear before the council. Explaining to Colonel Coursey the prior necessity of obtaining the governor-general's permission for their meeting, Carondondawe declared "that the Governr. Genll. and We are One, and One heart, & One head, for the Covenant that is betwixt the Governr. Genll. and us is Inviolable. Yea So strong that if the very Thundr. Should breake upon the Covenant Chain it would not break it asundr."

No Iroquois could challenge a more elemental force than the Thunderers to test the strength of the Covenant Chain. Having outdistanced the Onondaga both in intimacy of alliance with Andros and in devotion to the Covenant Chain (a metaphor Carondondawe was not too proud to adopt from Garacontié's speech), the Mohawk orator turned from the spirit world to the physical one to demonstrate both the Mohawk's special relationship to the Anglo-Iroquoian alliance and their superiority to the third of the elder brethren of the Iroquois, the Seneca. Carondondawe contrasted his people's presence in force at the council fire with the timorousness of their half-tamed backcountry brethren. The Seneca "were upon their Journey to come hither with Six hundred men but for feare turned back again, but we were not afraid to come here," said Carondondawe.

Once the Mohawk's oneness with the governor-general and their sophistication and courage relative to the other senior nations of the league, the Onondaga and the Seneca, were made clear, the Mohawk spokesman proceeded perfunctorily through the condolence-council formalities required to certify his nation's adherence to the present proposals. The Mohawk had, Carondondawe declared, listened with attention to the envoy's speech. They had prepared an answer for it. Its theme was that the Mohawk were entirely innocent of all injuries done to the Chesapeake Bay Christians. The Mohawk now repeated and so accepted the clauses of Colonel Coursey's proposal. They acknowledged his hospitality. They offered him a present to authenticate their words. Carondondawe went on to accept the system of mediation in cases of conflict and reparation in cases of injury that Coursey had suggested and Garacontié had amplified.

Then the assembled sachems of the Mohawk offered two chants to the council. They sang into the minds of their audience the fact of the council and the terms of the alliance; over and over again, their chant reiterated that this agreement, the Covenant Chain, unbreakable and eternal, had been forged "in this house ordained to that End by the Governr. Genll." If some other Iroquois nations should, now or afterwards, suggest a meeting place "in their own Countrey" (that is, at Onondaga, which Garacontié was proposing to the Chesapeake envoys as the place of next year's council fire), "we desire that it may not be Accepted but that this be and remaine the only appointed & prefixed place."

The essence of Mohawk might in aboriginal America had been its association with Albany, first as a source of advanced technology, now as the council fire of the Covenant Chain alliance systems. The Mohawk were as determined as ever to protect and to exploit their geopolitical advantage, even—indeed, especially—against the ritual, traditional, pan-Iroquoian center of Onondaga. "If you have a minde hereafter to Speake with us," Carondondawe told Coursey, "we desire that it may be here and noe where else."

To his powerful evocation of the Covenant Chain and to his reinforcement of that association with Albany and Andros which was its metal, the Mohawk sachem appended a personal note of thanks to Colonel Coursey "for ye Releasing of the two Sonnes of Carondondawe." He made a characteristically vindictive acknowledgment of his satisfaction "that yu beheaded the Sachem of the Susquehannohs . . . who was the cause of their being taken Prisoners." Carondondawe then gave Coursey much the most valuable present of the entire council, five beaver robes. Just as this present richly testified to Carondondawe's gratitude for the lives of his sons and to his gratification at the death of their enemy, so the uses, the conventions, the political rivalries of Iroquoian diplomacy, and its fundamental role in consolidating the great outcomes of 1676, all had been powerfully expressed by the "words" of the Wolf Clan's lord.[63]

"Put Aside All Mistakes"

The long consultations, trade, and festivities at Albany stretched on through the summer season—interminably, in Colonel Coursey's view. He began to see why the experienced Andros had refused all entreaties to come up to Albany in advance of the mid-August date he had chosen back in May. "White man's time" had then, as it has now, only relative impact upon the Iroquois. The governor-general was present, however, on 23 August when "The Sinnondowannes & Cajouges" replied to the "Propositions made to them the 22.º of Aug.ᵗ 1677 by the Honble: Coll. Henry Coursey." Six Seneca sachems from Sinnedowane (the town otherwise called Sonnontouan or Totiakton, located in the bend of the Honeoye Creek 2 miles north of its falls) had persisted in coming to the council, encouraged by Wentworth Greenhalgh, one of the "two Christians" sent west by the governor-general in May 1677 "to the furthest nations of Indians" with the wampum summons to the Covenant Chain council. The sachems' six hundred escorts, with the sachems of the three other central Seneca settlements, had retreated to defend the Seneca country in the face of Frontenac's reiterated threats and warnings.[64]

Sinnedowane's sachems alone were left to represent the most numerous nation of the Iroquois. The Sinnedowane speaker, the sachem Adondarechaa, began his speech with a Seneca definition of the Covenant

63. Quotations are from C.O. 1/40, 82–83. Variant printed versions are in Leder, ed., "Indian Records," Pa. Hist., 23: 45–47, and in Browne, ed., Archives of Maryland, V, 256–58.
64. Browne, ed., Archives of Maryland, V, 258–59. Leder, ed., "Indian Records," Pa. Hist., 23: 47–48. C.O. 1/40, 83. N.Y.C.D., III, 256.

Chain, he stressed the antiquity of its origins, and he recounted Edmund Andros' role in reshaping it. Adondarechaa observed that his nation had "never had warrs with this Governmt." either in its Dutch or its English period. Rather, with New York "we have alwaies had a firm Covenant . . . wch hath been faithfully kept by the Governor Genll. whom we have taken to be our greatest Lord." When the old association with the Albany market had become military and diplomatic as well as mercenary, Iroquoian thinking required it to become a personal relationship. For the Seneca, therefore, Corleaer had become a sachem, one of the *Hoyarnagówar* and the greatest of these league lords.

No Christian and European "father" image was about to be accepted by the Seneca stalwarts of traditional Iroquoian culture. Largest, least acculturated, most distant from the Europeans of the leagued peoples, the Seneca were still "feather-wearers," traditionalists. They had wondered at Wentworth Greenhalgh's horses. They had welcomed his party with feasts and dancing. They had offered him and his escorts "such maids as liked us to ly with." They had tortured prisoners from the Gulf Coast and the southwest before the envoys (for their edification, the warrior captives were made to sing their war songs and to confess their killings). Then "there were most cruelly burned four men, four women, and one boy, the cruelty lasted about seven hours, when they were almost dead, letting them loose to ye mercy of ye boys, and taking the hearts of such as were dead to feast on." No sooner had the exhausted envoys gone to sleep than they were shocked by "a great noyse, as if ye houses had all fallen butt it was onely ye Inhabitants driving away ye Ghosts of ye murthered." Such was unspoiled Iroquoia.[65]

Its greatest lord, the governor-general, was owed thanks, so the Seneca sachem Adondarechaa said, "for he hath put aside all mistakes" and so prevented the Seneca attacks on the Chesapeake colonists from coming home to them. In the presence of the governor-general, the Seneca were pleased to negotiate a peace with the envoy from Maryland and Virginia. The Seneca knew that "Our People have been Offensive unto yu," Adondarechaa said to Coursey, but the Seneca proposed to him as a model of future peace "ye Covenant we have with the Governr. Genll." The Seneca agreed that, if attacked by Chesapeake tribesmen, they would give the governments of Virginia and Maryland an opportunity to obtain satisfaction from their native clients for the injured Iroquois "before we take up the axe agt. them." The Seneca asked reciprocal treatment for themselves so that their greatest lord would be—as he afterwards often was—called on by the Chesapeake governments to negotiate settlements with the Seneca, rather than having to resort to hostil-

65. Greenhalgh's journal, 28 May–14 July 1677, *N.Y.C.D.*, III, 251–52.

ities. Adondarechaa explained, "the reason that we plundered the English was their Entertaining of those Indians that were our Enemies." Victory over the Susquehanna, however, made it easy for the Seneca to "promise never to do the like" again. Having accepted generous presents from Colonel Coursey, the Seneca would observe their promises to his government, Adondarechaa said. They expected the like from the envoy who took up their beaver on behalf of the colonists.[66]

Last, and least, of the Five Nations to speak at the Covenant Chain council were the Cayuga. Their seven sachems were grateful for wagon transportation to Albany from Schenectady, their spokesman said, but they were miffed that "the Smallest Belt of Wampum was sent to us" to call them to the conference. So they sealed their word of complaint with "a Small Beaver." Of course, the Cayuga "Absolutely approve and confirm the Sinnondowannes Answer for our Resolution was taken together" with that of their uncles the Seneca, just as the Oneida answer had been agreed on in council with their fathers the Onondaga. An independent people with a voice of their own, however, the Cayuga were entitled to speak their part in the condolence council. So their spokesman repeated Coursey's propositions and the Seneca response. The Cayuga added that they would publish the covenant to their people "as we come home." Ever polite, if a bit hurt, the Cayuga concluded the Covenant Chain council, the Anglo-Iroquoian alliance, with proper thanks to their hosts "for the Propositions yu. have made and for the presents given us for our farr Journey."[67]

"Diligence and Faithfulness"

A "farr Journey" was imminent for Edmund Andros as well as for his western Iroquoian allies. At the end of August 1677, while he was still receiving "reitterated assurances . . . of their faithfullness" from the assembled Iroquois, the governor-general also "received leave from his Rll Highnesse to goe for England." The nature of his reception in the imperial metropolis was forecast in the duke's letter of leave. This letter

---

66. C.O. 1/40, 83. Leder, ed., "Indian Records," *Pa. Hist.*, 23: 47–48. Browne, ed., *Archives of Maryland*, V, 258–59.

67. Browne, ed., *Archives of Maryland*, V, 259–60. Leder, ed., "Indian Records," *Pa. Hist.*, 23: 48–49. C.O. 1/40, 83–84.

was almost cordial, coming as it did from so cold a prince as James Stuart, and it was in violent contrast to his condemnation of Sir William Berkeley, the personification of the colonial era ended in 1676 and the scapegoat of the Chesapeake revolution. His royal highness was pleased that his lieutenant's government in New York, alone of all those on the continent, had been kept in peace during "the time of troubles" that had centered on 1676. He and, more expansively, his secretary were further gratified that Andros' accounts for 1676 actually showed a surplus in the duke's New York revenue, this despite the war and its attendant expenses for Indian presents and arms, and for the costs of four forts—Fort James, Fort Albany, Fort Charles (at Pemaquid, fabricated in January 1676/7), and the Newcastle-on-Delaware stockade—as well as for the relief of Rhode Island and the supply of the offshore islands and outlying settlements of the duke's dominions during King Philip's War. The duke therefore not only agreed to continue Andros' present customs rates and collectors, he even made him a gift of the £200 contingency money advanced at the outset of his government. This gift was an earnest of the duke's promise to Andros that "I shall on occasion be mindefull of your diligence and faithfulness in my service."[68]

The duke's secretary expanded upon the sources of the prince's pleasure with his lieutenant, boundary defense in particular. Andros' actions against Connecticut had been highly approved of. Connecticut's own aggression in patenting eastern New York lands had put the colony in the wrong. It would be kept there by the king-in-council's resolution—growing quickly as the dimensions of the disasters of 1676 were realized at Whitehall—"to enter upon a regulacon of matters in New England." All obstacles to the duke's present assertion of "all those rights intended him by . . . the crowne" would soon be removed, Andros was told. His actions against New England's independence would be not just confirmed but greatly enlarged upon, as it happened, by Andros himself in accordance with the recommendations he would make to the privy council.[69]

"As for the Northerne Bounds" of the duke's dominions, the duke's secretary agreed with his lieutenant that these were the lake and river of Canada. French pretensions south of them were to be rejected, as Andros and the Iroquois had done. James Stuart's southern boundary, won by conquest from the Dutch, was well beyond the Delaware. Andros had done well, he was told, to defend it from the Marylanders. As Sir John Werden wrote, the duke's household officers were concerned that the region was held for their master by no better title than conquest and by

68. Andros' "General Concerns," *N.Y.C.D.*, III, 256. His royal highness [York] to Major Andros, 7 May 1677, *ibid.*, 246; also in C.O. 5/1112, 24.
69. Werden to Andros, 7 May 1677, *ibid.*, 24–25; also in *N.Y.C.D.*, III, 246–47.

continual application of force, claims "wch indeed to an ordinary person would not be very secure."

His royal highness was no ordinary person, but even so Andros was warned that his colleagues in the duke's imperial household had not been able to have the acts of trade relaxed for the wife of Andros' partner, Frederick Phillips (as that anglicized merchant was now known). The governor-general was also warned that he would be coming home to an active, if not distracted, political season at Whitehall. Parliament was to be summoned in hopes that the crown could equal its successes of the 1676–77 session in obtaining ship money and excise taxes.

Thus briefed and encouraged, Edmund Andros made his preparations to take a brief leave from his government, fully aware that it was his drive, determination, and dogged adherence to the imperial interests of the English crown that had, in the three years centered upon 1676, made New York the dynamic center of English empire on the American continent.

As quickly as he could, the governor-general concluded the Covenant Chain council at Albany. Before he left the town, he amplified its trading privileges, taxes, and military discipline. Then he sailed down the Hudson and met the annual sessions of the "General Court of Assizes" for its mixture of judicial, legislative, and advisory business in October. To the general court and council the governor-general read (parts of) the duke's letter of leave. As it required, he asked his advisers, executives, and magistrates if, in their collective opinion, his absence "might be withoutt prejudice or inconvenience to his Duty or Country." Duly reassured that he could have the winter off, the governor-general instructed all of the civil magistrates and military officers of the duke in their duty, alerted the neighboring colonies to his departure, gave his lady a power of attorney for his personal affairs, and sailed from Sandy Hook for England on 17 November 1677.[70]

"Such Popular Governments"

O n 8 April 1678, the privy-council committee for foreign plantations met at Whitehall. "Taking notice of . . . the business of New Eng-

70. *N.Y.C.D.*, III, 256. For the cabinet's prior discussion of the New York–Amsterdam trade, see S.P. 104/176, 84, 85v.

land which hath long depended before them," they were told by Secretary Williamson that his royal highness was about "to despatch Sir Edmund Andros to his Government of New York." Before the king's new knight sailed, the royal duke had suggested that the imperial councilors learn the lessons of 1676 from the successful Sir Edmund. By exposing New York's concerns to the privy council, the duke again declared his proprietary possession to be a government of the king's. There the writ of Charles II had always run. Now New York was the most royal of American provinces.[71]

Obedient as always to the duke's commands, the council committee asked Sir Edmund in. He began his testimony by defining the boundaries of the ducal province. He described the challenges to them by corporate and proprietary colonies. Having opened the sad story of New England's aggression, Andros easily moved on to a central concern of the council by re-emphasizing his oft-reported judgment that Massachusetts had unnecessarily expanded, if it had not actually begun, King Philip's War. The leaders of the "Confederate Colonies" had compounded their error by spurning his assistance and that of the Mohawk, Andros reported. When they went ahead anyway and won the war despite the New Englanders, the ungrateful commonwealthsmen accused Albany of supplying Philip's armies. Spurned and slandered, the Anglo-Iroquoian allies had not only decided the war, they had negotiated the peace as well, Sir Edmund reported, for the racist and popular governments of the puritan colonies were not able to manage this for themselves.

Excited by this explicit confirmation of their anti-puritan, anti-popular, anti-corporate prejudices, the privy councilors asked the duke to have Sir Edmund expand his testimony from his discussion of the duke's dominions to report the impressions he had received of their bad neighbors in New England during the critical year 1676. The mere minutes of Sir Edmund's response fill ten large printed pages, but a few of his analyses and recommendations must be recounted here, for they had a special shaping power over the development of England's empire in America in the wake of the revolutions of 1676, red, white, and imperial.

First, Sir Edmund said, the events of 1676 had demonstrated that the confusion of boundaries and jurisdictions, rights and obligations, arising out of three-quarters of a century of conflicting colonial patents and possessions, a period of "almost continuall Warrs" during which rights could not be legally determined, meant that nothing short of the direct intervention of "the King's Royall authority" in America would ever produce either justice or security for his subjects there. "All my hopes is Regula-

71. Minutes of the privy-council plantations committee, 8 April 1678, *N.Y.C.D.*, III, 257.

tions and Orders from the King, as the only means to keep us well in peace and preserve or defend us if wars," Andros wrote.[72]

Imperial intervention would be easier because New England, numerous though its people were, had "noe noted experienced officer among them," Major Andros observed. (It is worth observing that the French delayed their planned assault on New York in 1676/7 as much because Major Andros "has some reputation" militarily as because of expected Iroquoian opposition and ongoing European negotiations.) Moreover, the puritan commonwealths were enfeebled by "disadvantages very greate" from the war "& likely to be more, even in the losse of sd Indians."[73]

New England's loss in native population had been New York's gain because of Andros' realization that the welfare of English empire in America depended upon careful, courteous, even cordial relations with the native nations. American peace, Andros observed, depended mostly on agreements, his covenants, with the Amerindians. Yet, during 1676, none of New York's colonial neighbors north of the Chesapeake, Maryland included, had accepted Andros' offers of diplomatic service, despite their "greatest occasions" for assistance. Nonetheless, all had benefited from his imperial efforts. The governor-general naturally concluded from this experience that peace with the Indians could not be maintained "so long as each petty Colony hath or assumes absolute power of Peace and Warr, which cannot be managed by such popular Governments, as was evident by the late Indian wars in New England."[74]

Union, "as one people and country," Sir Edmund said, was the only possible security for England's northern colonies. This, however, "(by reason of the severall distinct independen[t] collonys) cannot be but by His Mat[ies] asserting, & regulating the militia or force of ye severall collonyes." As unified defense required the elimination of the colonies' military independence, so their protection by the crown's orders and officers would secure the colonists' obedience to them "all for the future." Royal rule and regulation would impose colonial unity. Unified by the crown, as Sir Edmund Andros presciently observed a century before the fact,

72. "Answers to the Inquiries of Plantacions for New Yorke . . . Recd from Sr Edm. Andros on the 16th of Ap. 1678," *ibid.*, 260; also in C.O. 5/1111, 23. Andros to Blathwayt, 12 October 1678, *ibid.*, 43–44; also in *N.Y.C.D.*, III, 272–73.

73. M. Du Chesneau to M. de Seignelay, Quebec, 14 November 1679, *N.Y.C.D.*, IX, 137. See the same source's estimate of "Boston" as "a Republic, under the protection of England, faintly recognizing his Britannic Majesty," the elected governor of which, Leverett, "is an old man, ill qualified for war." Andros is quoted from his answer to inquiries, 9 April 1678, *ibid.*, III, 263.

74. Andros to William Blathwayt, New York, 16 September 1678, *ibid.*, 271; also in C.O. 5/1111, 42.

the English colonies in America could not only "bring any Indians to reason"; they could also make any effort to conquer the colonies from Europe more expensive "then [possession of] the country could compensate."[75]

He had declared a century beforehand what was to be the strategic determinant of the American Revolution of 1776, but what Sir Edmund immediately anticipated from the revolutions of 1676 was the Dominion of New England. In it, all the territories from the Delaware to the St. Croix, which the governor-general had protected and pacified in alliance with the Five Nations of the Iroquois during 1676, became a single viceroyalty under his command ten years later. A military coup in England was echoed in America before the dominion was three years old, sabotaging the only opportunity for a regional government of northeastern America. What was achieved under Sir Edmund's dominion government, and what has prevailed to the present as his legacy to America, was the political and cultural anglicization of New England.

As he looked back at his experience in 1676, Andros not only anticipated his creative command of 1686, but also commented on the peculiar nature of puritan rule with a penetration that gives the lie to the canards still current about his political perception. Contravening the prevalent prejudice of the English imperial authorities—that New Englanders were all regicides and republicans—Sir Edmund insisted that "the generality of the Magistrates and people are well affected to ye King & Kingdome." He had then to explain why they had rejected his much-needed aid, and every other imperial manifestation. Andros' answers were New England's commonwealth habits and corporate ignorance. The colonists, he explained, "knoweing noe other governmt then their owne, think it best, and are wedded to and opinionate for it." Elected within and sworn to uphold these colonial corporations, the magistrates "are obliged to assert & maintaine sd Governmt all they cann." As the ruling elite were congregationalists, so in religion as in government, Andros said, they "depend upon the people to justifie them in their actions." Sir Edmund's antidotes for commonwealth politics and congregational religion were obvious, given his prior career: royal rule and the Church of England; regional planning and command in defense and for trade; fair, firm, and, if absolutely necessary, forceful dealings with native nations and European populations alike. These were the hallmarks of Andros' imperialism. It was with good reason that, in 1686, the chief of the moderate, anglican, monarchical imperialists hoped for "a good account of New England, and much for the Kings advantage, if Sir Edmund Andros

75. *N.Y.C.D.*, III, 263.

goes thither: he understands the people and knows how to manage them." [76]

"He Certainly Did
Great Things"

Naturally, so aristocratic, so arrogant, so anglican, so royalist a soldier, diplomat, and magistrate made many enemies. When Andros left New York, the Connecticut government once again bitterly denounced his questioning of their colony's borders. They declared that they knew of no services performed for them in the late war either by him or by "his Indians." Massachusetts sourly concluded that Andros was, inexplicably, more concerned with the good will of the Mohawk than with theirs. From the opposite frontier of the ducal dominions, the baron Baltimore pronounced himself furious at Andros because of "the great obstruction he had given Colonel Coursey in his negotiation at Fort Albany." Against the ambitions of the Calverts, Andros had shielded settlers, Susquehanna, and the Seneca. Instead of leaving them subject to the proprietary power of the baron Baltimore, Andros had bound them all to the imperial interest of the duke of York. Sir Edmund, the angry proprietor said, "is both knave and coward." [77]

South across the Potomac, however, Baltimore's neighbors found nothing but good in Andros' creation, the Covenant Chain, that all-encompassing peace by which, as even Lord Baltimore admitted, the great wars of 1676 had been ended. The secretary of Virginia recorded both Virginia's adherence to the Covenant Chain and its people's gratitude to the primary peacemaker. Colonel Jeffreys' government, he wrote, had added to the treaty of May 1676 "one article by wch wee have included all the English and Indians in Maryland as they have done for us and New Yorke & New England soe that the peace at present is universall

---

76. *Ibid.*, 264. The earl of Clarendon, lord lieutenant of Ireland, to William Blaithwait, Dublin Castle, 15 May 1686, in Samuel W. Singer, ed., *The Correspondence of Henry Hyde, earl of Clarendon* . . . (London, 1828), I, 393.

77. Charles baron Baltemore to William Blathwait, 11 March 1681/2, in Browne, ed., *Archives of Maryland*, V, 349.

and we owe much of it to the great activity and dilligence of Major Andrews Governr. of New Yorke." [78]

William Penn's colonial success was also based upon the political and diplomatic achievements of Edmund Andros in 1676 (and on the generosity of "the duke, his master" five years afterwards). Pennsylvania's laudable record of peaceful relations with the Native Americans rested on the Anglo-Iroquoian alliance that Edmund Andros and Daniel Garacontié had engineered. Penn's "Great Experiment" in pacifism and social experimentation flourished only because it was sheltered on the one side by the military and diplomatic might of the English empire and on the other side by that of the Five Nations of the Iroquoian League, two powers associated by Edmund Andros for the development of mid-America.

On Andros' retirement from New York, William Penn wrote, "he has no easy game to play yt comes after Sr Ed. Andros for tho he was not without objection he certainly did great things more than both his predecessors," the famous founder of English New York, Richard Nicolls, and its failed defender, Francis Lovelace. Indeed, Penn wrote, he wanted to keep Andros in America and wished that he "had a place worthy of his Care." If Sir Edmund would go on in the government of what were now, thanks to him, "the middle colonies," William Penn offered to give him "ten thousand acres of Land & the Command of the Three Countys [of Delaware, which Andros had founded] and use him always as my Friend." [79]

Unfortunately for the political tranquillity of Penn's province, he could not secure Sir Edmund's services, for four successive English sovereigns felt as he did about Andros' abilities. They kept him constantly employed in the imperial executive for another twenty-eight years from the date of Penn's letter. When Penn wrote, Sir Edmund was groom of the bedchamber to King Charles, the heir apparent's servant at the side of the dying king. King James promoted Sir Edmund to colonel's rank in the royal cavalry when he rode west in 1685 to help repress Monmouth's rebellion. Immediately thereafter, Sir Edmund Andros became the governor-general of the new Dominion of New England. He emerged with difficulty, but in triumph, from the wreckage of King James' regime. Andros' acquaintance of thirty years before, the prince of Orange, now William III of England, commissioned Sir Edmund governor-general of Virginia. After six years in that command, the aged Andros accepted from

78. T. Ludwell to Sec. Coventry, 29 December 1677, Coventry Ms. 78, Longleat House, Wiltshire, England.
79. "W. P. Philada, 30th 5 mo. 1683," *Pennsylvania Magazine* 39 (1916), 233–34. This concludes with a P.S.: "Pray give my Salutes to Sr Ed. Andrews."

Queen Anne the government of his bailiwick, Guernsey. There, in 1711, after a term of seven years, Andros concluded his long lifetime of service to the Stuart sovereigns. In all of his imperial commands, Sir Edmund Andros still acted upon the principles and preserved the reputation he had won in 1676.

SOME SUGGESTED READING FOR BOOK THREE

The sketch of a great life, that of Daniel Garacontié of Onondaga, is based, as all such works must be, on inspired reporting. The supremely intelligent and insightful reports of the Jesuit fathers were collected, edited, translated, and republished by Ruben Gold Thwaites and his associates at the State Historical Society of Wisconsin (see note 1, page 251). Although there is in this splendid series of sources the material of many seventeenth-century Native-American lives, none, save for the pioneering articles in the *Dictionary of Canadian National Biography*, has been written. Bruce G. Trigger's two columns on "Garakontie" in the *Dictionary* (322–23) are by far the most extended work on the subject. It is based upon the *Relations*, and I have followed its authority whenever possible on the vexing questions of dating their collated contents. Also noteworthy is Louise Phelps Kellogg's interesting article in the *Dictionary of American Biography*, VII, 130–31. There are three lines on Garacontié in the extremely useful article by Elizabeth Tooker, "The League of the Iroquois: Its History, Politics, and Ritual," in Bruce G. Trigger, ed., *Northeast*, vol. 15 of *Handbook of North American Indians*, ed. William C. Sturtevant (Washington, 1978), 431.

I have also relied upon this splendid *Handbook* for synonymy, thus identifying most of the native nations with which Garacontié had dealings. For the French, one may still consult with pleasure Francis Parkman's great series *France and England in North America*, although the only mention of Garacontié, a few lines paraphrased from the *Relations*, is in *The Old Regime in Canada* (Boston, 1874), 184; in ed. of 1907, I, 245. Revision of Parkman's Bostonian prejudices in accordance with modern canons of scholarship has been undertaken by W. J. Eccles, who summarized his work in *The Canadian Frontier 1534–1760* (New York, 1969).

Anyone interested in Iroquoian culture will also consult Trigger's masterwork on the Huron Iroquois, *The Children of Aataenstic: A History of the Huron People to 1660* (Montreal, 1976), and its very readable compaction, *The Huron Farmers of the North* (New York, 1969). On the English relations with the Iroquois during this period, the standard work not cited in the notes is Allen W. Trelease, *Indian Affairs in Colonial New York* (Ithaca, 1960; Port Washington, 1971). On the Iroquois relations with the English, although it does not speak particularly to the period of Garacontié's life, Anthony F. C. Wallace's *The Death and Rebirth of the Seneca* (New York, 1970, 1972) is indispensable.

On Onondaga and its people, see the works by Bradley, Clark, and Tuck cited above (note 8, page 258). For Onondaga's place in the League of the Iroquois, see Parker (note 1, page 251) and Morgan (note 14, page 261). For the league's imperial career, Hunt (note 13, page 260) is still invaluable.

Garacontié's aboriginal obsession was the Susquehanna. On this nation, there is the brilliant study by Francis Jennings, "Glory, Death and Transfiguration: The Susquehannock Indians in the Seventeenth Century," cited above (note 44, page 382). Also fundamental is the same author's "The Constitutional Evolution of the Covenant Chain," *Proceedings of the American Philosophical Society* 115 (1971), 88–96, although this does not discuss the 1675–76 negotiations. Jennings' forthcoming work on Iroquois diplomacy has been cited (note 68, page 301). The literature on the Iroquois is a large one and may be reviewed in Trigger's *Northeast* (807–90) and in Elizabeth Tooker's *The Indians of the Northeast: A Critical Bibliography* (Bloomington, 1978).

Among the secondary sources on Edmund Andros' early career cited in the text, special attention should be paid to Edith F. Carey's pocket biographies of "Amias Andros and Sir Edmund His Son" (note 5, page 310), based upon sources that were burned in the Andros manor house. The role of the Guards in the Restoration cycle of plot and repression is treated in the second chapter of my *The Governors-General* (see pages 287–88). The political backgrounds of Major Andros' service in the West Indies are best described in Harlow's *Barbados* (note 12, page 315), but see also C. S. S. Higham's *The Development of the Leeward Islands Under the Restoration 1660–1688* (Cambridge, 1921). More generally, see A. P. Thornton's *West India Policy Under the Restoration* (Oxford, 1956). For social development, consult Richard S. Dunn's *Sugar and Slaves: The Rise of the Planter Class in the English West Indies, 1624–1713* (Chapel Hill, 1972).

Andros' New York years are the subject of the first part of Jeanne Gould Bloom's dissertation, "Sir Edmund Andros: A Study in Seventeenth Century Colonial Administration" (Yale University, 1962), which also treats his governments in New England and Virginia. Besides Brodhead's *History of the State of New York* (note 36, page 328) see also W. F. Craven's *Colonies in Transition*, which corrects what is otherwise the best single chapter on Andros' administration, in the third volume of Andrews, *Colonial Period* (see page 164). Some of the best of the more recent studies are Patricia U. Bonomi's *A Factious People* (New York, 1971); Michael Kammen's *Colonial New York* (New York, 1975); and Sung Bok Kim's *Landlord and Tenant in Colonial New York* (Chapel Hill, 1978). Especially valuable for the present work has been the meticulous scholarship of Robert C. Ritchie in *The Duke's Province* (Chapel Hill, 1977).

On Andros' subsequent career see Bloom's dissertation, my "The Trials of Sir Edmund Andros" (in *The Human Dimensions of Nation Making*, James Kirby Martin, ed. [Madison, 1976], 23–53, and the sources therein cited), and *The Governors-General*, index, s.v. "Andros, Sir Edmund."

CONCLUSIONS

THE REVOLUTIONS OF 1676
AND THE END OF
AMERICAN INDEPENDENCE

"Here's fine revolution,
an we had the trick to see 't."

HAMLET V.1.96–97

"**R**evolution" has three modern meanings related to sociopolitical transformation (none of them that astronomical analogy of cyclical change so beloved of recent historical reflection). The oldest meaning (c. 1450) is simply "a great change in affairs." Such was the alteration of the Amerindian balance of power in 1676, the consequence of King Philip's War in the north, the Susquehanna war in the south, and the advantage taken of both by the League of the Iroquois.

The second meaning (c. 1600) of "revolution" describes the second Anglo-American event of 1676. Consequent upon the Amerindian Revolution there was "a complete overthrow of the established government . . . by those who were previously subject to it." Nathaniel Bacon's Revolution in Virginia, first against a failure of frontier defense, then against the colonial regime of Sir William Berkeley, and finally against the empire of England, was such a revolution.

The third sort of "revolution" (c. 1600) which concerned contemporaries also occurred in 1676. This was "a forcible substitution of a new ruler or [here "and"] form of government." Such was the royal reaction to the failed autonomy of Sir William Berkeley, the independence asserted by Nathaniel Bacon, and the initial indications of the Amerindian Revolution.

The physical range and political profundity of the Imperial Revolution extended far beyond the imposition of a Guards colonel to replace Bacon and Berkeley and the installation of a garrison government to eliminate autonomy and independence in Virginia. Not only was a "new-model" government installed in the Old Dominion, but the imperial crown also exploited the effects of the Amerindian Revolution to challenge New England independence. That both New England and Virginia were weakened by the Amerindian Revolution and that its victors, the Five Nations, were located within the duke of York's dominions and allied with his lieutenant, shifted the gravity of American development from the older English colonies to the multi-ethnic settlements between the Hudson and the Delaware, to ducal "New York" and its successor provinces.

The Imperial Revolution altered the shape of American institutions; it redirected the course of colonial growth; it made autonomous colonial politics Anglo-American. Economic and social exchanges, as well as political culture, were anglicized in the wake of the crown's "forcible substitution" of royal rule for that of colonial oligarchs. American colonies thus became English provinces. The imperially instituted diplomatic union of the Anglo-American provinces encouraged even the most imperious Amerindians to become serviceable allies of "the Great King Charles over the great Lake." These alterations in America transformed Whitehall's view of the world. Now Eastern America was seen as a whole, with its political, diplomatic, strategic center not, as formerly, at Boston or at Jamestown, the capitals of the old colonial cultures, but, rather, at the headquarters of England's continental empire in America, Fort James, New York. The three revolutions of 1676 had ended American independence.

The independence asserted and assaulted in Virginia and New England in 1676 was proclaimed anew a century afterwards. Both the extinction of seventeenth-century autonomy and the foundations of eighteenth-century freedom were the work of many more years than the central and symbolic "'76." The alternative to American autonomy, the imperial constitution itself, was not decisively defined until the crown issued the Jamaica and Virginia instructions of 1681. The imposition of royal government on Virginia was not completed until 1683. The annulment of New England's corporate regimes waited until 1684. The Dominion of New England, although it was charted by Major Andros' actions in 1676 and called for in Sir Edmund's reports of 1678, was not operative under his command until 1686. The effects of the coup of 1688/9, which ostensibly undid much of the Imperial Revolution, were not repaired until 1691. Even then, it was more than a decade before the apogee of the Old Empire was reached.

No sooner was the work of imperialism and anglicization well established than it became clear to the governors-general that royal repression and English acculturation had themselves sown the seeds of subsequent revolution. Royally imposed social peace and physical protection permitted physical recovery in the provinces during the generation after 1676 and ensured actual advance in the subsequent, postwar, era after 1714. The very anglicization of politics first reformed and then revivified provincial institutions and ideology. For example, the imposition of tripartite provincial government—governor-general, royal council, representative body—destroyed the unarticulated institutions of American autonomy, but it structurally encouraged debates couched in terms of the executive-oriented ideology of court and country, tory and whig. These debates voiced Americans' search for imperial order, royal justice, and executive leadership on the one hand and yet, on the other, expressed their insistence upon measures of provincial self-sufficiency and self-government.

The eclipse of American independence after 1676 was an effect of the debilitation of its bases in the older English colonies. Their dramatic decline from American pre-eminence and their long subjection to English empire were a function of their failure to acknowledge the importance, or respect the integrity, of the Amerindians. New Englanders remained convinced, despite the dreadful lessons of 1676, that the only "reasonable" response to Indian self-assertion was "the utter extirpation" of the aborigines. The mass of Virginians wanted "to ruine and extirpate all Indians in Generall." Given such genocidal urges, the English colonists could not come to terms with King Philip, the Susquehanna sachems, or the Iroquoian lords. Yet it was their interaction, the Amerindian Revolution, that both instigated and determined the epochal events of 1676.

King Philip did more than any Englishman to end the independence of New England. His revenge on the puritans who invaded his homeland and violated his culture was multiplied many times by the other Algonquin antagonized by the godly colonists' aggression and bigotry, their greed and racism. In less than two years' time, the aggrieved Amerindians killed as many as two thousand five hundred colonists, erased a generation of settlement, and forestalled New England's expansion for almost a century. The Algonquin cost was catastrophic: six thousand dead, wounded, and enslaved meant the end of national existences for the native societies of southern New England. The puritan colonists (with the signal assistance of Jamaican buccaneers and Mohawk Iroquois) had found a "final solution" to their domestic Indian problem. Ironically, however, the puritan purge of the "heathen barbarians" from their midst not only externalized but also reinforced the native barrier to New England's growth. A frontier line, between colonists and natives, between

New England and Iroquoia, replaced the cellular structure of mixed Indian and colonial villages, and was a far more effective limit on New England expansion. King Philip's War had sapped the physical (and psychic) strength of puritanism, limited the territorial frontiers of New England, and dramatically reduced the corporate colonies' ability to resist the rising tide of English empire either politically or economically.

A parallel process produced even more dramatically damaging results to American independence in the continent's other early English center of isolated settlement and institutional autonomy, the "Old Dominion" of Virginia. Frontiersmen fed on the spoils of the beaten Powhatan peoples incautiously attacked the Susquehanna Iroquois. When these "roily water people" completed their ritual revenge, they had killed more than five hundred settlers to compensate for their five fallen sagamores and pushed the Virginia frontier back below the fall line. The frontier fighting that grew out of the Susquehanna revenge may have doubled the colonial casualties.

Their Iroquoian cousins not only fell upon the dispersed Susquehanna and "exterminated" them; they also attacked any Chesapeake colonists who crossed them in their scouring of the Susquehanna. The outraged colonists attacked every Indian they could find. Native reprisals were multiplied. The upshot of the Amerindian Revolution in the Old Dominion was that the Virginians lost most of their former frontier and much of its European population, virtually eliminated economically valuable native nations, and erased the interracial frontiers within the colony, only to find themselves—as the New Englanders had done—faced with a new frontier line defined and defended by the Iroquois.

The defeated and homogenized older colonies were confined by the victorious and diversified Five Nations. Their League of Peace and Power was now reinforced by refugee New England Algonquin and amalgamated Susquehanna Iroquois. The Amerindian losers of 1676 were successfully integrated into the socializing clans of the kinship league to defend the vastly expanded perimeters of its sphere of influence. These Iroquoian edges were now the frontiers of every English colony on the American continent. The league itself nonetheless remained divided between rival diplomatic and economic nexuses. The eastward-looking Mohawk shared the Albany headquarters of their associate "Corleaer," the governor-general of the duke of York's dominions (the territories between the New England and the Chesapeake colonies). The southern- and westward-oriented Onondaga's great town of Onnontagé was the traditional capital of Iroquoia, however, and the senior sachem of the Onondaga, the Sagochiendagehté, was the statesman and spokesman of the "Seneca" (the four western fires of the Lodge Extended Lengthwise).

Both the western and eastern Iroquois, their spokesmen, the Sagochiendagehté (Daniel Garacontié) and, for the Mohawk, Carondondawe, were brought together with Coursey for the Chesapeake colonies, Richards and Pynchon for New England, and Cospechy for the Algonquin refugees, by Corleaer, New York's governor-general, Edmund Andros, in the Covenant Chain conferences of 1677. These negotiations concluded the Amerindian Revolution of 1676. While exchanges exhibited the rivalries of the Iroquois, each of the Five Nations nonetheless accepted "the Absolute Covenant of Peace" proposed by Daniel Garacontié. This "universal peace," extending from Maine to the Carolinas, was symbolized by a silver "Covenant Chain." The chain was the senatorial Sagochiendagehté's metaphor for the association of the Iroquoian League with both the English colonies and the imperial crown, through the agency of Edmund Andros and in accord with the ancient league principles of reparation and reciprocity. By effectively extending the jurisdiction of the Iroquoian League from the national territories of the Five Nations, bounded on the east by the Falls of the Mohawk and on the west by the gorge of the Genesee, to a vast sphere of influence extending from the frontiers of English settlement westward to the Illinois, the Covenant Chain not only defined the present supremacy of the Iroquois, it also facilitated the future empire of the English. For a century and a half after 1676, American settlement would be concentrated in the confines charted by the Covenant Chain council. What the Iroquois claimed in 1676, the English largely acquired from them by 1768, and the Americans developed for generations after they dispersed the league.

That ultimate American development of the Iroquoian sphere also owed much to the second or political revolution of 1676. The state forms and political organization, the republican ideology and revolutionary institutions, considered characteristically American were most amply articulated in Virginia during 1676. There, colonial responses to the Amerindian Revolution successively produced frontier revolt, political reform, civil war, social revolution, and American independence.

The political revolution of 1676 was couched in the terms of English "country," commonwealth, civil-war ideology. Nathaniel Bacon's first reaction to Sir William Berkeley's failed frontier defenses, Bacon's followers' demands for more responsible government and more respectable governors, the civil-war justifications of both rebels and loyalists, the social leveling and political rationalizations of the domestic revolution in the Chesapeake, all were expressed in the language of the previous, revolutionary, generation in England. It was the partisan legacy of that generation, the "country's" fear of the "court's" military and monarchist conspiracy against liberty, localism, and legislatures, which inspired the triumphant revolutionaries to assert their independence from the English crown in 1676.

The institutional expressions of political revolution and American independence in 1676—the association of taxation with representation; the introduction of general elections and popular participation at every level of the extant government; revolutionary rule by committees of associators, bound by oath to resist oligarchy, monarchy, and empire—were 1676's inheritance from the English Revolution and its legacy to the American Revolution of 1776. So too was the public activity of otherwise repressed classes. Women, servants, and slaves organized and fought the revolution, which was excited by Indian attacks and made articulate by educated English emigrants.

These emigrants, sometimes themselves veterans of civil war and military dictatorship, otherwise their heirs, left many thousands of counterparts behind at home to resist the modern, militarized, monarchy. Naturally, their slogans, whether a 1676 London reprint of the *Historical Discourse* of that commonwealth and Cromwellian statesman Nathaniel Bacon—a defense of legislative and lawful government—or Francis Jenks' proto-whig speech of 1676 to the common hall of the City against the Franco-Catholic absolutist conspiracy—were echoed in Jamestown and Boston, examples of the unities of Anglo-American politics and of the "country" protest against the imperial prerogative. The "court" of Charles II knew that political revolution was as incipient in England as it was actual in the Chesapeake, and that republican ideology was as popular in Barbados or Bristol as it was in the corporations of Massachusetts Bay or the City of London.

Yet the English crown (as few but the most sanguine of absolutists predicted in 1676) had permanently ended British revolution. The instruments of the Imperial Revolution would be as effectively repressive in the British realm as they had been in the American dominions of the English crown. The Scots rising of 1679 would be crushed by the duke of Monmouth's royal regulars, and he himself would be defeated by the redcoats in 1685. The last upheaval in England itself, the so-called "revolution" of 1689, was a coup d'état, not a change of government, an event more reactionary than revolutionary. The same political and physical instruments—a bureaucratized privy council and a departmentalized executive; the "Guards and Garrisons"—which made the crown invulnerable in Britain by 1676 were either applied, by the privy council, or transported, in the case of garrison government, to America to undo independence in Virginia and confine it in New England.

Cases in point are the first two American regiments of the English army, the Barbados Regiment of 1667–78 and the Virginia Regiment of 1676–83. They embodied the military monopoly which underlay imperial monarchy in "Greater Britain." Edmund Andros had been major of the Barbados Regiment in its successive incarnations as marines, garrison companies, and dragoons; in its various posts, Barbados, the Leeward Islands, English ports, London's Hounslow Heath, Irish towns; in its wide-ranging duties in imperial assault, colonial and coastal defense, political and military police; in its dealings with American colonists and Caribs, English soldiers and subjects, Irish natives and recruits. Major Andros took his experience of this imperial corps, together with the staff and infantry characteristic of that garrison government by which the English crown controlled the British Isles, out to command New York, to confine New England, and, as it happened, to ally England with the Iroquois.

Full attention elsewhere has precluded much discussion here of the central role of the sovereign's Guards in imperial politics and social stabilization throughout the empire. Of all the Guards-based regiments, that sent to Virginia in 1676 to repress revolution and undo autonomy, under its colonel, the royal commissioner and imperial executive Herbert Jeffreys, has as obscure a history as any. Yet it was a fundamental force in the Imperial Revolution of 1676 and so has impressed the shape of American institutions and attitudes ever since.

Not only did the Virginia Regiment repress the revolution, still smoldering at its arrival in the Old Dominion, and oust the old regime, which had incited revolution and resisted royalization, the regiment's presence also enforced imperial orders to differentiate the government of Virginia into distinct branches, separate their responsibilities, and subject them all to direct supervision by the king-in-council at Whitehall. So the Guards of Charles II enforced the imposition on the political bellwether of early America of a tripartite, balanced, federal political model. Since assumed to be characteristically American, that political model is actually imperial in origin.

This Imperial Revolution and its armed authority was hateful to both revolutionaries and reactionaries in Virginia, just as the weight that the Guards gave the imperial executive in England was anathema to the country champions of aristocracy and locality, and their representatives at home. Thus the "standing army issue" was alive in both the metropolis and the provinces, in the realm and the dominions, and it remained controversial in the militarily contested and socially underdeveloped empire long after England itself had been physically secured and socially stabilized.

The focus of anti-military, anti-monarchical fears was James duke of York. The royal duke was the patron of both the colonel of the Virginia Regiment and the major of the Barbados Regiment. He was the chairman of the cabinet committee that directed the repression of the revolution and dictated the imperial reform of autonomous institutions in Virginia administered by Colonel Jeffreys. James Stuart was the proprietor of the province of New York, to which he dispatched Major Andros, ordering him to consolidate what became "The Middle Colonies," to establish socially responsible, politically authoritarian, militarily secure government there, and to use that government to ally the Iroquois to the empire and to isolate "the New England disease" of republican government and independence.

James Stuart's imperial role awaits a full assessment. Still, the story of a single year, 1676, has suggested the duke's manipulation of the developing imperial institution of the privy council of England during the crisis of 1676; his role in the transfer of garrison government to Virginia, New York, and New England; his dictation of the ensuing political definition, social development, military defense, and Amerindian alliance. Thus the royal duke was central to the creation of the cosmopolitan, continental provinces which asserted English empire and loyally supported it for more than a century. They dominated the region between the older, inherently independent, colonies that were eclipsed for a century by the Amerindian and Imperial revolutions of 1676. All of these momentous events and outcomes testify to the imperial importance of this vilified prince and his neglected, soldierly subordinates in the anglicization of America. During, after, and because of 1676, they put an end to American independence.

Maps and Decorations

The maps in *1676* are from *The Blathwayt Atlas*, a facsimile of the only unit surviving from the cartographic collections of the privy council's plantations committee. This geography of power was largely assembled and long possessed by that archetypal imperial bureaucrat, William Blathwayt. He began his Whitehall career in April 1676, when he took charge of the office staff of the plantations committee, and in May 1676 Blathwayt became the secretary attending their lordships' debates.[1]

His first reflection of the councilors' imperial attitudes was a Danbyite analysis of England's American priorities. In a world of warring empires, Blathwayt wrote, the colonies would be lost unless militarily organized and defended. Lost colonies only enhanced the strength of England's European rivals. Therefore, the first provincial priority was military protection. To this the public revenue of the provinces and their contributions to the English exchequer must be primarily devoted. To this all the demands of merchants or proprietors, traders or landholders, must be subordinated. The army and its officer-administrators first, the navy and its merchant auxiliaries second, and every private interest only afterwards: such were the imperial priorities Blathwayt parroted to his prime minister, the lord treasurer.

The young official (Blathwayt was twenty-seven in 1676) came naturally by these militant measures of empire and administration for he was the nephew and protégé of Thomas Povey, the Cromwellian civil servant and restoration imperial adviser. Under his uncle's patronage, Blathwayt began his official career, the only clerk in the English embassy at The Hague who was fluent in Dutch. His first official correspondence was with Major Edmund Andros about the gubernatorial politics of tin salvage. Their correspondence was to continue for thirty-five years. In immediate succession to Andros, Blathwayt served in the Swedish embassy, then entered the new plantations office shortly after its formation in 1675. On becoming office head in 1676, Blathwayt's first official act was to facilitate the payment of Andros' arrears as major of the Barbados Regiment. Blathwayt's first colonial correspondents were Andros' fellow-offi-

cers, now in command of Caribbean colonies. Acquiring a privy council
clerkship in July 1678—with special responsibility for the plantations
office—Blathwayt assured Governor-General Andros of the "great satisfaction" his recommendations for royalizing the government of New England had given the king in council and reported "their very great readiness" to impose on the puritan commonwealths "such a Settlement as
shall better sute with their Allegiance to the King." In May 1680, Blathwayt was commissioned auditor general of the plantations revenue and
he encouraged Sir Edmund Andros in his efforts to extend their joint
jurisdiction to New Jersey. King Charles next commissioned the colonial
secretary and auditor as secretary at war in August 1683. As "secretary of
war and plantations" (so the synthesis of 1676 had been institutionalized),
Blathwayt was instrumental in securing Sir Edmund Andros' commission
as governor-general of the Dominion of New England.[2]

It was in this era of imperial adolescence that Blathwayt collected,
both in his own special trips to The Hague and to Paris and from Governor-General Andros and his ilk, as well as from London mapmakers, the
cartographs which here chart the early career of Edmund Andros and of
the English empire c. 1676. This atlas of early English empire, like all the
English cartography of the period, demonstrates that English surveying,
drawing, engraving, and publishing were much inferior to Spanish geography, French rendering, and Dutch collection and distribution. Nonetheless, the *Atlas* summarizes Whitehall's world view, collecting the
pioneering productions of colonial surveyors, naval explorers, and the
"Thames School" of early English mapmakers, as well as French and
Dutch maps, in a volume largely compiled and intensely used by the
bureaucratic linchpin of imperial administration in the most politically
creative period of the English empire.

The vision of the known world and its European empires which
prevailed in England after 1676 is best expressed in John Thornton's "A
New Mapp of the World" (Map # 1 of the *Atlas*, reproduced on pages
174–175). It was issued in 1683 just as the outcomes of 1676 were being
written into the constitutions of England's overseas centers in the Caribbean, the Chesapeake, and along the littoral bisected by Cape Cod. As
these locations suggest, the English world view expressed by Thornton's
map was Atlantic-centered. And Thornton was especially concerned to
record the recent English contributions to Atlantic exploration—observations of compass variation for the ends of the Straits of Magellan—
which established Captain Wood's reputation. Thornton's dedication also
expresses England's Atlantic imperial orientation for the dedicatee, Sir
James Hayes, was, in 1676, deputy governor of the Hudson's Bay Company to Prince Rupert and was also a member of the Irish privy council.
Finally, Thornton's map "contains the best representation of American

colonial possessions to be shown on an English world map up to the time of its publication." [3]

Another of Thornton's productions, "A Mapp of Virginia Mary-land, New-Jarsey, New-York, & New England" (Map # 10 of the *Blathwayt Atlas*, partially reproduced facing page 23) is based in part on the survey of 1676 by James Wasse. This was conducted on behalf of the duke of York's favorite, William Penn, against the interests of Major John Fenwick and during Fenwick's imprisonment by Governor-General Andros. The surveyor's ship was that of Captain Samuel Groome, a capital unit of the York River squadron which fought against the Baconian revolutionaries. The map shows both end points of the Susquehanna migration of 1675/6 and many of the sites of the subsequent revolution in the Chesapeake region. Besides the direct correspondence of the sites named in the text with those on the map, see also West Point (Clayborgh) and King's Creek (at the "K" in "York"), rebel and loyalist headquarters, respectively, on the York River in 1676.

The Algonquin uprisings of 1675–1676, the Iroquoian counter-expansion, the relation of France to both, and the reports reaching England of all three, helped convince at least the Danbyite privy councilors that, even in aboriginal affairs (of which the king-in-council had previously taken but little notice), France was the root of enmity to English empire in America. The plantations committee sent Blathwayt off to Paris for intelligence of the imperial enemy. Map # 6 (partially reproduced at page 77) is presumably part of the parcel of books and maps which "the Elephant" (he never forgot) purchased for the committee. It was sadly dated even then, having been first printed in 1656, but Nicolas Sanson's "Le Canada, ou Nouvelle France, &c. . . ." nonetheless shows a knowledge of the interior geography and native inhabitants of America east of the Lakes unequaled by the English twenty years later.

In 1676, Robert Morden and William Berry published "A Map of New England New Yorke . . ." (Map # 12 of the *Blathwayt Atlas*, which is partially reproduced on page 220). Whether or not this map was drawn to illustrate Sanson's "Present State of New England" (with the continuation of which it was simultaneously published), the Morden and Berry publication illustrates that influential report of King Philip's successes against the New Englanders. The lost towns are located, the tribal territories labeled (including Philip's own "Mounthope") and the intrusive presence of "the Mowhawks"—whose invasion cost the Algonquins the war—is strongly engraved across southern New England.

Incited by Major Andros, the Mohawk not only eviscerated the Algonquin uprising in 1676/7, they exposed the military debility of the puritan governments. So much Andros made sure the crown comprehended. The result, as Blathwayt wrote Andros, was that "the Jurisdictions of the Massachusetts is somewhat lessened and I hope their Ambition will be so too. . . ." Blathwayt himself wrote the shrinkage of the puritan sphere onto his copy of the Morden and Berry map. He crossed out the over-extensive territorial claims of Massachusetts and Connecticut and he inscribed New Hampshire's boundaries instead. Blathwayt's young cousin and apprentice, John Povey, then colored in the western and northern restrictions on the colonial commonwealths imposed by Edmund Andros from the duke's dominions, New York and Maine. Povey also outlined the boundaries of Mason's New Hampshire and defined free-thinking Rhode Island. He vividly colored the edges of "the King's Province," the territory of the Narragansetts now preserved from the puritan expansionists, as Blathwayt wrote, by Andros' efforts. The end of puritan independence and expansion, the rise of the royalist proprietors, the annihilation of the Algonquin, the intrusion of the Mohawk Iroquois, all are memorialized on the Morden and Berry map.[4]

Prior concerns of Major Edmund Andros—and his imperial ilk—can be charted on Jean Baptiste du Tertre's elegant elevation of St. Christophers (Map # 27 of the *Blathwayt Atlas*, reproduced, minus its borders and surrounding seas, on page 316). This is an enlarged version of the map drawn by the former sailor, Orangist soldier, and Dominican priest for his *Histoire Générale des Antilles Habitée par les Francais* (note 16, page 317). Du Tertre's work underlies much of the description of the Barbados Regiment's failed assault on St. Kitts (pages 315–318). The sad site was seemingly southeast of "Pointe des Palmistes."

Not just the names of the places and the peoples of 1676 but their pictures as well are presented in this atlas of empire. These maps' "decorations"—cartouches and their supporters; exotic flora and fauna; ships, small craft, and seaports—all manifest the mind-set of European imperialists, express their racial assumptions, expose the technological and societal instruments of their empires, in short, chart the relation of geographic expansion to intellectual growth.

The technological marvels of the age of empire, the ships that conveyed the European invaders to America and fought their battles around the world, grace the margins of the *Blathwayt Atlas'* maps. Representations of the working ships of the seventeenth century are so few as to make these engravings valuable as records of the maritime instruments of European empire. The great *naus*, bound home to Portugal from India, round the Cape of Good Hope on Map # 46. Ships reach, run, and beat across the "Oceanus Aethiopicus" of Map # 47. They battle off of Guinea, Jamaica, and Montserrat (Maps # 45, 36, 30). They progress in rig and model from the broad-sailed, high-pooped Iberian galleons of Map # 40 to the tall-masted, low-decked English merchantmen of Maps # 10 and 25, utilitarian barks on Map # 23, and cut-down carriers on Map #13, while the heavily armed warships of England patrol the margins of the world on Map # 1.

The maps are also valuable for their depiction of several forms of European and Amerindian small craft. Illustrations of Dutch double-enders in New Amsterdam (Map # 9), an English sloop off the Virginia Capes (Map # 10), and shallops and wherries in the harbor of New York (Map # 13) show us the trucks and taxis of the maritime age. Rarer still are the maps' views of native vessels. Of these the most important are the Beothuk dugout—"Navis ex arboris trunco igne excavata"—and the Algonquin canoe—"Sine Navicule e corticibus arborum"—of Map # 9.

As well as their vessels, the Amerindians themselves are sketched on these maps. Given European physiognomies, the Indians are shown engaged in elemental acts—suckling or slaughtering—to evince their purported savagery. Exotic dress (or lack of it), and the weaponry of wood-armed warriors are also displayed to emphasize native otherness to Europeans. Yet native commerce is pictured, as is its medium, fur-bearing animals. Game is also illustrated, as are the native settlements fed by it. The double villages of Maps # 9 and 13 (derived from a Dutch original of 1627) could be classic Onondagan moiety settlements, dominant and subordinate, large and small, elder and younger, whose resident clans exchanged feasts and ceremonies, the condolence council chief among them. The movement of the Susquehanna capital south from the borders of the Five Nations to the great falls of the Susquehanna River and, finally, to the banks of the Potomac is mapped on # 10 and 12 of the *Blathwayt Atlas*. The final destruction of the valley fortress of the Susquehanna by the Five Nations in 1676, the tragic end of a once-preeminent people, is a terse note—"Susquehanna fort Demolished"—on Map # 15.

Unlike the Indians, the Africans drawn on the maps of the *Blathwayt Atlas* often exhibit physiological differences from Europeans, and frequently skin color is indicated by shading. In the African case, as in the Indian, however, cultural symbols did even more than somatic traits to illustrate alien character. The African slave of Map # 36, for example, is European in his features but his servile status is marked by his loincloth, his function expressed by the sugar cane he carries, and his humanity degraded by his association with plantation livestock. He was, as 1676 would show, a man ripe for revolution.

1. *The Blathwayt Atlas. A Collection of Forty-eight Manuscript and Printed Maps of the Seventeenth Century Relating to the British Overseas Empire in That Era, Brought Together About 1683 for the Use of the Lords of Trade and Plantations by William Blathwayt Secretary* (Provi-

dence, 1970), reproduced by the kind permission of the Librarian of the John Carter Brown Library.

2. Blathwayt to Andros, 10 Feb. 1678/9, Blathwayt Correspondence 3, no. 1, Colonial Williamsburg, Inc.; Stephen Saunders Webb, "William Blathwayt, Imperial Fixer: From Popish Plot to Glorious Revolution," *The William and Mary Quarterly*, 3rd ser., 25 (1968): 3–21.

3. Jeannette D. Black, *The Blathwayt Atlas Volume II. Commentary* (Providence, 1975), 32.

4. Blathwayt to Andros, 15 July 1679, Blathwayt Papers, Williamsburg, 3, No. 1.

Index